MICROSOFT® OFFICE

PowerPoint® 2003

Comprehensive Concepts and Techniques

Gary B. Shelly
Thomas J. Cashman
Susan L. Sebok

THOMSON
COURSE TECHNOLOGY

COURSE TECHNOLOGY
25 THOMSON PLACE
BOSTON MA 02210

SHELLY
CASHMAN
SERIES®

Australia • Canada • Denmark • Japan • Mexico • New Zealand • Philippines • Puerto Rico • Singapore
South Africa • Spain • United Kingdom • United States

THOMSON

COURSE TECHNOLOGY

Microsoft Office PowerPoint 2003:
Comprehensive Concepts and Techniques, CourseCard Edition

Gary B. Shelly
Thomas J. Cashman
Susan L. Sebok

Managing Editor:
Alexandra Arnold

Senior Acquisitions Editor:
Dana Merk

Product Manager:
Reed Cotter

Editorial Assistant:
Selena Coppock

Print Buyer:
Laura Burns

Series Consulting Editor:
Jim Quasney

Director of Production:
Patty Stephan

Production Editor:
Catherine G. DiMassa

Production Assistant:
Jill Klaffky

Development Editor:
Ginny Harvey

Copy Editor:
Nancy Lamm

Proofreader:
Lori Silfen

Interior Designer:
Becky Herrington

Cover Designers:
Ken Russo
Richard Herrera

Illustrators:
Richard Herrera
Andrew Bartel

Compositors:
Jeanne Black
Andrew Bartel
Kellee LaVars
Kenny Tran

Indexer:
Cristina Haley

Printer:
Banta Menasha

ISBN-13: 978-1-4188-4366-3
ISBN-10: 1-4188-4366-0

PHOTO CREDITS: Microsoft PowerPoint 2003 *Project 1, page PPT 6* laptop computer, Courtesy of PhotoDisc, Inc.

MICROSOFT° OFFICE

PowerPoint 2003

Comprehensive Concepts and Techniques

Contents

Appendix A

Microsoft PowerPoint Help System

Appendix B

Speech and Handwriting Recognition

Appendix C

Publishing Office Web Pages to a Web Server

Appendix D

Changing Screen Resolution and Resetting the PowerPoint Toolbars and Menus

Appendix E

Microsoft Office Specialist Certification

PowerPoint 2003 CourseCard

Preface

The Shelly Cashman Series® offers the finest textbooks in computer education. We are proud of the fact that our series of Microsoft Office 4.3, Microsoft Office 95, Microsoft Office 97, Microsoft Office 2000, and Microsoft Office XP textbooks have been the most widely used books in education. With each new edition of our Office books, we have made significant improvements based on the software and comments made by the instructors and students. The *Microsoft Office 2003* books continue with the innovation, quality, and reliability that you have come to expect from the Shelly Cashman Series.

In this *Microsoft Office PowerPoint 2003* book, you will find an educationally sound, highly visual, and easy-to-follow pedagogy that combines a vastly improved step-by-step approach with corresponding screens. All projects and exercises in this book are designed to take full advantage of the PowerPoint 2003 enhancements. The project material is developed to ensure that students will see the importance of learning PowerPoint for future coursework. The popular Other Ways and More About features offer in-depth knowledge of PowerPoint 2003, and the new Q&A feature offers students a way to solidify important slideshow concepts. The Learn It Online page presents a wealth of additional exercises to ensure your students have all the reinforcement they need.

Objectives of This Textbook

Microsoft Office PowerPoint 2003: Comprehensive Concepts and Techniques, CourseCard Edition is intended for a two- to three-unit course that presents Microsoft Office PowerPoint 2003. No experience with a computer is assumed, and no mathematics beyond the high school freshman level is required. The objectives of this book are:

- To teach the fundamentals of PowerPoint 2003
- To emphasize the presentation development cycle
- To expose students to practical examples of the computer as a useful tool
- To acquaint students with the proper procedures to create effective presentations
- To develop an exercise-oriented approach that allows learning by doing
- To introduce students to new input technologies
- To encourage independent study and help those who are working alone
- To assist students preparing to take the Microsoft Office Specialist examination for the Microsoft Office PowerPoint 2003 specialist-level certification

Approved by Microsoft as Courseware for Microsoft Office Specialist Certification

Microsoft Office PowerPoint 2003: Comprehensive Concepts and Techniques, CourseCard Edition has been approved by Microsoft as courseware for Microsoft Office Specialist certification. After completing the first four projects and corresponding exercises in this book, students will be prepared to take the specialist-level examination for Microsoft Office PowerPoint 2003.

By passing the certification exam for a Microsoft software application, students demonstrate their proficiency in that application to employers. This exam is offered at participating centers, corporations, and employment agencies. See Appendix E for additional information about obtaining Microsoft Office Specialist certification and for a table that includes the Microsoft Office PowerPoint 2003 skill sets and corresponding page numbers where a skill is discussed in the book, or visit the Web site microsoft.com/officespecialist.

The Shelly Cashman Series Microsoft Office Specialist Center (Figure 1) has links to valuable information about the certification program. The Web page (scsite.com/winoff2003/cert) includes links to general information on certification, choosing an application for certification, preparing for the certification exam, and taking and passing the certification exams.

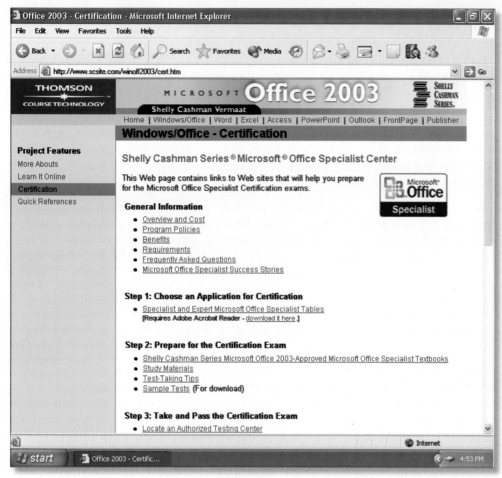

FIGURE 1

The Shelly Cashman Approach

Features of the Shelly Cashman Series *Microsoft Office PowerPoint 2003* books include:

- Project Orientation: Each project in the book presents a practical problem and complete solution using an easy-to-understand methodology.
- Step-by-Step, Screen-by-Screen Instructions: Each of the tasks required to complete a project is identified throughout the project. Full-color screens accompany the steps.
- Thoroughly Tested Projects: Unparalleled quality is ensured because every screen in the book is produced by the author only after performing a step, and then each project must pass Thomson Course Technology's award-winning Quality Assurance program.
- Other Ways Boxes and Quick Reference Summary: The Other Ways boxes displayed at the end of many of the step-by-step sequences specify the other ways to perform the task completed in the steps. Thus, the steps and the Other Ways box make a comprehensive reference unit.
- More About and Q&A Features: These marginal annotations provide background information, tips, and answers to common questions that complement the topics covered, adding depth and perspective to the learning process.
- Integration of the World Wide Web: The World Wide Web is integrated into the PowerPoint 2003 learning experience by (1) More About annotations that send students to Web sites for up-to-date information and alternative approaches to tasks; (2) a Microsoft Office Specialist Certification Web page so students can prepare for the certification examinations; (3) a PowerPoint 2003 Quick Reference Summary Web page that summarizes the ways to complete tasks (mouse, menu, shortcut menu, and keyboard); and (4) the Learn It Online page at the end of each project, which has project reinforcement exercises, learning games, and other types of student activities.

Organization of This Textbook

Microsoft Office PowerPoint 2003: Comprehensive Concepts and Techniques, CourseCard Edition provides basic instruction on how to use PowerPoint 2003. The material is divided into six projects, a Web feature, a Collaboration feature, an Online feature, five appendices, and a Quick Reference Summary.

Project 1 – Using a Design Template and Text Slide Layout to Create a Presentation   In Project 1, students are introduced to PowerPoint terminology, the PowerPoint window, and the basics of creating a bulleted list presentation. Topics include choosing a design template by using a task pane; creating a title slide and text slides with single and multi-level bulleted lists; changing the font size and font style; ending a slide show with a black slide; saving a presentation; viewing the slides in a presentation; checking a presentation for spelling errors; printing copies of the slides; and using the PowerPoint Help system.

Project 2 – Using the Outline Tab and Clip Art to Create a Slide Show   In Project 2, students create a presentation from an outline, insert clip art, and add animation effects. Topics include creating a slide presentation by indenting paragraphs on the Outline tab; changing slide layouts; inserting clip art; changing clip art size; adding an animation scheme; animating clip art; running an animated slide show; printing audience handouts from an outline; and e-mailing a slide show from within PowerPoint.

Web Feature – Creating a Presentation on the Web Using PowerPoint   In the Web feature, students are introduced to saving a presentation as a Web page. Topics include saving an existing PowerPoint presentation as an HTML file; viewing the presentation as a Web page; editing a Web page through a browser; and viewing the editing changes.

Project 3 – Using Visuals to Enhance a Slide Show   In Project 3, students create a presentation from a Microsoft Word outline and then enhance it with visuals. Topics include creating a slide background using a picture; modifying clips; deleting a slide; customizing bullets using the slide master; inserting and formatting a table; creating and formatting an organization chart; applying a new design template to a single slide; rearranging slides; adding animation schemes to selected slides, and printing slides as handouts.

Project 4 – Modifying Visual Elements and Presentation Formats   In Project 4, students create a presentation using the AutoContent Wizard and then customize this slide show. Topics include adding a graphical heading using WordArt; modifying the presentation by changing the color scheme; adding information to the slide master footer; adding data from other sources; including an Excel chart and a Word table; finding and replacing text; adding hyperlinks and sound effects; using the Thesaurus; adding an action button and action setting; rehearsing presentation timings; running a slide show with hyperlinks; using the grid and guides to position objects; hiding slides; delivering and navigating a presentation using the Slide Show toolbar; printing speaker notes; and saving the presentation as a Rich Text Format outline.

Collaboration Feature – Delivering Presentations to and Collaborating with Workgroups   In the Collaboration feature, students learn to use the Package for CD feature to save presentations along with the Microsoft Office PowerPoint Viewer. Topics include setting up a review cycle to track, accept, and reject changes in a presentation; reviewing presentation comments; comparing and merging presentations; and scheduling online broadcasts.

Project 5 – Working with Macros and Visual Basic for Applications (VBA)   In Project 5, students use VBA to develop a slide show customized for each presentation. The slides contain a template, digital picture, and video clip that vary depending on the presentation designer's selections. Topics include creating a new toolbar and adding buttons; using the macro recorder to create a macro that prints a handout of the slides; assigning the macro to a command on the File menu; and creating a form composed of controls.

Project 6 – Creating a Self-Running Presentation Containing Shapes   In Project 6, students create a self-running presentation. Topics include inserting a slide from another presentation; using the Format Painter; inserting and formatting a Venn diagram and an AutoShape; adding and formatting AutoShape text; applying a motion path animation effect to an AutoShape; creating and starting a self-running presentation; and adding and formatting slide numbers.

Microsoft Office Online Feature – Importing Files from the Microsoft Office Online Web Site   In this Online feature, students learn how to download design templates and clips from a source on the Internet and add them to a presentation. Topics include connecting to the Microsoft Office Online Web site; searching for templates and sound and animation clips; and importing a template and clips into a presentation.

Appendices   The book includes five appendices. Appendix A presents an introduction to the Microsoft PowerPoint Help system. Appendix B describes how to use the PowerPoint speech and handwriting recognition capabilities. Appendix C explains how to publish Web pages to a Web server. Appendix D shows how to change the screen resolution and reset the menus and toolbars. Appendix E introduces students to Microsoft Office Specialist certification.

Quick Reference Summary   In PowerPoint 2003, you can accomplish a task in a number of ways, such as using the mouse, menu, shortcut menu, and keyboard. The Quick Reference Summary at the back of the book provides a quick reference to each task presented.

PowerPoint 2003 CourseCard   New! Now includes a free, tear-off PowerPoint 2003 CourseCard that provides students with a great way to have PowerPoint skills at their fingertips.

End-of-Project Student Activities

A notable strength of the Shelly Cashman Series *Microsoft Office PowerPoint 2003* books is the extensive student activities at the end of each project. Well-structured student activities can make the difference between students merely participating in a class and students retaining the information they learn. The activities in the Shelly Cashman Series *Microsoft Office PowerPoint 2003* books include the following.

- **What You Should Know**   A listing of the tasks completed within a project together with the pages on which the step-by-step, screen-by-screen explanations appear.
- **Learn It Online**   Every project features a Learn It Online page that contains 12 exercises. These exercises include True/False, Multiple Choice, Short Answer, Flash Cards, Practice Test, Learning Games, Tips and Tricks, Newsgroup usage, Expanding Your Horizons, Search Sleuth, Office Online Training, and Office Marketplace.
- **Apply Your Knowledge**   This exercise usually requires students to open and manipulate a file on the Data Disk that parallels the activities learned in the project. To obtain a copy of the Data Disk, follow the instructions on the inside back cover of this textbook.
- **In the Lab**   Three in-depth assignments per project require students to utilize the project concepts and techniques to solve problems on a computer.
- **Cases and Places**   Five unique real-world case-study situations, including one small-group activity.

Instructor Resources CD-ROM

The Shelly Cashman Series is dedicated to providing you with all of the tools you need to make your class a success. Information on all supplementary materials is available through your Course Technology representative or by calling one of the following telephone numbers: Colleges and Universities, 1-800-648-7450; High Schools, 1-800-824-5179; Private Career Colleges, 1-800-347-7707; Canada, 1-800-268-2222; Corporations with IT Training Centers, 1-800-648-7450; and Government Agencies, Health-Care Organizations, and Correctional Facilities, 1-800-477-3692.

The Instructor Resources for this textbook include both teaching and testing aids. The contents of each item on the Instructor Resources CD-ROM (ISBN 0-619-20048-0) are described below.

INSTRUCTOR'S MANUAL   The Instructor's Manual is made up of Microsoft Word files, which include detailed lesson plans with page number references, lecture notes, teaching tips, classroom activities, discussion topics, projects to assign, and transparency references. The transparencies are available through the Figure Files described below.

LECTURE SUCCESS SYSTEM   The Lecture Success System consists of intermediate files that correspond to certain figures in the book, allowing you to step through the creation of an application in a project during a lecture without entering large amounts of data.

SYLLABUS   Sample syllabi, which can be customized easily to a course, are included. The syllabi cover policies, class and lab assignments and exams, and procedural information.

FIGURE FILES Illustrations for every figure in the textbook are available in electronic form. Use this ancillary to present a slide show in lecture or to print transparencies for use in lecture with an overhead projector. If you have a personal computer and LCD device, this ancillary can be an effective tool for presenting lectures.

POWERPOINT PRESENTATIONS PowerPoint Presentations is a multimedia lecture presentation system that provides slides for each project. Presentations are based on project objectives. Use this presentation system to present well-organized lectures that are both interesting and knowledge based. PowerPoint Presentations provides consistent coverage at schools that use multiple lecturers.

SOLUTIONS TO EXERCISES Solutions are included for the end-of-project exercises, as well as the Project Reinforcement Exercises.

RUBRICS AND ANNOTATED SOLUTION FILES The grading rubrics provide a customizable framework for assigning point values to the laboratory exercises. Annotated solution files that correspond to the grading rubrics make it easy for you to compare students' results with the correct solutions whether you receive their homework as hard copy or via e-mail.

TEST BANK & TEST ENGINE The ExamView test bank includes 110 questions for every project (25 multiple choice, 50 true/false, and 35 short answer) with page number references and, when appropriate, figure references. A version of the test bank you can print also is included. The test bank comes with a copy of the test engine, ExamView, the ultimate tool for your objective-based testing needs. ExamView is a state-of-the-art test builder that is easy to use. ExamView enables you to create paper-, LAN-, or Web-based tests from test banks designed specifically for your Course Technology textbook. Utilize the ultra-efficient QuickTest Wizard to create tests in less than five minutes by taking advantage of Course Technology's question banks, or customize your own exams from scratch.

LAB TESTS/TEST OUT The Lab Tests/Test Out exercises parallel the In the Lab assignments and are supplied for the purpose of testing students in the laboratory on the material covered in the project or testing students out of the course.

DATA FILES FOR STUDENTS All the files that are required by students to complete the exercises are included. You can distribute the files on the Instructor Resources CD-ROM to your students over a network, or you can have them follow the instructions on the inside back cover of this book to obtain a copy of the Data Disk.

ADDITIONAL ACTIVITIES FOR STUDENTS These additional activities consist of Project Reinforcement Exercises, which are true/false, multiple choice, and short answer questions that help students gain confidence in the material learned.

SAM 2003

SAM 2003 helps you energize your class exams and training assignments by allowing students to learn and test important computer skills in an active, hands-on environment.

SAM 2003 ASSESSMENT With SAM 2003 Assessment, you create powerful interactive exams on critical applications such as Word, Excel, Access, PowerPoint, Windows, Outlook, and the Internet.

SAM 2003 TRAINING Invigorate your lesson plan with SAM 2003 Training. Using highly interactive text, graphics, and sound, SAM 2003 Training gives your students the flexibility to learn computer applications by choosing the training method that fits them best. Create customized training units that employ various approaches to teaching computer skills.

SAM 2003 ASSESSMENT AND TRAINING Designed to be used with the Shelly Cashman Series, SAM 2003 Assessment and Training includes built-in page references so students can create study guides that match the Shelly Cashman Series textbooks you use in class.

Online Content

Course Technology offers textbook-based content for Blackboard, WebCT, and MyCourse 2.1.

BLACKBOARD AND WEBCT   As the leading provider of IT content for the Blackboard and WebCT platforms, Course Technology delivers rich content that enhances your textbook to give your students a unique learning experience.

MYCOURSE 2.1   MyCourse 2.1 is Course Technology's powerful online course management and content delivery system. MyCourse 2.1 allows nontechnical users to create, customize, and deliver Web-based courses; post content and assignments; manage student enrollment; administer exams; track results in the online grade book; and more.

To the Student... Getting the Most Out of Your Book

Welcome to *Microsoft Office PowerPoint 2003: Comprehensive Concepts and Techniques, CourseCard Edition.*
You can save yourself a lot of time and gain a better understanding of Microsoft Office PowerPoint 2003 if you
spend a few minutes reviewing the figures and callouts in this section.

1 Project Orientation

Each project presents a practical problem and
shows the solution in the first figure of the project.
The project orientation lets you see firsthand how
problems are solved from start to finish using
application software and computers.

2 Consistent Step-by-Step, Screen-by-Screen Presentation

Project solutions are built using a step-by-step,
screen-by-screen approach. This pedagogy allows
you to build the solution on a computer as you read
through the project. Generally, each step is followed
by an italic explanation that indicates the result of
the step.

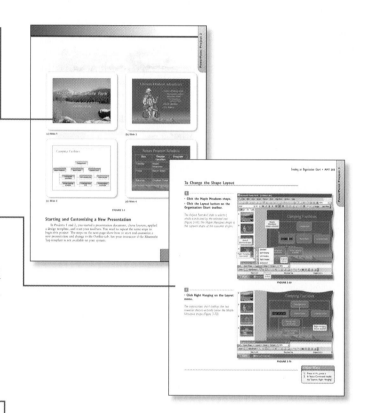

3 More Than Just Step-by-Step

More About and Q&A annotations in the margins
of the book and substantive text in the paragraphs
provide background information, tips, and answers
to common questions that complement the topics
covered, adding depth and perspective. When you
finish with this book, you will be ready to use
PowerPoint to solve problems on your own.

4 Other Ways Boxes and Quick Reference Summary

Other Ways boxes that follow many of the step
sequences and a Quick Reference Summary at the
back of the book explain the other ways to complete the task presented, such as using the mouse,
menu, shortcut menu, and keyboard.

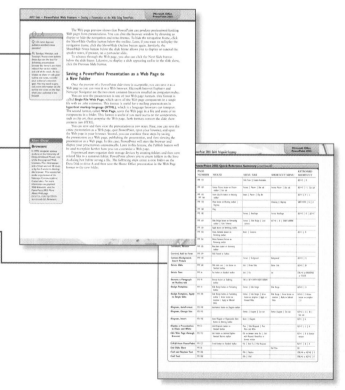

5 Emphasis on Getting Help When You Need It

The first project of each application and Appendix A show you how to use all the elements of the PowerPoint Help system. Being able to answer your own questions will increase your productivity and reduce your frustrations by minimizing the time it takes to learn how to complete a task.

6 Review

After you successfully step through a project, a section titled What You Should Know summarizes the project tasks with which you should be familiar. Terms you should know for test purposes are bold in the text.

7 Reinforcement and Extension

The Learn It Online page at the end of each project offers reinforcement in the form of review questions, learning games, and practice tests. Also included are Web-based exercises that require you to extend your learning beyond the book.

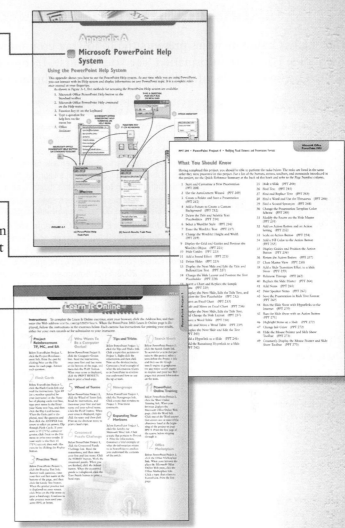

8 Laboratory Exercises

If you really want to learn how to use the applications, then you must design and implement solutions to problems on your own. Every project concludes with several carefully developed laboratory assignments that increase in complexity.

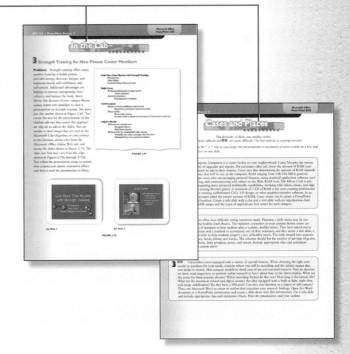

Shelly Cashman Series – Traditionally Bound Textbooks

The Shelly Cashman Series presents the following computer subjects in a variety of traditionally bound textbooks. For more information, see your Course Technology representative or call 1-800-648-7450. For Shelly Cashman Series information, visit Shelly Cashman Online at **scseries.com**

	COMPUTERS
Computers	Discovering Computers 2006: A Gateway to Information, Complete
	Discovering Computers 2006: A Gateway to Information, Introductory
	Discovering Computers 2006: A Gateway to Information, Brief
	Discovering Computers: Fundamentals, Second Edition
	Teachers Discovering Computers: Integrating Technology in the Classroom, Third Edition
	Essential Introduction to Computers, Sixth Edition (40-page)

	WINDOWS APPLICATIONS
Microsoft Office	Microsoft Office 2003: Essential Concepts and Techniques (5 projects)
	Microsoft Office 2003: Brief Concepts and Techniques (9 projects)
	Microsoft Office 2003: Introductory Concepts and Techniques, Second Edition (15 projects)
	Microsoft Office 2003: Advanced Concepts and Techniques (12 projects)
	Microsoft Office 2003: Post Advanced Concepts and Techniques (11 projects)
	Microsoft Office XP: Essential Concepts and Techniques (5 projects)
	Microsoft Office XP: Brief Concepts and Techniques (9 projects)
	Microsoft Office XP: Introductory Concepts and Techniques, Windows XP Edition (15 projects)
	Microsoft Office XP: Introductory Concepts and Techniques, Enhanced Edition (15 projects)
	Microsoft Office XP: Advanced Concepts and Techniques (11 projects)
	Microsoft Office XP: Post Advanced Concepts and Techniques (11 projects)
Integration	Teachers Discovering and Integrating Microsoft Office: Essential Concepts and Techniques, Second Edition
	Integrating Microsoft Office XP Applications and the World Wide Web: Essential Concepts and Techniques
PIM	Microsoft Outlook 2002: Essential Concepts and Techniques • Microsoft Office Outlook 2003: Introductory Concepts and Techniques
Microsoft Works	Microsoft Works 6: Complete Concepts and Techniques[1] • Microsoft Works 2000: Complete Concepts and Techniques[1]
Microsoft Windows	Microsoft Windows XP: Comprehensive Concepts and Techniques[2]
	Microsoft Windows XP: Brief Concepts and Techniques
	Microsoft Windows 2000: Comprehensive Concepts and Techniques[2]
	Microsoft Windows 2000: Brief Concepts and Techniques
	Microsoft Windows 98: Comprehensive Concepts and Techniques[2]
	Microsoft Windows 98: Essential Concepts and Techniques
	Introduction to Microsoft Windows NT Workstation 4
Notebook Organizer	Microsoft Office OneNote 2003: Introductory Concepts and Techniques
Word Processing	Microsoft Office Word 2003: Comprehensive Concepts and Techniques[2] • Microsoft Word 2002: Comprehensive Concepts and Techniques[2]
Spreadsheets	Microsoft Office Excel 2003: Comprehensive Concepts and Techniques[2] • Microsoft Excel 2002: Comprehensive Concepts and Techniques[2]
Database	Microsoft Office Access 2003: Comprehensive Concepts and Techniques[2] • Microsoft Access 2002: Comprehensive Concepts and Techniques[2]
Presentation Graphics	Microsoft Office PowerPoint 2003: Comprehensive Concepts and Techniques[2] • Microsoft PowerPoint 2002: Comprehensive Concepts and Techniques[2]
Desktop Publishing	Microsoft Office Publisher 2003: Comprehensive Concepts and Techniques[2] • Microsoft Publisher 2002: Comprehensive Concepts and Techniques[1]

	PROGRAMMING
Programming	Microsoft Visual Basic .NET: Comprehensive Concepts and Techniques[2] • Microsoft Visual Basic 6: Complete Concepts and Techniques[1] • Java Programming: Comprehensive Concepts and Techniques, Second Edition[2] • Structured COBOL Programming, Second Edition • Understanding and Troubleshooting Your PC • Programming Fundamentals Using Microsoft Visual Basic .NET

	INTERNET
Concepts	Discovering the Internet: Brief Concepts and Techniques • Discovering the Internet: Complete Concepts and Techniques
Browser	Microsoft Internet Explorer 6: Introductory Concepts and Techniques, Windows XP Edition • Microsoft Internet Explorer 5: An Introduction • Netscape Navigator 6: An Introduction
Web Page Creation	Web Design: Introductory Concepts and Techniques • HTML: Comprehensive Concepts and Techniques, Third Edition[2] • Microsoft Office FrontPage 2003: Comprehensive Concepts and Techniques[2] • Microsoft FrontPage 2002: Comprehensive Concepts and Techniques[2] • Microsoft FrontPage 2002: Essential Concepts and Techniques • JavaScript: Complete Concepts and Techniques, Second Edition[1] • Macromedia Dreamweaver MX: Comprehensive Concepts and Techniques[2]

	SYSTEMS ANALYSIS
Systems Analysis	Systems Analysis and Design, Sixth Edition

	DATA COMMUNICATIONS
Data Communications	Business Data Communications: Introductory Concepts and Techniques, Fourth Edition

[1] Also available as an Introductory Edition, which is a shortened version of the complete book, [2] Also available as an Introductory Edition and as a Complete Edition, which are shortened versions of the comprehensive book.

Using a Design Template and Text Slide Layout to Create a Presentation

PROJECT

1

CASE PERSPECTIVE

Do you use the 168 hours in each week effectively? From attending class, doing homework, attending school events, exercising, eating, watching television, and sleeping, juggling the demands of school and personal lives can be daunting. Odds are that one of every three students will fail a course at one point in their college career due to poor study habits.

The ability to learn effectively is the key to college success. What matters is not how long people study but how well they use their time in the classroom and while preparing for class assignments and tests. Students with good academic skills maximize their time and, consequently, achieve the highest grades on exams and homework assignments. They ultimately earn higher incomes than their less organized peers because good academic practices carry over to the working environment.

Advisers in the Academic Skills Center at your college are aware of this fact and are developing seminars to help students succeed. Their first presentation focuses on getting organized, enhancing listening skills, and taking tests effectively. Dr. Traci Johnson, the dean of the Academic Skills Center, has asked you to help her create a PowerPoint slide show to use at next month's lunchtime study skills session (Figure 1-1 on page PPT 5). In addition, she would like handouts of the slides to distribute to these students.

As you read through this project, you will learn how to use PowerPoint to create, save, and print a slide show that is composed of single- and multi-level bulleted lists.

Using a Design Template and Text Slide Layout to Create a Presentation

PROJECT

1

Objectives

You will have mastered the material in this project when you can:

- Start and customize PowerPoint
- Describe the PowerPoint window
- Select a design template
- Create a title slide and text slides with single- and multi-level bulleted lists
- Change the font size and font style

- Save a presentation
- End a slide show with a black slide
- View a presentation in slide show view
- Quit PowerPoint and then open a presentation
- Display and print a presentation in black and white
- Use the PowerPoint Help system

What Is Microsoft Office PowerPoint 2003?

Microsoft Office PowerPoint 2003 is a complete presentation graphics program that allows you to produce professional-looking presentations (Figure 1-1). A PowerPoint **presentation** also is called a **slide show**.

PowerPoint contains several features to simplify creating a slide show. For example, you can instruct PowerPoint to create a predesigned presentation, and then you can modify the presentation to fulfill your requirements. You quickly can format a slide show using one of the professionally designed presentation design templates. To make your presentation more impressive, you can add tables, charts, pictures, video, sound, and animation effects. Additional PowerPoint features include the following:

- **Word processing**   create bulleted lists, combine words and images, find and replace text, and use multiple fonts and type sizes.
- **Outlining**   develop your presentation using an outline format. You also can import outlines from Microsoft Word or other word processing programs.
- **Charting**   create and insert charts into your presentations. The two chart types are: standard, which includes bar, line, pie, and xy (scatter) charts; and custom, which shows such objects as floating bars and colored lines.
- **Drawing**   form and modify diagrams using shapes such as arcs, arrows, cubes, rectangles, stars, and triangles.
- **Inserting multimedia**   insert artwork and multimedia effects into your slide show. The Microsoft Clip Organizer contains hundreds of media files, including pictures, photos, sounds, and movies.

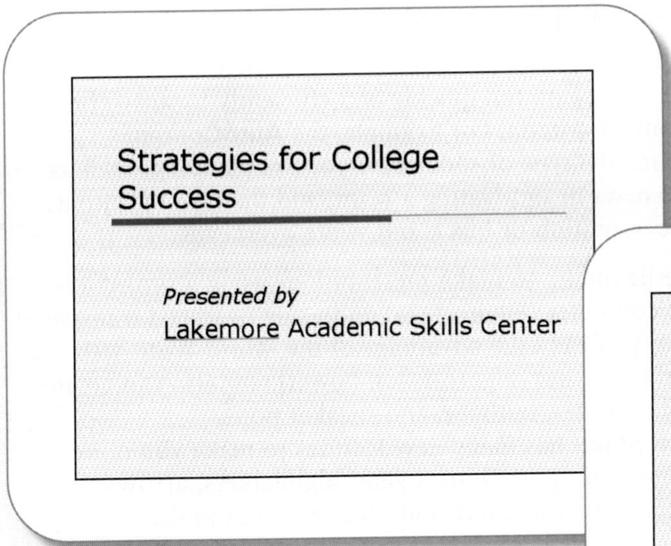

(a) Slide 1 (Title Slide)

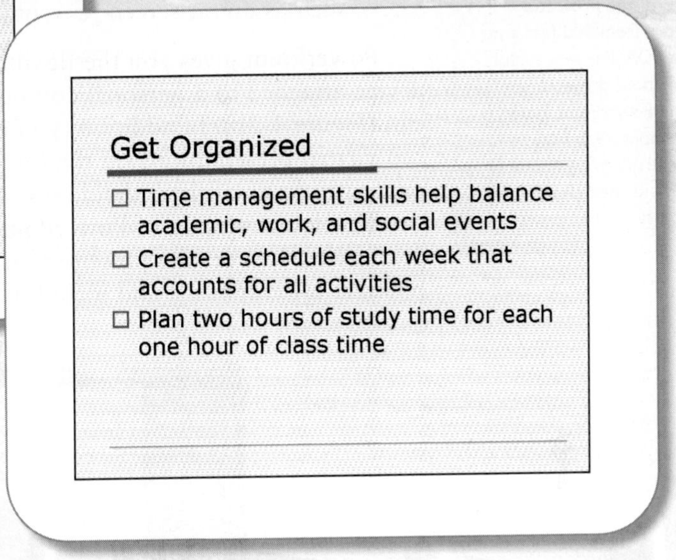

Strategies for College Success

Presented by
Lakemore Academic Skills Center

(b) Slide 2 (Single-Level Bulleted List)

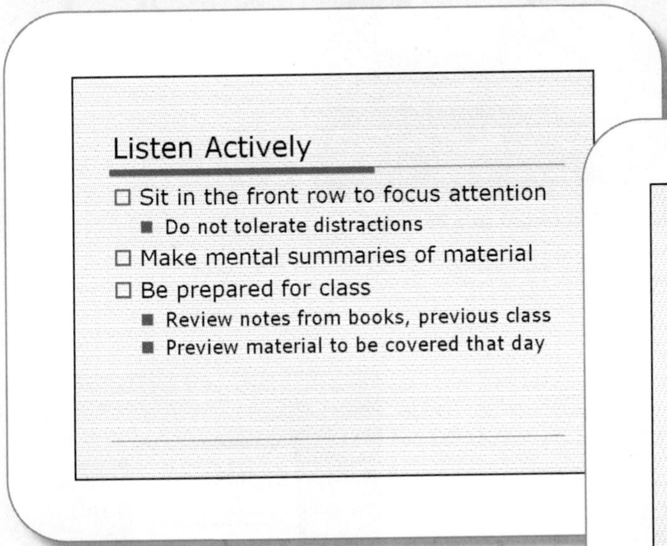

Get Organized

☐ Time management skills help balance academic, work, and social events
☐ Create a schedule each week that accounts for all activities
☐ Plan two hours of study time for each one hour of class time

(c) Slide 3 (Multi-Level Bulleted List)

Listen Actively

☐ Sit in the front row to focus attention
  ■ Do not tolerate distractions
☐ Make mental summaries of material
☐ Be prepared for class
  ■ Review notes from books, previous class
  ■ Preview material to be covered that day

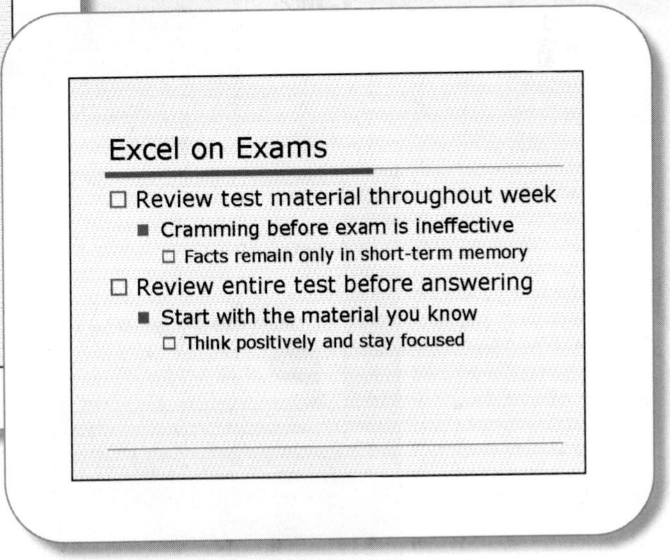

(d) Slide 4 (Multi-Level Bulleted List)

Excel on Exams

☐ Review test material throughout week
  ■ Cramming before exam is ineffective
    ☐ Facts remain only in short-term memory
☐ Review entire test before answering
  ■ Start with the material you know
    ☐ Think positively and stay focused

FIGURE 1-1

More About

Portable Projection Devices

New multimedia projectors weigh less than three pounds and can be held in one hand. Some projectors allow users to control the projector wirelessly from 300 feet away using a PDA. For more information about projectors, visit the PowerPoint 2003 More About Web page (scsite.com/ppt2003/more) and then click Projectors.

- **Web support** save presentations or parts of a presentation in HTML format so they can be viewed and manipulated using a browser. You can publish your slide show to the Internet or to an intranet.
- **E-mailing** send your entire slide show as an attachment to an e-mail message.
- **Using Wizards** create a presentation quickly and efficiently by answering prompts for specific content criteria. For example, the **AutoContent Wizard** gives prompts for the type of slide show you are planning, such as communicating serious news or motivating a team, and the type of output, such as an on-screen presentation or black and white overheads.

PowerPoint gives you the flexibility to make presentations using a projection device attached to a personal computer (Figure 1-2a) and using overhead transparencies (Figure 1-2b). In addition, you can take advantage of the World Wide Web and run virtual presentations on the Internet (Figure 1-2c). PowerPoint also can create paper printouts of the individual slides, outlines, and speaker notes.

This latest version of PowerPoint has many new features to make you more productive. It saves the presentation to a CD; uses pens, highlighters, arrows, and pointers for emphasis; and includes a thesaurus and other research tools.

(a) Projection Device Connected to a Personal Computer

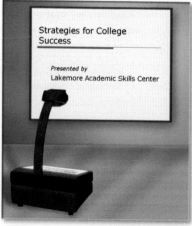

(b) Overhead Transparencies

(c) PowerPoint Presentation on the World Wide Web

FIGURE 1-2

Project One — Strategies for College Success

PowerPoint allows you to produce slides to use in an academic, business, or other environment. In Project 1, you create the presentation shown in Figures 1-1a through 1-1d. The objective is to produce a presentation, called Strategies for College Success, to be displayed using a projection device. As an introduction to PowerPoint, this project steps you through the most common type of presentation, which is a **text slide** consisting of a bulleted list. A **bulleted list** is a list of paragraphs, each preceded by a bullet. A **bullet** is a symbol such as a heavy dot (•) or other character that precedes text when the text warrants special emphasis.

Starting and Customizing PowerPoint

If you are stepping through this project on a computer and you want your screen to agree with the figures in this book, then you should change your computer's resolution to 800 × 600. To change the resolution on your computer, see Appendix D.

To start PowerPoint, Windows must be running. The quickest way to begin a new presentation is to use the Start button on the **Windows taskbar** at the bottom of the screen. The following steps show how to start PowerPoint and a new presentation.

Q: Can I change the bullet characters?

A: Yes. While default bullets are part of the design templates, they can be modified or deleted. You can use symbols, numbers, and picture files as revised bullets. You also can change their size and color.

To Start PowerPoint

1

• **Click the Start button on the Windows taskbar, point to All Programs on the Start menu, point to Microsoft Office on the All Programs submenu, and then point to Microsoft Office PowerPoint 2003 on the Microsoft Office submenu.**

Windows displays the commands on the Start menu above the Start button, the All Programs submenu, and the Microsoft Office submenu (Figure 1-3).

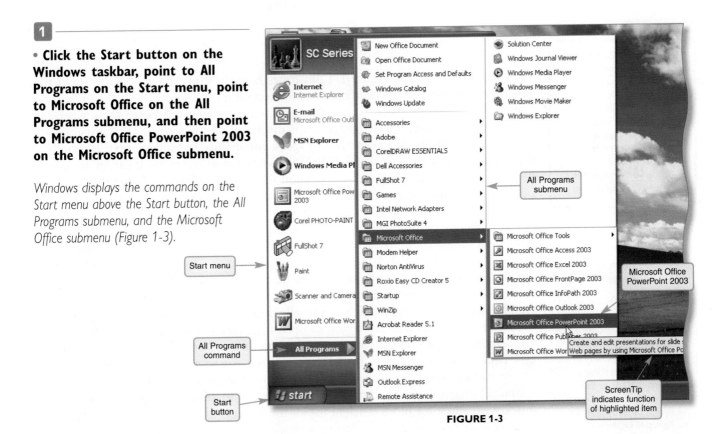

FIGURE 1-3

2

• **Click Microsoft Office PowerPoint 2003.**

PowerPoint starts. While PowerPoint is starting, the mouse pointer changes to the shape of an hourglass. After several seconds, PowerPoint displays a blank presentation titled Presentation1 in the PowerPoint window (Figure 1-4).

3

• **If the PowerPoint window is not maximized, double-click its title bar to maximize it.**

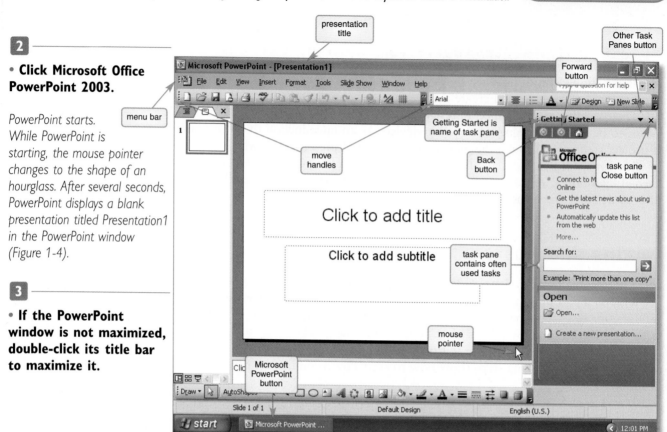

FIGURE 1-4

The screen shown in Figure 1-4 illustrates how the PowerPoint window looks the first time you start PowerPoint after installation on most computers. If the Office Speech Recognition software is installed and active on your computer, then, when you start PowerPoint, the Language bar is displayed on the screen. The **Language bar** contains buttons that allow you to speak commands and dictate text. It usually is located on the right side of the Windows taskbar next to the notification area, and it changes to include the speech recognition functions available in PowerPoint. In this book, the Language bar is closed because it takes up computer resources, and with the Language bar active, the microphone can be turned on accidentally by clicking the Microphone button, causing your computer to act in an unstable manner. For additional information about the Language bar, see page PPT 16 and Appendix B.

As shown in Figure 1-4, PowerPoint displays a task pane on the right side of the screen. A **task pane** is a separate window that enables users to carry out some PowerPoint tasks more efficiently. When you start PowerPoint, it displays the Getting Started task pane, which is a small window that provides commonly used links and commands that allow you to open files, create new files, or search Office-related topics on the Microsoft Web site. In this book, the Getting Started task pane is hidden to allow the maximum screen size to appear in PowerPoint.

At startup, PowerPoint also displays two toolbars on a single row. A **toolbar** contains buttons, boxes, and menus that allow you to perform frequent tasks quickly. To allow for more efficient use of the buttons, the toolbars should appear on two separate rows, instead of sharing a single row. The following steps show how to close the Language bar, close the Getting Started task pane, and instruct PowerPoint to display the toolbars on two separate rows.

To Customize the PowerPoint Window

1

• **If the Language bar appears, right-click it to display a list of commands.**

The Language bar shortcut menu appears (Figure 1-5).

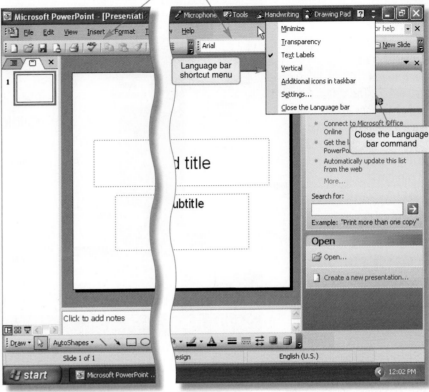

FIGURE 1-5

2

• **Click the Close the Language bar command.**

• **If necessary, click the OK button in the Language Bar dialog box.**

• **Click the Getting Started task pane Close button in the upper-right corner of the task pane.**

• **If the Standard and Formatting toolbars are positioned on the same row, click the Toolbar Options button on the Standard toolbar.**

The Language bar disappears. PowerPoint closes the Getting Started task pane and increases the size of the PowerPoint window. PowerPoint also displays the Toolbar Options list showing the buttons that do not fit on the toolbars when the toolbars are displayed on one row (Figure 1-6).

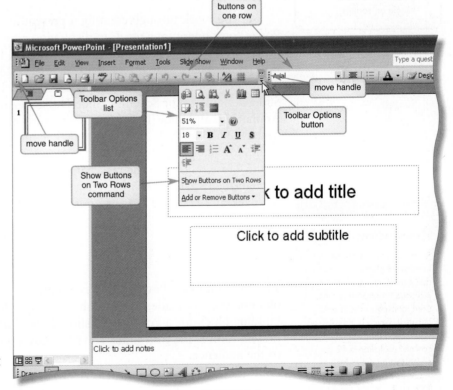

FIGURE 1-6

3

• **Click Show Buttons on Two Rows.**

PowerPoint displays the buttons on two separate rows (Figure 1-7). The Toolbar Options list shown in Figure 1-6 on the previous page is empty because all the buttons are displayed on two rows.

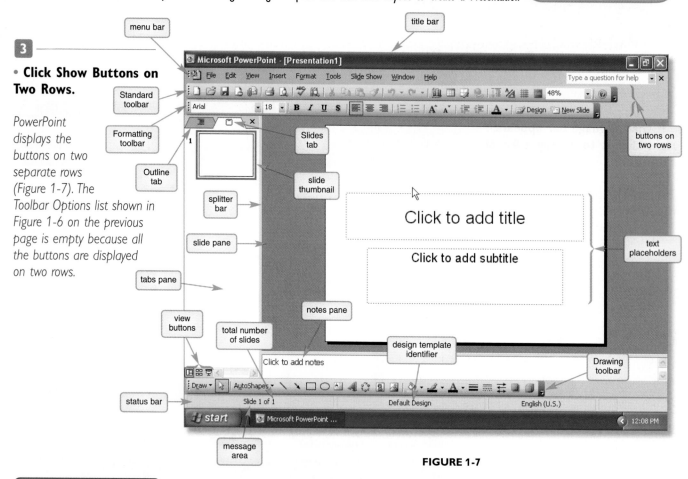

FIGURE 1-7

As you work through creating a presentation, you will find that certain PowerPoint operations result in displaying a task pane. Besides the Getting Started task pane shown in Figure 1-4 on page PPT 8, PowerPoint provides 15 additional task panes: Help, Search Results, Clip Art, Research, Clipboard, New Presentation, Template Help, Shared Workspace, Document Updates, Slide Layout, Slide Design, Slide Design - Color Schemes, Slide Design - Animation Schemes, Custom Animation, and Slide Transition. These task panes are discussed when they are used. You can show or hide a task pane by clicking the Task Pane command on the View menu. You can activate additional task panes by clicking the down arrow to the left of the Close button on the task pane title bar (Figure 1-4) and then selecting a task pane in the list. To switch between task panes that you opened during a session, use the Back and Forward buttons on the left side of the task pane title bar.

The PowerPoint Window

The basic unit of a PowerPoint presentation is a **slide**. A slide contains one or many **objects**, such as a title, text, graphics, tables, charts, and drawings. An object is the building block for a PowerPoint slide. PowerPoint assumes the first slide in a new presentation is the **title slide**. The title slide's purpose is to introduce the presentation to the audience.

In PowerPoint, you have the option of using the PowerPoint default settings or establishing your own. A **default setting** is a particular value for a variable that PowerPoint assigns initially. It controls the placement of objects, the color scheme, the transition between slides, and other slide attributes, and it remains in effect unless you cancel or override it. **Attributes** are the properties or characteristics of an object. For example, if you underline the title of a slide, the title is the object, and the underline is the attribute. When you start PowerPoint, the default **slide layout** is **landscape orientation**, where the slide width is greater than its height. In landscape orientation, the slide size is preset to 10 inches wide and 7.5 inches high. You can change the slide layout to **portrait orientation**, so the slide height is greater than its width, by clicking Page Setup on the File menu. In portrait orientation, the slide width is 7.5 inches, and the height is 10 inches.

When a PowerPoint window is open, its name appears in an icon on the Windows taskbar. The **active application** is the one displaying in the foreground of the desktop. That application's corresponding icon on the Windows taskbar is displayed recessed.

PowerPoint Views

PowerPoint has three main views: normal view, slide sorter view, and slide show view. A **view** is the mode in which the presentation appears on the screen. You may use any or all views when creating a presentation, but you can use only one at a time. You also can select one of these views to be the default view. Change views by clicking one of the view buttons located at the lower-left of the PowerPoint window above the Drawing toolbar (Figure 1-7). The PowerPoint window display varies depending on the view. Some views are graphical while others are textual.

You generally will use normal view and slide sorter view when you are creating a presentation. **Normal view** is composed of three working areas that allow you to work on various aspects of a presentation simultaneously (Figure 1-7). The left side of the screen has a tabs pane that consists of an **Outline tab** and a **Slides tab** that alternate between views of the presentation in an outline of the slide text and a thumbnail, or miniature, view of the slides. You can type the text of the presentation on the Outline tab and easily rearrange bulleted lists, paragraphs, and individual slides. As you type, you can view this text in the **slide pane**, which shows a large view of the current slide on the right side of the window. You also can enter text, graphics, animations, and hyperlinks directly in the slide pane. The **notes pane** at the bottom of the window is an area where you can type notes and additional information. This text can consist of notes to yourself or remarks to share with your audience.

In normal view, you can adjust the width of the slide pane by dragging the **splitter bar** and the height of the notes pane by dragging the pane borders. After you have created at least two slides, **scroll bars**, **scroll arrows**, and **scroll boxes** will be displayed below and to the right of the windows, and you can use them to view different parts of the panes.

Slide sorter view is helpful when you want to see all the slides in the presentation simultaneously. A thumbnail version of each slide is displayed, and you can rearrange their order, add transitions and timings to switch from one slide to the next in a presentation, add and delete slides, and preview animations.

Slide show view fills the entire screen and allows you to see the slide show just as your audience will view it. Transition effects, animation, graphics, movies, and timings are shown as they will appear during an actual presentation.

More About

Sizing Panes

The three panes in normal view allow you to work on all aspects of your presentation simultaneously. You can drag the splitter bar and the pane borders to make each area larger or smaller.

Table 1-1 identifies the view buttons and provides an explanation of each view.

Table 1-1	View Buttons and Functions	
BUTTON	BUTTON NAME	FUNCTION
	Normal View	Shows three panes: the tabs pane with either the Outline tab or the Slides tab, the slide pane, and the notes pane.
	Slide Sorter View	Shows thumbnail versions of all slides in a presentation. You then can copy, cut, paste, or otherwise change the slide position to modify the presentation. Slide sorter view also is used to add timings, to select animated transitions, and to preview animations.
	Slide Show View	Shows the slides as an electronic presentation on the full screen of your computer's monitor. Looking much like a slide projector display, this view can show you the effect of transitions, build effects, slide timings, and animations.

More About

The 7 × 7 Rule

All slide shows in the projects and exercises in this textbook follow the 7 x 7 rule. This guideline states that each slide should have a maximum of seven lines, and each of these lines should have a maximum of seven words. This rule requires PowerPoint designers to choose their words carefully and, in turn, helps viewers read the slides easily.

Placeholders, Text Areas, Mouse Pointer, and Scroll Bars

The PowerPoint window contains elements similar to the document windows in other Microsoft Office applications. Other features are unique to PowerPoint. The main elements are the placeholders, text areas, mouse pointer, and scroll bars.

PLACEHOLDERS **Placeholders** are boxes that are displayed when you create a new slide. All layouts except the Blank slide layout contain placeholders. Depending on the particular slide layout selected, placeholders are displayed for the slide title, body text, charts, tables, organization charts, media clips, and clip art. You type titles, body text, and bulleted lists in **text placeholders**; you place graphic elements in chart placeholders, table placeholders, organizational chart placeholders, and clip art placeholders. A placeholder is considered an **object**, which is a single element of a slide.

TEXT AREAS **Text areas** are surrounded by a dotted outline. The title slide in Figure 1-7 on page PPT 10 has two text areas that contain the text placeholders where you will type the main heading, or title, of a new slide and the subtitle, or other object. Other slides in a presentation may use a layout that contains text areas for a title and bulleted lists.

MOUSE POINTER The **mouse pointer** can become one of several different shapes depending on the task you are performing in PowerPoint and the pointer's location on the screen. The different shapes are discussed when they appear.

SCROLL BARS When you add a second slide to a presentation, a **vertical scroll bar** appears on the right side of the slide pane. PowerPoint allows you to use the scroll bar to move forward or backward through the presentation.

The **horizontal scroll bar** also may be displayed. It is located on the bottom of the slide pane and allows you to display a portion of the slide when the entire slide does not fit on the screen.

Status Bar, Menu Bar, Standard Toolbar, Formatting Toolbar, and Drawing Toolbar

The status bar is displayed at the bottom of the screen above the Windows taskbar (Figure 1-7). The menu bar, Standard toolbar, and Formatting toolbar are displayed at the top of the screen just below the title bar. The Drawing toolbar is displayed above the status bar.

STATUS BAR Immediately above the Windows taskbar at the bottom of the screen is the status bar. The **status bar** consists of a message area and a presentation design template identifier (Figure 1-7). Generally, the message area shows the current slide number and the total number of slides in the slide show. For example, in Figure 1-7 the message area shows Slide 1 of 1. Slide 1 is the current slide, and of 1 indicates the slide show contains only one slide. The template identifier shows Default Design, which is the template PowerPoint uses initially.

MENU BAR The **menu bar** is a special toolbar that includes the PowerPoint menu names (Figure 1-8a). Each **menu name** represents a menu of commands that you can use to perform tasks such as retrieving, storing, printing, and manipulating objects in a presentation. When you point to a menu name on the menu bar, the area of the menu bar containing the name changes to a button. To display a menu, such as the Edit menu, click the Edit menu name on the menu bar. A **menu** is a list of commands. If you point to a command on a menu that has an arrow to its right edge, a **submenu** shows another list of commands.

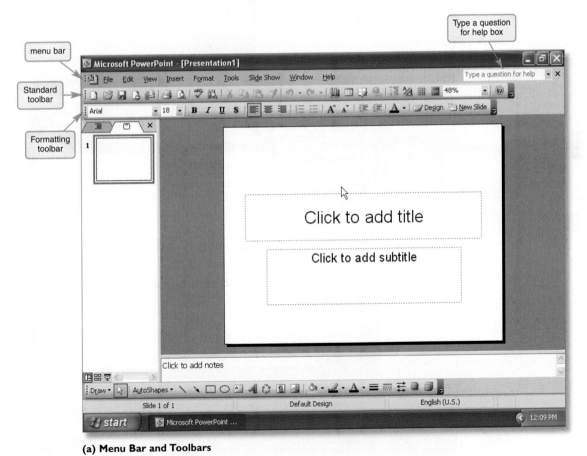

(a) Menu Bar and Toolbars

FIGURE 1-8

When you click a menu name on the menu bar, PowerPoint displays a **short menu** listing the most recently used commands (Figure 1-8b). If you wait a few seconds or click the arrows at the bottom of the short menu, it expands into a full menu. A **full menu** lists all the commands associated with a menu (Figure 1-8c). You also can display a full menu immediately by double-clicking the menu name on the menu bar. In this book, always have PowerPoint show the full menu by using one of the following techniques:

1. Click the menu name on the menu bar and then wait a few seconds.
2. Click the menu name on the menu bar and then click the arrows at the bottom of the short menu.
3. Click the menu name on the menu bar and then point to the arrows at the bottom of the short menu.
4. Double-click the menu name on the menu bar.

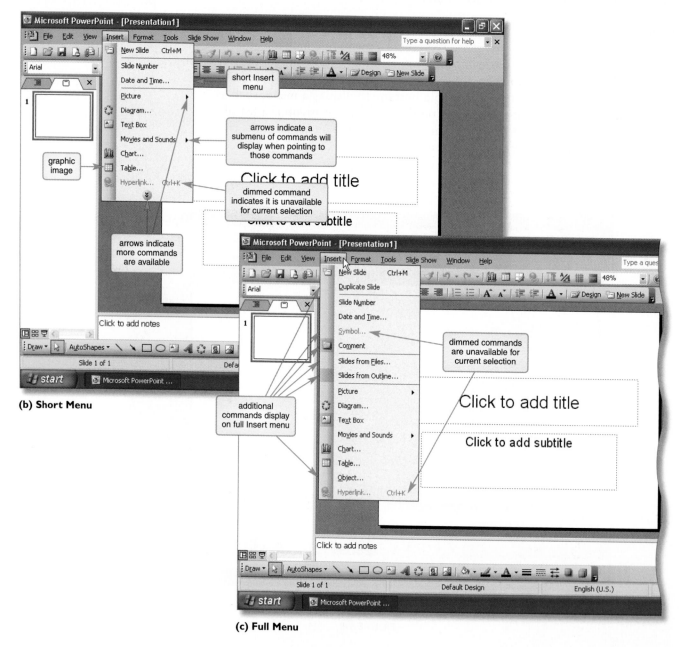

(b) Short Menu

(c) Full Menu

FIGURE 1-8 *(continued)*

Both short and full menus display some **dimmed commands** that appear gray, or dimmed, instead of black, which indicates they are not available for the current selection. A command with a dark gray shading to the left of it on a full menu is a **hidden command** because it does not appear on a short menu. As you use PowerPoint, it automatically personalizes the short menus for you based on how often you use commands. That is, as you use hidden commands, PowerPoint *unhides* them and places them on the short menu.

The menu bar can change to include other menu names depending on the type of work you are doing in PowerPoint. For example, if you are adding a chart to a slide, Data and Chart menu names are added to the menu bar with commands that reflect charting options.

STANDARD, FORMATTING, AND DRAWING TOOLBARS The **Standard toolbar** (Figure 1-9a), **Formatting toolbar** (Figure 1-9b), and **Drawing toolbar** (Figure 1-9c on the next page) contain buttons and boxes that allow you to perform frequent tasks more quickly than when using the menu bar. For example, to print a slide show, you click the Print button on the Standard toolbar. Each button has an image on the button face that helps you remember the button's function. Also, when you move the mouse pointer over a button or box, the name of the button or box appears below it in a ScreenTip. A **ScreenTip** is a short on-screen note associated with the object to which you are pointing. For examples of ScreenTips, see Figures 1-3 and 1-13 on pages PPT 7 and PPT 19.

Figure 1-9 illustrates the Standard, Formatting, and Drawing toolbars and describes the functions of the buttons. Each of the buttons and boxes will be explained in detail when they are used.

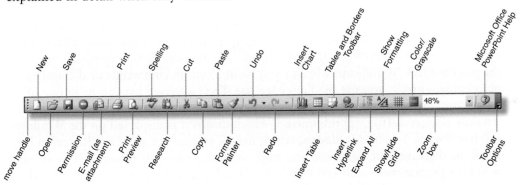

(a) Standard Toolbar

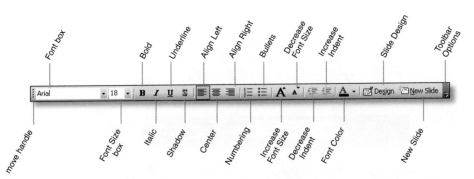

(b) Formatting Toolbar

FIGURE 1-9

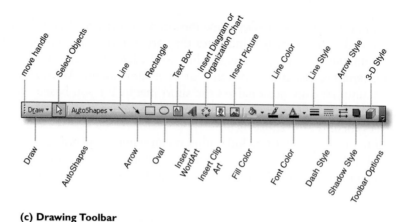

(c) Drawing Toolbar

FIGURE 1-9 (continued)

PowerPoint has several additional toolbars you can display by pointing to Toolbars on the View menu and then clicking the respective name on the Toolbars submenu. You also may display a toolbar by pointing to a toolbar and right-clicking to display a shortcut menu, which lists the available toolbars. A **shortcut menu** contains a list of commands or items that relate to the item to which you are pointing when you right-click.

Speech Recognition

With the **Office Speech Recognition software** installed and a microphone, you can speak the names of toolbar buttons, menus, menu commands, list items, alerts, and dialog box controls, such as OK and Cancel. You also can dictate words to fill the placeholders. To indicate whether you want to speak commands or dictate placeholder entries, you use the Language bar. The Language bar can be in one of four states: (1) **restored**, which means it is displayed somewhere in the PowerPoint window (Figure 1-10a); (2) **minimized**, which means it is displayed on the Windows taskbar (Figure 1-10b); (3) **hidden**, which means you do not see it on the screen but it will be displayed the next time you start your computer; (4) **closed**, which means it is hidden permanently until you enable it. If the Language bar is hidden or closed and you want it to display, then do the following:

1. Right-click an open area on the Windows taskbar at the bottom of the screen.
2. Point to Toolbars and then click Language bar on the Toolbars submenu.

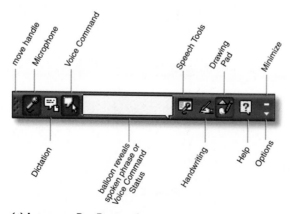

(a) Language Bar Restored

FIGURE 1-10

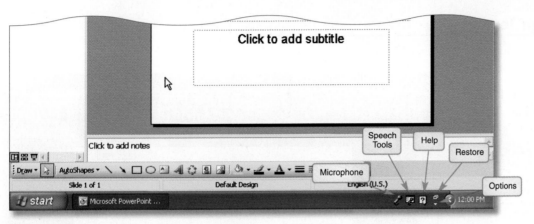

(b) Language Bar Minimized on Windows Taskbar

FIGURE 1-10 *(continued)*

If the Language bar command is dimmed on the Toolbars submenu or if the Speech command is dimmed on the Tools menu, the Office Speech Recognition software is not installed.

In this book, the Language bar does not appear in the figures. If you want to close the Language bar so that your screen is identical to what you see in the book, right-click the Language bar and then click Close the Language bar on the shortcut menu.

Additional information about the speech recognition capabilities of PowerPoint is available in Appendix B.

Choosing a Design Template

A **design template** provides consistency in design and color throughout the entire presentation. It determines the color scheme, font and font size, and layout of a presentation. PowerPoint has three Slide Design task panes that allow you to choose and change the appearance of slides in your presentation. The **Slide Design task pane** shows a variety of styles. You can alter the colors used in the design templates by using the **Slide Design – Color Schemes task pane**. In addition, you can animate elements of your presentation by using the **Slide Design – Animation Schemes task pane**.

In this project, you will select a particular design template by using the Slide Design task pane. The top section of the task pane, labeled Used in This Presentation, shows the template currently used in the slide show. PowerPoint uses the **Default Design** template until you select a different style. When you place your mouse over a template, the name of the template appears. Once a PowerPoint slide show has been created on the computer, the next section of the task pane displayed is the Recently Used templates. This area shows the four templates you have used in your newest slide shows. The Available For Use area shows additional templates. The templates are displayed in alphabetical order in the two columns.

You want to change the template for this presentation from the Default Design to Profile. The steps on the next page apply the Profile design template.

To Choose a Design Template

1

• **Point to the Slide Design button on the Formatting toolbar (Figure 1-11).**

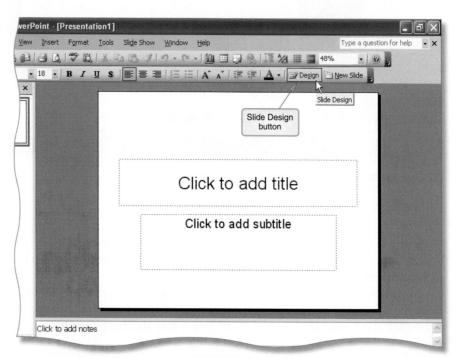

FIGURE 1-11

2

• **Click the Slide Design button and then point to the down scroll arrow in the Apply a design template list.**

The Slide Design task pane appears (Figure 1-12). The Apply a design template list shows thumbnail views of numerous design templates. Your list may look different depending on your computer. The Default Design template is highlighted in the Used in This Presentation area. Other templates display in the Available For Use area and possibly in the Recently Used area. The Close button in the Slide Design task pane can be used to close the task pane if you do not want to apply a new template.

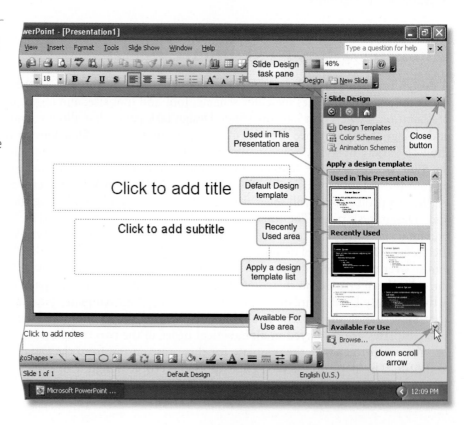

FIGURE 1-12

3

• **Click the down scroll arrow to scroll through the list of design templates until Profile appears in the Available For Use area. Point to the Profile template.**

The Profile template is selected, as indicated by the blue box around the template and the arrow button on the right side (Figure 1-13). PowerPoint provides 45 templates in the Available For Use area. Additional templates are available on the Microsoft Office Online Web site. A ScreenTip shows the template's name. Your system may display the ScreenTip, Profile.pot, which indicates the design template's file extension (.pot).

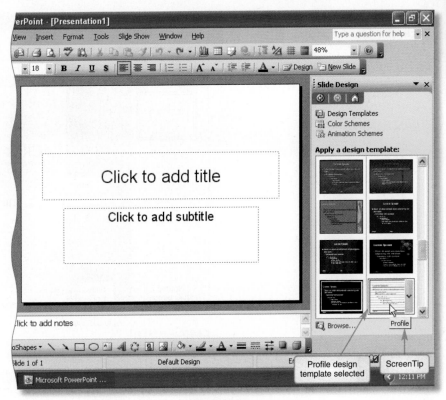

FIGURE 1-13

4

• **Click Profile.**

• **Point to the Close button in the Slide Design task pane.**

The template is applied to Slide 1, as shown in the slide pane and Slides tab (Figure 1-14).

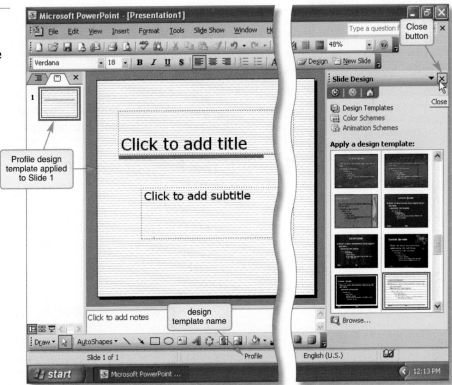

FIGURE 1-14

5

• **Click the Close button.**

Slide 1 is displayed in normal view with the Profile design template (Figure 1-15).

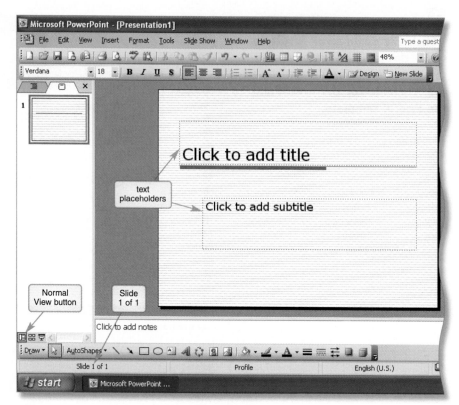

FIGURE 1-15

Creating a Title Slide

With the exception of a blank slide, PowerPoint assumes every new slide has a title. To make creating a presentation easier, any text you type after a new slide appears becomes title text in the title text placeholder.

Entering the Presentation Title

The presentation title for Project 1 is Strategies for College Success. To enter text in your slide, you type on the keyboard or speak into the microphone. As you begin entering text in the title text placeholder, the title text is displayed immediately in the Slide 1 thumbnail in the Slides tab. The following steps create the title slide for this presentation.

To Enter the Presentation Title

1

• **Click the label, Click to add title, located inside the title text placeholder.**

*The insertion point is in the title text placeholder (Figure 1-16). The **insertion point** is a blinking vertical line (|), which indicates where the next character will display. The mouse pointer changes to an I-beam. A **selection rectangle** appears around the title text placeholder. The placeholder is selected as indicated by the border and sizing handles displaying on the edges.*

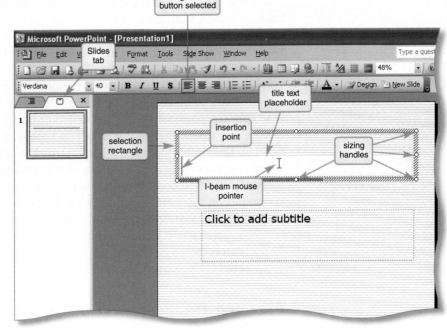

FIGURE 1-16

2

• **Type** Strategies for College Success **in the title text placeholder. Do not press the ENTER key.**

The title text, Strategies for College Success, appears on two lines in the title text placeholder and in the Slides tab (Figure 1-17). The insertion point appears after the final letter s in Success. The title text is displayed aligned left in the placeholder with the default text attributes of the Verdana font and font size 40.

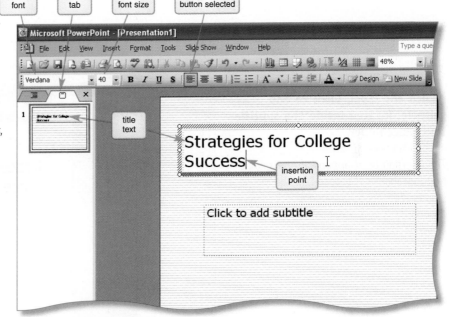

FIGURE 1-17

Other Ways

1. In Dictation mode, say "Strategies for College Success"

PowerPoint **line wraps** text that exceeds the width of the placeholder. One of PowerPoint's features is **text AutoFit**. If you are creating a slide and need to squeeze an extra line in the text placeholder, PowerPoint will prompt you to resize the existing text in the placeholder so the spillover text will fit on the slide.

Correcting a Mistake When Typing

If you type the wrong letter, press the BACKSPACE key to erase all the characters back to and including the one that is incorrect. If you mistakenly press the ENTER key after typing the title and the insertion point is on the new line, simply press the BACKSPACE key to return the insertion point to the right of the letter s in the word Success.

When you install PowerPoint, the default setting allows you to reverse up to the last 20 changes by clicking the Undo button on the Standard toolbar. The ScreenTip that appears when you point to the Undo button changes to indicate the type of change just made. For example, if you type text in the title text placeholder and then point to the Undo button, the ScreenTip that appears is Undo Typing. For clarity, when referencing the Undo button in this project, the name displaying in the ScreenTip is referenced. Another way to reverse changes is to click the Undo command on the Edit menu. As with the Undo button, the Undo command reflects the last type of change made to the presentation.

You can reapply a change that you reversed with the Undo button by clicking the Redo button on the Standard toolbar. Clicking the Redo button reverses the last undo action. The ScreenTip name reflects the type of reversal last performed.

Entering the Presentation Subtitle

The next step in creating the title slide is to enter the subtitle text into the subtitle text placeholder. Complete the following steps to enter the presentation subtitle.

To Enter the Presentation Subtitle

1

• **Click the label, Click to add subtitle, located inside the subtitle text placeholder.**

The insertion point appears in the subtitle text placeholder (Figure 1-18). The mouse pointer changes to an I-beam, indicating the mouse is in a text placeholder. The selection rectangle indicates the placeholder is selected.

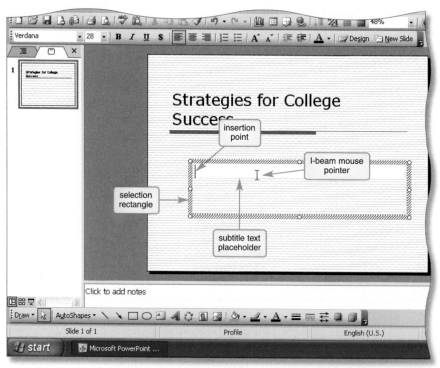

FIGURE 1-18

2

• **Type** Presented by **and then press the ENTER key.**

• **Type** Lakemore Academic Skills Center **but do not press the ENTER key.**

The subtitle text appears in the subtitle text placeholder and the Slides tab (Figure 1-19). The insertion point appears after the letter r in Center. A red wavy line appears below the word, Lakemore, to indicate a possible spelling error.

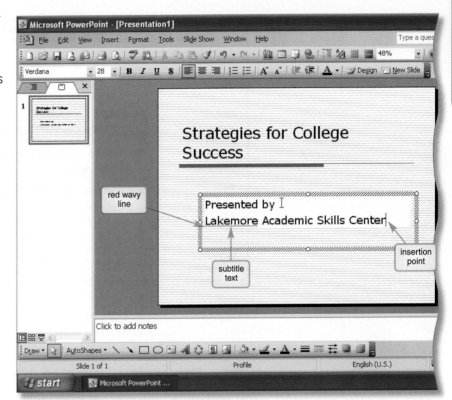

FIGURE 1-19

After pressing the ENTER key in Step 2, PowerPoint created a new line, which is the second paragraph in the placeholder. A **paragraph** is a segment of text with the same format that begins when you press the ENTER key and ends when you press the ENTER key again.

Text Attributes

This presentation uses the Profile design template. Each design template has its own text attributes. A **text attribute** is a characteristic of the text, such as font, font size, font style, or text color. You can adjust text attributes any time before, during, or after you type the text. Recall that a design template determines the color scheme, font and font size, and layout of a presentation. Most of the time, you use the design template's text attributes and color scheme. Occasionally, you may want to change the way a presentation looks, however, and still keep a particular design template. PowerPoint gives you that flexibility. You can use the design template and change the font and the font's color, effects, size, and style. Text may have one or more font styles and effects simultaneously. Table 1-2 on the next page explains the different text attributes available in PowerPoint.

Table 1-2	Design Template Text Attributes
ATTRIBUTE	**DESCRIPTION**
Color	Defines the color of text. Printing text in color requires a color printer or plotter.
Effects	Effects include underline, shadow, emboss, superscript, and subscript. Effects can be applied to most fonts.
Font	Defines the appearance and shape of letters, numbers, and special characters.
Size	Specifies the height of characters on the screen. Character size is gauged by a measurement system called points. A single point is about 1/72 of an inch in height. Thus, a character with a point size of 18 is about 18/72 (or 1/4) of an inch in height.
Style	Font styles include regular, bold, italic, and bold italic.

The next two sections explain how to change the font size and font style attributes.

Changing the Style of Text to Italic

Text font styles include plain, italic, bold, shadowed, and underlined. PowerPoint allows you to use one or more text font styles in a presentation. The following steps add emphasis to the first line of the subtitle text by changing regular text to italic text.

To Change the Text Font Style to Italic

1

• **Triple-click the paragraph, Presented by, in the subtitle text placeholder, and then point to the Italic button on the Formatting toolbar.**

The paragraph, Presented by, is highlighted (Figure 1-20). The Italic button is surrounded by a blue box. You select an entire paragraph quickly by triple-clicking any text within the paragraph.

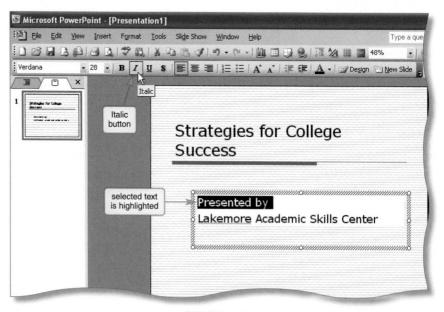

FIGURE 1-20

2

• **Click the Italic button.**

The text is italicized on the slide and the slide thumbnail (Figure 1-21).

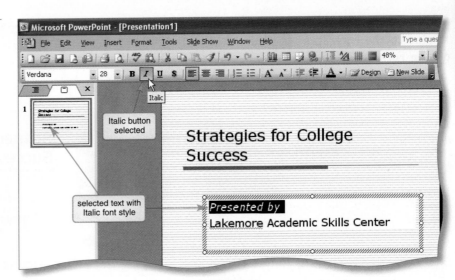

FIGURE 1-21

Other Ways

1. Right-click selected text, click Font on shortcut menu, click Italic in Font style list
2. On Format menu click Font, click Italic in Font style list
3. Press CTRL+I
4. In Voice Command mode, say "Italic"

To remove the italic style from text, select the italicized text and then click the Italic button. As a result, the Italic button is not selected, and the text does not have the italic font style.

Changing the Font Size

The Profile design template default font size is 40 point for title text and 28 point for body text. A point is 1/72 of an inch in height. Thus, a character with a point size of 40 is 40/72 (or 5/9) of an inch in height. Slide 1 requires you to increase the font size for the paragraph, Lakemore Academic Skills Center. The following steps illustrate how to increase the font size.

To Increase Font Size

1

• **Position the mouse pointer in the paragraph, Lakemore Academic Skills Center, and then triple-click.**

PowerPoint selects the entire paragraph (Figure 1-22).

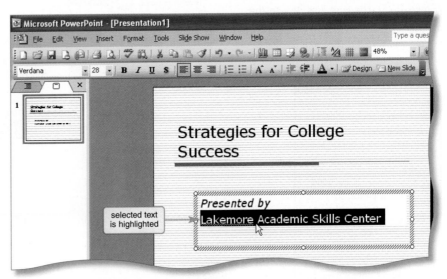

FIGURE 1-22

2

• **Point to the Font Size box arrow on the Formatting toolbar.**

*The ScreenTip shows the words, Font Size (Figure 1-23). The **Font Size box** is surrounded by a box and indicates that the subtitle text is 28 point.*

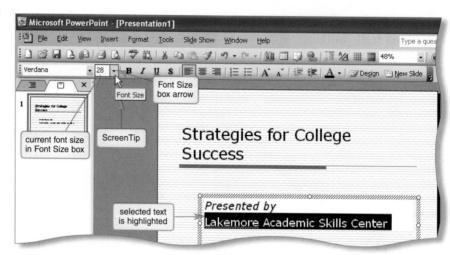

FIGURE 1-23

3

• **Click the Font Size box arrow, click the Font Size box scroll bar, and then point to 32 in the Font Size list.**

When you click the Font Size box, a list of available font sizes is displayed in the Font Size list (Figure 1-24). The font sizes displayed depend on the current font, which is Verdana. Font size 32 is highlighted.

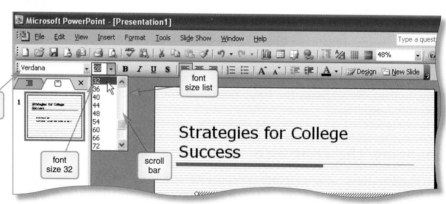

FIGURE 1-24

4

• **Click 32.**

The font size of the subtitle text, Lakemore Academic Skills Center, increases to 32 point (Figure 1-25). The Font Size box on the Formatting toolbar shows 32, indicating the selected text has a font size of 32.

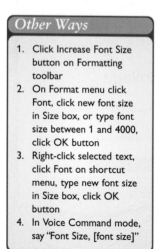

Other Ways

1. Click Increase Font Size button on Formatting toolbar
2. On Format menu click Font, click new font size in Size box, or type font size between 1 and 4000, click OK button
3. Right-click selected text, click Font on shortcut menu, type new font size in Size box, click OK button
4. In Voice Command mode, say "Font Size, [font size]"

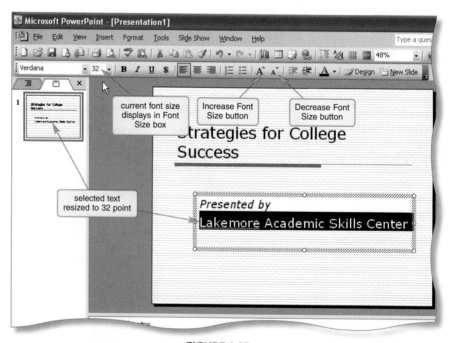

FIGURE 1-25

The Increase Font Size button on the Formatting toolbar (Figure 1-25) increases the font size in preset increments each time you click the button. If you need to decrease the font size, click the Font Size box arrow and then select a size smaller than 32. The Decrease Font Size button on the Formatting toolbar (Figure 1-25) also decreases the font size in preset increments each time you click the button.

Saving the Presentation on a Floppy Disk

While you are building a presentation, the computer stores it in memory. It is important to save the presentation frequently because the presentation will be lost if the computer is turned off or you lose electrical power. Another reason to save your work is that if you run out of lab time before completing your project, you may finish the project later without starting over. Therefore, always save any presentation you will use later on a floppy disk or hard disk. A saved presentation is referred to as a **file**. Before you continue with Project 1, save the work completed thus far. The following steps illustrate how to save a presentation on a floppy disk in drive A using the Save button on the Standard toolbar.

To Save a Presentation on a Floppy Disk

1

• **With a formatted floppy disk in drive A, click the Save button on the Standard toolbar.**

The Save As dialog box is displayed (Figure 1-26). The default folder, My Documents, appears in the Save in box. Strategies for College Success appears highlighted in the File name text box because PowerPoint uses the words in the title text placeholder as the default file name. Presentation appears in the Save as type box. The buttons on the top and on the side are used to select folders and change the appearance of file names and other information.

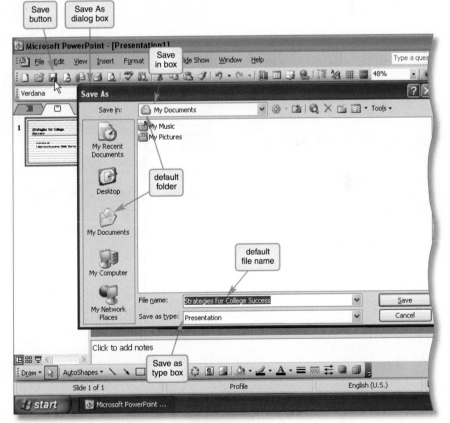

FIGURE 1-26

2

• **Type** College Success **in the File name text box. Do not press the ENTER key after typing the file name.**

• **Click the Save in box arrow.**

The name, College Success, appears in the File name text box (Figure 1-27). A file name can be up to 255 characters and can include spaces. The Save in list shows a list of locations in which to save a presentation. Your list may look different depending on the configuration of your system. Clicking the Cancel button closes the Save As dialog box.

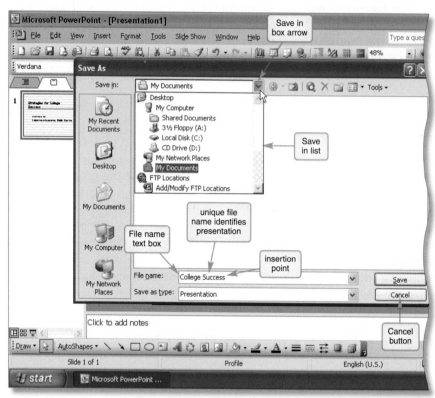

FIGURE 1-27

3

• **Click 3½ Floppy (A:) in the Save in list.**

Drive A becomes the selected drive (Figure 1-28).

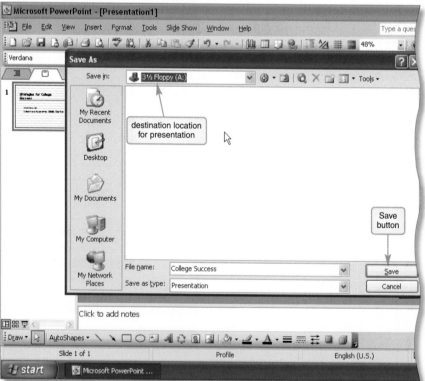

FIGURE 1-28

4

• **Click the Save button in the Save As dialog box.**

PowerPoint saves the presentation on the floppy disk in drive A. The title bar shows the file name used to save the presentation, College Success (Figure 1-29).

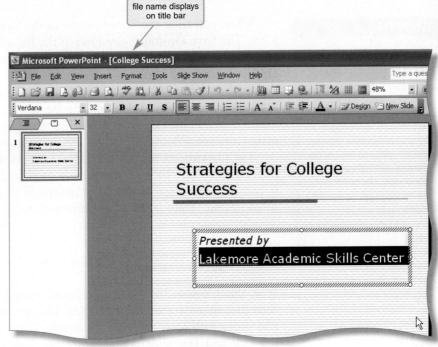

file name displays on title bar

FIGURE 1-29

PowerPoint automatically appends the extension .ppt to the file name, College Success. The **.ppt** extension stands for **P**ower**P**oin**t**. Although the slide show, College Success, is saved on a floppy disk, it also remains in memory and is displayed on the screen.

It is a good practice to save periodically while you are working on a project. By doing so, you protect yourself from losing all the work you have done since the last time you saved.

The seven buttons at the top and to the right in the Save As dialog box in Figure 1-28 and their functions are summarized in Table 1-3.

Other Ways

1. On File menu click Save As, type file name, select drive or folder, click Save button
2. On File menu click Save As, click My Computer button, select drive or folder, click Save button
3. Press CTRL+S or press SHIFT+F12, type file name, select drive or folder, click OK button
4. In Voice Command mode, say "File, Save As, [type desired file name], Save"

Table 1-3   Save As Dialog Box Toolbar Buttons

BUTTON	BUTTON NAME	FUNCTION
	Default File Location	Displays contents of default file location
	Up One Level	Displays contents of folder one level up from current folder
	Search the Web	Starts browser and displays search engine
	Delete	Deletes selected file or folder
	Create New Folder	Creates new folder
	Views	Changes view of files and folders
Tools ▾	Tools	Lists commands to print or modify file names and folders

More About

Passwords

The most common word
used for a password is the
word, password. When
choosing a password for your
files, experts recommend
using a combination of letters
and numbers and making the
word at least eight characters.
Avoid using your name and
the names of family members
or pets.

When you click the Tools button in the Save As dialog box, PowerPoint displays
a list. The Save Options command in the list allows you to save the presentation
automatically at a specified time interval and to reduce the file size. The Security
Options command allows you to modify the security level for opening files that may
contain harmful computer viruses and to assign a password to limit access to the file.
A password is case-sensitive and can be up to 15 characters long. **Case-sensitive**
means PowerPoint can differentiate between uppercase and lowercase letters. If you
assign a password and then forget the password, you cannot access the file.

The file buttons on the left of the Save As dialog box in Figure 1-28 on page
PPT 28 allow you to select frequently used folders. The My Recent Documents
button displays a list of shortcuts (pointers) to the most recently used files in a folder
titled Recent. You cannot save presentations to the Recent folder.

Adding a New Slide to a Presentation

With the title slide for the presentation created, the next step is to add the first text
slide immediately after the title slide. Usually, when you create a presentation, you
add slides with text, graphics, or charts. When you add a new slide, PowerPoint uses
the Title and Text slide layout. Some placeholders allow you to double-click the
placeholder and then access other objects, such as media clips, charts, diagrams, and
organization charts.

The following steps add a new Text slide layout with a bulleted list. The default
PowerPoint setting will display the Slide Layout task pane each time a new slide is
added. Your system may not display this task pane if the setting has been changed.

To Add a New Text Slide with a Bulleted List

1

• **Click the New Slide button on the
Formatting toolbar.**

*The Slide Layout task pane opens. The Title
and Text slide layout is selected. Slide 2 of 2
appears on the status bar (Figure 1-30).*

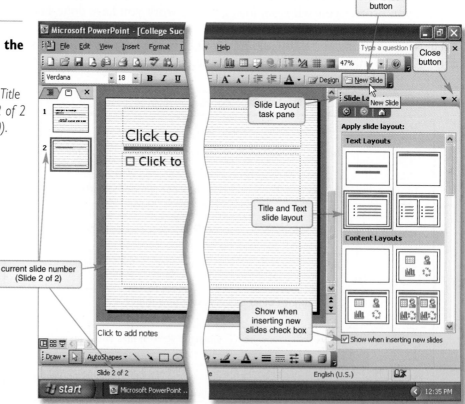

FIGURE 1-30

2

• **If necessary, click the Show when inserting new slides check box to remove the check mark, and then click the Close button on the Slide Layout task pane.**

Slide 2 appears in both the slide pane and Slides tab retaining the attributes of the Profile design template (Figure 1-31). The vertical scroll bar appears in the slide pane. The bullet appears as an outline square.

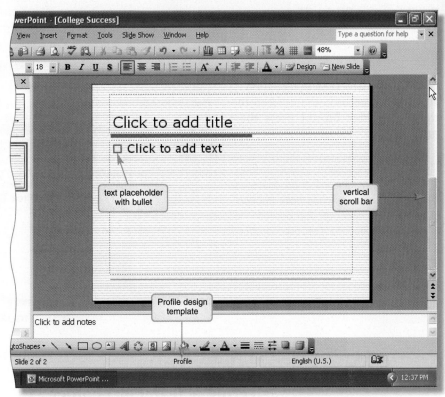

FIGURE 1-31

Slide 2 appears with a title text placeholder and a text placeholder with a bullet. You can change the layout for a slide at any time during the creation of a presentation by clicking Format on the menu bar and then clicking Slide Layout. You also can click View on the menu bar and then click Task Pane. You then can double-click the slide layout of your choice from the Slide Layout task pane.

Other Ways

1. On Insert menu click New Slide
2. Press CTRL+M
3. In Voice Command mode, say "New Slide"

Creating a Text Slide with a Single-Level Bulleted List

The information in the Slide 2 text placeholder is presented in a bulleted list. All the bullets appear on one level. A **level** is a position within a structure, such as an outline, that indicates the magnitude of importance. PowerPoint allows for five paragraph levels. Each paragraph level has an associated bullet. The bullet font is dependent on the design template.

Entering a Slide Title

PowerPoint assumes every new slide has a title. The title for Slide 2 is Get Organized. The step on the next page shows how to enter this title.

More About

Deleting Bullets

If you do not want bullets to display on a particular paragraph, select the paragraph and then click the Bullets button on the Formatting toolbar.

To Enter a Slide Title

1

• **Click the title text placeholder and then type** Get Organized **in the placeholder. Do not press the ENTER key.**

The title, Get Organized, appears in the title text placeholder and in the Slides tab (Figure 1-32). The insertion point appears after the d in Organized. The selection rectangle indicates the title text placeholder is selected.

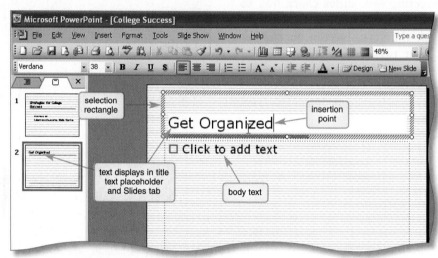

FIGURE 1-32

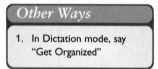

Other Ways

1. In Dictation mode, say "Get Organized"

Selecting a Text Placeholder

Before you can type text into the text placeholder, you first must select it. The following step selects the text placeholder on Slide 2.

To Select a Text Placeholder

1

• **Click the bulleted paragraph labeled, Click to add text.**

The insertion point appears immediately to the right of the bullet on Slide 2 (Figure 1-33). The mouse pointer may change shape if you move it away from the bullet. The selection rectangle indicates the text placeholder is selected.

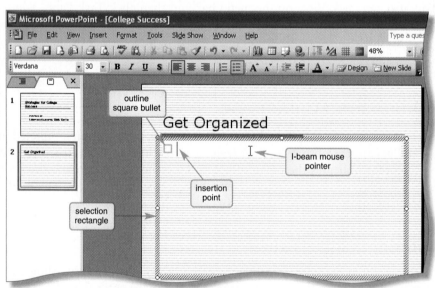

FIGURE 1-33

Other Ways

1. Press CTRL+ENTER

Typing a Single-Level Bulleted List

As discussed previously, a bulleted list is a list of paragraphs, each of which is preceded by a bullet. A paragraph is a segment of text ended by pressing the ENTER key. The next step is to type the single-level bulleted list, which consists of three entries (Figure 1-1b on page PPT 5). The following steps illustrate how to type a single-level bulleted list.

To Type a Single-Level Bulleted List

1

• **Type** Time management skills help balance academic, work, and social events **and then press the ENTER key.**

The paragraph, Time management skills help balance academic, work, and social events, appears (Figure 1-34). The font size is 30. The insertion point appears after the second bullet. When you press the ENTER key, PowerPoint ends one paragraph and begins a new paragraph. With the Title and Text slide layout, PowerPoint places an outline square bullet in front of the new paragraph.

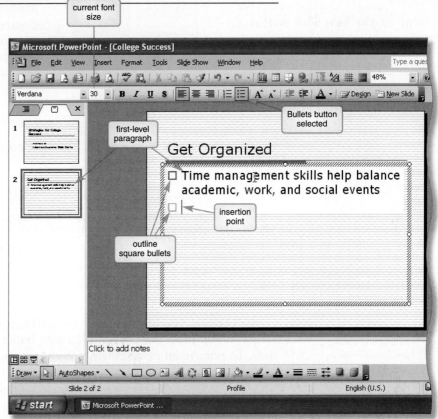

FIGURE 1-34

2

• **Type** Create a schedule each week that accounts for all activities **and then press the ENTER key.**

• **Type** Plan two hours of study time for each one hour of class time **but do not press the ENTER key.**

• **Point to the New Slide button on the Formatting toolbar.**

The insertion point is displayed after the e in time (Figure 1-35). Three new first-level paragraphs are displayed with outline square bullets in both the text placeholder and the Slides tab. When you press the ENTER key, PowerPoint adds a new paragraph at the same level as the previous paragraph.

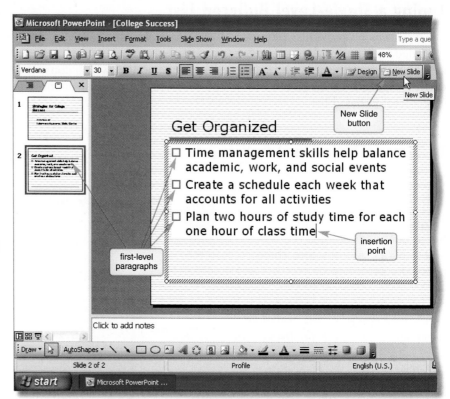

FIGURE 1-35

Notice that you did not press the ENTER key after typing the last paragraph in Step 2. If you press the ENTER key, a new bullet appears after the last entry on this slide. To remove an extra bullet, press the BACKSPACE key.

Creating a Text Slide with a Multi-Level Bulleted List

Slides 3 and 4 in Figure 1-1 on page PPT 5 contain more than one level of bulleted text. A slide that consists of more than one level of bulleted text is called a **multi-level bulleted list slide**. Beginning with the second level, each paragraph indents to the right of the preceding level and is pushed down to a lower level. For example, if you increase the indent of a first-level paragraph, it becomes a second-level paragraph. This lower-level paragraph is a subset of the higher-level paragraph. It usually contains information that supports the topic in the paragraph immediately above it. You increase the indent of a paragraph by clicking the Increase Indent button on the Formatting toolbar.

When you want to raise a paragraph from a lower level to a higher level, you click the Decrease Indent button on the Formatting toolbar.

Creating a text slide with a multi-level bulleted list requires several steps. Initially, you enter a slide title in the title text placeholder. Next, you select the body text placeholder. Then, you type the text for the multi-level bulleted list, increasing and decreasing the indents as needed. The next several sections explain how to add a slide with a multi-level bulleted list.

Adding New Slides and Entering Slide Titles

When you add a new slide to a presentation, PowerPoint keeps the same layout used on the previous slide. PowerPoint assumes every new slide has a title. The title for Slide 3 is Listen Actively. The following steps show how to add a new slide (Slide 3) and enter a title.

To Add a New Slide and Enter a Slide Title

1

• **Click the New Slide button.**

Slide 3 of 3 appears in the slide pane and Slides tab (Figure 1-36).

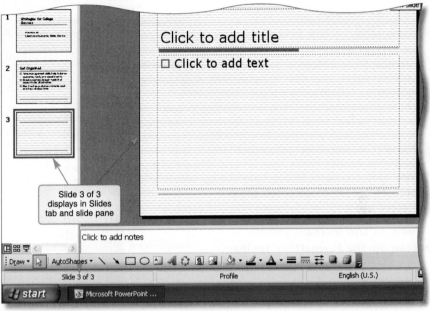

FIGURE 1-36

2

• **Type** Listen Actively **in the title text placeholder. Do not press the ENTER key.**

Slide 3 shows the Title and Text slide layout with the title, Listen Actively, in the title text placeholder and in the Slides tab (Figure 1-37). The insertion point appears after the y in Actively.

FIGURE 1-37

Slide 3 is added to the presentation with the desired title.

Other Ways

1. Press SHIFT+CTRL+M
2. In Dictation mode, say "New Slide, Listen Actively"

Typing a Multi-Level Bulleted List

The next step is to select the body text placeholder and then type the multi-level bulleted list, which consists of six entries (Figure 1-1c on page PPT 5). The following steps show how to create a list consisting of three levels.

To Type a Multi-Level Bulleted List

• **Click the bulleted paragraph labeled, Click to add text.**

The insertion point appears immediately to the right of the bullet on Slide 3. The mouse pointer may change shape if you move it away from the bullet.

• **Type** Sit in the front row to focus attention **and then press the ENTER key.**
• **Point to the Increase Indent button on the Formatting toolbar.**

The paragraph, Sit in the front row to focus attention, appears (Figure 1-38). The font size is 30. The insertion point appears to the right of the second bullet.

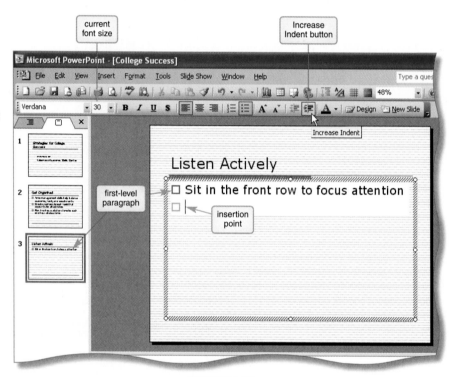

FIGURE 1-38

• **Click the Increase Indent button.**

The second paragraph indents below the first and becomes a second-level paragraph (Figure 1-39). The bullet to the left of the second paragraph changes from an outline square to a solid square, and the font size for the paragraph now is 26. The insertion point appears to the right of the solid square.

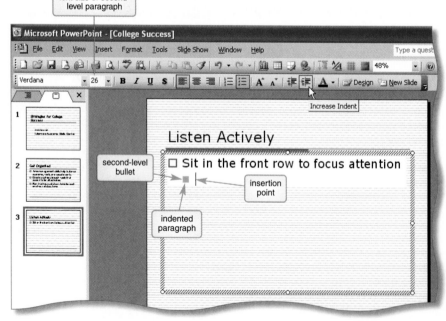

FIGURE 1-39

4

• **Type** Do not tolerate distractions **and then press the ENTER key.**

• **Point to the Decrease Indent button on the Formatting toolbar.**

The first second-level paragraph appears with a solid orange square bullet in both the slide pane and the Slides tab (Figure 1-40). When you press the ENTER key, PowerPoint adds a new paragraph at the same level as the previous paragraph.

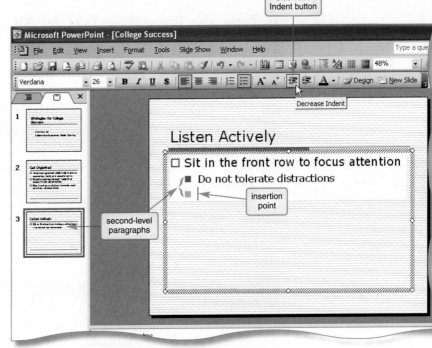

FIGURE 1-40

5

• **Click the Decrease Indent button.**

The second-level paragraph becomes a first-level paragraph (Figure 1-41). The bullet of the new paragraph changes from a solid orange square to an outline square, and the font size for the paragraph is 30. The insertion point appears to the right of the outline square bullet.

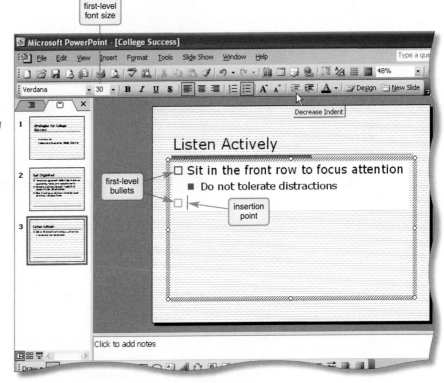

FIGURE 1-41

The steps on the next page complete the text for Slide 3.

Other Ways

1. In Dictation mode, say, "Sit in the front row to focus attention, New Line, Increase Indent, Do not tolerate distractions, New Line, Decrease Indent"

To Type the Remaining Text for Slide 3

1 **Type** `Make mental summaries of material` **and then press the ENTER key.**

2 **Type** `Be prepared for class` **and then press the ENTER key.**

3 **Click the Increase Indent button on the Formatting toolbar.**

4 **Type** `Review notes from books, previous class` **and then press the ENTER key.**

5 **Type** `Preview material to be covered that day` **but do not press the ENTER key.**

Slide 3 is displayed as shown in Figure 1-42. The insertion point appears after the y in day.

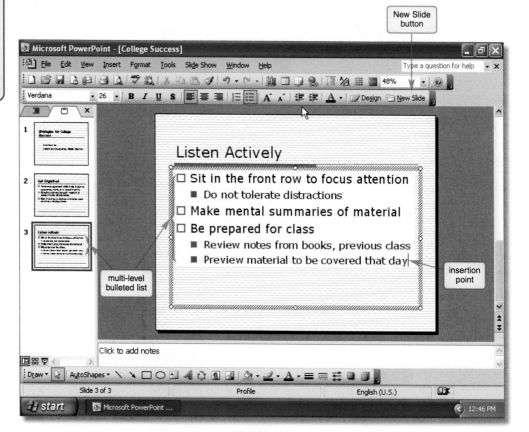

FIGURE 1-42

In Step 4 above, you did not press the ENTER key after typing the last paragraph. If you press the ENTER key, a new bullet appears after the last entry on this slide. To remove an extra bullet, press the BACKSPACE key.

Slide 4 is the last slide in this presentation. It also is a multi-level bulleted list and has three levels. The following steps create Slide 4.

To Create Slide 4

1 Click the **New Slide button on the Formatting toolbar.**

2 Type Excel on Exams **in the title text placeholder.**

3 Press CTRL+ENTER **to move the insertion point to the body text placeholder.**

4 Type Review test material throughout week **and then press the ENTER key.**

5 Click the **Increase Indent button on the Formatting toolbar. Type** Cramming before exams is ineffective **and then press the ENTER key.**

The title and first two levels of bullets are added to Slide 4 (Figure 1-43).

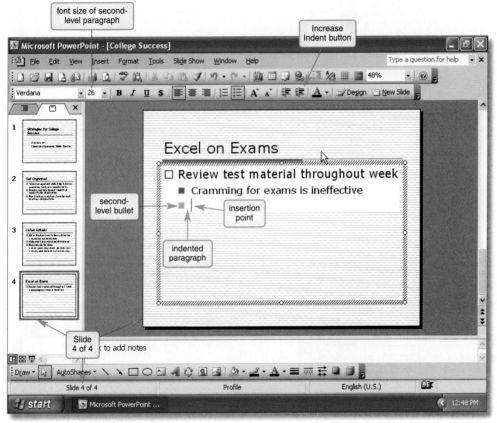

FIGURE 1-43

Other Ways

1. In Dictation mode, say "New Slide, Excel on Exams, [type CTRL+ENTER], Review test material throughout week, New Line, Increase Indent, Cramming before exams is ineffective"

Creating a Third-Level Paragraph

The next line in Slide 4 is indented an additional level, to the third level. The steps on the next page create an additional level.

To Create a Third-Level Paragraph

1

• **Click the Increase Indent button on the Formatting toolbar.**

The second-level paragraph becomes a third-level paragraph (Figure 1-44). The bullet to the left of the new paragraph changes from a solid square to an outline square, and the font size for the paragraph is 23. The insertion point appears after the outline square bullet.

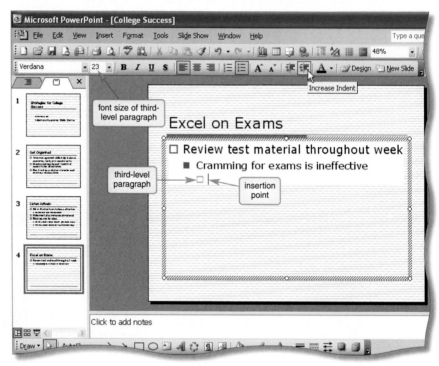

FIGURE 1-44

2

• **Type** Facts remain only in short-term memory **and then press the ENTER key.**

• **Point to the Decrease Indent button on the Formatting toolbar.**

The first third-level paragraph, Facts remain only in short-term memory, is displayed with the bullet for a second third-level paragraph (Figure 1-45).

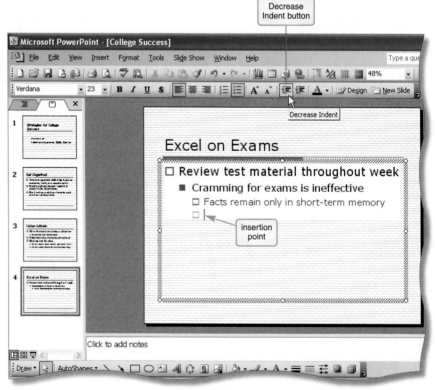

FIGURE 1-45

3

• **Click the Decrease Indent button two times.**

The insertion point appears at the first level (Figure 1-46).

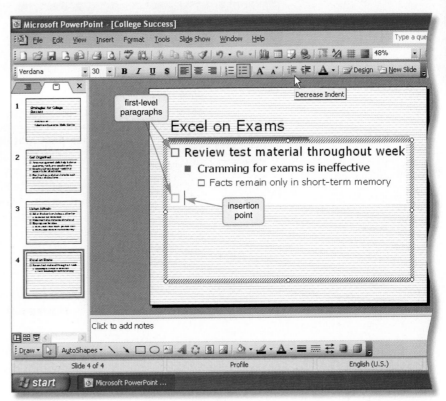

FIGURE 1-46

The title text and three levels of paragraphs discussing preparing for exams are complete. The next three paragraphs concern strategies for taking tests. As an alternative to clicking the Increase Indent button, you can press the TAB key. Likewise, instead of clicking the Decrease Indent button, you can press the SHIFT+TAB keys. The following steps illustrate how to type the remaining text for Slide 4.

To Type the Remaining Text for Slide 4

1 **Type** Review entire test before answering **and then press the ENTER key.**

2 **Press the TAB key to increase the indent to the second level.**

3 **Type** Start with the material you know **and then press the ENTER key.**

4 **Press the TAB key to increase the indent to the third level.**

5 **Type** Think positively and stay focused **but do not press the ENTER key.**

The Slide 4 title text and body text are displayed in the slide pane and Slides tabs (Figure 1-47 on the next page). The insertion point appears after the d in focused.

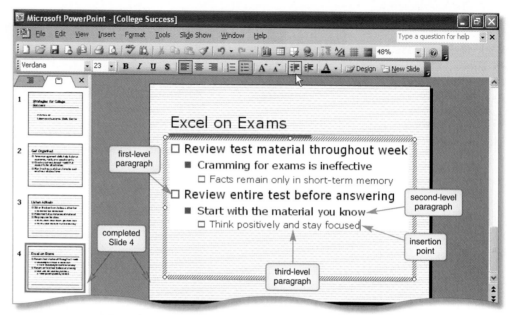

FIGURE 1-47

All the slides are created for the College Success slide show. This presentation consists of a title slide, one text slide with a single-level bulleted list, and two text slides with a multi-level bulleted list.

Ending a Slide Show with a Black Slide

After the last slide in the slide show appears, the default PowerPoint setting is to end the presentation with a black slide. This black slide appears only when the slide show is running and concludes the slide show gracefully so your audience never sees the PowerPoint window. A **black slide** ends all slide shows unless the option setting is deselected. The following steps verify that the End with black slide option is activated.

To End a Slide Show with a Black Slide

1

• **Click Tools on the menu bar and then point to Options (Figure 1-48).**

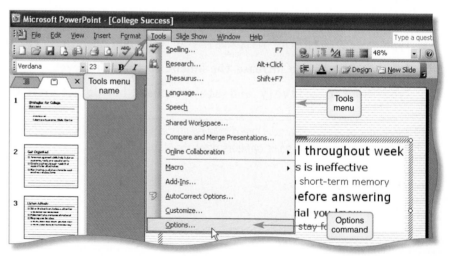

FIGURE 1-48

2

- **Click Options.**
- **If necessary, click the View tab when the Options dialog box appears.**
- **Verify that the End with black slide check box is selected.**
- **If a check mark does not show, click End with black slide.**
- **Point to the OK button.**

The Options dialog box appears (Figure 1-49). The View sheet contains settings for the overall PowerPoint display and for a particular slide show.

3

- **Click the OK button.**

The End with black slide option will cause the slide show to end with a black slide until it is deselected.

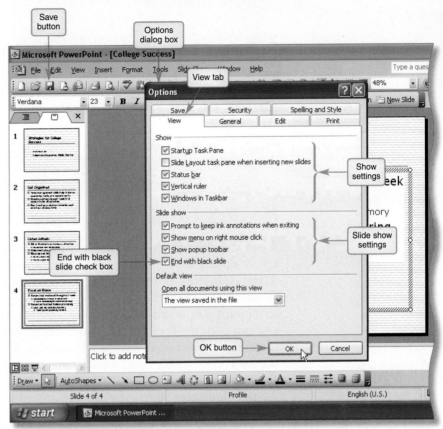

FIGURE 1-49

With all aspects of the presentation complete, it is important to save the additions and changes you have made to the College Success presentation.

Saving a Presentation with the Same File Name

Saving frequently cannot be overemphasized. When you first saved the presentation, you clicked the Save button on the Standard toolbar, and the Save dialog box appeared. When you want to save the changes made to the presentation after your last save, you again click the Save button. This time, however, the Save dialog box does not appear because PowerPoint updates the document called College Success.ppt on the floppy disk. The steps on the next page illustrate how to save the presentation again.

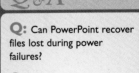
Q: Can PowerPoint recover files lost during power failures?

A: Yes. If PowerPoint's AutoRecover feature is turned on, files that were open when PowerPoint stopped responding may be displayed in the Document Recovery task pane. This task pane allows you to open the files, view the contents, and compare versions. You then can save the most complete version of your presentation.

To Save a Presentation with the Same File Name

1 Be certain your floppy disk is in drive A.

2 Click the Save button on the Standard toolbar.

PowerPoint overwrites the old College Success.ppt document on the floppy disk in drive A with the revised presentation document. Slide 4 is displayed in the PowerPoint window.

Moving to Another Slide in Normal View

When creating or editing a presentation in normal view, you often want to display a slide other than the current one. You can move to another slide using several methods. In the Outline tab, you can point to any of the text in a particular slide to display that slide in the slide pane, or you can drag the scroll box on the vertical scroll bar up or down to move through the text in the presentation. In the slide pane, you can click the Previous Slide or Next Slide button on the vertical scroll bar. Clicking the Next Slide button advances to the next slide in the presentation. Clicking the Previous Slide button backs up to the slide preceding the current slide. You also can drag the scroll box on the vertical scroll bar. When you drag the scroll box, the **slide indicator** shows the number and title of the slide you are about to display. Releasing the mouse button shows the slide.

A slide's **Zoom setting** affects the portion of the slide displaying in the slide pane. PowerPoint defaults to a setting of approximately 50 percent so the entire slide is displayed. This percentage depends on the size and type of your monitor. If you want to display a small portion of the current slide, you would zoom in by clicking the **Zoom box arrow** and then clicking the desired magnification. You can display the entire slide in the slide pane by clicking **Fit** in the Zoom list. The Zoom setting affects the action of the vertical and horizontal scroll bars. If Zoom is set so the entire slide is not visible in the slide pane, clicking the up scroll arrow on the vertical scroll bar shows the next portion of the slide, not the previous slide.

Using the Scroll Box on the Slide Pane to Move to Another Slide

Before continuing with Project 1, you want to display the title slide. The following steps show how to move from Slide 4 to Slide 1 using the scroll box on the slide pane vertical scroll bar.

To Use the Scroll Box on the Slide Pane to Move to Another Slide

1

• **Position the mouse pointer on the scroll box.**

• **Press and hold down the mouse button.**

Slide: 4 of 4 Excel on Exams appears in the slide indicator (Figure 1-50). When you click the scroll box, the Slide 4 thumbnail has no gray border in the Slides tab.

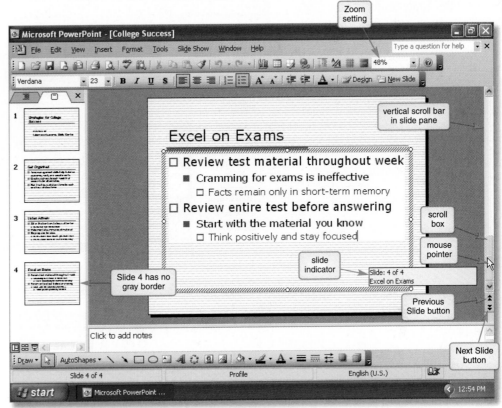

FIGURE 1-50

2

• **Drag the scroll box up the vertical scroll bar until Slide: 1 of 4 Strategies for College Success appears in the slide indicator.**

Slide: 1 of 4 Strategies for College Success appears in the slide indicator (Figure 1-51). Slide 4 still is displayed in the PowerPoint window.

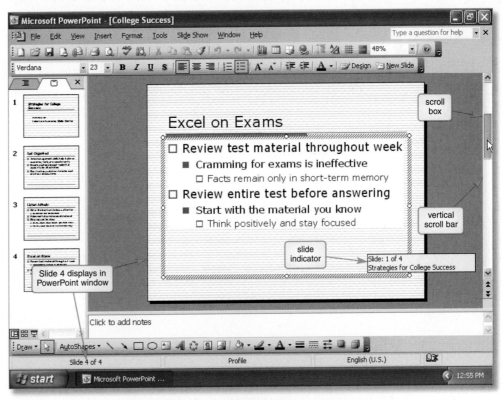

FIGURE 1-51

3

• **Release the mouse button.**

Slide 1, titled Strategies for College Success, appears in the PowerPoint window (Figure 1-52). The Slide 1 thumbnail has a gray border in the Slides tab, indicating it is selected.

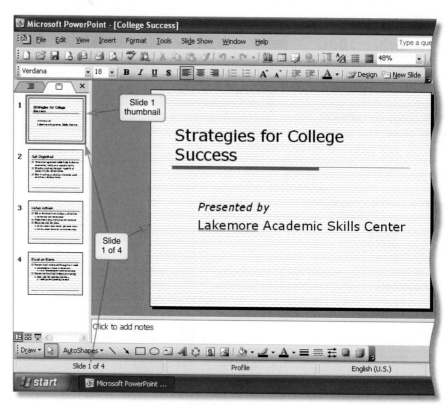

FIGURE 1-52

Viewing the Presentation in Slide Show View

The Slide Show button, located in the lower-left of the PowerPoint window above the status bar, allows you to show a presentation using a computer. The computer acts like a slide projector, displaying each slide on a full screen. The full-screen slide hides the toolbars, menus, and other PowerPoint window elements. When making a presentation, you use **slide show view**. You can start slide show view from normal view or slide sorter view.

Starting Slide Show View

Slide show view begins when you click the Slide Show button in the lower-left of the PowerPoint window above the status bar. PowerPoint then shows the current slide on the full screen without any of the PowerPoint window objects, such as the menu bar or toolbars. The following steps show how to start slide show view.

To Start Slide Show View

1

• **Point to the Slide Show button in the lower-left corner of the PowerPoint window above the status bar (Figure 1-53).**

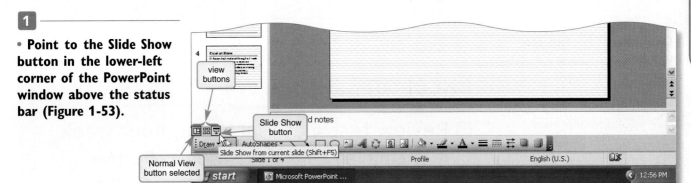

FIGURE 1-53

2

• **Click the Slide Show button.**

A starting slide show message may display momentarily, and then the title slide fills the screen (Figure 1-54). The PowerPoint window is hidden.

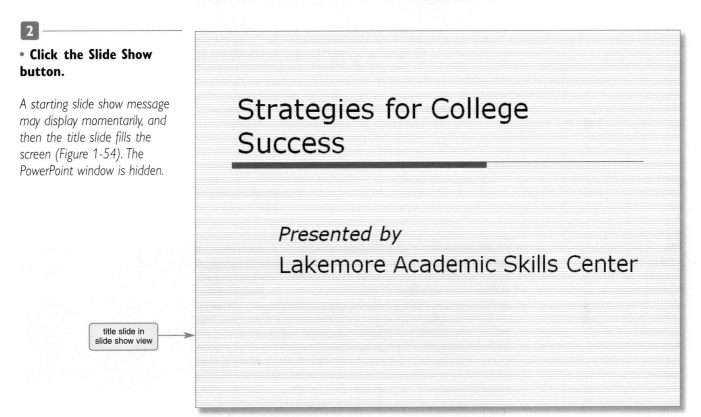

Strategies for College Success

Presented by
Lakemore Academic Skills Center

FIGURE 1-54

Other Ways

1. On View menu click Slide Show
2. Press F5
3. In Voice Command mode, say "View show"

Advancing Through a Slide Show Manually

After you begin slide show view, you can move forward or backward through the slides. PowerPoint allows you to advance through the slides manually or automatically. The steps on the next page illustrate how to move manually through the slides.

To Move Manually Through Slides in a Slide Show

1

• **Click each slide until the Excel on Exams slide (Slide 4) is displayed.**

Slide 4 is displayed (Figure 1-55). Each slide in the presentation shows on the screen, one slide at a time. Each time you click the mouse button, the next slide appears.

Slide 4 displays in slide show view

Excel on Exams

☐ Review test material throughout week
  ■ Cramming before exams is ineffective
    ☐ Facts remain only in short-term memory
☐ Review entire test before answering
  ■ Start with the material you know
    ☐ Think positively and stay focused

FIGURE 1-55

2

• **Click Slide 4.**

The black slide appears (Figure 1-56). The message at the top of the slide announces the end of the slide show. If you wanted to end the presentation at this point and return to normal view, you would click the black slide.

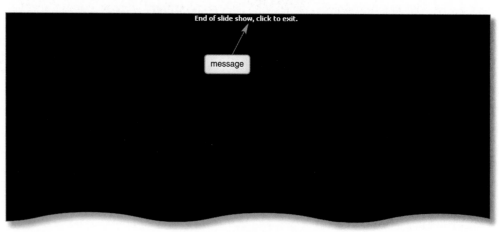

End of slide show, click to exit.

message

FIGURE 1-56

Using the Popup Menu to Go to a Specific Slide

Slide show view has a shortcut menu, called the Popup menu, that appears when you right-click a slide in slide show view. This menu contains commands to assist you during a slide show. For example, clicking the Next command moves to the next slide. Clicking the Previous command moves to the previous slide. Pointing to the Go to Slide command and then clicking the desired slide allows you to move to any slide in the presentation. The Go to Slide submenu contains a list of the slides in the presentation. You can go to the requested slide by clicking the name of that slide. The following steps illustrate how to go to the title slide (Slide 1) in the College Success presentation.

To Display the Popup Menu and Go to a Specific Slide

1

• **With the black slide displaying in slide show view, right-click the slide.**

• **Point to Go to Slide on the Popup menu, and then point to 1 Strategies for College Success in the Go to Slide submenu.**

The Popup menu appears on the black slide, and the Go to Slide submenu shows a list of slides in the presentation (Figure 1-57). Your screen may look different because the Popup menu appears near the location of the mouse pointer at the time you right-click.

2

• **Click 1 Strategies for College Success.**

The title slide, Strategies for College Success (shown in Figure 1-54 on page PPT 47), is displayed.

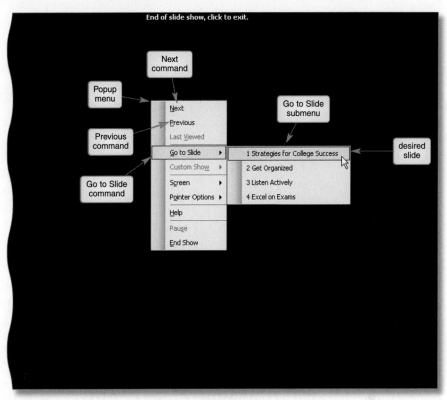

FIGURE 1-57

Additional Popup menu commands allow you to change the mouse pointer to a ballpoint or felt tip pen or highlighter that draws in various colors, make the screen black or white, create speaker notes, and end the slide show. Popup menu commands are discussed as they are used.

Using the Popup Menu to End a Slide Show

The End Show command on the Popup menu ends slide show view and returns to the same view as when you clicked the Slide Show button. The steps on the next page show how to end slide show view and return to normal view.

To Use the Popup Menu to End a Slide Show

1

• **Right-click the title slide and then point to End Show on the Popup menu.**

The Popup menu appears on Slide 1 (Figure 1-58).

2

• **Click End Show.**

• **If the Microsoft Office PowerPoint dialog box appears, click the Yes button.**

PowerPoint ends slide show view and returns to normal view (shown in Figure 1-59 below). Slide 1 is displayed because it is the last slide displayed in slide show view.

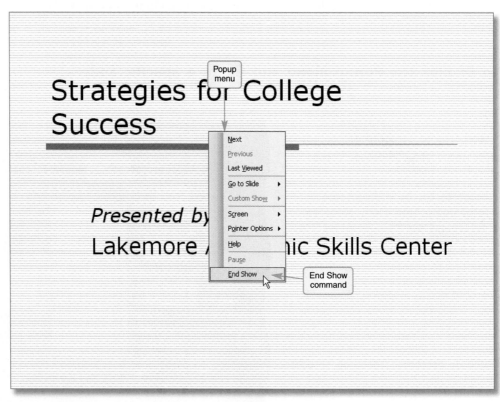

FIGURE 1-58

Quitting PowerPoint

The College Success presentation now is complete. When you quit PowerPoint, you are prompted to save any changes made to the presentation since the last save. The program then closes all PowerPoint windows, quits, and returns control to the desktop. The following steps quit PowerPoint.

To Quit PowerPoint

1

• **Point to the Close button on the PowerPoint title bar (Figure 1-59).**

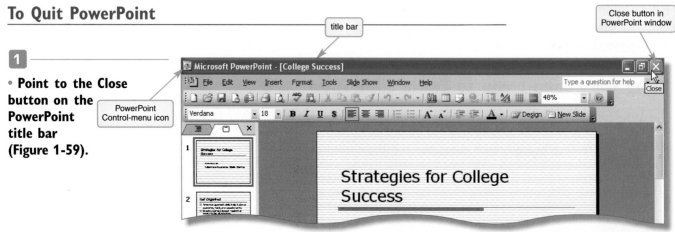

FIGURE 1-59

2

• **Click the Close button.**

PowerPoint closes and the Windows desktop is displayed (Figure 1-60). If you made changes to the presentation since your last save, a Microsoft Office PowerPoint dialog box appears asking if you want to save changes. Clicking the Yes button saves the changes to the presentation before quitting PowerPoint. Clicking the No button quits PowerPoint without saving the changes. Clicking the Cancel button cancels the exit and returns control to the presentation.

FIGURE 1-60

Starting PowerPoint and Opening a Presentation

Once you have created and saved a presentation, you may need to retrieve it from the floppy disk to make changes. For example, you may want to replace the design template or modify some text. The steps on the next page assume PowerPoint is not running.

To Start PowerPoint and Open an Existing Presentation

1

• **With your floppy disk in drive A, click the Start button on the taskbar, point to All Programs, point to Microsoft Office, and then click Microsoft Office PowerPoint 2003 on the Microsoft Office submenu.**

• **When the Getting Started task pane opens, point to the Open link in the Open area.**

PowerPoint starts. The Getting Started task pane opens (Figure 1-61).

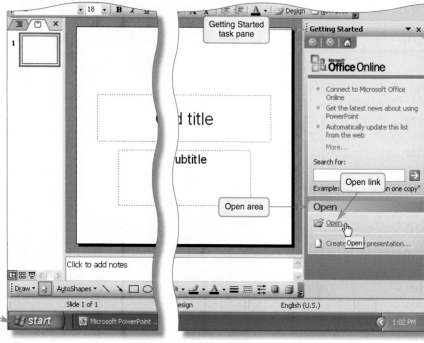

FIGURE 1-61

2

• **Click the Open link. Click the Look in box arrow, click 3½ Floppy (A:), and then double-click College Success.**

PowerPoint opens the presentation College Success and shows the first slide in the PowerPoint window (Figure 1-62). The presentation is displayed in normal view because PowerPoint opens a presentation in the same view in which it was saved. The Getting Started task pane disappears.

Other Ways

1. Right-click Start button, click Explore, display contents of drive A, double-click file name
2. Click Open button on Standard toolbar, select file name, click Open button in Open Office Document dialog box
3. On File menu click Open, select file name, click Open button in Open dialog box
4. In Voice Command mode, say "Open, [file name], Open"

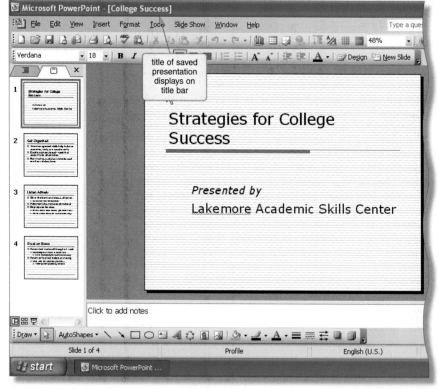

FIGURE 1-62

When you start PowerPoint and open the College Success file, the application name and file name are displayed on a recessed button on the Windows taskbar. When more than one application is open, you can switch between applications by clicking the appropriate application button. If you want to open a presentation other than a recent one, click the Open button on the Standard toolbar or in the Getting Started task pane. Either button lets you navigate to a slide show stored on a disk.

Checking a Presentation for Spelling and Consistency

After you create a presentation, you should check it visually for spelling errors and style consistency. In addition, you can use PowerPoint's Spelling and Style tools to identify possible misspellings and inconsistencies.

Checking a Presentation for Spelling Errors

PowerPoint checks the entire presentation for spelling mistakes using a standard dictionary contained in the Microsoft Office group. This dictionary is shared with the other Microsoft Office applications such as Word and Excel. A **custom dictionary** is available if you want to add special words such as proper names, cities, and acronyms. When checking a presentation for spelling errors, PowerPoint opens the standard dictionary and the custom dictionary file, if one exists. When a word appears in the Spelling dialog box, you perform one of the actions listed in Table 1-4.

Q&A

Q: Can I rely on the spelling checker?

A: While PowerPoint's Spelling checker is a valuable tool, it is not infallible. You should proofread your presentation carefully by pointing to each word and saying it aloud as you point to it. Be mindful of commonly misused words such as its and it's, through and though, and to and too.

Table 1-4 Summary of Spelling Checker Actions	
ACTION	**DESCRIPTION**
Ignore the word	Click the Ignore button when the word is spelled correctly but not found in the dictionaries. PowerPoint continues checking the rest of the presentation.
Ignore all occurrences of the word	Click the Ignore All button when the word is spelled correctly but not found in the dictionaries. PowerPoint ignores all occurrences of the word and continues checking the rest of the presentation.
Select a different spelling	Click the proper spelling of the word from the list in the Suggestions box. Click the Change button. PowerPoint corrects the word and continues checking the rest of the presentation.
Change all occurrences of the misspelling to a different spelling	Click the proper spelling of the word from the list in the Suggestions box. Click the Change All button. PowerPoint changes all occurrences of the misspelled word and continues checking the rest of the presentation.
Add a word to the custom dictionary	Click the Add button. PowerPoint opens the custom dictionary, adds the word, and continues checking the rest of the presentation.
View alternative spellings	Click the Suggest button. PowerPoint lists suggested spellings. Click the correct word from the Suggestions box or type the proper spelling. Then click the Change button. PowerPoint continues checking the rest of the presentation.
Add spelling error to AutoCorrect list	Click the AutoCorrect button. PowerPoint adds the spelling error and its correction to the AutoCorrect list. Any future misspelling of the word is corrected automatically as you type.
Close	Click the Close button to close the Spelling checker and return to the PowerPoint window.

The standard dictionary contains commonly used English words. It does not, however, contain proper names, abbreviations, technical terms, poetic contractions, or antiquated terms. PowerPoint treats words not found in the dictionaries as misspellings.

Starting the Spelling Checker

The following steps illustrate how to start the Spelling checker and check the entire presentation.

To Start the Spelling Checker

1

• **Point to the Spelling button on the Standard toolbar (Figure 1-63).**

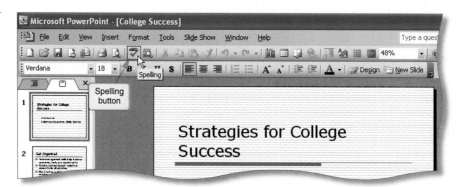

FIGURE 1-63

2

• **Click the Spelling button.**

• **When the Spelling dialog box appears, point to the Ignore button.**

PowerPoint starts the Spelling checker and displays the Spelling dialog box (Figure 1-64). The word, Lakemore, appears in the Not in Dictionary box. Depending on the custom dictionary, Lakemore may not be recognized as a misspelled word.

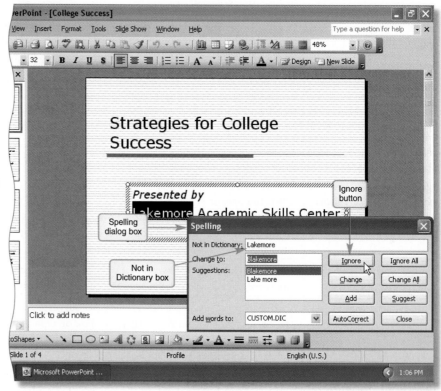

FIGURE 1-64

3

• **Click the Ignore button.**

• **When the Microsoft Office PowerPoint dialog box appears, point to the OK button.**

PowerPoint ignores the word, Lakemore, and continues searching for additional misspelled words. PowerPoint may stop on additional words depending on your typing accuracy. When PowerPoint has checked all slides for misspellings, the Microsoft Office PowerPoint dialog box informs you that the spelling check is complete (Figure 1-65).

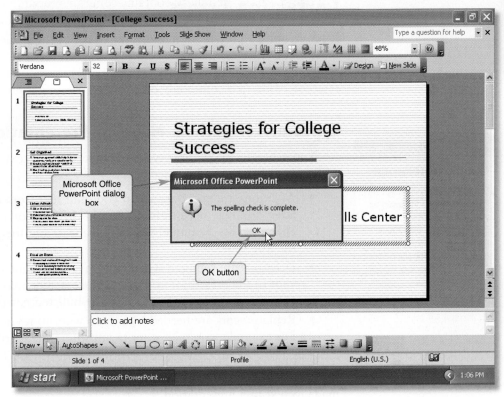

FIGURE 1-65

4

• **Click the OK button.**

• **Click the slide to remove the highlight from the word, Lakemore.**

PowerPoint closes the Spelling checker and returns to the current slide, Slide 1 (Figure 1-66), or to the slide where a possible misspelled word displayed.

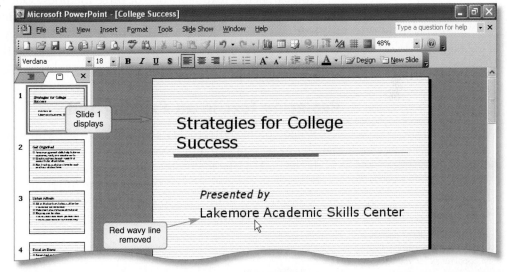

FIGURE 1-66

The red wavy line below the word, Lakemore, is gone because you instructed PowerPoint to ignore that word, which does not appear in the standard dictionary. You also could have added that word to the dictionary so it would not be flagged as a possible misspelled word in subsequent presentations you create using that word.

Other Ways

1. On Tools menu click Spelling
2. Press ALT+T, press S; when finished, press ENTER
3. Press F7
4. In Voice Command mode, say "Spelling"

Correcting Errors

After creating a presentation and running the Spelling checker, you may find that you must make changes. Changes may be required because a slide contains an error, the scope of the presentation shifts, or the style is inconsistent. This section explains the types of errors that commonly occur when creating a presentation.

Types of Corrections Made to Presentations

You generally make three types of corrections to text in a presentation: additions, deletions, and replacements.

- Additions are necessary when you omit text from a slide and need to add it later. You may need to insert text in the form of a sentence, word, or single character. For example, you may want to add the presenter's middle name on the title slide.
- Deletions are required when text on a slide is incorrect or no longer is relevant to the presentation. For example, a slide may look cluttered. Therefore, you may want to remove one of the bulleted paragraphs to add more space.
- Replacements are needed when you want to revise the text in a presentation. For example, you may want to substitute the word, their, for the word, there.

Editing text in PowerPoint basically is the same as editing text in a word processing package. The following sections illustrate the most common changes made to text in a presentation.

Deleting Text

You can delete text using one of three methods. One is to use the BACKSPACE key to remove text just typed. The second is to position the insertion point to the left of the text you wish to delete and then press the DELETE key. The third method is to drag through the text you wish to delete and then press the DELETE key. (Use the third method when deleting large sections of text.)

Replacing Text in an Existing Slide

When you need to correct a word or phrase, you can replace the text by selecting the text to be replaced and then typing the new text. As soon as you press any key on the keyboard, the highlighted text is deleted and the new text is displayed.

PowerPoint inserts text to the left of the insertion point. The text to the right of the insertion point moves to the right (and shifts downward if necessary) to accommodate the added text.

Displaying a Presentation in Black and White

Printing handouts of a presentation allows you to use them to make overhead transparencies. The Color/Grayscale button on the Standard toolbar shows the presentation in black and white before you print. Table 1-5 identifies how PowerPoint objects display in black and white.

OBJECT	APPEARANCE IN BLACK AND WHITE VIEW
Bitmaps	Grayscale
Embossing	Hidden
Fills	Grayscale
Frame	Black
Lines	Black
Object shadows	Grayscale
Pattern fills	Grayscale
Slide backgrounds	White
Text	Black
Text shadows	Hidden

Table 1-5 Appearance in Black and White View

The following steps show how to display the presentation in black and white.

To Display a Presentation in Black and White

1

• **Click the Color/Grayscale button on the Standard toolbar and then point to Pure Black and White in the list.**

The Color/Grayscale list is displayed (Figure 1-67). Pure Black and White alters the slides' appearance so that only black lines display on a white background. Grayscale shows varying degrees of gray.

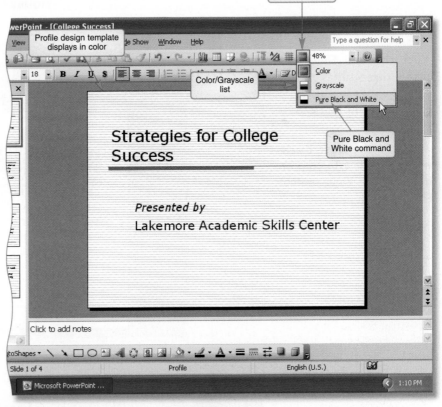

FIGURE 1-67

2

- **Click Pure Black and White.**

Slide 1 is displayed in black and white in the slide pane (Figure 1-68). The four thumbnail slides are displayed in color in the Slides tab. The Grayscale View toolbar appears. The Color/Grayscale button on the Standard toolbar changes from color bars to black and white.

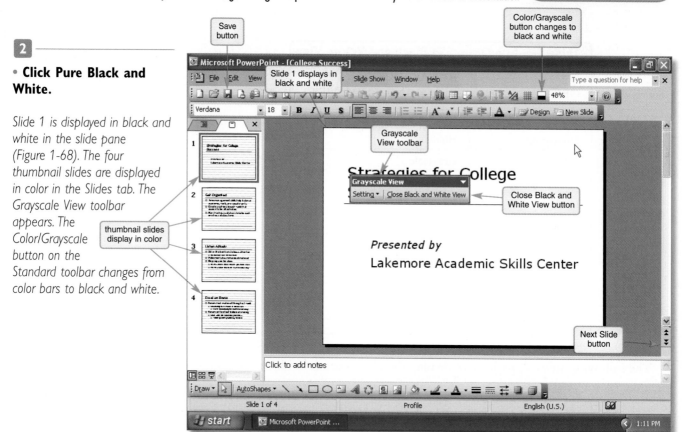

FIGURE 1-68

3

- **Click the Next Slide button three times to view all slides in the presentation in black and white.**

- **Point to the Close Black and White View button on the Grayscale View toolbar (Figure 1-69).**

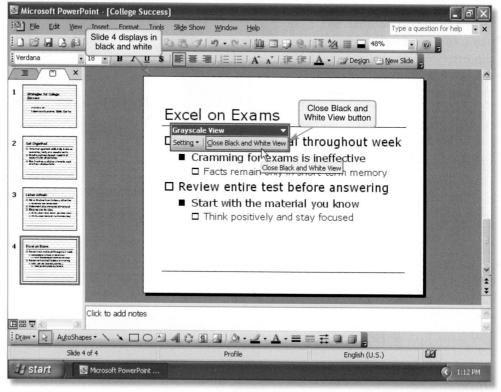

FIGURE 1-69

4

• **Click the Close Black and White View button.**

Slide 4 is displayed with the default Profile color scheme (Figure 1-70).

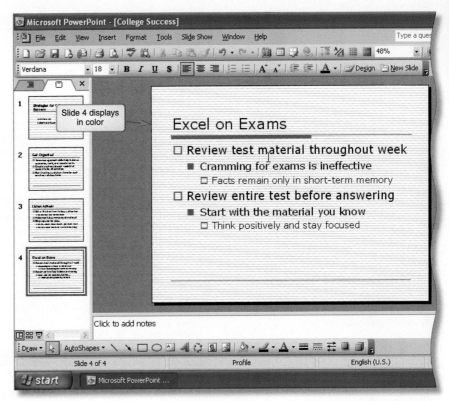

FIGURE 1-70

After you view the text objects in the presentation in black and white, you can make any changes that will enhance printouts produced from a black and white printer or photocopier.

Printing a Presentation

After you create a presentation, you often want to print it. A printed version of the presentation is called a **hard copy**, or **printout**. The first printing of the presentation is called a **rough draft**. The rough draft allows you to proofread the presentation to check for errors and readability. After correcting errors, you print the final copy of the presentation.

Saving Before Printing

Before printing a presentation, you should save your work in the event you experience difficulties with the printer. You occasionally may encounter system problems that can be resolved only by restarting the computer. In such an instance, you will need to reopen the presentation. As a precaution, always save the presentation before you print. The steps on the next page save the presentation before printing.

To Save a Presentation Before Printing

1 **Verify that the floppy disk is in drive A.**

2 **Click the Save button on the Standard toolbar.**

All changes made after your last save now are saved on the floppy disk.

Printing the Presentation

After saving the presentation, you are ready to print. Clicking the Print button on the Standard toolbar causes PowerPoint to print all slides in the presentation. The following steps illustrate how to print the presentation slides.

To Print a Presentation

1

• **Ready the printer according to the printer instructions.**

• **Click the Print button on the Standard toolbar.**

The printer icon in the tray status area on the Windows taskbar indicates a print job is processing (Figure 1-71). This icon may not display on your system, or it may display on your status bar. After several moments, the slide show begins printing on the printer. When the presentation is finished printing, the printer icon in the tray status area on the Windows taskbar no longer is displayed.

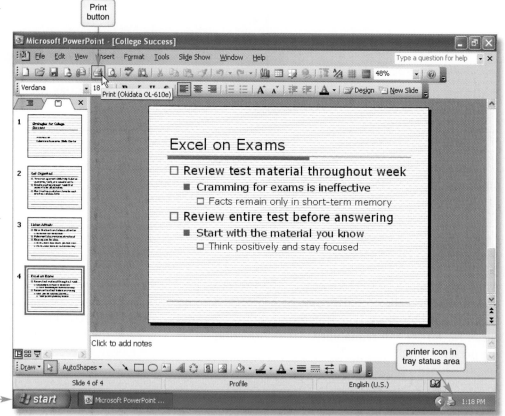

FIGURE 1-71

2

• **When the printer stops, retrieve the printouts of the slides.**

The presentation, College Success, prints on four pages (Figures 1-72a through 1-72d).

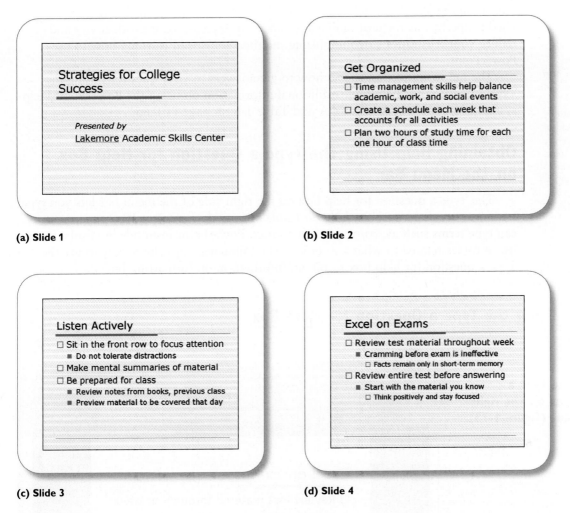

(a) Slide 1

(b) Slide 2

(c) Slide 3

(d) Slide 4

FIGURE 1-72

Other Ways

1. On File menu click Print
2. Press CTRL+P or press CTRL+SHIFT+F12
3. In Voice Command mode, say "Print"

You can click the printer icon next to the clock in the tray status area on the Windows taskbar to obtain information about the presentations printing on your printer and to delete files in the print queue that are waiting to be printed.

Making a Transparency

With the handouts printed, you now can make overhead transparencies using one of several devices. One device is a printer attached to your computer, such as an inkjet printer or a laser printer. Transparencies produced on a printer may be in black and white or color, depending on the printer. Another device is a photocopier. Because each of these devices requires a special transparency film, check the user's manual for the film requirement of your specific device, or ask your instructor.

PowerPoint Help System

More About

The PowerPoint Help System

Need Help? It is no further away than the Type a question for help box on the menu bar in the upper-right corner of the window. Click the box that contains the text, Type a question for help (Figure 1-73), type `help`, and then press the ENTER key. PowerPoint responds with a list of topics you can click to learn about obtaining help on any PowerPoint-related topic. To find out what is new in PowerPoint 2003, type `what is new in PowerPoint` in the Type a question for help box.

You can get answers to PowerPoint questions at any time by using the PowerPoint Help system. You can activate the PowerPoint Help system by using the Type a question for help box on the menu bar, by using the Microsoft PowerPoint Help button on the Standard toolbar, or by clicking Help on the menu bar (Figure 1-73). Used properly, this form of online assistance can increase your productivity and reduce your frustrations by minimizing the time you spend learning how to use PowerPoint.

The following section shows how to get answers to your questions using the Type a question for help box. Additional information on using the PowerPoint Help system is available in Appendix A and Table 1-6 on page PPT 65.

Obtaining Help Using the Type a Question for Help Box on the Menu Bar

The Type a question for help box on the right side of the menu bar lets you type free-form questions such as, *how do I save* or *how do I create a Web page*, or you can type terms such as, *copy*, *save*, or *format*. PowerPoint responds by displaying a list of topics related to what you typed. The following steps show how to use the Type a question for help box to obtain information on formatting bullets.

To Obtain Help Using the Type a Question for Help Box

1

• **Type** `bullet` **in the Type a question for help box on the right side of the menu bar (Figure 1-73).**

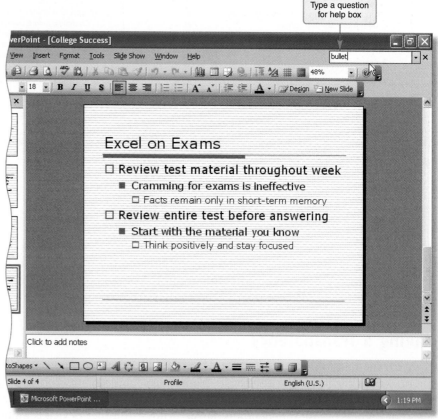

FIGURE 1-73

2

• **Press the ENTER key.**

• **When PowerPoint displays the Search Results task pane, scroll down and then point to the topic, Change the bullet style in a list.**

PowerPoint displays the Search Results task pane with a list of topics relating to the term, bullet. PowerPoint found 30 results from Microsoft Office Online. The mouse pointer changes to a hand, which indicates it is pointing to a link (Figure 1-74).

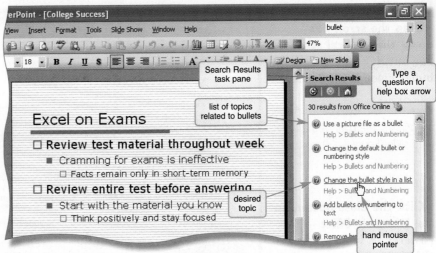

FIGURE 1-74

3

• **Click Change the bullet style in a list.**

• **When the Microsoft Office PowerPoint Help window is displayed, double-click its title bar to maximize it.**

A Microsoft Office PowerPoint Help window provides Help information about changing the bullet style in a list (Figure 1-75).

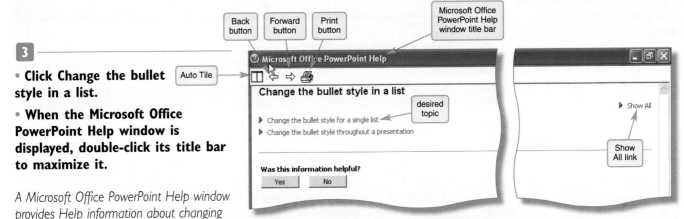

FIGURE 1-75

4

• **Click the Show All link.**

Directions for changing a bullet style for a single list are displayed. Options include change the bullet character, change the bullet size, and change the bullet color (Figure 1-76).

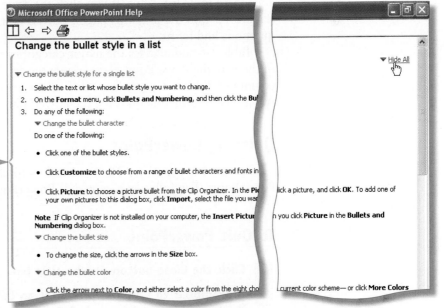

FIGURE 1-76

5

• **Drag the scroll box down the vertical scroll bar until Change the bullet color is displayed.**

PowerPoint displays specific details of changing the color of the bullets on a slide (Figure 1-77).

6

• **Click the Close button on the Microsoft Office PowerPoint Help window title bar.**

• **Click the Close button on the Search Results task pane.**

The PowerPoint Help window closes, and the PowerPoint presentation is displayed.

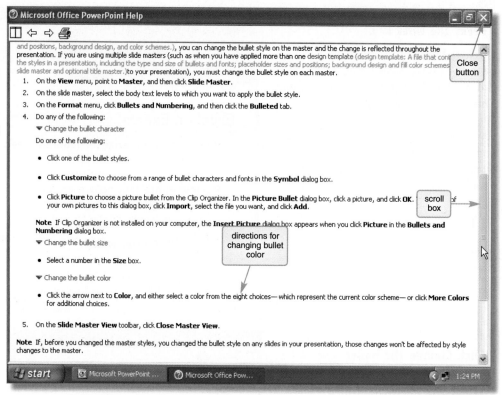

FIGURE 1-77

Other Ways

1. Click Microsoft Office PowerPoint Help button on Standard toolbar; or on Help menu click Microsoft Office PowerPoint Help
2. Press F1

Use the buttons in the upper-left corner of the Microsoft Office PowerPoint Help window (Figure 1-75 on the previous page) to navigate through the Help system, change the display, and print the contents of the window.

As you enter questions and terms in the Type a question for help box, PowerPoint adds them to its list. Thus, if you click the Type a question for help box arrow (Figure 1-74 on the previous page), PowerPoint will display a list of previously asked questions and terms.

Table 1-6 summarizes the major categories of Help available to you. Because of the way the PowerPoint Help system works, be certain to review the rightmost column of Table 1-6 if you have difficulties activating the desired category of Help. Additional information on using the PowerPoint Help system is available in Appendix A.

Quitting PowerPoint

Project 1 is complete. The final task is to close the presentation and quit PowerPoint. The following steps quit PowerPoint.

To Quit PowerPoint

1 **Click the Close button on the title bar.**

2 **If prompted to save the presentation before quitting PowerPoint, click the Yes button in the Microsoft Office PowerPoint dialog box.**

Table 1-6   PowerPoint Help System

TYPE	DESCRIPTION	HOW TO ACTIVATE
Microsoft Office PowerPoint Help	Displays PowerPoint Help task pane. Answers questions or searches for terms that you type in your own words.	Click the Microsoft Office PowerPoint Help button on the Standard toolbar or click Microsoft Office PowerPoint Help on the Help menu.
Office Assistant	Similar to the Type a question for help box. The Office Assistant answers questions that you type in your own words, offers tips, and provides help for a variety of PowerPoint features.	Click the Office Assistant icon. If the Office Assistant does not display, click Show the Office Assistant on the Help menu.
Type a question for help box	Answers questions or searches for terms that you type in your own words.	Type a question or term in the Type a question for help box on the menu bar and then press the ENTER key.
Table of Contents	Groups Help topics by general categories. Use when you know only the general category of the topic in question.	Click the Microsoft Office PowerPoint Help button on the Standard toolbar or click Microsoft Office PowerPoint Help on the Help menu, and then click the Table of Contents link on the PowerPoint Help task pane.
Microsoft Office Online	Used to access technical resources and download free product enhancements on the Web.	Click Microsoft Office Online on the Help menu.
Detect and Repair	Automatically finds and fixes errors in the application.	Click Detect and Repair on the Help menu.

Project Summary

In creating the Strategies for College Success slide show in this project, you gained a broad knowledge of PowerPoint. First, you were introduced to starting PowerPoint and creating a presentation consisting of a title slide and single- and multi-level bulleted lists. You learned about PowerPoint design templates, objects, and attributes.

This project illustrated how to create an interesting introduction to a presentation by changing the text font style to italic and increasing font size on the title slide. Completing these tasks, you saved the presentation. Then, you created three text slides with bulleted lists, two with multi-level bullets, to explain effective academic skills. Next, you learned how to view the presentation in slide show view. Then, you learned how to quit PowerPoint and how to open an existing presentation. You used the Spelling checker to search for spelling errors. You learned how to display the presentation in black and white. You also learned how to print hard copies of the slides in order to make handouts and overhead transparencies. Finally, you learned how to use the PowerPoint Help system to answer your questions.

If you have a SAM user profile, you may have access to hands-on instruction, practice, and assessment of the skills covered in this project. Log in to your SAM account and go to your assignments page to see what your instructor has assigned.

What You Should Know

Having completed this project, you should be able to perform the tasks below. The tasks are listed in the same order they were presented in this project. For a list of the buttons, menus, toolbars, and commands introduced in this project, see the Quick Reference Summary at the back of this book and refer to the Page Number column.

1. Start PowerPoint (PPT 7)
2. Customize the PowerPoint Window (PPT 9)
3. Choose a Design Template (PPT 18)
4. Enter the Presentation Title (PPT 21)
5. Enter the Presentation Subtitle (PPT 22)
6. Change the Text Font Style to Italic (PPT 24)
7. Increase Font Size (PPT 25)
8. Save a Presentation on a Floppy Disk (PPT 27)
9. Add a New Text Slide with a Bulleted List (PPT 30)
10. Enter a Slide Title (PPT 32)
11. Select a Text Placeholder (PPT 32)
12. Type a Single-Level Bulleted List (PPT 33)
13. Add a New Slide and Enter a Slide Title (PPT 35)
14. Type a Multi-Level Bulleted List (PPT 36)
15. Type the Remaining Text for Slide 3 (PPT 38)
16. Create Slide 4 (PPT 39)
17. Create a Third-Level Paragraph (PPT 40)
18. Type the Remaining Text for Slide 4 (PPT 41)
19. End a Slide Show with a Black Slide (PPT 42)
20. Save a Presentation with the Same File Name (PPT 44)
21. Use the Scroll Box on the Slide Pane to Move to Another Slide (PPT 45)
22. Start Slide Show View (PPT 47)
23. Move Manually Through Slides in a Slide Show (PPT 48)
24. Display the Popup Menu and Go to a Specific Slide (PPT 49)
25. Use the Popup Menu to End a Slide Show (PPT 50)
26. Quit PowerPoint (PPT 50)
27. Start PowerPoint and Open an Existing Presentation (PPT 52)
28. Start the Spelling Checker (PPT 54)
29. Display a Presentation in Black and White (PPT 57)
30. Save a Presentation Before Printing (PPT 60)
31. Print a Presentation (PPT 60)
32. Obtain Help Using the Type a Question for Help Box (PPT 62)
33. Quit PowerPoint (PPT 64)

Learn It Online

Instructions: To complete the Learn It Online exercises, start your browser, click the Address bar, and then enter the Web address scsite.com/ppt2003/learn. When the PowerPoint 2003 Learn It Online page is displayed, follow the instructions in the exercises below. Each exercise has instructions for printing your results, either for your own records or for submission to your instructor.

1 Project Reinforcement TF, MC, and SA

Below PowerPoint Project 1, click the Project Reinforcement link. Print the quiz by clicking Print on the File menu for each page. Answer each question.

2 Flash Cards

Below PowerPoint Project 1, click the Flash Cards link and read the instructions. Type 20 (or a number specified by your instructor) in the Number of playing cards text box, type your name in the Enter your Name text box, and then click the Flip Card button. When the flash card is displayed, read the question and then click the ANSWER box arrow to select an answer. Flip through Flash Cards. If your score is 15 (75%) correct or greater, click Print on the File menu to print your results. If your score is less than 15 (75%) correct, then redo this exercise by clicking the Replay button.

3 Practice Test

Below PowerPoint Project 1, click the Practice Test link. Answer each question, enter your first and last name at the bottom of the page, and then click the Grade Test button. When the graded practice test is displayed on your screen, click Print on the File menu to print a hard copy. Continue to take practice tests until you score 80% or better.

4 Who Wants To Be a Computer Genius?

Below PowerPoint Project 1, click the Computer Genius link. Read the instructions, enter your first and last name at the bottom of the page, and then click the PLAY button. When your score is displayed, click the PRINT RESULTS link to print a hard copy.

5 Wheel of Terms

Below PowerPoint Project 1, click the Wheel of Terms link. Read the instructions, and then enter your first and last name and your school name. Click the PLAY button. When your score is displayed, right-click the score and then click Print on the shortcut menu to print a hard copy.

6 Crossword Puzzle Challenge

Below PowerPoint Project 1, click the Crossword Puzzle Challenge link. Read the instructions, and then enter your first and last name. Click the SUBMIT button. Work the crossword puzzle. When you are finished, click the Submit button. When the crossword puzzle is redisplayed, click the Print Puzzle button to print a hard copy.

7 Tips and Tricks

Below PowerPoint Project 1, click the Tips and Tricks link. Click a topic that pertains to Project 1. Right-click the information and then click Print on the shortcut menu. Construct a brief example of what the information relates to in PowerPoint to confirm you understand how to use the tip or trick.

8 Newsgroups

Below PowerPoint Project 1, click the Newsgroups link. Click a topic that pertains to Project 1. Print three comments.

9 Expanding Your Horizons

Below PowerPoint Project 1, click the Expanding Your Horizons link. Click a topic that pertains to Project 1. Print the information. Construct a brief example of what the information relates to in PowerPoint to confirm you understand the contents of the article.

10 Search Sleuth

Below PowerPoint Project 1, click the Search Sleuth link. To search for a term that pertains to this project, select a term below the Project 1 title and then use the Google search engine at google.com (or any major search engine) to display and print two Web pages that present information on the term.

11 PowerPoint Online Training

Below PowerPoint Project 1, click the PowerPoint Online Training link. When your browser displays the Microsoft Office Online Web page, click the PowerPoint link. Click one of the PowerPoint courses that covers one or more of the objectives listed at the beginning of the project on page PPT 4. Print the first page of the course before stepping through it.

12 Office Marketplace

Below PowerPoint Project 1, click the Office Marketplace link. When your browser displays the Microsoft Office Online Web page, click the Office Marketplace link. Click a topic that relates to PowerPoint. Print the first page.

Apply Your Knowledge

1 Searching on the World Wide Web

Instructions: Start PowerPoint. Open the presentation Apply 1-1 Internet Searching from the Data Disk. See the inside back cover of this book for instructions for downloading the Data Disk or see your instructor for information on accessing the files required for this book. The two slides in the presentation give information on tools to search the Web. Make the following changes to the slides so they appear as shown in Figure 1-78.

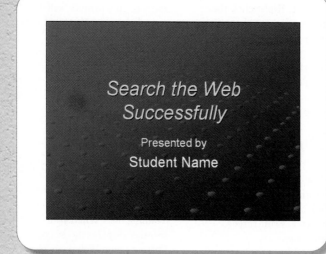

(a) Slide 1 (Title Slide)

(b) Slide 2 (Multi-Level Bulleted List)

FIGURE 1-78

Change the design template to Digital Dots. On the title slide, use your name in place of Student Name and change the font size to 40. Italicize the title text.

On Slide 2, increase the indent of the second and fourth paragraphs, Categorized lists of links arranged by subject and displayed in series of menus, and Requires search text: a word, words, phrase, to second-level paragraphs. Then change the last paragraph, Carefully craft keywords to limit search, to a third-level paragraph.

Display the revised presentation in black and white, and then print the two slides.

Save the presentation using the file name, Apply 1-1 Search Tools. Hand in the hard copy to your instructor.

Note: These labs require you to create presentations based on notes. When you design these slide shows, use the 7 × 7 rule, which states that each line should have a maximum of seven words, and each slide should have a maximum of seven lines.

1 Common Cold Concerns Presentation

Problem: The common cold is one of the most frequent health problems; more than one billion cases are reported each year. Although no remedy cures the runny nose or sore throat that accompany this illness, students can reduce their chances of catching a cold and feel better when they are sick. Dr. Larry Hopper is the head physician at your campus's health clinic. He has asked you to prepare a short PowerPoint presentation and handouts to educate students about how to thwart the common cold. He hands you the outline shown in Figure 1-79 and asks you to create the presentation shown in Figures 1-80a through 1-80f on the following pages.

I.) Coping with the Common Cold
Presented by
Larry Hopper, M.D.

II.) Cold Facts
■ We have more than 1 billion colds annually
■ No remedy cures the common cold
■ You can reduce the chances of catching a cold
■ You can feel better when you are sick

III.) When You Are Feeling Sick
■ Get plenty of rest
■ Drink lots of fluids
■ Consume chicken soup

IV.) If Your Throat Is Sore
■ Gargle with warm salt water
■ Let a lozenge dissolve slowly in your mouth
  – Choose one with menthol and mild anesthetic

V.) If Your Nose Is Stuffy
■ Try a decongestant
  – Shrinks blood vessels
  – Do not take for more than three days
■ Try an antihistamine
  – Relieves a runny nose, itching, and sneezing
  – Has a drying effect

VI.) Avoid a Cold
■ Stay away from other people with colds
■ Wash your hands frequently
■ Keep your hands away from your mouth and nose
■ Dispose of tissues promptly

FIGURE 1-79

(continued)

Common Cold Concerns Presentation *(continued)*

(a) Slide 1

(b) Slide 2

(c) Slide 3

(d) Slide 4

FIGURE 1-80

In the Lab

If Your Nose Is Stuffy

- Try a decongestant
  - Shrinks blood vessels
  - Do not take for more than three days
- Try an antihistamine
  - Relieves a runny nose, itching, and sneezing
  - Has a drying effect

(e) Slide 5

Avoid a Cold

- Stay away from other people with colds
- Wash your hands frequently
- Keep your hands away from your mouth and nose
- Dispose of tissues promptly

(f) Slide 6

FIGURE 1-80 *(continued)*

Instructions: Perform the following tasks.

1. Create a new presentation using the Network design template (row 14, column 2).
2. Using the typed notes illustrated in Figure 1-79 on page PPT 69, create the title slide shown in Figure 1-80a using your name in place of Larry Hopper. Italicize the title paragraph, Coping with the Common Cold, and increase the font size to 60. Increase the font size of the first paragraph of the subtitle text, Presented by, to 36. Italicize your name.
3. Using the typed notes in Figure 1-79, create the five text slides with bulleted lists shown in Figures 1-80b through 1-80f.
4. Click the Spelling button on the Standard toolbar. Correct any errors.
5. Drag the scroll box to display Slide 1. Click the Slide Show button to start slide show view. Then click to display each slide.
6. Save the presentation using the file name, Lab 1-1 Common Cold Concerns.
7. Display and print the presentation in black and white. Close the presentation. Hand in the hard copy to your instructor.

In the Lab

2 Computers 4 U Repair Store Presentation

Problem: Computers 4 U is a computer repair store near your campus. The co-owners, Elliott Dane and Lynn Verone, specialize in repairing computer systems and building custom computers. Elliott and Lynn want to attract new customers, and they have asked you to help them design a PowerPoint advertising campaign. Having graduated from your college, they are familiar with the hardware and software students need for their classes. They have typed information on their services for you (Figure 1-81), and they have asked you to create the presentation shown in Figures 1-82a through 1-82d.

1) Computers 4 U
Complete Repairs and Service
Elliott Dane and Lynn Verone

2) Hardware and Software
- Convenient in-store appointments
- On-site service
  - 24 hours a day
- Plan for future computer purchases
- Arrange financing for new systems

3) Complete Supplies
- Toner cartridges
  - All major printer brands in-stock
- Paper
  - Wide variety of patterns and colors
- Labels
  - Complete selection of sizes

4) Convenient Location
- Bremen Mall
  - 15800 South Wabash Street
  - Napier, Washington
  - 555-1123

FIGURE 1-81

In the Lab

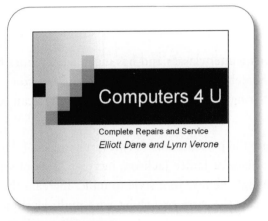

(a) Slide 1 (Title Slide)

(b) Slide 2

Hardware and Software

- Convenient in-store appointments
- On-site service
  - 24 hours a day
- Plan for future computer purchases
- Arrange financing for new systems

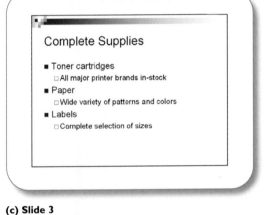

(c) Slide 3

Complete Supplies

- Toner cartridges
  - All major printer brands in-stock
- Paper
  - Wide variety of patterns and colors
- Labels
  - Complete selection of sizes

(d) Slide 4

Convenient Location

- Bremen Mall
  - 15800 South Wabash Street
  - Napier, Washington
  - 555-1123

FIGURE 1-82

Instructions: Perform the following tasks.

1. Create a new presentation using the Pixel design template (row 16, column 1).
2. Using the typed notes illustrated in Figure 1-81, create the title slide shown in Figure 1-82a using your name in place of Elliott Dane. Italicize both names. Increase the font size of the title paragraph, Computers 4 U, to 68. Decrease the font size of the first paragraph of the subtitle text, Complete Repairs and Service, to 30.
3. Using the typed notes in Figure 1-81, create the three text slides with bulleted lists shown in Figures 1-82b through 1-82d.
4. Click the Spelling button on the Standard toolbar. Correct any errors.
5. Save the presentation using the file name, Lab 1-2 Computers 4 U.
6. Display the presentation in black and white.
7. Print the black and white presentation. Close the presentation. Hand in the hard copy to your instructor.

3 Community Center Course Update

Problem: The Rivercrest Community Center has updated its winter classes and has included activities for town residents of all ages. For children, the new classes are Skateboarding Fundamentals, Tumbling for Toddlers, and Basketball Boot Camp. For adults, the new offerings are Yoga and Spinning. Seniors can enroll in Self-Defense and Flexibility.

Instructions Part 1: Using the outline in Figure 1-83, create the presentation shown in Figure 1-84. Use the Radial design template. On the title slide, type your name in place of Janice Jackson, increase the font size of the title paragraph, Rivercrest Community Center, to 50, and change the text font style to italic. Increase the font size of the subtitle paragraph, New Winter Classes, to 40. Create the three text slides with multi-level bulleted lists shown in Figures 1-84b through 1-84d.

Correct any spelling mistakes, and then view the slide show. Save the presentation using the file name, Lab 1-3 Part One Winter Classes. Display and print the presentation in black and white.

1. Rivercrest Community Center
New Winter Classes
Janice Jackson, Director

2. Children's Classes
- Skateboarding Fundamentals
    - Emphasizes safety and control
- Tumbling for Toddlers
    - Learn coordination while having fun
- Basketball Boot Camp
    - Features game strategies and conditioning

3. Adults' Classes
- Yoga
    - Enjoy a mind-body experience
        - Release external tensions and chaos
- Spinning
    - Learn proper bike set-up
    - Involves series of cycling techniques

4. Seniors' Classes
- Self-defense
    - Learn to avoid dangerous situations
- Flexibility
    - Improve range of motion, balance, posture
        - Helps to prevent falls
    - Instill your body with grace and movement

FIGURE 1-83

In the Lab

(a) Slide 1 (Title Slide)

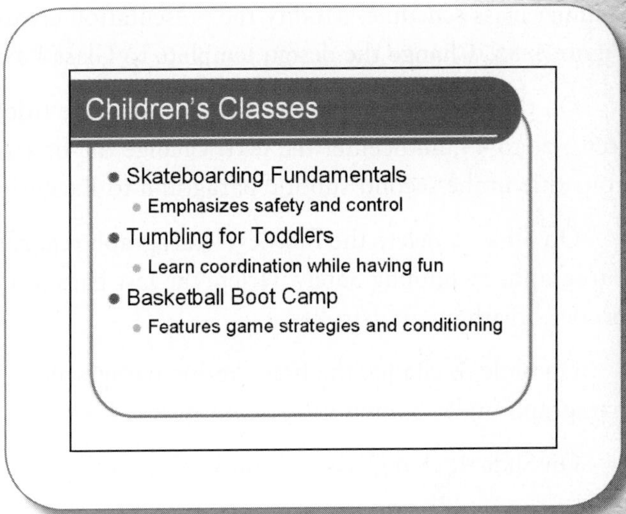

Rivercrest Community Center

New Winter Classes
Janice Jackson, Director

(b) Slide 2

Children's Classes

- Skateboarding Fundamentals
  - Emphasizes safety and control
- Tumbling for Toddlers
  - Learn coordination while having fun
- Basketball Boot Camp
  - Features game strategies and conditioning

(c) Slide 3

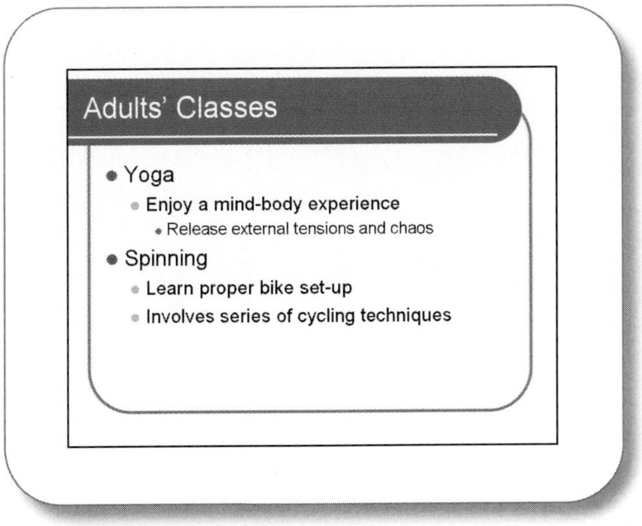

Adults' Classes

- Yoga
  - Enjoy a mind-body experience
    - Release external tensions and chaos
- Spinning
  - Learn proper bike set-up
  - Involves series of cycling techniques

(d) Slide 4

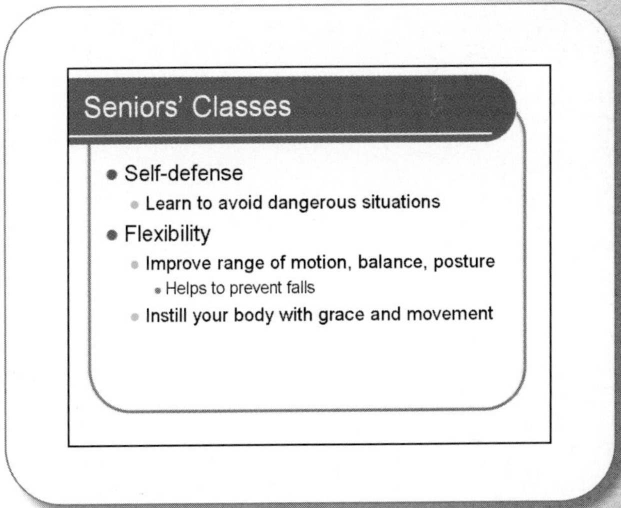

Seniors' Classes

- Self-defense
  - Learn to avoid dangerous situations
- Flexibility
  - Improve range of motion, balance, posture
    - Helps to prevent falls
  - Instill your body with grace and movement

FIGURE 1-84

(continued)

Community Center Course Update *(continued)*

Instructions Part 2: The Rivercrest Community Center wants to update this presentation to promote the summer class schedule. Modify the presentation created in Part 1 to create the presentation shown in Figure 1-85. Change the design template to Glass Layers.

On the title slide, remove the italics from the title paragraph, Rivercrest Community Center, decrease the font size to 44, and center the text. Change the first subtitle paragraph to New Summer Classes. Then change your title in the second subtitle paragraph to Executive Director and decrease the font size to 28.

On Slide 2, delete the first-level paragraph regarding the basketball boot camp and replace it with the paragraph, Swimming Safely. Delete the last paragraph on the slide and replace it with the paragraph, Practice proper breathing and strokes.

On Slide 3, change the first subtitle paragraph to Yoga and Tai Chi. Then change the first first-level paragraph under Spinning to, Learn proper bike set-up and form.

On Slide 4, change the second-level paragraph under Self-Defense to, Learn to escape from an attacker.

Correct any spelling mistakes, and then view the slide show. Save the presentation using the file name, Lab 1-3 Part Two Summer Classes. Display and print the presentation in black and white. Close the presentation. Hand in both presentation printouts to your instructor.

In the Lab

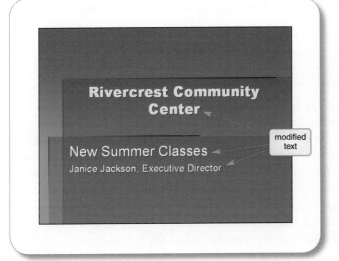

(a) Slide 1

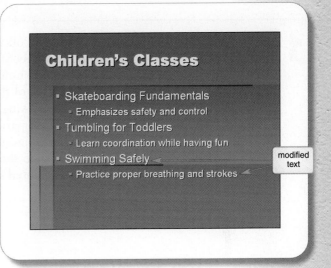

(b) Slide 2

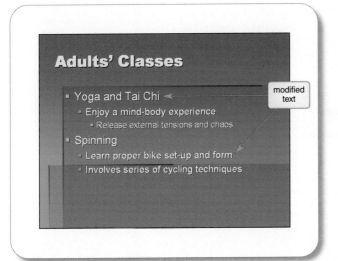

(c) Slide 3

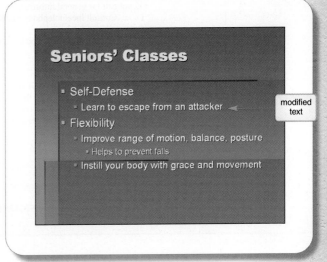

(d) Slide 4

FIGURE 1-85

Cases and Places

The difficulty of these case studies varies:
■ are the least difficult and ■■ are more difficult. The last exercise is a group exercise.

Note: Remember to use the 7 × 7 rule as you design the presentations: a maximum of seven words on a line and a maximum of seven lines on one slide.

1 ■ The dispatcher at the Imperial Grove Police Station is noticing an increase in the number of calls made to the emergency 911 telephone number. These calls, unfortunately, are not always emergencies. Community residents have been calling the number to obtain information on everything from the times of movies at the local theatre to the names of the local city trustees. Police Chief Gina Colatta wants to inform homeowners of the importance of using the 911 service correctly. She created the outline shown in Figure 1-86 and asks you to help her prepare an accompanying PowerPoint presentation to show at the local mall and food stores. Using the concepts and techniques introduced in this project, together with Chief Colatta's outline, develop a slide show with a title slide and three text slides with bulleted lists. Print the slides so they can be distributed to residents at the conclusion of the presentation.

1) 911 – A Call for Help
　Presented by
　Chief Gina Colatta
　Imperial Grove Police Department

2) What It Is For
　When you need an emergency response
　　Fire
　　Police
　　Emergency Medical Personnel
　When disaster occurs
　　Tornadoes, earthquakes, floods

3) How to Help
　Do not call for general information
　　Consult local telephone directories
　If you call by mistake:
　　Tell the dispatcher you have misdialed
　Wait if you hear a recording

4) Other Information
　Tell the telephone company if you change your name or address
　　This info displays on the dispatcher's screen
　　The dispatcher relies on this information
　Be certain your house number can be seen from the street

FIGURE 1-86

Cases and Places

2 Your school is planning a job fair to occur during the week of midterm exams. The Placement Office has invited 100 companies and local businesses to promote its current and anticipated job openings. The Placement Office director, Latasha Prince, hands you the outline shown in Figure 1-87 and asks you to prepare a presentation and handouts to promote the event. Use this list to design and create a presentation with a title slide and three text slides with bulleted lists.

1. Brookville College Career Fair
Presented by
Brookville College Placement Office
Latasha Prince, Director

2. Who Is Coming?
National corporations
    Progressive companies looking for high-quality candidates
Local companies
    Full-time and part-time
     - Hundreds of jobs

3. When Is It?
Midterm week
    Monday through Friday
Brookville College Cafeteria
Convenient hours
    9:00 a.m. to 8:00 p.m.

4. How Should I Prepare?
Bring plenty of resumes
    More than 100 companies expected
Dress neatly
View the Placement Office Web site
    Up-to-date information
    Company profiles

FIGURE 1-87

Cases and Places

3 ■■ In-line skating is a popular recreational sport throughout the world. In 1989, three million skaters spent $20 million on these skates and protective gear. In 1994, sales soared when nearly 14 million skaters spent $250 million. Today, the more than 27 million in-line skaters are purchasing more than $300 million in equipment yearly. Females account for 52 percent of skaters, and youths ranging in age from 7 to 17 are 58 percent of the total skaters. In-line skaters can participate more safely if they follow these steps: Wear full protective gear, including a helmet, wrist guards, and knee and elbow pads; practice basic skills, including braking, turning, and balancing, in a parking lot or other flat surface; always skate under control; and avoid hills until mastering speed control. The public relations director of your local park district has asked you to prepare a slide show emphasizing these safety tips and illustrating the in-line skating popularity surge. You decide to develop a slide show to run at the sporting goods store. Prepare a short presentation aimed at encouraging skaters to practice safe skating.

4 ■■ About 25 percent of the population suffers from the flu each year from October through May. Flu-related symptoms generally last for two weeks and include sudden headaches, chills, dry coughs, high fevers, and body aches. Serious complications are common, and an estimated 20,000 Americans die each year from the disease. Annual flu shots can help prevent the illness, and they are recommended for high-risk individuals such as the elderly and healthcare workers. Some drugs will help shorten the duration of the illness and decrease its severity if given within 48 hours after symptoms appear. General health tips include eating a balanced diet, getting enough rest, staying home when ill, exercising frequently, and washing hands frequently with warm, soapy water. Your campus' health services department wants to develop a presentation for students informing them about the flu and giving advice to stay healthy. Using the techniques introduced in the project, create a presentation about the flu.

5 ■■ **Working Together** Volunteers can make a contribution to society while they gain much fulfillment in return. Community organizations and non-for-profit businesses frequently seek volunteers for various projects. Have each member of your team visit or telephone several local civic groups to determine volunteer opportunities. Gather data about:

1) Required duties
2) Number of required hours
3) Contact person
4) Address
5) Telephone number

After coordinating the data, create a presentation with at least one slide showcasing the charitable organization. As a group, critique each slide. Hand in a hard copy of the final presentation.

Using the Outline Tab and Clip Art to Create a Slide Show

CASE PERSPECTIVE

For some students, the Healthy Eating Pyramid developed by the Harvard School of Public Health is as foreign as the Great Pyramid of Egypt. Eating a balanced diet seems as impossible as solving a quadratic formula. Obesity, hypertension, heart disease, and diabetes are soaring as a consequence of poor eating and lack of exercise, as two of every three Americans are classified as overweight or obese. Moreover, 25 percent of the U.S. population leads a completely sedentary lifestyle.

Cultural and social factors contribute to this unhealthy existence, so health care and fitness professionals need to educate adults and adolescents about adopting nutritious meals and daily exercise as the basis of a healthy lifestyle. Jessica Cantero, the Fitness Director at your college, realizes that students need to understand and apply simple measures they can take to help promote a healthy body. She wants to develop a series of workshops to motivate students to control their weight, exercise moderately, and release stress.

She knows that PowerPoint slide shows enhance speakers' presentations, so she asks you to assist her in developing a slide show to accompany her first workshop. This presentation will include nutritional information based on the Healthy Eating Pyramid, daily exercise guidelines, relaxation principles, and the advantages of maintaining a healthy lifestyle.

As you read through this project, you will learn how to use PowerPoint to add clip art and animation to increase the presentation's visual interest. You also will e-mail the completed presentation to Jessica.

Using the Outline Tab and Clip Art to Create a Slide Show

P R O J E C T

Objectives

You will have mastered the material in this project when you can:

- Start and customize a new slide show from an outline
- Add a slide and create a closing slide on the Outline tab
- Create text slides with multi-level bulleted lists on the Outline tab
- Save and review a presentation

- Insert and move clip art and change its size
- Add a header and footer to outline pages
- Animate clip art
- Add an animation scheme and run an animated slide show
- Print a presentation outline
- E-mail a slide show from within PowerPoint

Introduction

At some time during either your academic or business life, you probably will make a presentation. The presentation may be informative by providing detailed information about a specific topic. Other presentations may be persuasive by selling a proposal or a product to a client, convincing management to approve a new project, or influencing the board of directors to accept the new fiscal budget. As an alternative to creating your presentation in the slide pane in normal view, as you did in Project 1, PowerPoint provides an outlining feature to help you organize your thoughts. When the outline is complete, it becomes the foundation for your presentation.

Project Two — Healthy Eating, Healthy Living

Project 2 uses PowerPoint to create the five-slide Healthy Eating, Healthy Living presentation shown in Figures 2-1a through 2-1e. You create the presentation from the outline shown in Figure 2-2 on page PPT 84.

**Healthy Eating
Healthy Living**

Nutrition and Fitness Basics
Clark College Fitness Center

(a) Slide 1

Nutrition Guidelines

- Healthy Eating
  Pyramid
  - Eat more vegetable
    oils, whole grains
  - Eat less pasta,
    white bread

(b) Slide 2

Recommended Exercise

- 30 minutes of daily
  moderate-intensity
  activity
  - Brisk walking
  - Bicycling
  - Gardening

(c) Slide 3

Relaxation Techniques

- Quiet the mind and body
  - Visualize a tranquil setting
  - Concentrate on positive thoughts
- Build strength and refresh the body
  - Practice yoga or Pilates basics
  - Improve balance through core training

(d) Slide 4

Healthy Living Benefits

- Lowers cholesterol, blood pressure
- Reduces heart disease risk
- Helps prevent adult-onset diabetes
  - Affects 8% of adults
- Maintains body weight
  - Helps avoid excess gain

(e) Slide 5

FIGURE 2-1

I. Healthy Eating Healthy Living
    A. Nutrition and Fitness Basics
    B. Clark College Fitness Center
II. Nutrition Guidelines
    A. Healthy Eating Pyramid
        1. Eat more vegetable oils, whole grains
        2. Eat less pasta, white bread
III. Recommended Exercise
    A. 30 minutes of daily moderate-intensity activity
        1. Brisk walking
        2. Bicycling
        3. Gardening
IV. Relaxation Techniques
    A. Quiet the mind and body
        1. Visualize a tranquil setting
        2. Concentrate on positive thoughts
    B. Build strength and refresh the body
        1. Practice yoga or Pilates basics
        2. Improve balance through core training
V. Healthy Living Benefits
    A. Lowers cholesterol, blood pressure
    B. Reduces heart disease risk
    C. Helps prevent adult-onset diabetes
        1. Affects 8% of adults
    D. Maintains body weight
        1. Helps avoid excess gain

FIGURE 2-2

You can create your presentation outline using the Outline tab. When you create an outline, you type all the text at one time, as if you were typing an outline on a sheet of paper. This technique differs from creating a presentation in the slide pane in normal view, where you type text as you create each individual slide and the text is displayed both in the slide pane and on the Outline tab. PowerPoint creates the presentation as you type the outline by evaluating the outline structure and displaying a miniature view of the slide. Regardless of how you build a presentation, PowerPoint automatically creates the three views discussed in Project 1: normal, slide sorter, and slide show.

The first step in creating a presentation on the Outline tab is to type a title for the outline. The **outline title** is the subject of the presentation and later becomes the presentation title text. Then, you type the remainder of the outline, indenting appropriately to establish a structure, or hierarchy. Once the outline is complete, you make your presentation more persuasive by adding **clips**, which are media files of art, animation, sound, and movies. This project uses outlining to create the presentation and clip art to support the text visually.

Starting and Customizing PowerPoint

Project 1 introduced you to starting a presentation document, choosing a layout, and applying a design template. The following steps summarize how to start a new presentation, customize the PowerPoint window, choose a layout, and apply a design template. To start and customize PowerPoint, Windows must be running. If you are stepping through this project on a computer and you want your screen to match the figures in this book, then you should change your computer's resolution to 800 × 600. For more information on how to change the resolution on your computer, see Appendix B.

More About

Outlining

Outlining helps you plan, organize, and design your presentation. When you start to create an outline, you often begin to see new possibilities and find new ways to divide and group your ideas. You also find gaps where additional information is needed. A final glance at an outline can tell you if your plan is appropriate. For more information on outlining, visit the PowerPoint 2003 More About Web page (scsite.com/ppt2003 /more) and click Outlining.

To Start and Customize PowerPoint

1 Click the Start button on the Windows taskbar, point to All Programs on the Start menu, point to Microsoft Office on the All Programs submenu, and then click Microsoft Office PowerPoint 2003 on the Microsoft Office submenu.

2 If the PowerPoint window is not maximized, double-click its title bar to maximize it.

3 If the Language bar appears, right-click it and then click Close the Language bar on the shortcut menu.

4 If the Getting Started task pane appears in the PowerPoint window, click its Close button in the upper-right corner.

5 If the Standard and Formatting toolbars are positioned on the same row, click the Toolbar Options button and then click Show Buttons on Two Rows.

6 Click the Slide Design button on the Formatting toolbar. When the Slide Design task pane is displayed, click the down scroll arrow in the Apply a design template list, and then click the Axis template in the Available For Use area.

7 Click the Close button in the Slide Design task pane.

If the Axis template is not displayed in the Slide Design task pane, ask your instructor about installing additional templates. The PowerPoint window with the Standard and Formatting toolbars on two rows appears as shown in Figure 2-3. PowerPoint displays the Title Slide layout and the Axis template on Slide 1 in normal view.

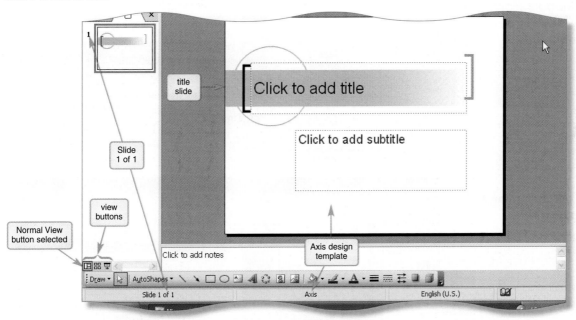

FIGURE 2-3

Using the Outline Tab

The **Outline tab** provides a quick, easy way to create a presentation. **Outlining** allows you to organize your thoughts in a structured format. An outline uses indentation to establish a **hierarchy**, which denotes levels of importance to the main topic. An outline is a summary of thoughts, presented as headings and subheadings, often used as a preliminary draft when you create a presentation.

The three panes — tabs, slide, and notes — shown in normal view also display when you click the Outline tab. The notes pane is displayed below the slide pane. In the tabs pane, the slide text appears along with a slide number and a slide icon. Body text is indented below the title text. Objects, such as pictures, graphs, or tables, do not display. The slide icon is blank when a slide does not contain objects. The attributes for text on the Outline tab are the same as in normal view except for color and paragraph style.

PowerPoint formats a title style and five levels of body text in an outline. The outline begins with the slide title, which is not indented. The title is the main topic of the slide. Body text supporting the main topic begins on the first level and also is not indented. If desired, additional supporting text can be added on the second through fifth levels. Each level is indented. Levels four and five generally are used for very detailed scientific and engineering presentations. Business and sales presentations usually focus on summary information and use the first, second, and third levels.

PowerPoint initially displays in normal view when you start a new presentation. To type the outline, click the Outline tab in the tabs pane. The following steps show how to change to the Outline tab and display the Outlining toolbar.

To Change to the Outline Tab and Display the Outlining Toolbar

1

• **Click the Outline tab located in the tabs pane.**

The Outline tab is selected. The tabs pane increases and the slide pane decreases in size. The tabs pane consists of the Outline tab and the Slides tab (Figure 2-4).

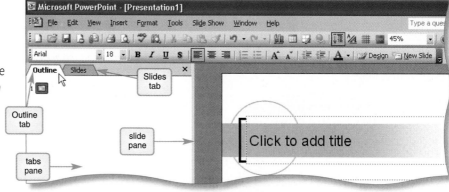

FIGURE 2-4

2

• **Click View on the menu bar and then point to Toolbars.**

• **Point to Outlining on the Toolbars submenu.**

The View menu and Toolbars submenu are displayed (Figure 2-5).

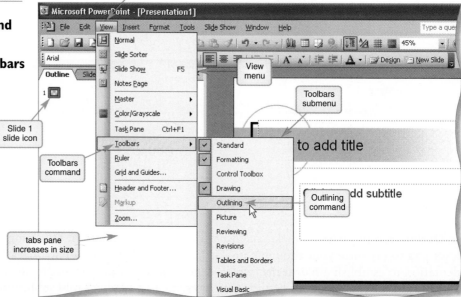

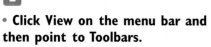

FIGURE 2-5

3

• **Click Outlining.**

The Outlining toolbar is displayed (Figure 2-6).

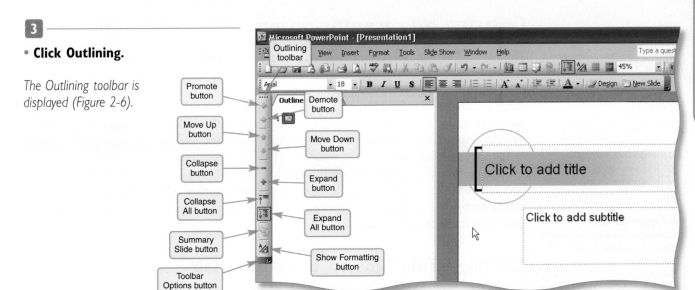

Promote button

Move Up button

Collapse button

Collapse All button

Summary Slide button

Toolbar Options button

Demote button

Move Down button

Expand button

Expand All button

Show Formatting button

FIGURE 2-6

You can create and edit your presentation on the Outline tab. This tab also makes it easy to sequence slides and to relocate title text and body text from one slide to another. In addition to typing text to create a new presentation on the Outline tab, PowerPoint can produce slides from an outline created in Microsoft Word or another word processing application if you save the outline as an RTF file or as a plain text file. The file extension **RTF** stands for **R**ich **T**ext **F**ormat.

Table 2-1 describes the buttons on the Outlining toolbar.

	Table 2-1	Buttons on the Outlining Toolbar
BUTTON	**BUTTON NAME**	**DESCRIPTION**
	Promote	Moves the selected paragraph to the next-higher level (up one level, to the left).
	Demote	Moves the selected paragraph to the next-lower level (down one level, to the right).
	Move Up	Moves a selected paragraph and its collapsed (temporarily hidden) subordinate text above the preceding displayed paragraph.
	Move Down	Moves a selected paragraph and its collapsed (temporarily hidden) subordinate text down, below the following displayed paragraph.
	Collapse	Hides all but the titles of selected slides. Collapsed text is represented by a gray line.
	Expand	Displays the titles and all collapsed text of selected slides.
	Collapse All	Displays only the title of each slide. Text other than the title is represented by a gray line below the title.
	Expand All	Displays the titles and all the body text for each slide.
	Summary Slide	Creates a new slide from the titles of the slides you select in slide sorter or normal view. The summary slide creates a bulleted list from the titles of the selected slides. PowerPoint inserts the summary slide in front of the first selected slide.
	Show Formatting	Shows or hides character formatting (such as bold and italic) in normal view. In slide sorter view, switches between showing all text and objects on each slide and displaying titles only.
	Toolbar Options	Allows you to select the particular buttons you want to display on the toolbar.

Creating a Presentation on the Outline Tab

The Outline tab enables you to view title and body text, add and delete slides, drag and drop slide text, drag and drop individual slides, promote and demote text, save a presentation, print an outline, print slides, copy and paste slides or text to and from other presentations, apply a design template, and import an outline. When you **drag and drop** slide text or individual slides, you change the order of the text or the slides by selecting the text or slide you want to move or copy and then dragging the text or slide to its new location.

Developing a presentation on the Outline tab is quick because you type the text for all slides on one screen. Once you type the outline, the presentation fundamentally is complete. If you choose, you then can enhance your presentation with objects in the slide pane.

Creating a Title Slide on the Outline Tab

Recall from Project 1 that the title slide introduces the presentation to the audience. In addition to introducing the presentation, Project 2 uses the title slide to capture the audience's attention by using a design template with an interesting title. The following steps show how to create a title slide on the Outline tab.

To Create a Title Slide on the Outline Tab

1

• **Click the Slide 1 slide icon on the Outline tab.**

The Slide 1 slide icon is selected. You also could click anywhere in the tabs pane to select the slide icon (Figure 2-7).

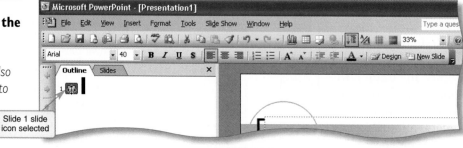

FIGURE 2-7

2

• **Type** Healthy Eating **and then press the SHIFT+ENTER keys.**

• **Type** Healthy Living **and then press the ENTER key.**

• **Point to the Demote button on the Outlining toolbar.**

The Demote ScreenTip is displayed (Figure 2-8). Pressing the SHIFT+ENTER keys moves the insertion point to the next line and maintains the same first level. The insertion point is in position for typing the title for Slide 2. The first-level font is Arial and the font size is 40 point.

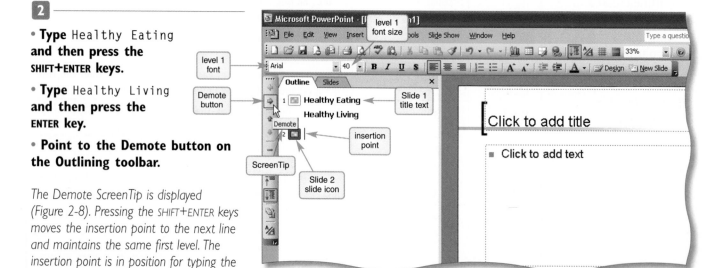

FIGURE 2-8

3

- **Click the Demote button on the Outlining toolbar.**
- **Type** Nutrition and Fitness Basics **and then press the ENTER key.**
- **Type** Clark College Fitness Center **and then press the ENTER key.**

The paragraphs, Nutrition and Fitness Basics and Clark College Fitness Center, are subtitles on the title slide (Slide 1) and demote to the second level (Figure 2-9). The second level is indented to the right below the first-level paragraph. The second-level font is Arial and the font size is 32 point.

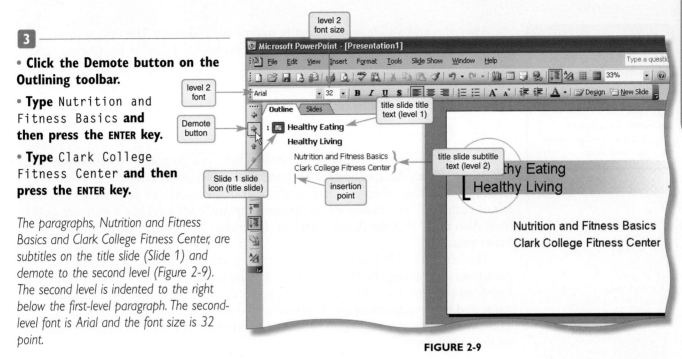

FIGURE 2-9

The title slide text for the Healthy Eating, Healthy Living presentation is complete. The next section explains how to add a slide on the Outline tab.

Adding a Slide on the Outline Tab

Recall from Project 1 that when you add a new slide in normal view, PowerPoint defaults to a Text slide layout with a bulleted list. This action occurs on the Outline tab as well. One way to add a new slide on the Outline tab is to promote a paragraph to the first level by clicking the Promote button on the Outlining toolbar until the insertion point or the paragraph is displayed at the first level. A slide icon is displayed when the insertion point or paragraph reaches this level. The following step shows how to add a slide on the Outline tab.

To Add a Slide on the Outline Tab

1

- **Click the Promote button on the Outlining toolbar.**

The Slide 2 slide icon is displayed, indicating a new slide is added to the presentation (Figure 2-10). The insertion point is in position to type the title for Slide 2 at the first level.

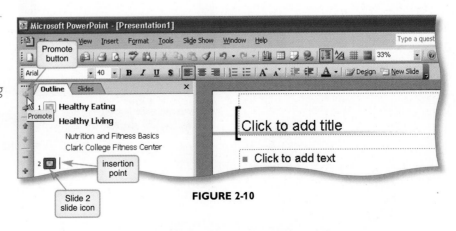

FIGURE 2-10

Other Ways

1. Type title text, press ENTER, click Demote button on Formatting toolbar, type subtitle text, press ENTER
2. Type title text, press ENTER, press TAB, type subtitle text, press ENTER

Other Ways

1. Click New Slide button on Formatting toolbar
2. On Insert menu click New Slide
3. Press CTRL+M, press ENTER
4. Press ALT+I, press N
5. In Voice Command mode, say "New Slide"

After you add a slide, you are ready to type the slide text. The next section explains how to create text slides with multi-level bulleted lists on the Outline tab.

Creating Text Slides with Multi-Level Bulleted Lists on the Outline Tab

To create a text slide with multi-level bulleted lists, you demote or promote the insertion point to the appropriate level and then type the paragraph text. Recall from Project 1 that when you demote a paragraph, PowerPoint adds a bullet to the left of each level. Depending on the design template, each level has a different bullet font. Also recall that the design template determines font attributes, including the bullet font.

The first text slide you create in Project 2 describes the basic nutritional guidelines comprising the Healthy Eating Pyramid. The slide title is displayed as a first-level paragraph on the Outline tab and in the slide pane, and the Pyramid name and food suggestions are displayed as second- and third-level paragraphs. The following steps explain how to create a text slide with a multi-level bulleted list on the Outline tab.

To Create a Text Slide with a Multi-Level Bulleted List on the Outline Tab

1

• **Type** Nutrition Guidelines **and then press the ENTER key.**

• **Click the Demote button on the Outlining toolbar to demote to the second level.**

The title for Slide 2, Nutrition Guidelines, is displayed and the insertion point is in position to type the first bulleted paragraph (Figure 2-11). A bullet is displayed to the left of the insertion point.

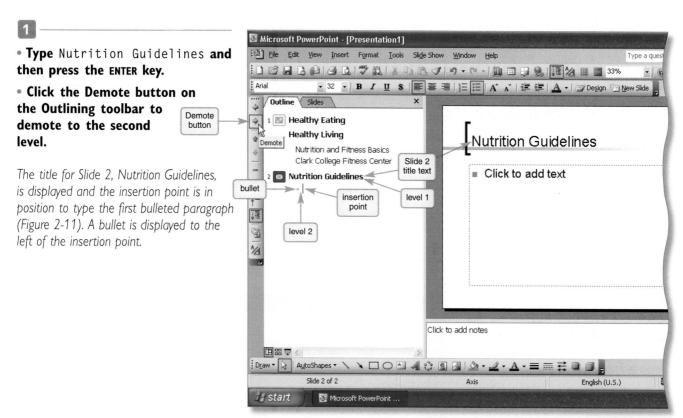

FIGURE 2-11

2

• **Type** Healthy Eating Pyramid **and then press the ENTER key.**

• **Click the Demote button on the Outlining toolbar to demote to the third level.**

• **Type** Eat more vegetable oils, whole grains **and then press the ENTER key.**

• **Type** Eat less pasta, white bread **and then press the ENTER key.**

Slide 2 is displayed with three levels: the title, Nutrition Guidelines, on the first level; the Pyramid name on the second level; and two bulleted paragraphs and the insertion point on the third level (Figure 2-12).

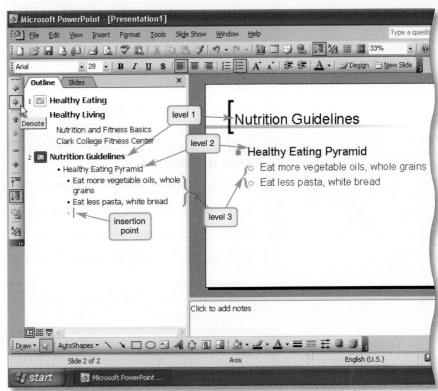

FIGURE 2-12

Slide 2 is complete. The text on this slide abides by the 7 × 7 rule. As you learned in Project 1, this rule recommends that each line should have a maximum of seven words, and each slide should have a maximum of seven lines. All slides in this slide show use the 7 × 7 rule.

The remaining three slides in the presentation contain multi-level bulleted lists. Slide 3 provides information about exercise guidelines, Slide 4 gives details about relaxation procedures, and Slide 5 lists the benefits of adhering to a healthy lifestyle. It is easy and efficient to type the text for these slides on the Outline tab because you can view all the text you type in the outline in the tabs pane to check organization.

Creating a Second Text Slide with a Multi-Level Bulleted List

The next slide, Slide 3, provides details about daily exercise. Experts recommend exercising moderately for 30 minutes each day. The steps on the next page show how to create this slide.

Q&A

Q: How many levels should a slide have?

A: Three. Graphic designers recommend limiting the levels to three although PowerPoint gives you five levels of body text to use on each slide. Details on all five levels may overwhelm audiences. If you find yourself needing more than three levels, consider combining content in one level or using two different slides.

To Create a Second Text Slide with a Multi-Level Bulleted List

1 Click the Promote button on the Outlining toolbar two times so that Slide 3 is added after Slide 2.

2 Type Recommended Exercise and then press the ENTER key.

3 Click the Demote button on the Outlining toolbar to demote to the second level.

4 Type 30 minutes of daily moderate-intensity activity and then press the ENTER key.

5 Click the Demote button to demote to the third level.

6 Type Brisk walking and then press the ENTER key.

7 Type Bicycling and then press the ENTER key.

8 Type Gardening and then press the ENTER key.

The completed Slide 3 is displayed (Figure 2-13).

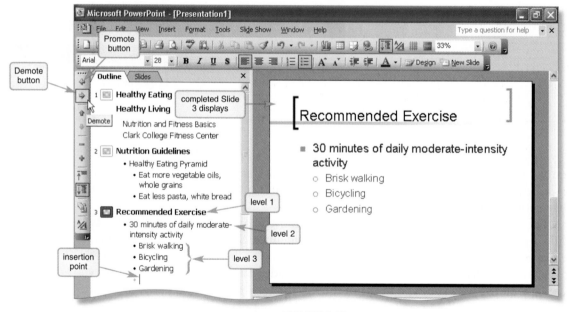

FIGURE 2-13

Creating a Third Text Slide with a Multi-Level Bulleted List

Slide 4 describes recommended relaxation techniques that should be practiced in conjunction with eating nutritional meals and exercising daily. The following steps show how to create this slide.

To Create a Third Text Slide with a Multi-Level Bulleted List

1 Click the Promote button on the Outlining toolbar two times so that Slide 4 is added after Slide 3.

2 Type Relaxation Techniques and then press the ENTER key.

3 Click the Demote button on the Outlining toolbar to demote to the second level.

4 **Type** Quiet the mind and body **and then press the ENTER key.**

5 **Click the Demote button to demote to the third level.**

6 **Type** Visualize a tranquil setting **and then press the ENTER key.**

7 **Type** Concentrate on positive thoughts **and then press the ENTER key.**

8 **Click the Promote button to promote to the second level.**

9 **Type** Build strength and refresh the body **and then press the ENTER key.**

10 **Click the Demote button to demote to the third level.**

11 **Type** Practice yoga or Pilates basics **and then press the ENTER key.**

12 **Type** Improve balance through core training **and then press the ENTER key.**

The completed Slide 4 is displayed (Figure 2-14).

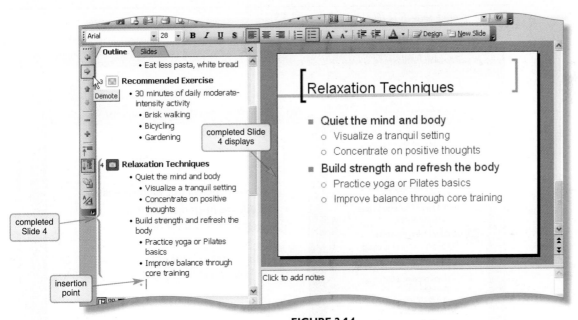

FIGURE 2-14

Creating a Closing Slide on the Outline Tab

The last slide in a presentation is the closing slide. A **closing slide** gracefully ends a presentation. Often used during a question and answer session, the closing slide usually remains on the screen to reinforce the message delivered during the presentation. Professional speakers design the closing slide with one or more of these methods:

1. List important information. Tell the audience what to do next.
2. Provide a memorable illustration or example to make a point.
3. Appeal to emotions. Remind the audience to take action or accept responsibility.
4. Summarize the main point of the presentation.
5. Cite a quotation that directly relates to the main point of the presentation. This technique is most effective if the presentation started with a quotation.

The last text slide you create in Project 2 describes the benefits of practicing a healthy lifestyle. The steps on the next page show how to create this closing slide.

To Create a Closing Slide on the Outline Tab

1 **Click the Promote button on the Outlining toolbar two times to add Slide 5 after Slide 4. Type** Healthy Living Benefits **and then press the ENTER key.**

2 **Click the Demote button on the Outlining toolbar to demote to the second level. Type** Lowers cholesterol, blood pressure **and then press the ENTER key.**

3 **Type** Reduces heart disease risk **and then press the ENTER key.**

4 **Type** Helps prevent adult-onset diabetes **and then press the ENTER key.**

5 **Click the Demote button to demote to the third level. Type** Affects 8% of adults **and then press the ENTER key.**

6 **Click the Promote button to promote to the second level. Type** Maintains body weight **and then press the ENTER key.**

7 **Click the Demote button. Type** Helps avoid excess gain **but do not press the ENTER key.**

The completed Slide 5 is displayed (Figure 2-15).

FIGURE 2-15

The outline now is complete and you should save the presentation. The next section explains how to save the presentation.

Saving a Presentation

Recall from Project 1 that it is wise to save your presentation frequently. With all the text for your presentation created, save the presentation using the following steps.

To Save a Presentation

1 Insert a formatted floppy disk in drive A and then click the Save button on the Standard toolbar.

2 Type Nutrition and Fitness in the File name text box. Do not press the ENTER key after typing the file name. Click the Save in box arrow.

3 Click 3½ Floppy (A:) in the Save in list.

4 Click the Save button in the Save As dialog box.

The presentation is saved with the file name, Nutrition and Fitness, on the floppy disk in drive A. PowerPoint uses the first text line in a presentation as the default file name. The file name is displayed on the title bar.

Reviewing a Presentation in Slide Sorter View

In Project 1, you displayed slides in slide show view to evaluate the presentation. Slide show view, however, restricts your evaluation to one slide at a time. The Outline tab is best for quickly reviewing all the text for a presentation. Recall from Project 1 that slide sorter view allows you to look at several slides at one time, which is why it is the best view to use to evaluate a presentation for content, organization, and overall appearance. The following step shows how to change from the Outline tab to slide sorter view.

To Change the View to Slide Sorter View

1

• **Click the Slide Sorter View button at the lower left of the PowerPoint window.**

PowerPoint displays the presentation in slide sorter view (Figure 2-16). Slide 5 is selected because it was the current slide on the Outline tab. The Slide Sorter View button is selected.

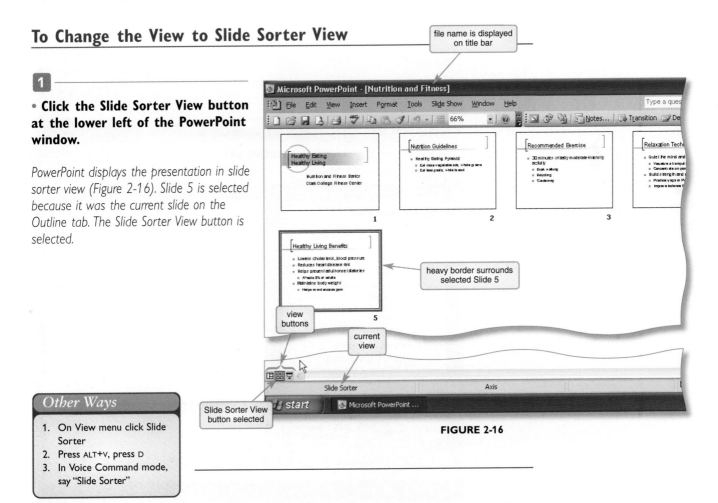

FIGURE 2-16

You can review the five slides in this presentation all in one window. Notice the slides have a significant amount of space and look plain. These observations indicate a need to add visual interest to the slides by using clips. The next several sections explain how to improve the presentation by changing slide layouts and adding clip art.

You can make changes to text in normal view and on the Outline tab. It is best, however, to change the view to normal view when altering the slide layouts so you can see the results of your changes. The following steps show how to change the view from slide sorter view to normal view.

To Change the View to Normal View

1

• **Click the Slide 2 slide thumbnail.**

• **Point to the Normal View button at the lower left of the PowerPoint window.**

Slide 2 is selected, as indicated by the thick blue border around that slide (Figure 2-17).

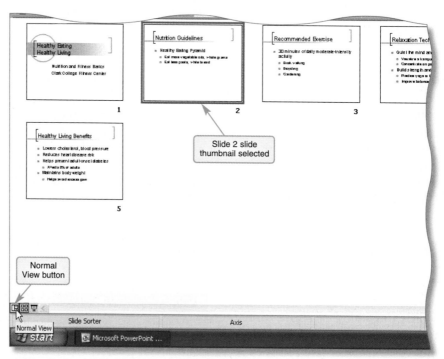

FIGURE 2-17

2

• **Click the Normal View button.**

The Normal View button is selected at the lower left of the PowerPoint window. The Slide 2 slide icon is selected in the tabs pane, and Slide 2 is displayed in the slide pane (Figure 2-18).

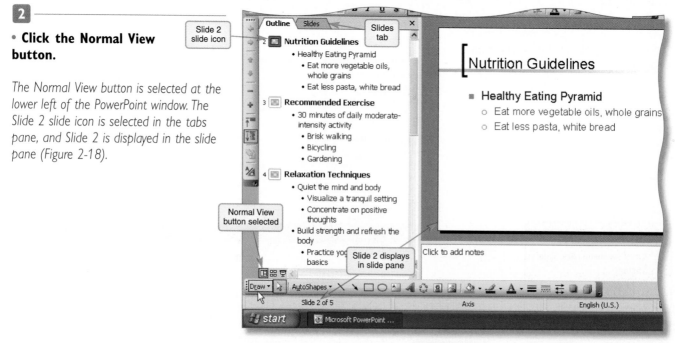

FIGURE 2-18

3

• **Click the Slides tab in the tabs pane.**

The tabs pane reduces in size. Slide thumbnails of the five slides are displayed (Figure 2-19).

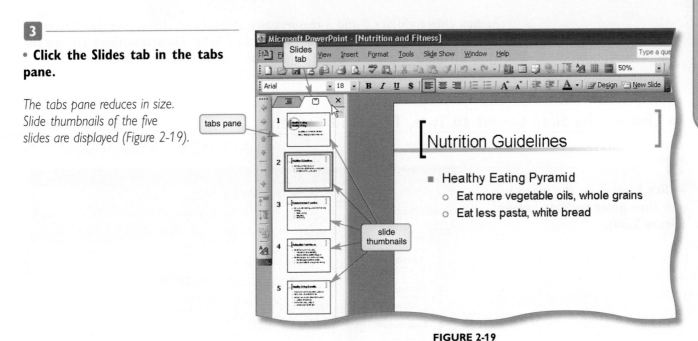

FIGURE 2-19

Switching between slide sorter view and normal view helps you review your presentation and assess whether the slides have an attractive design and adequate content.

Changing Slide Layout

When you developed this presentation, PowerPoint applied the Title Slide layout for Slide 1 and the Title and Text layout for the other four slides in the presentation. These layouts are the default styles. A **layout** specifies the arrangement of placeholders on a slide. These placeholders are arranged in various configurations and can contain text, such as the slide title or a bulleted list, or they can contain content, such as clips, pictures, charts, tables, and shapes. The placement of the text, in relationship to content, depends on the slide layout. The content placeholders may be to the right or left of the text, above the text, or below the text. You can specify a particular slide layout when you add a new slide to a presentation or after you have created the slide.

Using the **Slide Layout task pane**, you can choose a slide layout. The layouts in this task pane are arranged in four areas: Text Layouts, Content Layouts, Text and Content Layouts, and Other Layouts. The two layouts you have used in this project — Title Slide and Title and Text — are included in the Text Layouts area, along with the Title Only and Title and 2-Column Text layouts. The Content Layouts area contains a blank slide and a variety of placeholder groupings for charts, tables, clip art, pictures, diagrams, and media clips. The Text and Content Layouts have placeholders for a title, a bulleted list, and content. The Other Layouts area has layouts with placeholders for a title and one object, such as clip art, charts, media clips, tables, organization charts, and charts.

When you change the layout of a slide, PowerPoint retains the text and objects and repositions them into the appropriate placeholders. Using slide layouts eliminates the need to resize objects and the font size because PowerPoint automatically sizes the objects and text to fit the placeholders. If the objects are in **landscape orientation**, meaning their width is greater than their height, PowerPoint sizes them to the width of the placeholders. If the objects are in **portrait orientation**, meaning their height is greater than their width, PowerPoint sizes them to the height of the placeholders.

More About

Slide Content

Indentation identifies levels of importance. The more important the item, the closer it should be displayed to the left edge of the slide. Subordinate items must support the main topic under which they are placed. This means they must be less important in meaning while being related logically.

Adding clips to Slides 2 and 3 requires two steps. First, change the slide layout to Title, Text, and Content or to Title, 2 Content and Text. Then, insert clip art into the content placeholders. The following steps show how to change the slide layout on Slide 2 from Title and Text to Title, Text, and Content.

To Change the Slide Layout to Title, Text, and Content

1

• **Click Format on the menu bar and then point to Slide Layout (Figure 2-20).**

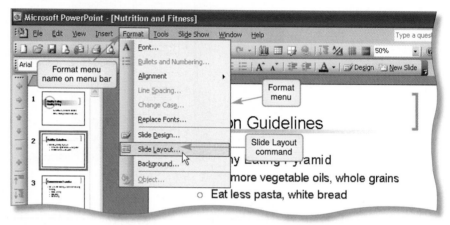

FIGURE 2-20

2

• **Click Slide Layout.**

• **Click the down arrow in the Apply slide layout area and scroll down until the Text and Content Layouts area displays.**

• **Point to the Title, Text, and Content layout in the Text and Content Layouts area.**

The Slide Layout task pane is displayed (Figure 2-21). The Title, Text, and Content layout is selected, as indicated by the blue box around the template, the ScreenTip, and the down arrow on the right side.

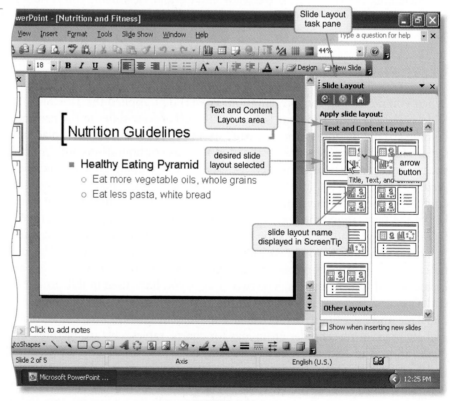

FIGURE 2-21

3

• **Click Title, Text, and Content.**

The layout is applied to Slide 2 (Figure 2-22). PowerPoint moves the text placeholder containing the bulleted list to the left side of the slide and automatically resizes the text. The content placeholder on the right side of the slide has the message, Click icon to add content.

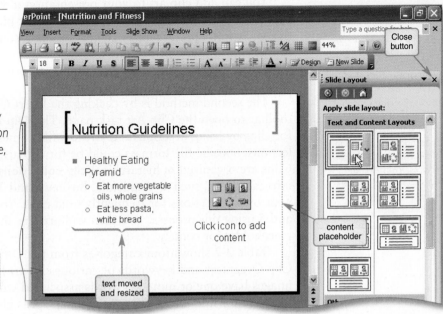

FIGURE 2-22

4

• **Click the Close button in the Slide Layout task pane.**

Slide 2 is displayed in normal view with the new slide layout applied (Figure 2-23).

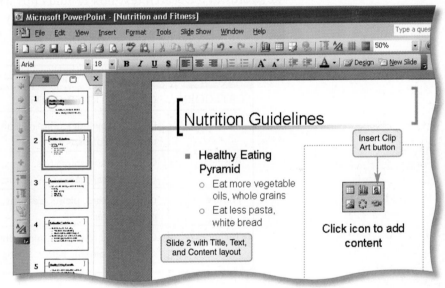

FIGURE 2-23

PowerPoint reduced the second-level text in the Slide 2 text placeholder from a font size of 32 point to 28 point so all the words fit into the placeholder.

Adding Clip Art to a Slide

Clip art helps the visual appeal of the Nutrition and Fitness slide show and offers a quick way to add professional-looking graphic images to a presentation without creating the images yourself. This art is contained in the **Microsoft Clip Organizer**, a collection of drawings, photographs, sounds, videos, and other media files shared with Microsoft Office applications.

Other Ways

1. Right-click slide anywhere except text placeholders, click Slide Layout on shortcut menu, double-click desired slide layout
2. Press ALT+O, press L, press ARROW keys to select desired slide layout, press ENTER
3. In Voice Command mode, say "Format, Slide Layout, Title Text and Content, Close"

Q: Can I add clips to the Clip Organizer?

A: Yes. You can add media files and objects created in Microsoft Office programs. The media files are stored in a new subcollection in the My Collections clip collection folder. The objects can be pictures, WordArt, and AutoShapes, and you can store them in any desired collection folder.

You can add clip art to your presentation in two ways. One way is by selecting one of the slide layouts that includes a content placeholder with instructions to open the Microsoft Clip Organizer to add content. You will add art to Slides 2 and 3 in this manner. Double-clicking a button in the content placeholder activates the instructions to open the Select Picture dialog box, which allows you to enter keywords to search for clips.

The second method is by clicking the Insert Clip Art button on the Drawing toolbar to open the Clip Art task pane. The **Clip Art task pane** allows you to search for clips by using descriptive keywords, file names, media file formats, and clip collections. Specific file formats could be for clip art, photographs, movies, and sounds. Clips are organized in hierarchical **clip collections**, which combine topic-related clips into categories, such as Academic, Business, and Technology. You also can create your own collections for frequently used clips. You will insert clip art into Slides 4 and 5 using this process. You then will arrange the clips on the slides without using a placeholder for content.

Table 2-2 shows four categories from the Office Collections in the Microsoft Clip Organizer and keywords of various clip art files in those categories. Clip art images have one or more keywords associated with various entities, activities, labels, and emotions. In most instances, the keywords give the name of the clip and related categories. For example, an image of a cow in the Animals category has the keywords animals, cattle, cows, dairies, farms, and Holsteins. You can enter these keywords in the Search text box to find clips when you know one of the words associated with the image. Otherwise, you may find it necessary to scroll through several categories to find an appropriate clip.

Table 2-2	Microsoft Clip Organizer Category and Keyword Examples
CATEGORY	**CLIP ART KEYWORDS**
Academic	Books, knowledge, information, schools, school buses, apple for the teacher, professors
Business	Computers, inspirations, ideas, currencies, board meetings, conferences, teamwork, profits
Nature	Lakes, flowers, plants, seasons, wildlife, weather, trees, sunshine, rivers, leaves
Technology	Computers, diskettes, microchips, cellular telephones, e-commerce, office equipment, data exchanges

Depending on the installation of the Microsoft Clip Organizer on your computer, you may not have the clip art used in this project. Contact your instructor if you are missing clips used in the following steps. If you have an open connection to the Internet, clips from the Microsoft Web site will display automatically as the result of your search results.

Inserting Clip Art into a Content Placeholder

With the Title, Text, and Content layout applied to Slide 2, you insert clip art into the content placeholder. The following steps show how to insert clip art of a cornucopia into the content placeholder on Slide 2.

To Insert Clip Art into a Content Placeholder

1

• **Point to the Insert Clip Art button in the content placeholder.**

The Insert Clip Art button is selected (Figure 2-24). A ScreenTip describes its function.

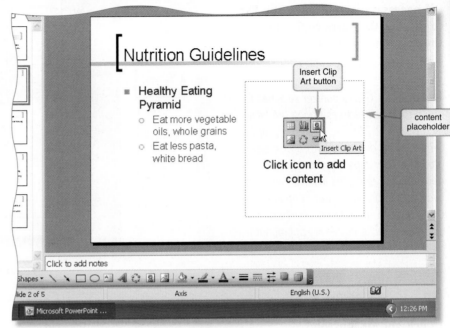

FIGURE 2-24

2

• **Click the Insert Clip Art button.**

• **Type** food **in the Search text text box and then point to the Go button.**

The Select Picture dialog box is displayed (Figure 2-25). The clips displaying on your computer may vary.

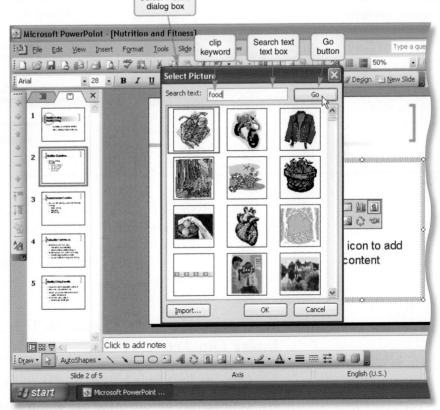

FIGURE 2-25

3

- **Click the Go button.**
- **If necessary, scroll down the list to display the cornucopia clip shown in Figure 2-26.**
- **Click the clip to select it.**

The Microsoft Clip Organizer searches for and displays all pictures having the keyword, food (Figure 2-26). The desired clip of a cornucopia is displayed with a blue box around it. Your clips may be different depending on the clips installed on your computer and if you have an open connection to the Internet, in which case you may need to obtain an appropriate clip from the Internet.

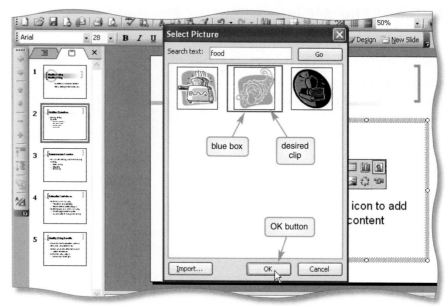

FIGURE 2-26

4

- **Click the OK button.**
- **If the Picture toolbar is displayed, click the Close button on the Picture toolbar.**

The selected clip is inserted into the top content placeholder on Slide 2 (Figure 2-27). PowerPoint sizes the clip automatically to fit the placeholder.

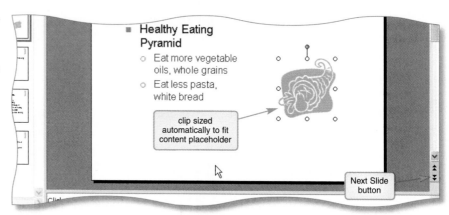

FIGURE 2-27

Slide 2 is complete. The next step is to change the Slide 3 layout and then add two clips. This slide uses the Title, 2 Content and Text slide layout so the two clips display vertically on the left side of the slide and the bulleted list is displayed on the right side. The following steps show how to change the slide layout and then add clip art to Slide 3.

To Change the Slide Layout to Title, 2 Content and Text and Insert Clip Art

1 Click the Next Slide button on the vertical scroll bar to display Slide 3.

2 Click Format on the menu bar and then click Slide Layout.

3 Scroll to display the Title, 2 Content and Text slide layout located in the Text and Content Layouts area of the Slide Layout task pane.

4 Click the Title, 2 Content and Text slide layout and then click the Close button in the Slide Layout task pane.

5 Click the Insert Clip Art button in the top content placeholder. **Type** woman in the Search text text box and then click the Go button.

6 If necessary, scroll down the list to display the desired clip of a woman walking and then click the clip to select it. Click the OK button.

The selected clip is inserted into the content placeholder on Slide 3 (Figure 2-28). The slide has the Title, 2 Content and Text slide layout.

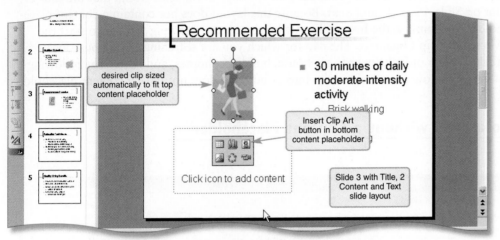

FIGURE 2-28

Inserting a Second Clip into a Slide

Another clip on Slide 3 is required to fill the bottom content placeholder. This clip should be the image of roses. The following steps show how to insert the roses clip into the bottom placeholder on Slide 3.

To Insert a Second Clip into a Slide

1 Click the Insert Clip Art button in the bottom content placeholder.

2 Type flowers in the Search text text box and then click the Go button.

3 If necessary, scroll down the list to display the desired clip of yellow roses, click the clip to select it, and then click the OK button.

The selected clip is inserted into the bottom content placeholder on Slide 3 (Figure 2-29). PowerPoint automatically sizes the clip to fit the placeholder.

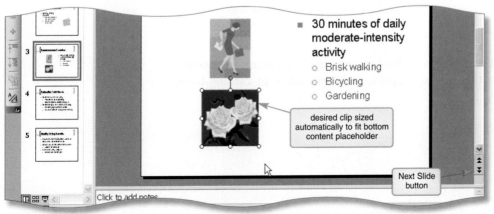

FIGURE 2-29

Slide 3 is complete. Your next step is to add a clip to Slide 4 without changing the slide layout.

Inserting Clip Art into a Slide without a Content Placeholder

PowerPoint does not require you to use a content placeholder to add clips to a slide. You can insert clips on any slide regardless of its slide layout. On Slides 2 and 3, you added clips that enhanced the message in the text. Recall that the slide layout on Slide 4 is Title and Text. Because this layout does not contain a content placeholder, you can use the Insert Clip Art button on the Drawing toolbar to start the Microsoft Clip Organizer. The clip for which you are searching has a house located by a lake. A few of its keywords are house, buildings, homes, and lakes. The following steps show how to insert this clip into a slide that does not have a content placeholder.

To Insert Clip Art into a Slide without a Content Placeholder

1

• **Click the Next Slide button on the vertical scroll bar to display Slide 4.**

• **Click Tools on the menu bar and then click AutoCorrect Options.**

• **If necessary, when the AutoCorrect dialog box displays, click the AutoFormat As You Type tab.**

• **Click Automatic layout for inserted objects in the Apply as you work area if a check mark does not display.**

• **Click OK.**

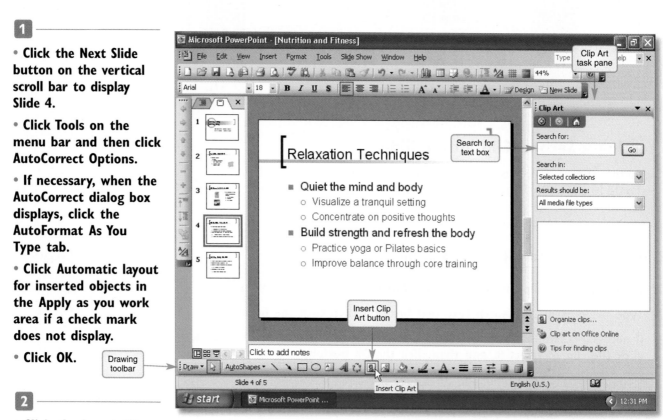

FIGURE 2-30

2

• **Click the Insert Clip Art button on the Drawing toolbar.**

• **If the Add Clips to Organizer dialog box displays asking if you want to catalog media files, click Don't show this message again, or, if you want to catalog later, click the Later button.**

The Clip Art task pane is displayed (Figure 2-30).

3

• **Click the Search for text box.**

• **Type** house **and then press the ENTER key.**

• **If necessary, scroll to display the desired clip of a house located beside a lake.**

• **Point to this image.**

The clip of a lake and house is displayed with any other clips sharing the house keyword (Figure 2-31). Your clips may be different. The clip's keywords, size in pixels (260 x 223), file size (33 KB), and file type (WMF) are displayed.

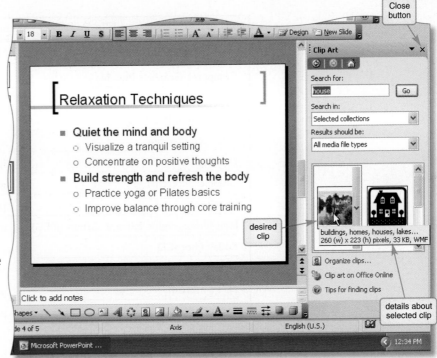

FIGURE 2-31

4

• **Click the desired clip.**

• **Click the Close button on the Clip Art task pane title bar.**

PowerPoint inserts the clip into Slide 4 (Figure 2-32). The slide layout changes automatically to Title, Text, and Content. The Automatic Layout Options button is displayed. If your slide layout does not change, then continue this project using the Moving Clip Art section on page PPT 108.

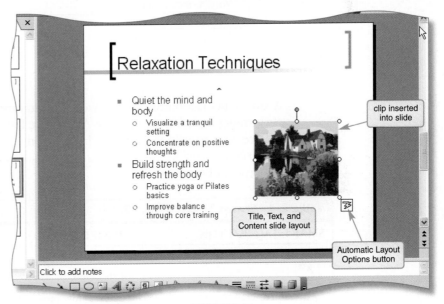

FIGURE 2-32

In addition to clip art, you can insert pictures into a presentation. These may include scanned photographs, line art, and artwork from compact discs. To insert a picture into a presentation, the picture must be saved in a format that PowerPoint can recognize. Table 2-3 (on the next page) identifies some of the formats PowerPoint recognizes.

You can import files saved with the .emf, .gif, .jpg, .png, .bmp, .rle, .dib, and .wmf formats directly into PowerPoint presentations. All other file formats require separate filters that are shipped with the PowerPoint installation software and must be installed. You can download additional filters from the Microsoft Office Online Web site.

Table 2-3 Primary File Formats PowerPoint Recognizes	
FORMAT	**FILE EXTENSION**
Computer Graphics Metafile	.cgm
CorelDRAW	.cdr, .cdt, .cmx, and .pat
Encapsulated PostScript	.eps
Enhanced Metafile	.emf
FlashPix	.fpx
Graphics Interchange Format	.gif
Hanako	.jsh, .jah, and .jbh
Joint Photographic Experts Group (JPEG)	.jpg
Kodak PhotoCD	.pcd
Macintosh PICT	.pct
PC Paintbrush	.pcx
Portable Network Graphics	.png
Tagged Image File Format	.tif
Windows Bitmap	.bmp, .rle, .dib
Microsoft Windows Metafile	.wmf
WordPerfect Graphics	.wpg

Smart Tags

A **smart tag** is a button that PowerPoint automatically displays on the screen when performing a certain action. The Automatic Layout Options button in Figure 2-32 on the previous page is a smart tag. In addition to the Automatic Layout Options button, PowerPoint provides three other smart tags. Table 2-4 summarizes the smart tags available in PowerPoint.

Table 2-4 Smart Tags in PowerPoint		
SMART TAG BUTTON		**MENU FUNCTION**
[icon]	AutoCorrect Options	Undoes an automatic correction, stops future automatic corrections of this type, or displays the AutoCorrect Options dialog box.
[icon]	Paste Options	Specifies how moved or pasted items should display, e.g., with original formatting, without formatting, or with different formatting.
[icon]	AutoFit Options	Undoes automatic text resizing to fit the current placeholder or changes single-column layouts to two-column layouts, inserts a new slide, or splits the text between two slides.
[icon]	Automatic Layout Options	Adjusts the slide layout to accommodate an inserted object.

Clicking a smart tag button shows a menu that contains commands relative to the action performed at the location of the smart tag. For example, if you want PowerPoint to undo the layout change when you add a clip to a slide, click the Automatic Layout Options button to display the Smart Tag Actions menu, and then click Undo Automatic Layout on the Smart Tag Actions menu to display the initial layout.

Using the Automatic Layout Options Button to Undo a Layout Change

The Title and Text layout used in Slide 4 did not provide a content placeholder for the clip you inserted, so PowerPoint automatically changed the layout to Title, Text, and Content. If your slide layout did not change, then disregard this section and continue the project on the next page with the Moving Clip Art section. Because the text now violates the 7 × 7 rule with this layout and because you want to place the clip in a location other than the areas specified, you should change the layout to the Title and Text layout.

The Automatic Layout Options button is displayed because PowerPoint changed the layout automatically. If you move your mouse pointer near the changed object or text, the Automatic Layout Options button is displayed as an arrow, indicating that a list of options is available that allow you to undo the new layout, stop the automatic layout of inserted objects, or alter the AutoCorrect Options settings. The following steps show how to undo the layout change.

To Use the Automatic Layout Options Button to Undo a Layout Change

1

• **If your slide layout automatically changed to Title, Text, and Content, click the Automatic Layout Options button.**

• **Point to Undo Automatic Layout.**

The Automatic Layout Options list is displayed (Figure 2-33). Clicking Undo Automatic Layout will reverse the layout change.

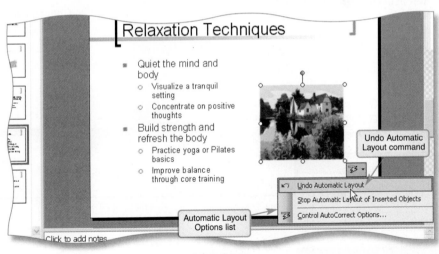

FIGURE 2-33

2

• **Click Undo Automatic Layout.**

The layout reverts to Title and Text (Figure 2-34).

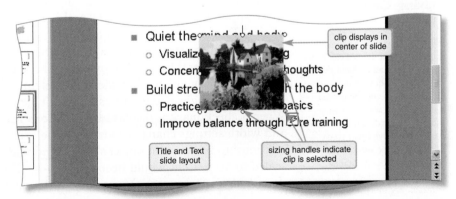

FIGURE 2-34

The desired clip is displayed in the center of Slide 4, which has the original Title and Text slide layout. The next step is to move the clip to the top-right corner of the slide.

Moving Clip Art

After you insert a clip into a slide, you may want to reposition it. The house clip on Slide 4 overlays the bulleted list. You want to move the clip away from the text to the upper-right corner of the slide. The following steps show how to move the clip to the upper-right corner of the slide.

To Move Clip Art

1

• **With the clip selected, point to the clip and then press and hold down the mouse button.**

• **Drag the clip to the upper-right corner of the slide.**

• **Release the mouse button.**

When you drag a clip, a dotted box is displayed. The dotted box indicates the clip's new position. When you release the left mouse button, the clip of the house is displayed in the new location and the dotted line disappears (Figure 2-35). Sizing handles display at the corners and along its edges.

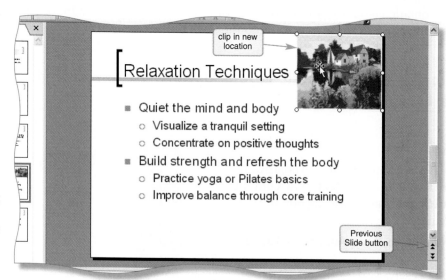

FIGURE 2-35

Changing the Size of Clip Art

Sometimes it is necessary to change the size of clip art. For example, on Slide 2 much space appears around the clip. To make this object fit onto the slide, you increase its size. To change the size of a clip by an exact percentage, use the Format Picture command on the shortcut menu. The Format Picture dialog box contains six tabbed sheets with several formatting options. The **Size sheet** contains options for changing a clip's size. You either enter the exact height and width in the Size and rotate area, or enter the height and width as a percentage of the original clip in the Scale area. When a check mark is displayed in the **Lock aspect ratio check box**, the height and width settings change to maintain the original aspect ratio. **Aspect ratio** is the relationship between an object's height and width. For example, a 3-by-5-inch object scaled to 50 percent would become a 1½-by-2½-inch object. The following steps describe how to increase the size of the clip using the Format Picture dialog box.

To Change the Size of Clip Art

1

- **Click the Previous Slide button on the vertical scroll bar two times to display Slide 2.**
- **Right-click the clip.**
- **Point to Format Picture on the shortcut menu.**

Sizing handles display at the clip's corners and along its edges (Figure 2-36).

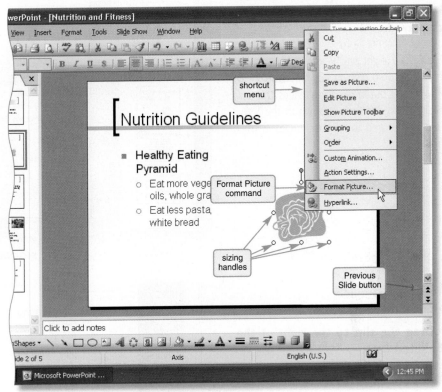

FIGURE 2-36

2

- **Click Format Picture.**
- **Click the Size tab when the Format Picture dialog box is displayed.**

The Size sheet in the Format Picture dialog box is displayed (Figure 2-37). The Height and Width text boxes in the Scale area display the current percentage of the clip, 100%. Check marks are displayed in the Lock aspect ratio and Relative to original picture size check boxes.

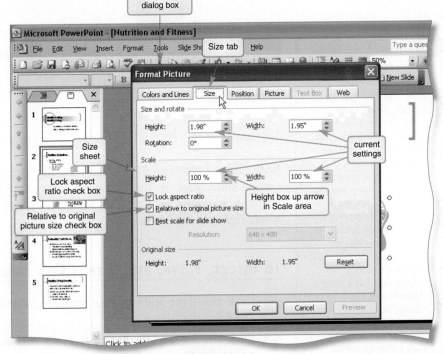

FIGURE 2-37

3

• **Click and hold down the mouse button on the Height box up arrow in the Scale area until 135% is displayed.**

Both the Height and Width text boxes in the Scale area display 135% (Figure 2-38). PowerPoint automatically changes the Height and Width text boxes in the Size and rotate area to reflect changes in the Scale area.

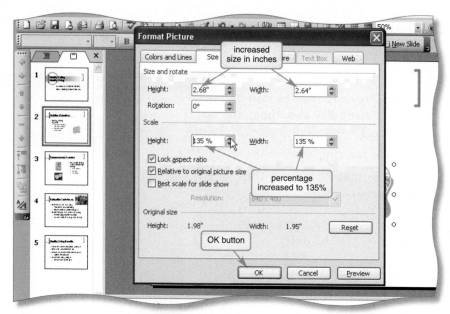

FIGURE 2-38

4

• **Click the OK button.**

• **Drag the clip to the right of the bulleted list.**

PowerPoint closes the Format Picture dialog box and displays the enlarged clip in the desired location (Figure 2-39).

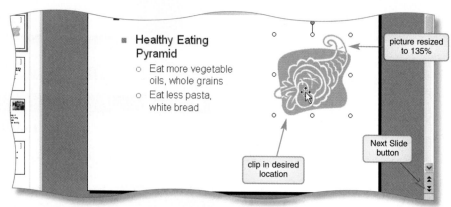

FIGURE 2-39

Other Ways

1. Click clip, on Format menu click Picture, click Size tab, click and hold down mouse button on Height box up or down arrow in Scale area until desired size is reached, click OK button

2. Press ALT+O, press I, press CTRL+TAB three times to select Size tab, press TAB to select Height text box in Scale area, press up or down arrow keys to increase or decrease size, press ENTER

3. Click clip, drag a sizing handle until clip is desired shape and size

4. Right-click slide anywhere except text placeholders, click Slide Layout on shortcut menu, double-click desired slide layout

Inserting, Moving, and Sizing a Clip into a Slide

With Slides 1 through 4 complete, the final step is to add the stethoscope clip to the closing slide, Slide 5. The following steps show how to add a stethoscope to Slide 5 without changing the Title and Text layout, size the clip, and then move it to the lower-right corner of the slide.

To Insert, Move, and Size a Clip into a Slide

1 Click the Next Slide button on the vertical scroll bar three times to display Slide 5.

2 Click the Insert Clip Art button on the Drawing toolbar. Delete the word, house, in the Search for text box, type stethoscope, and then press the ENTER key. Click the stethoscope shown in Figure 2-40 or another appropriate clip. Click the Close button on the Clip Art task pane title bar.

3 If the layout changes, click the Automatic Layout Options button and then click Undo Automatic Layout.

4 Right-click the stethoscope and then click Format Picture on the shortcut menu. Click the Size tab in the Format Picture dialog box, click and hold down the mouse button on the Height box up arrow in the Scale area until 160% is displayed, and then click the OK button.

5 Drag the stethoscope to the lower-right corner of the slide.

The stethoscope is inserted, moved, and sized into Slide 5 (Figure 2-40).

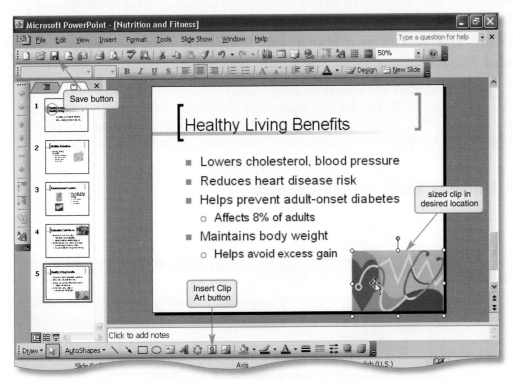

FIGURE 2-40

Saving the Presentation Again

To preserve the work completed, perform the following step to save the presentation again.

To Save a Presentation

1 Click the Save button on the Standard toolbar.

The changes made to the presentation after the previous save are saved on the floppy disk.

A default setting in PowerPoint allows for **fast saves**, which saves only the changes made since the last time you saved. To save a full copy of the complete presentation, click Tools on the menu bar, click Options on the Tools menu, and then click the Save tab. Remove the check mark in the Allow fast saves check box by clicking the check box and then click the OK button.

Adding a Header and Footer to Outline Pages

A printout of the presentation outline often is used as an audience handout. Distributing a copy of the outline provides the audience with paper on which to write notes or comments. Another benefit of distributing a copy of the outline is to help the audience see the text on the slides when lighting is poor or the room is too large. To help identify the source of the printed outline, add a descriptive header and footer. A **header** is displayed at the top of the sheet of paper or slide, and a **footer** is displayed at the bottom. Both contain specific information, such as the presenter's name or the company's telephone number. In addition, the current date and time and the slide or page number can display beside the header or footer information.

Using the Notes and Handouts Sheet to Add Headers and Footers

You add headers and footers to outline pages by clicking the Notes and Handouts sheet in the Header and Footer dialog box and entering the information you want to print. The following steps show how to add the current date, header information, the page number, and footer information to the printed outline.

To Use the Notes and Handouts Sheet to Add Headers and Footers

1

• **Click View on the menu bar and then point to Header and Footer (Figure 2-41).**

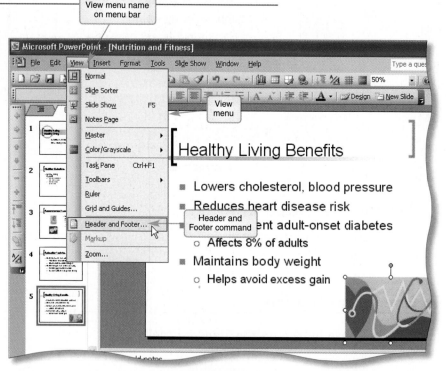

FIGURE 2-41

2

• **Click Header and Footer.**

• **Click the Notes and Handouts tab when the Header and Footer dialog box is displayed.**

The Notes and Handouts sheet in the Header and Footer dialog box is displayed (Figure 2-42). Check marks display in the Date and time, Header, Page number, and Footer check boxes. The Fixed option button is selected.

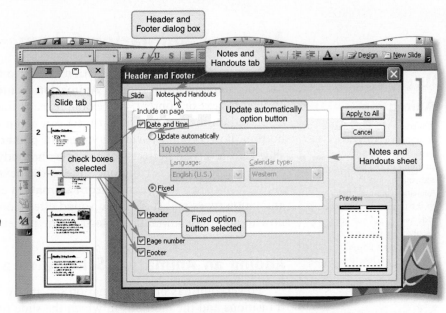

FIGURE 2-42

3

• **Click the Update automatically option button and then click the Header text box.**

• **Type** Healthy Eating, Healthy Living **in the Header text box.**

• **Click the Footer text box.**

• **Type** Clark College Fitness Center **in the Footer text box (Figure 2-43).**

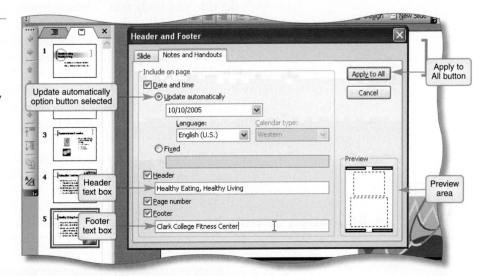

FIGURE 2-43

4

• **Click the Apply to All button.**

PowerPoint applies the header and footer text to the outline, closes the Header and Footer dialog box, and displays Slide 5 (Figure 2-44). You cannot see header and footer text until you print the outline (shown in Figure 2-60 on page PPT 124).

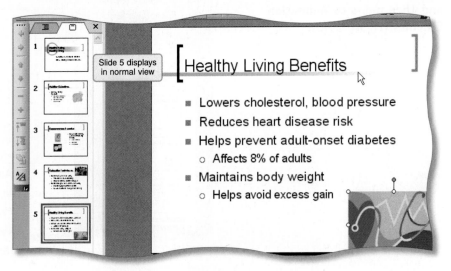

FIGURE 2-44

**Microsoft Office
PowerPoint 2003**

Applying Animation Schemes

PowerPoint provides many animation effects to add interest and make a slide show presentation look professional. **Animation** includes special visual and sound effects applied to text or content. For example, each line on the slide can swivel as it is displayed on the screen. Or an object can zoom in from the top of the screen to the bottom. PowerPoint provides a variety of **preset animation schemes** that determine slide transitions and effects for the title and body text. A **slide transition** is a special effect used to progress from one slide to the next in a slide show. PowerPoint also allows you to set your own **custom animation** effects by defining your own animation types and speeds and sound effects on a slide. The following pages discuss how to add these animation effects to the presentation.

Adding an Animation Scheme to a Slide Show

PowerPoint has preset animation schemes with visual effects that vary the slide transitions and the methods in which the slide title and bullets or paragraphs display on the slides. Not all animation schemes have the slide transition element or effects for both the title and body text. These schemes are grouped in three categories: Subtle, Moderate, and Exciting. The name of the animation scheme characterizes the visual effects used. For example, the Unfold animation scheme in the Moderate category uses the Push Right slide transition effect, the Fly In effect for the title text, and the Unfold effect for the body text. The Pinwheel scheme in the Exciting category does not use a slide transition effect, but it uses the Pinwheel effect for the title text and the Peek In effect for the body text.

In this presentation, you apply the Float animation scheme to all slides. This effect is added easily by using the Slide Design task pane, which you used earlier in this project to select a design template. The following steps show how to apply the Float animation scheme to the Nutrition and Fitness presentation.

To Add an Animation Scheme to a Slide Show

1

• **Click Slide Show on the menu bar and then point to Animation Schemes (Figure 2-45).**

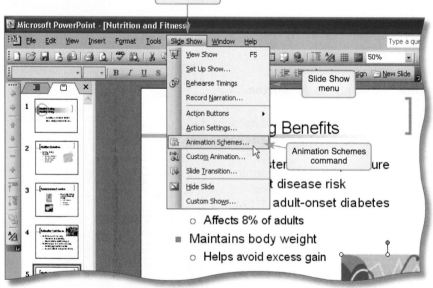

FIGURE 2-45

2

• **Click Animation Schemes.**

• **Scroll down the Apply to selected slides list and then point to Float in the Exciting category.**

The Slide Design task pane is displayed (Figure 2-46). The list of possible slide transition effects is displayed in the Apply to selected slides area. The Float ScreenTip shows that the Float animation scheme uses the Comb Horizontal slide transition, the Float effect for the title text, and the Descend effect for the body text.

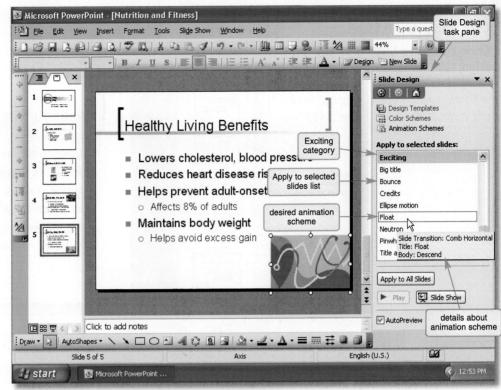

FIGURE 2-46

3

• **Click Float.**

• **Point to the Apply to All Slides button.**

PowerPoint applies the Float animation effect to Slide 5, as indicated by the animation icon on the left side of the Slide 5 slide thumbnail on the Slides tab (Figure 2-47). The Float animation effect is previewed because the AutoPreview check box is selected.

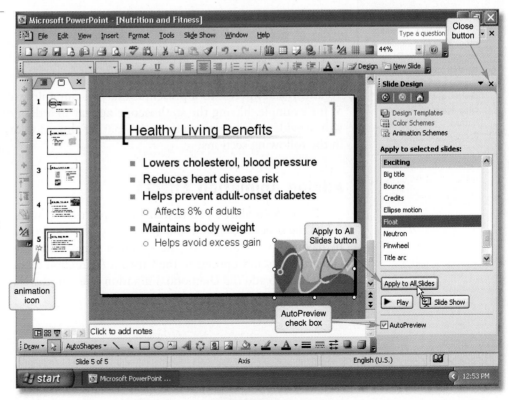

FIGURE 2-47

4

• **Click Apply to All Slides.**

• **Click the Close button in the Slide Design task pane.**

The Float animation effect is applied to all slides in the presentation (Figure 2-48).

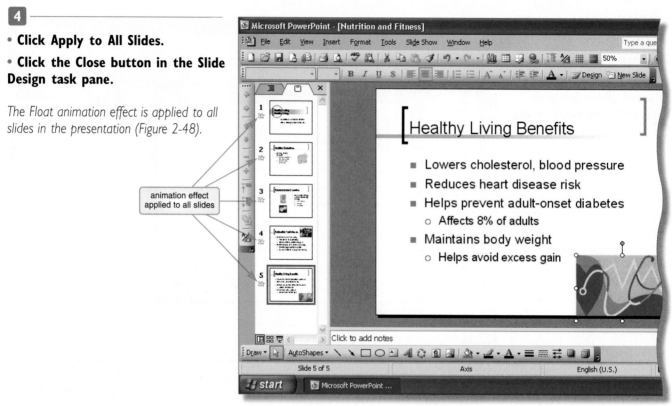

FIGURE 2-48

Animating Clip Art

To add visual interest to a presentation, you can **animate** certain content. On Slide 5, for example, having the stethoscope appear in a diamond pattern on the screen will provide an interesting effect. Animating clip art takes several steps as described in the following sections.

Adding Animation Effects

PowerPoint allows you to animate clip art along with animating text. Because Slide 5 lists the benefits of maintaining a healthy lifestyle, you want to emphasize these facts by having the clip appear on the screen in a diamond pattern. One way of animating clip art is to select options in the Custom Animation dialog box. The following steps show how to add the Diamond animation effect to the clip on Slide 5.

To Animate Clip Art

1

• **Right-click the clip and then point to Custom Animation on the shortcut menu.**

The shortcut menu is displayed (Figure 2-49). The clip is selected, as indicated by the sizing handles that display at the corners and along its edges.

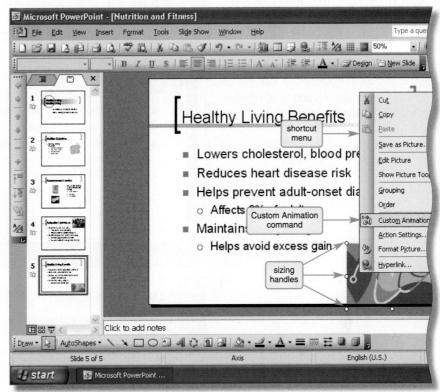

FIGURE 2-49

2

• **Click Custom Animation.**
• **Point to the Add Effect button.**

The Custom Animation task pane is displayed (Figure 2-50). Two animation effects have been applied to the title and body of the slide previously.

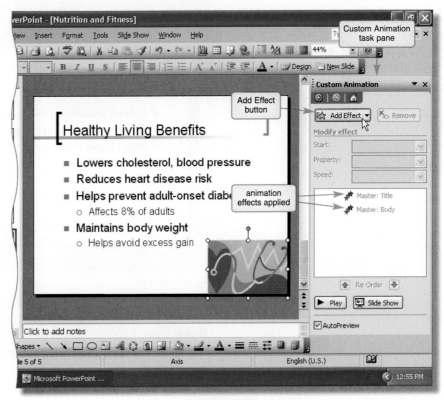

FIGURE 2-50

3

• **Click the Add Effect button, point to Entrance, and then point to Diamond in the Entrance effects list.**

A list of possible effects for the Entrance option is displayed (Figure 2-51). Your list may vary. You can apply a variety of effects to the clip, including how it enters and exits the slide.

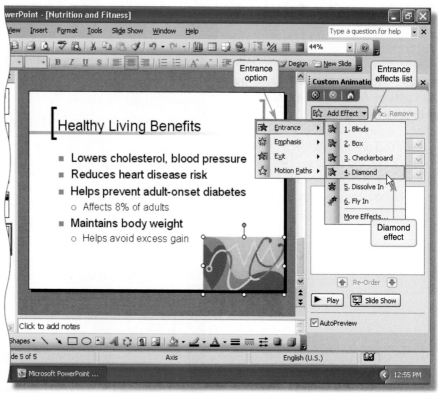

FIGURE 2-51

4

• **Click Diamond.**

The animation effect is applied to the stethoscope, as indicated by the number 1 icon displaying to the left of the clip and the corresponding 1 displaying in the Custom Animation list (Figure 2-52). You will see this effect when you click the mouse on that slide during your slide show.

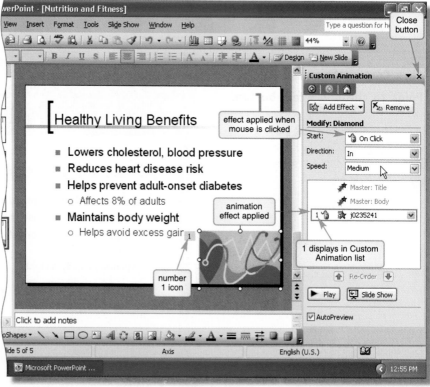

FIGURE 2-52

5

• **Click the Close button on the Custom Animation task pane title bar (Figure 2-53).**

The stethoscope clip will appear in the presentation using the Diamond animation effect during the slide show.

FIGURE 2-53

When you run the slide show, the bulleted-list paragraphs are displayed, and then the clip art will begin displaying on the slide in a diamond shape at the position where you inserted it into Slide 5.

Animation effects are complete for this presentation. You now can review the presentation in slide show view and correct any spelling errors.

Saving the Presentation Again

The presentation is complete. The following step shows how to save the finished presentation on a floppy disk before running the slide show.

To Save a Presentation

1 **Click the Save button on the Standard toolbar.**

PowerPoint saves the presentation on your floppy disk by saving the changes made to the presentation since the last save.

Running an Animated Slide Show

Project 1 introduced you to using slide show view to look at your presentation one slide at a time. This project introduces you to running a slide show with preset and custom animation effects. When you run a slide show with slide transition effects, PowerPoint displays the slide transition effect when you click the mouse button to advance to the next slide. When a slide has text animation effects, each paragraph level is displayed in the sequence specified by the animation settings in the Custom Animation dialog box. The following steps show how to run the animated Nutrition and Fitness presentation.

To Run an Animated Slide Show

1

• **Click the Slide 1 slide thumbnail on the Slides tab.**

• **Click the Slide Show button at the lower left of the PowerPoint window.**

• **When Slide 1 is displayed in slide show view, click the slide anywhere.**

PowerPoint applies the Comb Horizontal slide transition effect and shows the title slide title text, Healthy Eating, Healthy Living (Figure 2-54), using the Float animation effect. When you click the slide, the first paragraph in the subtitle text placeholder, Nutrition and Fitness Basics, is displayed using the Descend animation effect.

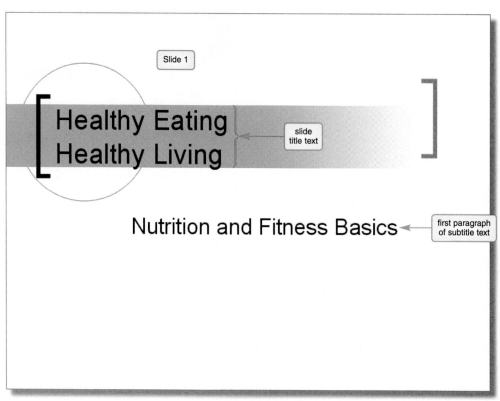

FIGURE 2-54

2

• **Click the slide again.**

PowerPoint displays the second paragraph in the subtitle text placeholder, Clark College Fitness Center, using the Float animation effect (Figure 2-55). If the Popup Menu buttons are displayed when you move the mouse pointer, do not click them.

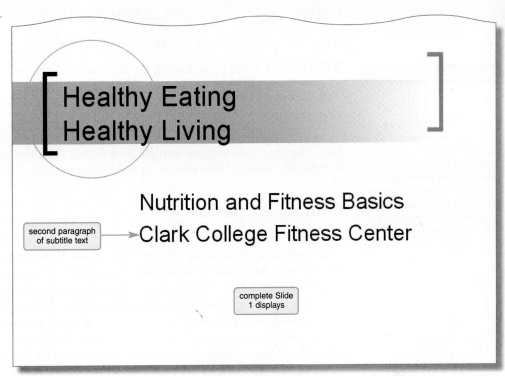

FIGURE 2-55

3

• **Continue clicking to finish running the slide show and return to normal view.**

Each time a new slide is displayed, PowerPoint first displays the Comb Horizontal slide transition effect and only the slide title using the Float effect. Then, PowerPoint builds each slide based on the animation settings. When you click the slide after the last paragraph is displayed on the last slide of the presentation, PowerPoint displays a blank slide. When you click again, PowerPoint exits slide show view and returns to normal view (Figure 2-56).

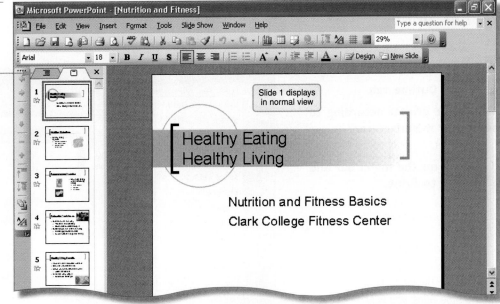

FIGURE 2-56

With the presentation complete and animation effects tested, the last step is to print the presentation outline and slides.

Printing a Presentation Created on the Outline Tab

When you click the Print button on the Standard toolbar, PowerPoint prints a hard copy of the presentation component last selected in the Print what box in the Print dialog box. To be certain to print the component you want, such as the presentation outline, use the Print command on the File menu. When the Print dialog box is displayed, you can select the appropriate presentation component in the Print what box. The next two sections explain how to use the Print command on the File menu to print the presentation outline and the presentation slides.

Printing an Outline

During the development of a lengthy presentation, it often is easier to review your outline in print rather than on the screen. Printing your outline also is useful for audience handouts or when your supervisor or instructor wants to review your subject matter before you develop your presentation fully.

Recall that the Print dialog box shows print options. When you want to print your outline, select Outline View in the Print what list in the Print dialog box. The outline, however, prints as last viewed on the Outline tab. This means that you must select the Zoom setting to display the outline text as you want it to print. If you are uncertain of the Zoom setting, you should return to the Outline tab and review it before printing. The following steps show how to print an outline from normal view.

To Print an Outline

1

• **Click the Outline tab.**

• **Ready the printer according to the printer manufacturer's instructions.**

• **Click File on the menu bar and then point to Print.**

The File menu is displayed (Figure 2-57). The Expand All button on the Outlining toolbar is selected, so the entire outline will print. If you want to print only the slide titles, you would click the Collapse All button.

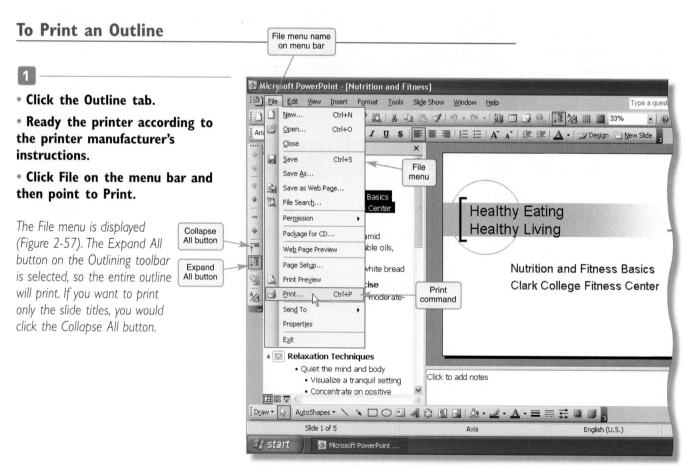

FIGURE 2-57

2

• **Click Print on the File menu.**

• **When the Print dialog box is displayed, click the Print what box arrow and then point to Outline View.**

The Print dialog box is displayed (Figure 2-58). Outline View is displayed highlighted in the Print what list.

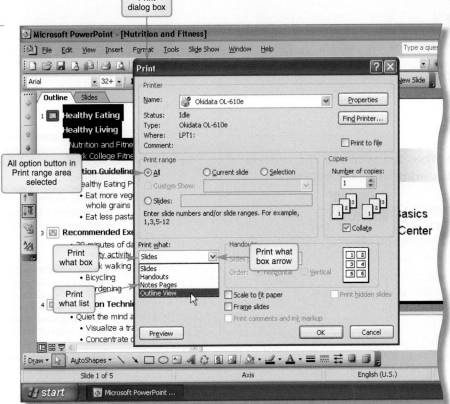

FIGURE 2-58

3

• **Click Outline View in the list (Figure 2-59).**

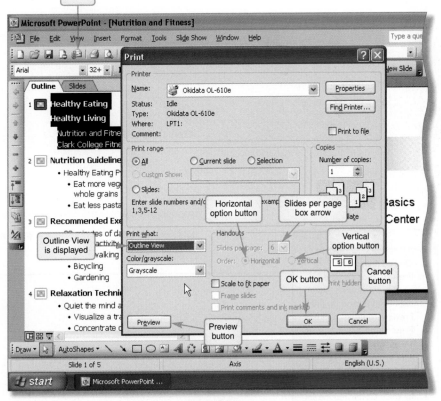

FIGURE 2-59

4

• **Click the OK button.**

To cancel the print request, click the Cancel button.

5

• **When the printer stops, retrieve the printout of the outline.**

PowerPoint displays the five slides in outline form (Figure 2-60). The words, Healthy Eating, Healthy Living, and the current date display in the header, and the words, Clark College Fitness Center, and the page number display in the footer.

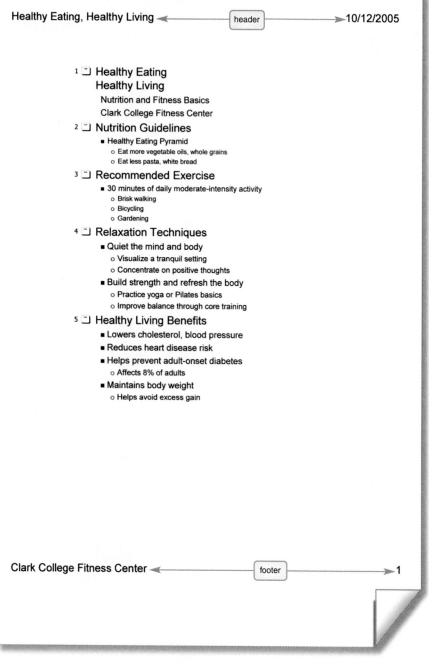

FIGURE 2-60

Other Ways

1. On File menu click Print Preview, click Outline View in Print what list, click Print button on Print Preview toolbar
2. Press ALT+F, press P, press TAB, press W, press DOWN ARROW until Outline View is selected, press ENTER, press ENTER
3. In Voice Command mode, say "File, Print, Print What, Outline View, OK"

The **Print what list** in the Print dialog box contains options for printing slides, handouts, notes, and an outline. The Handouts area allows you to specify whether you want one, two, three, four, six, or nine slide images to display on each page. Printing handouts is useful for reviewing a presentation because you can analyze several slides displayed simultaneously on one page. Additionally, many businesses distribute handouts of the slide show before a presentation so the attendees can refer to a copy. To print handouts, click Handouts in the Print what box, click the Slides per page box arrow in the Handouts area, and then click 1, 2, 3, 4, 6, or 9. You can change the order in which the Nutrition and Fitness slides display on a page by clicking the Horizontal option button for Order in the Handouts area, which shows Slides 1 and 2, 3 and 4, and 5 and 6 adjacent to each other, or the Vertical option button for Order, which shows Slides 1 and 4, 2 and 5, and 3 and 6 adjacent to each other.

You also can click the Preview button if you want to see how your printout will look. After viewing the preview, click the Close button on the Preview window toolbar to return to normal view.

Printing Presentation Slides

At this point, you may want to check the spelling in the entire presentation and instruct PowerPoint to ignore any words spelled correctly. After correcting errors, you will want to print a final copy of your presentation. If you made any changes to your presentation since your last save, be certain to save your presentation before you print.

The following steps show how to print the presentation.

To Print Presentation Slides

1 Ready the printer according to the printer manufacturer's instructions.

2 Click File on the menu bar and then click Print.

3 When the Print dialog box is displayed, click the Print what box arrow.

4 Click Slides in the list.

5 Click the OK button. When the printer stops, retrieve the slide printouts.

The printouts should resemble the slides in Figures 2-61a through 2-61e.

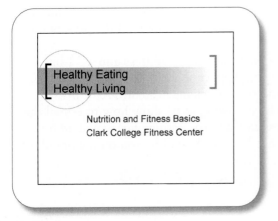

(a) Slide 1

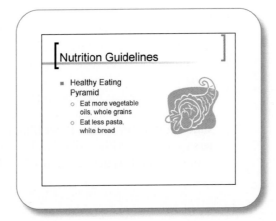

(b) Slide 2

FIGURE 2-61

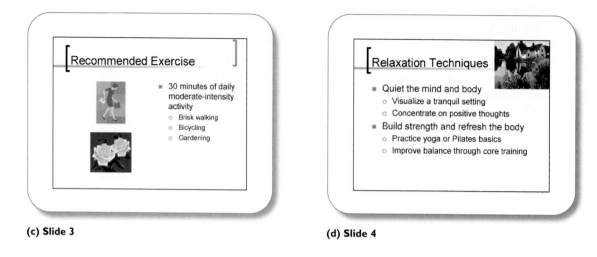

(c) Slide 3

(d) Slide 4

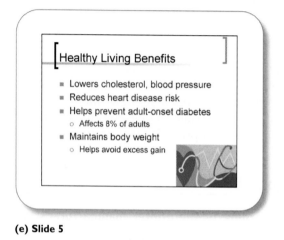

(e) Slide 5

FIGURE 2-61 *(continued)*

E-Mailing a Slide Show from within PowerPoint

More About

The Quick Reference

For more information, see the Quick Reference Summary at the back of this book, or visit the PowerPoint 2003 Quick Reference Web page (scsite.com/ ppt2003/qr).

Billions of e-mail messages are sent throughout the world each day. Computer users use this popular service on the Internet to send and receive plain text e-mail or to send and receive e-mail content that includes objects, links to other Web pages, and file attachments. These attachments can include Office files, such as PowerPoint slide shows or Word documents. Using Microsoft Office, you can e-mail the presentation directly from within PowerPoint.

For these steps to work properly, users need an e-mail address and a 32-bit e-mail program compatible with a Messaging Application Programming Interface, such as Outlook, Outlook Express, or Microsoft Exchange Client. Free e-mail accounts are available at hotmail.com. The following steps show how to e-mail the slide show from within PowerPoint to Jessica Cantero. Assume her e-mail address is jessica_cantero@hotmail.com. If you do not have an E-mail button on the Standard toolbar, then this activity is not available to you.

To E-Mail a Slide Show from within PowerPoint

1

• **Click the E-mail (as Attachment) button on the Standard toolbar. See your instructor if the Choose Profile dialog box displays.**

• **When the e-mail Message window is displayed, type** jessica_cantero @hotmail.com **in the To text box.**

• **Select the text in the Subject text box and then type** Nutrition and Fitness slide show **in the Subject text box.**

• **Click the message body.**

PowerPoint displays the e-mail Message window (Figure 2-62). The insertion point is in the message body so you can type a message to Jessica Cantero.

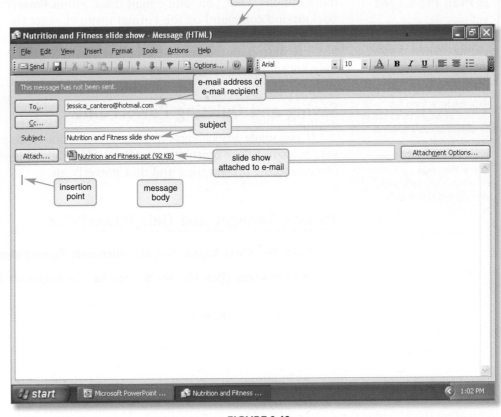

FIGURE 2-62

2

• **Type** Attached is the PowerPoint presentation you can use for your first workshop. **in the message body.**

• **Point to the Send button.**

The message is intended to help the recipient of the e-mail understand the purpose of your e-mail (Figure 2-63).

3

• **Click the Send button on the Standard toolbar.**

The e-mail with the attached presentation is sent to jessica_cantero@hotmail.com.

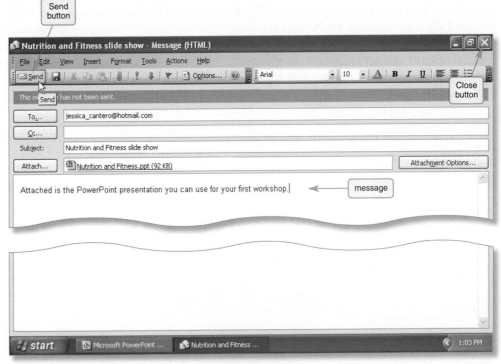

FIGURE 2-63

More About

E-Mail Messages

The first e-mail message was sent in 1969 from Professor Leonard Kleinrock to a colleague at Stanford University. Researchers estimate the number of messages sent daily will jump from the current 31 billion to 60 billion by 2006. For more information on e-mail messages, visit the PowerPoint 2003 More About Web page (scsite.com/ppt2003 /more) and click E-Mail.

Because the slide show was sent as an attachment, Jessica Cantero can save the attachment and then open the presentation in PowerPoint. You can choose many more options when you send e-mail from within PowerPoint. For example, the Background command on the Format menu changes the colors of the message background and lets you add a picture to use as the background. In addition, the Security button on the Standard toolbar allows you to send secure messages that only your intended recipient can read.

Saving and Quitting PowerPoint

If you made any changes to your presentation since your last save, you should save it again before quitting PowerPoint. The following steps show how to save changes to the presentation and quit PowerPoint.

To Save Changes and Quit PowerPoint

1 Click the Close button on the Microsoft PowerPoint window title bar.

2 If prompted, click the Yes button in the Microsoft PowerPoint dialog box.

PowerPoint saves any changes made to the presentation since the last save and then quits PowerPoint.

Project Summary

In creating the Healthy Eating, Healthy Living slide show in this project, you increased your knowledge of PowerPoint. You created a slide presentation on the Outline tab where you entered all the text in the form of an outline. You arranged the text using the Promote and Demote buttons. Once the outline was complete, you changed slide layouts and added clip art. After adding clip art to slides without using a content placeholder, you moved and sized the clips. You added preset animation effects and applied animation effects to a clip. You learned how to run an animated slide show demonstrating slide transition and animation effects. Finally, you printed the presentation outline and slides using the Print command on the File menu and e-mailed the presentation.

If you have a SAM user profile, you may have access to hands-on instruction, practice, and assessment of the skills covered in this project. Log in to your SAM account and go to your assignments page to see what your instructor has assigned.

What You Should Know

Having completed this project, you should be able to perform the tasks below. The tasks are listed in the same order they were presented in this project. For a list of the buttons, menus, toolbars, and commands introduced in this project, see the Quick Reference Summary at the back of this book and refer to the Page Number column.

1. Start and Customize PowerPoint   (PPT 85)
2. Change to the Outline Tab and Display the Outlining Toolbar   (PPT 86)
3. Create a Title Slide on the Outline Tab   (PPT 88)
4. Add a Slide on the Outline Tab   (PPT 89)
5. Create a Text Slide with a Multi-Level Bulleted List on the Outline Tab   (PPT 90)
6. Create a Second Text Slide with a Multi-Level Bulleted List   (PPT 92)
7. Create a Third Text Slide with a Multi-Level Bulleted List   (PPT 92)
8. Create a Closing Slide on the Outline Tab   (PPT 94)
9. Save a Presentation   (PPT 95)
10. Change the View to Slide Sorter View   (PPT 95)
11. Change the View to Normal View   (PPT 96)
12. Change the Slide Layout to Title, Text, and Content   (PPT 98)
13. Insert Clip Art into a Content Placeholder   (PPT 101)
14. Change the Slide Layout to Title, 2 Content and Text and Insert Clip Art   (PPT 102)
15. Insert a Second Clip into a Slide   (PPT 103)
16. Insert Clip Art into a Slide without a Content Placeholder   (PPT 104)
17. Use the Automatic Layout Options Button to Undo a Layout Change   (PPT 107)
18. Move Clip Art   (PPT 108)
19. Change the Size of Clip Art   (PPT 109)
20. Insert, Move, and Size a Clip into a Slide   (PPT 110)
21. Save a Presentation   (PPT 111)
22. Use the Notes and Handouts Sheet to Add Headers and Footers   (PPT 112)
23. Add an Animation Scheme to a Slide Show   (PPT 114)
24. Animate Clip Art   (PPT 117)
25. Save a Presentation   (PPT 119)
26. Run an Animated Slide Show   (PPT 120)
27. Print an Outline   (PPT 122)
28. Print Presentation Slides   (PPT 125)
29. E-Mail a Slide Show from within PowerPoint   (PPT 127)
30. Save Changes and Quit PowerPoint   (PPT 128)

Learn It Online

Instructions: To complete the Learn It Online exercises, start your browser, click the Address bar, and then enter the Web address scsite.com/ppt2003/learn. When the PowerPoint 2003 Learn It Online page is displayed, follow the instructions in the exercises below. Each exercise has instructions for printing your results, either for your own records or for submission to your instructor.

1 Project Reinforcement TF, MC, and SA

Below PowerPoint Project 2, click the Project Reinforcement link. Print the quiz by clicking Print on the File menu for each page. Answer each question.

2 Flash Cards

Below PowerPoint Project 2, click the Flash Cards link and read the instructions. Type 20 (or a number specified by your instructor) in the Number of playing cards text box, type your name in the Enter your Name text box, and then click the Flip Card button. When the flash card is displayed, read the question and then click the ANSWER box arrow to select an answer. Flip through Flash Cards. If your score is 15 (75%) correct or greater, click Print on the File menu to print your results. If your score is less than 15 (75%) correct, then redo this exercise by clicking the Replay button.

3 Practice Test

Below PowerPoint Project 2, click the Practice Test link. Answer each question, enter your first and last name at the bottom of the page, and then click the Grade Test button. When the graded practice test is displayed on your screen, click Print on the File menu to print a hard copy. Continue to take practice tests until you score 80% or better.

4 Who Wants To Be a Computer Genius?

Below PowerPoint Project 2, click the Computer Genius link. Read the instructions, enter your first and last name at the bottom of the page, and then click the PLAY button. When your score is displayed, click the PRINT RESULTS link to print a hard copy.

5 Wheel of Terms

Below PowerPoint Project 2, click the Wheel of Terms link. Read the instructions, and then enter your first and last name and your school name. Click the PLAY button. When your score is displayed, right-click the score and then click Print on the shortcut menu to print a hard copy.

6 Crossword Puzzle Challenge

Below PowerPoint Project 2, click the Crossword Puzzle Challenge link. Read the instructions, and then enter your first and last name. Click the SUBMIT button. Work the crossword puzzle. When you are finished, click the Submit button. When the crossword puzzle is redisplayed, click the Print Puzzle button to print a hard copy.

7 Tips and Tricks

Below PowerPoint Project 2, click the Tips and Tricks link. Click a topic that pertains to Project 2. Right-click the information and then click Print on the shortcut menu. Construct a brief example of what the information relates to in PowerPoint to confirm you understand how to use the tip or trick.

8 Newsgroups

Below PowerPoint Project 2, click the Newsgroups link. Click a topic that pertains to Project 2. Print three comments.

9 Expanding Your Horizons

Below PowerPoint Project 2, click the Expanding Your Horizons link. Click a topic that pertains to Project 2. Print the information. Construct a brief example of what the information relates to in PowerPoint to confirm you understand the contents of the article.

10 Search Sleuth

Below PowerPoint Project 2, click the Search Sleuth link. To search for a term that pertains to this project, select a term below the Project 2 title and then use the Google search engine at google.com (or any major search engine) to display and print two Web pages that present information on the term.

11 PowerPoint Online Training

Below PowerPoint Project 2, click the PowerPoint Online Training link. When your browser displays the Microsoft Office Online Web page, click the PowerPoint link. Click one of the PowerPoint courses that covers one or more of the objectives listed at the beginning of the project on page PPT 82. Print the first page of the course before stepping through it.

12 Office Marketplace

Below PowerPoint Project 2, click the Office Marketplace link. When your browser displays the Microsoft Office Online Web page, click the Office Marketplace link. Click a topic that relates to PowerPoint. Print the first page.

Apply Your Knowledge

1 Hiking for Family Fitness

Instructions: Start PowerPoint. Open the presentation Apply 2-1 Hiking Adventure from the Data Disk. See the inside back cover of this book for instructions for downloading the Data Disk or see your instructor for information on accessing the files required for this book. The four slides in the presentation give information on helping families plan for a hike through forest preserves and parks. Make the following changes to the slides so they appear as shown in Figure 2-64.

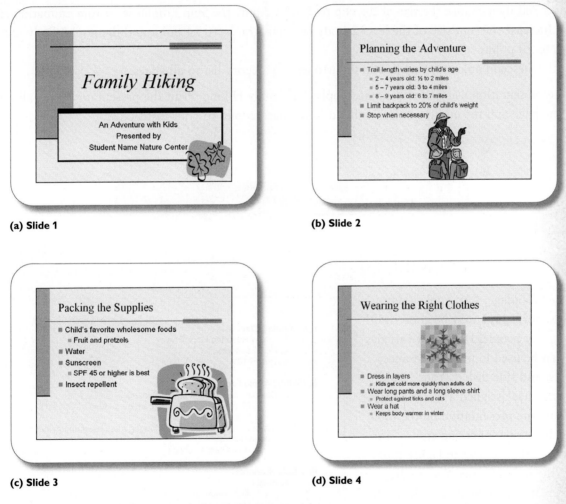

(a) Slide 1

(b) Slide 2

(c) Slide 3

(d) Slide 4

FIGURE 2-64

Change the design template to Layers. On the title slide, replace the words, Student Name, with your name. Then add the current date, page number, and your name to the notes and handouts footer.

On Slide 1, increase the font size of the Family Hiking paragraph to 72 point and then italicize this text. Insert the leaves clip shown in Figure 2-64a. Scale the clip art to 118% and then drag the clip to the bottom-right corner of the slide. Apply the Box Entrance custom animation effect to the clip.

(continued)

Apply Your Knowledge

Hiking for Family Fitness *(continued)*

On Slide 2, change the slide layout to Title and Text over Content. Insert the backpacking clip shown in Figure 2-64b on the previous page. Change the size of the clip to 167% and then drag the clip to the bottom center of the slide.

On Slide 3, insert the toaster clip shown in Figure 2-64c. Undo the Automatic Layout if necessary, increase the clip size to 207%, and then drag it to the bottom-right corner of the slide. Apply the Blinds Entrance custom animation effect to the clip.

On Slide 4, change the slide layout to Title and Content over Text. Insert the snowflake clip shown in Figure 2-64d and then change the size of the clip to 120%. Apply the Spin Emphasis custom animation effect to the clip. Increase the font size of the level 2 body text paragraphs to 24 point and the level 3 body text paragraphs to 20 point.

Apply the Descend animation scheme in the Moderate category list to all slides.

Save the presentation using the file name, Apply 2-1 Family Hiking. Print the presentation with all four slides on one page and the outline, and then hand in the hard copies to your instructor.

In the Lab

1 An Apple a Day Presentation

Problem: The adage, "An apple a day keeps the doctor away" may be good health advice for many people. Dozens of varieties of apples can be used in pies, applesauce, juice, salads, and side dishes. Your Health 101 instructor has assigned a research paper and a five-minute presentation on the topic of the health benefits of eating apples. You generate the outline shown in Figure 2-65 to prepare the presentation. You use the outline to create the presentation shown in Figures 2-66a through 2-66d.

I. An Apple a Day...
    A. ...May Keep the Doctor Away
    B. Nick Saunders
    C. Health 101

II. Healthy Apple Facts
    A. Contains cancer-fighting antioxidants
        1. More than a 1,500 milligram megadose of Vitamin C
        2. Fight bad cholesterol
    B. Complex carbohydrates give longer, more even energy boost
    C. Contains boron
        1. Helps harden bones

III. Apple Nutrients
    A. Pectin
        1. Aids digestion
        2. May help reduce cancer, heart disease
    B. Fiber
        1. Equal to bran cereal

IV. Cook or Baking Quantities
    A. 3 medium-sized apples equal 1 pound
    B. 6-8 medium-sized apples fill a 9-inch pie
    C. 1 pound makes 1½ cups applesauce

FIGURE 2-65

In the Lab

(a) Slide 1

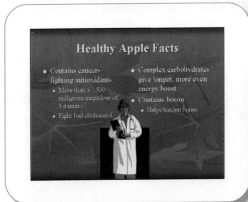

(b) Slide 2

(c) Slide 3

(d) Slide 4

FIGURE 2-66

Instructions: Perform the following tasks.

1. Use the Outline tab to create a new presentation. Apply the Maple design template.

2. Using the outline shown in Figure 2-65, create the title slide shown in Figure 2-66a. Use your name instead of the text, Nick Saunders. Decrease the font size of the class name to 24 point. Insert the caduceus clip art. Scale the clip to 150% and then drag the clip to the lower-left corner of the slide. Add the Blinds Entrance custom animation effect to the clip.

3. Insert a new slide. Change the slide layout on Slide 2 to Title and 2-Column Text. Using the outline in Figure 2-65, type the text for Slide 2. Insert the doctor clip art shown in Figure 2-66b. Scale the clip to 200% and then drag the clip between the two columns of text.

4. Using the outline shown in Figure 2-65, create the Slides 3 and 4 with the bulleted lists shown in Figures 2-66c and 2-66d.

5. Change the slide layout on Slide 3 to Title, Text, and Content. Insert the medicine clip art shown in Figure 2-66c. Scale the clip art to 210% and then center it in the space beside the text. Add the Diamond Entrance custom animation effect to the clip.

6. On Slide 4, change the slide layout to Title, Content and Text. Insert the apple clip art shown in Figure 2-66d, scale it to 200%, and then center it in the space beside the text. Add the Box Entrance custom animation effect.

(continued)

In the Lab

An Apple a Day Presentation *(continued)*

7. Add your name to the outline header and your school's name to the outline footer.
8. Apply the Title arc animation scheme in the Exciting category to all slides in the presentation.
9. Save the presentation using the file name, Lab 2-1 Apples.
10. Display and print the presentation with two slides on one page and the outline. Close the presentation. Hand in the hard copy to your instructor.

2 Financial Planning Advice

Problem: Credit card debt is at an all-time high, and many people are nearing retirement age with inadequate savings. Many students at your school have asked their instructors and members of the Accounting Club for advice on helping them gain financial security. To assist these students, the Accounting Club members have decided to prepare a PowerPoint presentation to show to these students. They have given you the outline shown in Figure 2-67. You create the text for the presentation on the Outline tab, and you decide to add animation effects to the slide show. The completed slides are shown in Figures 2-68a through 2-68d.

1. It Figures: Your Financial Future
   Build a Secure Fiscal Plan
   Midwest College Accounting Club

2. Prepare for Retirement Now
   Eliminate all debt
   Follow the 20/80 rule
      Live on 20 percent
      Save 80 percent
   Develop a financial plan

3. Realize Importance of Financial Planning
   Establish a monthly budget
   Develop an investment strategy
      Savings
      Low-risk investments
      High-risk investments

4. Use a Certified Financial Planner
   Helps prepare taxes
   Gives insurance advice
   Develops debt-reduction strategies
   Assists with estate planning

FIGURE 2-67

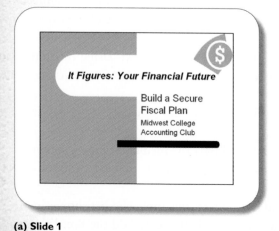

(a) Slide 1

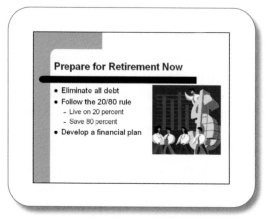

(b) Slide 2

FIGURE 2-68

(c) Slide 3

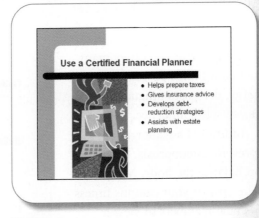

(d) Slide 4

FIGURE 2-68 *(continued)*

Instructions: Perform the following tasks.

1. Use the Outline tab to create a new presentation from the outline shown in Figure 2-67. Apply the Capsules design template.

2. On the title slide, italicize the title text, It Figures: Your Financial Future. Increase the font size of the text, Build a Secure Fiscal Plan, to 36 point. Using Figure 2-68a as a reference, insert the dollar clip art shown, scale it to 105%, and then drag it to the upper-right corner of the slide.

3. On Slide 2, insert the clip art shown in Figure 2-68b and then, if necessary, click the AutoCorrect Options button to undo the layout change. Scale the clip to 230% and then drag it to the right of the text.

4. On Slide 3, change the slide layout to Title, Text, and Content. Insert the clip art shown in Figure 2-68c. Scale the clip to 160% and then move it to the location shown in the figure.

5. On Slide 4, change the slide layout to Title, Content and Text. Insert the clip art shown in Figure 2-68d, scale the clip to 195%, and then move it to the location shown in the figure.

6. Add the current date and your name to the outline header. Include Accounting Club and the page number in the outline footer.

7. Apply the Compress animation scheme in the Moderate category to all slides.

8. Animate the clip on Slide 1 using the Spin Emphasis custom animation effect, the clip on Slide 2 using the Fly In Entrance effect, and the clip on Slide 3 using the Box Entrance effect. Do not animate the clip on Slide 4.

9. Save the presentation using the file name, Lab 2-2 Financial Future.

10. Display and print the presentation with two slides on one page and the outline. Close the presentation. Hand in the hard copy to your instructor.

In the Lab

3 Strength Training for New Fitness Center Members

Problem: Strength training offers many positive benefits: it builds power, provides energy, decreases fatigue, and improves mood, self-confidence, and self-esteem. Additional advantages are helping to prevent osteoporosis, burn calories, and balance the body. Mary Halen, the director of your campus fitness center, wants new members to view a presentation on strength training. She gives you the outline shown in Figure 2-69. You create the text for the presentation on the Outline tab and then search for appropriate clip art to add to the slides. You are unable to find images that are part of the Microsoft Clip Organizer, so you connect to the Internet, obtain clips from the Microsoft Office Online Web site, and create the slides shown in Figure 2-70. The clips you find may vary from the clips shown in Figures 2-70a through 2-70d. You refine the presentation using an animation scheme and custom animation effects and then e-mail the presentation to Mary.

Gain More Than Muscles with Strength Training
   Presented by
   Mary Halen
   Central College Fitness Center

Build Power
   Increase performance in many sports
      Tennis and golf
   Increase endurance
      Running and swimming

Feel Energized
   Improve mood, confidence, and esteem
      Expand beyond sports into personal life
   Burn calories
      Even while resting
      Increase body's metabolism for up to 12 hours after exercising

Improve Health
   Help prevent osteoporosis
      Strengthen bones
      Build bone density
   Balance body by making both sides strong
      Normally one side is stronger than the other
      Balanced body is less prone to injuries

FIGURE 2-69

(a) Slide 1

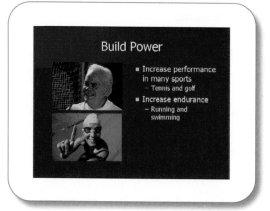

(b) Slide 2

FIGURE 2-70

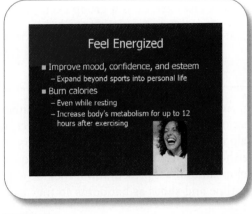

(c) Slide 3

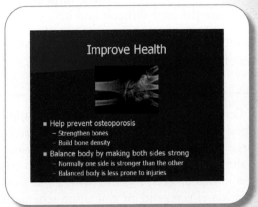

(d) Slide 4

FIGURE 2-70 *(continued)*

Instructions: Perform the following tasks.

1. Create a new presentation using the Slit design template and the outline in Figure 2-69.
2. On the title slide, insert and size both clip art images shown in Figure 2-70a. Add the Fly In Entrance custom animation effect and change the speed to Medium.
3. On Slide 2, change the slide layout to Title, 2 Content and Text. Insert the clips shown in Figure 2-70b. Add the Fly In Entrance custom animation effect for the top image and change the direction to From Top. Add the Fly In Entrance custom animation effect for the bottom image. Size the clips if necessary.
4. On Slide 3, insert the clip shown in Figure 2-70c. Add the Spin Emphasis custom animation effect. Size the clip if necessary.
5. Change the slide layout on Slide 4 (Figure 2-70d) to Title and Content over Text. Insert the clip art image shown. Add the Box Entrance custom animation effect. Size the clip if necessary.
6. Display your name and the current date in the outline header, and display the page number and the name of your school in the outline footer.
7. Apply the Unfold animation scheme in the Moderate category to all slides.
8. Save the presentation using the file name, Lab 2-3 Strength Training.
9. Display and print the presentation with all four slides on one page and the outline. Close the presentation. Hand in the hard copy to your instructor.
10. E-mail the presentation to Mary using the address mary_halen@hotmail.com.

Cases and Places

The difficulty of these case studies varies:
■ are the least difficult and ■■ are more difficult. The last exercise is a group exercise.

Note: Remember to use the 7 × 7 rule as you design the presentations: a maximum of seven words on a line and a maximum of seven lines on one slide.

1 ■ One of the easiest methods of exercising is walking. Active walkers know that walking enhances the body and spirit. Paula Pearson, the director of recreation at your community's park district, wants to organize a walking club, and she has asked you to help her promote the idea. She hands you the outline shown in Figure 2-71 and asks you to create a slide show. Using the concepts and techniques introduced in this project, together with Paula's outline, develop slides for a presentation. Include clip art, animation effects, and an animation scheme. Print the outline and slides as handouts so they can be distributed to presentation attendees.

1. Walk On
  Walk Your Way to Health
      Presented by
      Paula Pearson
      West Haven Park District

2. Walking Benefits
  - Enhances both body and spirit
  - Prolongs life, according to leading researchers

3. Training Techniques
  - Try interval training
      Increase walking speed for 30 seconds
      Return to normal speed for one minute

4. Walking Techniques
  - Walk with a friend
      Adds motivation
      Helps pass the time
      Gives motivation to walk in inclement weather
  - Swing arms
      Increases heart rate, burns more calories

FIGURE 2-71

Cases and Places

2 ■ The community theater company in the town of Northern Shores is seeking subscribers and volunteers for the upcoming season. The public relations director has supplied the outline shown in Figure 2-72. You have been asked to help with the recruiting efforts. You decide to develop a presentation that includes information about the newly renovated theater, volunteer opportunities, and upcoming performances. Using the concepts and techniques introduced in this project, together with the outline, develop slides for a presentation. Include clip art, animation effects, and an animation scheme. Display the presentation title in the outline header and your name in the outline footer. Print the outline and slides as handouts.

A. Northern Shores Center for the Performing Arts
   The area's newest and finest theater company

B. Northern Shores Theater Venue
   Newly renovated building
      More than $7 million spent
      Improved sight lines and acoustics
      Full symphony orchestra pit
   Comfortable seating
      Accommodations for the disabled

C. Volunteer Opportunities
      Developing and distributing promotional materials
      Ushering at performances
      Participating in social activities throughout the year
      Assisting with Children's Theater

D. Upcoming Performances
      February 14 - Music for the Heart
      March 17 - Irish Favorites
      July 1 - Americana Folk Tales
      December 16 - Holiday Spectacular

FIGURE 2-72

Cases and Places

3 ■■ Many students on your campus visit the Health Clinic asking for antibiotics prescriptions. The doctors and nurses spend much time explaining that antibiotics are not necessarily the best medicine for the illnesses. You work in the clinic part time and volunteer to create a PowerPoint presentation that answers many of the students' common questions. You speak with the doctors on staff and learn that antibiotics are credited with changing modern medicine. They are used to kill bacteria, not viruses, and can control infectious diseases. Many bacteria, however, have become resistant to these drugs. Antibiotics are prescribed for bacterial infections, not viruses such as flu, colds, most coughs, and sore throats. Students can take antibiotics prudently by taking all doses of the medications exactly as prescribed. They should not stop taking drugs early, even if they feel fine. Antibiotic resistance occurs when the medications are taken unnecessarily. When the illness persists, additional drugs may be required to kill the germ. Some bacteria refuse to die, and super strains have been bred by overuse and misuse of antiobiotics. Using this information, develop a slide show. Choose an appropriate design template and add clip art, animation effects, and an animation scheme. Print the presentation slides and outline to distribute as handouts for patients.

4 ■■ The Healthy Eating Pyramid shows that a balanced diet contains daily servings of fruit and vegetables. Although fruit and vegetables are less costly than snack foods, many adults and children buy junk food rather than the vitamin-laden fruit and vegetable alternatives. Your school cafeteria manager has asked you to prepare a PowerPoint presentation explaining the ABCs of fruits and vegetables to students. Using the techniques introduced in the project, create a presentation about the virtues of eating these foods. Include clip art, animation effects, and an animation scheme to add interest. Print the outline and slides as handouts so they can be distributed to cafeteria diners.

5 ■■ **Working Together** Prospective employees often focus on salary and job responsibilities when they consider job offers. One area they often neglect, however, is benefit packages. Career counselors emphasize that these benefits can contribute significantly to salary levels and should be given serious consideration. Have each member of your team visit or telephone several local businesses, your campus placement center, or companies' Web sites to determine benefit packages. Gather data about:

1) Retirement plans

2) Stock options

3) Life insurance coverage

4) Health coverage

5) Tuition reimbursement

6) Signing bonuses

7) On-site fitness facilities

After coordinating the data, create a presentation with at least one slide showcasing each company's benefit packages. As a group, critique each slide. Hand in a hard copy of the final presentation.

Creating a Presentation on the Web Using PowerPoint

CASE PERSPECTIVE

A home office can be the key to redefining the way we work. More than 54 percent of American households have a home office, and more than 46 million Americans work at home at least part time. These offices range from a desk and chair in the kitchen to a separate room complete with storage and ergonomic furniture.

Many people attempt to create an effective workspace only to realize that the space lacks comfort, connectivity, and convenience. The most important step in developing the home office is planning. Start by developing a budget, analyzing electrical needs such as the placement of outlets, and listing computer hardware and office equipment. Decisions need to be made about the optimal type of lighting, whether to buy modular or built-in furniture, and the arrangement of work materials to increase efficiency and minimize body strain.

Making these decisions can be daunting. Professional space planners know how to make functional and ergonomic workspaces. By analyzing their clients' unique needs, they can design environments that help workers be productive and comfortable. They arrange the equipment and furniture based on the clients' tasks and the rooms' dimensions and constraints.

Comfort @ Home, Inc., is a local business specializing in assisting home workers to develop the best office design for their needs. Kendra Linder, the owner of this business, wants to provide community residents with the guidelines for an effective home office design. She decides the most effective way to disseminate this information is to create a PowerPoint slide show (Figure 1 on the next page) and then have you publish the presentation on the World Wide Web.

As you read through this Web feature, you will learn how to create and display a Web page from a PowerPoint presentation, edit the results using a browser, and then publish the presentation.

Objectives

You will have mastered the material in this project when you can:

- Preview and save a presentation as a Web page
- Create a new folder using file management tools
- View a Web page using a browser
- Edit the Web page content through a browser
- Publish a presentation as a Web page

Introduction

The graphic design power of PowerPoint allows you to create vibrant presentations that convey information in a clear, interesting manner. Some of these presentations are created for small, specific audiences, such as a subcommittee planning a department retreat. In this case, the presentation may be shown in an office conference room. Other presentations are designed for large, general audiences, such as workers at a corporation's various offices across the country learning about a new insurance benefits package. These employees can view the presentation on their company's **intranet**, which is an internal network that uses Internet technologies. On a grand scale, you can inform the entire world about the contents of your presentation by posting your slide show to the World Wide Web. To publish to the World Wide Web, you need a **File Transfer Protocol (FTP)** program to copy your presentation and related files to an **Internet service provider (ISP)** computer.

PowerPoint provides you with two ways to create a Web page. First, you can start a new presentation, as you did in Projects 1 and 2 when you produced the Strategies for College Success and the Healthy

Eating, Healthy Living presentations. PowerPoint provides a Web Presentation template in the **AutoContent Wizard** option when you start PowerPoint. The wizard provides design and content ideas to help you develop an effective slide show for an intranet or for the Internet by opening a sample presentation that you can alter by adding your own text and graphics.

Second, the Save as Web Page command on the File menu allows you to **publish** presentations, which is the process of making existing presentations available to others on the World Wide Web or on a company's intranet. If you have access to a Web server, you can publish Web pages by saving them to a Web folder or to an FTP location. To learn more about publishing Web pages to a Web folder or FTP location using Microsoft Office applications, refer to Appendix C.

The Publish command allows you to create a Web page from a single slide or from a multiple-slide presentation. This Web Feature illustrates opening the Home Office presentation on the Data Disk (Figure 1a) and then saving the presentation as

FIGURE 1

a Web page using the Save as Web Page command. You will save the Web pages and associated folders on a floppy disk rather than to a Web server. At times, this saving process may be slow and requires patience. See the inside back cover of this book for instructions for downloading the Data Disk or see your instructor for information on accessing the files required in this book.

Then, you will edit the presentation, save it again, and view it again in your default browser. Finally, you will publish your presentation, and PowerPoint will start your default browser and open your file so you can view the presentation (Figures 1b through 1e).

Using Web Page Preview and Saving a PowerPoint Presentation as a Web Page

PowerPoint makes it easy to create a presentation and then preview how it will display on an intranet or on the World Wide Web. This action opens the presentation in your default Web browser without saving files. By previewing your slide show, you can decide which features look good and which need modification. The left side of the window includes the navigation frame, which is the outline of the presentation. The outline contains a table of contents consisting of each slide's title text. You can click the Expand/Collapse Outline button below the navigation frame to view the complete slide text. The right side of the window shows the complete slide in the slide frame. The speaker notes, if present, are displayed in the notes frame below the slide frame. Once the preview is acceptable, you then can save the presentation as a Web page.

Previewing the Presentation as a Web Page

Because you are converting the Home Office presentation on the Data Disk to a Web page, the first step in this project is to open the Home Office file. At any time while developing a presentation, you can preview it as a Web page by using the Web Page Preview command on the File menu. When you use the Web Page Preview command, your browser starts and the presentation is displayed as a Web page. The steps on the next page show how to use the Web Page Preview command.

More About

Home Office Planning

Assistance for designing an effective home office is available on various Web sites. Furniture companies, space planners, and ergonomics experts provide helpful advice for developing comfortable and useful workspaces. For more information on home office planning, visit the PowerPoint 2003 More About Web page (scsite.com/ppt2003/more) and click Offices.

More About

Viewing a Presentation

Saving the presentation in Web page format is an excellent vehicle for distributing the slide show to many viewers. Another method of sharing your file is by broadcasting, which allows audience members to view the slide show in real time on their computers while you control precisely what they see. You also can record a broadcast so viewers can watch the presentation at their convenience.

To Preview the Presentation as a Web Page

1

• **Insert the Data Disk in drive A.**

• **Start PowerPoint and then open the presentation, Home Office, on the Data Disk in drive A.**

• **Click File on the menu bar.**

PowerPoint starts and opens the slide show, Home Office, in normal view. The presentation is composed of four slides. PowerPoint displays the File menu (Figure 2).

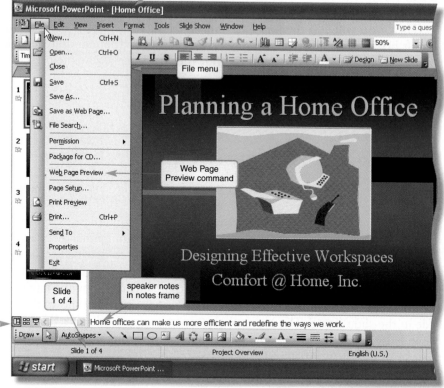

FIGURE 2

2

• **Click Web Page Preview.**

PowerPoint starts your browser. The browser displays a Web page preview of Slide 1 of the Home Office presentation in the slide frame in the browser window (Figure 3). The navigation frame contains the table of contents, which consists of the title text of each slide. The speaker notes are displayed in the notes frame. The Microsoft PowerPoint button on the taskbar no longer is selected. Windows displays a selected browser button on the taskbar, indicating it is active.

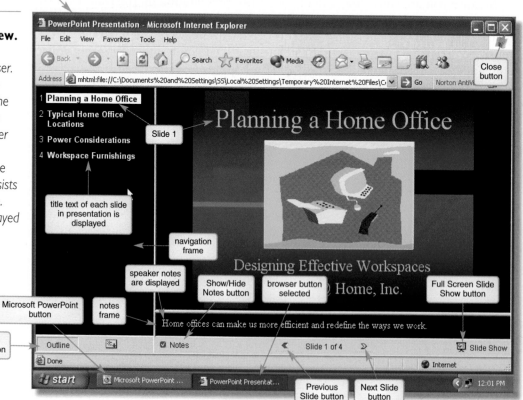

FIGURE 3

3

• **Click the Full Screen Slide Show button.**

Slide 1 fills the entire screen (Figure 4). The Slide 1 title text and clip art are displayed. The Web Page preview in the browser is nearly identical to the display of the presentation in PowerPoint.

FIGURE 4

4

• **Click to display the first line of the subtitle text.**

The first line of the Slide 1 subtitle text is displayed.

5

• **Continue clicking each slide in the presentation.**

• **When the black slide is displayed, click it.**

Each of the four slides in the Home Office presentation is displayed. The message on the black slide, End of slide show, click to exit, indicates the conclusion of the slide show.

6

• **Click the Close button on the right side of the browser title bar.**

The browser closes, PowerPoint becomes active, and PowerPoint displays Slide 1 (Figure 5).

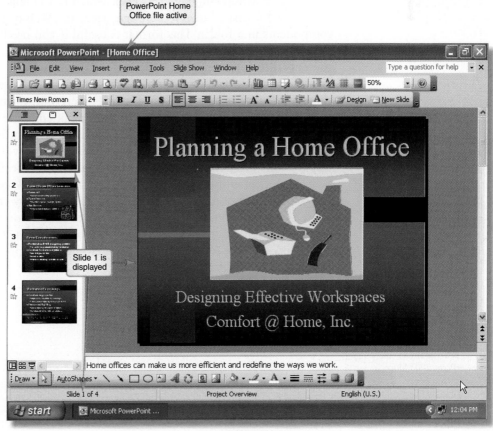

FIGURE 5

The Web page preview shows that PowerPoint can produce professional-looking Web pages from presentations. You can alter the browser window by choosing to display or hide the navigation and notes frames. To hide the navigation frame, click the Show/Hide Outline button below the outline. Later, if you want to redisplay the navigation frame, click the Show/Hide Outline button again. Similarly, the Show/Hide Notes button below the slide frame allows you to display or conceal the speaker notes, if present, on a particular slide.

To advance through the Web page, you also can click the Next Slide button below the slide frame. Likewise, to display a slide appearing earlier in the slide show, click the Previous Slide button.

Saving a PowerPoint Presentation as a Web Page to a New Folder

Once the preview of a PowerPoint slide show is acceptable, you can save it as a Web page so you can view it in a Web browser. Microsoft Internet Explorer and Netscape Navigator are the two more common browsers installed on computers today.

You can save the presentation in one of two Web page formats. One format is called **Single File Web Page**, which saves all the Web page components in a single file with an .mht extension. This format is useful for e-mailing presentations in **hypertext markup language (HTML)**, which is a language browsers can interpret. The second format, called **Web Page**, saves the Web page in a file and some of its components in a folder. This format is useful if you need access to the components, such as clip art, that comprise the Web page. Both formats convert the slide show contents into HTML.

You can save and then view the presentation in two ways. First, you can save the entire presentation as a Web page, quit PowerPoint, open your browser, and open the Web page in your browser. Second, you can combine these steps by saving the presentation as a Web page, publishing the presentation, and then viewing the presentation as a Web page. In this case, PowerPoint will start the browser and display your presentation automatically. Later in this feature, the Publish button will be used to explain further how you can customize a Web page.

Experienced users organize their storage devices by creating folders and then save related files to a common folder. PowerPoint allows you to create folders in the Save As dialog box before saving a file. The following steps create a new folder on the Data Disk in drive A and then save the Home Office presentation in the Web Page format to the new folder.

To Save a Presentation in Web Page Format to a New Folder

1

• **With the Home Office presentation open, click the Next Slide button twice to view Slide 3.**

• **Click the notes pane and then type** More than 46 million Americans work at home at least part time; more than 54 percent of American households have a home office. **as the note.**

• **Click File on the menu bar.**

PowerPoint displays the File menu (Figure 6). The last four words of the speaker notes you typed appear in the notes pane.

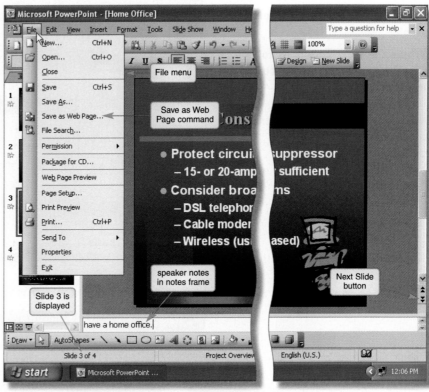

FIGURE 6

2

• **Click Save as Web Page.**

• **When the Save As dialog box is displayed, type** Home Office Web Page **in the File name text box.**

• **Click the Save as type box arrow and then click Web Page.**

PowerPoint displays the Save As dialog box (Figure 7). The default file format type is Single File Web Page.

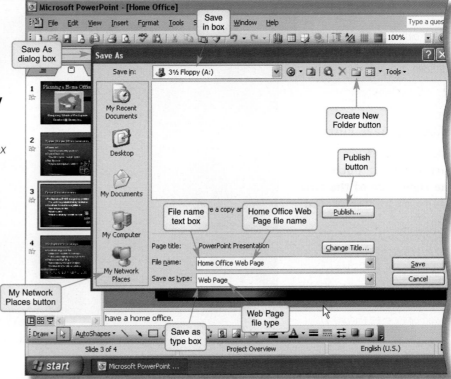

FIGURE 7

3

• **If necessary, click the Save in box arrow and select 3½ Floppy (A:).**

• **Click the Create New Folder button.**

• **When the New Folder dialog box is displayed, type** Web Feature **in the Name text box.**

PowerPoint displays the New Folder dialog box (Figure 8).

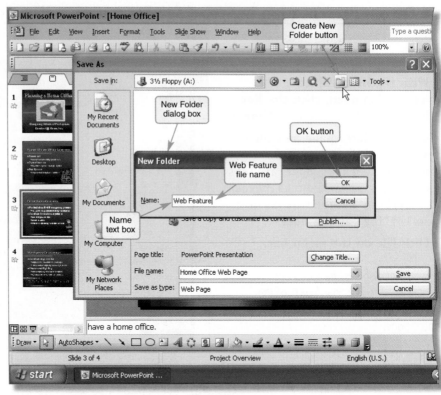

FIGURE 8

4

• **Click the OK button in the New Folder dialog box.**

PowerPoint automatically selects the new Web Feature folder in the Save in box.

5

• **Click the Save button.**

• **After all files are saved, click the Close button on the right side of the title bar to close PowerPoint.**

PowerPoint saves the presentation in HTML format on the Data Disk in drive A in the Web Feature folder using the file name Home Office Web Page.htm. PowerPoint closes (Figure 9).

FIGURE 9

The Save As dialog box that displays when you use the Save as Web Page command is slightly different from the Save As dialog box that displays when you use the Save As command. The Publish button in the Save As dialog box in Figure 7 on page PPT 147 is an alternative to the Save button and allows you to customize the Web page further. In the previous set of steps, the Save button was used to complete the save. Later in this feature, the Publish button will be used to explain further how you can customize a Web page.

File Management Tools in PowerPoint

Creating a new folder allows you to organize your work. PowerPoint automatically inserts the new folder name in the Save in box when you click the OK button in the New Folder dialog box (Figure 8). Once you create a folder, you can right-click it while the Save As dialog box is active and perform many file manager tasks directly in PowerPoint. For example, once the shortcut menu is displayed, you can rename the selected folder, delete it, copy it, display its properties, and perform other file management functions.

If you have access to a Web server that allows you to save files to a Web folder, then you can save the Web page directly to the Web server by clicking the My Network Places button in the lower-left corner of the Save As dialog box (Figure 7). If you have access to a Web server that allows you to save to an FTP site, then you can select the FTP site under FTP locations in the Save in box just as you select any folder in which to save a file. To save a presentation to a Web server, see Appendix C.

After PowerPoint saves the presentation in Step 5, it displays the HTML file — not the presentation — in the PowerPoint window. PowerPoint can continue to display the presentation in HTML format because within the HTML file that was created, PowerPoint also saved the formats to display the HTML file. This is referred to as **round tripping** the HTML file back to the application in which it was created.

Viewing the Web Page Using Your Browser

With the Home Office Web page saved to the folder, Web Feature, on the Data Disk in drive A, the next step is to view it using a browser, such as Microsoft Internet Explorer or Netscape, as shown in the steps on the next page.

> ### More About
>
> ### Saving Files
>
> PowerPoint provides many file formats for saving presentations. One useful format that allows viewers to see, but not alter, a presentation is the PowerPoint Show (.pps) format. A slide show saved as a PowerPoint Show always will open as a slide show presentation.

> ### More About
>
> ### Viewing Web Presentations
>
> Several PowerPoint features do not work when a presentation is viewed as a Web page. These features include embossed and shadow effects for fonts, text that is animated by the letter or word rather than by the paragraph, and special effects on charts. In addition, music will not play throughout a Web presentation because moving to another slide stops the sound.

To View the Web Page Using Your Browser

1

• **If necessary, insert the Data Disk in drive A.**

• **Click the Start button on the taskbar, point to All Programs, and then click Internet Explorer.**

• **When the Internet Explorer window displays, type** a:\web feature\home office web page.htm **in the Address bar and then press the ENTER key.**

The browser displays Slide 1 in the Web page, Home Office Web Page.htm (Figure 10).

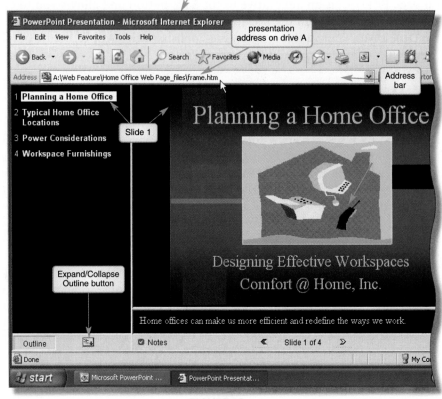

FIGURE 10

2

• **Click the Expand/ Collapse Outline button at the bottom of the window.**

The text of each slide in an outline appears in the navigation frame (Figure 11). To display only the title of each slide, you would click the Expand/Collapse Outline button again.

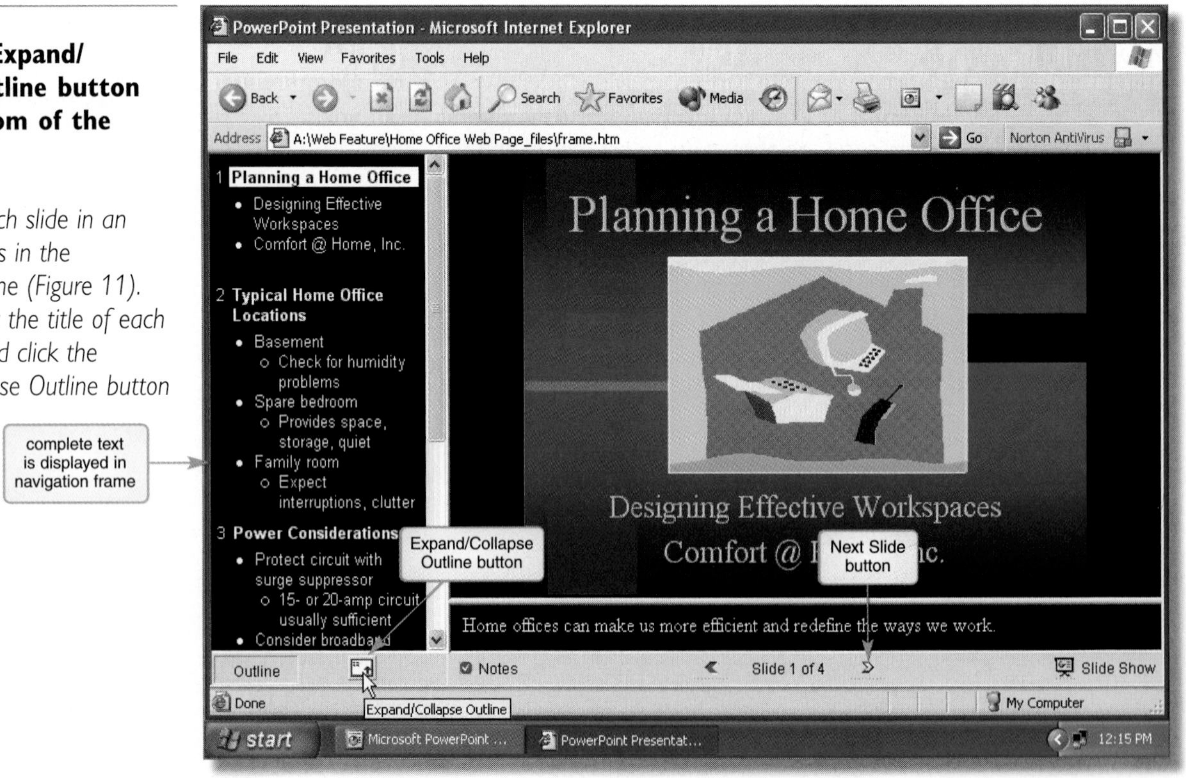

FIGURE 11

3

• **Click the Next Slide button three times to view all four slides.**

The browser displays each of the slides in the Home Office presentation. Slide 4 is displayed in the browser (Figure 12).

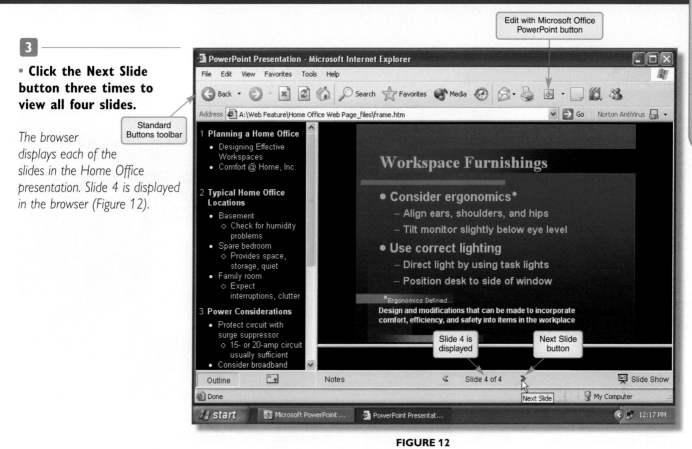

FIGURE 12

Figures 11 and 12 show that a Web page is an ideal medium for distributing information to a large group of people. The Web page can be made available to anyone with a computer, browser, and the address. The Web page also can be e-mailed easily because it resides in a single file, rather than in a file and folder.

If you want, you can use the Print command on the File menu in your browser to print the slides one at a time. You also can view the HTML source PowerPoint created by clicking Source on the View menu in Internet Explorer or Page Source on the View menu in Netscape.

Editing a Web Page through a Browser

You may want to modify your Web page by making small changes to the text or art on some slides. In this presentation, you want to change the title text in Slide 1 to reflect the fact that a home office can provide comfort as well as efficiency. You can modify the presentation using PowerPoint directly in the browser window. Your computer may indicate other editing options, such as using Windows Notepad. The steps on the next page modify the Title Slide title text.

More About

Printing

If your printer seems to print slowly, Microsoft suggests clearing at least two megabytes of space on your hard drive and also closing any unnecessary programs that are running simultaneously.

To Edit a Web Page through a Browser

1

• **Click the Edit with Microsoft Office PowerPoint button on the Standard Buttons toolbar.**

• **Select the words, Planning a Home Office, in the title text placeholder.**

When you click the Edit button, PowerPoint opens a new presentation with the same file name as the Web presentation file name, as indicated by the title bar and the selected Microsoft PowerPoint - [Home Office Web Page] button on the Windows taskbar (Figure 13). A selection rectangle appears around the title text place-holder. The four words are highlighted.

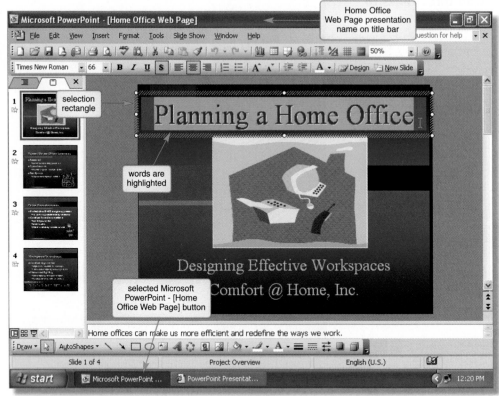

FIGURE 13

2

• **Type** The Comforts of Home **in the title text placeholder.**

The title text is modified (Figure 14).

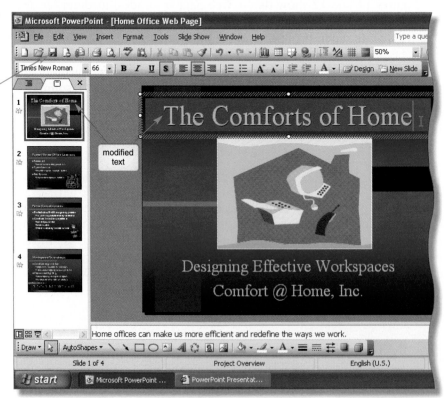

FIGURE 14

3

- **Click the Save button on the Standard toolbar.**

It takes several minutes for PowerPoint to save the changes to the Home Office Web Page.htm file on the Data Disk in drive A. The buttons on the taskbar indicate that the PowerPoint presentation and the browser are open.

4

- **Click the PowerPoint Presentation - Microsoft Internet Explorer button on the taskbar.**
- **Click the Previous Slide button three times to display Slide 1.**

The browser displays the revised title text on Slide 1 (Figure 15). If the revised text does not display, click the Refresh button on the Standard Buttons toolbar.

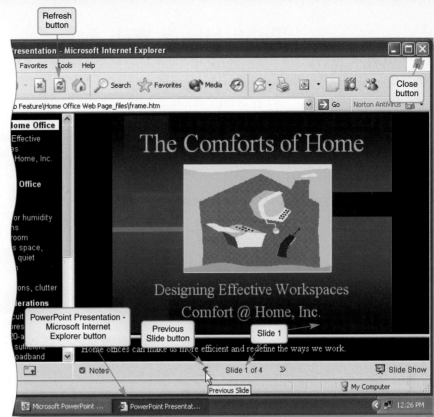

FIGURE 15

5

- **Click the Close button on the browser title bar.**
- **Click the Save button to save the revised PowerPoint Home Office Web Page.**

The browser closes, and the PowerPoint window displays in normal view with the modified Slide 1 of the Home Office Web Page presentation active (Figure 16).

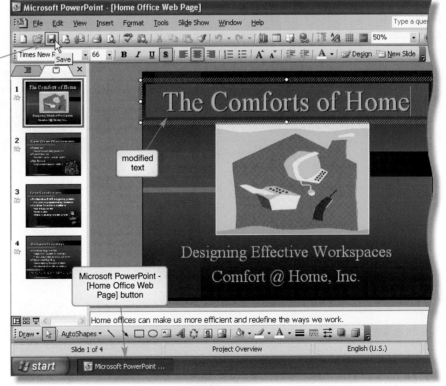

FIGURE 16

Publishing a Web Page

PowerPoint allows you to publish the presentation by saving the pages to a Web folder or to an FTP location. When you publish your presentation, it is available for other computer users to view on the Internet or by other means. Publishing a Web page of a presentation is an alternative to distributing printed copies of the slides. The following section uses the Publish button in the Save As dialog box, rather than the Save button, to illustrate PowerPoint's additional publishing capabilities.

To Publish a PowerPoint Presentation

1

• **Click File on the menu bar and then click Save as Web Page.**

• **Click the Save as type box arrow and then click Single File Web Page.**

• **Type** Home Office Single File Web Page **in the File name text box.**

• **If necessary, click the Save in box arrow, select 3½ Floppy (A:) in the Save in list, and then select the folder, Web Feature.**

The Save As dialog box is displayed (Figure 17). When you use the Publish button, PowerPoint will save the Web page in a single file.

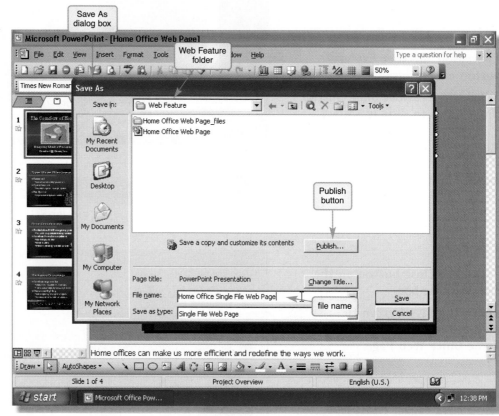

FIGURE 17

2

- **Click the Publish button.**
- **If the Office Assistant appears, click No, don't provide help now.**
- **If necessary, click Open published Web page in browser to select it.**

The Publish as Web Page dialog box is displayed (Figure 18). PowerPoint defaults to publishing the complete presentation, although you can choose to publish one or a range of slides. The Open published Web page in browser check box is selected, which means the Home Office Single File Web Page presentation will open in your default browser when you click the Publish button.

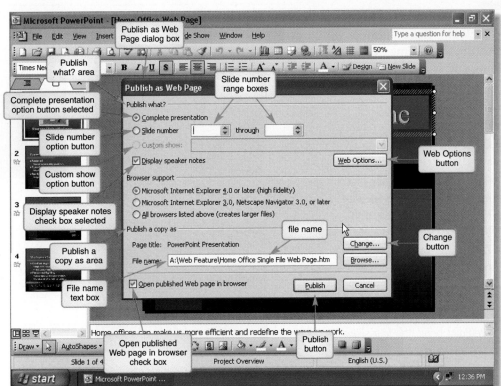

FIGURE 18

3

- **Click the Publish button.**

PowerPoint saves the presentation as a single file, Home Office Single File Web Page.mht, in the Web Feature folder on the Data Disk in drive A. After a few minutes, PowerPoint opens your default Web browser in a separate window (Figure 19). If the browser does not open, click the PowerPoint Presentation - Microsoft Internet Explorer button on the Windows taskbar.

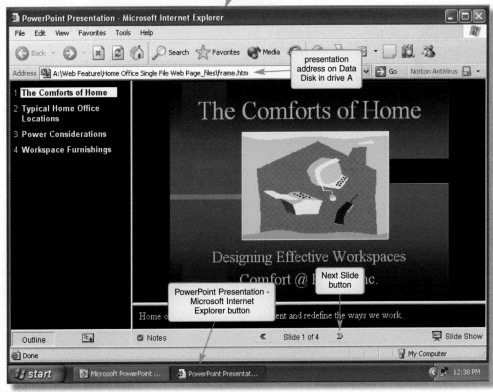

FIGURE 19

4

• **Click the Next Slide button three times to view the four slides.**

• **Click the Close button in the upper-right corner of the browser window.**

• **Click File on the menu bar, click Print, click the Print what arrow, click Handouts, click Vertical in the Handouts area, and then click the OK button.**

• **Click the Save button to save the revised Home Office Web Page.**

The browser closes, and PowerPoint prints the four slides as a handout (Figure 20). PowerPoint takes a few minutes to save the file to the Data Disk.

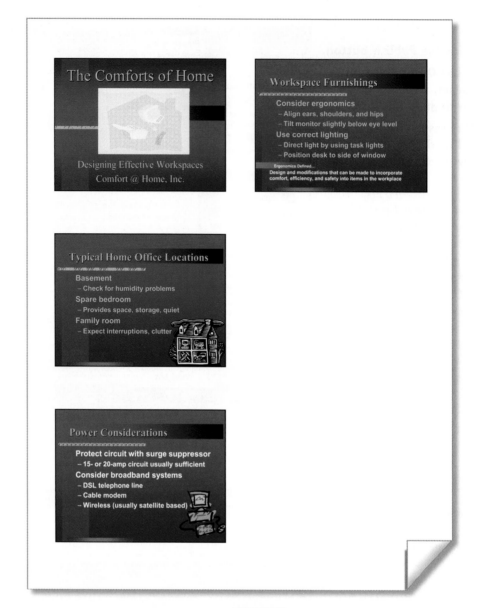

FIGURE 20

Publishing provides customizing options that are not available when you simply save the entire presentation and then start your browser. The Publish as Web Page dialog box provides several options to customize your Web page. For example, you can change the page title that displays on the browser's title bar and in the history list. People visiting your Web site can store a link to your Web page, which will display in their favorites list. To change the page title, you click the Change button in the Publish a copy as area (Figure 18 on the previous page) and then type a new title.

The Publish what? area of the Publish as Web Page dialog box allows you to publish parts of your presentation. PowerPoint defaults to publishing the complete presentation, but you can select specific slides by clicking the Slide number option button and then entering the range of desired slide numbers in the range boxes. In addition, you can publish a custom show you have created previously. A **custom show** is a subset of your presentation that contains slides tailored for a specific audience. For example, you may want to show Slides 1, 2, and 4 to one group and Slides 1, 3, and 4 to another group.

You can choose to publish only the publication slides and not the accompanying speaker notes. By default, the Display speaker notes check box is selected in the Publish what? area. You typed speaker notes for Slide 1 of this presentation, so the speaker notes will appear in the browser window. If you do not want to make your notes available to users, click the Display speaker notes check box to remove the check mark.

The Web Options button in the Publish what? area allows you to select options to determine how your presentation will look when viewed in a Web browser. You can choose options such as allowing slide animation to show, selecting the screen size, and having the notes and outline panes display when viewing the presentation in a Web browser.

The Web page now is complete. The next step is to make your Web presentation available to others on your network, an intranet, or the World Wide Web. Ask your instructor how you can post your presentation.

Web Feature Summary

This Web feature introduced you to creating a Web page by viewing an existing presentation as a Web page in your default browser. The presentation then was saved as an HTML file. Next, you modified Slide 1. You then reviewed the Slide 1 change using your default browser and then published the slide show. With the Home Office presentation converted to a Web page, you can post the file to an intranet or to the World Wide Web.

If you have a SAM user profile, you may have access to hands-on instruction, practice, and assessment of the skills covered in this project. Log in to your SAM account and go to your assignments page to see what your instructor has assigned.

What You Should Know

Having completed this project, you should be able to perform the tasks below. The tasks are listed in the same order they were presented in this project. For a list of the buttons, menus, toolbars, and commands introduced in this project, see the Quick Reference Summary at the back of this book and refer to the Page Number column.

1. Preview the Presentation as a Web Page (PPT 144)
2. Save a Presentation in Web Page Format to a New Folder (PPT 147)
3. View the Web Page Using Your Browser (PPT 150)
4. Edit a Web Page through a Browser (PPT 152)
5. Publish a PowerPoint Presentation (PPT 154)

In the Lab

1 Creating a Web Page from the College Success Presentation

Problem: Dr. Traci Johnson, the dean of the Academic Skills Center at Lakemore College, wants to expand the visibility of the College Success presentation you created for the Academic Skills Center in Project 1. Dr. Johnson believes the World Wide Web would be an excellent vehicle to help students throughout the campus and at other colleges, and she has asked you to help transfer the presentation to the Internet.

Instructions: Start PowerPoint and then perform the following steps with a computer.

1. Open the College Success presentation shown in Figure 1-1 on page PPT 5 that you created in Project 1. (If you did not complete Project 1, see your instructor for a copy of the presentation.)
2. Use the Save as Web Page command on the File menu to save the presentation in Web page format. Create a new folder called College Success Exercise and then save the Web page with the file name, Lab WF 1-1 Lakemore.
3. View the presentation in a browser.
4. Edit the Web page by using the words, Achieve Your Academic Personal Best, as the Slide 1 title text.
5. Change the last paragraph to the words, Turn off cellular telephone, on Slide 3.
6. View the modified Web page in a browser.
7. Print the modified presentation as a handout with the slides arranged vertically.
8. Ask your instructor for instructions on how to post your Web page so others may have access to it.

2 Creating a Web Page from the Nutrition and Fitness Presentation

Problem: The Nutrition and Fitness presentation you developed in Project 2 for Jessica Cantero, the Fitness director at your college, is generating much interest. Students are registering for the first workshop and are inquiring about additional seminars. Jessica has asked you to post the presentation to the school's intranet.

Instructions: Start PowerPoint and then perform the following steps with a computer.

1. Open the Nutrition and Fitness presentation shown in Figures 2-1a through 2-1e on page PPT 83 that you created in Project 2. (If you did not complete Project 2, see your instructor for a copy of the presentation.)
2. Use the Save as Web Page command on the File menu to save the presentation in Web Page format. Create a new folder called Healthy Exercise and then save the Web page using the file name, Lab WF 1-2 Nutrition.
3. View the presentation in a browser.
4. Modify Slide 1 by italicizing both subtitle lines.
5. On Slide 1, type Workshops are scheduled each Monday at 7 p.m. and Friday at noon. as the note.
6. Modify Slide 3 by changing the word, Bicycling, to the word, Golfing.
7. On Slide 4, type Yoga has been practiced actively for more than 5,000 years. as the note.
8. View the modified Web page in a browser.
9. Print the modified presentation as a handout with the slides arranged horizontally.
10. Ask your instructor for instructions on how to post your Web page so others may have access to it.

3 Creating a Personal Presentation

Problem: You have decided to apply for a position as a tutor in your college's academic assistance center. You are preparing to send your resume and cover letter to the dean of this area in your school, and you want to develop a unique way to publicize your academic skills and personality traits. You decide to create a personalized PowerPoint presentation emphasizing your scholarly achievements and your interpersonal communication skills. You refer to this presentation in your cover letter and inform the executive director that she can view this presentation because you have saved the presentation as a Web page and posted the pages on your school's Web server.

Instructions: Start PowerPoint and then perform the following steps with a computer.

1. Prepare a presentation highlighting your scholarly skills and personality strengths. Create a title slide and at least three additional slides. Use appropriate clip art and an animation scheme.
2. Use the Save as Web Page command to convert and publish the presentation as a single file Web page. Save the Web page in a folder named Tutoring Web File using the file name, Lab WF 1-3 Tutor Position.
3. View the presentation in a browser.
4. Print the Web page.
5. Ask your instructor for instructions on how to post your Web page so others may have access to it.

Using Visuals to Enhance a Slide Show

PROJECT

3

CASE PERSPECTIVE

Vacationers are turning toward campgrounds instead of hotel rooms. In an effort to travel to destinations near home, save money, and bond with family and friends, travelers are finding that camping is a pleasurable alternative to costly resorts and airfares.

Whether the campground is located in state parks or private land, the areas have been swamped since the mid-1990s with requests for campsite activity reservations. Choice areas often are booked for the entire season, so vacation planners need to begin their search for the ideal spot early and earnestly. Computers enter into the camping picture, too, for handheld global positioning system receivers can survey hiking trail terrain and elevation and the campsite reservations can be made via the Internet.

The rangers at Hidden Lake State Park also are experiencing an upturn in camping activity. In an effort to assist camping planners, they want to create a PowerPoint presentation that describes the three campgrounds in the park. The presentation also could list the outdoor activities available, including hiking, rock climbing, and fly fishing. Each campground has an amphitheater where lectures are held three times weekly. Wally Freeman, the campground director of activities, has asked you to help with the marketing efforts. He knows you have extensive computer experience and wants you to develop a PowerPoint slide show that promotes Hidden Lake and describes its campgrounds, activities, and programs. He has asked you to use a variety of visuals, including clip art, a table, and an organization chart. You agree to create the presentation.

As you read through this project, you will learn how to use PowerPoint to add clip art and animation to increase the presentation's visual interest.

Using Visuals to Enhance a Slide Show

Objectives

You will have mastered the material in this project when you can:

- Create presentations using visuals
- Open a Microsoft Word outline as a presentation
- Add a picture to create a custom background
- Format text-based content
- Insert and modify a clip
- Customize bullets using the slide master

- Insert and format a table
- Create and format an organization chart
- Apply a new design template to a single slide
- Rearrange slides
- Add an animation scheme to selected slides
- Print slides as handouts

Introduction

Bulleted lists and simple graphics are the starting point for most presentations, but they can become boring. Advanced PowerPoint users want exciting presentations — something to impress their audiences. With PowerPoint, it is easy to develop impressive presentations by modifying slide backgrounds, customizing bullets, embedding organization charts and tables, and creating new graphics.

One problem you may experience when developing a presentation is finding the proper graphic to convey your message. One way to overcome this obstacle is to modify clip art from the Microsoft Clip Organizer. Another solution is to create a table and an organization chart.

This project introduces several techniques to make your presentations more exciting.

Project Three — Hidden Lake Camping and Outdoor Activities

Project 3 expands on PowerPoint's basic presentation features by importing existing files and embedding objects. This project creates a presentation that is used to promote the camping and nature activities at Hidden Lake State Park (Figures 3-1a through 3-1d). The project begins by building the presentation from an outline created in Microsoft Word. Then, several objects are inserted to customize the presentation. These objects include customized bullets, an organization chart, a table, and clip art.

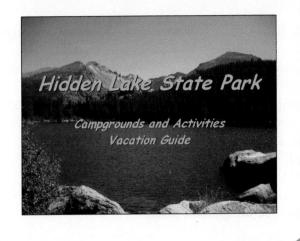

(a) Slide 1

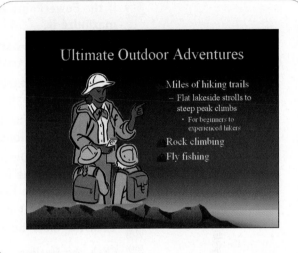

(b) Slide 2

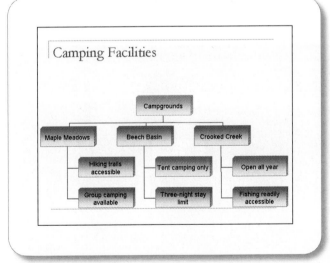

(c) Slide 3

Day	Theater Location	Program
Tuesday	Maple Meadows	It's a Wild, Wild World
Friday	Beech Basin	Mountain Highs and Lows
Saturday	Crooked Creek	Wildflower Wilderness

Nature Program Schedule

(d) Slide 4

FIGURE 3-1

Starting and Customizing a New Presentation

In Projects 1 and 2, you started a presentation document, chose layouts, applied a design template, and reset your toolbars. You need to repeat the same steps to begin this project. The steps on the next page show how to start and customize a new presentation and change to the Outline tab. See your instructor if the Mountain Top template is not available on your system.

To Start and Customize a New Presentation and Change to the Outline Tab

1 Click the Start button on the Windows taskbar, point to All Programs on the Start menu, point to Microsoft Office on the All Programs submenu, and then click Microsoft Office PowerPoint 2003 on the Microsoft Office submenu.

2 If the PowerPoint window is not maximized, double-click its title bar to maximize it.

3 If the Language bar appears, right-click it and then click Close the Language bar on the shortcut menu.

4 If the Getting Started task pane appears in the PowerPoint window, click its Close button in the upper-right corner.

5 If the Standard and Formatting toolbars are positioned on the same row, click the Toolbar Options button and then click Show Buttons on Two Rows.

6 Click the Slide Design button on the Formatting toolbar. When the Slide Design task pane is displayed, click the down scroll arrow in the Apply a design template list, and then click the Mountain Top template in the Available For Use area.

7 Click the Close button in the Slide Design task pane.

8 Click the Outline tab in the tabs pane.

The PowerPoint window with the Standard and Formatting toolbars on two rows appears as shown in Figure 3-2. PowerPoint displays the Title Slide slide layout and the Mountain Top template on Slide 1 in normal view.

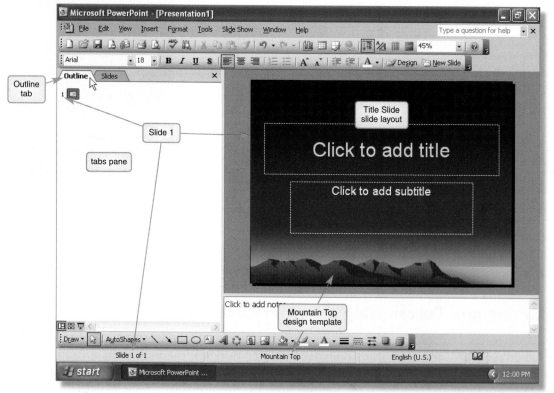

FIGURE 3-2

Importing Text Created in Another Application

In your classes, you may be asked to make an oral presentation. For example, in your English composition class, your instructor may require you to summarize verbally a research paper you wrote. You can use a PowerPoint presentation to help you construct and deliver your presentation.

PowerPoint can use text created in other programs to create a new slide show. This text may have originated in Microsoft Word or another word processing program, or it may have appeared on a Web page. Microsoft Word files use the file extension **.doc** in their file names. Text originating in other word processing programs should be saved in Rich Text Format (.rtf) or plain text format (.txt), and Web page documents should have an HTML extension (.htm).

An outline created in Microsoft Word or another word processing program works well as a shell for a PowerPoint presentation. Instead of typing text in PowerPoint, as you did in Projects 1 and 2, you can import this outline; add visual elements such as clip art, photos, graphical bullets, and animation schemes; and ultimately create an impressive slide show. If you did not create an outline to help you write your word processing document, you can create one by saving your paper with a new file name, removing all text except the topic headings, and then saving the file again.

PowerPoint automatically opens Microsoft Office files, and many other types of files, in PowerPoint format. The **rich text format** file type is used to transfer formatted documents between applications, even if the programs are running on different platforms, such as IBM-compatible and Macintosh. When a Word or Rich Text Format document is inserted, PowerPoint creates an outline structure based on heading styles in the document. A Heading 1 in a source document becomes a slide title in PowerPoint, a Heading 2 becomes the first level of body text on the slide, a Heading 3 the second level of text on the slide, and so on.

If the original document contains no heading styles, PowerPoint creates an outline based on paragraphs. For example, in a .doc or .rtf file, for several lines of text styled as Normal and broken by paragraphs, PowerPoint turns each paragraph into a slide title.

To create a presentation using an existing outline, select **Slides from Outline** on the Insert menu. PowerPoint opens the Insert Outline dialog box, displays All Outlines in the Files of type box, and displays a list of outlines. Next, you select the file that contains the outline. PowerPoint then creates a presentation using your outline. Each major heading in your outline becomes a slide title, and subheadings become a bulleted list.

Opening a Microsoft Word Outline as a Presentation

The next step in this project is to import an outline created in Microsoft Word. PowerPoint can produce slides based on an outline created in Microsoft Word or another word processing program if the outline was saved in a format that PowerPoint can recognize. The outline you import in this project was saved as a file with an .rtf extension.

Importing an outline into PowerPoint requires two steps. First, you must tell PowerPoint you are opening an existing document. Then, to open the outline, you need to select the proper file in the Insert Outline dialog box. The steps on the next page open a Microsoft Word outline as a presentation.

More About

File Conversion

PowerPoint uses converters to open Microsoft Office files automatically. These converters are installed when PowerPoint is installed. If PowerPoint recognizes the file extension, such as .doc or .xls, it converts the file to the correct format. If PowerPoint does not recognize the file extension, you can run Office Setup to add additional converters.

More About

Sending Outlines to Word

While you can open Microsoft Word outlines in PowerPoint, you also can send your PowerPoint outline to Word and then use the text to create handouts and other documents. To perform this action, click File on the menu bar, point to Send To, click Microsoft Office Word, and then click Outline only.

To Open a Microsoft Word Outline as a Presentation

1

• **Insert your Data Disk into drive A.**

• **Click Insert on the menu bar and then point to Slides from Outline.**

The Insert menu is displayed (Figure 3-3). You want to open the outline created in Microsoft Word and saved on your Data Disk.

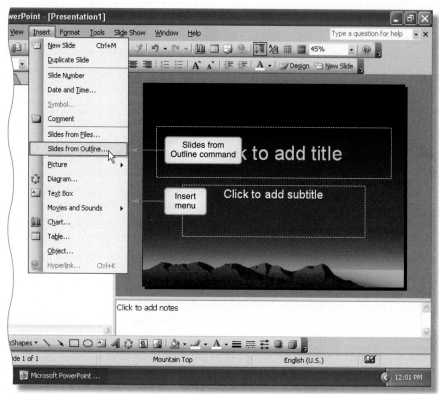

FIGURE 3-3

2

• **Click Slides from Outline.**

• **Click the Look in box arrow and then click 3½ Floppy (A:).**

• **Click Hidden Lake Outline in the Look in list.**

The Insert Outline dialog box is displayed (Figure 3-4). A list displays the outline files that PowerPoint can open. Your list may be different depending on the files stored on your floppy disk.

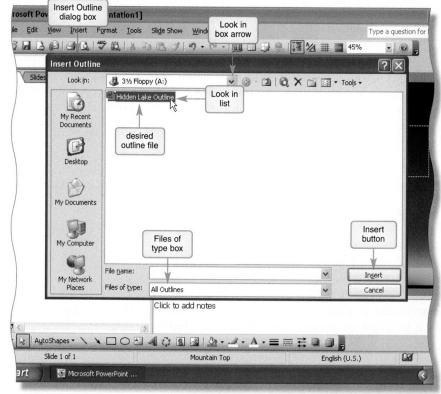

FIGURE 3-4

3

• **Click the Insert button.**

PowerPoint opens the Hidden Lake Outline and creates Slides 2 through 5 (Figure 3-5). The outline is displayed in the tabs pane, and Slide 2 is displayed in the slide pane. The outline text on Slides 2 and 3 is displayed bulleted, indicating the slide layout is a bulleted list.

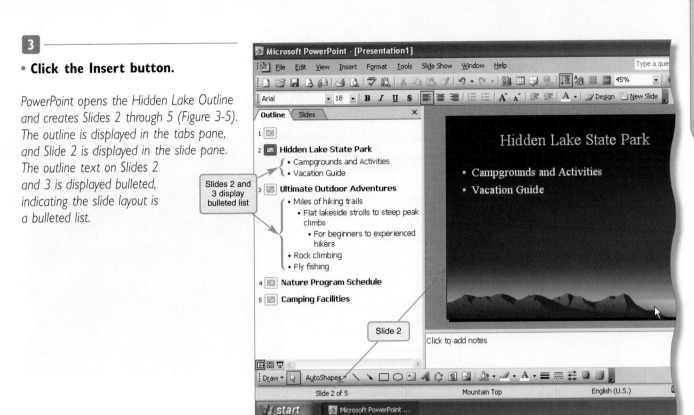

FIGURE 3-5

Imported outlines can contain up to nine outline levels, whereas PowerPoint outlines are limited to six levels (one for the title text and five for body paragraph text). When you import an outline, all text in outline levels six through nine is treated as a fifth-level paragraph.

Deleting a Slide

PowerPoint added Slides 2 through 5 when you imported the Microsoft Word outline. Slide 1 is blank and should be deleted. The steps on the next page delete Slide 1.

To Delete a Slide

1

- **Click the Slide 1 slide icon on the Outline tab.**

The Slide 1 slide icon is selected, and Slide 1 is displayed (Figure 3-6).

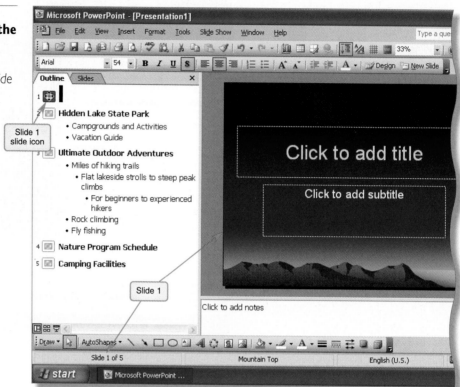

FIGURE 3-6

2

- **Click Edit on the menu bar and then point to Delete Slide (Figure 3-7).**

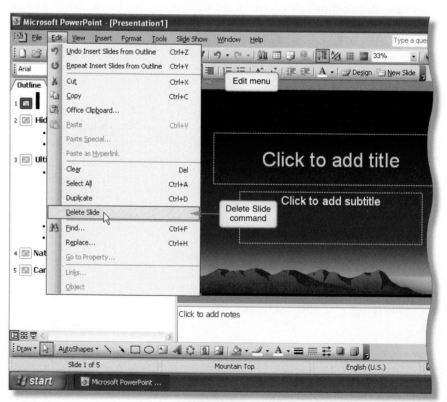

FIGURE 3-7

3

• **Click Delete Slide.**

The blank Slide 1 is deleted and is replaced with the original Slide 2 (Figure 3-8).

FIGURE 3-8

The current slides in the presentation have the Title and Text slide layout. The following steps show how to apply the Title Slide layout to Slide 1.

Changing the Slide 1 Layout to Title Slide

When you started the new presentation, PowerPoint created Slide 1 and applied the Title Slide slide layout. Now that the original Slide 2 is the new Slide 1, you want to apply the Title Slide slide layout to introduce the presentation. The following steps change the Slide 1 slide layout.

To Change the Slide Layout to Title Slide

1 **Click Format on the menu bar and then click Slide Layout.**

2 **Click the Title Slide slide layout located in the Text Layouts area in the Slide Layout task pane.**

3 **Click the Close button in the Slide Layout task pane.**

Slide 1 has the desired Title Slide slide layout (Figure 3-9).

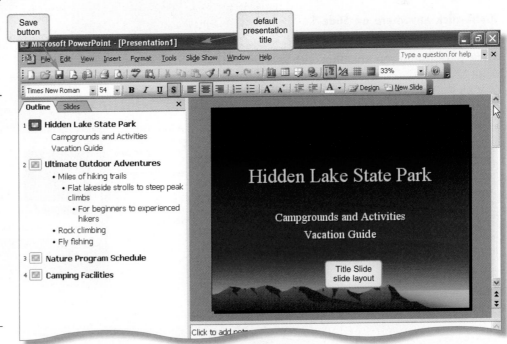

FIGURE 3-9

Saving the Presentation

You now should save the presentation because you applied a design template, created a presentation from an outline file, deleted a slide, and applied a new slide layout. The following steps summarize how to save a presentation.

To Save a Presentation

1 Click the Save button on the Standard toolbar.

2 Type Hidden Lake in the File name text box.

3 Click the Save in box arrow. Click 3½ Floppy (A:) in the Save in list.

4 Click the Save button in the Save As dialog box.

The presentation is saved on the floppy disk in drive A with the file name Hidden Lake. This file name is displayed on the title bar.

Adding a Picture to Create a Custom Background

To generate audience interest in a presentation, you can add pictures. The next step is to insert a picture of Hidden Lake to create a custom background. This picture is stored on the Data Disk. See the inside back cover of this book for instructions for downloading the Data Disk or see your instructor for information about accessing the files required for this book. The following steps add this picture to the Slide 1 background.

To Add a Picture to Create a Custom Background

1

• **Right-click anywhere on Slide 1 except the title text placeholder.**

• **Click Background on the shortcut menu.**

The Background dialog box is displayed (Figure 3-10).

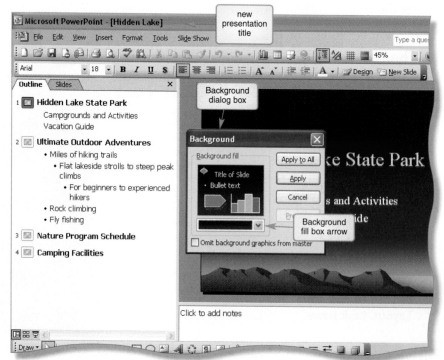

FIGURE 3-10

2

• **Click the Background fill box arrow in the Background dialog box.**

• **Point to Fill Effects on the menu.**

The Background fill menu containing commands and options for filling the slide background is displayed (Figure 3-11). The current background fill color is light purple, which is the Mountain Top design template default. The eight colors in the top row are for the Mountain Top color scheme. Fill Effects is highlighted.

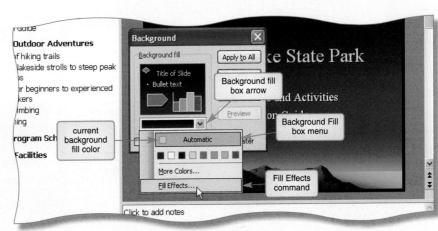

FIGURE 3-11

3

• **Click Fill Effects.**

• **If necessary, when the Fill Effects dialog box is displayed, click the Picture tab.**

The Fill Effects dialog box is displayed (Figure 3-12).

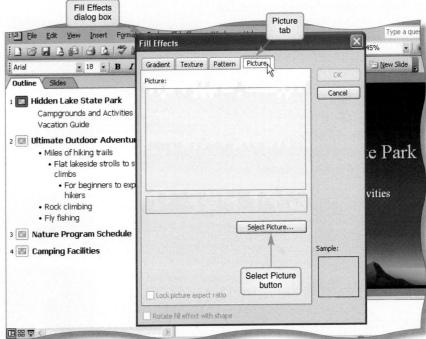

FIGURE 3-12

4

• **Click the Select Picture button.**

• **When the Select Picture dialog box is displayed, click the Look in box arrow and then click 3½ Floppy (A:).**

• **Click the Hidden Lake thumbnail.**

The Select Picture dialog box is displayed (Figure 3-13). The selected file, Hidden Lake, is displayed in the Preview box.

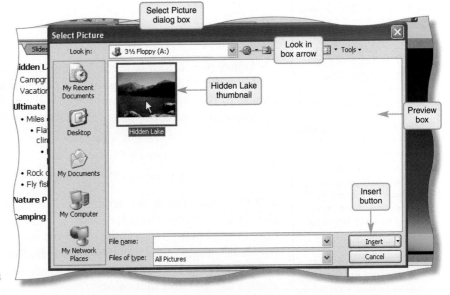

FIGURE 3-13

5

- **Click the Insert button.**
- **When the picture is displayed in the Fill Effects dialog box, click the OK button.**
- **When the Background dialog box is displayed, click the Omit background graphics from master check box.**

The Background dialog box displays the Hidden Lake picture in the Background fill area (Figure 3-14). You do not want the mountains that are part of the Mountain Top design template to display, so you click the Omit background graphics from master box to have only the Hidden Lake photograph and outline text display on Slide 1.

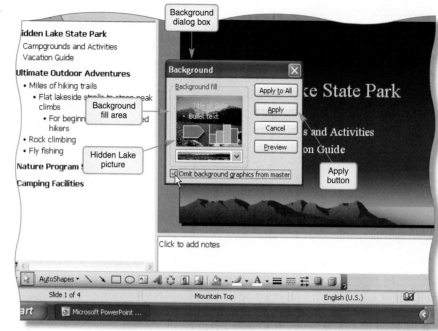

FIGURE 3-14

6

- **Click the Apply button.**

The Hidden Lake picture is displayed as the Slide 1 background (Figure 3-15). You could add the picture to Slide 1 or to all slides in the presentation. The Mountain Top design template text attributes are displayed on the slide.

FIGURE 3-15

Other Ways

1. On Format menu click Background, click Background fill box arrow, click Fill Effects, click Select Picture button, click Look in box arrow, click 3½ Floppy (A:), click desired picture, click Insert button, click OK button, click Apply button
2. Press ALT+O, press K, press DOWN ARROW, press F, if necessary press LEFT ARROW, press ALT+L, press ALT+I, press arrow key to select 3½ Floppy (A:), press ENTER, press TAB three times, press arrow keys to select desired picture, press ALT+S, press ENTER, press ENTER
3. In Voice Command mode, say "Format, Background"

When you customize the background, the design template text attributes remain the same, but the slide background changes. For example, adding the Hidden Lake picture to the slide background changes the appearance of the slide background but maintains the text attributes of the Mountain Top design template.

Formatting Text-Based Content

The Mountain Top design template has text attributes for the title slide and each text slide that determine the color scheme, font and font size, and layout of a presentation. PowerPoint gives you the ability to format the slide text content but still keep a particular design template by changing the font and the font's color, effects, size, and style. In Project 1 you changed the font style and size. In the next section, you will change the font and font color.

Changing the Font and Font Attributes

Text font attributes include styles (regular, bold, italic, and bold italic), size, effects, and color. PowerPoint allows you to use one or more text attributes on a slide. The following steps add emphasis to the title text by changing the font, font style, and font color.

To Change the Title Slide Font and Font Attributes

1

- **Position the mouse pointer before the word, Hidden, in Slide 1 on the Outline tab.**
- **Click and then drag through the title slide title and subtitle text.**

PowerPoint highlights the title and subtitle text paragraphs (Figure 3-16).

FIGURE 3-16

2

- **Right-click the highlighted text and then click Font on the shortcut menu.**

The Font dialog box is displayed (Figure 3-17). Times New Roman is the default font for the Mountain Top slide template.

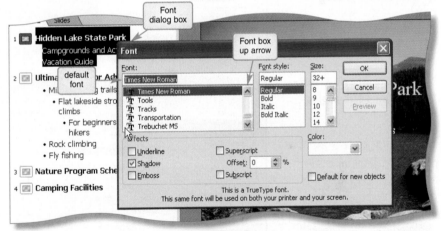

FIGURE 3-17

3

- **Click the Font box up arrow.**
- **Scroll up the list until the font name, Comic Sans MS, is displayed in the Font list.**
- **Click Comic Sans MS.**

Comic Sans is the new title slide font.

4

- **Click Bold Italic in the Font style list.**

The title slide text will display with bold and italic attributes (Figure 3-18).

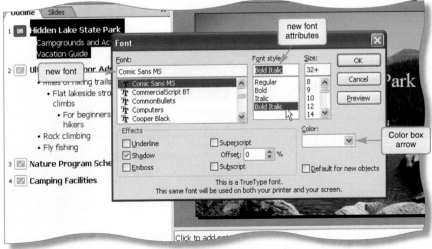

FIGURE 3-18

5

- **Click the Color box arrow.**
- **Click More Colors in the Color list.**
- **If necessary, click the Standard tab in the Colors dialog box.**
- **Click the color, gold, on the Standard tab (row 11, color 4).**

Light purple is the default title text font color in the Mountain Top color scheme (Figure 3-19). The color, gold, is not part of the Mountain Top color scheme. You also can mix your own color by clicking the Custom tab.

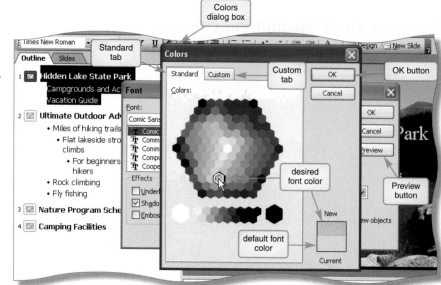

FIGURE 3-19

6

- **Click the OK button in the Colors dialog box.**

7

- **Click the Preview button in the Font dialog box.**

The text on Slide 1 is displayed with the Comic Sans MS font with bold italic and gold font attributes (Figure 3-20). If the Font dialog box is displayed over the slide, click the Font dialog box title bar and then drag the box to a new location.

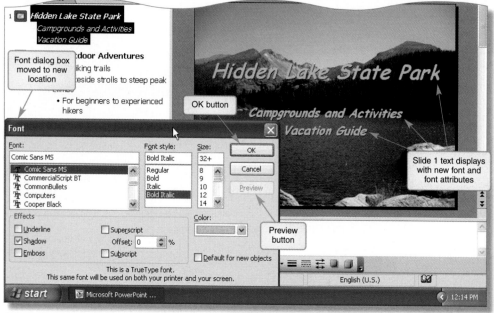

FIGURE 3-20

8

- **Click the OK button in the Font dialog box.**

The modified Slide 1 font and attributes are displayed (Figure 3-21).

FIGURE 3-21

To remove the bold and italic styles from text, select the text and then click the Italic and Bold buttons. As a result, the Italic and Bold buttons are not selected, and the text does not have the bold italic font attributes.

Inserting and Modifying Clips

A **clip art picture** is composed of many objects grouped together to form one object. PowerPoint allows you to modify and enhance the clip by disassembling it into the objects. **Disassembling** a clip art picture, also called **ungrouping**, separates one object into multiple objects. Once ungrouped, you can manipulate the individual objects as needed to form a new object. When you ungroup a clip art picture in PowerPoint, it becomes a **drawing object** and loses its link to the Microsoft Clip Organizer. In addition to clips, other drawing objects are curves, lines, AutoShapes, and WordArt.

Objects usually are saved in one of two **graphic formats**: vector or bitmap. A **vector graphic** is a piece of art that has been created by a drawing program such as CorelDRAW or Adobe Illustrator. The clip art pictures used in this project are vector graphic objects and are created as a collection of lines. Vector graphic files store data either as picture descriptions or as calculations. These files describe a picture mathematically as a set of instructions for creating the objects in the picture. These mathematical descriptions determine the position, length, and direction in which the lines are drawn. These calculations allow the drawing program to re-create the picture on the screen as necessary. Because vector graphic objects are described mathematically, they also can be layered, rotated, and magnified with relative ease. Vector graphics also are known as **object-oriented pictures**. Clip art pictures in the Microsoft Clip Organizer that have the file extension of **.wmf** are examples of vector files. Vector files can be ungrouped and manipulated by their component objects. You will ungroup the hiking clips used on Slide 2 in this project.

PowerPoint allows you to insert vector files because it uses **graphic filters** to convert the various graphic formats into a format PowerPoint can use. These filters are installed with the initial PowerPoint installation or can be added later by running the Setup program.

A **bitmap graphic** is the other major format used to store objects. These art pieces are composed of a series of small dots, called pixels, which form shapes and lines. A **pixel**, short for **picture element**, is one dot in a grid. A picture that is produced on the computer screen or on paper by a printer is composed of thousands of these dots. Just as a bit is the smallest unit of information a computer can process, a pixel is the smallest element that can display or that print hardware and software can manipulate in creating letters, numbers, or graphics.

Bitmap graphics are created by digital cameras or in paint programs such as Microsoft Paint. Bitmap graphics also can be produced from **digitizing** art, pictures, or photographs by passing the artwork through a scanner. A **scanner** is a hardware device that converts lines and shading into combinations of the binary digits 0 and 1 by sensing different intensities of light and dark. The scanner shines a beam of light on the picture being scanned. The beam passes back and forth across the picture, sending a digitized signal to the computer's memory. A **digitized signal** is the conversion of input, such as the lines in a drawing, into a series of discrete units represented by the binary digits 0 and 1. **Scanned pictures** are bitmap pictures and have jagged edges. The jagged edges are caused by the individual pixels that create the picture. Bitmap graphics also are known as **raster images**. Pictures in the Microsoft Clip Organizer that have the file extensions of **.jpg** (Joint Photographic Experts Group), **.bmp** (Windows Bitmap), **.gif** (Graphics Interchange Format), and **.png** (Portable Network Graphics) are examples of bitmap graphic files.

More About

Modifying and Using Art

If you change a clip, be certain you have the legal right to do so. For example, corporate logos are designed using specific colors and shapes and often cannot be altered. In addition, you cannot use photographs and illustrations to damage people's reputations by representing them falsely. For example, you cannot insert a photograph of a former boyfriend or girlfriend in a slide that gives information about students who have been arrested on campus for committing criminal acts.

Q&A

Q: Can I Import Macintosh PICT Files?

A: Yes. PowerPoint uses the Macintosh PICT graphics filter (Pictim32.flt) to convert Macintosh files. You should rename these files using the .pct extension so Microsoft Office for Windows recognizes the files as PICT graphics.

More About

Cropping Pictures

Use the Crop command to cut unwanted areas from any picture except an animated GIF picture. Select the picture, click the Crop button on the Picture toolbar, position the cropping tool over a center cropping handle, and then drag the handle inward. Click the Crop button again to turn off the cropping command.

Bitmap files cannot be ungrouped and converted to smaller PowerPoint object groups. They can be manipulated, however, in an imaging program such as Microsoft Photo Editor. This program allows you to rotate or flip the pictures and then insert them in your slides.

Slide 2 contains a modified version of three people: an adult leader and two child hikers. This clip is from the Microsoft Clip Organizer. You may want to modify a clip art picture for various reasons. Many times you cannot find a clip art picture that precisely illustrates your topic. For example, you want a picture of a man and woman shaking hands, but the only available clip art picture has two men and a woman shaking hands.

Occasionally you may want to remove or change a portion of a clip art picture or you might want to combine two or more clip art pictures. For example, you can use one clip art picture for the background and another picture as the foreground. Still other times, you may want to combine a clip art picture with another type of object. The types of objects you can combine with a clip art picture depend on the software installed on your computer. The **Object type list** in the Insert Object dialog box identifies the types of objects you can combine with a clip art picture. In this presentation, the picture with three people hiking contains a background that is not required to display on the slide, so you will ungroup the clip art picture and remove the background.

Modifying the clip on Slide 2 requires several steps. First, you display Slide 2 and change the slide layout. Then, you insert the hiking picture into the slide. In the next step, you scale the picture to increase its size. Finally, you ungroup the clip, change the color of the backpacks and hats, and then regroup the component objects. The following steps explain in detail how to insert, scale, ungroup, modify, and regroup a clip art image.

Changing the Slide 2 Layout to Title, Content and Text

For aesthetic reasons, you want the bulleted list to display on the right side of the slide. The following steps change the slide layout.

To Change the Slide Layout to Title, Content and Text

1 Click the Next Slide button to display Slide 2.

2 Click Format on the menu bar and then click Slide Layout.

3 Scroll down and then click the Title, Content and Text slide layout in the Text and Content Layouts area in the Slide Layout task pane.

4 Click the Close button in the Slide Layout task pane.

5 Click the Slides tab in the tabs pane.

Slide 2 has the desired Title, Content and Text slide layout (Figure 3-22). The slide thumbnails display in the tabs pane.

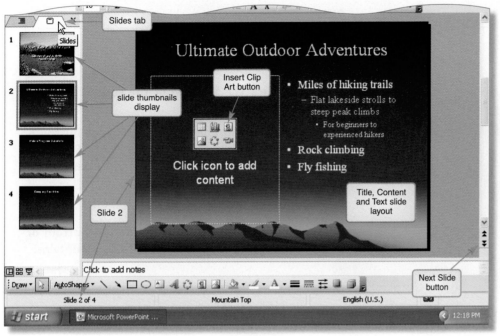

FIGURE 3-22

Inserting a Clip into a Content Placeholder

The first step in modifying a clip is to insert the picture into a slide. You insert the hiking clip from the Microsoft Clip Organizer. In later steps, you modify the clip.

The following steps explain how to insert the clip of the three hikers. See your instructor if this clip is not available on your system.

To Insert a Clip into a Content Placeholder

1 Click the **Insert Clip Art button** in the content placeholder (row 1, column 3).

2 Type backpackers **in the Search text text box and then click the Go button.**

3 If necessary, scroll down the list to display the desired clip shown in Figure 3-1b on page PPT 163, click the clip to select it, and then click the OK button.

The selected clip is inserted into the content placeholder on Slide 2 (Figure 3-23). If the desired clip does not display on your system, see your instructor.

FIGURE 3-23

Sizing and Moving Clips

With the hiking clip inserted on Slide 2, the next step is to increase its size. The steps on the next page size and move the clip.

To Size and Move a Clip

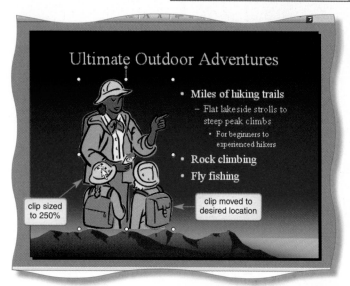

FIGURE 3-24

1 Right-click the clip and then click Format Picture on the shortcut menu.

2 Click the Size tab in the Format Picture dialog box.

3 Click and hold down the mouse button on the Height box up arrow in the Scale area until 250 % is displayed and then release the mouse button.

4 Click the OK button.

5 Drag the hiking clip up so the bottom of the clip is on the top of the mountains.

The hiking clip art picture increases in size and is displayed in the desired location (Figure 3-24).

Ungrouping a Clip

The next step is to ungroup the hiking clip on Slide 2. When you **ungroup** a clip art picture, PowerPoint breaks it into its component objects. A clip may be composed of a few individual objects or several complex groups of objects. These groups can be ungrouped repeatedly until they decompose into individual objects.

The following steps ungroup a clip.

To Ungroup a Clip

1

• **With the hiking clip selected, right-click the clip.**

• **Point to Grouping on the shortcut menu, and then point to Ungroup on the Grouping submenu.**

Sizing handles indicate the clip is selected (Figure 3-25).

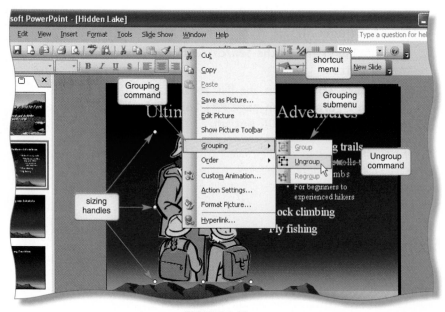

FIGURE 3-25

2

- **Click Ungroup.**

- **Click the Yes button in the Microsoft PowerPoint dialog box.**

The message in the Microsoft PowerPoint dialog box explains that this clip is an imported picture. Converting it to a Microsoft Office drawing permanently discards any embedded data or linking information it contains.

3

- **Right-click the clip, point to Grouping on the shortcut menu, and then click Ungroup.**

The clip now displays as many objects, and sizing handles display around the ungrouped objects (Figure 3-26).

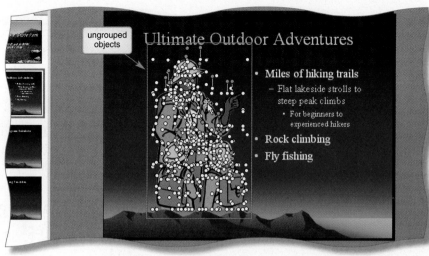

FIGURE 3-26

Other Ways

1. On Draw menu click Ungroup
2. In Voice Command mode, say "Draw, Ungroup"

Because a clip art picture is a collection of complex groups of objects, you may need to ungroup a complex object into less complex objects before being able to modify a specific object. When you ungroup a clip and click the Yes button in the Microsoft PowerPoint dialog box (Step 2 above), PowerPoint converts the clip to a PowerPoint object. Recall that a PowerPoint object is an object not associated with a supplementary application.

If for some reason you decide not to ungroup the clip art picture, click the No button in the Microsoft PowerPoint dialog box. Clicking the No button terminates the Ungroup command, and the clip art picture is displayed on the slide as a clip art picture.

Recall that a clip art picture is an object imported from the Microsoft Clip Organizer. Disassembling imported, embedded, or linked objects eliminates the embedding data or linking information the object contains that ties it back to its original source. Use caution when objects are not completely regrouped. Dragging or scaling affects only the selected object, not the entire collection of objects. To **regroup** the individual objects, select all the objects, click the Draw button on the Drawing toolbar, and then click Group.

More About

Adding Pictures to Notes

If you want to see your pictures on your printed notes, you can add the images to these pages. Click Notes Page on the View menu and then add the picture or object. Then click the Normal View button at the lower-left corner of the Microsoft PowerPoint window to return to normal view.

Deselecting Clip Art Objects

All of the ungrouped objects in Figure 3-26 are selected. Before you can manipulate an individual object, you must deselect all selected objects to remove the selection rectangles, and then you must select the object you want to manipulate. For example, on this slide, you will change the colors of the hats and backpacks. The step on the next page explains how to deselect objects.

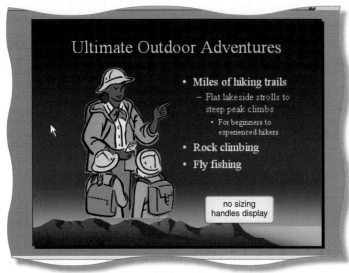

FIGURE 3-27

To Deselect Clip Art Objects

1 **Click outside the clip area.**

Slide 2 displays without the sizing handles around the objects (Figure 3-27).

The hiking clip now is ungrouped into many objects. The next section explains how to change the color of objects.

Changing the Color of a PowerPoint Object

Now that the hiking picture is ungrouped, you can change the color of the objects. The clip is composed of hundreds of objects, so you must exercise care when selecting the correct object to modify. If sizing handles are displayed around the incorrect object, click outside of the clip art and then retry. The following steps change the color of the hikers' hats.

To Change the Color of a PowerPoint Object

1

• **Click the adult hiker's hat.**

Sizing handles display around the hat (Figure 3-28). If you inadvertently select a different area, click outside of the clip and retry.

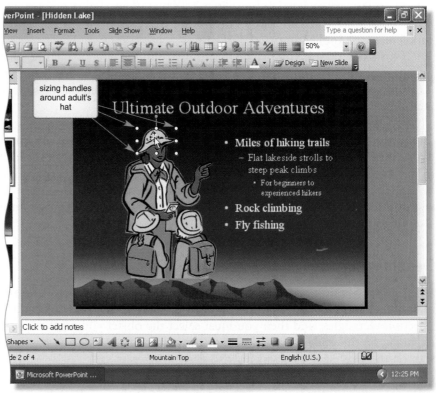

FIGURE 3-28

2

• **Right-click the hat and then point to Format AutoShape on the shortcut menu.**

The shortcut menu displays (Figure 3-29).

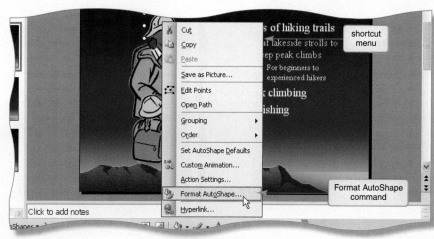

FIGURE 3-29

3

• **Click Format AutoShape.**

• **When the Format AutoShape dialog box displays, click the Colors and Lines tab, and then click the Color box arrow in the Fill area.**

The Format AutoShape dialog box displays (Figure 3-30). The blue hat color is displayed in the Automatic area. The colors displayed in the row directly below the Automatic area are the default colors associated with the Mountain Top design template.

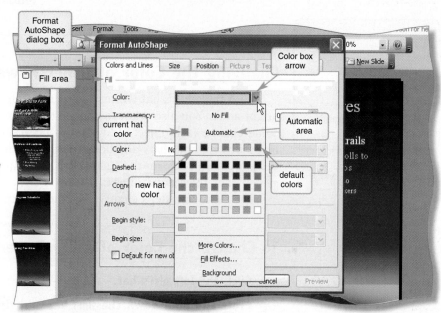

FIGURE 3-30

4

• **Click the color, white, in the row of colors directly below the Automatic area (row 1, column 2).**

White is the default text and lines color for the Mountain Top design template (Figure 3-31). The white color displays in the Color box in the Format AutoShape dialog box.

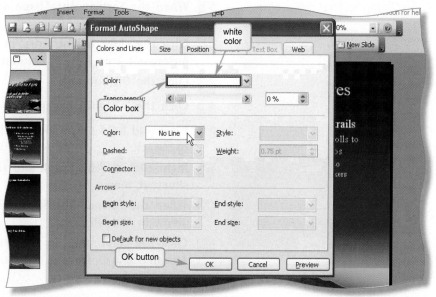

FIGURE 3-31

5

• **Click the OK button.**

The Format AutoShape dialog box closes, and the adult's hat is white (Figure 3-32).

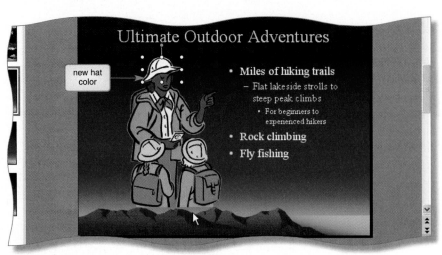

FIGURE 3-32

Changing the Color of Other PowerPoint Objects

With the adult's hat white, you want to change the color of the girls' hats to bright aqua. You also want to change the color of their backpacks to pink. You could change each object individually, but you can perform this task more efficiently by modifying both hats and both backpacks simultaneously using the **SHIFT+click technique**. To perform the SHIFT+click technique, press and hold down the SHIFT key as you click the second object. After you click the second object, release the SHIFT key.

The following steps change the colors of the girls' hats and backpacks.

To Change the Color of Other PowerPoint Objects

1 Click the left girl's hat.

2 Press and hold down the SHIFT key and then click the right girl's hat.

3 Right-click one hat and then click Format AutoShape on the shortcut menu.

4 When the Format AutoShape dialog box displays, click the Color box arrow in the Fill area.

5 Click the color, bright aqua, in the row of colors directly below the Automatic area (row 1, column 7).

6 Click the OK button.

7 Click the left girl's backpack.

8 Press and hold down the SHIFT key and then click the right girl's backpack.

9 Right-click one backpack and then click Format AutoShape on the shortcut menu.

10 When the Format AutoShape dialog box displays, click the Color box arrow in the Fill area.

11 Click the color, pink, in the first column of colors directly below the Automatic area (row 5, column 1).

12 Click the OK button.

FIGURE 3-33

The PowerPoint object displays with the girls' bright aqua hats and pink backpacks (Figure 3-33).

Regrouping Objects

All of the ungrouped objects in the hikers' picture must be regrouped so they are not accidentally moved or manipulated. The following steps regroup these objects.

To Regroup Objects

1

• **Click outside the lower-right corner of the clip and then drag diagonally to the upper-left corner of the clip above the woman's hat.**

A dotted-line rectangle is displayed around the hiking clip as you drag (Figure 3-34). You want to group the objects within this area. The mouse pointer should be a block arrow only, not an arrow overlaying a double two-headed arrow.

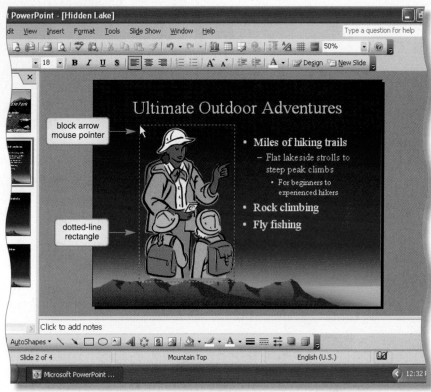

FIGURE 3-34

2

• **Release the mouse button.**
• **Click the Draw button on the Drawing toolbar and then point to Regroup on the Draw menu.**

Sizing handles display on all the selected components of the hiking clip (Figure 3-35).

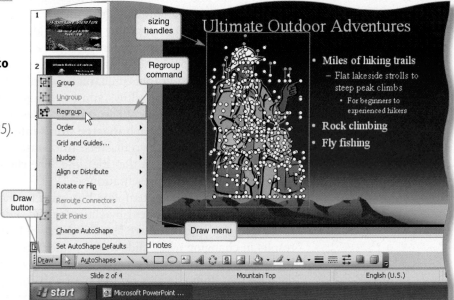

FIGURE 3-35

3

• **Click Regroup.**

The eight sizing handles displaying around the entire clip indicate the object is regrouped (Figure 3-36).

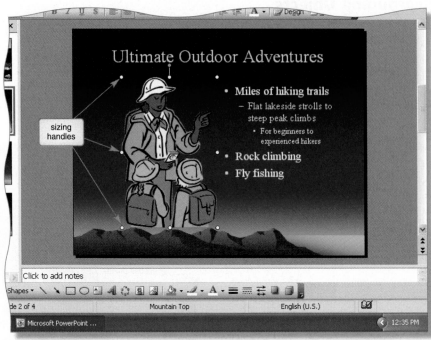

FIGURE 3-36

All the components of the hiking picture now are grouped into one object. The next change you want to make to Slide 2 is to modify bullets in the list.

Customizing Graphical Bullets Using the Slide Master

PowerPoint allows you to change the appearance of bullets in a slide show. Slide 2's Title, Content and Text slide layout uses the default bullet styles determined by the Mountain Top design template. You may want to change these characters, however, to add visual interest and variety to your slide show.

The Mountain Top design template uses white dots for the first-level paragraphs and white dashes for the second-level paragraphs. Changing the solid white round bullet to a mountain graphical character would enhance the visual nature of your presentation. PowerPoint allows you to change the bullet style for a single list or throughout a presentation. When several slides need to be changed, you should change the slide master. Each **master** stores information about the design template's appearance. Slides have two masters: title master and slide master. The **title master** controls the appearance of the title slide. The **slide master** controls the appearance of the other slides in a presentation.

If you select a design template but want to change one of its components, you can override that component by changing the slide master. The slide master components frequently changed are listed in Table 3-1. Any change to the slide master results in changing every slide in the presentation, except the title slide. For example, if you change the level-2 bullet on the slide master, each slide (except the title slide) changes that bullet. In this project, you will change the bullet style on the slide master to reflect the change throughout the presentation, so the new symbol will display in the bulleted list on Slide 2.

Bullet styles have three components: character, size, and color. A **bullet character** can be a predefined style, a variety of fonts and characters displayed in the Symbol dialog box, or a picture from the Clip Organizer. **Bullet size** is measured as a percentage of the text size and can range from 25 to 400 percent. **Bullet color** is based on the eight colors in the design template's color scheme. Additional standard and custom colors also are available.

To emphasize the nature message in the slide show, you want to change the bullet style in the first-level paragraphs from a solid round bullet to the mountain symbol and from white to brown. You will make these changes on the slide master.

Displaying the Slide Master

Table 3-1 Summary of Slide Master Components	
COMPONENT	**DESCRIPTION**
Background items	Any object other than the title object or text object. Typical items include borders and graphics such as a company logo, page number, date, and time.
Color scheme	A coordinated set of eight colors designed to complement each other. Color schemes consist of background color, line and text color, shadow color, title text color, object fill color, and three different accent colors.
Date	Inserts the special symbol used to print the date the presentation was printed.
Font	Defines the appearance and shape of letters, numbers, and special characters.
Size	Specifies the size of the characters on the screen in a measurement system called points.
Slide number	Inserts the special symbol used to print the slide number.
Style	Font styles include regular, bold, italic, and bold italic. Effects include underline, shadow, emboss, superscript, and subscript. Effects can be applied to most fonts.
Text alignment	Position of text in a paragraph is left-aligned, right-aligned, centered, or justified. Justified text is spaced proportionally across the object.
Time	Inserts the special symbol used to print the time the presentation was printed.

To change all first-level bullets throughout the presentation, the bullet should be changed on the slide master. The following steps display the slide master.

To Display the Slide Master

1

• **Click View on the menu bar, point to Master, and then point to Slide Master on the Master submenu.**

The View menu and Master submenu display (Figure 3-37). Each PowerPoint component — slides (both title and text), audience handouts, and notes pages — has a master that controls its appearance.

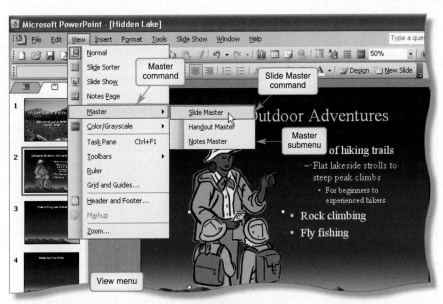

FIGURE 3-37

2

• **Click the Slide Master command.**

The Mountain Top slide master and Slide Master View toolbar display (Figure 3-38). The Mountain Top Title Master slide thumbnail and Mountain Top Slide Master slide thumbnail display on the left edge of the screen. The Mountain Top Slide Master slide thumbnail is selected.

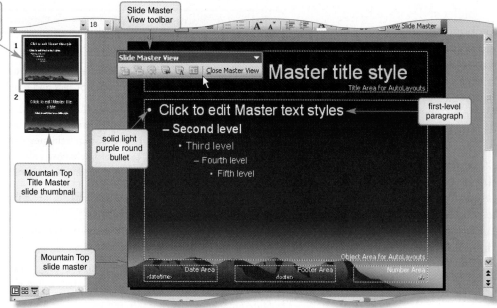

FIGURE 3-38

Other Ways

1. Press and hold down SHIFT, click Slide Master View button
2. In Voice Command mode, say "View, Master, Slide Master"

The **Slide Master View toolbar** contains buttons that are useful when inserting multiple slide masters or title masters in a slide show. Table 3-2 describes the buttons on the Slide Master View toolbar. You will use some of these buttons in Project 4.

Once the slide master is displayed, any changes to the components are reflected throughout the slide show except on the title slide. In Figure 3-38, the text styles and bullets for the five paragraph levels and for the title are shown. The first-level paragraph has a solid light purple round bullet, the Arial font, a font size of 32, and it is left-aligned. These slide master text attributes are modified in a manner similar to changing attributes on an individual slide.

Changing a Bullet Character on the Slide Master

The first bullet style change replaces the solid light purple round bullet with the mountain symbol. The following steps change the level-1 bullet character.

Table 3-2 Buttons on the Slide Master View Toolbar		
BUTTON	**BUTTON NAME**	**DESCRIPTION**
	Insert New Slide Master	Adds multiple slide masters to a slide show.
	Insert New Title Master	Adds multiple title masters to a slide show.
	Delete Master	Deletes a slide master from a slide show. When a slide master is deleted, the title master is deleted automatically.
	Preserve Master	Protects a slide master so it is not deleted automatically when all slides following that master are deleted or when another design template is applied to all slides that follow that master.
	Rename Master	Gives a slide master a customized name.
	Master Layout	Displays the elements on the master, such as the title and subtitle text, header and footer placeholders, lists, pictures, tables, charts, AutoShapes, and movies.
	Close Master View	Hides the Slide Master View toolbar.

To Change a Bullet Character on the Slide Master

1

• **On the slide master, click the paragraph, Click to edit Master text styles.**

• **Click Format on the menu bar.**

The Format menu is displayed (Figure 3-39).

FIGURE 3-39

2

• **Click Bullets and Numbering on the Format menu.**

• **If necessary, click the Bulleted tab when the Bullets and Numbering dialog box is displayed.**

The Bullets and Numbering dialog box is displayed (Figure 3-40). The Bulleted tab has a variety of bullets and the options of no bullets or custom bullets.

FIGURE 3-40

3

• **Click the Customize button in the Bullets and Numbering dialog box.**

• **Click the Font box arrow in the Symbol dialog box.**

The round bullet symbol is selected in the Symbol dialog box because it is the default level-1 bullet style for the Mountain Top design template (Figure 3-41). The round bullet is part of the General Punctuation subset of symbols for the Arial font.

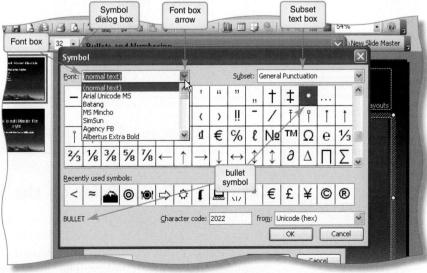

FIGURE 3-41

4

• **Scroll through the list until Webdings is displayed.**

• **Click Webdings.**

• **Click the mountain symbol.**

The symbols for the Webdings font are displayed, and the mountain symbol is selected (Figure 3-42). You may have to scroll through the symbols to locate the mountain symbol. Your list of available fonts may differ depending on the type of printer you are using and the fonts that are installed on your system. Any Webdings symbol can be used as a bullet.

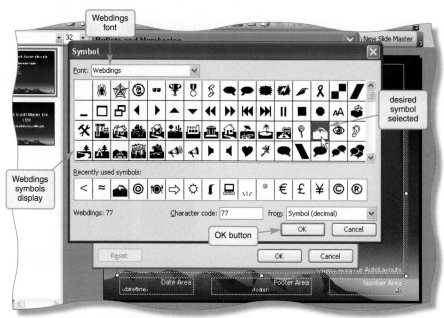

FIGURE 3-42

5

• **Click the OK button in the Symbol dialog box.**

The Bullets and Numbering dialog box is displayed (Figure 3-43). PowerPoint applies the mountain symbol to the first-level paragraph, which you will see when the dialog box closes.

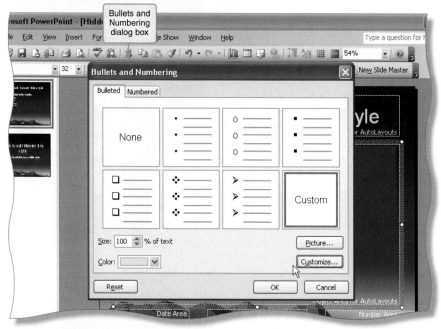

FIGURE 3-43

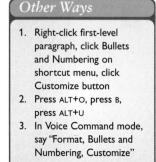

Other Ways

1. Right-click first-level paragraph, click Bullets and Numbering on shortcut menu, click Customize button
2. Press ALT+O, press B, press ALT+U
3. In Voice Command mode, say "Format, Bullets and Numbering, Customize"

The mountain symbol now will display as the level-1 bullet throughout the slide show. The next step is to change the color of the mountain bullet.

Changing a Bullet Color on the Slide Master

The new white bullet blends with the other bullets. To add contrast to the symbol, a brown bullet works well with the blue background and brown mountains at the bottom of the slide. The color brown is one of the eight default colors of the Mountain Top design template. The following steps change the level-1 bullet color.

To Change a Bullet Color on the Slide Master

1

• **With the Bullets and Numbering dialog box displaying, click the Color box arrow.**

The color light purple is displayed in the Color box and is selected in the row of available colors because it is the default bullet color in the Mountain Top design template (Figure 3-44).

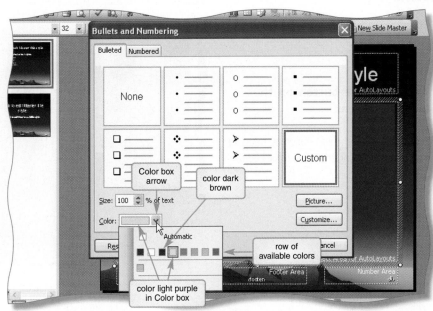

FIGURE 3-44

2

• **Click the color dark brown in the row of available colors (row 1, column 3).**

The color dark brown is displayed in the Color box (Figure 3-45).

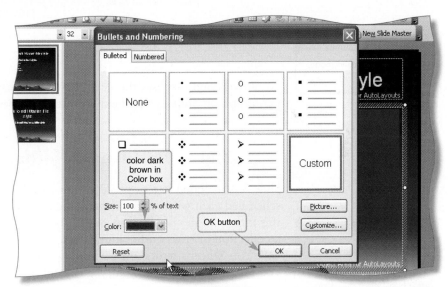

FIGURE 3-45

3

• **Click the OK button.**

• **Point to the Close Master View button on the Slide Master View toolbar.**

The dark brown mountain custom bullet is displayed in the level-1 paragraph (Figure 3-46). All changes to the slide master are complete. After closing the slide master view, the presentation returns to normal view.

FIGURE 3-46

4

• **Click the Close Master View
button.**

Slide 2 is complete (Figure 3-47).

5

• **Click the Save button on the
Standard toolbar.**

*PowerPoint saves the file. You may need to
insert a new disk or save the file to your
hard drive.*

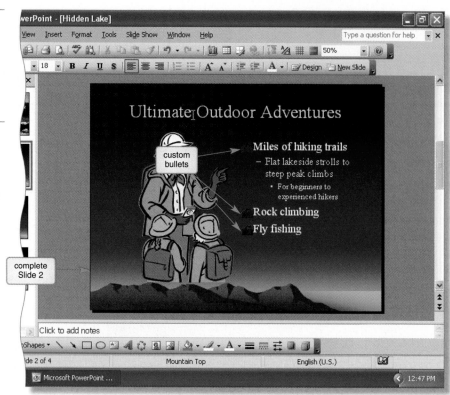

FIGURE 3-47

PowerPoint displays the new brown bullet symbol in front of each level-1
paragraph on Slide 2. The next section describes how to add a table to a slide.

Creating a Table on a Slide

Slide 3 is included in this presentation to inform campers of the three programs
scheduled each week at the three Hidden Lake State Park campgrounds. To make
this information visually appealing, you can arrange the figures in a table. A **table** is
a collection of rows and columns. The intersection of a row and a column is called a
cell. You fill cells with data pertaining to the Hidden Lake nature programs. Then
you format the table by changing the column heading alignment, font style, and size.

Inserting a Basic Table

PowerPoint provides two major methods of creating a table. If the table is basic
and has the same number of rows in each column, such as the one for this presentation, use the **Insert Table button** on the Standard toolbar and specify the number of
desired rows and columns. If the table is more complex, use the **Tables and Borders
toolbar** to draw and format the table. The following steps insert a basic table.

To Insert a Basic Table

1

- **Click the Next Slide button to display Slide 3.**
- **Click the Insert Table button on the Standard toolbar.**
- **Point to the upper-left square in the grid.**

Slide 3 displays the slide title and a text placeholder. The first square is dark blue, meaning it is selected. The message at the bottom of the grid states that the table has one row and one column (Figure 3-48).

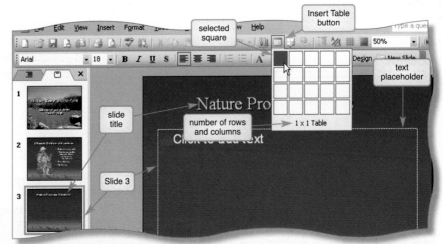

FIGURE 3-48

2

- **Move the mouse pointer two squares to the right so the first three squares in the grid are selected.**
- **Move the mouse pointer down to select four rows in the grid.**

Four rows and three columns are selected, as indicated by the dark blue squares and the message at the bottom of the grid (Figure 3-49).

FIGURE 3-49

3

- **Click the selected square at the bottom-right corner of the grid.**
- **If necessary, click the Close button on the Tables and Borders toolbar.**

PowerPoint displays a table with four rows and three columns. The insertion point is in the upper-left cell, which is selected (Figure 3-50).

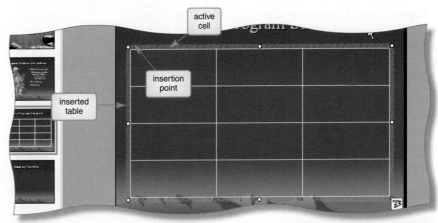

FIGURE 3-50

Other Ways

1. On Insert menu click Table, type desired number of rows and columns, click OK button
2. Press ALT+I, press B, type desired number of columns, press TAB, type desired number of rows, press ENTER

Table 3-3 Nature Program Schedule Data		
Day	Theater Location	Program
Tuesday	Maple Meadows	It's a Wild, Wild World
Friday	Beech Basin	Mountain Highs and Lows
Saturday	Crooked Creek	Wildflower Wilderness

Entering Data in a Table

The table on Slide 3 consists of three columns: one for the day of the week, one for the location of the theater, and one for the program name. A **heading** identifies each column. The days, locations, and programs are summarized in Table 3-3.

The following steps enter data in the table.

To Enter Data in a Table

1

• **Type** Day **and then press the RIGHT ARROW key.**

The first column title, Day, is displayed in the top-left cell. The middle cell in the first row is the active cell (Figure 3-51). You also can press the TAB key to advance to the next cell.

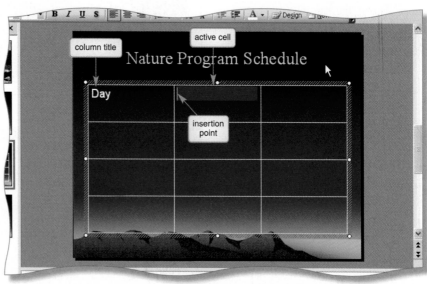

FIGURE 3-51

2

• **Repeat Step 1 to enter the remaining column titles and for the other table cells by using Table 3-3 as a guide.**

The three days of the week and the corresponding theater locations and programs display (Figure 3-52). All entries are left-aligned and display in 28-point Arial font.

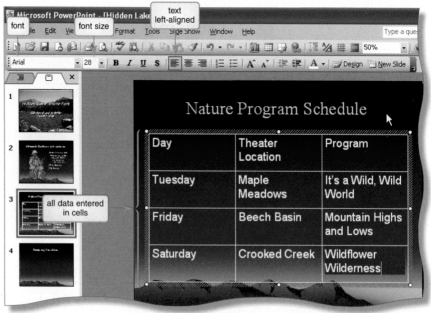

FIGURE 3-52

The next step is to format the table. You **format** the table to emphasize certain entries and to make it easier to read and understand. In this project, you will change the column heading alignment and font style and size. The process required to format the table is explained in the remainder of this section. Although the format procedures will be carried out in a particular manner, you should be aware that you can make these format changes in any order.

Formatting a Table Cell

You format an entry in a cell to emphasize it or to make it stand out from the rest of the table. The following steps bold and center the column headings and then increase the font size.

To Format a Table Cell

More About

Embedding Tables

If the data in your table changes frequently, consider using an embedded table. This table can be created in another Microsoft Office program, such as Word or Excel, and then added to a PowerPoint slide. Once embedded, the table becomes part of the original file. When the information changes in the original file, it also changes in your PowerPoint table.

1

• **Click the top-left cell, Day.**

• **Press and hold the SHIFT key and then click the top-right cell, Program.**

• **Release the SHIFT key.**

The three column headings, Day, Theater Location, and Program, are selected (Figure 3-53).

FIGURE 3-53

2

• **Click the Font box arrow on the Formatting toolbar.**

• **Scroll down and then click Times New Roman.**

The text in the heading cells is displayed in 28-point Times New Roman font (Figure 3-54).

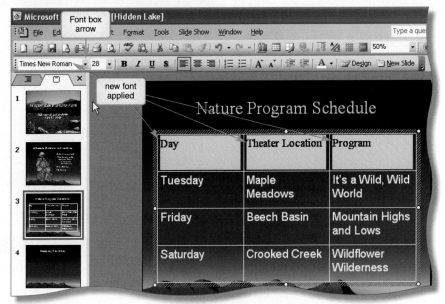

FIGURE 3-54

3

• **Click the Bold button on the Formatting toolbar.**

The text is displayed in bold and is left-aligned in the cells (Figure 3-55).

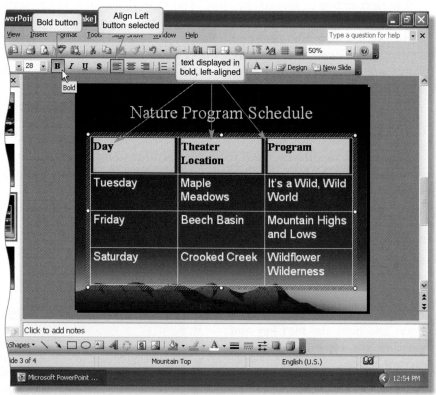

FIGURE 3-55

4

• **Click the Center button on the Formatting toolbar.**

The text is centered in the cells (Figure 3-56).

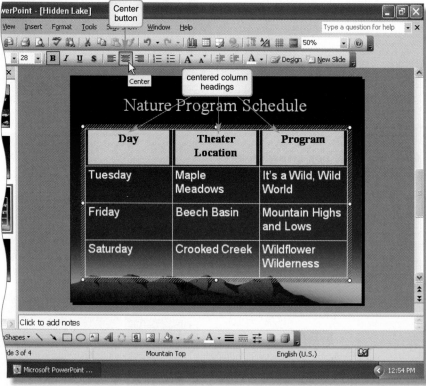

FIGURE 3-56

5

• **Click the Increase Font Size button on the Formatting toolbar twice.**

The text is enlarged to a font size of 36 point (Figure 3-57).

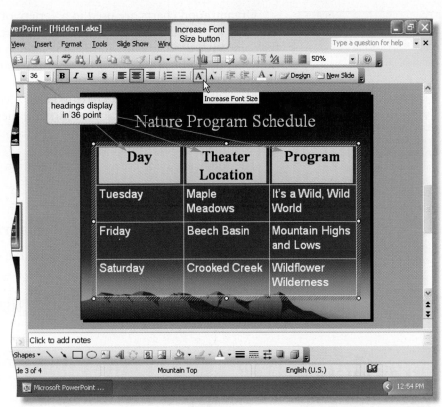

FIGURE 3-57

You can change the font type, style, or size at any time while the table is selected. Some PowerPoint users prefer to change font and cell alignments before they enter any data. Others change the font and alignment while they are building the table or after they have entered all the data.

Slide 3 now is complete. Again, because you have made some significant changes to the presentation, save the slide show by clicking the Save button on the Standard toolbar. The next section shows how to create an organization chart that describes the three campgrounds at Hidden Lake.

Creating an Organization Chart

Slide 4 contains a chart that elaborates on the campgrounds available at Hidden Lake, as shown in Figure 3-58. This type of chart is called an **organization chart**, which is a hierarchical collection of elements depicting various functions or responsibilities that contribute to an organization or to a collective function. Typically, you would use an organization chart to show the structure of people or departments within an organization, hence the name, organization chart.

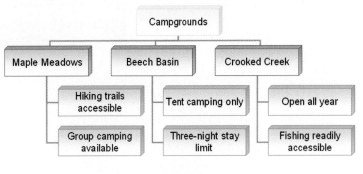

FIGURE 3-58

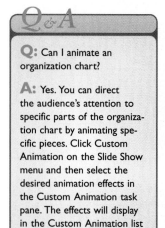

Q&A

Q: Can I animate an organization chart?

A: Yes. You can direct the audience's attention to specific parts of the organization chart by animating specific pieces. Click Custom Animation on the Slide Show menu and then select the desired animation effects in the Custom Animation task pane. The effects will display in the Custom Animation list in the order in which they were applied.

Organization charts are used in a variety of ways to depict relationships. For example, a company uses an organization chart to describe the relationships between the company's departments. In the information sciences, often organization charts show the decomposition of a process or program. When used in this manner, the chart is called a **hierarchy chart**.

Creating an organization chart requires several steps. First, you display the slide that will contain the organization chart and then select the Organization Chart diagram from the Diagram Gallery. Then you enter and format the contents of the shapes in the organization chart.

The following steps create the organization chart for this project.

Displaying the Next Slide and the Organization Chart Diagram

The following steps display Slide 4 and the organization chart diagram.

To Display the Next Slide and the Organization Chart Diagram

1

• **Click the Next Slide button to display Slide 4.**

• **Click the Insert Diagram or Organization Chart button on the Drawing toolbar.**

Slide 4 displays the slide title, a text placeholder, and the Diagram Gallery dialog box (Figure 3-59). The Organization Chart diagram type is selected. The other diagram types are Cycle Diagram, Radial Diagram, Pyramid Diagram, Venn Diagram, and Target Diagram.

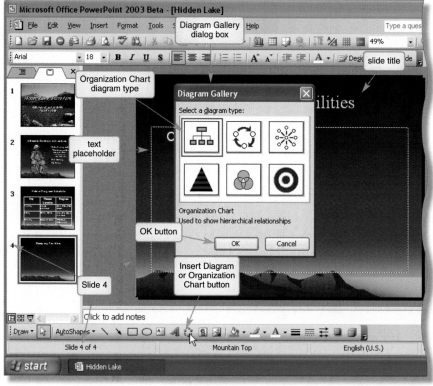

FIGURE 3-59

2

• **Click the OK button.**

A sample organization chart and the Organization Chart toolbar display (Figure 3-60). The organization chart is composed of four shapes connected by lines. The top shape, called the superior shape, is selected automatically.

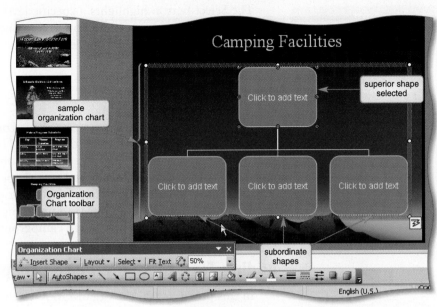

FIGURE 3-60

PowerPoint displays a sample organization chart to help create the chart. The sample is located in a work area called the **canvas** and is composed of one **superior shape**, located at the top of the chart, and three **subordinate shapes**. Lines to one or more subordinates connect a superior shape, also called a manager. A subordinate shape is located at a lower level than its manager and has only one manager. When a lower-level subordinate shape is added to a higher-level subordinate shape, the higher-level subordinate shape becomes the manager of the lower-level subordinate shape. A whole section of an organization chart is referred to as a **branch**, or an appendage, of the chart.

The Organization Chart toolbar (Figure 3-61) contains buttons to help you create and design your chart. The Insert Shape button allows you to add three different shapes to your chart: subordinate, coworker, and assistant. Three subordinate shapes are displayed by default in the sample organization chart. A **coworker shape** is located next to another shape and is connected to the same superior shape. An **assistant shape** is located below another shape and is connected to any other shape with an elbow connector.

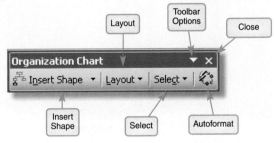

FIGURE 3-61

The Layout button changes the location of the lines connecting the subordinate branches. Layout options include Standard, Both Hanging, Left Hanging, and Right Hanging. It also has options to change the size of the entire organization chart by shrinking, expanding, or scaling.

More About

Organization Chart Shapes

To create a unique look, change the superior, assistant, subordinate, or coworker shapes, or the lines and connectors. AutoShapes include stars, banners, callouts, flow-charting symbols, and basic shapes, such as a heart, lightning bolt, sun, and moon.

The Select button highlights a specific level or branch in the chart. It also allows you to select all assistants or all connecting lines. Once these areas are selected, you easily can change their visual elements, such as text color, fill colors, line style, or line color.

The Autoformat button allows you to add a preset design scheme by selecting a style from the Organization Chart Style Gallery. These designs have a variety of colors, background shades, and borders.

Hidden Lake State Park has three campgrounds: Maple Meadows, Beech Basin, and Crooked Creek. Each campground varies in the type of camping allowed and nearby activities. As a result, your organization chart will consist of three shapes immediately below the manager and two shapes immediately below each subordinate manager. These organization chart layouts for each activity are identical, so you create the structure for the Maple Meadows campground and then repeat the steps for the Beech Basin and Crooked Creek campgrounds.

Adding Text to the Superior Shape

In this presentation, the organization chart is used to describe the three Hidden Lake campgrounds. The topmost shape, called the superior, identifies the purpose of this organization chart: Campgrounds. Recall that when you inserted the Organization Chart diagram, the superior shape is selected. The following step explains how to create the title for this shape.

To Add Text to the Superior Shape

1

• **Type** Campgrounds **in the superior shape.**

Campgrounds is displayed in the superior shape (Figure 3-62).

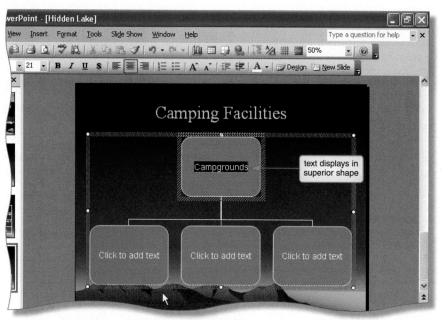

FIGURE 3-62

The text for the superior shape is entered. The next steps are to add text to the three subordinate shapes and then insert and add text to the subordinate and coworker shapes.

Adding Text to the Subordinate Shapes

The process of adding text to a subordinate shape is the same as adding text to the superior shape except that first you must select the subordinate shape. The following steps explain how to add text to subordinate shapes.

To Add Text to the Subordinate Shapes

1

• **Click the left subordinate shape.**

• **Type** Maple Meadows **in the shape.**

Maple Meadows is displayed as the text for the left subordinate shape (Figure 3-63).

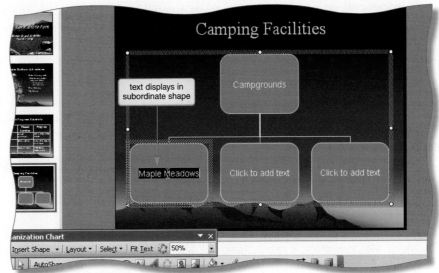

FIGURE 3-63

2

• **Click the middle subordinate shape.**

• **Type** Beech Basin **in the shape.**

Beech Basin is displayed as the text for the middle subordinate shape.

3

• **Click the right subordinate shape.**

• **Type** Crooked Creek **in the shape.**

Crooked Creek is displayed as the text for the right subordinate shape (Figure 3-64).

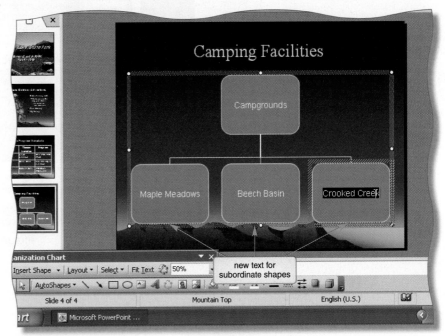

FIGURE 3-64

Inserting Subordinate and Coworker Shapes

More About

Choosing Colors

More than eight percent of males have color perception difficulties, with the most common problem being distinguishing red and green. For more information about this color deficiency, visit the Microsoft PowerPoint 2003 More About Web page (scsite.com/ppt2003/more) and click Colors.

You can add three types of shapes to the organization chart: subordinate, coworker, and assistant. Because each of the three Hidden Lake campgrounds has two qualities, you need to add two subordinate shapes to each of the campgrounds.

To add a single subordinate shape to the chart, click the Insert Shape button on the Organization Chart toolbar. The subordinate shape is the default shape. To add a coworker or assistant shape, click the Insert Shape button arrow and then click the desired shape.

In this organization chart, the two features of the Maple Meadows campground — hiking trails accessible and group camping available — are subordinate to the Maple Meadows shape. These two features are coworkers because they both are connected to the same manager. The following steps explain how to use the Insert Shape button to add these two shapes below the Maple Meadows shape.

To Insert Subordinate and Coworker Shapes

1

• **Click the Maple Meadows shape.**

• **Click the Insert Shape button on the Organization Chart toolbar.**

The Maple Meadows shape is selected and the new subordinate shape is displayed (Figure 3-65).

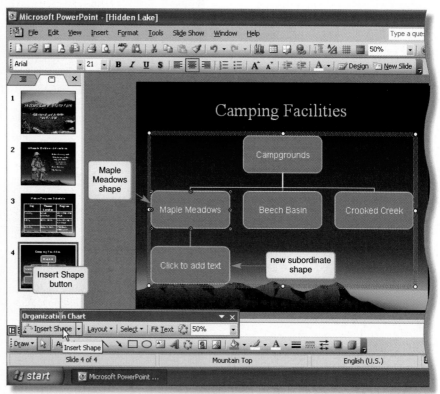

FIGURE 3-65

2

• **Click the new subordinate shape.**

• **Click the Insert Shape button arrow on the Organization Chart toolbar.**

The new subordinate shape is selected below the Maple Meadows shape. Maple Meadows now is the manager to the new subordinate shapes. Three possible shapes display on the Insert Shape menu (Figure 3-66).

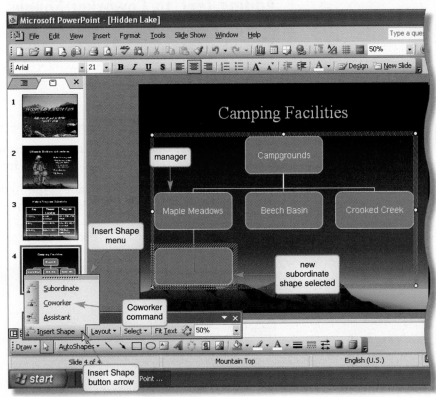

FIGURE 3-66

3

• **Click Coworker on the Insert Shape menu.**

A new coworker shape is added to the right of the subordinate shape (Figure 3-67).

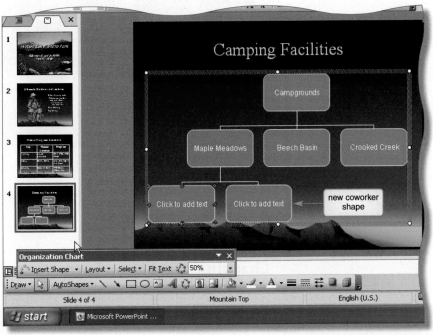

FIGURE 3-67

The basic structure of the left side of the organization chart is complete. You now will add text to the coworker shapes in the chart.

Other Ways

1. Press ALT+N, press DOWN ARROW, press C
2. In Voice Command mode, say "Insert Shape, Coworker"

Adding Text to Coworker Shapes

The next step in creating the organization chart is to add text to the two new shapes that are subordinate to the Maple Meadows shape. The following steps summarize adding text to each coworker shape.

To Add Text to Coworker Shapes

1 **If necessary, click the left coworker shape. Type** Hiking trails **and then press the ENTER key. Type** accessible **in the shape.**

2 **Click the right coworker shape. Type** Group camping **and then press the ENTER key. Type** available **in the shape.**

Both coworker shapes contain text related to the Maple Meadows campground (Figure 3-68).

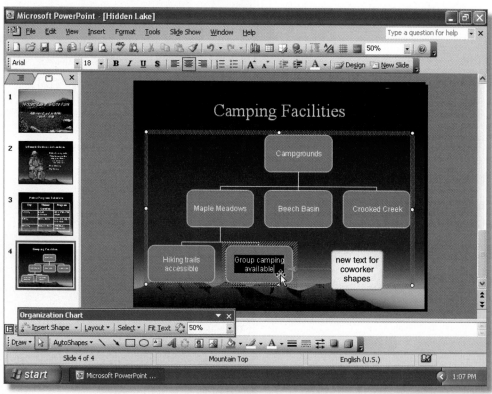

FIGURE 3-68

Changing the Shape Layout

Now that the shapes for the Maple Meadows branch are labeled, you want to change the way the organization chart looks. With the addition of each new shape, the chart expanded horizontally, which is the default layout. Before you add the Beech Basin campground qualities, you will change the layout of the coworker shapes from Standard to Right Hanging. To change the layout, you must select the most superior shape of the branch to which you want to apply the new layout. The following steps change the shape layout.

More About

Layouts

An effective presentation has objects, text, and graphics placed in appropriate locations. You can find many resources, tips, and articles on making clear and interesting presentations on the Internet. For more information about presentation design resources, visit the Microsoft PowerPoint 2003 More About Web page (scsite.com/ppt2003/more) and click Layouts.

To Change the Shape Layout

1

- **Click the Maple Meadows shape.**
- **Click the Layout button on the Organization Chart toolbar.**

The default Standard style is selected, which is indicated by the selected icon (Figure 3-69). The Maple Meadows shape is the superior shape of the coworker shapes.

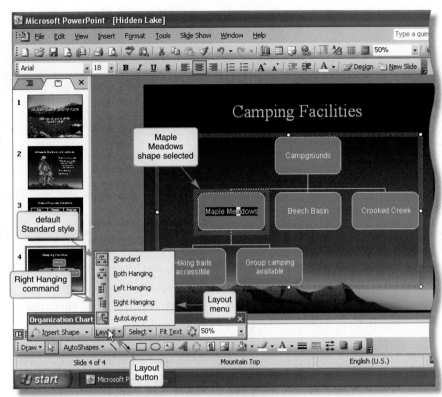

FIGURE 3-69

2

- **Click Right Hanging on the Layout menu.**

The organization chart displays the two coworker shapes vertically below the Maple Meadows shape (Figure 3-70).

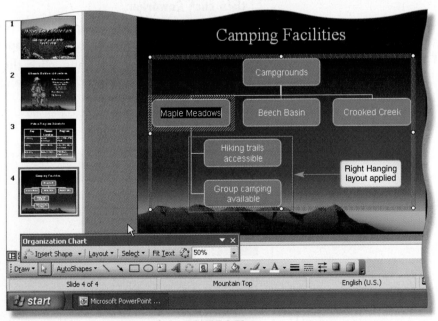

FIGURE 3-70

Other Ways

1. Press ALT+L, press R
2. In Voice Command mode, say "Layout, Right Hanging"

If you select an incorrect style or want to return to the previous style, click the Undo Change Layout command on the Edit menu or press CTRL+Z.

Inserting Additional Subordinate and Coworker Shapes

With the Maple Meadows campground features added to the organization chart, you need to create the Beech Basin and Crooked Creek components of the chart. The following steps add four shapes, enter text, and change the layout.

To Insert Additional Subordinate and Coworker Shapes

1 Click the Beech Basin shape and then click the Insert Shape button on the Organization Chart toolbar.

2 Click the new subordinate shape and then type Tent camping only in the shape.

3 Click the Insert Shape button arrow on the Organization Chart toolbar and then click Coworker.

4 Click the new coworker shape, type Three-night stay and then press the ENTER key. Type limit in the shape.

5 Click the Beech Basin shape, click the Layout button, and then click Right Hanging.

6 Click the Crooked Creek shape and then click the Insert Shape button on the Organization Chart toolbar.

7 Click the new subordinate shape and then type Open all year in the shape.

8 Click the Insert Shape button arrow on the Organization Chart toolbar and then click Coworker.

9 Click the new coworker shape, type Fishing readily and then press the ENTER key. Type accessible in the shape.

10 Click the Crooked Creek shape, click the Layout button on the Organization Chart toolbar, and then click Right Hanging.

Four shapes contain text related to the campground facilities at Hidden Lake (Figure 3-71).

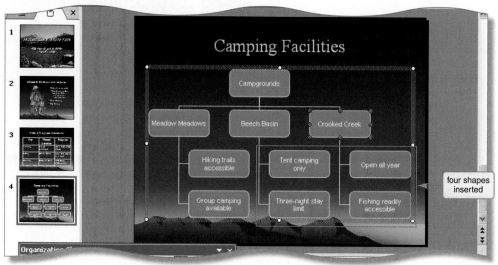

FIGURE 3-71

All the desired text now is displayed on the organization chart. The next section explains how to change the organization chart style.

Changing the Preset Design Scheme

To format the organization chart so it looks like the chart shown in Figure 3-58 on page PPT 195, select a diagram style in the Organization Chart Style Gallery. The **Organization Chart Style Gallery** contains a variety of styles that use assorted colors, border styles, and shadow effects. The following steps describe how to change the default design scheme.

To Change the Preset Design Scheme

1

• **Point to the Autoformat button on the Organization Chart toolbar (Figure 3-72).**

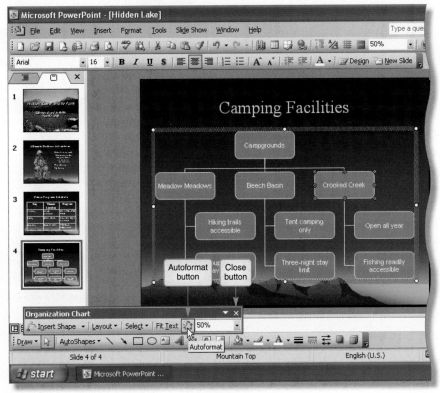

FIGURE 3-72

2

• **Click the Autoformat button and then click the 3-D Color diagram style in the Diagram Style list.**

Diagram Style names display in the list. When you click a name, PowerPoint previews that style (Figure 3-73).

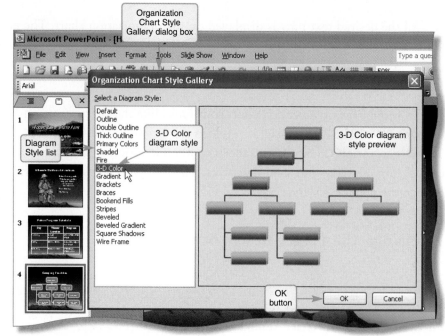

FIGURE 3-73

3

• **Click the OK button in the Organization Chart Style Gallery dialog box.**

• **Click the Close button on the Organization Chart toolbar.**

PowerPoint applies the 3-D Color diagram style to all the shapes and lines in the chart (Figure 3-74).

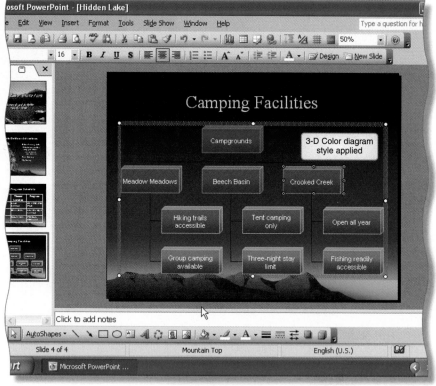

FIGURE 3-74

Other Ways

1. Press SHIFT+ALT+C, press RIGHT ARROW, press ENTER, press DOWN ARROW or UP ARROW to scroll through styles, press ENTER
2. In Voice Command mode, say "Autoformat, 3-D Color, Apply"

Scaling an Organization Chart

The organization chart on Slide 4 would be easier to read if it were enlarged. **Scaling** allows you to enlarge or reduce an object by very precise amounts while retaining the object's original proportions.

The following steps scale an organization chart object.

To Scale an Organization Chart

1 Right-click a blank area of the chart placeholder and then right-click Format Organization Chart on the shortcut menu.

2 Click the Size tab. In the Scale area, double-click **100** in the Height text box. Type **110** as the entry.

3 Click the OK button.

4 Use the UP and LEFT ARROW keys to move the organization chart to the desired location on the slide.

The organization chart is scaled to 110 percent of its original size (Figure 3-75). If necessary, adjust the chart size by repeating Steps 1–4 with a different percentage or by dragging a corner sizing handle.

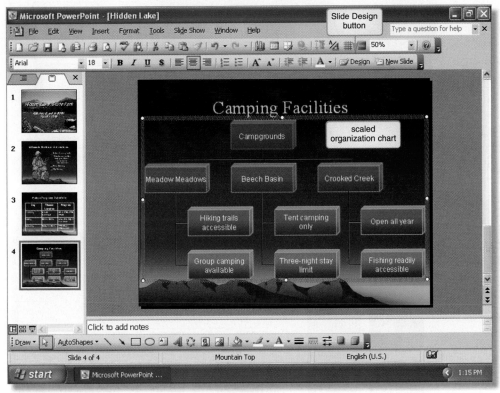

FIGURE 3-75

Applying a New Design Template

You can see that the information in the organization chart will display more prominently if the slide has a different background. One method of changing the look of an individual slide is to change the design template. The steps on the next page change the design template on Slide 4 from Mountain Top to Quadrant.

More About

The PowerPoint Help System

Need Help? It is no further away than the Type a question for help box on the menu bar in the upper-right corner of the window. Click the box that contains the text, Type a question for help (Figure 3-75), type help, and then press the ENTER key. PowerPoint responds with a list of topics you can click to learn about obtaining help on any PowerPoint-related topic. To find out what is new in PowerPoint 2003, type what is new in PowerPoint in the Type a question for help box.

To Apply a New Design Template to a Single Slide

1

• **With Slide 4 displaying, click the Slide Design button on the Formatting toolbar.**

• **When the Slide Design task pane is displayed, click the down scroll arrow in the Apply a design template list until the Edge template is displayed in the Available For Use area.**

• **Click the button arrow on the right side of the Edge template.**

The Edge template menu is displayed with options for applying the template to all slides, the selected slide, or to view a larger preview (Figure 3-76).

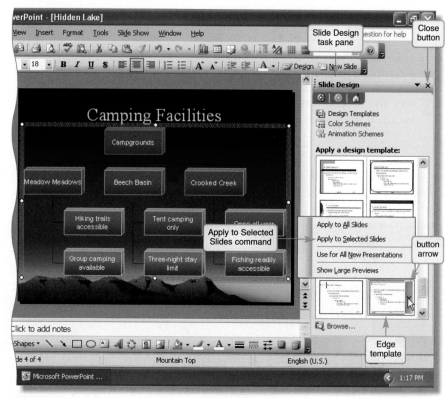

FIGURE 3-76

2

• **Click Apply to Selected Slides.**

• **Click the Close button in the Slide Design task pane.**

PowerPoint applies the Edge template to only Slide 4 (Figure 3-77).

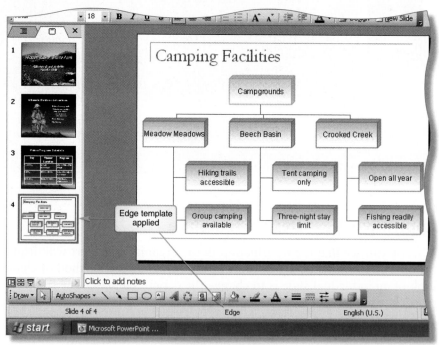

FIGURE 3-77

Slide 4 now is complete. The next section describes how to change the order of individual slides.

Rearranging Slides

The Slide 4 organization chart should display before the Slide 3 table in a slide show. Changing slide order is an easy process. The following steps rearrange Slides 3 and 4.

To Rearrange Slides

1

• **Click the Slide 3 slide thumbnail in the tabs pane.**

The Slide 3 slide thumbnail is selected (Figure 3-78).

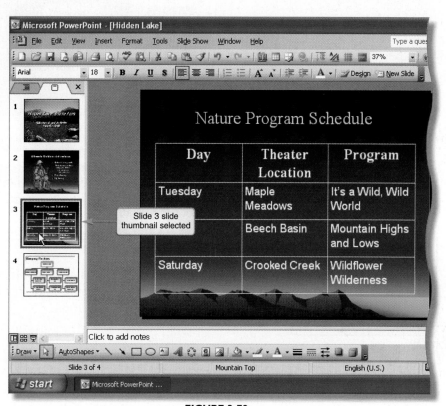

FIGURE 3-78

Microsoft Office
PowerPoint 2003

2

• **Drag the Slide 3 slide thumbnail below the Slide 4 slide thumbnail.**

The slide with the organization chart is displayed above the slide with the table (Figure 3-79). When you are dragging the slide thumbnail, a line indicates the new location of the selected slide.

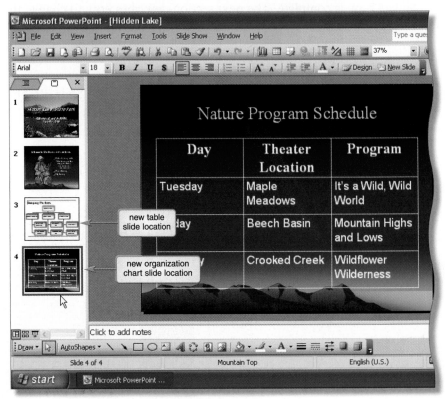

FIGURE 3-79

The order of Slides 3 and 4 is changed. If you want to change the order of multiple consecutive slides, press the SHIFT key before clicking each slide icon or slide thumbnail. Save the presentation.

Adding an Animation Scheme to Selected Slides

The final step in preparing the Hidden Lake presentation is to add an animation scheme to Slides 1, 2, and 4. The following steps add the Rise Up animation scheme to these three slides.

To Add an Animation Scheme to Selected Slides

1 **If necessary, click the Slide 4 thumbnail to select it. Press and hold down the CTRL key and then click the Slide 2 and Slide 1 slide thumbnails. Release the CTRL key.**

2 **Click Slide Show on the menu bar and then click Animation Schemes.**

3 **Scroll down the Apply to selected slides list and then click Rise Up in the Moderate category.**

4 **Click the Close button in the Slide Design task pane.**

The Rise Up animation scheme is applied to Slides 1, 2, and 4 in the Hidden Lake presentation (Figure 3-80).

FIGURE 3-80

Printing Slides as Handouts

The following steps print the presentation slides as handouts, four slides per page.

To Print Slides as Handouts

1 Ready the printer.

2 Click File on the menu bar and then click Print.

3 Click the Print what box arrow and then click Handouts in the list.

4 Click the Slides per page box arrow in the Handouts area and then click 4 in the list. Verify the Horizontal option button is selected. If it is not selected, then click to select it.

5 If Grayscale is not displayed in the Color/grayscale box, click the Color/grayscale arrow and then click Grayscale.

6 Click the OK button.

The handout prints as shown in Figure 3-81 on the next page.

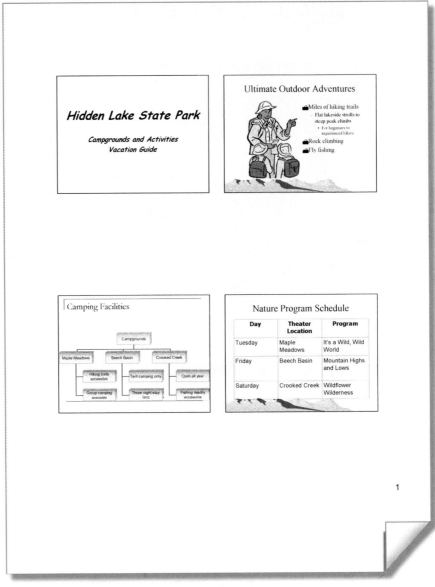

FIGURE 3-81

Creating and Presenting a Custom Show

A **custom show** is a presentation within a presentation. You can group slides in an existing presentation so that you can show that section of a presentation to a particular audience. To create a custom show, you would follow these steps.

To Create a Custom Show

1 Click Slide Show on the menu bar and then click Custom Shows.

2 When the Custom Shows dialog box is displayed, click the New button.

3 In the Slides in presentation area, select a slide you want to include in the custom show. To select multiple slides, hold down the CTRL key as you click the slide titles.

4 Click the Add button.

5 Type a name in the Slide show name text box.

6 Click the OK button.

If you decide to add or remove slides from a custom show, you can click the Edit button in the Custom Shows dialog box, add or remove the desired slide, and then click the OK button. Once the custom show has been finalized, you can display these slides rather than the entire presentation. To present the custom show, you would follow these steps.

To Present a Custom Show

1 Click Slide Show on the menu bar and then click Set Up Show.

2 When the Set Up Show dialog box is displayed, click the Custom show option button in the Show Slides area, click the Custom show arrow, and then select the show you want to display.

3 Click the OK button.

4 Start the slide show.

Running the Slide Show, Saving, and Quitting PowerPoint

With the slide show complete, click the Slide Show button and run the presentation to ensure that you are satisfied with the slide content and animation scheme.

If you made any changes to your presentation since your last save, you should save it again before quitting PowerPoint. The following steps save changes to the presentation and quit PowerPoint.

To Save Changes and Quit PowerPoint

1 Click the Close button on the Microsoft PowerPoint window title bar.

2 If prompted, click the Yes button in the Microsoft PowerPoint dialog box.

PowerPoint saves any changes made to the presentation since the last save and then quits PowerPoint.

> ### More About
>
> #### Custom Shows
>
> If you decide you no longer need a custom show, you can remove it. To remove a custom show, click Slide Show on the menu bar and then click Custom Shows. When the Custom Shows dialog box is displayed, click the name of the custom show you want to remove and then click the Remove button. Click the Close button.

Project Summary

Project 3 introduced you to several methods of enhancing a presentation with visuals. You began the project by creating the presentation from an outline that was created in Word. Then, when you created Slide 2, you learned how to ungroup and customize clip art. You also learned how to change the bullet character on the slide master. You learned to create and format a table on Slide 3. Slide 4 introduced you to creating an organization chart and applying a design template to a single slide and changing the order of slides in the presentation. Finally, you printed your presentation slides as handouts.

If you have a SAM user profile, you may have access to hands-on instruction, practice, and assessment of the skills covered in this project. Log in to your SAM account and go to your assignments page to see what your instructor has assigned.

What You Should Know

Having completed this project, you should be able to perform the tasks below. For a list of the buttons, menus, toolbars, and commands introduced in this project, see the Quick Reference Summary at the back of this book and refer to the Page Number column.

1. Start and Customize a New Presentation and Change to the Outline Tab   (PPT 164)
2. Open a Microsoft Word Outline as a Presentation   (PPT 166)
3. Delete a Slide   (PPT 168)
4. Change the Slide Layout to Title Slide (PPT 169)
5. Save a Presentation   (PPT 170)
6. Add a Picture to Create a Custom Background (PPT 170)
7. Change the Title Slide Font and Font Attributes (PPT 173)
8. Change the Slide Layout to Title, Content and Text   (PPT 176)
9. Insert a Clip into a Content Placeholder (PPT 177)
10. Size and Move a Clip   (PPT 178)
11. Ungroup a Clip   (PPT 178)
12. Deselect Clip Art Objects   (PPT 180)
13. Change the Color of a PowerPoint Object (PPT 180)
14. Change the Color of Other PowerPoint Objects (PPT 182)
15. Regroup Objects   (PPT 183)
16. Display the Slide Master   (PPT 185)
17. Change a Bullet Character on the Slide Master (PPT 187)

18. Change a Bullet Color on the Slide Master (PPT 189)
19. Insert a Basic Table   (PPT 191)
20. Enter Data in a Table   (PPT 192)
21. Format a Table Cell   (PPT 193)
22. Display the Next Slide and the Organization Chart Diagram   (PPT 196)
23. Add Text to the Superior Shape   (PPT 198)
24. Add Text to the Subordinate Shapes   (PPT 199)
25. Insert Subordinate and Coworker Shapes (PPT 200)
26. Add Text to Coworker Shapes   (PPT 202)
27. Change the Shape Layout   (PPT 203)
28. Insert Additional Subordinate and Coworker Shapes   (PPT 204)
29. Change the Preset Design Scheme   (PPT 205)
30. Scale an Organization Chart   (PPT 207)
31. Apply a New Design Template to a Single Slide (PPT 208)
32. Rearrange Slides   (PPT 209)
33. Add an Animation Scheme to Selected Slides (PPT 210)
34. Print Slides as Handouts   (PPT 211)
35. Create a Custom Show   (PPT 212)
36. Present a Custom Show   (PPT 213)
37. Save Changes and Quit PowerPoint   (PPT 213)

Learn It Online

Instructions: To complete the Learn It Online exercises, start your browser, click the Address bar, and then enter the Web address scsite.com/ppt2003/learn. When the PowerPoint 2003 Learn It Online page is displayed, follow the instructions in the exercises below. Each exercise has instructions for printing your results, either for your own records or for submission to your instructor.

1 Project Reinforcement TF, MC, and SA

Below PowerPoint Project 3, click the Project Reinforcement link. Print the quiz by clicking Print on the File menu for each page. Answer each question.

2 Flash Cards

Below PowerPoint Project 3, click the Flash Cards link and read the instructions. Type 20 (or a number specified by your instructor) in the Number of playing cards text box, type your name in the Enter your Name text box, and then click the Flip Card button. When the flash card is displayed, read the question and then click the ANSWER box arrow to select an answer. Flip through Flash Cards. If your score is 15 (75%) correct or greater, click Print on the File menu to print your results. If your score is less than 15 (75%) correct, then redo this exercise by clicking the Replay button.

3 Practice Test

Below PowerPoint Project 3, click the Practice Test link. Answer each question, enter your first and last name at the bottom of the page, and then click the Grade Test button. When the graded practice test is displayed on your screen, click Print on the File menu to print a hard copy. Continue to take practice tests until you score 80% or better.

4 Who Wants To Be a Computer Genius?

Below PowerPoint Project 3, click the Computer Genius link. Read the instructions, enter your first and last name at the bottom of the page, and then click the PLAY button. When your score is displayed, click the PRINT RESULTS link to print a hard copy.

5 Wheel of Terms

Below PowerPoint Project 3, click the Wheel of Terms link. Read the instructions, and then enter your first and last name and your school name. Click the PLAY button. When your score is displayed, right-click the score and then click Print on the shortcut menu to print a hard copy.

6 Crossword Puzzle Challenge

Below PowerPoint Project 3, click the Crossword Puzzle Challenge link. Read the instructions, and then enter your first and last name. Click the SUBMIT button. Work the crossword puzzle. When you are finished, click the Submit button. When the crossword puzzle is redisplayed, click the Print Puzzle button to print a hard copy.

7 Tips and Tricks

Below PowerPoint Project 3, click the Tips and Tricks link. Click a topic that pertains to Project 3. Right-click the information and then click Print on the shortcut menu. Construct a brief example of what the information relates to in PowerPoint to confirm you understand how to use the tip or trick.

8 Newsgroups

Below PowerPoint Project 3, click the Newsgroups link. Click a topic that pertains to Project 3. Print three comments.

9 Expanding Your Horizons

Below PowerPoint Project 3, click the Expanding Your Horizons link. Click a topic that pertains to Project 3. Print the information. Construct a brief example of what the information relates to in PowerPoint to confirm you understand the contents of the article.

10 Search Sleuth

Below PowerPoint Project 3, click the Search Sleuth link. To search for a term that pertains to this project, select a term below the Project 3 title and then use the Google search engine at google.com (or any major search engine) to display and print two Web pages that present information on the term.

11 Word Online Training

Below PowerPoint Project 3, click the PowerPoint Online Training link. When your browser displays the Microsoft Office Online Web page, click the PowerPoint link. Click one of the PowerPoint courses that covers one or more of the objectives listed at the beginning of the project on page PPT 162. Print the first page of the course before stepping through it.

12 Office Marketplace

Below PowerPoint Project 3, click the Office Marketplace link. When your browser displays the Microsoft Office Online Web page, click the Office Marketplace link. Click a topic that relates to PowerPoint. Print the first page.

Apply Your Knowledge

1 Computer Security

Instructions: Start PowerPoint. Open the outline, Apply 3-1 Security Risks, from the Data Disk. See the inside back cover of this book for instructions for downloading the Data Disk or see your instructor for information on accessing the clips and files required for this book. The outline gives three specific methods for safeguarding a computer. Make the following changes to the slides so they appear as shown in Figure 3-82.

Apply the Glass Layers design template. Delete the blank Slide 1. Change the slide layout for Slide 1 to Title Slide (Figure 3-82a).

On Slide 1, insert the computer inoculation clip. Size the clip to 43%. Ungroup the clip and change the man's shirt to red. Regroup the clip. On Slide 2, insert the computer clip shown in Figure 3-82b. Size the clip to 295%. Ungroup the clip and delete the flames from the right and top. Regroup the clip.

Change the first-level paragraph bullets on the slide master to the computer symbol located in the Wingdings font. Change the bullet color to red.

Apply the Zoom animation scheme in the Moderate category list to both slides. Save the presentation with the file name, Apply 3-1 Computer Security. Print the slides as a handout with both slides on one page. Hand in the hard copy to your instructor.

(a) Slide 1

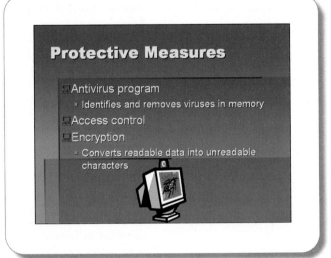

(b) Slide 2

FIGURE 3-82

In the Lab

1 Dino-mite Dash

Problem: The volunteers at the natural history society in your community are sponsoring a 5K run on St. Patrick's Day. You decide to participate by helping with event promotion and encouraging local businesses to donate prizes. The volunteers ask you to create a presentation describing the run to community residents. You decide to begin the assignment by creating a title slide with a clip showing a dinosaur jogging. You import a clip, modify it, and then import and modify another clip with a shamrock and leprechaun hat to create the slide shown in Figure 3-83. See your instructor if the clips are not available on your system.

Instructions: Perform the following tasks:

1. Start PowerPoint and apply the Quadrant design template to the Title Only slide layout.
2. Type Dino-mite Dash for the slide title. Center the title, change the font size to 60, and change the font color to black.
3. Insert the jogging dinosaur clip shown in Figure 3-83. Size the clip to 85%.
4. Ungroup the picture. Then change the blue parts of the top of the shoes and the socks to sea green.

FIGURE 3-83

5. Insert the leprechaun hat clip. Size the clip to 85%.
6. Ungroup this clip and delete all pieces except the hat and shamrock.
7. Regroup the hat object, and then move the hat to the top of the dinosaur's head. Regroup both clips together as one object.
8. Apply the Faded zoom motion animation scheme.
9. Save the presentation with the file name, Lab 3-1 Race.
10. Print the slide.
11. Quit PowerPoint.

2 Fruit and Vegetable Nutrition

Problem: Nutritionists are discovering the increased health benefits of eating fruits and vegetables. The vitamins, antioxidants, minerals, and fiber that occur naturally in these foods can help prevent disease and help increase the quality of life. Five servings are recommended each day, but the average adult eats only three servings daily. In an effort to urge students to have a healthier diet, nutritionists at your campus fitness center have asked you to help them create a presentation describing fruit and vegetable nutrition facts. They want you to include one table listing the serving size and calories of three fruits and another listing the serving size and calories of three vegetables. Create the presentation shown in Figures 3-84a, 3-84b, 3-84c, and 3-84d.

Instructions: Perform the following tasks:

1. Start PowerPoint. Open the outline, Lab 3-2 Fruits and Vegetables, from the Data Disk. Apply the Ripple design template. Delete Slide 1, which is blank.

2. On Slide 1, apply the Title Slide slide layout. Increase the title font size to 80 point, italicize the text, and change the font color to red. Replace the nutritionist's name with your name.

3. Insert the apple clip shown in Figure 3-84a and size it to 250%. Ungroup the clip and then delete the brown border from the top. Regroup the clip.

4. View the slides in slide sorter view and then move Slide 2 so that it displays after Slide 4.

5. On Slide 2, insert the oranges photograph as a background. Create the table shown in Figure 3-84b. Format the table by changing all the text to Baskerville Old Face or a similar font if your system does not have this font. Change the font color to bright blue. Change the column headings to 40 point. Center and bold these headings.

6. On Slide 3, insert the tomatoes photograph as a background. Create the table shown in Figure 3-84c. Format the table by changing all the text to Baskerville Old Face. Change the column headings to 40 point. Center and bold these headings.

7. On Slide 4, use the slide master to change the first-level bullet to the fork, plate, and knife shown in Figure 3-84d. Increase the bullet size to 125% of text. Change the bullet color to red.

8. Insert the clip shown in Figure 3-84d. Size the clip to 200% and then delete the person from the clip. Change the placemat color to red.

9. Apply the Title arc animation scheme to Slides 1 and 4.

10. Save the presentation with the file name, Lab 3-2 Five a Day.

11. Create a custom show using Slides 1 and 4. Name the custom show Fruits and Vegetables 2. Run both the custom and full slide shows. Save the file again.

12. Print handouts with two slides on one page. Quit PowerPoint.

In the Lab

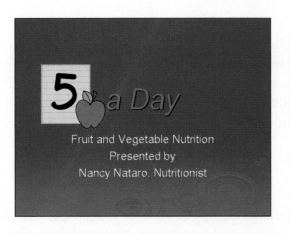

5 a Day

Fruit and Vegetable Nutrition
Presented by
Nancy Nataro, Nutritionist

(a) Slide 1

Fruit Servings

Fruit	Serving	Calories
Banana	1 medium	110
Cherries	1 cup	90
Grapes	1.5 cups	90

(b) Slide 2

Vegetable Servings

Vegetable	Serving	Calories
Carrot	7-inch long	35
Leaf Lettuce	1.5 cups	15
Tomato	1 medium	35

(c) Slide 3

What Is on Your Plate?

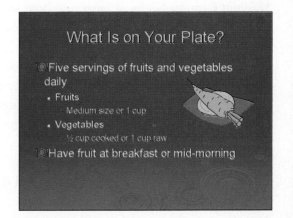

- Five servings of fruits and vegetables daily
  - Fruits
    - Medium size or 1 cup
  - Vegetables
    - ½ cup cooked or 1 cup raw
- Have fruit at breakfast or mid-morning

(d) Slide 4

FIGURE 3-84

3 Westwood Wolf Exhibit

Problem: The zoo in the town of Westwood is refurbishing its wolf exhibit. You have been asked to help with the publicity efforts and donations. You decide to develop a presentation that includes information about the wolves, wolf packs, and zoo seminars. Create the presentation starting with the Wolf outline on your Data Disk. Then insert the photograph and table and create the organization chart shown in Figures 3-85a, 3-85b, 3-85c, and 3-85d. See your instructor if the photo and clip art are not available on your system.

Instructions: Perform the following tasks:

1. Start PowerPoint. Open the outline, Lab 3-3 Wolf Outline, on your Data Disk.
2. Apply the Edge design template. Delete Slide 1, which is blank.
3. On Slide 1, apply the Title Slide slide layout. Insert the Wolf photograph as the slide background. Change the title and subtitle text font color to white. Right-align the title and subtitle text. Replace the director's name with your name.
4. View the slides in slide sorter view and then change the order of Slides 2 and 3.
5. On Slide 2, insert the table shown in Figure 3-85b. Format the table by changing the column headings to 38-point Century Gothic. Center and bold the headings.
6. On Slide 3, create the organization chart shown in Figure 3-85c. Apply the Shaded diagram style. Scale the chart to 115% or to another size so that the chart fills the slide.
7. On Slide 4, use the slide master to change the first-level bullets to the sun symbol shown in Figure 3-85d that is part of the Webdings font. Change the bullet color to dark green. Change the second-level bullets to the arrow symbol that is part of the Wingdings 3 font. Change the bullet color to brown.
8. On Slide 4, insert the wolf clip shown in Figure 3-85d. Size the clip to 135%. Ungroup this clip and delete the blue background. Regroup the clip.
9. Apply the Unfold animation scheme to Slides 1 and 4.
10. Create a custom show using Slides 1, 3, and 4. Name the custom show Wolf 2. Run both the full and custom shows.
11. Save the presentation with the file name, Lab 3-3 Wolf Exhibit. Print the presentation and then quit PowerPoint.

In the Lab

(a) Slide 1

Westwood Zoo Wolf Seminars

Date	Program
March 22	Photographing the Animals
June 8	Anatomy and Physiology
September 15	Folklore and History

(b) Slide 2

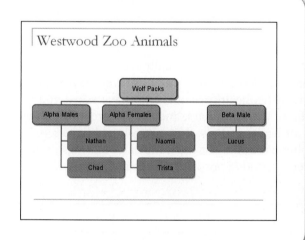

(c) Slide 3

Westwood Zoo Wolf Exhibition

○ Five animals on display
　⇨ Two acquired from Wyoming
○ Fed twice weekly
　⇨ Mondays and Fridays at noon
○ Adult wolves weigh more than 100 pounds
○ Howling is method of communicating

(d) Slide 4

FIGURE 3-

Cases and Places

The difficulty of these case studies varies:
■ are the least difficult and ■■ are more difficult. The last exercise is a group exercise.

Note: Remember to use the 7 × 7 rule as you design the presentations: a maximum of seven words on a line and a maximum of seven lines on one slide.

1 ■ Casey's Complete Computers is a repair facility in your neighborhood. Casey Murphy, the owner, performs a variety of upgrades and repairs. His customers often ask about the amount of RAM (random access memory) to add to their systems. Casey says that determining the amount of RAM depends on the applications that will be run on the computer. RAM ranging from 128–256 MB is good for home and business users who are managing personal finances, using standard application software such as word processing, and communicating with others on the Web. RAM from 256 MB to 1 GB is adequate for users requiring more advanced multimedia capabilities, working with videos, music, and digital imaging, and playing Internet games. A minimum of 1 GB of RAM is for users creating professional Web sites and for running sophisticated CAD, 3-D design, or other graphics-intensive software. In an effort to help customers select the proper amount of RAM, Casey wants you to create a PowerPoint presentation and handout. Create a title slide with a clip and a text slide with an organization chart describing the RAM ranges and the types of applications best suited for each category.

2 ■ Busy students often have difficulty eating nutritious meals. Planning a daily menu may be one method of making healthy food choices. The nutrition counselors at your campus fitness center are planning a series of seminars to help students plan a realistic, healthy menu. They have asked you to create a presentation and a handout to accompany one of their seminars, and they desire a title slide, a bulleted list, and table to help students prepare a day of healthy meals. The table should have separate rows for breakfast, lunch, dinner, and snacks. The columns should list the number of servings of grains, vegetables and fruits, dairy products, meats, and sweets. Include appropriate clips and animation effects. Create a custom show.

3 ■■ Camcorders come equipped with a variety of special features. When choosing the right camcorder to purchase for your needs, consider where you will be recording and the subject matter that you desire to record. Also compare models to check ease of use and essential features. Visit an electronics store, read magazines, or perform online research to learn about four of the latest models. What are the prices for these popular devices? Which recording format do they use? How long is the battery life? What are the maximum optical and digital zooms? Are they equipped with a built-in light, night shot, and image stabilization? Do they have a USB port? Can they also function as a digital or still camera? Then, use Microsoft Word to create an outline that organizes your research findings. Open this Word document as a PowerPoint presentation and create a slide show with this information. Use a title slide and include appropriate clips and animation effects. Print the presentation and your outline.

Cases and Places

4 Many students are scheduling massage therapy treatments to relieve the stress they encounter and to improve circulation. The fitness center at your school offers four different massages, each designed for a specific purpose. Jessica Cantero, the Fitness Center director, has asked you to prepare a PowerPoint presentation, and she gives you the data shown in Table 3-4. Select a design template and create a slide show using this data. Introduce the presentation with a title slide.

Table 3-4 Massage Therapy Treatment Data		
TREATMENT	BENEFIT	COST
Stone Massage Therapy	Heat penetrates deep into muscle tissue	1 hour - $65
Sports Massage	Reduces chance of injury	½ hour - $40
Shiatsu	Strengthens immune system	1 hour - $55
Reflexology	Stimulates body's natural ability to heal itself	½ hour - $45

For Slide 2, list information promoting massage therapy treatment benefits. Use the row headings in Table 3-4 to create Slides 3 through 6. Modify the slide layouts using the slide master. Choose appropriate clip art and animation effects. Display the presentation title in the outline header and your name in the outline footer. Print the slides and the presentation outline.

5 **Working Together** Discussing eating habits with a nutrition counselor is one of the first steps people can make toward enhancing their diets. These counselors generally are available in a variety of locations, including fitness centers and clinics. Have each member of your team visit or telephone several local nutrition counselors to gather information about:

1) Healthy eating during the holidays
2) Essential vitamins for males
3) Essential vitamins for females
4) Special diets for marathon runners
5) Tips for effective weight loss

After coordinating the data, create a presentation with at least one slide describing specific nutrition advice. Introduce the presentation with a title slide. Include clip art and animation effects. Create a custom show. As a group, critique each slide. Hand in a hard copy of the final presentation.

Modifying Visual Elements and Presentation Formats

PROJECT

4

CASE PERSPECTIVE

College costs are rising dramatically. In recent years, higher education expenses have increased nearly twice as quickly as the inflation rate. Depending on the type of college chosen, students can expect their tuition bills and fees to be more than $1,000 higher than the previous year's total. Almost one-half of students attend two-year public colleges, where the average tuition can be less than $2,000 for a full-time class load. Tuition at a four-year private school can exceed $18,000, and the total bill can add to more than $40,000.

When planning a budget for college, students need to consider expenses for tuition, fees, books and supplies, and other miscellaneous costs. Of these expenses, tuition is the largest, amounting to nearly two-thirds of the total college bill. Room and board averages another $7,000.

Despite the high costs of higher education, the expense generally pays for itself. The U.S. Census Bureau reports that students earning a bachelor's degree earn, on average, more than 80 percent more than high school graduates. During a lifetime, this additional income can amount to more than $1 million.

Financial aid counselors at Eastwood State College assist prospective and current students prepare for college expenses. The director, Melissa Jackson, wants to offer a seminar for groups of students and community residents regarding paying for a college education. She has asked you to help with this project by developing a PowerPoint presentation. You recommend using a variety of graphics to help the audience visualize the monetary aspects of college.

As you read through this project, you will learn how to use PowerPoint to add these visual elements, including charts and tables.

Microsoft Office PowerPoint 2003

Modifying Visual Elements and Presentation Formats

OBJECTIVES

You will have mastered the material in this project when you can:

- Create a presentation using the AutoContent Wizard
- Create and scale a WordArt element and add it to a slide
- Add sound effects and hyperlinks to slides
- Insert a chart, an Excel chart, and a Word table
- Revise and customize individual slides
- Use the Thesaurus
- Modify a presentation template by changing the color scheme

- Add information to the slide master Footer Area
- Add an action button and action setting
- Apply transition effects to a presentation
- Rehearse presentation timings and run a slide show with hyperlinks
- Print speaker notes and save slide presentations as Rich Text Format outlines

Introduction

"Variety's the very spice of life that gives it all its flavour," according to the British poet William Cowper. A PowerPoint presentation shows variety by selecting design templates, appropriate colors, and slide layouts for specific audiences. The beginning of a PowerPoint slide show sets the tone, announces the topic, and generates interest.

All this variety may result in confusion when starting to compose a presentation. Microsoft designers recognize this undertaking and have developed the AutoContent Wizard to help begin a presentation. This wizard creates up to 12 slides with suggested content about specific topics, such as selling a new product or reporting the status of a project. Based on the user's responses to questions about the presentation type, style, and options, the wizard selects a design template and creates slides with varying layouts and content that can be modified to fit the audience's needs.

Project Four — College Finances

Project 4 customizes the slide show generated by the AutoContent Wizard. You will add a graphical heading and change the background on Slide 1 to call attention to the college finances slide show topic. You also will add data from other sources, including an Excel chart and a Word table, and insert visual elements to create the slide show shown in Figures 4-1a through 4-1e.

(a) Slide 1

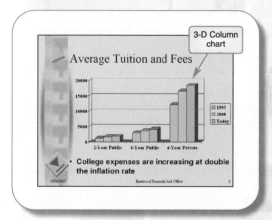

(b) Slide 2

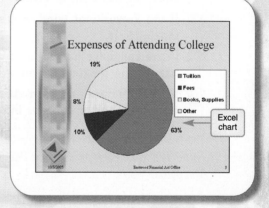

(c) Slide 3

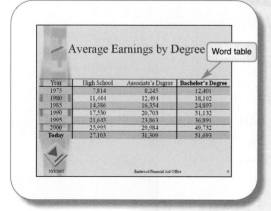

(d) Slide 4

(e) Slide 5

FIGURE 4-1

More About

Presentation Design

The key to a successful presentation is organization, and the AutoContent Wizard can help organize your ideas. As you review the 18 presentations, formulate the context of your slide show and decide which topic best fits your slide show plan. Then, select the slides that support your major topic and eliminate the slides that are not relevant.

Starting a New Presentation Using the AutoContent Wizard

Beginning the college finances slide show is made easier by using the AutoContent Wizard. This feature helps you get started by supplying organization and ideas for the slides. The 18 presentations are organized in five categories: All, General, Corporate, Projects, and Sales / Marketing. After starting a new presentation, use the AutoContent Wizard to generate slides for the college finances presentation.

Starting and Customizing a New Presentation

In Projects 1 and 2, you started a presentation document, chose layouts, applied a design template, and reset your toolbars. You need to repeat the same steps to begin this project. The following steps show how to start and customize a new presentation.

To Start and Customize a New Presentation

1 **Click the Start button on the Windows taskbar, point to All Programs on the Start menu, point to Microsoft Office on the All Programs submenu, and then click Microsoft Office PowerPoint 2003 on the Microsoft Office submenu.**

2 **If the PowerPoint window is not maximized, double-click its title bar to maximize it.**

3 **If the Language bar appears, right-click it and then click Close the Language bar on the shortcut menu.**

4 **If the Standard and Formatting toolbars are positioned on the same row, click the Toolbar Options button and then click Show Buttons on Two Rows.**

The PowerPoint window with the Standard and Formatting toolbars on two rows appears as shown in Figure 4-2. PowerPoint displays the Title Slide slide layout and the Default Design template on Slide 1 in normal view.

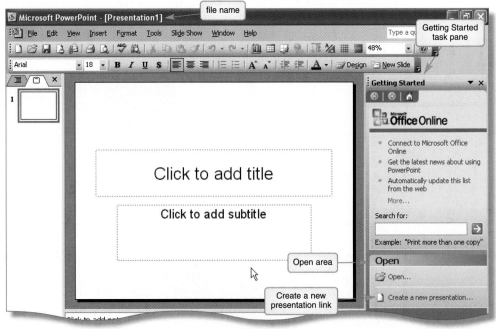

FIGURE 4-2

Using the AutoContent Wizard

With the presentation created, you can use the AutoContent Wizard to generate content. Because the topic of your slide show involves marketing a college finances seminar, the **Marketing Plan presentation** that is part of the Sales / Marketing presentation type creates useful ideas to begin developing the presentation. The wizard also will create a footer that is displayed at the bottom of each slide. The following steps use the AutoContent Wizard.

To Use the AutoContent Wizard

1

• **Click the Create a new presentation link in the Open area of the Getting Started task pane.**

The New Presentation task pane is displayed (Figure 4-3).

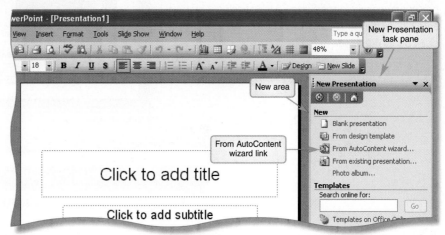

FIGURE 4-3

2

• **Click From AutoContent wizard.**

• **If the Office Assistant is displayed, right-click the Office Assistant and then click Hide on the shortcut menu.**

PowerPoint opens the AutoContent Wizard dialog box and displays the Start panel, describing the function of the AutoContent Wizard (Figure 4-4).

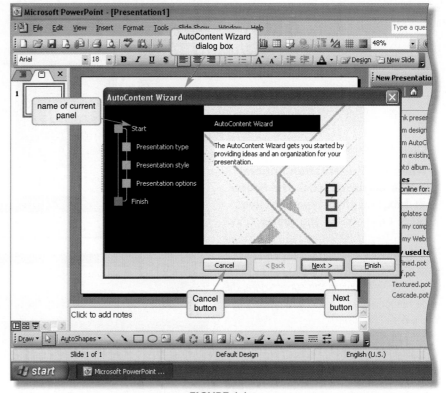

FIGURE 4-4

• **Click the Next button.**

• **When the Presentation type panel is displayed, click the Sales / Marketing button.**

• **Click the Marketing Plan presentation type.**

The 24 presentations are grouped in five categories (Figure 4-5). General is the default category. The names of the presentations within the Sales / Marketing category display in a list. You can click the Back button to review previous panels.

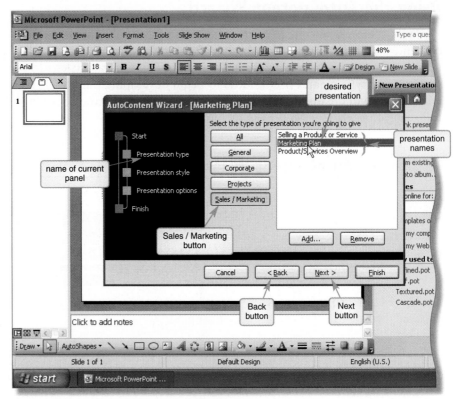

FIGURE 4-5

• **Click the Next button.**

The Presentation style panel is displayed. PowerPoint defaults to developing an on-screen presentation. You could select alternate outputs, such as a Web presentation, overheads, or slides.

• **Click the Next button.**

• **When the Presentation options panel is displayed, click the Footer text box and then type** Eastwood State College **as the footer text.**

The AutoContent Wizard creates a footer that will display at the bottom of each slide. The footer will contain the current date, the slide number, and the text you typed (Figure 4-6).

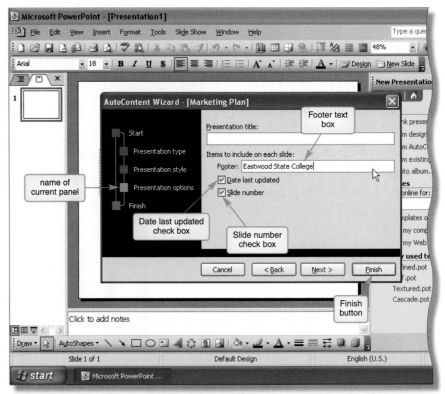

FIGURE 4-6

6

• **Click the Next button.**

The Finish panel displays a message that the AutoContent Wizard has all the necessary information to develop the slides.

7

• **Click the Finish button.**

PowerPoint closes the AutoContent Wizard and displays Slide 1 in the presentation (Figure 4-7). Melissa Jackson's name is displayed because her name was entered as the software user when PowerPoint was installed on the system for this project; a different name will display on your slide. The footer displays the current date, the Eastwood State College text, and the slide number. The AutoContent Wizard created a new presentation, so Presentation2 is displayed as the presentation title in the PowerPoint window.

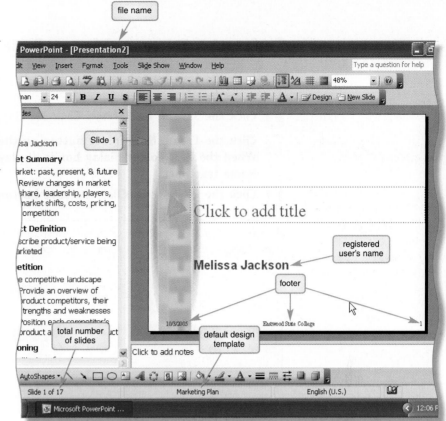

FIGURE 4-7

The AutoContent Wizard developed seventeen slides in the Marketing Plan theme. You will modify these slides to fit the college finances topic by changing the presentation color scheme, changing the slide backgrounds, adding a bitmap graphic, creating a WordArt element, inserting an Excel chart and a Word table, and adding a chart, hyperlinks, sound, and transitions.

Creating a Folder and Saving a Presentation

You now should create a folder and save the presentation. The steps on the next page create a folder and save the presentation.

To Create a Folder and Save a Presentation

1 Click the Save button on the Standard toolbar. When the Save As dialog box is displayed, type `College Finances` in the File name text box.

2 Click the Save in box arrow. Click 3½ Floppy (A:) in the Save in list.

3 Click the Create New Folder button on the toolbar in the Save As dialog box. When the New Folder dialog box is displayed, type `Cash for College` in the Name text box.

4 Click the OK button. Click the Save button in the Save As dialog box.

The presentation is saved in the Cash for College folder on the floppy disk in drive A with the file name College Finances. This file name is displayed on the title bar (Figure 4-8).

file name

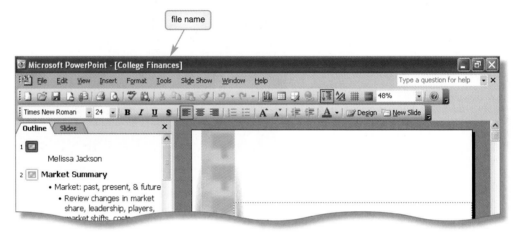

FIGURE 4-8

Adding a Picture to Create a Custom Background

To add variety to the presentation, you can insert a photograph to a slide background. As in Project 3, you decide to add a photograph to the Slide 1 background. This photograph is stored on the Data Disk. See the inside back cover of this book for instructions for downloading the Data Disk or see your instructor for information about accessing the files required for this book. The following steps add this picture to the Slide 1 background.

To Add a Picture to Create a Custom Background

1 Right-click anywhere on Slide 1 except the title text placeholder. Click Background on the shortcut menu. When the Background dialog box is displayed, click the Background fill box arrow.

2 Click Fill Effects on the menu. When the Fill Effects dialog box is displayed, click the Picture tab and then click the Select Picture button.

3 When the Select Picture dialog box is displayed, click the Look in box arrow and then click 3½ Floppy (A:). Click the Student thumbnail.

4 Click the Insert button. When the picture is displayed in the Fill Effects dialog box, click the OK button.

5   **Click Omit background graphics from master.**

6   **Click the Apply button.**

Slide 1 displays the Student picture as the slide background (Figure 4-9). The Marketing Plan design template text attributes display on the slide. The vertical stripe on the left side of the slide does not display because you clicked the Omit background graphics from master check box.

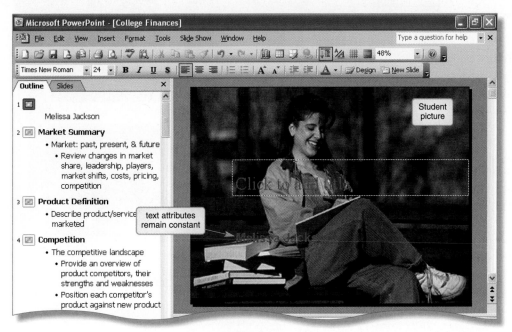

FIGURE 4-9

Creating a WordArt Element and Adding It to a Slide

The Student picture on Slide 1 is intended to generate interest in the presentation. Another method of attracting viewers is by using a **WordArt element**, which is text that has been altered with special effects. PowerPoint supplies 30 predefined WordArt styles that vary in shape and color.

Creating and adding the Cash for College WordArt element shown in Figure 4-1a on page PPT 227 requires several steps. First, you delete the title text placeholder because you are going to use the WordArt element as the presentation title. Then, you create the WordArt object. Finally, you position and size the element on the title slide. The next several sections explain how to create the WordArt element and then add it to Slide 1.

Deleting the Title and Subtitle Text Placeholders

The Cash for College WordArt object will display in the middle of Slide 1 as a substitution for title text. You need to delete the title text and subtitle text placeholders because you are not going to use them in this presentation. The steps on the next page delete the title and subtitle text placeholders.

To Delete the Title and Subtitle Text Placeholders

1

• **Click the title text placeholder's selection rectangle.**

The mouse pointer changes to a four-headed arrow (Figure 4-10).

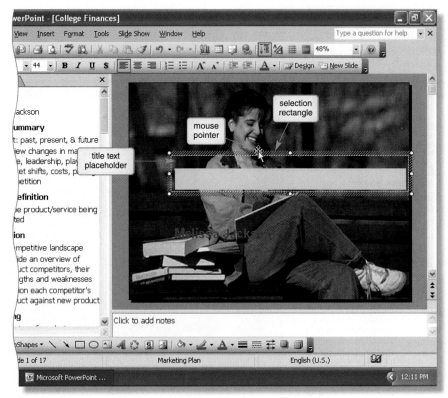

FIGURE 4-10

2

• **Right-click the selection rectangle.**

• **Point to Cut on the shortcut menu (Figure 4-11).**

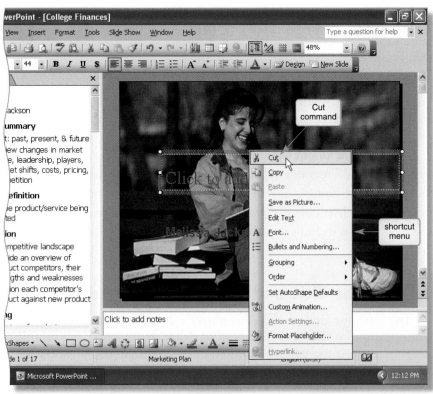

FIGURE 4-11

3

• **Click Cut.**

• **Click the subtitle text placeholder and then click the placeholder's selection rectangle.**

The mouse pointer changes to a four-headed arrow (Figure 4-12). Slide 1 is displayed without the title text placeholder.

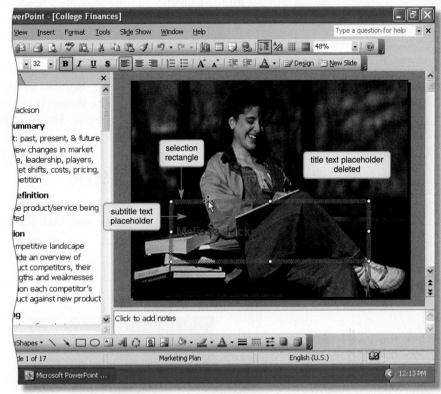

FIGURE 4-12

4

• **Right-click the selection rectangle.**

• **Click Cut.**

• **Press the DELETE key.**

Slide 1 is displayed without the subtitle text placeholder (Figure 4-13).

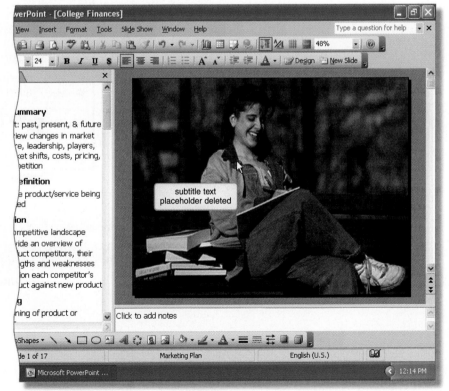

FIGURE 4-13

With the title and subtitle text placeholders deleted, you can create the WordArt element. The Cash for College title on Slide 1, shown in Figure 4-1a on page PPT 227, contains letters that have been altered with special text effects. Using WordArt, first you will select a letter style for this text. Then, you will type the name of the presentation and select a unique shape for its layout, although many other predefined shapes could be used. Buttons on the WordArt toolbar allow you to rotate, slant, curve, and alter the shape of letters. WordArt also can be used in the other Microsoft Office applications. The next several sections explain how to create the text WordArt element.

Selecting a WordArt Style

PowerPoint supplies WordArt styles with a variety of shapes and colors. The following steps select a style for the Cash for College text.

To Select a WordArt Style

1

• **Click the Insert WordArt button on the Drawing toolbar.**

• **When the WordArt Gallery dialog box is displayed, click the WordArt style in row 5, column 4.**

The WordArt Gallery dialog box is displayed (Figure 4-14).

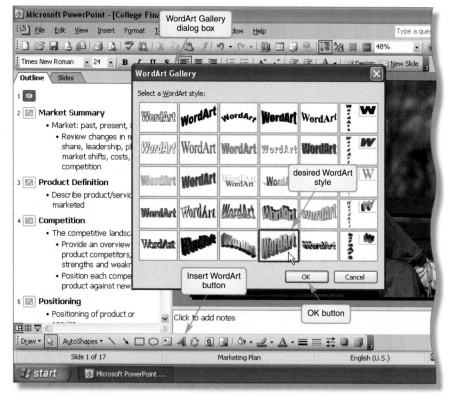

FIGURE 4-14

2

• **Click the OK button.**

The Edit WordArt Text dialog box is displayed (Figure 4-15). The default text, Your Text Here, in the Text text box is selected.

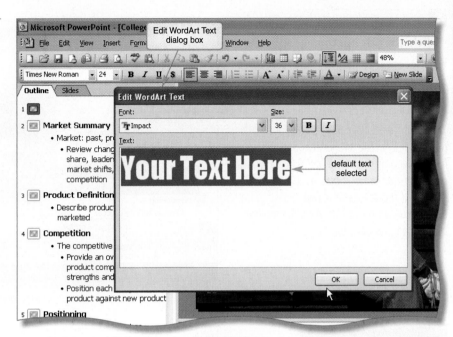

FIGURE 4-15

Other Ways

1. On Insert menu point to Picture, click WordArt, click desired style, click OK
2. Press ALT+I, press P, press W, press arrow keys to select desired style, press ENTER
3. In Voice Command mode, say "Insert, Picture, WordArt, [click desired style], OK"

Entering the WordArt Text

To create a text element, you must enter text in the Edit WordArt Text dialog box. By default, the words, Your Text Here, in the Text text box are selected. When you type the text for your title object, it replaces the selected text. When you want to start a new line, press the ENTER key. The following steps enter the text for the Cash for College heading.

To Enter the WordArt Text

1

• **If necessary, select the text in the Edit WordArt Text dialog box.**

• **Type** Cash for College **in the Text text box.**

The text is displayed in the Text text box in the Edit WordArt Text dialog box (Figure 4-16). The default font is Impact, and the font size is 36.

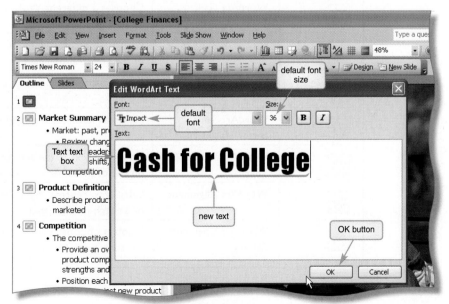

FIGURE 4-16

2

• **Click the OK button.**

• **If necessary, display the WordArt toolbar by right-clicking a toolbar and then clicking WordArt.**

The Cash for College text is displayed (Figure 4-17). The WordArt toolbar is displayed in the same location and with the same shape as it displayed the last time it was used. You can move the WordArt toolbar by dragging its title bar.

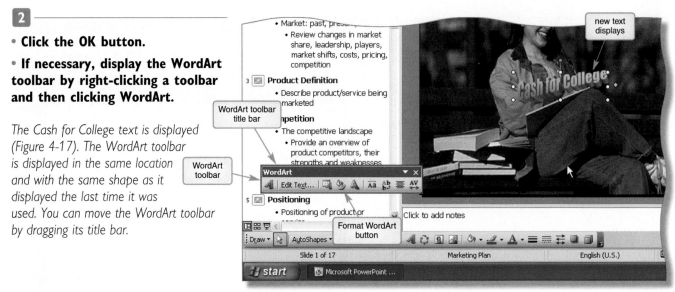

FIGURE 4-17

Other Ways

1. Type text, press ENTER
2. In Dictation mode, say "Cash for College"

The WordArt toolbar contains buttons that allow you to change an object's appearance. For example, you can rotate the letters, change the character spacing and alignment, scale the size, and add different fill and line colors. Table 4-1 explains the purpose of each button on the WordArt toolbar.

Table 4-1	**WordArt Toolbar Button Functions**	
BUTTON	**NAME**	**FUNCTION**
	Insert WordArt	Creates a WordArt element
Edit Text...	Edit Text	Changes the text characters, font, and font size
	WordArt Gallery	Chooses a different WordArt style for the selected WordArt object
	Format WordArt	Formats the color, lines, size, pattern, position, and other properties of the selected object
	WordArt Shape	Modifies the text into one of 40 shapes
Aa	WordArt Same Letter Heights	Makes all letters the same height, regardless of case
Ab b	WordArt Vertical Text	Stacks the text in the selected WordArt object vertically — one letter on top of the other — for reading from top to bottom
	WordArt Alignment	Left-aligns, centers, right-aligns, word-justifies, letter-justifies, or stretch-justifies text
AV	WordArt Character Spacing	Displays options (Very Tight, Tight, Normal, Loose, Very Loose, Custom, Kern Character Pairs) for adjusting spacing between text

The next section explains how to shape the WordArt text.

Changing the WordArt Height and Width

WordArt objects actually are drawing objects, not text. Consequently, WordArt objects can be modified in various ways, including changing their height, width, line style, fill color, and shadows. Unlike text, however, they neither can display in outline view nor be spell checked. In this project, you will increase the height and width of the WordArt object. The Size tab in the Format WordArt dialog box contains two areas used to change an object's size. The first, the **Size and rotate area**, allows you to enlarge or reduce an object, and the rotate area allows you to turn an object around its axis. The second, the **Scale area**, allows you to change an object's size while maintaining its height-to-width ratio, or **aspect ratio**. If you want to retain the object's original settings, you click the Reset button in the **Original size area**. The following steps change the height and width of the WordArt object.

More About

Saving a Slide as a Graphic

You can insert a PowerPoint slide into another file or into a Web page. To save a slide as a graphic, display the slide, click Save As on the File menu, and then click Windows Metafile or GIF Graphics Interchange Format in the Save as type box.

To Change the WordArt Height and Width

1

- **Click the Format WordArt button on the WordArt toolbar.**
- **If necessary, click the Size tab in the Format WordArt dialog box.**
- **Click Lock aspect ratio.**

The Size sheet is displayed in the Format WordArt dialog box (Figure 4-18). The Cash for College text currently is .96 inches high and 3.38 inches wide.

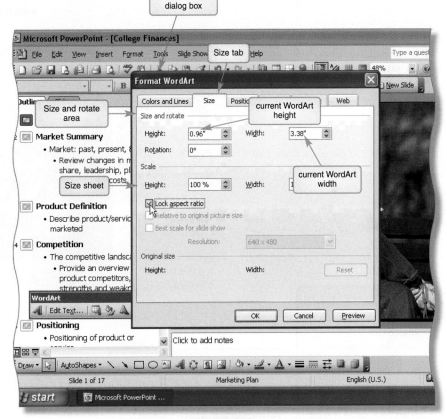

FIGURE 4-18

2

• **Triple-click the Height text box in the Size and rotate area.**

• **Type** 2.5 **in the Height text box.**

The Height text box displays the new entry (Figure 4-19). The width will change proportionally when you click the OK button.

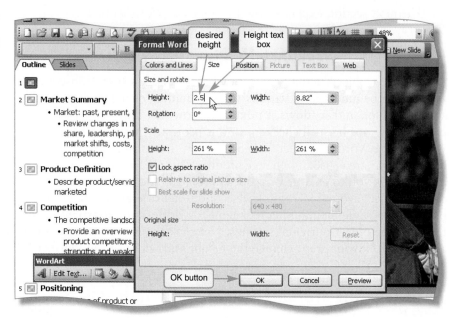

FIGURE 4-19

3

• **Click the OK button.**

The resized WordArt text object is displayed (Figure 4-20).

FIGURE 4-20

The Cash for College WordArt text object is created. The next step is to display it in a precise location on the slide. The grids and guides help you align objects in exact locations on slides.

Displaying Grids and Guides and Positioning a WordArt Object

In this project, you use the PowerPoint grid and guides to help position the WordArt object on Slide 1. The **grid** is a set of intersecting lines, and the **guides** are two straight dotted lines, one horizontal and one vertical. When an object is close to a guide, its corner or its center (whichever is closer) **snaps,** or attaches itself, to the guide. You can drag a guide to a new location to meet your alignment requirements.

When you point to a guide and then press and hold the mouse button, Power-Point displays a box containing the exact position of the guide on the slide in inches. The center of a slide is 0.00 on both the vertical and the horizontal guides. An arrow displays below the guide position to indicate the vertical guide is either left or right of center. An arrow displays to the right of the guide position to indicate the horizontal guide is either above or below center. The following steps display the grid and guides and position the Cash for College WordArt text object on Slide 1.

To Display the Grid and Guides and Position the WordArt Object

1

• **With Slide 1 selected, right-click anywhere on the slide except the WordArt text object.**

• **Point to Grid and Guides on the shortcut menu (Figure 4-21).**

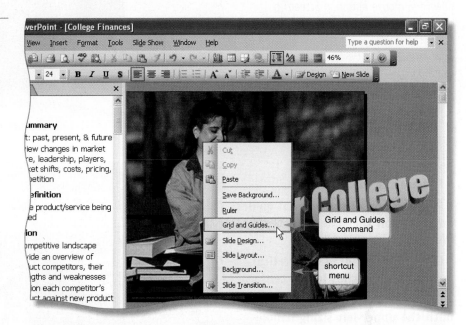

FIGURE 4-21

2

• **Click Grid and Guides.**

• **When the Grid and Guides dialog box displays, click the Spacing box arrow in the Grid settings area and then click 1/10".**

• **Click Display grid on screen in the Grid settings area.**

• **Click Display drawing guides on screen in the Guide settings area.**

Once you click 1/10" in the Grid settings area, the value changes to 0.1. The Snap object to grid check box indicates the action buttons and other objects will snap to the drawing guides that display on the screen (Figure 4-22).

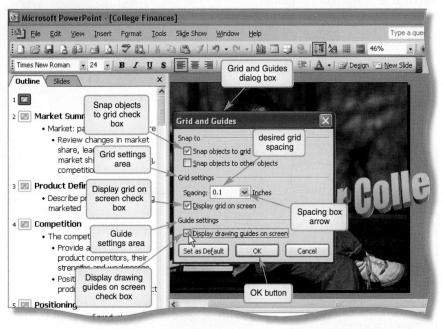

FIGURE 4-22

3

• **Click the OK button.**

• **Point to one of the horizontal guides anywhere on the slide except the WordArt text object.**

• **Click and then drag the horizontal guide to .60 inches above center. Do not release the mouse button.**

The grid and the horizontal and vertical guides display (Figure 4-23). While holding down the mouse button, a ScreenTip displays indicating the position of the horizontal guide. This guide will be used to position the top-left edge of the WordArt text object.

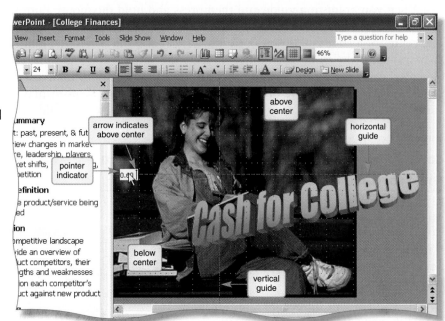

FIGURE 4-23

4

• **Release the mouse button.**

• **Point to one of the vertical guides anywhere on the slide except the WordArt text object.**

• **Click and then drag the vertical guide to 4.50 inches left of center.**

• **Drag the WordArt text object until the upper-left sizing handle snaps to the intersection of the vertical and horizontal guides.**

The WordArt text object is positioned correctly (Figure 4-24). The top of the WordArt text object aligns with the horizontal guide, and the left edge of the object aligns with the vertical guide.

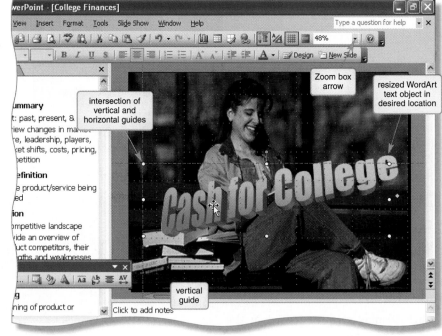

FIGURE 4-24

The Cash for College WordArt object displays in the desired location.

Hiding Guides

When you no longer want to control the exact placement of objects on the slide, you can **hide guides**. The following steps hide guides.

To Hide Guides

1 Right-click Slide 1 anywhere except the WordArt text object. Click Grid and Guides on the shortcut menu.

2 When the Grid and Guides dialog box displays, click Display grid on screen in the Grid settings area.

3 Click Display drawing guides on screen in the Guide settings area.

4 Click the OK button.

The guides are hidden.

Adding a Sound Effect

The final modification to the title slide is adding music to play when Slide 1 is displayed during a slide show. Using a **sound effect** calls attention to areas of interest or importance to which a presenter may want to call attention. PowerPoint allows you to add sounds and music to a presentation. These sounds can be from the Microsoft Clip Organizer, files you have stored on your computer, a CD, and the Internet. To hear the sound effects, you need speakers and a sound card on your system. During the slide show, the sound clip, Marketing Music, should play when Slide 1 is displayed. This clip is available on the Microsoft Office Clip Art and Media Web site and is on your Data Disk. Marketing Music is a **Musical Instrument Digital Interface** (**MIDI**) file, which uses a standard format to encode and communicate music and sound between computers, music synthesizers, and instruments. The following steps add the music to Slide 1.

To Add a Sound Effect

1

• **Click Insert on the menu bar and then point to Movies and Sounds.**

• **Point to Sound from File on the Movies and Sounds submenu.**

The Insert menu and Movies and Sounds submenu display (Figure 4-25).

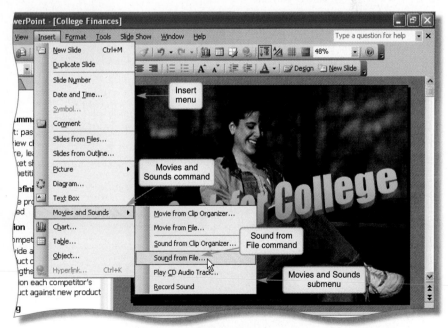

FIGURE 4-25

2

• **Click Sound from File.**

• **If necessary, when the Insert Sound dialog box is displayed, click the Look in box arrow and then click 3½ Floppy (A:).**

• **Click Marketing Music.**

The Marketing Music file in the Insert Sound dialog box is displayed (Figure 4-26). Your list of file names may vary.

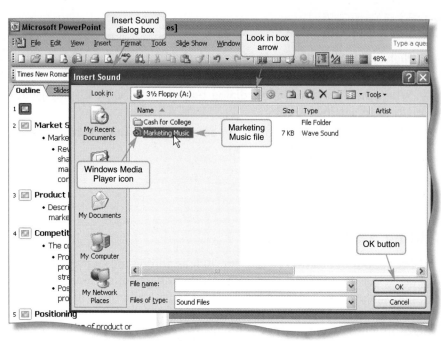

FIGURE 4-26

3

• **Click the OK button.**

• **When the Microsoft Office PowerPoint dialog box is displayed, click the Automatically button.**

The speaker icon indicates the sound is added to Slide 1. Clicking the Automatically button instructs PowerPoint to play the Marketing Music sound file automatically when the slide show starts. Clicking the When Clicked button tells PowerPoint to play the sound when you click Slide 1.

4

• **Drag the speaker icon off the slide to the lower-right corner of the screen.**

You cannot hide the speaker icon, but you can drag it off the slide because it is set to play automatically during the slide show (Figure 4-27). If you had not selected the automatic option, you would have to click the speaker icon to play the sound effect.

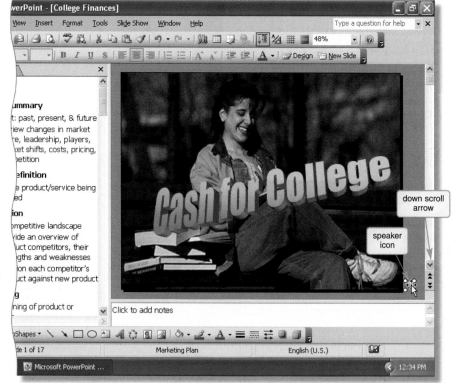

FIGURE 4-27

Deleting Slides

The financing college presentation will have five slides. You will add a chart on Slide 3, an Excel chart on Slide 5, a Word table on Slide 7, and resource information on Slide 8. Slides 2, 4, 6, and 9 through 17 are not needed in this presentation. One quick method of deleting multiple adjacent slides is to use the SHIFT+click technique. You used this technique in Project 3 to select multiple clip art objects before changing their colors. One quick method of deleting multiple slides that are not consecutive is to use the **CTRL+click technique**. You perform the CTRL+click technique by pressing and holding down the CTRL key as you click the desired slides to delete. In this project, the SHIFT+click technique can be used to delete Slides 9 through 17 and the CTRL+click technique can be used to delete Slides 2, 4, and 6. The slides can be deleted when viewing the tabs pane in normal view or when using slide sorter view. This presentation consists of 17 slides, so it is easier and more efficient to use slide sorter view because many slide thumbnails are visible simultaneously in this view. The following steps delete the slides.

To Delete Slides

1 Click the Slide Sorter View button at the lower left of the PowerPoint window.

2 Click the Slide 9 thumbnail. Click the down scroll arrow until Slide 17 is displayed. Press and hold down the SHIFT key and then click slide 17.

3 Press the DELETE key.

4 Click the Slide 2 thumbnail. Press and hold down the CTRL key and then click Slides 4 and 6.

5 Press the DELETE key.

6 Click the Normal View button at the lower left of the PowerPoint window.

Slides 2, 4, 6, and 9 through 17 are deleted (Figure 4-28). The presentation now is composed of five slides.

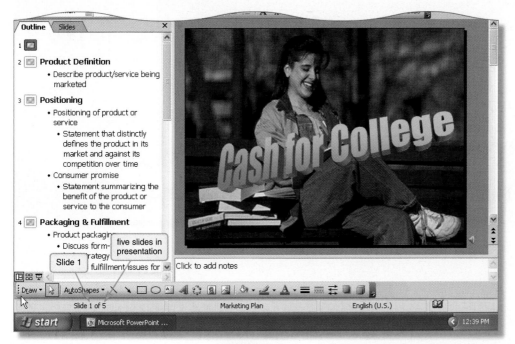

FIGURE 4-28

You now should save the presentation again because you inserted a picture to create a custom background, deleted the title and subtitle text placeholders and replaced them with a WordArt object, and deleted several slides.

The next steps will change the content and graphics on individual slides.

Adding a Chart to a Slide

Financial aid counselors at Eastwood State College have surveyed neighboring institutions to determine the tuition and fees charges. The chart on Slide 2 shows the average total tuition and fees expenses for full-time students attending area two-year and four-year public colleges and four-year private colleges. The findings denote that students at public community colleges generally spend less than $2,000 yearly for their education, and students at four-year public schools spend twice that amount. In contrast, students at nearby private colleges are incurring approximately $18,000 in tuition and fees expenses. The costs at all three types of colleges have increased steadily during the past decade. You will build the chart on Slide 2, shown in Figure 4-29, directly within the PowerPoint presentation using the supplementary application called **Microsoft Graph**, which is installed automatically with Power-Point.

When you start to create this tuition and fees chart, Microsoft Graph opens and displays a chart and associated data. The default Microsoft Graph chart style is a **3-D Column chart**. This style compares values across categories and across series. The 3-D Column chart is appropriate when comparing two or more items in specified intervals, such as in this Slide 2 chart depicting how college students have faced rising costs from 1995 to the present.

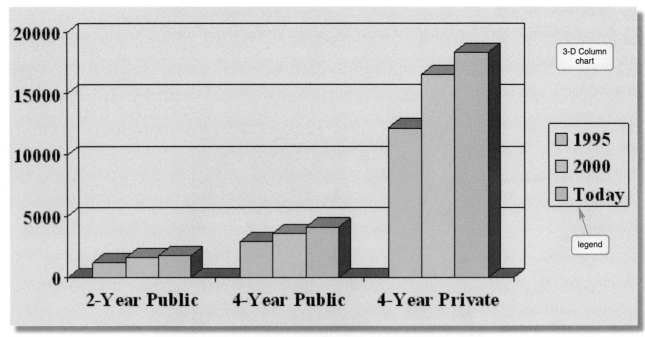

FIGURE 4-29

The figures for the chart are entered in a corresponding **datasheet**, which is a rectangular grid containing columns (vertical) and rows (horizontal). Column letters display above the grid to identify particular **columns**, and row numbers display on the left side of the grid to identify particular **rows**. **Cells** are the intersections of rows and columns, and they are the locations for the chart data and text labels. For example, cell A1 is the intersection of column A and row 1. Numeric and text data are entered in the **active cell**, which is the one cell surrounded by a heavy border. You will replace the sample data in the datasheet by typing entries in the cells, but you also can import data from a text file or Lotus 1-2-3 file, import a Microsoft Excel worksheet or chart, or paste data obtained in another program.

Displaying the Next Slide and Editing the Title and Bulleted List Text

Before you create the 3-D Column chart, you first must display Slide 2 and edit the text generated by the AutoContent Wizard. The following steps describe these tasks.

To Display the Next Slide and Edit the Title and Bulleted List Text

1 Click the Next Slide button to display Slide 2. Triple-click the title text, **Product Definition. Type** `Average Tuition and Fees` **in the title text placeholder.**

2 Triple-click the first first-level paragraph in the text placeholder.

3 **Type** `College expenses are increasing at double the inflation rate` **as the new text.**

Slide 2 is displayed with the edited text (Figure 4-30).

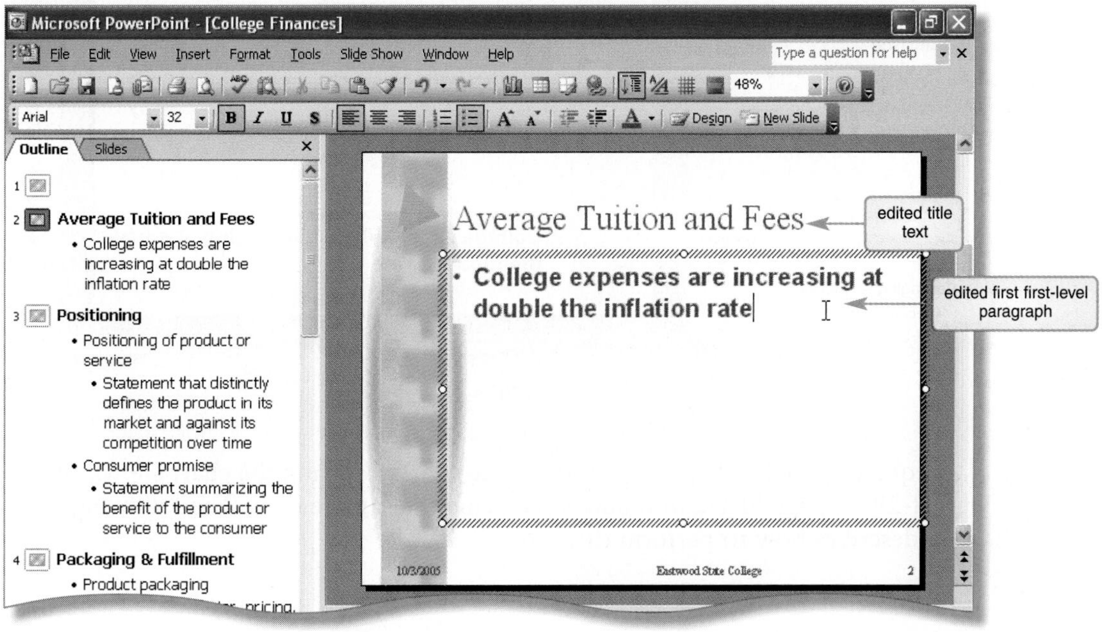

More About

AutoNumber Bullets

PowerPoint's AutoNumber feature adds numbers to the beginning of each slide paragraph. To use this feature on all slides, display the slide master. Then, remove any bullets by pressing the BACKSPACE key. Type 1. (the number 1 and a period) or I) (the Roman numeral one and a closing parenthesis). When you press the ENTER key, PowerPoint will add the next consecutive number or Roman numeral.

FIGURE 4-30

Changing the Slide Layout and Positioning the Text Placeholder

The next steps require changing the layout so the chart is displayed above the text placeholder and then positioning the text placeholder above the footer. The following steps describe this procedure.

To Change the Slide Layout and Position the Text Placeholder

1 Click Format on the menu bar and then click Slide Layout.

2 Click the Title and Content over Text slide layout in the Text and Content Layouts area in the Slide Layout task pane.

3 Click the Close button in the Slide Layout task pane.

4 Click the text placeholder border. Drag the middle sizing handle on the bottom edge of the text placeholder up until it is below the paragraph.

5 Drag the text placeholder down until it is displayed above the footer text. If the AutoFit Options smart tag is displayed, click it and then click Stop Fitting Text to This Placeholder.

Slide 2 has the desired Title and Content over Text slide layout. The text placeholder is displayed in the desired position (Figure 4-31).

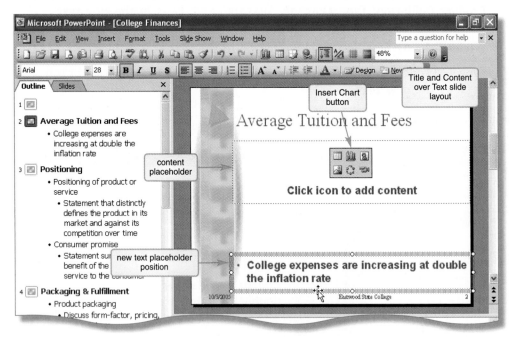

FIGURE 4-31

Adequate space has been allocated for the chart. Creating the chart shown in Figure 4-29 on page PPT 246 requires replacing the sample data. The following section describes how to perform this action.

Inserting a Chart and Replacing the Sample Data

Microsoft Graph provides sample data to create the default chart. You need to change these figures to the numbers representing the costs at area two-year public, four-year public, and four-year private colleges in 1995, in 2000, and today. Table 4-2 summarizes the survey data. Each column represents the tuition and fees at these higher education institutions in three specific years. The numbers are entered into rows 1 through 3, and the titles are entered above the data rows in columns A, B, and C. The legend titles are entered in the first column. The chart **legend** identifies each bar in the chart. In this case, the aqua bar identifies the 1st quarter results, the pink bar identifies the 2nd quarter, and the purple bar identifies the 3rd quarter. The sample data is displayed in four columns; the tuition and fees chart requires only three categories: two-year public, four-year public, and four-year private. You therefore need to delete one column of sample data. The following steps describe how to replace the sample data.

Q&A

Q: Can I add more rows and columns to the datasheet?

A: Yes. The Microsoft Graph sample datasheet displays five rows and six columns. To display additional rows and columns, click the scroll boxes and scroll arrows. Drag the window corner in the lower-right corner of the datasheet to increase the datasheet size.

Table 4-2 Tuition and Fees Survey Data			
	2-Year Public	4-Year Public	4-Year Private
1995	1234	2901	12224
2000	1624	3592	16542
Today	1802	4125	18352

More About

Changing Chart Styles

Give your chart a different style by clicking Chart Type on the Chart menu and then selecting a new style on the Standard Types or Custom Types tab.

To Insert a Chart and Replace the Sample Data

1

• **Click the Insert Chart button in the content placeholder.**

• **Right-click the letter D at the top of column D in the datasheet and then point to Clear Contents on the shortcut menu.**

Microsoft Graph displays the sample datasheet and chart (Figure 4-32). The cells in column D are selected.

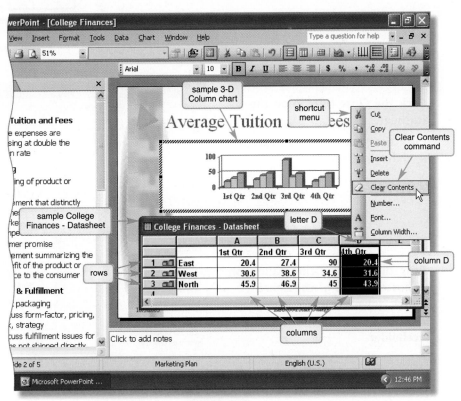

FIGURE 4-32

2

• **Click Clear Contents.**

• **Click cell A1, which is the intersection of column A and row 1.**

Cell A1 is selected (Figure 4-33). The mouse pointer changes to a block plus sign.

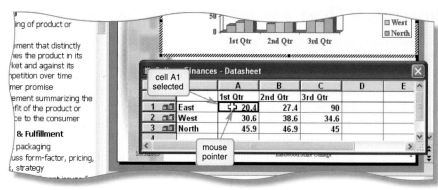

FIGURE 4-33

3

• **Type** 1234 **in cell A1 and then press the RIGHT ARROW key.**

• **Enter the remaining figures and data labels by using Table 4-2 on the previous page as a guide.**

As you type these figures and data labels in the datasheet, they modify the chart (Figure 4-34).

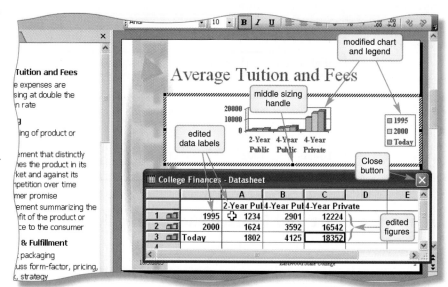

FIGURE 4-34

4

• **Click the Close button on the datasheet.**

• **Click the slide anywhere except the chart window.**

The datasheet closes and the revised chart and legend display.

5

• **Drag the middle sizing handle on the bottom edge of the chart window down until it is above the bulleted paragraph in the text placeholder.**

The chart and legend display in the desired location on Slide 2 (Figure 4-35).

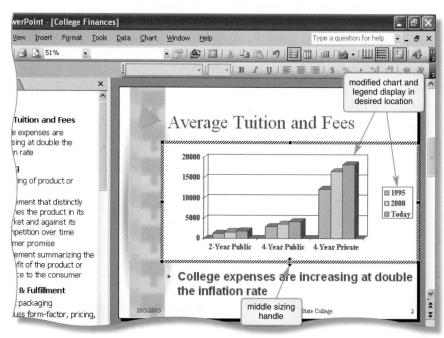

FIGURE 4-35

The tuition and fees data has been entered in the Microsoft Graph datasheet. The three categories surveyed — two-year public, four-year public, and four-year private — display. Slide 2 is complete. You should save the presentation by clicking the Save button on the Standard toolbar.

The next slide in the presentation also will have a chart. Unlike the chart you just created using Microsoft Graph, this chart was created in Microsoft Excel. You will insert this chart into Slide 3. This graphic depicts the percentages of the four categories of college expenses: tuition, fees, books and supplies, and other.

Inserting an Excel Chart

Tuition accounts for nearly two-thirds of Eastwood State College students' academic expenses. Fees are another 10 percent of the bill, and books and supplies are 8 percent. Miscellaneous fees comprise the remaining 20 percent of the total expenses. The proportion of these expenses should be of interest to students and community residents attending the seminar, and a chart created in Microsoft Excel can depict these percentages. A **Clustered Bar chart** compares values across categories. Similarly, the college expenses chart shown in Figure 4-36 illustrates the proportion of tuition, fees, books and supplies, and other expenses.

Other Ways

1. On Insert menu click Chart, click column D, on Edit menu point to Clear, click All, enter data, on View menu click Datasheet

2. Press ALT+I, press H, click column D, press ALT+E, press A, press A, enter data, press ALT+V, press D

3. In Voice Command mode, say "Insert, Chart, [click column D], Edit, Clear, All, [enter data], View, Datasheet"

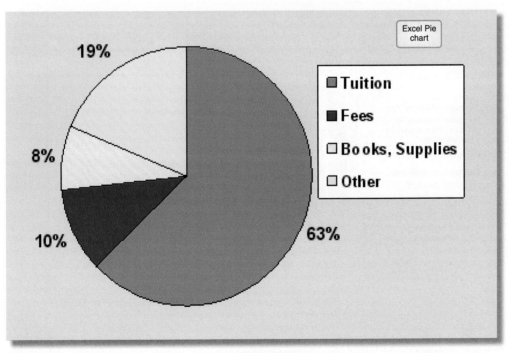

FIGURE 4-36

PowerPoint allows you to insert, or **embed**, many types of objects into a presentation. You inserted clips into slides in Projects 2 and 3, and you will embed a Microsoft Word table into Slide 4. Other objects you can embed include video clips, Microsoft PhotoDraw pictures, and Adobe Acrobat documents.

More About

Formatting Chart Text

You can format the font used for the legend and axes. To format the legend, right-click the legend, click Format Legend on the shortcut menu, click the Font tab, and then select Font attributes, such as font style, size, color, and effects. To format the axes, right-click on an axis, click Format Axis on the shortcut menu, click the Font tab, and then make the selections.

Displaying the Next Slide, Editing the Title Text, and Deleting the Text Placeholder

Before you insert the Excel chart from the Data Disk, you need to display the next slide, change the title text, and delete the text placeholder. The following steps describe how to display the slide, enter a title, and delete the text placeholder.

To Display the Next Slide, Edit the Title Text, and Delete the Text Placeholder

1 Click the Next Slide button to display Slide 3.

2 Double-click the title text, Positioning. Type Costs of Attending College in the title text placeholder.

3 Click in the text placeholder. Click the text placeholder selection rectangle.

4 Press the DELETE key twice.

Slide 3 is displayed with the new title text and deleted text placeholder (Figure 4-37).

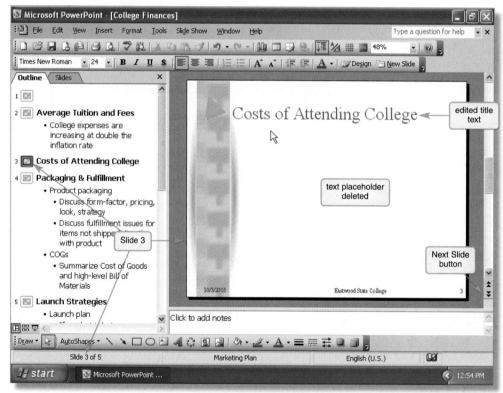

FIGURE 4-37

The slide title and a blank area for the Excel chart now are displayed in Slide 3. The next section explains how to insert this Excel chart.

Inserting an Excel Chart

The Clustered Bar chart on the Data Disk shows the proportion of expenses incurred while attending college. The following steps embed this chart.

To Insert an Excel Chart

1

- **Click Insert on the menu bar and then point to Object.**

The Insert menu is displayed (Figure 4-38). You want to insert the chart created in Microsoft Excel and saved on your Data Disk.

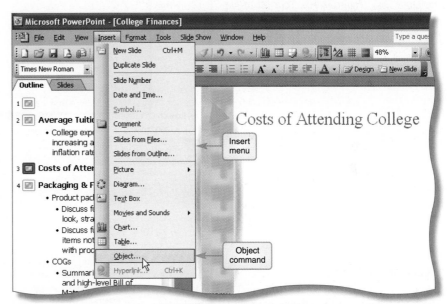

FIGURE 4-38

2

- **Click Object.**
- **When the Insert Object dialog box is displayed, click Create from file.**

The Insert Object dialog box is displayed (Figure 4-39). The Create from file option allows you to select an object created in another application or in PowerPoint.

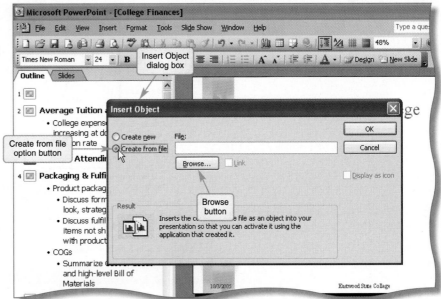

FIGURE 4-39

3

• **Click the Browse button.**

• **When the Browse dialog box is displayed, click the Look in box arrow and then click 3½ Floppy (A:).**

• **Click College Expenses in the Look in list.**

The Browse dialog box shows the files on the Data Disk (Figure 4-40). Your list of file names may vary. College Expenses is the Excel file you will insert into Slide 3.

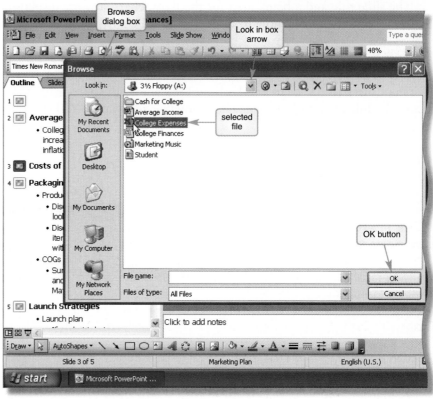

FIGURE 4-40

4

• **Click the OK button.**

The Insert Object dialog box now appears with A:\College Expenses.xls in the File text box (Figure 4-41). The .xls extension indicates the file is a Microsoft Excel file.

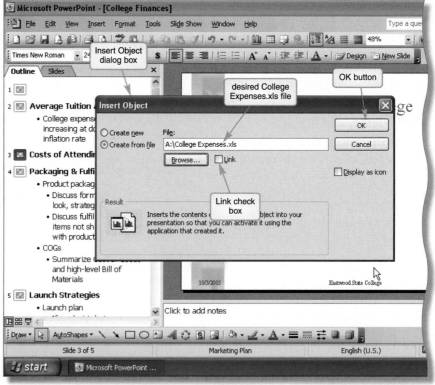

FIGURE 4-41

5

• **When the Insert Object dialog box is redisplayed, click the OK button.**

Slide 3 includes the College Expenses chart (Figure 4-42).

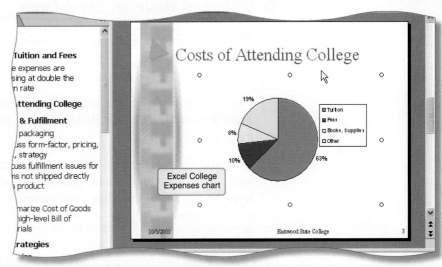

FIGURE 4-42

Other Ways

1. On Insert menu click Object, click Create from file, type file name, click OK button
2. Press ALT+I, press O, press ALT+F, type file name, click OK button
3. In Voice Command mode, say "Insert, Object, Create from file, [type file name], OK"

When you click the Create from file option button in the Insert Object dialog box, the dialog box changes. The File box replaces the Object type box. Another change to the dialog box is the addition of the Link check box. If the **Link check box** is selected, the object is inserted as a linked, instead of an embedded, object. Similar to an embedded object, a **linked object** also is created in another application; however, the linked object maintains a connection to its source. If the original object is changed, the linked object on the slide also changes. The linked object is stored in the **source file**, the file in which the object was created.

For example, the Excel chart you embedded into the slide is stored on the Data Disk. If you were to link rather than embed the College Expenses file, then every time the College Expenses file changes in Excel, the changes would display on the chart in Slide 3. Your PowerPoint presentation would store a representation of the original College Expenses file and information about its location. If you later moved or deleted the source file, the link would be broken, and the object would not be available. Consequently, if you make a presentation on a computer other than the one on which the presentation was created and the presentation contains a linked object, be certain to include a copy of the source files. The source files must be stored in the exact location as originally specified when you linked them to your presentation.

When you select a source file from the Browse dialog box, PowerPoint associates the file with a specific application, which is based on the file extension. For example, if you select a source file with the file extension **.doc**, PowerPoint recognizes the file as a Microsoft Word file. Additionally, if you select a source file with the file extension **.xls**, PowerPoint recognizes the file as a Microsoft Excel file.

Scaling and Moving an Excel Chart

Sufficient space exists on Slide 3 to enlarge the chart. The steps on the next page scale the chart object.

Q&A

Q: Can I edit an Excel chart?

A: Yes. If you want to change the chart that you imported into your slide, double-click the chart, use the Excel tools and menus to modify the chart, and then click outside the chart to return to PowerPoint.

To Scale and Move an Excel Chart

1 **Right-click the College Expenses chart and then click Format Object on the shortcut menu.**

2 **If necessary, click the Size tab in the Format Object dialog box.**

3 **Click and hold down the mouse button on the Height box up arrow in the Scale area until 110 % is displayed and then release the mouse button.**

4 **Click the OK button.**

5 **Drag the College Expenses chart up and to the left so it is centered on the slide. If necessary, you can make small adjustments by pressing the arrow keys on the keyboard that correspond to the direction in which to move.**

The Excel chart is enlarged and moved to the desired position (Figure 4-43).

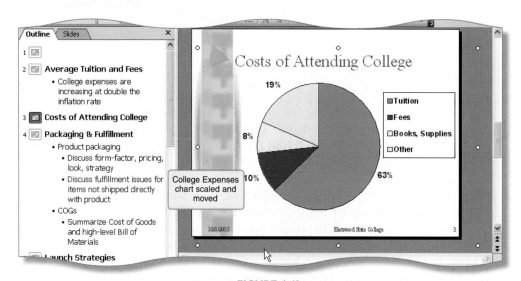

FIGURE 4-43

Slide 3 now is complete. Again, because you have changed the presentation significantly, save the slide show by clicking the Save button on the Standard toolbar. The next slide also will have a graphic, and it will show the average salary Eastwood State College community residents have earned since 1975 based on the amount of education they have completed.

Adding a Table from Word

The College Finances presentation now shows how community members' salaries have increased since 1975 based on their education levels. Figure 4-44 shows a Microsoft Word table that lists the yearly income earned by high school graduates, community residents who have earned only an associate's degree, and residents with a bachelor's degree. Eastwood State College administrators have been tracking these numbers since 1975. The Average Income file was created using Microsoft Word and enhanced with Word's Table AutoFormat feature. PowerPoint allows you to embed this table into a presentation. The same steps used to insert the Excel College Expenses chart into a slide are used to insert a Microsoft Word table. In the following sections, you will display the next slide, edit the title text, and insert the Word table from the Data Disk.

Year	High School	Associate's Degree	**Bachelor's Degree**
1975	7,814	8,245	12,401
1980	11,444	12,494	18,102
1985	14,386	16,354	24,893
1990	17,530	20,703	31,132
1995	21,643	23,863	36,891
2000	25,995	29,984	49,732
Today	27,103	31,309	51,693

Word Average Income table

FIGURE 4-44

Displaying the Next Slide, Editing the Title Text, and Changing the Slide Layout

Before you insert the Word table, you need to display the next slide, edit the slide title text, and change the slide layout.

To Display the Next Slide, Edit the Title Text, and Change the Slide Layout

1 Click the Next Slide button to display Slide 4.

2 Triple-click the title text, Packaging & Fulfillment. Type Average Income by Degree in the title text placeholder.

3 Click in the text placeholder. Click the text placeholder selection rectangle.

4 Press the DELETE key twice.

Slide 4 has a new title and the desired Title Only slide layout (Figure 4-45).

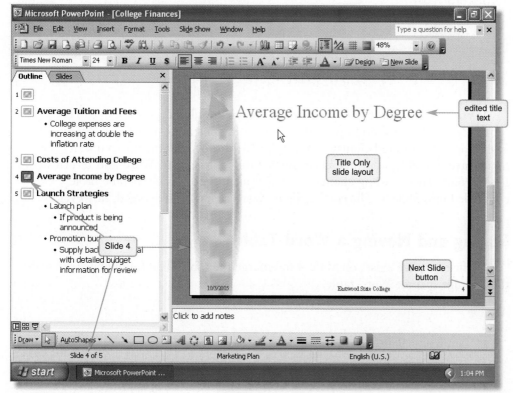

FIGURE 4-45

Inserting a Word Table

Slide 4 now appears with the slide title and a blank area for the Average Income table. The following steps explain how to insert this Word table, which has the file name Average Income.doc.

To Insert a Word Table

1 **Click Insert on the menu bar and then click Object.**

2 **When the Insert Object dialog box is displayed, click Create from file. Click the Browse button.**

3 **When the Browse dialog box is displayed, click the Look in box arrow and then click 3½ Floppy (A:). Click Average Income in the Look in list. Click the OK button.**

4 **When the Insert Object dialog box is displayed, click the OK button.**

Slide 4 appears with the Average Income table (Figure 4-46).

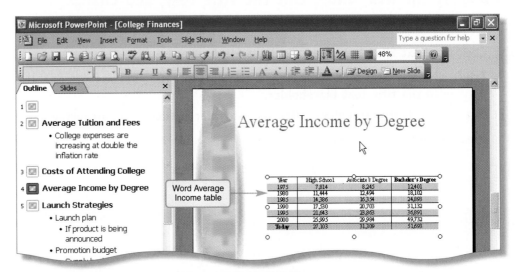

FIGURE 4-46

If you want to edit the Average Income table, double-click the table. This action starts Microsoft Word and opens the Average Income table as a Word document. Then, make the desired changes or use the Word tools and menus to modify the table, save the table, and then click outside the table to quit Word and return to PowerPoint. These editing changes will appear in the Average Income table embedded into Slide 4. The source file in Word remains unchanged, however.

Scaling and Moving a Word Table

Sufficient space exists on Slide 4 to enlarge the table. The following steps scale the Average Income Word table.

To Scale and Move a Word Table

1 Right-click the Average Income table and then click Format Object on the shortcut menu.

2 If necessary, click the Size tab in the Format Object dialog box.

3 Click and hold down the mouse button on the Height box up arrow in the Scale area until 160 % is displayed and then release the mouse button.

4 Click the OK button.

5 Drag the Average Income table up and to the left so it is centered on the slide. If necessary, you can make small adjustments by pressing the arrow keys on the keyboard that correspond to the direction in which to move.

The Average Income table is enlarged and moved to the desired position (Figure 4-47).

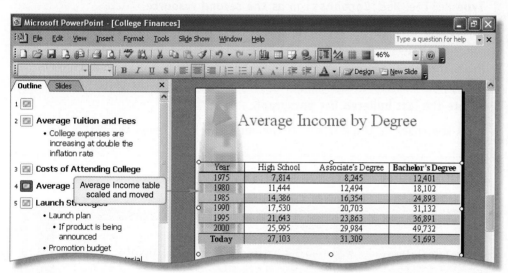

FIGURE 4-47

Slide 4 is complete, so you should save the slide show by clicking the Save button on the Standard toolbar. The College Finances presentation informs Eastwood State College seminar attendees viewing the slide show about the need to save for the various college expenses. The final slide in the presentation will give information on locating additional information on financial topics.

Adding Hyperlinks

Slide 5 in the College Finances slide show presents resources for additional information. Eastwood State College audience members can refer to these sources to learn more about the topics presented in the slide show or to obtain specific information that would benefit them personally.

Part of this slide will contain hyperlinks. A **hyperlink**, also called a **link**, is a connection from one slide to a Web page, another slide, a custom show consisting of specific slides in a presentation, or a file. Hyperlinks can be text or an object, such as a picture, graph, shape, or WordArt. On Slide 5, the text hyperlinks will be **absolute links** because they will specify the exact location of a page on the World Wide Web. This location is encoded as a **Uniform Resource Locator** (**URL**), also called a **Web address**. The following sections explain how to create the hyperlinks.

Other Ways

1. On Format menu click Object, if necessary click Size tab, click Scale Height box up arrow to display desired height, click OK button

2. Press ALT+O, press O, if necessary press RIGHT ARROW KEY, press ALT+H, press UP ARROW key to display desired height, press ENTER

3. In Voice Command mode, say "Format, Object, Height, [type height], OK"

Displaying the Next Slide and Editing the Text

Before you create the hyperlinks to the World Wide Web, you need to display the next slide and edit the slide text.

To Display the Next Slide and Edit the Text

1 Click the Next Slide button to display Slide 5.

2 Triple-click the title text, Launch Strategies. **Type** `College Financial Assets` **in the title text placeholder.**

3 Triple-click the first bullet text paragraph in the text placeholder. **Type** `Obtain additional information from` **and then press the ENTER key.**

4 Press the TAB key. **Type** `The College Board` **and then press the ENTER key.**

5 **Type** `Nellie Mae Corporation` **as the second resource.**

6 Select and then delete the second first-level paragraph. **Type** `Consider scholarships and loans` **as the bulleted text and then press the ENTER key.**

7 Press the TAB key and then type `More than 75% of public-college students receive financial aid` **but do not press the ENTER key.**

8 Delete the last bulleted list paragraph.

9 Click the chart at the bottom of the slide and then press the DELETE key.

The edited bulleted list is displayed in Slide 5 (Figure 4-48).

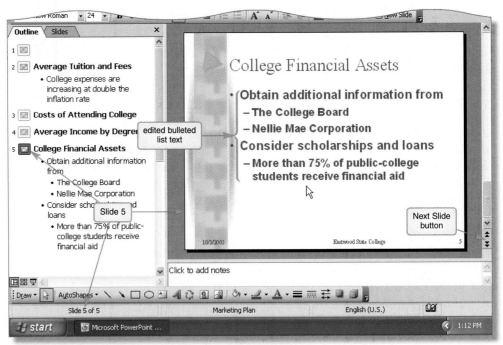

FIGURE 4-48

All editing changes are complete. The next step is to create hyperlinks for the two second-level paragraphs to receive additional information.

Adding a Hyperlink to a Slide

Each of the first two second-level paragraphs will be a hyperlink to an organization's Web page. If you are connected to the Internet when you run your presentation, you can click a hyperlink, and your default Web browser will access the URL you specified. The following steps describe how to create the first hyperlink.

To Add a Hyperlink to a Slide

1

• **Triple-click the first second-level paragraph, The College Board.**

• **Click the Insert Hyperlink button on the Standard toolbar.**

The Insert Hyperlink dialog box is displayed (Figure 4-49). The first second-level paragraph is selected.

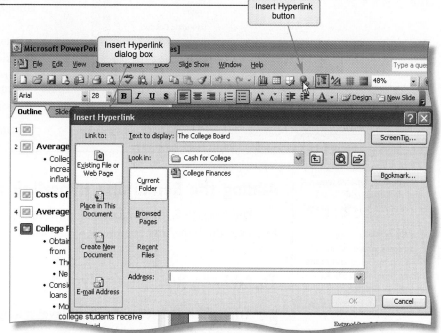

FIGURE 4-49

2

• **If necessary, click the Existing File or Web Page button on the Link to bar.**

• **Type** www.collegeboard.com **in the Address text box.**

The URL for The College Board hyperlink text is http://www.collegeboard.com (Figure 4-50). PowerPoint automatically appends the http:// to the URL.

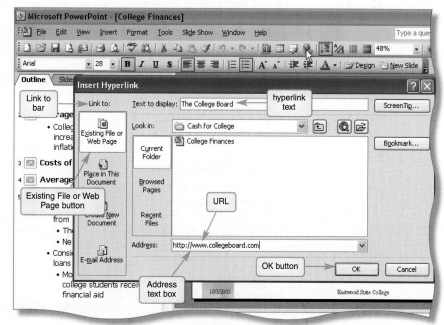

FIGURE 4-50

3

- **Click the OK button.**
- **Click Slide 5 anywhere except the text placeholder.**

The College Board hyperlink text is underlined and has the font color light purple (Figure 4-51).

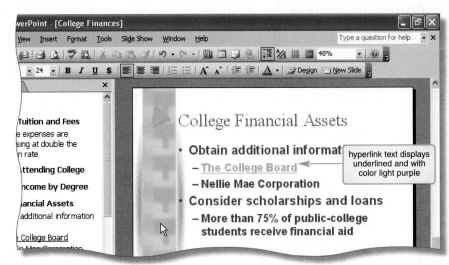

FIGURE 4-51

Adding the Remaining Hyperlink to the Slide

The hyperlink for the first second-level paragraph is complete. The next task is to create the hyperlink for the other second-level paragraph on Slide 5.

To Add the Remaining Hyperlink to a Slide

1 **Triple-click the second second-level paragraph, Nellie Mae Corporation.**

2 **Click the Insert Hyperlink button and then type** www.nelliemae.org **in the Address text box. Click the OK button.**

3 **Click Slide 5 anywhere except the text placeholder.**

The hyperlink for the second second-level paragraph is added (Figure 4-52).

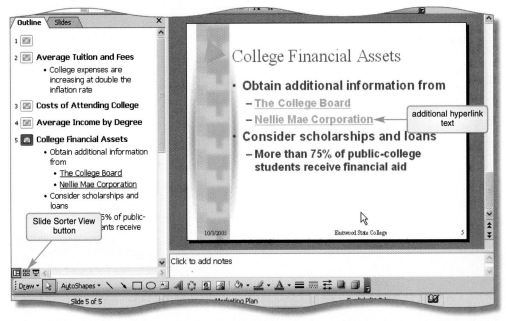

FIGURE 4-52

When you point to a hyperlink, the pointer becomes the shape of a hand to indicate it is something you can click. Hyperlinked text displays underlined and in a color that is part of the color scheme. Pictures, shapes, and objects also can serve as hyperlinks.

Hyperlinks are active only when you run the presentation, not when you are creating it in normal or slide sorter view. If you are connected to the Internet when you run the presentation, you will click each of the two second-level paragraphs. Your browser will display the corresponding Web page for each paragraph.

Revising and Customizing Individual Slides

The text for all five slides in the College Finances presentation has been entered. Once you complete a slide show, you might decide to change elements. PowerPoint provides several tools to assist you with making changes. The following pages discuss these tools.

Hiding Slides

Slides 2, 3, and 4 present technical information in graphical form. Depending on the audience's needs and the time constraints, you may decide not to display Slide 5 because it is a supporting slide. A supporting slide provides detailed information to supplement another slide in the presentation. For example, in a presentation to academic deans about the increase in student enrollment, one slide displays a graph representing the current year's enrollment and the previous three years' enrollment figures. A supporting slide might display a table showing each department's enrollment figures for every year in the graph.

When running a slide show, you may not want to display the supporting slide. You would want to display it when time permits and when you want to show the audience more details about a topic. You should insert the supporting slide after the slide you anticipate may warrant more detail. Then, you use the Hide Slide command to hide the supporting slide. The Hide Slide command hides the supporting slide from the audience during the normal running of a slide show. When you want to display the supporting hidden slide, press the H key. No visible indicator displays to show that a hidden slide exists. You must be aware of the content of the presentation to know where the supporting slide is located.

Slide 5 is a slide that supports information presented in the entire presentation. If time permits, or if the audience requires more information, you can display Slide 5. As the presenter, you decide whether to show Slide 5. You hide a slide in slide sorter view so you can see the slashed square surrounding the slide number, which indicates a slide is hidden. The steps on the next page hide Slide 5.

More About

Removing Hyperlinks

If you decide you no longer want a hyperlink in your presentation but you want to keep the text or object that represents the hyperlink, right-click the text or object and then click Remove Hyperlink on the shortcut menu. If you want to delete the hyperlink and the corresponding text or object, select the text or object and then press the DELETE key.

More About

Closing Slides

When you have created your final slide, review all the slides in slide sorter view to see if each slide fits the slide show theme. Some PowerPoint experts recommend starting to design a slide show by developing the closing slide first. Knowing how you want the slide show to end helps you focus on reaching this conclusion. You can create each slide in the presentation with this goal in mind. To learn more about developing presentations, visit the PowerPoint 2003 More About Web page (scsite.com/ppt2003/more) and click Developing.

To Hide a Slide

1

• **Click the Slide Sorter View button at the lower left of the PowerPoint window.**

• **Right-click Slide 5 and then point to Hide Slide on the shortcut menu.**

The shortcut menu is displayed in Slide Sorter view (Figure 4-53).

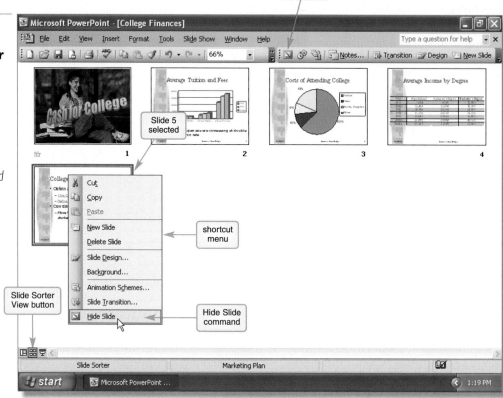

FIGURE 4-53

2

• **Click Hide Slide.**

A square with a slash surrounds the slide number to indicate Slide 5 is a hidden slide (Figure 4-54). The Hide Slide button is selected on the Slide Sorter toolbar.

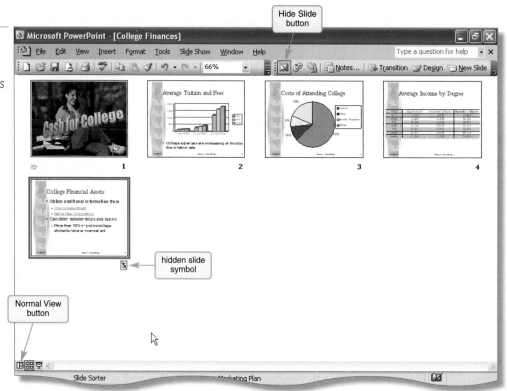

FIGURE 4-54

The Hide Slide button is a toggle — it either hides or displays a slide. The button also applies or removes a square with a slash surrounding the slide number. When you no longer want to hide a slide, change view to slide sorter view, right-click the slide, and then click Hide Slide on the shortcut menu. This action removes the square with the slash surrounding the slide number.

An alternative to hiding a slide in slide sorter view is to hide a slide in normal view. In this view, however, no visible indication is given that the slide is hidden. To hide a slide in normal view, display the slide you want to hide, click Slide Show on the menu bar, and then click Hide Slide.

When you run your presentation, the hidden slide does not display unless you press the H key when the slide preceding the hidden slide is displaying. For example, Slide 5 does not display unless you press the H key when Slide 4 is displayed in slide show view. You continue your presentation by clicking the mouse or pressing any of the keys associated with running a slide show. You skip the hidden slide by clicking the mouse and advancing to the next slide.

Other Ways

1. Click Hide Slide button on Slide Sorter toolbar
2. On Slide Show menu click Hide Slide
3. Press ALT+D, press H
4. In Voice Command mode, say "Slide Show, Hide Slide"

Finding Text

If you want to find a particular word on a slide, you can use PowerPoint's Find feature, which automatically locates each occurrence of a word or phrase. To search for a word, you would follow these steps.

To Find Text

1 **Click Edit on the menu bar and then click Find on the Edit menu.**

2 **Type the text to locate in the Find what text box and then click the Find Next button. To find the next occurrence of the text, click the Find Next button.**

Finding and Replacing Text

If you want to change all occurrences of a particular word or phrase throughout the slide show, you can use PowerPoint's Find and Replace feature. This function locates each desired word or phrase and then replaces it with specified text. To find and replace a word or phrase, you would follow these steps.

Other Ways

1. Press CTRL+F
2. Press ALT+E, press F
3. In Voice Command mode, say "Edit, Find"

To Find and Replace Text

1 **Click Edit on the menu bar and then click Replace on the Edit menu.**

2 **Type the text to locate in the Find what text box. Type the replacement text in the Replace with box. Click the Find Next button.**

3 **To replace all occurrences of the word or phrase, click the Replace All button.**

You occasionally might want to replace only certain occurrences of the word or phrase, not all of them. To instruct PowerPoint to confirm each change, click the Find Next button in the Replace dialog box instead of the Replace all button. When PowerPoint locates an occurrence of the text, it pauses and waits for you to click either the Replace button or the Find Next button. Clicking the Replace button changes the text; clicking the Find Next button instructs PowerPoint to disregard the replacement and look for the next occurrence of the Find what text.

If you accidentally replace the wrong text, you can undo a replacement by clicking the Undo button on the Standard toolbar. If you used the Replace All button, Word undoes all replacements. If you used the Replace button, Word undoes only the most recent replacement.

Using the Thesaurus

When reviewing your slide show, you may decide that a particular word does not express the exact usage you intended or that you used the same word on multiple slides. In these cases, you could find a **synonym**, or word similar in meaning, to replace the inappropriate or duplicate word. PowerPoint provides a **thesaurus**, which is a list of synonyms, to help you find a replacement word.

In this project, you want to find synonyms to replace the word, Costs, on Slide 3 and the word, Income, on Slide 4. The following steps locate appropriate synonyms.

Other Ways

1. On Edit menu click Find, type Find what text, click Replace button, type Replace with text
2. Press CTRL+H
3. Press ALT+E, press E
4. In Voice Command mode, say "Edit, Replace"

To Find a Word and Use the Thesaurus

1

• **Click the Normal View button at the lower left of the PowerPoint window.**

• **Click Edit on the menu bar and then click Find.**

• **When the Find dialog box is displayed, type** Costs **in the Find what box.**

PowerPoint displays the Find dialog box (Figure 4-55).

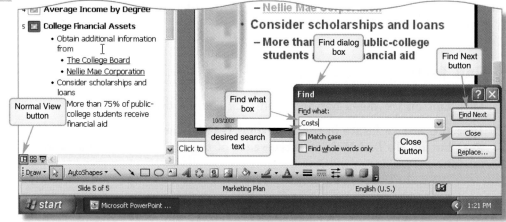

FIGURE 4-55

2

• **Click the Find Next button.**

• **Click the Close button in the Find dialog box.**

Slide 3 is displayed and the word, Costs, is selected (Figure 4-56).

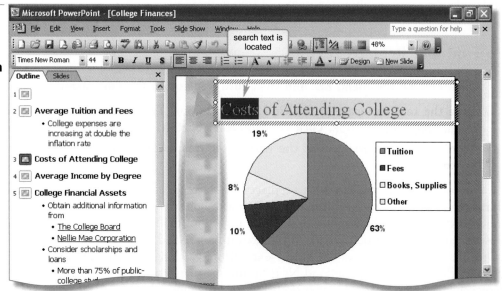

FIGURE 4-56

3

• **Click Tools on the menu bar and then point to Thesaurus.**

The Tools menu is displayed (Figure 4-57).

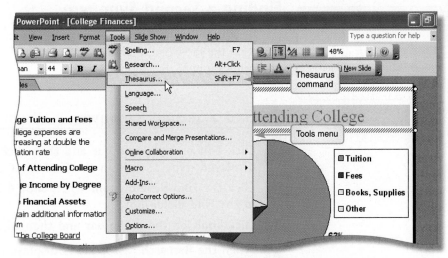

FIGURE 4-57

4

• **Click Thesaurus.**

• **When the Research task pane is displayed, point to the word, expenses, in the Thesaurus list and then click the arrow to the right of that word.**

• **Point to Insert.**

A list of synonyms for the word, Costs, displays in the Thesaurus area of the Research task pane (Figure 4-58).

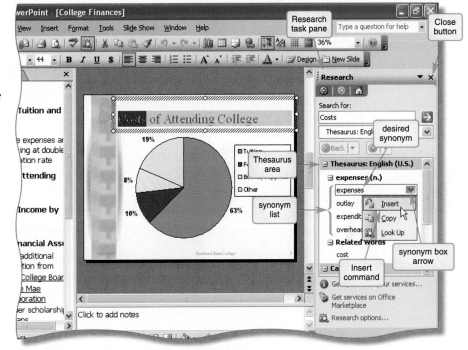

FIGURE 4-58

5

• **Click Insert.**

• **Click the Close button in the Research task pane.**

The word, Costs, is replaced by the synonym, Expenses, on Slide 3 (Figure 4-59).

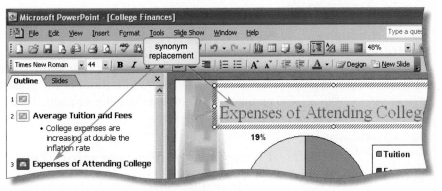

FIGURE 4-59

Finding a Second Synonym

Now that you have found a synonym for the word, Costs, you want to find a synonym for the word, Income, on Slide 4. The following steps replace that word with the synonym, Earnings.

To Find a Second Synonym

1 Click Edit on the menu bar and then click Find. When the Find dialog box is displayed, type `Income` in the Find what box.

2 Click the Find Next button. When Slide 4 is displayed, click the Close button in the Find dialog box.

3 Click Tools on the menu bar and then click Thesaurus.

4 When the Research task pane is displayed, point to the word, earnings, and then click the arrow to the right of that word. Click Insert.

5 Click the Close button in the Research task pane.

The word, Income, is replaced by the synonym, Earnings, on Slide 4 (Figure 4-60).

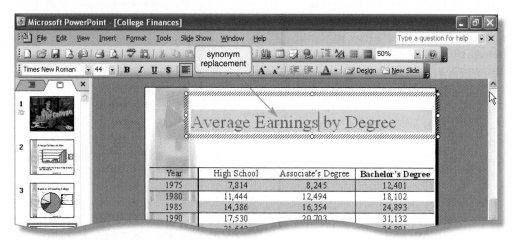

FIGURE 4-60

Using these steps, you revised individual slides. In the following section, you now will add variety to the entire presentation by changing the color scheme and using the title and slide masters to modify the footer text and add action buttons.

Customizing Entire Presentation Elements

With the basic elements of the slide show created, you need to modify two default elements that display on all slides in the presentation. First, you will modify the template by changing the color scheme. Then, you will add information to the slide master Footer Area.

Changing the Presentation Template Color Scheme

The first modification to make is to change the color scheme throughout the presentation. The **color scheme** of each slide template consists of eight balanced colors you can apply to all slides, an individual slide, notes pages, or audience handouts. A color scheme consists of colors for a background, text and lines, shadows, title text, fills, accent, accent and hyperlink, and accent and followed hyperlink. Table 4-3 explains the components of a color scheme.

Table 4-3 Color Scheme Components	
COMPONENT	DESCRIPTION
Background color	The background color is the fundamental color of a PowerPoint slide. For example, if the background color is black, you can place any other color on top of it, but the fundamental color remains black. The black background shows everywhere you do not add color or other objects.
Text and lines color	The text and lines color contrasts with the background color of the slide. Together with the background color, the text and lines color sets the tone for a presentation. For example, a gray background with a black text and lines color sets a dramatic tone. In contrast, a red background with a yellow text and lines color sets a vibrant tone.
Title text color	The title text color contrasts with the background color in a manner similar to the text and lines color. Title text is displayed in the title text placeholder on a slide.
Shadow color	The shadow color is applied when you color an object. This color usually is a darker shade of the background color.
Fill color	The fill color contrasts with both the background color and the text and lines color. The fill color is used for graphs and charts.
Accent colors	Accent colors are designed as colors for secondary features on a slide. Additionally, accent colors are used as colors on graphs.

The following steps change the color scheme for the template from a white background and blue letters to a blue background with purple title text.

To Change the Presentation Template Color Scheme

1

• **Click the Slide Design button on the Formatting toolbar.**

• **Point to Color Schemes in the Slide Design task pane.**

The Slide Design task pane is displayed (Figure 4-61).

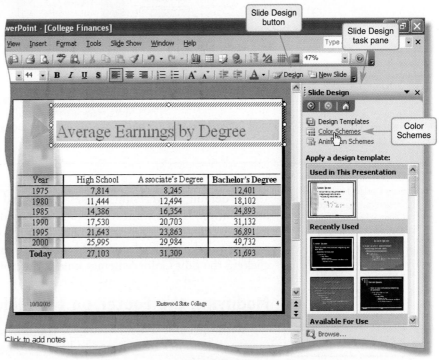

FIGURE 4-61

2

• **Click Color Schemes.**

• **Click the top-right color scheme template.**

Three color schemes are available (Figure 4-62). The top-right color scheme is selected and will be applied to all slides in the presentation.

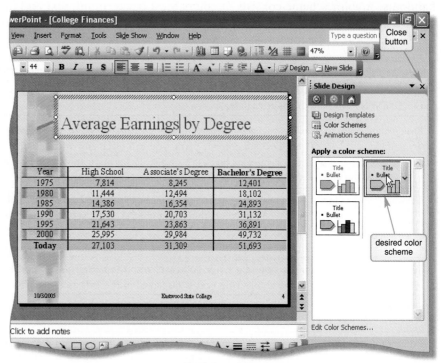

FIGURE 4-62

3

• **Click the Close button in the Slide Design task pane title bar.**

Slide 4 is displayed with the new color scheme (Figure 4-63). Slide thumbnails of the slides in the presentation display in the tabs pane.

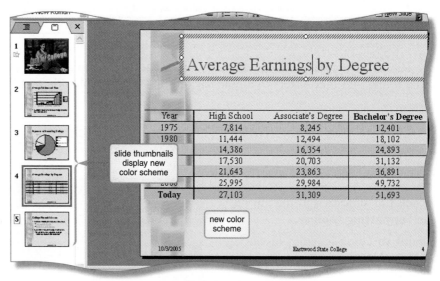

FIGURE 4-63

By default, PowerPoint applies the desired color scheme to all slides in the presentation. If you want to apply it to individual slides or want to see a larger template thumbnail, you would click the arrow button of the selected color scheme and then make your selections. In addition, you can edit the current color scheme by clicking the Edit Color Schemes link at the bottom of the task pane.

Modifying the Footer on the Slide Master

With the color scheme changed, you now can revise the text on the slide master slide footer from Eastwood State College to Eastwood Financial Aid Office.

One method of making this change is to modify the footer on the slide master. In Project 3, you modified the slide master when you customized bullets. In this project, you will display the slide master to add information to the Footer Area of that slide. The following steps modify the slide master footer.

To Modify the Footer on the Slide Master

1

• **Click View on the menu bar, point to Master, and then click Slide Master on the Master submenu.**

The Marketing Plan Title Master and Slide Master View toolbar display (Figure 4-64). The title master and slide master slide thumbnails display on the left edge of the screen. The slide master thumbnail is selected.

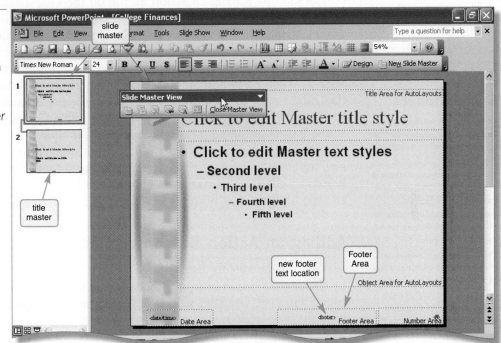

FIGURE 4-64

2

• **If necessary, click the Marketing Plan Slide master thumbnail on the left slide of the screen.**

• **Click the word, <footer>, in the Footer Area on the slide master.**

• **Type** Eastwood Financial Aid Office **in the footer text box.**

The Marketing Plan title master and slide master slide thumbnails display (Figure 4-65). The new footer text is displayed in the slide master Footer Area.

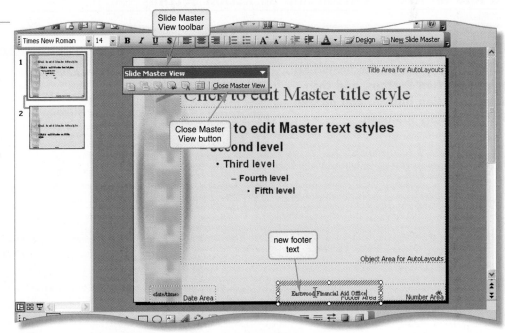

FIGURE 4-65

You have made a color scheme change on all five slides in the presentation and a footer change on the title slide in the presentation. The next steps will add an action button to the slide master.

Adding an Action Button on the Slide Master

With the footer changed on the title master, you now can add variety to your presentation by placing an action button on the slide master. An **action button** is a built-in 3-D button that can perform specific tasks such as display the next slide, provide help, give information, and play a sound. In addition, the action button can activate a hyperlink that allows users to jump to a specific slide in the presentation.

In this presentation, you will associate the action button with a hyperlink to Slide 5. When Eastwood State College speakers are lecturing about college costs, they might want to jump to the last slide in the presentation and then access a Web site for further information. One method of jumping easily to Slide 5 is to click the action button at the bottom-right corner of the slide.

Creating the action button and hyperlink requires several steps. First, add an action button and create a link to Slide 5. Then, to add variety, modify the action button by changing its size and color. The following sections describe how to add and modify an action button.

Adding an Action Button and an Action Setting

You will be able to display Slide 5 easily at any point in the presentation simply by clicking the action button. When you click the action button, a cash register sound will play. The next section describes how to create the action button and place it on the slide master.

To Add an Action Button and an Action Setting

1

• **Click Slide Show on the menu bar, point to Action Buttons, and then point to Action Button: End on the Action Buttons submenu.**

The Action Buttons submenu displays 12 built-in 3-D buttons (Figure 4-66).

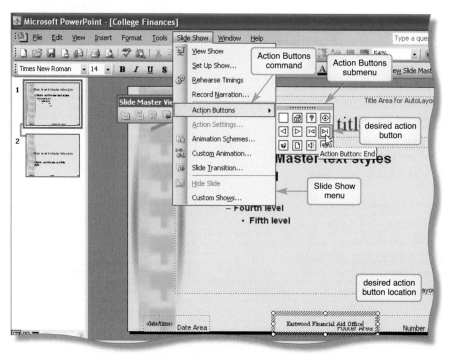

FIGURE 4-66

2

- **Click Action Button: End.**
- **Click the bottom-right corner of the slide master.**
- **If necessary, when the Action Settings dialog box is displayed, click the Mouse Click tab.**

The Action Settings dialog box is displayed (Figure 4-67) with the action button placed on Slide 2. Hyperlink to is the default Action on click. Last Slide displays in the Hyperlink to list box because the End action button is selected. The hyperlink can be established in other locations in the slide show or elsewhere.

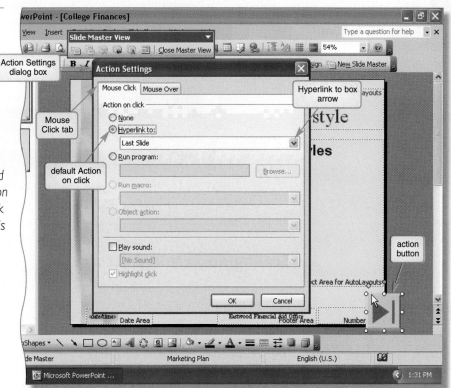

FIGURE 4-67

3

- **Click Play sound.**
- **Click the Play sound box arrow, click the down scroll arrow, and then click Cash Register.**

A check mark displays in the Play sound check box, and the Cash Register sound is selected (Figure 4-68). The Play sound list displays sounds that can play when you click the action button. You may have to install the Sound Effects feature to enable this sound function; if a Microsoft Office PowerPoint dialog box is displayed asking if you want to install the Sound Effects feature, click the Yes button.

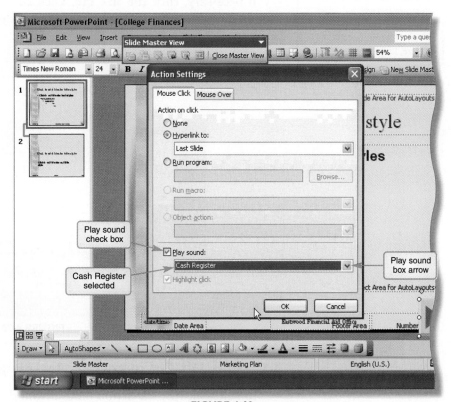

FIGURE 4-68

4

• **Click the OK button.**

The action button is highlighted on the slide master as indicated by the sizing handles (Figure 4-69).

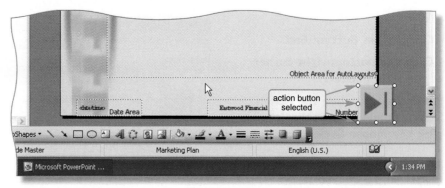

FIGURE 4-69

Scaling an Action Button

The size of the action button can be decreased. The following steps scale the action button.

To Scale an Action Button

1 **With the slide master displaying, right-click the action button and then click Format AutoShape on the shortcut menu.**

2 **If necessary, click the Size tab. Click Lock aspect ratio in the Scale area and then triple-click the Height text box in the Scale area. Type** 80 **in the Height box.**

3 **Click the OK button.**

The action button is resized to 80 percent of its original size (Figure 4-70).

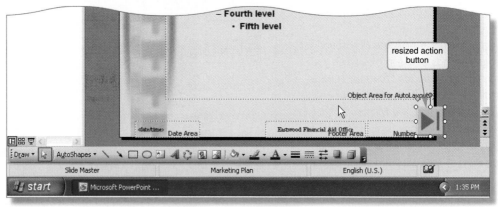

FIGURE 4-70

Adding a Fill Color to the Action Button

To better identify the action button from the slide background, you can add fill color. **Fill color** is the interior color of a selected object. The following steps add fill color to the action button on the slide master.

To Add a Fill Color to the Action Button

1

• **With the action button selected on the slide master, click the Fill Color button arrow on the Drawing toolbar.**

The Fill Color palette is displayed (Figure 4-71). Automatic is selected, indicating that medium blue is the current default fill color based on the Marketing Plan design template color scheme. Light purple is the default Follow Accent and Hyperlink Scheme Color.

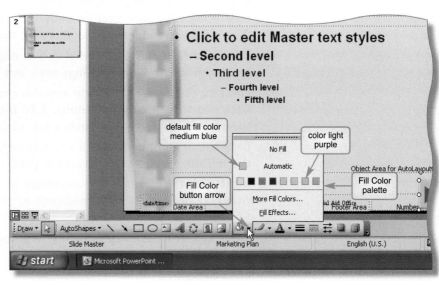

FIGURE 4-71

2

• **Click the color light purple (row 1, column 7).**

The action button displays filled with the color light purple (Figure 4-72).

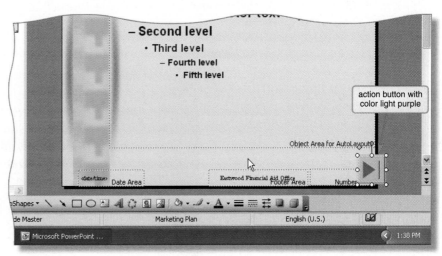

FIGURE 4-72

The slide master action button is filled with the color light purple. The fill color now is set to this color. The next step is to position the action button precisely in a desired location on the slide master.

Displaying Guides and Positioning the Action Button

Earlier in this project you used the PowerPoint grid and guides to align the WordArt text object on Slide 1. The guides will help you position the action button on the slide master. The steps on the next page will display the guides and align the action button.

Other Ways

1. On Format menu click AutoShape, click Colors tab and Lines tab
2. Right-click action button, click Format AutoShape on shortcut menu, click Colors and Lines tab
3. Press ALT+O, press O
4. In Voice Command mode, say "Format, AutoShape, Colors and Lines"

To Display Guides and Position the Action Button

1 With the slide master visible, right-click anywhere in the blue area of the slide except the title text or body text placeholders or the action button. Click Grid and Guides on the shortcut menu.

2 When the Grid and Guides dialog box displays, click Display drawing guides on screen in the Guide settings area and then click the OK button.

3 Point to the horizontal guide anywhere in the gray area outside of the slide. Click and then drag the guide to 2.20 inches below center. If necessary, drag the vertical guide to 4.50 inches left of center.

4 Drag the action button until the top edge snaps to the horizontal guide and the left edge snaps to the vertical guide.

5 Right-click the slide master anywhere in the blue area of the slide except the title text or body text placeholders or the action button. Click Grid and Guides on the shortcut menu.

6 When the Grid and Guides dialog box displays, click Display drawing guides on screen in the Guide settings area.

7 Click the OK button.

The action button is positioned in the lower-left corner of the slide (Figure 4-73). The guides are hidden.

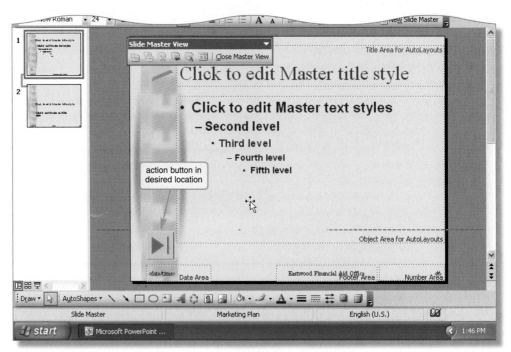

FIGURE 4-73

The action button displays in the desired location.

Rotating the Action Button

The Marketing Plan design template has a vertical purple and green stripe on the left side of the slide. Near the top of this stripe is a triangle positioned on an angle with one end pointing toward the upper-left corner of the slide. To add variety to your presentation, you want to balance the visual element of the stripe by rotating the action button so one end points toward the lower-right slide corner. Many PowerPoint objects can be rotated, including AutoShapes, pictures, and WordArt. The objects can be rotated in two ways. To rotate the object to any angle, drag the green rotate handle on the object in the direction you want it to rotate. The following steps describe how to rotate the action button on the slide master.

To Rotate the Action Button

1

• **With the slide master active, click the action button to select it.**

• **Drag the rotate handle on the action button to the right approximately 45 degrees.**

The action button turns toward the lower-right corner of the slide (Figure 4-74).

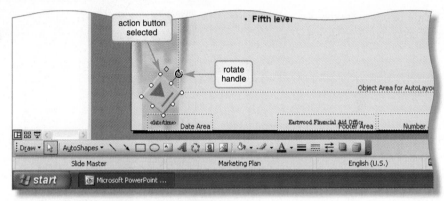

FIGURE 4-74

2

• **Click outside the rotate handle.**

The action button rotation is set (Figure 4-75).

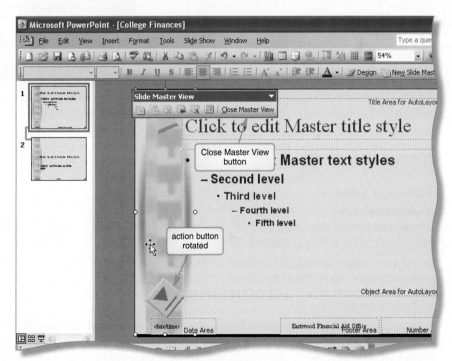

FIGURE 4-75

Other Ways

1. Click Draw button on the Drawing toolbar, point to Rotate or Flip, click Rotate Left 90° or Rotate Right 90°

Closing Master View

Now that all the changes to the slide master are complete, you can exit master view and return to normal view. All slides in the presentation have a new color scheme, a revised footer has been added to Slide 1, and an action button has been added to Slides 2 through 5. The following step closes master view.

To Close Master View

1

• **Click the Close Master View button on the Slide Master View toolbar.**

Slide 4 displays with the new color scheme and action button (Figure 4-76).

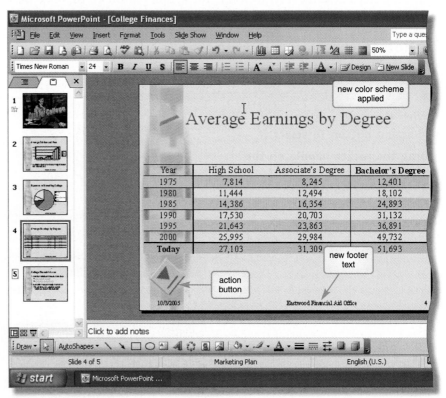

FIGURE 4-76

More About

Rotating Objects

Rotating objects on your slides can create an interesting effect. Once you select the AutoShape, picture, or WordArt object, you can rotate the object 90 degrees to the left or to the right by clicking the Draw button on the Drawing toolbar, pointing to Rotate or Flip, and then clicking Rotate Left or Rotate Right. If you press the SHIFT key while dragging the rotate handle, you will constrain the object's rotation to 15-degree angles.

You now should save your presentation because you have done a substantial amount of work.

All text and graphical elements have been added to the five slides in the presentation. You now will modify the presentation format by adding transition and sound effects and rehearsing the presentation timing.

Modifying the Presentation Format

PowerPoint allows you to control the way you advance from one slide to another by adding a **slide transition**. The AutoContent Wizard added animations to the slides, but it did not apply a slide transition. Some animation schemes include transitions, but if the one you select does not or if you want to change the transition, Power-Point allows you to apply this effect using the Slide Transition task pane. A slide transition can be applied to a single slide, a group of slides, or an entire presentation.

The second modification you will make is to rehearse the slide timing. When you **rehearse timings**, you start the slide show in **rehearsal mode** and then specify the number of seconds you want each slide to display on the screen when you run the slide show.

Adding a Slide Transition Effect to a Slide Show

PowerPoint has more than 50 unique slide transition effects, and you can vary the speed of each in a presentation. The name of the slide transition characterizes the visual effect that is displayed. For example, the slide transition effect, Split Vertical Out, displays the next slide by covering the previous slide with two vertical boxes moving from the center of the screen until the two boxes reach the left and right edges of the screen. The effect is similar to opening draw drapes over a window.

PowerPoint requires you to select at least one slide before applying slide transition effects. In this presentation, you apply slide transition effects to all slides except the title slide. Because Slide 5 already is selected, you must select Slides 2, 3, and 4. The quickest method of selecting these slides is by using the SHIFT+click technique you used to delete slides in this project.

The slide show includes the **Shape Diamond slide transition effect** between slides. That is, all slides begin stacked on top of one another, like a deck of cards. As you click the mouse button to view the next slide, the new slide enters the screen by starting at the center of the slide and opening up in a circle to the edges.

The following steps apply the Shape Diamond slide transition effect to the College Finances presentation.

More About

Delivering Presentations

If you want to be a better public speaker, consider joining Toastmasters International. This non-profit organization has helped more than three million people lose their fears of public speaking, become better listeners, and advance in their careers. Toastmasters members meet frequently and practice various types of public speaking, including giving prepared and impromptu speeches, conducting meetings, and giving and receiving constructive feedback. To learn more about this organization and to find a local chapter near you, visit the PowerPoint 2003 More About Web page (scsite.com/ppt2003/more) and click Delivering.

To Add a Slide Transition Effect to a Slide Show

1

• **Click Slide 5 on the Slides tab.**

• **Press and hold down the SHIFT key and then click Slide 2.**

• **Release the SHIFT key.**

Slides 2 through 5 are selected, as indicated by the heavy border around each slide.

2

• **Point to Slide 2 and right-click.**

• **Point to Slide Transition on the shortcut menu (Figure 4-77).**

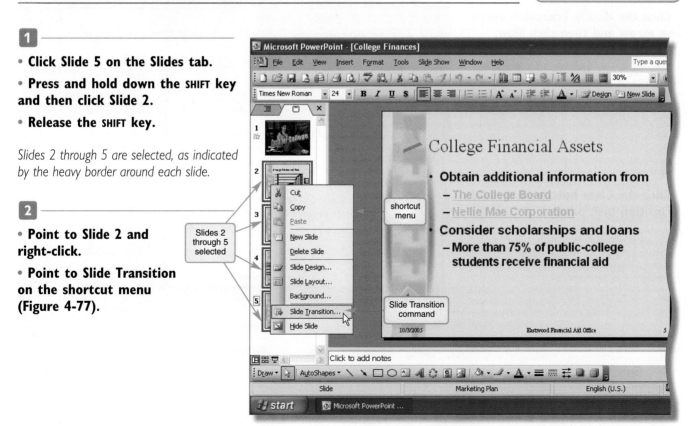

FIGURE 4-77

3

• **Click Slide Transition.**

• **When the Slide Transition task pane is displayed, click the down scroll arrow in the Apply to selected slides list until Shape Diamond is displayed.**

• **Click Shape Diamond.**

The Slide Transition task pane is displayed (Figure 4-78). The Apply to selected slides list displays available slide transition effects. The effect is previewed in the slide pane because the AutoPreview check box is checked. To see the preview again, click the Play button. To preview the effect on all slides in the presentation, click the Slide Show button.

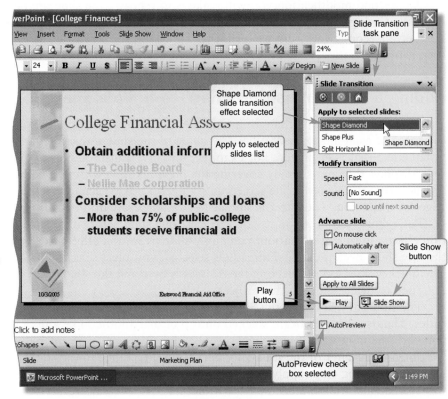

FIGURE 4-78

4

• **Click the Modify Transition Speed box arrow and then click Slow.**

The effect is previewed again in the slide pane. Slow is displayed in the Modify Transition Speed box (Figure 4-79). You can select a transition speed of Slow, Medium, or Fast.

5

• **Click the Close button in the Slide Transition task pane.**

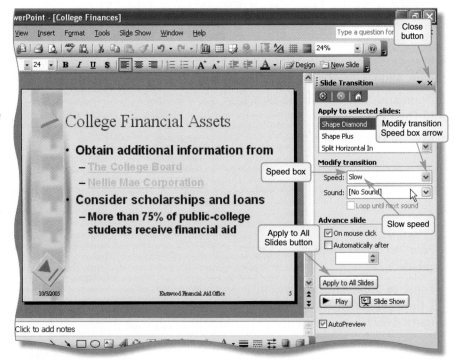

FIGURE 4-79

To apply slide transition effects to every slide in the presentation, right-click a slide, click Slide Transition on the shortcut menu, choose the desired slide transition effect, and then click the Apply to All Slides button in the Slide Transition task pane. To remove slide transition effects, select the slides to which slide transition effects are applied, click the up scroll arrow in the Apply to selected slides list until No Transition is displayed, and then click No Transition.

The Shape Diamond slide transition effect has been applied to the presentation. You should save the slide show again. The next step in creating this slide show is to set timings for the slide show.

Rehearsing Timings

In previous slide shows, you clicked to advance from one slide to the next. Because all slide components have been added to the five slides in the presentation, you now can set the time each slide is displayed on the screen. You can set these times in two ways. One method is to specify each slide's display time manually in the Slide Transition task pane. The second method is to use PowerPoint's **rehearsal feature**, which allows you to advance through the slides at your own pace, and the amount of time you view each slide is recorded. You will use the second technique in this project.

When you begin rehearsing a presentation, the Rehearsal toolbar is displayed. The **Rehearsal toolbar** contains buttons that allow you to start, pause, and repeat viewing the slides in the slide show and to view the times for each slide and the elapsed time. Table 4-4 describes the buttons on the Rehearsal toolbar.

Other Ways

1. Select slides, on Slide Show menu click Slide Transition, select desired transition, select desired transition speed, click Close button
2. Select slides, press ALT+D, press T, press arrow keys to select desired transition, press ENTER, press arrows keys to select desired transition speed, click Close button
3. In Voice Command mode, say "Slide Show, Slide Transition"

Table 4-4 Rehearsal Toolbar Buttons

BUTTON	BUTTON NAME	DESCRIPTION
→	Next	Displays the next slide or next animated element on the slide.
‖	Pause	Stops the timer. Click the Next or Pause button to resume timing.
0:00:19	Slide Time	Indicates the length of time a slide has displayed. You can enter a slide time directly in the Slide Time box.
↺	Repeat	Clears the Slide Time box and resets the timer to 0:00.
0:00:19	Elapsed Time	Indicates slide show total time.

Table 4-5 indicates the desired timings for the five slides in the College Finances presentation. Slide 1 is displayed and the effect plays for 40 seconds. Slide 5 has the two hyperlinks, so you need to allow time to view the Web sites if you decide to display that slide.

Table 4-5 Slide Rehearsal Timings

SLIDE NUMBER	DISPLAY TIME	ELAPSED TIME
1	0:00	0:40
2	0:20	1:00
3	0:20	1:20
4	0:20	1:40
5	0:50	2:30

The following steps add slide timings to the slide show.

To Rehearse Timings

1

• **Click Slide Show on the menu bar and then click Rehearse Timings.**

• **Point to the Next button on the Rehearsal toolbar.**

Slide 1 is displayed and the Marketing Music sound effect plays (Figure 4-80).

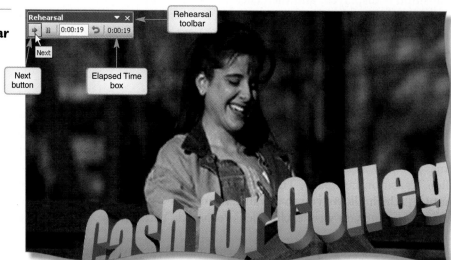

FIGURE 4-80

2

• **When the Elapsed Time box displays 0:40, click the Next button.**

Slide 2 is displayed.

3

• **When the Elapsed Time box displays 1:00, click the Next button to display Slide 3.**

• **When the Elapsed Time box displays 1:20, click the Next button to display Slide 4.**

• **When the Elapsed Time box displays 1:40, press H to display Slide 5.**

• **When the Elapsed Time box displays 2:30, click the Next button to display the black slide.**

• **Point to the Yes button in the Microsoft Office PowerPoint dialog box.**

The Microsoft Office PowerPoint dialog box displays the total time and asks if you want to keep the new slide timings with a total elapsed time of 0:02:30 (Figure 4-81).

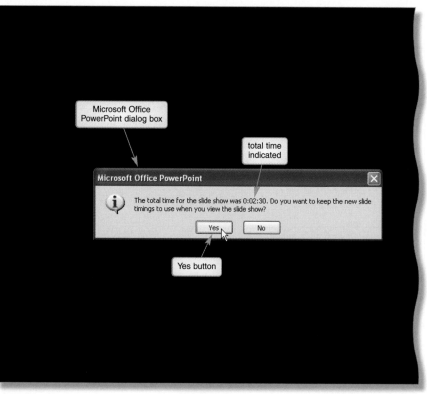

FIGURE 4-81

4

• **Click the Yes button.**

Each slide's timing is displayed in the lower-left corner in slide sorter view (Figure 4-82).

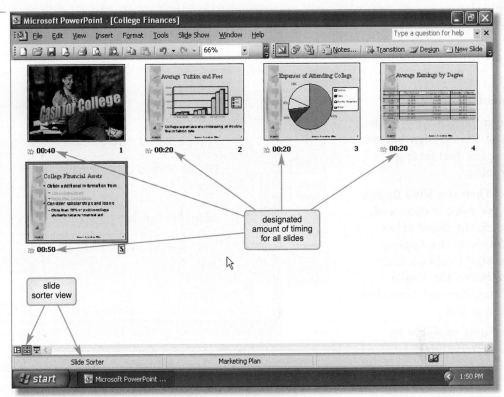

designated amount of timing for all slides

slide sorter view

FIGURE 4-82

The College Finances slide timing is complete. The presentation will run two minutes and thirty seconds.

Replacing the Slide Master

To add more variety to the presentation, you want to apply more than one design template. This feature is referred to as support for multiple masters. Each design template inserts a title and slide master automatically into the presentation, so more than one set of slide-title master pairs is displayed in Slide Master view. The steps on the next page describe how to apply a second design template to the College Finances presentation.

To Replace the Slide Master

1

• **In slide sorter view, double-click Slide 5.**

• **In normal view, click the Slide Design button on the Formatting toolbar.**

• **When the Slide Design task pane is displayed, click the down scroll arrow in the Apply a design template list, point to the Radial template, and then click the arrow.**

• **Point to Apply to Selected Slides.**

Radial is the desired design template for Slide 5 (Figure 4-83). If the Radial template is not displayed in the Apply a design template list, click the Additional Design Templates template to install additional templates or see your instructor.

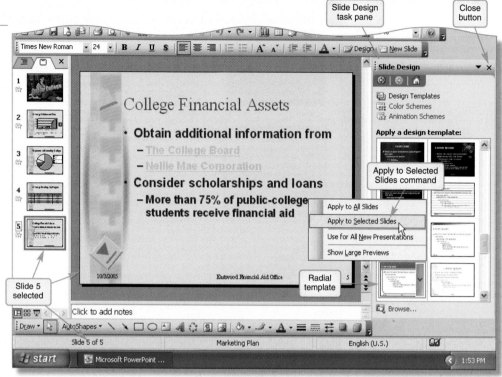

FIGURE 4-83

2

• **Click Apply to Selected Slides.**

• **Click the Close button in the Slide Design task pane.**

Slide 5 is displayed with the Radial design template (Figure 4-84).

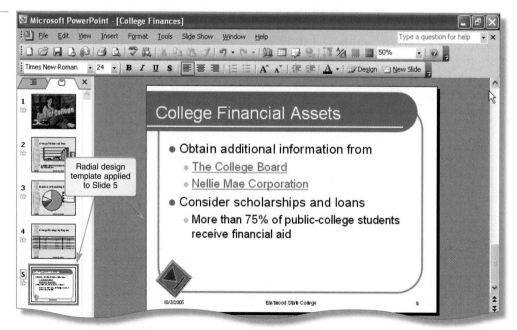

FIGURE 4-84

Slides 1 through 4 in the presentation have the Marketing Plan design template, and Slide 5 has the Radial design template. You should save these changes by clicking the Save button on the Formatting toolbar.

Adding Notes and Printing Speaker Notes

Slides and handouts usually are printed to distribute to audience members. These printouts also are helpful to speakers so they can write notes that will guide them through a presentation. As you create slides, you may find material you want to state verbally and do not want to include on the slide. You can type and format notes in the **notes pane** as you work in normal view and then print this information as **notes pages**. Notes pages print with a small image of the slide at the top and the comments below the slide. Charts, tables, and pictures added to the notes pane also print on these pages. You can make changes to the **notes master** if you want to alter the default settings, such as the font or the position of page elements, such as the slide area and notes area.

Adding Notes

In this project, comments are added to Slides 2, 4, and 5. After adding comments, you can print a set of speaker notes. The following steps add text to the notes pane on these slides and then print the notes.

To Add Notes

1

• **With Slide 5 displaying, click the notes pane and then type** More than $90 billion in financial aid is available in the form of grants, loans, and jobs.

The notes provide supplementary information for a speaker at a presentation (Figure 4-85)

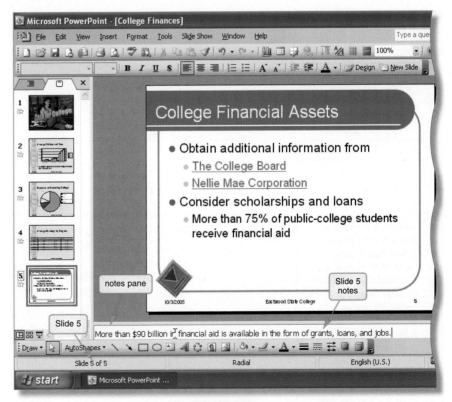

FIGURE 4-85

2

• **Click the Previous Slide button to display Slide 4.**

• **Click the notes pane and then type** Most graduates state that their increased earnings make their bachelor's degree a worthwhile investment.

3

• **Click the Previous Slide button two times to display Slide 2.**

• **Click the notes pane and then type** Every year it becomes increasingly difficult for students to afford attending college. Many students use their credit cards to fund their educations.

Only the last line of these notes is displayed (Figure 4–86). Dragging the splitter bar up enlarges the notes pane. Clicking the notes pane scroll arrows allows you to view all of the text.

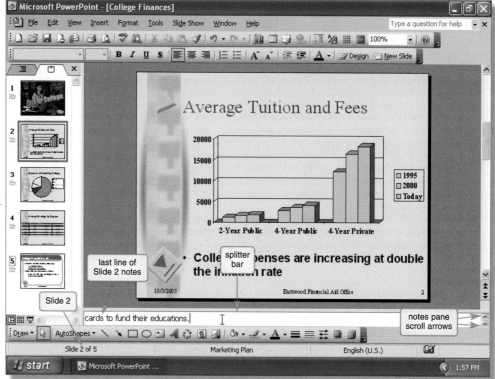

FIGURE 4-86

Other Ways

1. In Dictation mode, say "[select Slide 5 notes pane], More than $90 billion in financial aid is available in the form of grants, loans, and jobs., [select Slide 4 notes pane], Most graduates state that their increased earnings make their bachelor's degree a worthwhile investment., [select Slide 2 notes pane], Every year it becomes increasingly difficult for students to afford attending college. Many students use their credit cards to fund their educations."

Printing Speaker Notes

These notes give additional information that supplements the text on the slides. The following steps print the speaker notes.

To Print Speaker Notes

1

• **Click File on the menu bar and then click Print.**

• **When the Print dialog box is displayed, click the Print what box arrow and then click Notes Pages.**

The Print dialog box is displayed (Figure 4-87). Notes Pages appears highlighted in the Print what box.

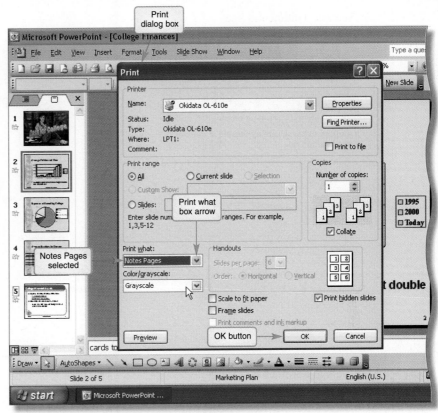

FIGURE 4-87

2

• **Click the OK button.**

PowerPoint displays the five notes pages (Figure 4-88). The notes appear on Slides 2, 4, and 5.

(a) Page 1

FIGURE 4-88

(continued)

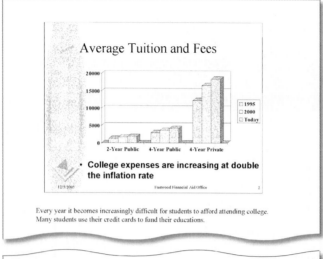

Every year it becomes increasingly difficult for students to afford attending college. Many students use their credit cards to fund their educations.

(b) Page 2

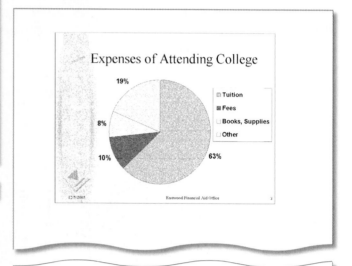

(c) Page 3

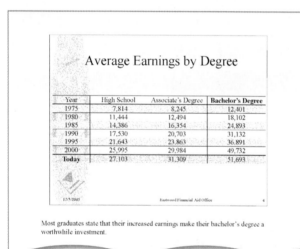

Most graduates state that their increased earnings make their bachelor's degree a worthwhile investment.

(d) Page 4

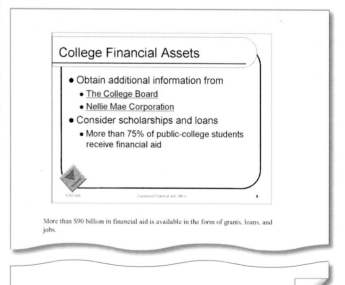

More than $90 billion in financial aid is available in the form of grants, loans, and jobs.

(e) Page 5

Other Ways

1. On File menu click Print Preview, click Notes Pages in Print What list, click Print button on Print Preview toolbar
2. Press ALT+F, press P, press TAB, press W, press DOWN ARROW key until Notes Pages is selected, press ENTER, press ENTER
3. In Voice Command mode, say "File, Print, Print What, Notes Pages, OK"

FIGURE 4-88 *(continued)*

Saving the Presentation in Rich Text Format

The presentation is complete. You now should spell check and then save it again by clicking the Spelling and Save buttons, respectively, on the Standard toolbar. So you can import the text into a Word document or another word processing package, you will save the presentation in **Rich Text Format (.rtf)**. When you save the file as an .rtf outline, you lose any graphics, such as the Word table and Excel worksheet. The following steps save the presentation as an .rtf outline.

More About

Page Orientation

Once you change the page orientation for slides or for the outline, handouts, and notes pages, you may discover that your text placeholders or other slide objects are not proportional or no longer look balanced on the slide. If this occurs, consider changing the shape or placement of these slide elements on each slide. If the change needs to be made on every slide, make the modifications on the slide master.

To Save the Presentation in Rich Text Format

1

• **Click File on the menu bar and then click Save As.**

2

• **When the Save As dialog box is displayed, click the Save as type box arrow, scroll down, and then click Outline/RTF.**

You can save the presentation in a variety of formats (Figure 4-89).

3

• **Click the Save button.**

PowerPoint saves the text of the presentation with the file name College Finances.rtf. If no more space remains on your Data Disk, insert another floppy disk.

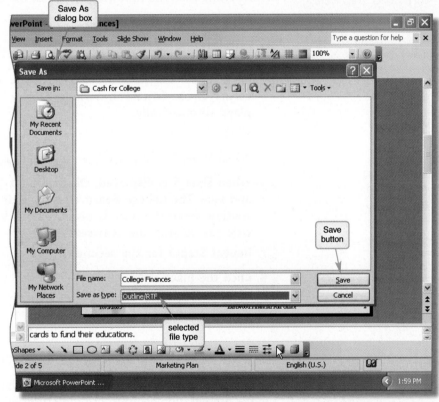

FIGURE 4-89

Other Ways

1. Press ALT+F, press A, press ALT+T, press DOWN ARROW key, press ENTER, press ENTER
2. In Voice Command mode, say "File, Save As, Save as type, Outline RTF, Save"

Running a Slide Show with Hyperlinks and an Action Button

The College Finances presentation contains a variety of useful features that provide value to an audience. The hyperlinks on Slide 5 show useful Web sites that give current information on finding cash to finance a college education. In addition, the action button allows a presenter to jump to Slide 5 while Slides 2, 3, or 4 are being displayed. If an audience member asks a question or if the presenter needs to answer specific questions regarding financial aid, the information on Slide 5 can be accessed immediately by clicking the action button.

Running a Slide Show with Hyperlinks to the Internet

Running a slide show that contains hyperlinks is the same as running any other slide show. When a presentation contains hyperlinks and you are connected to the Internet, you can click the hyperlink text to command your default browser to locate the hyperlink file. The following steps run the College Finances presentation.

To Run the Slide Show with Hyperlinks to the Internet

1 **Click Slide 1 on the Slides tab. Click the Slide Show button at the lower-left corner of the PowerPoint window. Slide 1 is displayed and the sound effect plays automatically.**

2 **Slides 2, 3, and 4 are displayed according to the slide timings.**

3 **When Slide 4 is displayed, press the H key.**

4 **When Slide 5 is displayed, click the first hyperlink to start your browser and view The College Board Web page. If necessary, maximize the Web page window when the page is displayed. Click the Close button on the Web page title bar to stop the browser.**

5 **Repeat Step 3 for the second hyperlink.**

6 **Click the black slide.**

Slide 1 is displayed in normal view.

Running a Slide Show with an Action Button

Once you have run the presentation and have seen all slides display, you should run the presentation again to use the action button. When you click the action button in the College Finances slide show, PowerPoint will display Slide 5 because you hyperlinked the button to the last slide in the presentation. When Slide 5 is displayed and you view the information and Web sites, you want to return to one of the other slides in the presentation. Jumping to particular slides in a presentation is called **navigating**. PowerPoint provides a set of keyboard shortcuts to help you navigate to various slides during the slide show. These navigational features are listed in Table 4-6.

Table 4-6 Navigation Shortcut Keys	
KEYBOARD SHORTCUT	**PURPOSE**
N Click SPACEBAR RIGHT ARROW DOWN ARROW ENTER PAGE DOWN	Advance to the next slide
P BACKSPACE LEFT ARROW UP ARROW PAGE UP	Return to the previous slide
Number followed by ENTER	Go to a specific slide
B	Display a black screen
PERIOD	Return to slide show from a black screen
W	Display a white screen
COMMA	Return to slide show from a white screen
ESC CTRL+BREAK HYPHEN	End a slide show

When running a slide show, you can press the F1 key to see a list of these keyboard controls. The following steps describe how the action button can be used to enhance a slide show being displayed in front of an audience.

To Run the Slide Show with an Action Button

1 **If necessary, click Slide 1 on the Slides tab. Click the Slide Show button at the lower-left corner of the PowerPoint window.**

2 **When Slide 3 is displayed, click the action button.**

3 **When Slide 5 is displayed, type the number 3 and then press the ENTER key to return to Slide 3.**

More About

The PowerPoint Help System

Need Help? It is no further than the Type a question for help box on the menu bar in the upper-right corner of the window. Click the box that contains the text, Type a question for help (Figure 4-89 on page PPT 289), type help, and then press the ENTER key. PowerPoint responds with a list of topics you can click to learn about obtaining help on any PowerPoint-related topic. To find out what is new in PowerPoint 2003, type what is new in PowerPoint in the Type a question for help box.

Delivering and Navigating a Presentation Using the Slide Show Toolbar

When you begin running a slide show and move the mouse pointer, the Slide Show toolbar is displayed. The **Slide Show toolbar** contains buttons that allow you to navigate to the next side or previous slide, mark up the current slide, or change the current display. When you move the mouse, the toolbar is displayed in the lower-left corner of the slide; it disappears after the mouse has not been moved for three seconds. Table 4-7 describes the buttons on the Slide Show toolbar.

Table 4-7   Slide Show Toolbar Buttons

BUTTON	DESCRIPTION	FUNCTION
	previous slide	Previous slide or previous animated element on the slide
	pointer arrow	Shortcut menu for arrows, pens, and highlighters
	slide show options	Shortcut menu for slide navigation and screen displays
	next slide	Next slide or next animated element on the slide

You click the arrow buttons on either end of the toolbar to navigate backward or forward through the slide show. The pointer arrow button has a variety of functions, most often to add **ink** notes or drawings to your presentation to emphasize aspects of slides or make handwritten notes. This feature is available in all views except Slide Sorter view. To highlight items on a slide in Slide Show view, you would follow these steps.

To Highlight Items on a Slide

1 If the Slide Show toolbar is not visible, rest the mouse pointer on the slide or click Options on the Tools menu, click the View tab and then click Show popup toolbar.

2 On the Slide Show toolbar, click the pointer arrow and then click Highlighter.

3 Move the mouse to highlight any area of the slide.

Instead of the Highlighter, you also can click Ballpoint Pen and Felt Tip Pen to draw or write notes on the slides. To change the color of ink during the presentation, you would perform the following step.

To Change Ink Color

1 Click the pointer arrow, point to Ink Color, and the select the desired color.

When the presentation ends, PowerPoint will prompt you to keep or discard the ink annotations.

To hide the mouse pointer and Slide Show toolbar during the slide show, you would perform the following step.

To Hide the Mouse Pointer and Slide Show Toolbar

1 **Click the pointer arrow on the Slide Show toolbar, point to Arrow Options, and then click Hidden.**

By default, the mouse pointer and toolbar are set at Automatic, which means they are hidden after three seconds of no movement. After you hide the mouse pointer and toolbar, they remain hidden until you choose one of the other commands on the Pointer Options submenu. They are displayed again when you move the mouse.

To keep the mouse pointer and toolbar displayed at all times during a slide show, you would perform the following step.

To Constantly Display the Mouse Pointer and Slide Show Toolbar

1 **Click the pointer arrow on the Slide Show toolbar, point to Arrow Options, and then click Visible.**

When you click the slide show options button on the Slide Show toolbar, PowerPoint displays the Popup menu that appears when you right-click a slide in slide sorter view. This menu is described on pages PPT 48 – 50.

The College Finances presentation now is complete. If you made any changes to your presentation since your last save, you now should save it again before quitting PowerPoint.

Project Summary

Project 4 started by using the AutoContent Wizard to generate some text and graphics using the Marketing Plan design template. After adding a picture to the title slide background, you created a WordArt title and added a sound effect to that slide. Next, you used Microsoft Graph to create a chart and then inserted an Excel chart and added a Word table. You then created a slide containing hyperlinks to Web sites containing additional financial aid information. You then customized presentation elements by changing the color scheme, modifying the footer, and adding an action button. You used the Thesaurus to change the slide wording. After adding and modifying the slide elements, you added slide transitions, rehearsed timings, and inserted a second slide master. To assist the individual who is presenting the slide show, you added notes to the slides and printed speaker notes. Finally, you saved the presentation in Rich Text Format and then ran the slide show to display the hyperlinks.

 If you have a SAM user profile, you may have access to hands-on instruction, practice, and assessment of the skills covered in this project. Log in to your SAM account and go to your assignments page to see what your instructor has assigned.

What You Should Know

Having completed this project, you should be able to perform the tasks below. The tasks are listed in the same order they were presented in this project. For a list of the buttons, menus, toolbars, and commands introduced in this project, see the Quick Reference Summary at the back of this book and refer to the Page Number column.

1. Start and Customize a New Presentation (PPT 228)
2. Use the AutoContent Wizard (PPT 229)
3. Create a Folder and Save a Presentation (PPT 232)
4. Add a Picture to Create a Custom Background (PPT 232)
5. Delete the Title and Subtitle Text Placeholders (PPT 234)
6. Select a WordArt Style (PPT 236)
7. Enter the WordArt Text (PPT 237)
8. Change the WordArt Height and Width (PPT 239)
9. Display the Grid and Guides and Position the WordArt Object (PPT 241)
10. Hide Guides (PPT 243)
11. Add a Sound Effect (PPT 243)
12. Delete Slides (PPT 245)
13. Display the Next Slide and Edit the Title and Bulleted List Text (PPT 247)
14. Change the Slide Layout and Position the Text Placeholder (PPT 248)
15. Insert a Chart and Replace the Sample Data (PPT 249)
16. Display the Next Slide, Edit the Title Text, and Delete the Text Placeholder (PPT 252)
17. Insert an Excel Chart (PPT 253)
18. Scale and Move an Excel Chart (PPT 256)
19. Display the Next Slide, Edit the Title Text, and Change the Slide Layout (PPT 257)
20. Insert a Word Table (PPT 258)
21. Scale and Move a Word Table (PPT 259)
22. Display the Next Slide and Edit the Text (PPT 260)
23. Add a Hyperlink to a Slide (PPT 261)
24. Add the Remaining Hyperlink to a Slide (PPT 262)
25. Hide a Slide (PPT 264)
26. Find Text (PPT 265)
27. Find and Replace Text (PPT 265)
28. Find a Word and Use the Thesaurus (PPT 266)
29. Find a Second Synonym (PPT 268)
30. Change the Presentation Template Color Scheme (PPT 269)
31. Modify the Footer on the Slide Master (PPT 271)
32. Add an Action Button and an Action Setting (PPT 272)
33. Scale an Action Button (PPT 274)
34. Add a Fill Color to the Action Button (PPT 275)
35. Display Guides and Position the Action Button (PPT 276)
36. Rotate the Action Button (PPT 277)
37. Close Master View (PPT 278)
38. Add a Slide Transition Effect to a Slide Show (PPT 279)
39. Rehearse Timings (PPT 282)
40. Replace the Slide Master (PPT 284)
41. Add Notes (PPT 285)
42. Print Speaker Notes (PPT 287)
43. Save the Presentation in Rich Text Format (PPT 289)
44. Run the Slide Show with Hyperlinks to the Internet (PPT 290)
45. Run the Slide Show with an Action Button (PPT 291)
46. Highlight Items on a Slide (PPT 292)
47. Change Ink Color (PPT 292)
48. Hide the Mouse Pointer and Slide Show Toolbar (PPT 293)
49. Constantly Display the Mouse Pointer and Slide Show Toolbar (PPT 293)

Learn It Online

Instructions: To complete the Learn It Online exercises, start your browser, click the Address bar, and then enter the Web address scsite.com/ppt2003/learn. When the PowerPoint 2003 Learn It Online page is displayed, follow the instructions in the exercises below. Each exercise has instructions for printing your results, either for your own records or for submission to your instructor.

1 Project Reinforcement TF, MC, and SA

Below PowerPoint Project 4, click the Project Reinforcement link. Print the quiz by clicking Print on the File menu for each page. Answer each question.

2 Flash Cards

Below PowerPoint Project 4, click the Flash Cards link and read the instructions. Type 20 (or a number specified by your instructor) in the Number of playing cards text box, type your name in the Enter your Name text box, and then click the Flip Card button. When the flash card is displayed, read the question and then click the ANSWER box arrow to select an answer. Flip through Flash Cards. If your score is 15 (75%) correct or greater, click Print on the File menu to print your results. If your score is less than 15 (75%) correct, then redo this exercise by clicking the Replay button.

3 Practice Test

Below PowerPoint Project 4, click the Practice Test link. Answer each question, enter your first and last name at the bottom of the page, and then click the Grade Test button. When the graded practice test is displayed on your screen, click Print on the File menu to print a hard copy. Continue to take practice tests until you score 80% or better.

4 Who Wants To Be a Computer Genius?

Below PowerPoint Project 4, click the Computer Genius link. Read the instructions, enter your first and last name at the bottom of the page, and then click the PLAY button. When your score is displayed, click the PRINT RESULTS link to print a hard copy.

5 Wheel of Terms

Below PowerPoint Project 4, click the Wheel of Terms link. Read the instructions, and then enter your first and last name and your school name. Click the PLAY button. When your score is displayed, right-click the score and then click Print on the shortcut menu to print a hard copy.

6 Crossword Puzzle Challenge

Below PowerPoint Project 4, click the Crossword Puzzle Challenge link. Read the instructions, and then enter your first and last name. Click the SUBMIT button. Work the crossword puzzle. When you are finished, click the Submit button. When the crossword puzzle is redisplayed, click the Print Puzzle button to print a hard copy.

7 Tips and Tricks

Below PowerPoint Project 4, click the Tips and Tricks link. Click a topic that pertains to Project 4. Right-click the information and then click Print on the shortcut menu. Construct a brief example of what the information relates to in PowerPoint to confirm you understand how to use the tip or trick.

8 Newsgroups

Below PowerPoint Project 4, click the Newsgroups link. Click a topic that pertains to Project 4. Print three comments.

9 Expanding Your Horizons

Below PowerPoint Project 4, click the Expanding Your Horizons link. Click a topic that pertains to Project 4. Print the information. Construct a brief example of what the information relates to in PowerPoint to confirm you understand the contents of the article.

10 Search Sleuth

Below PowerPoint Project 4, click the Search Sleuth link. To search for a term that pertains to this project, select a term below the Project 4 title and then use the Google search engine at google.com (or any major search engine) to display and print two Web pages that present information on the term.

11 PowerPoint Online Training

Below PowerPoint Project 4, click the PowerPoint Online Training link. When your browser displays the Microsoft Office Online Web page, click the PowerPoint link. Click one of the PowerPoint courses that covers one or more of the objectives listed at the beginning of the project on page PPT 226. Print the first page of the course before stepping through it.

12 Office Marketplace

Below PowerPoint Project 4, click the Office Marketplace link. When your browser displays the Microsoft Office Online Web page, click the Office Marketplace link. Click a topic that relates to PowerPoint. Print the first page.

Apply Your Knowledge

1 Seattle Fish Facts

Instructions: Start PowerPoint. Open the presentation Apply 4-1 Fish on the Data Disk. See the inside back cover of this book for instructions for downloading the Data Disk or see your instructor for information on accessing the clips and files required for this book. The two slides in the presentation give information on fish, with the background of The Seattle Aquarium on Slide 1 for interest. Make the following changes to the slides so they appear as shown in Figure 4-90.

(a) Slide 1

Category	Examples	Facts
Crustaceans	Crabs Lobster Prawns Shrimp	Smallest is the water flea, which is .0098 inch long
Saltwater	Shark Tuna Swordfish	Largest is the whale shark; it can weigh more than 20 tons
Shellfish	Clams Mussels Oysters Scallops	Some clams live more than 100 years

(b) Slide 2

FIGURE 4-90

Create a new folder with the name, Fish. Save the presentation with the file name, Apply 4-1 Seattle, in the new folder.

On Slide 1, apply the Network design template to the Title Slide slide layout and change the color scheme to the scheme in row 5, column 1. Add the picture, Seattle, from the Data Disk to the Slide 1 background and omit the background graphics from the master. Move the subtitle text placeholder down to the bottom of the slide. Change the subtitle text color to red (color 6 in the palette of available colors).

Delete the title text placeholder. Create the WordArt Object by selecting the WordArt style in row 1, column 3. Scale the WordArt height and width to 130 %. Change the WordArt object color by clicking the Fill Color button arrow on the Drawing toolbar and then clicking the color gold (color 5 in the palette of available colors). Drag the WordArt object to the position shown in Figure 4-90a.

Create a hyperlink for the WordArt object with a Seattle visitor's Web site. To create this hyperlink, select the WordArt object, click the Insert Hyperlink button on the Formatting toolbar, and then type `www.seeseattle.org` in the Address text box when the Insert Hyperlink dialog box is displayed. Click the OK button.

In the Slide 1 notes pane, type `Seattle is a scenic waterfront city with views of the Olympic and Cascade Mountains`.

Using the Slide master, add your name to the Slide 2 Footer Area. On Slide 2, apply the Ripple design template. Insert the Word table, Fish Facts, from the Data Disk. Scale the table to 160 % and then center the table under the title text placeholder.

In the Slide 2 notes pane, type The Seattle Aquarium features a Pacific coral reef, a salmon ladder, sea otters, and other fish and mammals.

Apply the Fade Smoothly slide transition effect to both slides with the Slow transition speed and the Breeze sound.

Save the presentation again and then run the slide show. Mark up the slides using the highlighter and orange ink and keep the ink annotations. Print speaker notes and then hand in the hard copies to your instructor.

In the Lab

1 Credit Card Debt

Problem: The College Finances presentation in the project explores the costs of attending college and finding monetary support for meeting the expenses. The notes on Slide 2 indicate that many students use credit cards to fund their college bills. While credit cards are convenient and generally easily accessible, they can become a burden when the balance exceeds household income. Credit card debt has risen dramatically in recent years as unemployment has increased and college expenses have increased more quickly than inflation rates. Your campus credit union offers services for students and staff and also offers a credit card. The manager, Danny Dollars, wants to emphasize that the near-record level of debt compared to disposable income is reaching dangerous levels for many students. He has surveyed the credit union members and found that the average amount of debt per household has risen for both undergraduate and graduate students in the past 15 years. The statistics from his survey are summarized in Table 4-8.

Table 4-8 Debt Percent Per Household				
	15 YEARS AGO	10 YEARS AGO	5 YEARS AGO	TODAY
Undergraduate Students	52.3	67.3	74.2	81.2
Graduate Students	63.4	76.8	81.2	87.3

You have a part-time job as a teller, and Danny has asked you to help him with seminars he is scheduling with incoming students. You have agreed to create a PowerPoint presentation to accompany his lectures and to run on a computer in the credit union office. Danny wants to approve the title slide before you work on the entire project, and you agree to create the title slide and slide showing the debt percent chart. The title slide contains a WordArt Object and a picture as the background. You create the slides shown in Figures 4-91a and 4-91b on pages PPT 298 and PPT 299.

(continued)

Credit Card Debt *(continued)*

Instructions: Perform the following tasks:

1. Start PowerPoint, open a new presentation, and apply the Slit design template. Change the color scheme to the gray scheme in row 4, column 2. Add the ATM picture from the Data Disk to the Slide 1 background and omit the background graphics from the master.

2. On Slide 1, delete the subtitle text placeholder. Create the WordArt element shown in Figure 4-91a. Use the WordArt style in row 3, column 1. Change the WordArt height to 2.5". Display the grid and guides and then position the object above the hand as shown in Figure 4-91a.

3. Type and then italicize the title text, change the font to Century Schoolbook, decrease the font size to 48, and change the font color to green (color 8 in the palette of available colors).

4. Drag the middle sizing handle on the top edge of the title text placeholder down to the top edge of the title text. Drag the title text placeholder to the bottom of the slide as shown in Figure 4-91a.

5. Insert a new slide and apply the Title and Content slide layout. Type Debt Percent Per Household in the title text placeholder. Add a chart using the data in Table 4-8 on the previous page. Scale the chart to 110 % and position the chart as shown in Figure 4-91b.

6. Add the Cover Right-Down slide transition effect to both slides. Modify the transition speed to Medium.

7. In the Slide 1 notes pane, type Use your charge card in emergencies and shop with cash. In the Slide 2 notes pane, type One of your classmates had $207,000 in credit card debt before graduation by charging tuition, books, rent, and educational expenses.

8. Save the presentation with the file name, Lab 4-1 Credit Card.

9. Display and print speaker notes. Close the presentation. Hand in the hard copy to your instructor.

FIGURE 4-91a

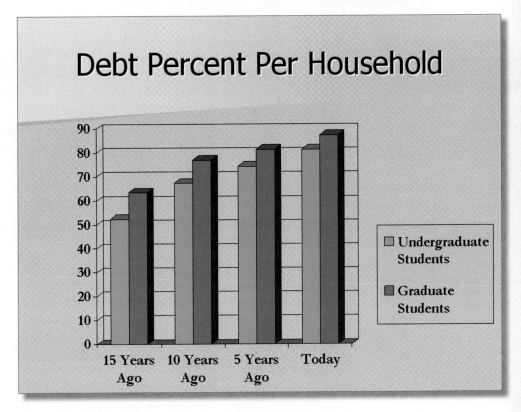

FIGURE 4-91b

2 Campus Job Fair

Problem: Every spring the Placement Office at your campus sponsors a job fair for upcoming graduates. This year the placement director wants to add interest to the event by showing a PowerPoint presentation with interesting information about the world of work. You have been asked to create this slide show that will run on a computer at a registration table on the day of the job fair. The slide show will focus on workplace facts and figures. It will include WordArt on the title slide and a chart showing the percentage of jobs in the healthcare field.

Instructions: Perform the following tasks:

1. Open a new presentation and use the AutoContent Wizard to generate content for the on-screen presentation. Use the Product/Services Overview presentation type in the Sales / Marketing category. When the Presentation options panel is displayed in the AutoContent Wizard, type Northlake College Job Fair as the presentation title and your name as the footer text. Include only the date last updated in the footer.

2. On Slide 1, modify the title text, Northlake College Job Fair, by changing the font to Bookman Old Style and italicizing and centering the text.

3. Delete the Your Logo Here placeholder in the upper-left corner and replace it with the WordArt object shown in Figure 4-92a on page PPT 301. Create this object using the WordArt style in row 5, column 1. Scale the WordArt object to 125 %.

(continued)

Campus Job Fair *(continued)*

4. Replace the subtitle text with the text shown in Figure 4-92a. Increase the subtitle text font size to 60 and bold the text. Change the font color to dark brown (color 6 in the palette of available colors).

5. Insert the sound file, Happy Urban, from the Data Disk and instruct PowerPoint to play the sound automatically. Drag the speaker icon off the slide to the lower-right corner of the screen.

6. On Slide 2, Overview, replace the bulleted text with the text shown in Figure 4-92b. Change the title text font to Bookman Old Style. Bold the title and bulleted text. Change the color scheme only for this slide to the scheme in row 2, column 1.

7. On Slide 3, replace the title text, Features & Benefits, with the title text shown in Figure 4-92c. Bold this text and change the font to Bookman Old Style. Delete the bulleted text, change the slide layout to Title Only, and then insert the Excel chart, Health Employment.xls, from the Data Disk. Scale this chart to 175 %, display the grid and guides, and position it as shown in Figure 4-92c. Insert the sound file, Heartbeat, from your Data Disk and instruct PowerPoint to play the sound automatically. Drag the speaker icon off the slide to the lower-right corner of the screen. If desired, delete the bullets.

8. On Slide 4, Applications, enter the title text shown in Figure 4-92d. Change the title text font to Bookman Old Style. Bold the text. Apply the Title and Content slide layout. If desired, delete the bullets.

9. Add a chart using the data in Table 4-9. Dr. Scholl's and the American Podiatry Association compiled these figures. Scale the chart to 105 % and position the chart as shown in Figure 4-91d.

10. Delete Slides 5, 6, and 7.

11. Use the Slide master to change the first-level paragraph bullet to a bull's eye, which is part of the Wingdings font. Increase the bullet size to 110 percent of text and change the color to black (color 2 in the palette of available colors).

12. Apply the Faded zoom animation scheme to all slides; the Cover Left-Down slide transition effect to Slides 2, 3, and 4; and the Fade Smoothly slide transition effect to Slide 1.

13. Use the Thesaurus to find a synonym for the word, positions.

14. Hide Slide 3.

15. Create a new folder with the name, Northlake College. Save the presentation with the file name, Lab 4-2 Job Fair, in the new folder. Save the presentation as a Rich Text Format outline and then send the presentation to Microsoft Word.

16. Run the Job Fair presentation. Hide Slide 2. Run the presentation again displaying all slides. Mark up the slides using the Ballpoint Pen and blue ink and keep the ink annotations.

17. Print the slides as a handout with two slides on one page.

Table 4-9	Walking Professionals
PROFESSION	**MILES WALKED YEARLY**
Police Officer	1,632
Letter Carrier	1,056
TV Reporter	1,008
Nurse	942
Doctor	840

In the Lab

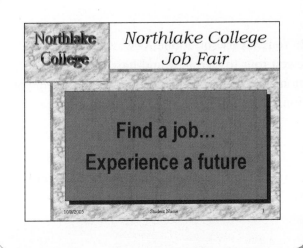

(a) Slide 1

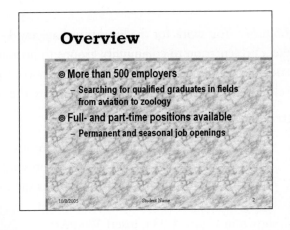

(b) Slide 2

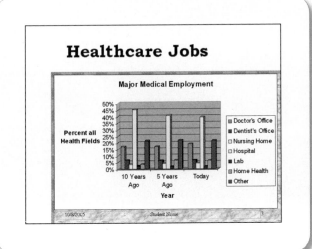

(c) Slide 3

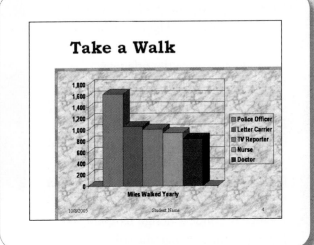

(d) Slide 4

FIGURE 4-92

In the Lab

3 U Travel 2 Travel Agency's European Tour

Problem: You work for the local travel agency, U Travel 2. Your supervisor, Annie Airway, has asked you to make a presentation to community groups to promote the newest tour to Germany and Italy. You decide to create a PowerPoint slide show to accompany your presentation and use the AutoContent Wizard to help you develop the key ideas for the slides. You create the presentation shown in Figures 4-93a through 4-93d.

Instructions: Perform the following tasks:

1. Create a new presentation, and use the AutoContent Wizard to generate content for the on-screen presentation. Use the Project Overview presentation type in the Project category. Include the date and slide number in the footer. Enter your name as the footer text.

2. On Slide 1, type the title and subtitle text shown in Figure 4-93a. Insert WordArt with the text, Book Now!, using the WordArt style in row 5, column 3. Scale the WordArt height and width to 215 %. Display the grid and guides, and position the art as shown in Figure 4-93a.

3. Delete Slides 3 and 6 through 11.

4. On Slide 2, replace the title text, Project Goals, with the text shown in Figure 4-93b. Italicize and bold this text. Delete the text placeholder. Change the slide layout to Title only. Insert the Word table, Travel Program, from the Data Disk. Scale the table to 205 % and center the table under the title text placeholder.

5. Change the Slide 2 design template to Echo and then change the color scheme to the scheme in row 5, column 2.

6. Insert an Information action button to the right of the Day 1 highlight table text, Explore Heidelberg Castle. Hyperlink the button to Slide 3 (Next Slide). Play the Wind sound when the mouse is clicked. Change the action button fill color to blue (color 7 in the palette of available colors) and scale it to 35 %.

FIGURE 4-93a

Tour Highlights

Day	City	Highlight	
1	Heidelberg	Explore Schloss Castle	ⓘ
2	Munich	Two-hour walking tour	
3	Munich	Visit Nymphenburg Palace	
4	Venice	Tour Piazza San Marco	ⓘ
5	Venice	Gondola ride on Grand Canal	
6	Lucerne	View medieval prosperity	
7	Lucerne	Boat trip to Mt. Pilatus	

2   Student Name   11/22/2005

FIGURE 4-93b

In the Lab

7. Insert an Information action button to the right of the Day 4 highlight table text, Tour Piazza San Marco. Hyperlink the button to Slide 4 (Last Slide). Play the Arrow sound when the mouse is clicked. Change the action button fill color to blue (color 7 in the palette of available colors) and scale it to 35 %.

8. On Slide 3, replace the title text with the title text, Historic Heidelberg, and then italicize and bold this text and change the font color to red (color 7 in the palette of available colors). Change the slide layout to Title, Text, and Content and replace the bulleted text with the text shown in Figure 4-93c. Insert the Heidelberg picture from the Data Disk, scale it to 25 %, display the grid and guides, and move it to the location shown in the figure. Create a hyperlink for the word, Heidelberg, with the URL, www.heidelberg.de.

9. Create a hyperlink for the Heidelberg picture to Slide 2 by selecting the picture and clicking the Insert Hyperlink button. When the Insert Hyperlink dialog box is displayed, click the Place in This Document button in the Link to list, click the 2. Tour Highlights slide title in the Select a place in this document list, and then click the OK button.

10. On Slide 4, replace the title text with the title text, Venice Vistas, and then italicize and bold this text and change the font color to red (color 7 in the palette of available colors). Change the slide layout to Title, Content, and Text and replace the bulleted text with the text shown in Figure 4-93d. Insert the Venice picture from the Data Disk, display the grid and guides, and move it to the location shown in the figure. Create a hyperlink for the word, Venice, with the URL, www.doge.it.

FIGURE 4-93c

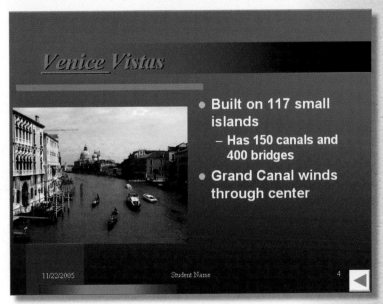

FIGURE 4-93d

(continued)

U Travel 2 Travel Agency's European Tour *(continued)*

11. On both Slide 3 and Slide 4, insert a Back or Previous action button in the lower-right corner of the slide. Hyperlink the button to Slide 2 by clicking the Hyperlink to arrow in the Action Settings dialog box, scrolling down and then clicking Slide, clicking 2. Tour Highlights in the Hyperlink to Slide dialog box, and then clicking the OK button. Change the action button fill color to white (color 2 in the row of available colors) and scale it to 50 %.

12. Apply the Comb Horizontal slide transition effect to Slides 2, 3, and 4. Modify the transition speed to Slow. Hide Slide 2.

13. Use the Thesaurus to find a synonym for the word, winds.

14. Rehearse timings for the slide show. Have Slide 1 display for 30 seconds, Slide 2 for 40 seconds, Slide 3 for 20 seconds, and Slide 4 for 20 seconds.

15. In the Slide 2 notes pane, type `Tour price includes airfare, hotels, admission to all attractions, and guided tours`. In the Slide 3 notes pane, type `This city blends old-world charm and modern-day excitement. Scholoss Castle's half-demolished state adds to its picturesque and romantic appeal`. In the Slide 4 notes pane, type `The Piazza and Basilica di San Marco are the undisputed symbols of the city. A gondola ride represents the classic romantic Venice`.

16. Run the presentation. Hide Slide 2. Run the presentation again displaying Slide 2 and using all hyperlinks.

17. Create a folder with the name, Europe. Save the presentation with the file name, Lab 4-3 Europe. Save the presentation as a Rich Text Format outline and then send the presentation to Microsoft Word. Print speaker notes. Change the page setup so that the pages print in landscape orientation, and print the presentation as a handout. Quit PowerPoint.

Cases and Places

The difficulty of these case studies varies:
■ are the least difficult and ■■ are more difficult. The last exercise is a group exercise.

Note: Remember to use the 7×7 rule as you design the presentations: a maximum of seven words on a line and a maximum of seven lines on one slide.

1 ■ Bicycling is an excellent method of achieving a low-impact cardiovascular workout while viewing the scenic outdoors. Pedaling for one hour on a flat road burns approximately 50 calories. Nearly 60 million people ride their bikes at least once a year, and 15 million bikers ride at least once weekly. Obviously the basic piece of equipment is an appropriate bike, and the key is finding the best bike for the rider's budget and recreational needs. Bikes can be grouped into three categories: comfort, fitness, and road. Comfort bikes are best suited for short rides. They cost approximately $300, have wide tires and a large seat, and weigh about 30 pounds. A rider sits upright because the handlebars are curved upwards. Fitness bikes range from $600 to $900 and are good for long, invigorating rides. The seat and tires are narrow and the handlebars are straight, so the rider's torso is slightly forward. They weigh between 22 and 29 pounds. Devoted riders prefer road bikes, which weigh less than 22 pounds. The downward-curving handlebars, thin tires, and narrow seat enhance aerodynamics. You work at Bobby's Bodacious Bikes, which carries a wide variety of bikes. Customers often have many questions about the styles and models of bikes, so you decide to simplify their purchasing decisions by developing a slide show. You start by designing a title slide that captures the spirit of biking. Modify the template color scheme and default font. Use a picture as the background on Slide 1 and add a WordArt element. Create a Word table that organizes the information in the categories of comfort, fitness, and road bikes. Use the Thesaurus to change at least 2 words. Enhance the presentation by adding sound clips and slide transition effects.

2 ■ Internet dating services were practically nonexistent in 1997 but now are the fastest growing segment of the industry. Many online services users formerly placed personal ads in newspapers, which once were the largest segment of the industry. While some of the online dating companies claim that 75 percent of their members have found a date by using the sites, some independent analysts claim that as many as 30 percent of the people who register misrepresent their age, weight, or marital status. Likewise, traditional independent dating services also are experiencing an increase in business. Sole proprietors with home-based offices run many of these operations, and their customers often have six-figure salaries. The Office of Student Activities at your college is considering starting a matchmaking program, and the director has surveyed students to see what dating services they have used throughout the years. Table 4-10 lists the survey results.

Table 4-10	Dating Services			
	1995	1998	2001	2004
Independent	120	105	90	231
Newspaper	480	360	290	210
Internet	—	16	270	315

One of the requirements in your sociology class is to write a research paper and then give an oral report on your findings. You decide to study the dating services industry and want to prepare a PowerPoint presentation explaining the major concepts. Using the techniques introduced in this project, create a short slide show. Use the statistics in Table 4-10 to add a chart to one slide. Include WordArt on the title slide, sound effects, and transition effects. When you run the presentation, use pens and highlighters for emphasis, and then keep the ink annotations. Add action buttons to jump to the first slide when you are displaying Slide 3 and to jump to Slide 4 when you are displaying Slide 2. Format the action buttons with shadows and bold lines. Use the Thesaurus to change at least 2 words.

Cases and Places

The difficulty of these case studies varies:
■ are the least difficult and ■■ are more difficult. The last exercise is a group exercise.

3 ■■ Copyrights are given to authors and other people who create original works, such as books, photographs, and music. These legal protections prevent having third parties reproduce the works without the copyright holders' consent. Only copyright holders can reproduce their copyrighted works. Copyrights last for a specific number of years depending on when the works were created. If the work was created and published on or after January 1, 1978, the copyright begins when the work was created and endures for the life of the creator plus 50 years after the creator's death. If the work was created prior to January 1, 1978, it is protected for 28 years with an option to renew the copyright for another 47 years. The copy center at your college wants to prepare a slide show and handouts emphasizing these copyright rules in an effort to prevent students and staff from photocopying copyrighted works. You decide to develop a slide show to run at the front counter. Prepare a short presentation aimed at encouraging customers to follow the copyright guidelines. Include a chart showing the length of time a copyright lasts. The title slide should include WordArt for visual appeal. Hide one slide. The final slide should have hyperlinks to copyright information on the United States Copyright Office and The Bureau of National Affairs, Inc. Web sites.

4 ■■ Energy bars have found their way into many athletes' workout bags. Recently, Americans spent more than $1.4 million on these bars, which range in price from $1 to more than $2.50 each. The bars have various nutritional elements, including protein, carbohydrates, soy, and fiber. Visit your local sporting goods or nutrition store and compare the ingredients in five different energy bars. Compare price, serving size, calories, protein, carbohydrates, fat, saturated fat, fiber, and sugars. Then read articles or search the Internet to find nutrition experts' reviews and opinions of these bars' nutritional quality. Develop a PowerPoint slide show reporting your findings. Include a chart comparing the energy bars. Enhance the presentation by adding slide transition effects, an animation scheme, and timings. Include hyperlinks to three of the bars' Web sites. Add speaker notes to the slides and print these notes.

5 ■■ **Working Together** Hybrid cars use both an electric motor and a small gas engine. They are environmentally friendly because they get approximately 50 miles per gallon and have low emissions. Compared with a base model four-door car, they cost about $5,000 more, but their upkeep costs are about equal. Have each member of your team visit or telephone several local car dealers to obtain information about a particular hybrid car and its competitors. Gather data about:

1) Sticker price
2) Rebates
3) Required and recommended maintenance
4) Gas mileage
5) Estimated expenses for five years
6) Insurance rates
7) Horsepower

After coordinating the data, create a presentation with at least one slide showcasing each vehicle. Summarize your findings in a Word table. As a group, critique each slide. Enhance the presentation by modifying the slide background, adding clips, applying animation schemes and transition effects, and rehearsing timings. Include hyperlinks to three Web sites. Add speaker notes to the slides and print these notes. Hand in a hard copy of the final presentation.

Delivering Presentations to and Collaborating with Workgroups

CASE PERSPECTIVE

Motorcycle sales have been climbing steadily in recent years as riders yearn for the adventure and freedom offered by this form of transportation. With this popularity, however, has come an increase in the number of motorcyclists' accidents. In an effort to promote motorcycle safety, the local motorcycle dealer is planning to present a series of seminars. John Jamison, the owner of Cycles Unlimited, wants to offer workshops on riding and street skills. The speaker at the seminars will be Andy Andreessen, who is an experienced motorcycle rider and instructor.

John has asked you to help him develop a PowerPoint presentation that gives an overview of the seminars. He would like you to develop the presentation and then deliver it to Andy and two members of his staff for review. You set up a review cycle so Andy and two members of his staff can comment on your presentation. When you have incorporated their comments in your final document, you will schedule and deliver an online broadcast to these three reviewers.

In addition, John wants to put this PowerPoint presentation on a compact disc to take to speaking engagements in the community. You agree to help by using PowerPoint's Package for CD feature, which includes the Microsoft Office PowerPoint Viewer so the packaged presentation can run on any computer that does not have PowerPoint installed.

As you read through this Collaboration Feature, you will learn how to develop a review cycle to track, accept, and reject changes in a presentation; add, edit, and delete comments in a presentation; and compare and merge presentations. In addition, you will learn how to prepare the presentation for a remote delivery by scheduling and defining settings for online broadcasts and packaging the presentation to a folder for storage on a compact disc.

Objectives

You will have mastered the material in this project when you can:

- Merge slide shows
- Insert, review, accept, and reject comments
- Schedule and deliver online broadcasts
- Save presentations using the Package for CD option

Introduction

The phrase, the whole is greater than the sum of its parts, certainly can apply to a PowerPoint slide show. Often presentations are enhanced when individuals collaborate to fine-tune text, visuals, and design elements on the slides. PowerPoint offers an effective method of sending presentations for review and for sharing comments. A **review cycle** occurs when a slide show author e-mails a file to multiple reviewers so they can make comments and changes to their copies of the slides and then return the file to the author. If the author uses Microsoft Outlook to send the presentation for review, this e-mail program automatically **tracks changes** to the file by displaying who made the changes and comments.

Another method of collaborating with colleagues is by broadcasting the presentation over the Web. **Presentation broadcasting** delivers the slide show to remote audiences who are on the same intranet or are using the Internet. An **intranet** is an internal network that applies Internet technologies and is used to distribute company information to employees.

PowerPoint file sizes often are much larger than those produced by other Microsoft Office programs, such as Word and Excel. Presentations with embedded pictures and video easily can grow beyond the 1.44 MB capacity of floppy disks. The large file size may present difficulties if you need to transport your presentation to show on another computer. One solution to this file size limitation is to use PowerPoint's **Package for CD** option. This element saves all the components of a presentation so it can be delivered on a computer other than the one on which it was created. Linked documents and multimedia files automatically are included in this packaged file, but they can be excluded if desired. The feature can embed any TrueType font that is included in Windows; however, it cannot embed other TrueType fonts that have built-in copyright restrictions.

Part 1: Workgroup Collaboration Using a Review Cycle

The slide show consists of four slides that provide guidelines for motorcycle riders and motorists. Topics address clothing for comfort and safety, factors leading to accidents, and riding and driving advice. The presentation uses a picture, clips, and WordArt to add visual interest. Figures 1a through 1d show the four original slides, and Figures 1e through 1h show slides that were modified after receiving comments from three people who reviewed the original slide show.

ORIGINAL PRESENTATION

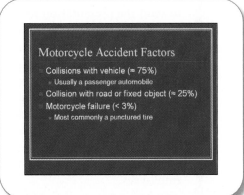

(a) Slide 1

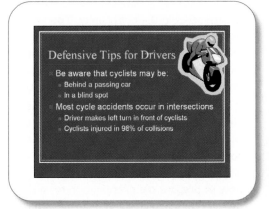

(b) Slide 2

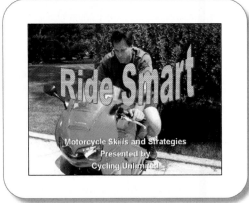

(c) Slide 3

(d) Slide 4

FIGURE 1

REVISED PRESENTATION

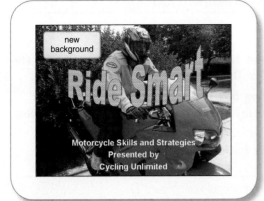

(e) Slide 1

(f) Slide 2

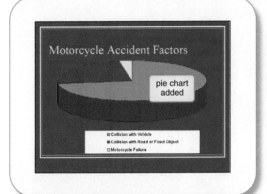

(g) Slide 3

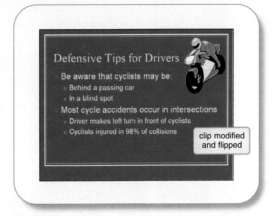

(h) Slide 4

FIGURE 1 *(continued)*

To avoid reading notes and changes made on printouts of a presentation, you can send the PowerPoint file to reviewers using Microsoft Outlook or any other 32-bit e-mail program that is compatible with the Messaging Application Programming Interface (MAPI), a network or Microsoft Exchange server, or a disk. Reviewers can edit the file using any version of PowerPoint.

The review cycle consists of inserting a comment on a slide, sending the presentation to reviewers, receiving the edited file, and evaluating the reviewers' suggestions by accepting and rejecting each comment using the Revisions task pane and Reviewing toolbar.

Starting PowerPoint and Opening a File

The steps on the next page illustrate how to start PowerPoint and open the presentation, Ride Smart, from the Data Disk. See the inside back cover for instructions for downloading the Data Disk or see your instructor for information about accessing the files required for this book.

To Start PowerPoint and Open a Presentation

1 Insert your Data Disk into drive A.

2 Click the Start button on the Windows taskbar, point to All Programs on the Start menu, and then click Open Office Document.

3 When the Open Office Document dialog box is displayed, click the Look in box arrow and then click 3½ Floppy (A:) in the Look in list. Double-click the file name, Ride Smart.

4 If the Language bar is displayed, click its Minimize button.

Slide 1 of the Ride Smart presentation is displayed in normal view (Figure 2).

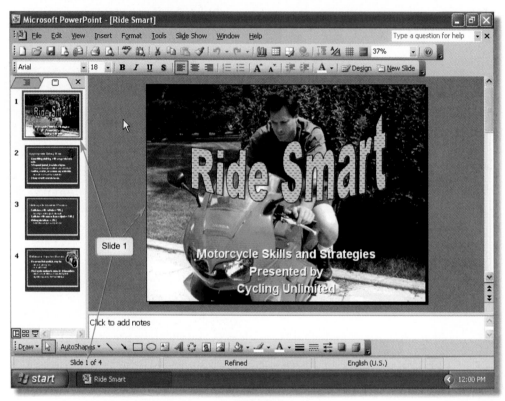

FIGURE 2

Displaying the Reviewing Toolbar and Inserting a Comment

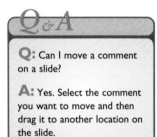

Q: Can I move a comment on a slide?

A: Yes. Select the comment you want to move and then drag it to another location on the slide.

To prepare a presentation for review, you might want to insert a comment containing information for the reviewers. A **comment** is a description that normally does not display as part of the slide show. The comment can be used to clarify information that may be difficult to understand, to pose questions, or to communicate suggestions. The first step in the review cycle for this project is to display the Reviewing toolbar and then insert a comment on Slide 1 asking the reviewers to express their opinions openly.

One method of inserting a comment is by clicking the Insert Comment button on the Reviewing toolbar. This toolbar is shown in Figure 4 on page PPT 312, and the buttons are described in Table 1.

Table 1   Buttons on the Reviewing Toolbar

BUTTON	BUTTON NAME	DESCRIPTION
	Show/Hide Markup	Displays comments on slides. It is activated when the first comment is entered.
Reviewers...	Reviewers	Displays the user names for all presentation reviewers.
	Previous Item	Selects the previous comment.
	Next Item	Selects the next comment.
	Apply	Incorporates the change into the presentation. Also applies all changes to the current slide or presentation.
	Unapply	Reverses the change made to the document. Also reverses all changes made to the current slide or presentation.
	Insert Comment	Adds a comment to a slide.
	Edit Comment	Changes the comment text.
	Delete Comment	Deletes a comment from a slide.
End Review...	End Review	Stops the reviewing process. All unapplied changes are lost.
	Revisions Pane	Displays or hides the Revisions task pane.
	Toolbar Options	Allow you to select the particular buttons you want to display on the toolbar.

The steps on the next page show how to display this toolbar and insert a comment on Slide 1.

To Display the Reviewing Toolbar and Insert a Comment

1

• **Click View on the menu bar and then point to Toolbars.**

• **Point to Reviewing on the Toolbars submenu.**

The View menu and Toolbars submenu are displayed (Figure 3).

FIGURE 3

2

• **Click Reviewing.**

• **Click the Insert Comment button on the Reviewing toolbar.**

*The Reviewing toolbar is displayed, and PowerPoint opens a **comment box** at the top of the slide (Figure 4). The presentation author's name is John Jamison, and his initials are JJ. The initials reflect the name that was entered when Microsoft Office 2003 was installed. Your author's initials may differ from those in this figure. PowerPoint adds a small rectangle, called a **comment marker**, to the upper-left corner of the slide. The number, 1, following the author's initials indicates the comment is the first comment made by this reviewer.*

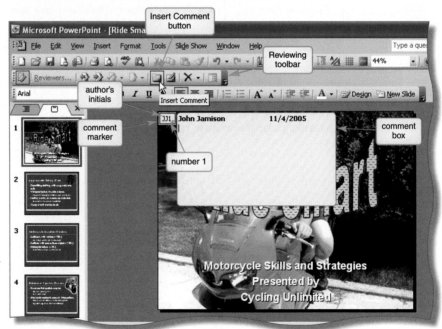

FIGURE 4

3

• **Type** Please review this presentation and make suggestions about the art and text. Thanks. **in the comment box.**

The author's name, date, and comment are displayed in the comment box (Figure 5).

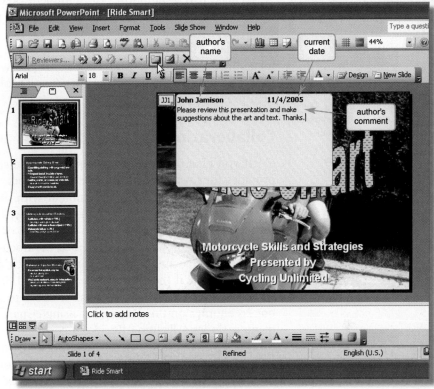

FIGURE 5

4

• **Click anywhere outside the comment box and then click the Save button on the Standard toolbar to save the presentation.**

*Clicking outside the comment box hides the text and **locks in** the comment. Your initials and the comment number are displayed (Figure 6).*

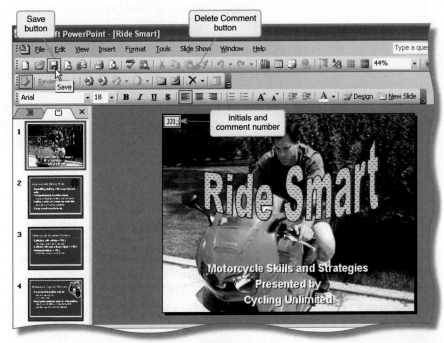

FIGURE 6

Other Ways

1. On Insert menu click Comment
2. Press ALT+I, press M
3. In Voice Command mode, say "Insert, Comment"

More About

Routing Presentations

Options for deadlines, deliveries, and status checks are available when you prepare a presentation for routing. The Add Routing Slip dialog box allow you to select whether the presentation should be sent to all the recipients simultaneously or if they should receive it sequentially in the order you specify. Reviewers make changes and insert comments using any version of PowerPoint. The presentation eventually returns to you.

When PowerPoint closes the comment box, the comment disappears from the screen. If you want to redisplay the comment, point to the comment marker. You can drag the comment to move its position on the slide. To change the reviewer's name and initials, click Tools on the menu bar, click Options, click the General tab, and then edit the Name and Initials fields. If you want to delete a comment, click the Delete Comment button on the Reviewing toolbar or click the comment marker and then press the DELETE key.

Collaborating with Workgroups

If you plan to have others edit your slide show or suggest changes, PowerPoint provides four ways to collaborate with others. **Collaborating** means working together in cooperation on a document with other PowerPoint users.

First, you can **distribute** your slide show to others, physically on a disk or through e-mail using the Send To command on the File menu. With the Send To command, you may choose to embed the document as part of the e-mail message or attach the file as an e-mail attachment, which allows recipients of the e-mail message to open the file if the application is installed on their systems.

Second, you can **route** your slide show to a list of people who pass it along from one to another on the routing list using e-mail. The Send To command on the File menu includes a Routing Recipient command. You specify e-mail addresses, the subject, and the message in the **routing slip**, which is similar to an e-mail message. PowerPoint creates the e-mail message with routing instructions and reminds people who open the document to pass it along to the next person in the routing list when they are finished.

Third, you can **collaborate** interactively with other people through discussion threads or online meetings. The integration of **NetMeeting** with Microsoft Office 2003 allows you to share and exchange files with people at different locations. When you start an online meeting from within PowerPoint, NetMeeting automatically starts in the background and allows you to share the contents of your file(s).

Fourth, you can collaborate by sharing the slide show. **Sharing** means more than simply giving another user a copy of your file. Sharing implies that multiple people can work independently on the same slide show simultaneously.

With any of the collaboration choices, you should keep track of the changes that others make to your slide show.

Distributing the Slide Show for Review

The next step is to send the slide show to Andy Andreessen and two of his assistants, Brianna Brooke and Christi Clarke. If you are completing this project on a personal computer, you will be prompted to choose the e-mail addresses of the recipients. You can use the recipients specified in the steps in this project, or you can substitute the e-mail addresses shown with e-mail addresses from your address book or class. Your return e-mail contact information must be valid to round trip the file back to yourself. The term **round trip** refers to sending a document to recipients and then receiving it back at some point in time.

More About

Using NetMeeting

Collaborate with and receive feedback from other people simultaneously as you complete your presentation. Microsoft has integrated its Office and NetMeeting programs so a number of people can view a presentation and share the contents of a file. You can schedule the meeting in advance by using Microsoft Outlook or start an impromptu online meeting from within an active PowerPoint presentation. If your colleagues are available and they decide to accept your invitation, the online meeting begins. They can use such tools as a whiteboard, video, and audio to present their opinions and comments. To learn more about NetMeeting, visit the PowerPoint 2003 More About Web page (scsite.com/ppt2003/more) and click NetMeeting.

The following steps illustrate how to distribute the presentation for review.

To Send the Presentation for Review

1

• **Click File on the menu bar, point to Send To, and then point to Mail Recipient (for Review).**

The File menu and Send To submenu are displayed (Figure 7).

2

• **Click Mail Recipient (for Review).**

• **If the Choose Profile dialog box is displayed, choose your user profile and then click the OK button. If the Office Assistant is displayed, click No thanks.**

• **When the e-mail Message window is displayed, type** Andy_Andreessen@hotmail.com; Brianna_Brooke@hotmail.com; Christi_Clarke@hotmail.com **in the To text box.**

PowerPoint displays the e-mail Message window (Figure 8). If you are working on a networked system, see your instructor or network administrator for the correct e-mail account to use.

3

• **Click the Send button on the Standard toolbar.**

The e-mail with the attached presentation is sent to the three reviewers.

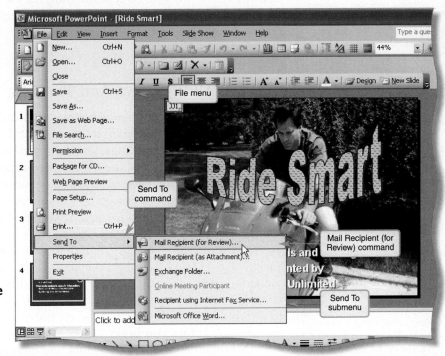

FIGURE 7

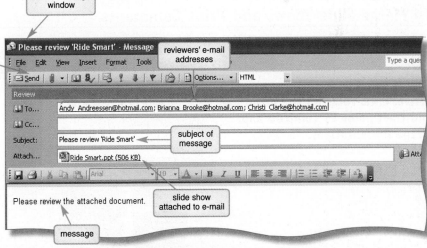

FIGURE 8

Other Ways

1. Press ALT+F, press D, press C, enter addresses, press ALT+S
2. In Voice Command mode, say "File, Send To, Mail Recipient for Review, [type addresses], Send"

More About

Print Preview Options

The Options button on the Print Preview toolbar allows you to adjust print preview options. For example, clicking the Color/Grayscale command shows how the slides will print on a black and white printer. The Frame Slides command adds a border around each slide, and the Scale to Fit Paper command enlarges or reduces the slide image to fill the paper.

Each of the reviewers opens the presentation and makes comments and suggestions about the presentation. Andy Andreessen's comments include changes to the Slide 1 background and a suggestion about the clip on Slide 4. Brianna Brooke's comments suggest a change to the text on Slide 2 to make the presentation conform to the 7 × 7 rule and recommend a slide transition on each slide. Christi Clarke's comments discuss repositioning the clip on Slide 2 and replacing the figures on Slide 3 with a chart. All the reviewers make the proposed changes to the presentation. The next section describes how you will merge these files and review the suggestions.

Merging Slide Shows and Printing Comments

PowerPoint keeps a **change history** with each shared slide show. The slide show owner reviews each presentation comment and then makes a decision about whether to accept the suggested change. After the reviewers commented on the Ride Smart presentation, they changed the file name to include their last names and then e-mailed the revised file back to you. If you and your reviewers use Microsoft Outlook as your e-mail program, PowerPoint automatically combines the reviewed presentations with your original slide show. If you used another e-mail program, a server, or a hard disk, you must merge the reviewers' files with your original.

Three slide shows — Ride Smart-Andreessen, Ride Smart-Brooke, and Ride Smart-Clarke — are stored on the Data Disk. As the owner of the original presentation, you review their comments and modifications and make decisions about whether to accept these suggestions. In this Collaboration Feature, you will see a printout of each slide and the comments each reviewer has made about the presentation before you begin to accept and reject each suggestion.

PowerPoint can print these slides and comments on individual pages. The following steps use this slide show to illustrate printing these suggestions.

To Merge Slide Shows and Print Comments

1

• **With the Ride Smart presentation active, click Tools on the menu bar and then point to Compare and Merge Presentations.**

The Tools menu is displayed (Figure 9).

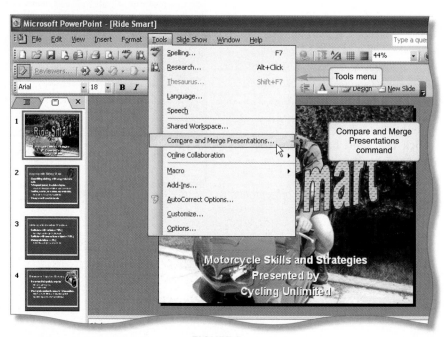

FIGURE 9

2

- **Click Compare and Merge Presentations.**

- **If necessary, when the Choose Files to Merge with Current Presentation dialog box is displayed, click the Look in box arrow and then click 3½ Floppy (A:).**

- **Click Ride Smart-Andreessen.**

- **Press the CTRL key, click Ride Smart-Brooke and Ride Smart-Clarke.**

- **Release the CTRL key.**

The Choose Files to Merge with Current Presentation dialog box is displayed (Figure 10). The files displayed on your computer may vary. The three selected files contain comments and revisions from the three reviewers. The steps instructed you to select the files to merge in the order they were sent to the reviewers, but you can merge files in any order.

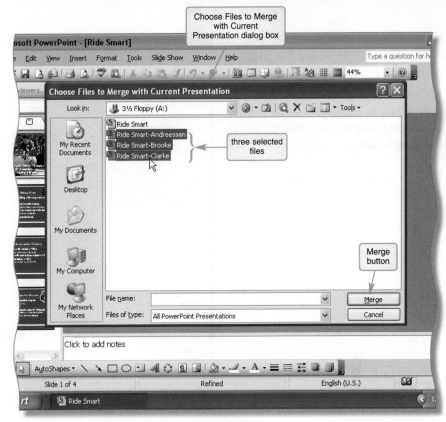

FIGURE 10

3

- **Click the Merge button.**

- **If a Microsoft Office PowerPoint dialog box is displayed asking if you want to browse your presentation, click the Continue button. If a Microsoft Office PowerPoint dialog box is displayed asking if you want to merge these changes with your original presentation, click the Yes button.**

The Revisions task pane is displayed (Figure 11). Each reviewer's comments in the Slide changes area are marked in a distinct color, which helps identify the author of each suggestion. The order of the comments in the list depends on the order in which the files were merged with the original presentation. PowerPoint may display your comments in a different sequence.

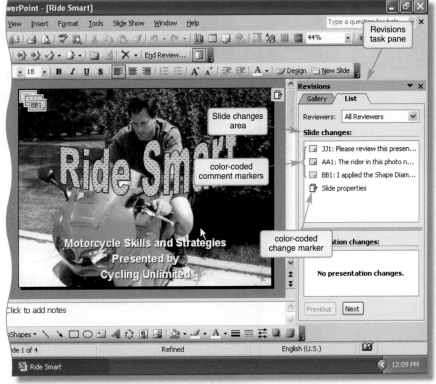

FIGURE 11

4

• **Click File on the menu bar and then click Print.**

• **If necessary, when the Print dialog box is displayed, click Print comments and ink markup to select the check box.**

The Print dialog box is displayed (Figure 12).

FIGURE 12

5

• **Click the Preview button.**

Slide 1 is displayed in the Print Preview window (Figure 13). To preview each of the eight pages, click the Next Page button.

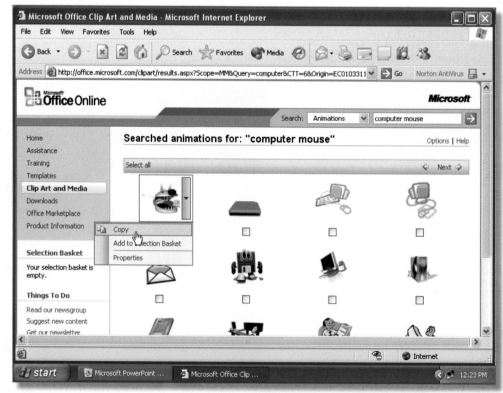

FIGURE 13

6

- **Click the Print button.**
- **Click the OK button.**

The four slides and four comment pages print, as shown in Figure 14.

7

- **Click the Close Preview button.**

The Close Preview button closes the Print Preview window. PowerPoint returns to normal view.

Ride Smart

(a) page 1

Motorcycle Skills and Strategies
Presented by
Cycling Unlimited

Slide 1

JJ1	Please review this presentation and make suggestions about the art and text. Thanks. John Jamison, 11/4/2005
AA1	The rider in this photo needs appropriate riding gear for safety and comfort. I recommend you substitute this slide. Andy Andreessen, 11/1/2005
BB1	I applied the Shape Diamond transition effect to all slides in the presentation. Brianna Brooke, 11/2/2005

(b) page 2

Appropriate Riding Gear

- Good-fitting clothing with snug waist and cuffs
- Windproof jacket; insulated layers
    - Zippered-front jacket offers wind resistance
- Leather, denim, and corduroy materials
    - Durable and abrasion-protective
- Sturdy over-the-ankle boots

BB2

CC1

(c) page 3

Slide 2

CC1	I moved the leather jacket clip to the bottom of the slide and then enlarged it. I think it looks good in this corner. Christi Clarke, 11/3/2005
BB2	I changed the first first-level paragraph by deleting the word, and, and adding a comma. The slide now follows the 7 x 7 rule. Brianna Brooke, 11/2/2005

(d) page 4

FIGURE 14

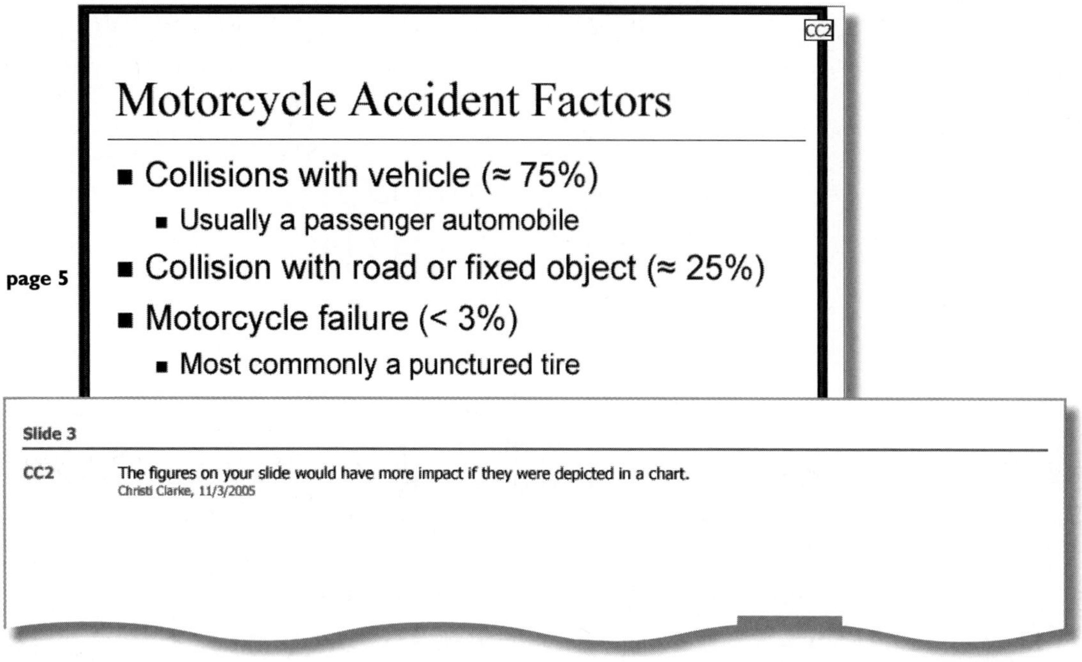

CC2

Motorcycle Accident Factors

- Collisions with vehicle (≈ 75%)
  - Usually a passenger automobile
- Collision with road or fixed object (≈ 25%)
- Motorcycle failure (< 3%)
  - Most commonly a punctured tire

(e) page 5

Slide 3

CC2   The figures on your slide would have more impact if they were depicted in a chart.
Christi Clarke, 11/3/2005

(f) page 6

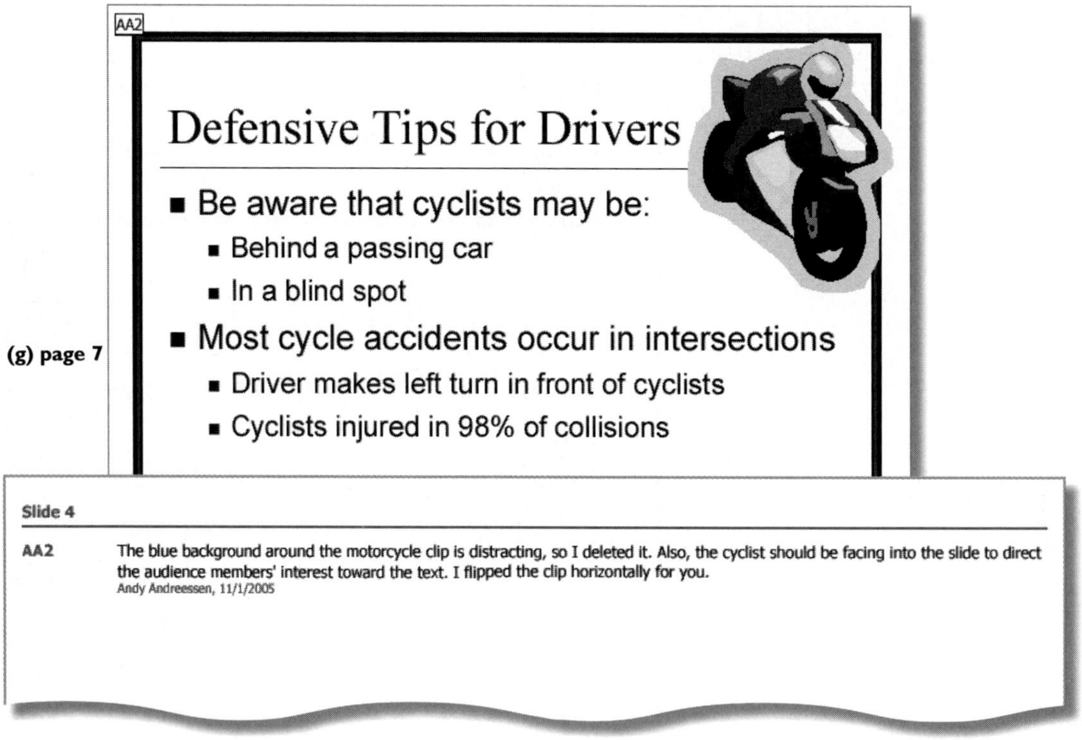

AA2

Defensive Tips for Drivers

- Be aware that cyclists may be:
  - Behind a passing car
  - In a blind spot
- Most cycle accidents occur in intersections
  - Driver makes left turn in front of cyclists
  - Cyclists injured in 98% of collisions

(g) page 7

Slide 4

AA2   The blue background around the motorcycle clip is distracting, so I deleted it. Also, the cyclist should be facing into the slide to direct the audience members' interest toward the text. I flipped the clip horizontally for you.
Andy Andreessen, 11/1/2005

(h) page 8

FIGURE 14 *(continued)*

Other Ways

1. In Voice Command mode, say "Tools, Compare and Merge Presentations, [select file names], Merge, Continue, File, Print, Include comment pages, Preview, Print, Close"

The eight printouts show each of the four slides and the comments each reviewer made about the slides. These pages are helpful to reference as you evaluate the reviewers' suggestions and changes.

Reviewing, Accepting, and Rejecting Comments

The Revisions task pane and Reviewing toolbar help you review each comment and then decide whether to accept the change or delete the suggestion. Color-coded comment and change markers are displayed in the Revisions task pane. The following steps show how to view each reviewer's comments for each slide in the presentation.

To Review and Accept Comments on Slide 1

More About

Print Preview in Grayscale

The Grayscale mode displays slides with some of the background switched to white. This modified grayscale sometimes creates a more readable printed version than you would see with color printed in true grayscale. To view a slide in true grayscale while using print preview, point to the Color/Grayscale command on the Options menu and then click Color.

1

• **With Slide 1 displaying, click the JJ1 comment marker on the List tab in the Revisions task pane.**

• **Point to the Delete Comment button on the Reviewing toolbar.**

The JJ1 comment box is displayed (Figure 15). The presentation author's name is John Jamison, and his initials are JJ. The initials in your comment box and color of your comment marker may vary. The comment marker indicates the first comment inserted before sending the presentation to the reviewers. Clicking the comment marker displays the comment.

FIGURE 15

2

• **Click the Delete Comment button on the Reviewing toolbar.**

• **Click the AA1 comment marker on the List tab in the Revisions task pane.**

John Jamison's comment is deleted from Slide 1 (Figure 16). Andy Andreessen's first comment regarding substituting a background photo is displayed. The Slide properties change marker is blank, which indicates you have not applied any changes to the slide.

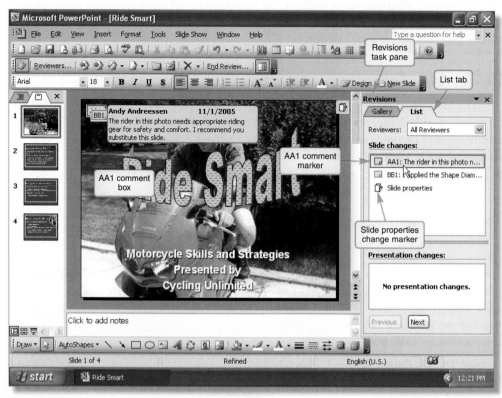

FIGURE 16

3

• **Click the Gallery tab in the Revisions task pane.**

The Gallery tab is displayed (Figure 17). The original Slide 1 does not have an appropriately dressed rider.

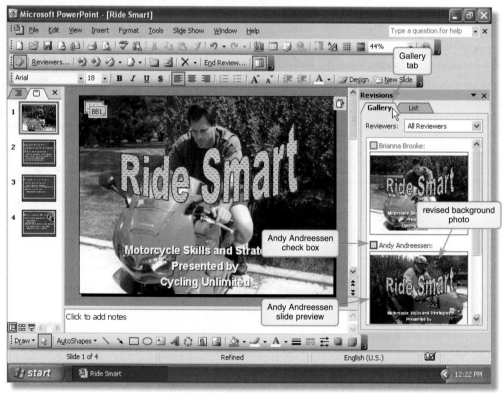

FIGURE 17

4

• **Click the Andy Andreessen check box above the Andy Andreessen slide preview.**

Slide 1 is displayed with the new background (Figure 18). Clicking the check box above the Andy Andreessen slide preview applies the revised slide he added to the presentation. You can accept the slide change by clicking the check box, clicking the slide preview, or clicking the Apply button on the Reviewing toolbar.

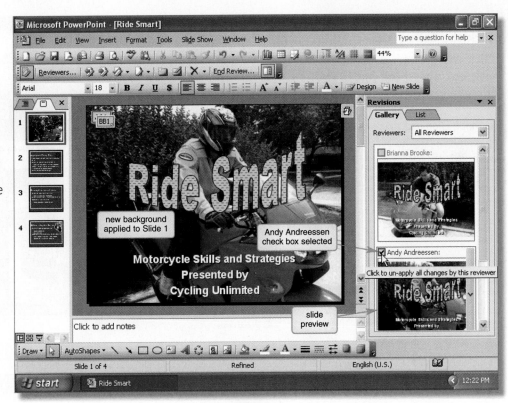

FIGURE 18

5

• **Click the List tab and then click the Delete Comment button on the Reviewing toolbar.**

• **Click the red BB1 comment marker.**

The Andy Andreessen change marker is deleted and the first Brianna Brooke comment is displayed (Figure 19).

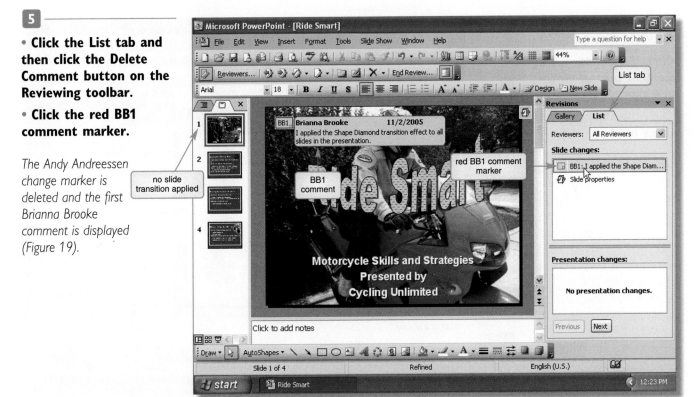

FIGURE 19

6

• **Click the Gallery tab.**

• **Click the Brianna Brooke check box above the Andy Andreessen slide preview.**

The Shape Diamond slide transition is applied to Slide 1 (Figure 20).

FIGURE 20

7

• **Click the List tab.**

• **Click the Delete Comment button on the Reviewing toolbar.**

• **Click the Slide properties change marker.**

Brianna Brooke's first comment is deleted from Slide 1. The checks indicate the changes you have applied (Figure 21). If you decide to unapply one or both of the Slide 1 changes, click the check boxes. A check mark is displayed in the Slide properties change marker, which indicates you have applied at least one change to the slide.

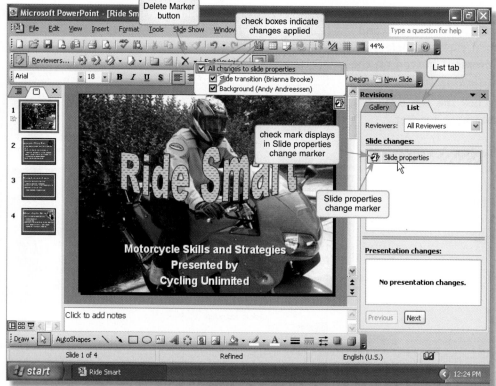

FIGURE 21

8 ─────────────

• **Click the Delete Marker button on the Reviewing toolbar.**

The new background and slide transition effect changes remain (Figure 22). The message in the Slide changes area in the Revisions task pane indicates that no more changes from the reviewers are available for Slide 1 and that the next comments are on Slide 2.

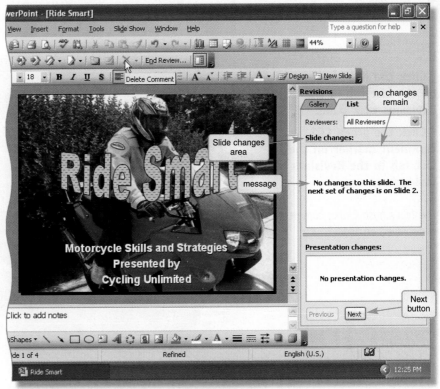

FIGURE 22

All the desired changes from the reviewers have been made to Slide 1. You now can review additional suggestions on the remaining slides in the slide show.

Reviewing, Accepting, and Rejecting Comments on Slides 2, 3, and 4

The three reviewers have made suggestions regarding the text and clip art on the next three slides. The steps on the next page illustrate how to review and accept comments on Slide 2.

More About

Personal Information

The three reviewers' names and initials display in the Revisions Pane. You may, however, not want your personal information displayed in a comment or macro or saved in a presentation. This information includes your name, initials, and company. To remove this information, click Tools on the menu bar and then click Options. When the Options dialog box displays, click the Security tab. In the Privacy options area, click Remove personal information from this file on save.

To Review and Accept or Reject Comments on Slide 2

1

- **Click the Next button on the List tab in the Revisions task pane.**
- **Click the green CC1 comment marker on the List tab in the Revisions task pane.**

The first Christi Clarke comment is displayed on Slide 2 (Figure 23).

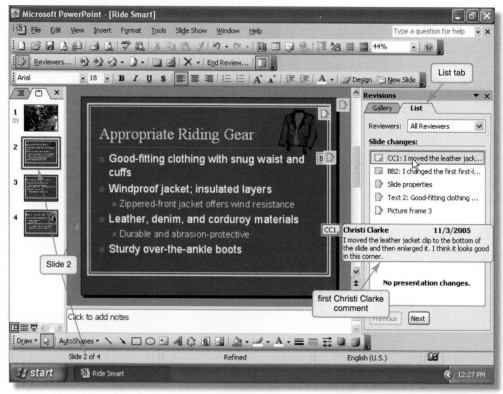

FIGURE 23

2

- **Click the Delete Comment button.**
- **Click the red BB2 comment marker.**

The Christi Clarke comment is deleted from Slide 2 and the second Brianna Brooke comment is displayed (Figure 24).

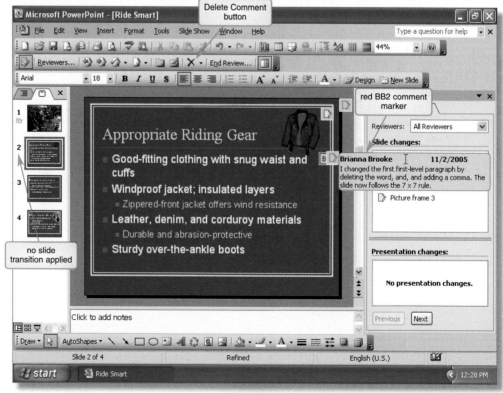

FIGURE 24

3

- **Click the Gallery tab.**

- **Click the Brianna Brooke check box above the Brianna Brooke slide preview.**

The Brianna Brooke revision is made to the first line of bulleted text in Slide 2 (Figure 25). The revision is displayed on the slide preview and on Slide 2. The first Brianna Brooke comment suggested and then applied a slide transition to all slides in the presentation. Clicking the check box accepts the changes. The animation icon indicates the Shape Diamond transition effect is applied to the slide.

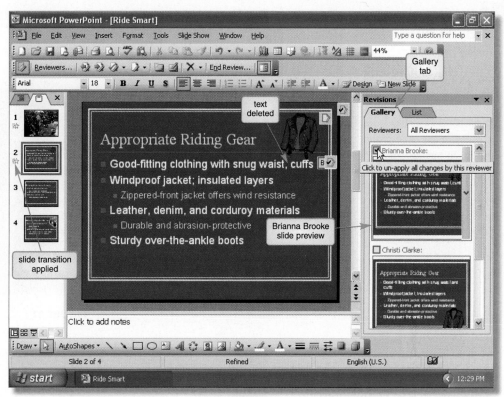

FIGURE 25

4

- **Click the List tab.**

- **Click the Delete Comment marker.**

- **Click the Slide properties change marker and then click the Delete Marker button.**

- **Click the Text 2 change marker and then click the Delete Marker button.**

All of the Brianna Brooke changes have been made to the slide (Figure 26).

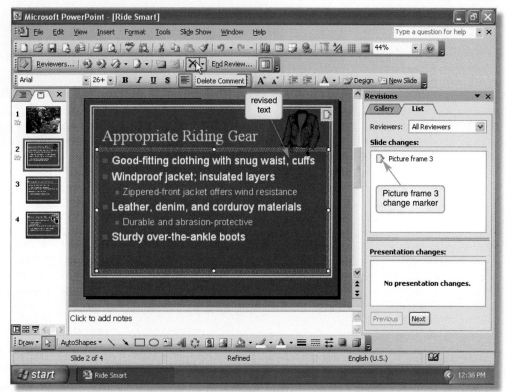

FIGURE 26

5

• **Click the Picture frame 3 change marker.**

• **Click the Gallery tab.**

The Christi Clarke slide modification to move and enlarge the leather jacket clip is displayed in the slide preview (Figure 27). If the Picture toolbar opens, click the Close button on the toolbar.

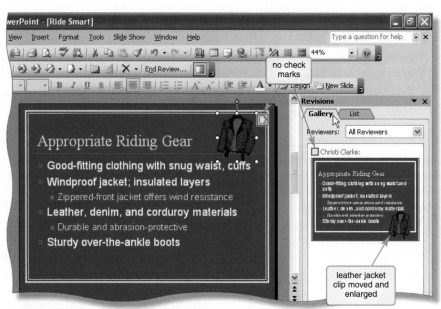

FIGURE 27

6

• **Click the List tab.**

• **Click the Delete Marker button.**

The message in the Slide changes area in the Revisions task pane indicates that no more changes from the reviewers are available for Slide 2 and that the next comments are on Slide 3 (Figure 28).

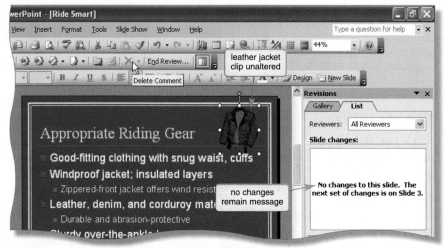

FIGURE 28

All the desired changes from the reviewers have been made to Slide 2. You accepted all the changes except moving the leather jacket to the lower-right corner of the slide. You now can review additional suggestions for the two remaining slides. The following steps illustrate how to review the comments on Slides 3 and 4 of the presentation using the instructions in Table 2.

To Review and Accept Comments on Slides 3 and 4

1 Click the Next button on the List tab in the Revisions task pane.

2 Be certain to delete each comment marker or change marker after you have performed the action in Table 2.

3 Review the additional comments in the slide show and perform the actions indicated in Table 2.

4 When you have reviewed all the comments, click the Close button in the Revisions task pane.

5 Save the Ride Smart presentation.

6 Run the Ride Smart presentation to see the modifications.

7 If the Reviewing toolbar is displayed, hide it by clicking View on the menu bar, pointing to Toolbars, and then clicking Reviewing on the Toolbars submenu.

The process of reviewing and accepting the changes to the slide show is complete. The Ride Smart presentation has been updated with suggestions from the three reviewers (Figure 29). You may need to use a second disk to save the file.

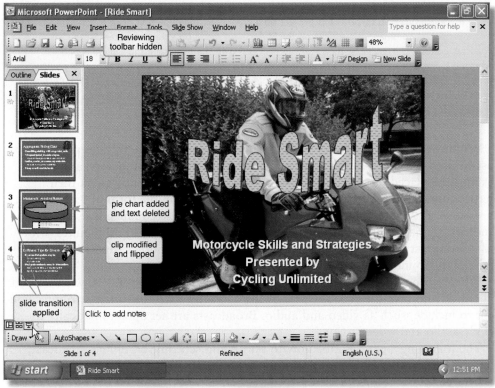

FIGURE 29

Table 2 Changes for Slides 3 and 4			
SLIDE NUMBER	**COMMENT MARKER**	**CHANGE MARKER**	**ACTION**
3	CC2		Read and then delete the comment.
		Slide properties	Apply only the Brianna Brooke slide transition.
		Object 2	Apply the Christi Clarke Inserted Object.
		Text 2	Apply the Christi Clarke Deleted Text 3.
4	AA2		Read and then delete the comment.
		Slide properties	Apply the Brianna Brooke slide transition.
		Group 3	Apply the Andy Andreessen Inserted Group.
		Picture frame 3	Apply the change to delete Picture frame 35.

These changes complete the Ride Smart slide show. The next step is to schedule and deliver this presentation as a broadcast to remote audiences.

Part 2: Scheduling and Delivering Online Broadcasts

PowerPoint's **broadcasting feature** allows remote viewers to see live performances of presentations. While saving slide shows as Web pages creates static versions of presentations, **delivering** broadcasts actually allows presenters to give presentations and include their voices and video.

Note: If you plan to step through this project on a computer, then you first need to confirm that the Online Broadcast command is available on the Slide Show menu on your computer. If the Online Broadcast command is available, then you can proceed with the project. If the Online Broadcast command is not available on the Slide Show menu, then you must download this feature from the Microsoft Office Online Web site. To display the Microsoft Office Online home page, click Microsoft Office Online on the Help menu. For additional information, enter Online Broadcast in the Type a question for help box or see your instructor for download instructions.

Windows Media Services or a third-party Windows Media Services provider must be used if a presentation is broadcast to more than 10 computers, and the files must be placed on a shared network server for viewers to access via their Internet connections. The file location must be specified in the form of \\servername\ sharename\. If the presentation includes video, Microsoft recommends using Windows Media Services. Prepare to deliver the broadcast about 30 minutes prior to the broadcast time so you can upload the file to the Windows Media Server and send e-mail reminder messages to your audience.

When setting up a broadcast, you must decide when to schedule it, whether you will record and save the broadcast for airing at a later date, and what attributes you want to include, such as video and audio. Broadcasts are set up automatically to include audio and video streams.

The following steps describe how to set up and schedule an online broadcast, which requires a connection to a network or to the Internet.

To Set Up and Schedule an Online Broadcast

1

• **Click Slide Show on the menu bar, point to Online Broadcast, and then point to Schedule a Live Broadcast.**

The Slide Show menu and Online Broadcast submenu are displayed (Figure 30).

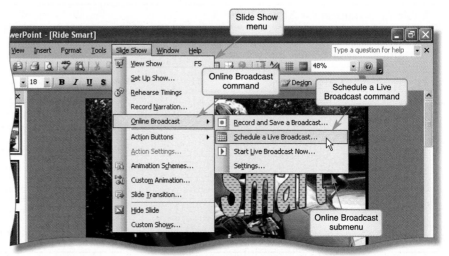

FIGURE 30

2

• **Click Schedule a Live Broadcast on the Online Broadcast submenu.**

• **When the Schedule Presentation Broadcast dialog box is displayed, click the Description text box and then type** This presentation will inform motorcyclists and automobile drivers about defensive techniques to reduce the occurrence and severity of motorcycle accidents.

• **Select the current name in the Speaker text box, and then type** Andy Andreessen **as the speaker name.**

• **If necessary, type a semicolon and your name in the Keywords text box.**

• **Delete any text in the Copyright and Email text boxes.**

The Schedule Presentation Broadcast dialog box is displayed as shown (Figure 31). The information in the text boxes will be displayed in the e-mail message sent to audience members.

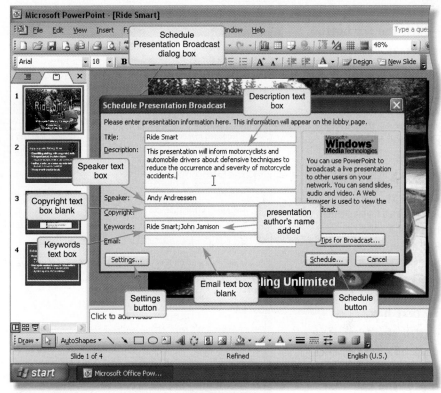

FIGURE 31

3

• **Click the Settings button.**

• **If necessary, when the Broadcast Settings dialog box is displayed, click None in the Audio/Video area on the Presenter tab.**

• **If necessary, click Display speaker notes with the presentation in the Presentation options area to remove the check mark.**

• **Ask your instructor where the broadcast files will be stored on your computer network, and then, in the Save broadcast files in text box, enter the location where these broadcast files will be stored by typing the location or browsing to the file.**

This presentation does not have audio or video components or speaker notes (Figure 32).

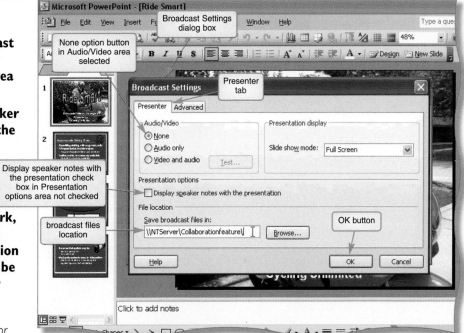

FIGURE 32

4

- **Click the OK button.**

- **Click the Schedule button.**

- **When the Ride Smart - Meeting window is displayed, click the Maximize button.**

- **On the Appointment tab, type**
Andy_Andreessen@
hotmail.com;
Brianna_Brooke@
hotmail.com;
Christi_Clarke@
hotmail.com **in the To text box.**

- **Click the Start time date box arrow, click the right arrow at the top of the calendar until the desired month is displayed, and then click the desired date.**

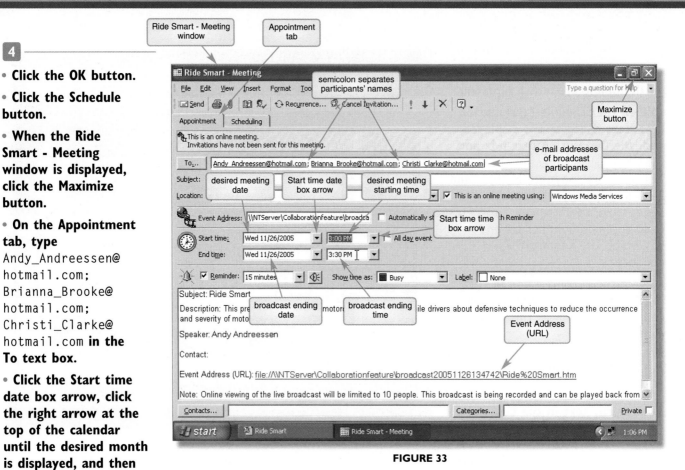

FIGURE 33

- **Click the Start time time box arrow and then click the desired time in the list.**

You may need to click a blinking Ride Smart - Meeting button on the taskbar to open the window. The Ride Smart - Meeting window is displayed as shown (Figure 33). Semicolons or commas can separate recipients' names. Sending the e-mail notifies the three reviewers that the broadcast has been scheduled for a particular date and time and can be viewed at the Event Address (URL) listed in the message. Meetings are scheduled automatically for 30 minutes on the same date.

5

• **Click the Send button on the Standard toolbar.**

• **When the Microsoft Office PowerPoint dialog box is displayed indicating the broadcast has been scheduled successfully and the broadcast settings have been saved, point to the OK button.**

The message indicates the broadcast settings have been saved in your Ride Smart file (Figure 34).

6

• **Click the OK button.**

Andy Andreessen, Brianna Brooke, and Christi Clarke will receive an e-mail message indicating that the Ride Smart broadcast has been scheduled.

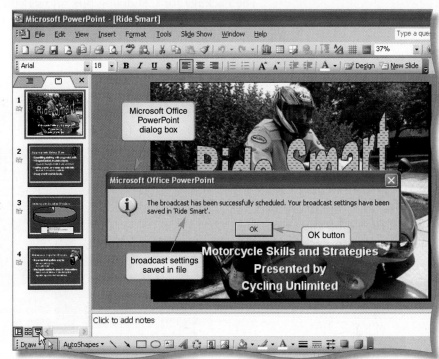

FIGURE 34

Other Ways

1. Press ALT+D, press O, press S
2. In Voice Command mode, say "Slide Show, Online Broadcast, Schedule a Live Broadcast"

The presentation has been set up and scheduled. When you are ready to begin the broadcast, click Slide Show on the menu bar, point to Online Broadcast, and then click Start Live Broadcast Now on the Online Broadcast submenu. When the Live Presentation Broadcast dialog box is displayed, click the Ride Smart broadcast and then click the Broadcast button. Andy Andreessen, Brianna Brooke, and Christi Clarke can view the slides by launching their Internet browsers and typing the link listed in their e-mail message invitations.

Broadcasting is one method of sharing a presentation with viewers. The next part of this project prepares the Ride Smart presentation so you can present the slide show with audience members at remote locations.

Part 3: Saving the Presentation Using the Package for CD Option

If your computer has compact disc (CD) burning hardware, the Package for CD option will copy a PowerPoint presentation and linked files onto a CD. Two types of CDs can be used: recordable (CD-R) and rewritable (CD-RW). If the CD-RW has existing content, these files will be overwritten. The PowerPoint Viewer is included so you can show the presentation on another computer that has Microsoft Windows but does not have PowerPoint installed. The **PowerPoint Viewer** also allows users to view presentations created with PowerPoint 2002, 2000, and 97.

More About

The PowerPoint Viewer

The PowerPoint Viewer is installed by default when Microsoft Office 2003 is installed. In addition, it is available for download from the Microsoft Office Online Web site. It supports opening presentations created using Microsoft PowerPoint 97 and later.

The Package for CD dialog box allows you to select the presentation files to copy, linking and embedding options, whether to add the Viewer, and passwords to open and modify the files. The following steps show how to save a presentation and related files to a CD using the Package for CD feature.

To Package a Presentation for Storage on a Compact Disc

1

• **Insert a CD-RW or a blank CD-R into your CD drive.**

• **With the Ride Smart presentation active, click File on the menu bar and then point to Package for CD.**

The File menu is displayed (Figure 35).

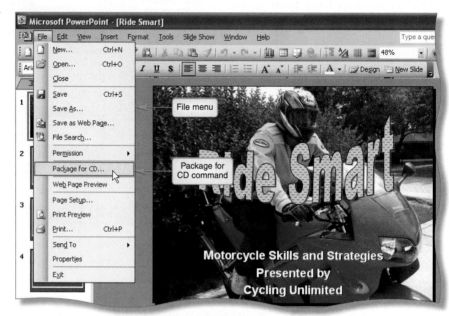

FIGURE 35

2

• **Click Package for CD.**

When the Package for CD dialog box is displayed, type Collaboration **in the Name the CD text box.**

PresentationCD is the default CD name. Ride Smart is the file that PowerPoint will copy to the CD (Figure 36). If desired, you can click the Add Files button to save additional files. You also can click the Options button if you do not want to include the PowerPoint Viewer and linked files, if you want to embed TrueType fonts, or if you want to use passwords to open or modify the files. You can click the Close button to exit the Package for CD dialog box.

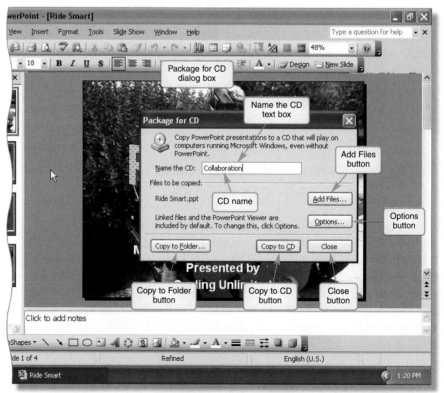

FIGURE 36

3

• **Click the Copy to CD button.**

PowerPoint packages the presentation files and displays status messages of which files are being added to the package. When all files have been copied successfully to the CD, PowerPoint displays a message asking if you want to copy the same files to another CD (Figure 37).

4

• **Click the No button in the Microsoft Office PowerPoint dialog box.**

• **Click the Close button in the Package for CD dialog box.**

PowerPoint closes the Package for CD dialog box and displays the Ride Smart presentation in normal view.

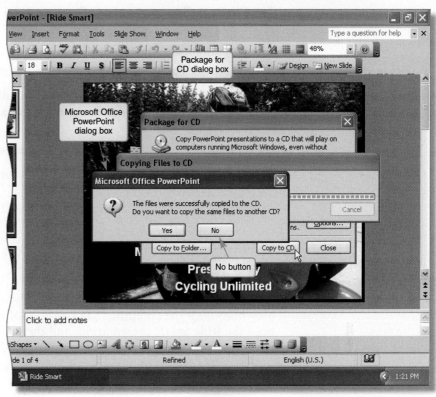

FIGURE 37

The Package for CD feature saves the presentation and related files on your CD. You now are ready to transport the presentation to a remote site.

Copying a Presentation Package to a Folder

The Package for CD option also allows you to save the presentation and related files to a folder on your computer or a network. If you do not include the viewer, the feature also allows you to save the files to a folder on a floppy disk. You then can use CD burning software to transfer these files to a CD. The steps on the next page describe how to copy the presentation and viewer to a folder on your computer.

Other Ways

1. Press ALT+F, press K, type CD name, press ALT+C
2. In Voice Command mode, say "File, Package for CD"

More About

Passwords

You can protect your slide content on CDs by using passwords on all packaged presentations. The passwords specify whether a user can look at or modify a file. In addition, you can add Information Rights Management to files that require more security. Only users with Office PowerPoint 2003 or later can view presentations protected by Information Rights Management, and these files cannot be viewed in the PowerPoint viewer.

To Copy a Presentation Package to a Folder

1 Click Package for CD on the File menu.

2 When the Package for CD dialog box is displayed, click Copy to Folder.

3 When the Copy to Folder dialog box is displayed, type the desired name for the folder in the Folder name text box and the desired folder location in the Location text box.

4 Click the OK button in the Copy to Folder dialog box.

5 Click the Close button in the Package for CD dialog box.

PowerPoint saves the presentation in a folder on the CD.

Viewing a Packaged Presentation Using the PowerPoint Viewer

When you arrive at a remote location, you will need to open the packed presentation. If the computer has PowerPoint installed, you can start PowerPoint, open the Ride Smart presentation, and then click the Slide Show button. If PowerPoint is not installed or if you simply want to run the presentation, the following steps explain how to run the presentation using the PowerPoint Viewer.

To View a Packaged Presentation Using the PowerPoint Viewer

1 Insert your Collaboration CD in the CD drive. Right-click the Start button on the taskbar and then click Open on the shortcut menu.

2 Click the Up button on the Standard Buttons toolbar until the My Computer window is displayed. Double-click the Collaboration CD drive icon.

PowerPoint opens the Ride Smart presentation and runs the slide show.

This project is complete. You now should close the Ride Smart presentation.

Closing the Presentation

The following step illustrates how to close the presentation but leave PowerPoint running.

To Close the Presentation

1 Click File on the menu bar and then click Close on the File menu.

PowerPoint closes the Ride Smart presentation.

Other Ways

1. Press ALT+F, press C
2. In Voice Command mode, say "File, Close"

Collaboration Feature Summary

This Collaboration Feature demonstrated three methods of sharing a presentation with others. In Part 1, you set up a review cycle and sent the presentation for review. In Part 2, you learned to set up and schedule an online broadcast. In Part 3, you learned to use the Package for CD feature to save and transport files.

 If you have a SAM user profile, you may have access to hands-on instruction, practice, and assessment of the skills covered in this project. Log in to your SAM account and go to your assignments page to see what your instructor has assigned.

What You Should Know

Having completed this project, you should be able to perform the tasks below. The tasks are listed in the same order they were presented in this project. For a list of the buttons, menus, toolbars, and commands introduced in this project, see the Quick Reference Summary at the back of this book and refer to the Page Number column.

1. Start PowerPoint and Open a Presentation (PPT 310)
2. Display the Reviewing Toolbar and Insert a Comment   (PPT 312)
3. Send the Presentation for Review   (PPT 315)
4. Merge Slide Shows and Print Comments (PPT 316)
5. Review and Accept Comments on Slide 1 (PPT 321)
6. Review and Accept or Reject Comments on Slide 2   (PPT 326)
7. Review and Accept Comments on Slides 3 and 4 (PPT 328)
8. Set Up and Schedule an Online Broadcast (PPT 330)
9. Package a Presentation for Storage on a Compact Disc   (PPT 334)
10. Copy a Presentation Package to a Folder (PPT 336)
11. View a Packaged Presentation Using the PowerPoint Viewer   (PPT 336)
12. Close the Presentation   (PPT 336)

1 Reviewing and Accepting Comments, Scheduling a Broadcast, and Using
the Package for CD Option

Problem: Your geology class is studying the Rocky Mountains. Your instructor has asked students to prepare
a report on one aspect of this topic, and you have decided to prepare a PowerPoint presentation on the tundra
that exists in Rocky Mountain National Park (RMNP). You visited RMNP this past summer and have several
photographs you can insert in your slide show. You prepare the Rocky Mountain Tundra presentation, which is
shown in Figures 38a through 38d, and then ask your professor and your lab partner to review the slide show
and to send you comments. You create the final presentation shown in Figures 38e through 38h on page
PPT 340. In addition, your professor wants you to broadcast the revised presentation to students enrolled
in another section of the class. She also requests that you use the Package for CD feature to transfer the
presentation so she can run the slide show on computers in the Geology Lab.

Instructions: Perform the following tasks:

1. Open the presentation, Lab CF-1 Rocky Mountain Tundra, from the Data Disk. The slides are shown in
   Figures 38a through 38d.
2. Merge the instructor's revised file, Rocky Mountain Tundra-Professor Jackson, and your lab partner's file,
   Rocky Mountain Tundra-Beth, on the Data Disk. Preview the slides and then increase the Zoom percent to
   150% to view the tundra on Slide 1. Print the slides and the comments.
3. Accept all transitions and template changes throughout the presentation.
4. On Slide 1, accept all the changes and delete the markers.
5. On Slide 2, reject Jackson's clip art and accept Beth's photo and delete the markers.
6. On Slide 3, accept Jackson's changes and reject Beth's editing change and delete the markers.
7. On Slide 4, accept all changes and delete the markers.
8. Schedule the broadcast for October 28 at 10:00 a.m. Invite your instructor to the broadcast.
9. Save the presentation with the file name, Lab CF-1 New Rocky Mountain Tundra. Print handouts with two
   slides per page.
10. Save the presentation using the Package for CD feature. Do not embed TrueType fonts, and do not include
    the Viewer.
11. Close the presentation. Hand in the printouts of the original slides, the comments, and the handouts of the
    revised slides and the CD containing the presentation to your instructor.

In the Lab

ORIGINAL PRESENTATION

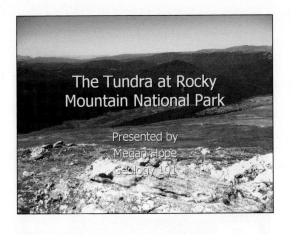

The Tundra at Rocky
Mountain National Park

Presented by
Megan Hope
Geology 101

(a) Slide 1

Defining a Tundra

- Treeless area
- Permanently frozen subsoil
- Low-growing vegetation
- Generally found in arctic regions

(b) Slide 2

Seeing the RMNP Tundra

- Unique area south of the Arctic Circle
- Old Fall River Road cuts through area
  - Open only during summer
  - Old one-way gravel road
  - 15 m.p.h. speed limit

(c) Slide 3

RMNP Tundra Facts

- Footsteps damage fragile vegetation
- Cache la Poudre river flows 1,600 feet below
  - Snowmelt causes fast-flowing waters
  - Temperatures less than 50 degrees

(d) Slide 4

FIGURE 38

(continued)

Reviewing and Accepting Comments, Scheduling a Broadcast, and Using the Package for CD Option *(continued)*

REVISED PRESENTATION

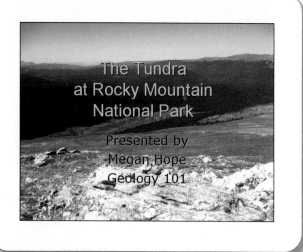

(e) Slide 1

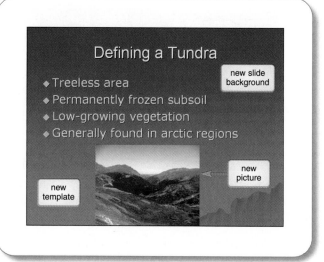

(f) Slide 2

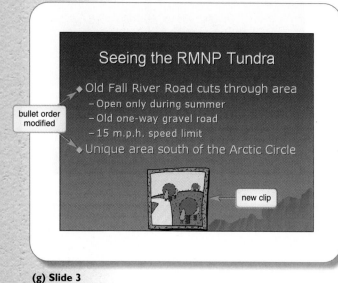

(g) Slide 3

(h) Slide 4

FIGURE 38 *(continued)*

In the Lab

2 Reviewing a Presentation and Saving Changes Using the Package for CD Option

Problem: Jessica Cantero successfully has shown the Nutrition and Fitness slide show you created for her in Project 2 to several groups of students at your college. She has made a few changes to the presentation and has e-mailed you her revised file, Lab CF-2 Nutrition and Fitness-Cantero. She informs you that she would like to present the slide show at the local health food store and at the library. Both of these locations have computers, so she would like to transport the slide show on a CD and install it on the computers at these sites instead of taking her notebook computer to these events. You agree to make her suggested changes to the presentation and to help her by using the Package for CD feature to transfer the slide show. Create the final presentation shown in Figures 39a through 39e.

Instructions: Perform the following tasks:

1. Open the Nutrition and Fitness presentation shown in Figures 2-1a through 2-1e on page PPT 83. (If you did not complete Project 2, see your instructor for a copy of the presentation.)
2. Merge the Lab CF-2 Nutrition and Fitness-Cantero file on your Data Disk. Print the slides and her comments. Accept all of Jessica's changes except the clip art change on Slide 5 and the animation settings. Delete the markers.
3. Create a new folder with the name, Revised Nutrition and Fitness. Save the presentation with the file name, Lab CF-2 Nutrition and Fitness Revised. Preview the slides, and then print Notes Pages.
4. Save the file using the Package for CD option. Include the linked files and embed TrueType fonts.
5. Close the presentation. Hand in the printouts of the original slides, the comments, and the Notes Pages and the CD containing the presentation to your instructor.

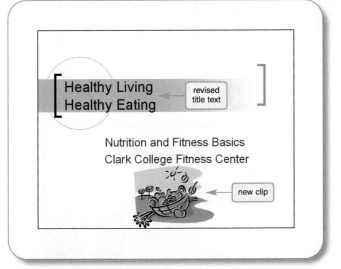

(a) Slide 1

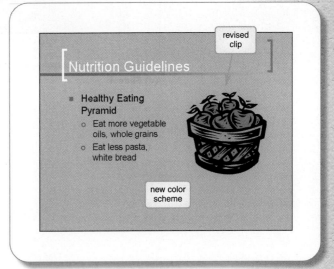

(b) Slide 2

FIGURE 39

(continued)

In the Lab

Reviewing a Presentation and Saving Changes Using the Package for CD Option *(continued)*

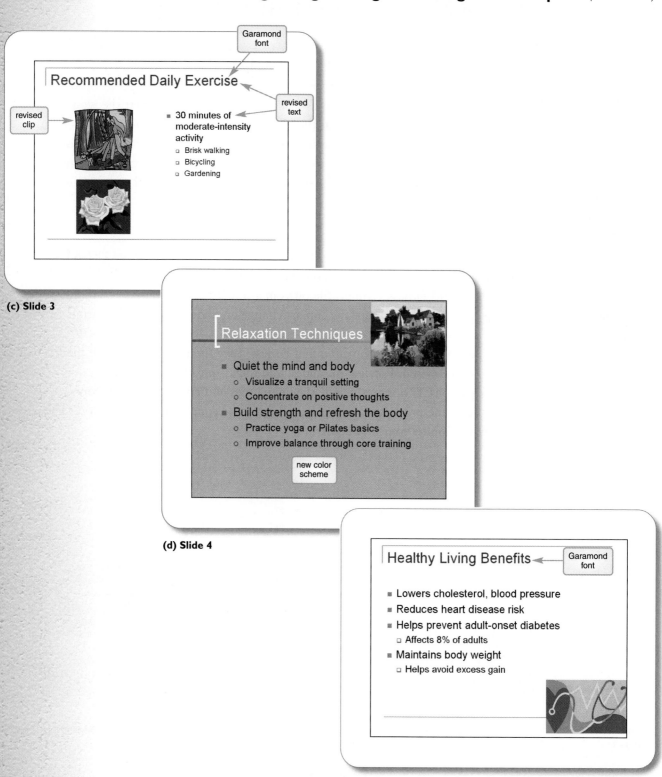

(c) Slide 3

(d) Slide 4

(e) Slide 5

FIGURE 39 *(continued)*

3 Broadcasting a Presentation and Reviewing Comments

Problem: After viewing the College Finances presentation in Project 4, you decide to create a similar presentation highlighting specific financial aid guidelines and policies at your college. You create the slide show and decide to solicit comments regarding the presentation from your professors, friends, classmates, or family members. You ask your network administrator or instructor to upload this file to a shared folder on your school's Web server.

Instructions: Perform the following tasks:

1. Invite two people and your instructor to view the online broadcast. Schedule the broadcast for 2:00 p.m. next Tuesday or a day and time that is convenient for the three invitees.

2. Insert a comment on Slide 1 of the presentation. Send the presentation to two professors, friends, classmates, or family members. Ask the reviewers to make comments and changes to the presentation and have them send their files back to you.

3. Merge their files with your original presentation. Preview the slides, and then preview them in Grayscale mode. Print the slides and their comments.

4. Review their comments and accept or reject their suggestions. Create a new folder with the name, Finances Broadcast. Save the presentation with the file name, Lab CF-3 Financial Aid. Print the revised slides.

5. Close the presentation. Hand in the printed original slides, comments, and revised slides to your instructor.

MICROSOFT
Office PowerPoint 2003

Working with Macros and Visual Basic for Applications (VBA)

PROJECT

5

CASE PERSPECTIVE

Vacations offer the opportunity to relax, meet new people, and explore interesting destinations. Numerous studies have shown that time away from school and a job allows students and employees to recharge and refresh themselves, thereby reducing stress while improving health and productivity. Some business experts believe that employers receive a $3 return on each dollar of vacation benefits they provide to employees in terms of increased morale and productivity.

Americans spend billions of dollars each year in search of the perfect destination. Travel agencies can help travelers choose the best type of trip that fits their needs and budget, and they often can develop travel packages for groups that minimize expenses and hassles. The Student Activities Office at your campus has teamed with the Vacation Central Travel Agency to sponsor four trips to Honolulu, Seattle, Chicago, and Denver. Ramon Cruz, the Student Activities Office director, has asked you to help him develop a slide show to generate interest in the trips. He wants to vary his slide show when he runs it at different locations and times during the school day. He has two video clips and two digital photographs highlighting the travel destinations.

After examining the information Ramon wants to emphasize, you determine that the best method for customizing each presentation is to use a form you develop using Visual Basic for Applications. Ramon's responses on the form will create a unique slide show for each presentation.

As you read through this project, you will learn how to create a toolbar with buttons and then add a command to the File menu to simplify these tasks: save the presentation as a Web page, use the Package for CD option, print a handout of slides, and display a form.

Working with Macros and Visual Basic for Applications (VBA)

PROJECT

5

Objectives

You will have mastered the material in this project when you can:

- Create a toolbar
- Customize a toolbar by adding buttons
- Use the macro recorder to create a macro
- Customize a menu by adding a command
- Open a presentation and print it by executing a macro
- Create a form to customize a presentation
- Create a user interface
- Add controls, such as command buttons and combo boxes, to a form
- Assign properties to controls
- Write VBA code to create a unique presentation

Introduction

Before a computer can take an action and produce a desired result, it must have a step-by-step description of the task to be accomplished. This series of precise instructions is called a **procedure**, which also is called a **program** or **code**. The process of writing a procedure is called **computer programming**. Every PowerPoint command on a menu and button on a toolbar has a corresponding procedure that executes when the command or button is clicked. When the computer **executes** a procedure, it carries out the step-by-step instructions. In a Windows environment, the instructions associated with a task are executed when an **event** takes place, such as clicking a button, an option button, or a check box.

Because a command or button in PowerPoint does not exist for every possible task, Microsoft has included a powerful programming language called **Visual Basic for Applications (VBA)**. This programming language allows you to customize and extend the capabilities of PowerPoint.

In this project, you will learn how to create macros using a code generator called a **macro recorder**. A **macro** is a procedure composed of VBA code that automates multi-step tasks. By simply executing a macro, the user can perform tasks that otherwise would require many keystrokes. You also will learn how to add buttons to toolbars. You will add a command to a menu and associate it with a print macro. Finally, you will learn the basics of VBA as you create an interface, set properties, and write the code.

The slide show you create in this project is intended to help the user, Ramon Cruz, promote the vacations. The goal is that he will open the Vacation Central file on his notebook computer at each presentation, open the form, and then make selections on the form to indicate which slide template, video clip, and picture to insert. VBA will create the presentation corresponding to these selections. Two possible slide shows are shown in Figures 5-1a through 5-1h.

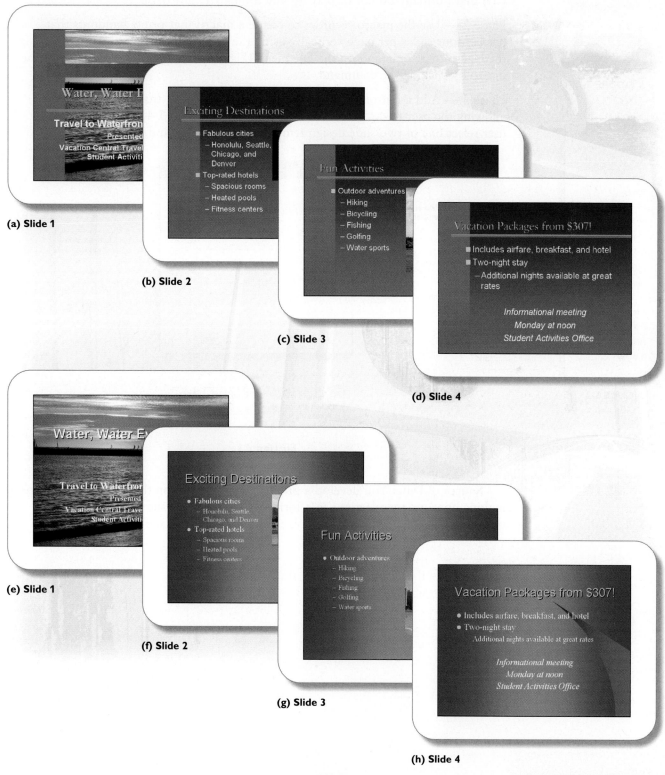

(a) Slide 1

(b) Slide 2

(c) Slide 3

(d) Slide 4

(e) Slide 1

(f) Slide 2

(g) Slide 3

(h) Slide 4

FIGURE 5-1

Project Five — Vacation Central

The following requirements are necessary to create the Vacation Central slide show:

Needs: The slide show requires an easy-to-use interface. This interface will be implemented in three phases:

Phase 1 — Create a toolbar and add two buttons (Save as Web Page and Package for CD) that normally do not display on any toolbar (Figure 5-2).

Phase 2 — Use the macro recorder to create a macro that prints handouts that display four slides per page vertically using the Pure Black and White option. Assign the macro to a command on the File menu (Figure 5-3) so the user can execute the macro by clicking the command.

Phase 3 — Add a button to the toolbar created in Phase 1 that displays a form allowing the user to design a custom presentation (Figure 5-4). This form lets the user select one of two slide design templates, video clips, and pictures.

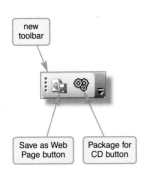

FIGURE 5-2

FIGURE 5-3

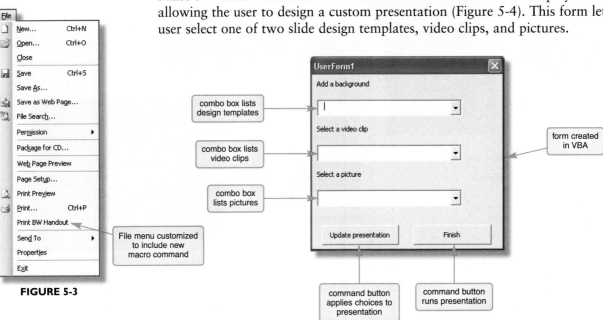

FIGURE 5-4

Source of Data: You develop a preliminary presentation the user will complete by making appropriate selections in a form. This slide show, shown in Figures 5-5a through 5-5d, has the file name, Travel, and is located on the Data Disk.

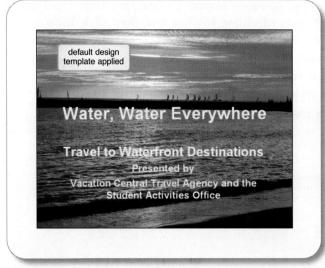

(a) Slide 1

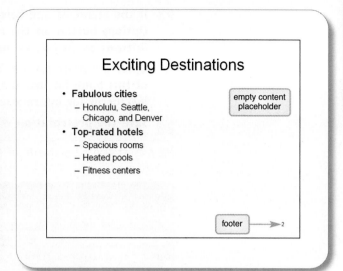

(b) Slide 2

(c) Slide 3

(d) Slide 4

FIGURE 5-5

Opening a Presentation and Saving it with a New File Name

To begin, start PowerPoint and open the Travel file on the Data Disk. Then reset the toolbars and menus so they display exactly as shown in this book (see Appendix D). The following steps illustrate how to open a presentation and save it with a new file name.

To Open a Presentation and Save it with a New File Name

1. Click the Start button on the Windows taskbar, point to All Programs on the Start menu, point to Microsoft Office on the All Programs submenu, and then click Microsoft Office PowerPoint 2003 on the Microsoft Office submenu.

2. If the Getting Started task pane is displayed, click the Close button on the task pane title bar.

3. If the Language bar is displayed, click its Minimize button.

4 If the Standard and Formatting toolbars display on one row, click the Toolbar Options button on the right side of either toolbar and then click Show Buttons on Two Rows on the Toolbar Options menu.

5 Open the presentation, Travel, from the Data Disk. See the inside back cover of this book for instructions for downloading the Data Disk or see your instructor for information on accessing the files required for this book.

6 Save the presentation with the file name, Vacation Central.

The presentation is saved with the file name, Vacation Central (Figure 5-6).

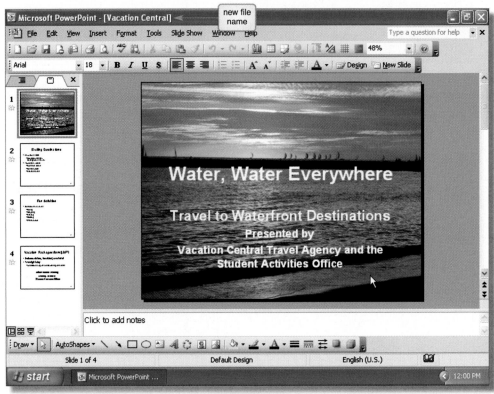

FIGURE 5-6

The Vacation Central presentation is composed of four slides (Figures 5-5a through 5-5d on the previous page). The first is a title slide with a picture of sailboats and a sunset as the background. The subtitle text mentions that all the vacation destinations involve viewing bodies of water and also shows the trips' sponsors. First, select one of two slide design templates, Green or Blue, to format the text and position the placeholders.

Slide 2 lists the four cities and the accommodation features, and it uses the Title, Text, and Content slide layout. The content placeholder is empty, but it will contain one of two possible video clips, a river in Rocky Mountain National Park near Denver or Buckingham Fountain in Chicago, based on the selection made in the Visual Basic form. A digital video camera was used to shoot this video, and then later the images were edited to use in this presentation.

Slide 3 highlights the activities travelers will find at the vacation locations. The outdoor adventures include a wide variety of sports. The slide also uses the Title, Text, and Content slide layout; one of two photos of Diamond Head in Hawaii or the Seattle skyline will be inserted into the content placeholder.

Slide 4 emphasizes the trips' details. Further information will be available at a meeting held in the Student Activities Office on Monday.

Slides 2, 3, and 4 have a footer that contains the slide number, as seen in Figure 5-7. In addition, they use the Faded Zoom animation scheme. Slide 1 automatically advances in 10 seconds or when you click the mouse, and Slides 2, 3, and 4 advance 15 seconds after they display or when you click the mouse.

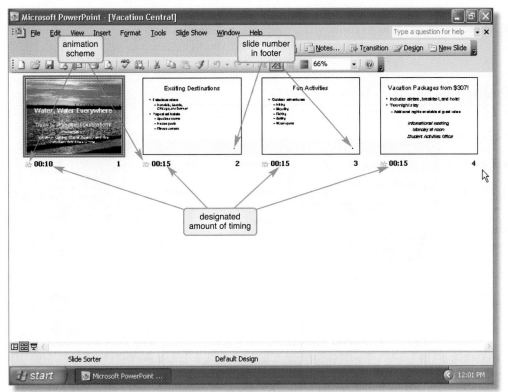

FIGURE 5-7

Phase 1 — Creating a Toolbar and Adding Two Buttons

The first phase of this project creates a toolbar that displays in the lower-right corner of the screen beside the Drawing toolbar. PowerPoint provides more than a dozen toolbars for a variety of purposes, but a **custom toolbar** allows you to display the buttons specific to your needs.

Creating and Customizing a Toolbar

One of the buttons you will add to the custom toolbar is the Save as Web Page button. Although users can save a file as a Web page by clicking the Save as Web Page command on the File menu, they also can click a button to make the presentation available to view on the Internet. The second button you will add to the custom toolbar in this phase of the project will launch the Package for CD Wizard. Users can click this button to compress and store the presentation files and the Microsoft Office PowerPoint Viewer. Users then can transport the presentation on a CD to show on a computer at the presentation site, rather than view it on their personal computers.

You can customize toolbars and menus by adding, deleting, and changing the functions of buttons and commands. Once you add a button to a toolbar or a command to a menu, you can assign a macro to the button or command. You customize a toolbar or menu by invoking the Customize command on the Tools menu. The key to understanding how to customize a toolbar or menu is to recognize that when the Customize dialog box is open, PowerPoint's toolbars and menus are in edit mode. **Edit mode** allows you to modify the toolbars and menus.

The following steps demonstrate how to create a custom toolbar.

To Create a Custom Toolbar

1

• **Click Tools on the menu bar and then point to Customize.**

The Tools menu is displayed (Figure 5-8). Your Tools menu may display different commands.

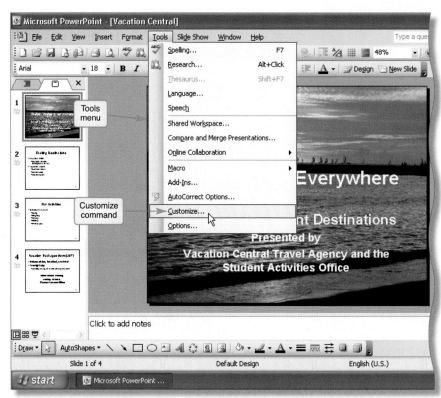

FIGURE 5-8

2

• **Click Customize.**

• **If necessary, when the Customize dialog box is displayed, click the Toolbars tab.**

The Toolbars sheet in the Customize dialog box is displayed (Figure 5-9).

FIGURE 5-9

3

• **Click the New button.**

• **When the New Toolbar dialog box is displayed, type** Vacation **in the Toolbar name text box.**

Vacation will be the name of the new toolbar (Figure 5-10).

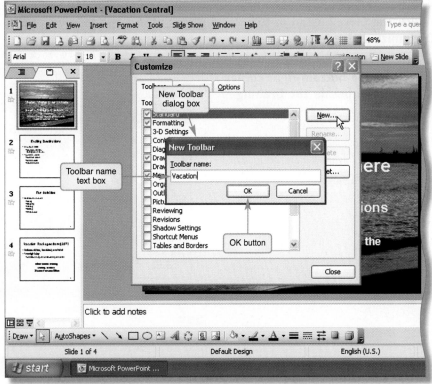

FIGURE 5-10

Microsoft Office
PowerPoint 2003

4

• **Click the OK button.**

The Vacation toolbar is displayed (Figure 5-11).

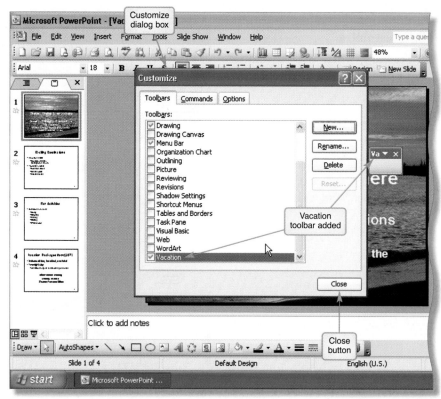

FIGURE 5-11

5

• **Click the Close button in the Customize dialog box.**
• **Click the Vacation toolbar and drag it to the bottom-right corner of the screen beside the Drawing toolbar.**

The Vacation toolbar is displayed in the desired location (Figure 5-12). The toolbar title does not display.

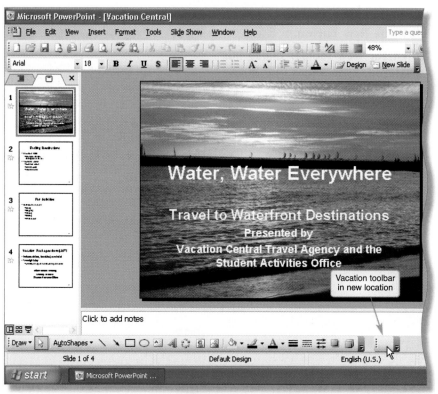

FIGURE 5-12

The Vacation toolbar is positioned beside the Drawing toolbar. The next step is to add two buttons to it. One button will save the presentation as a Web page, and the second will start the Package for CD Wizard. The following steps show how to add these buttons to the Vacation toolbar.

To Add Two Buttons to the Vacation Toolbar

1

• **Click the Toolbar Options button on the new toolbar.**

• **Point to Add or Remove Buttons, and then point to Customize on the Add or Remove Buttons submenu.**

The Add or Remove Buttons submenu is displayed (Figure 5-13).

FIGURE 5-13

2

• **Click Customize.**

• **When the Customize dialog box is displayed, click the Commands tab.**

• **Scroll down in the Commands list and then click Save as Web Page.**

You can select buttons from several categories, and each category has a variety of commands (Figure 5-14). File is the default category. Some commands have images associated with them.

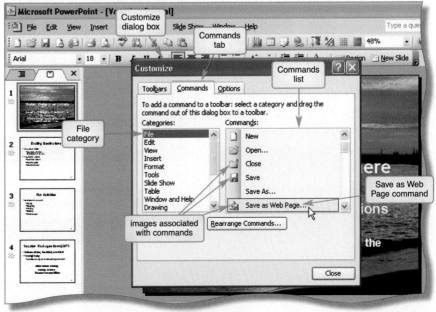

FIGURE 5-14

3

• **Drag the Save as Web Page command from the Commands list to the new Vacation toolbar.**

The Save as Web Page button displays with an image on the Vacation toolbar (Figure 5-15). The heavy border surrounding the button indicates PowerPoint is in edit mode.

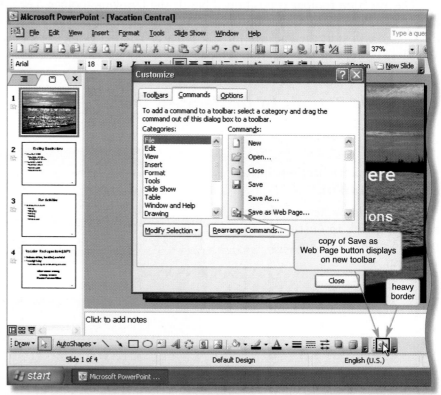

FIGURE 5-15

4

• **Scroll down in the Commands list and then click Package for CD.**

• **Drag the Package for CD command from the Commands list to the right of the Save as Web Page button on the Vacation toolbar.**

The Package for CD button is displayed on the Vacation toolbar with its name displaying on the face of the button (Figure 5-16). A heavy border surrounds the button, indicating that PowerPoint is in edit mode.

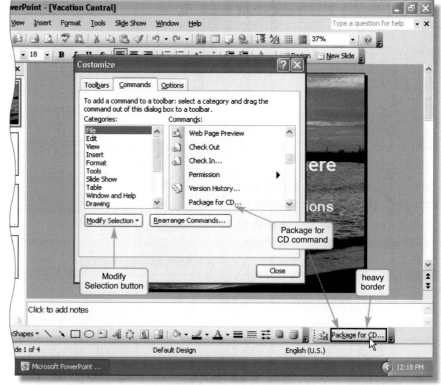

FIGURE 5-16

5

• **Click the Modify Selection button and then point to Change Button Image.**

• **When the Change Button Image palette is displayed, point to the button with three circles (row 6, column 4).**

PowerPoint displays a palette of button images from which to choose (Figure 5-17).

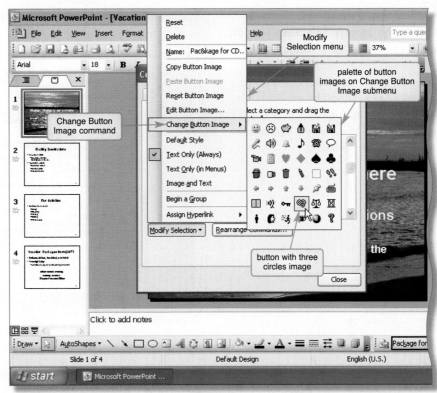

FIGURE 5-17

6

• **Click the button with the three circles image.**

The Package for CD button is displayed on the toolbar with the three circles image and the text, Package for CD (Figure 5-18).

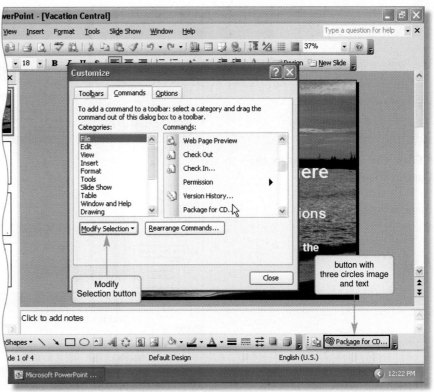

FIGURE 5-18

7

• **Click the Modify Selection button and then point to Default Style.**

The default style includes only the image, not text (Figure 5-19). The ampersand in the Name text box, Pac&kage for CD, underlines the letter k on the button, indicating a keyboard shortcut.

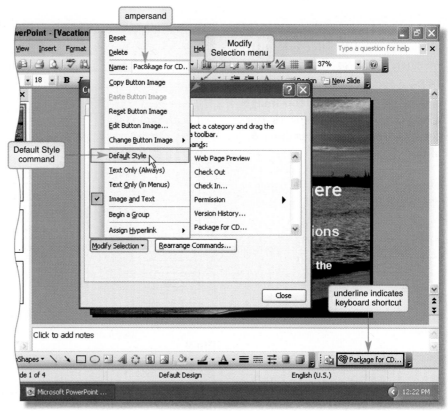

FIGURE 5-19

8

• **Click Default Style.**

The Package for CD button image is displayed with the three circles only (Figure 5-20).

9

• **Click the Close button in the Customize dialog box.**

PowerPoint quits edit mode.

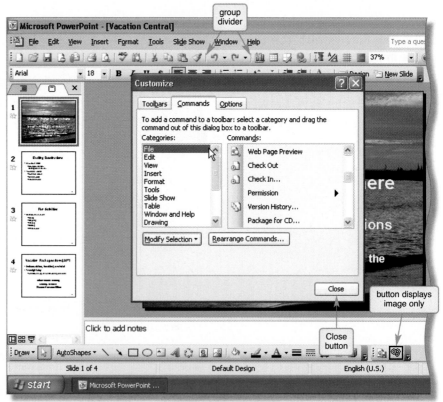

FIGURE 5-20

The previous steps illustrate how a toolbar is created easily and how buttons are added. PowerPoint includes a complete repertoire of commands for editing buttons on a toolbar, as shown on the Modify Selection menu in Figure 5-19. Table 5-1 briefly describes each of the commands on this menu.

Table 5-1 Summary of Commands on the Modify Selection Menu	
COMMAND	DESCRIPTION
Reset	Changes the image on the selected button to the original image and disassociates the macro with the button
Delete	Deletes the selected button
Name box	Changes the ScreenTip for a button and changes the command name for a command on a menu
Copy Button Image	Copies the button image to the Office Clipboard
Paste Button Image	Pastes the button image on the Office Clipboard onto the selected button
Reset Button Image	Changes the button image back to the original image
Edit Button Image	Allows you to edit the button image
Change Button Image	Allows you to choose a new button image
Default Style; Text Only (Always); Text Only (in Menus); Image and Text	Allows you to choose one of the four styles to indicate how the button should display
Begin a Group	Groups buttons by drawing a vertical line (divider) on the toolbar (see the group dividing lines in Figure 5-20)
Assign Hyperlink	Assigns a hyperlink to a Web page or document

You can add as many buttons as you want to a toolbar. You also can change any button's function. For example, when in edit mode with the Customize dialog box displaying, you can right-click the Save button on the Standard toolbar and assign it a macro or hyperlink. The next time you click the Save button, the macro will execute, or PowerPoint will launch the application associated with the hyperlink rather than save the presentation.

Reset any toolbar to its installation default by clicking the Toolbars tab in the Customize dialog box, selecting the toolbar in the Toolbars list, and clicking the Reset button. Because it is so easy to change the buttons on a toolbar, each project in this book begins by resetting the toolbars.

Saving the Presentation

The changes for Phase 1 of the presentation are complete. The following step describes how to save the presentation before recording a macro in Phase 2 of this project.

To Save a Presentation

1 **Click the Save button on the Standard toolbar.**

PowerPoint saves the presentation by saving the changes made to the presentation since the last save.

More About

Renaming ScreenTips

Once you have added a button to a toolbar, you can change its ScreenTip. To make this change, click Customize on the Tools menu, right-click the toolbar button, type the new name in the Name text box, and then press the ENTER key. You will see the name change when you view the ScreenTip.

More About

Presentation Design

The black and white handout in Figure 5-21 helps focus attention on slide content. Some designers recommend designing a presentation in black and white and then adding color to emphasize particular areas on the slide. By starting with black letters on a white background, you can concentrate on basic design principles, such as balance, contrast, rhythm, and harmony.

Phase 2 — Recording a Macro and Assigning it to a Menu Command

The second phase of the project creates a macro to print a handout displaying four slides per page vertically using the Pure Black and White option. The default PowerPoint print setting is Slides, with one slide printing on each sheet of paper. When the Print what setting is changed to handouts, the default setting is 6 slides per page in a horizontal order, meaning Slides 1 and 2 display at the top of the page, Slides 3 and 4 display in the middle of the page, and Slides 5 and 6 display at the bottom of the page. The user can distribute a one-page handout, shown in Figure 5-21, of the four slides in this presentation printed using the Pure Black and White option and displayed vertically, meaning Slides 1 and 3 display on the top, and Slides 2 and 4 display below.

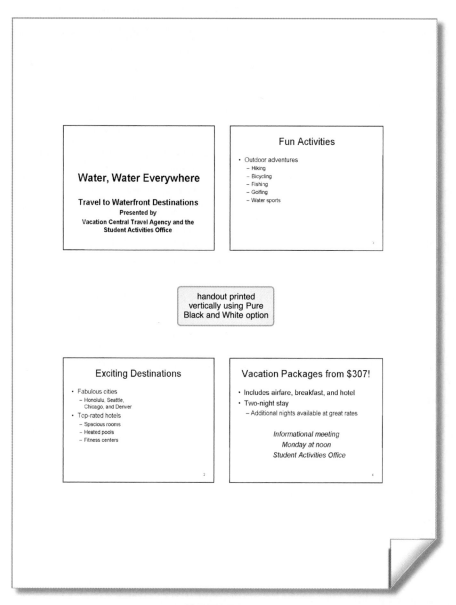

FIGURE 5-21

The planned macro will change the output from slides to handouts and will change the slide order on the handout from horizontal to vertical. The handout will print using the Pure Black and White option instead of Grayscale or another default setting on your computer, so all shades of gray will change to either black or white. Then, the macro will reset the Print dialog box to its original settings.

With the macro, users can print a one-page handout by executing a single command, rather than performing the several steps otherwise required. The users can click the Print button on the Standard toolbar and change the settings in the Print dialog box to print the handout, or they can execute the macro to print the handout. Once the macro is created, it will be assigned to a command on the File menu.

Recording a Macro

PowerPoint has a macro recorder that creates a macro automatically based on a series of actions performed while it is recording. Like a video recorder, the macro recorder records everything you do to a presentation over a period of time. The macro recorder can be turned on, during which time it records your activities, and then turned off to stop the recording. Once the macro is recorded, it can be **played back** or executed as often as desired.

It is easy to create a macro. All you have to do is turn on the macro recorder and perform these steps:

1. Start the macro recorder.
2. Change the output settings from slides to handouts, the slides per page from six to four, the slide order on the handout from horizontal to vertical, and the print option from Grayscale (or the default print setting on your computer) to Pure Black and White.
3. Print the handout.
4. Restore the output settings from four slides per page to six, from vertical to horizontal slide order, from handouts to slides, and from Pure Black and White to Grayscale (or the default print setting on your computer).
5. Stop the macro recorder.

What is impressive about the macro recorder is that you actually step through the task as you create the macro. You will see exactly what the macro will do before using it.

When you create the macro, you first must name it. The name is used to reference the macro when you want to execute it. The name PrintHandout is used for the macro. **Macro names** can be up to 255 characters long; they can contain numbers, letters, and underscores; and they cannot contain spaces and other punctuation. The steps on the next page show how to record the macro.

More About

Creating Presentations

People who are under a deadline to create a presentation say they frequently must seek solitude to finish the task. They find it nearly impossible to concentrate on organizing and developing a slide show when they are in a noisy environment filled with interruptions. Answering a ringing telephone, constantly checking e-mail, and talking with cohorts all interfere with staying on task. Researchers at the University of Michigan found that productivity drops 20 to 40 percent every time a worker multitasks. To learn more about working smartly, visit the PowerPoint 2003 More About Web page (scsite.com/ppt2003/more) and click Productivity.

More About

Digitizing Photographs

Ramon Cruz supplied the digitized Hawaii and Seattle pictures that will be inserted in Slide 3. Digitizing produces some dazzling objects that add interest to presentations. Many artists have traded their paintbrushes and easels for the mouse and monitor. To learn more about digital objects, visit the PowerPoint 2003 More About Web page (scsite.com/ppt2003/more) and click Digitizing.

To Record a Macro to Print Handouts in Vertical Slide Order in Pure Black and White

1

• **Click Tools on the menu bar, point to Macro, and then point to Record New Macro on the Macro submenu.**

The Tools menu and Macro submenu display (Figure 5-22).

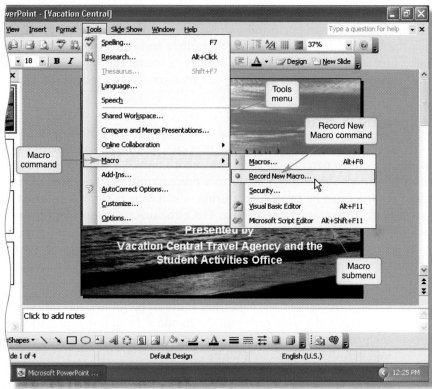

FIGURE 5-22

2

• **Click Record New Macro.**

• **When the Record Macro dialog box is displayed, type** PrintHandout **in the Macro name text box.**

• **Type** Macro prints Pure Black and White handouts in vertical slide order **in the Description text box.**

• **Make sure the Store macro in box displays Vacation Central.**

The Record Macro dialog box is displayed as shown in Figure 5-23.

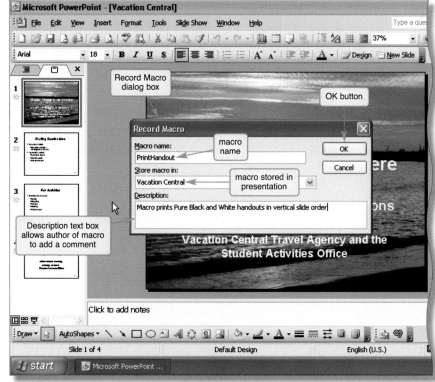

FIGURE 5-23

3

• **Click the OK button.**

The Stop Recording toolbar is displayed (Figure 5-24). Any task you perform after the Stop Recording toolbar is displayed will be part of the macro. When you are finished recording the macro, you will click the Stop Recording button on the Stop Recording toolbar to end the recording.

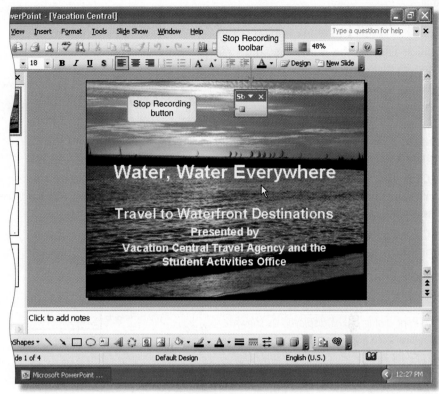

FIGURE 5-24

4

• **Click File on the menu bar and then click Print.**

• **When the Print dialog box is displayed, click the Print what box arrow and then click Handouts.**

• **Click the Slides per page box arrow in the Handouts area and then click 4.**

• **Click Vertical order in the Handouts area.**

• **Click the Color/grayscale box arrow and then click Pure Black and White.**

The Print dialog box is displayed as shown in Figure 5-25.

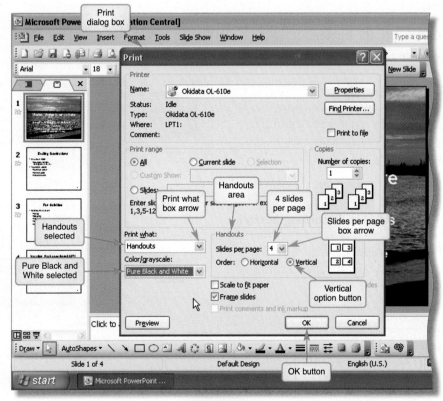

FIGURE 5-25

5

• **Click the OK button.**

• **Click File on the menu bar and then click Print.**

• **When the Print dialog box is displayed, click the Color/grayscale box arrow and then click Grayscale (or your computer's default print option).**

• **Click the Slides per page box arrow in the Handouts area and then click 6.**

• **Click Horizontal order in the Handouts area.**

• **Click the Print what box arrow and then click Slides.**

The Print dialog box is displayed as shown in Figure 5-26. Your computer is restored to its default print settings. The printout resembles the handout shown in Figure 5-21 on page PPT 360.

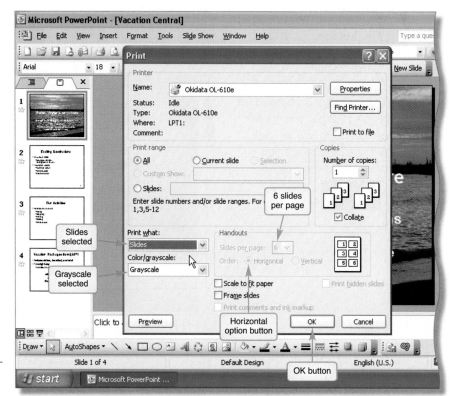

FIGURE 5-26

6

• **Click the OK button.**

• **Point to the Stop Recording button.**

The Print dialog box closes (Figure 5-27). The four slides in the presentation print in grayscale or your computer's default print option.

7

• **Click the Stop Recording button.**

PowerPoint stops recording the printing activities and hides the Stop Recording toolbar.

Other Ways

1. Click Record Macro button on Visual Basic toolbar
2. Press ALT+T, press M, press R
3. In Voice Command mode, say "Tools, Macro, Record New Macro"

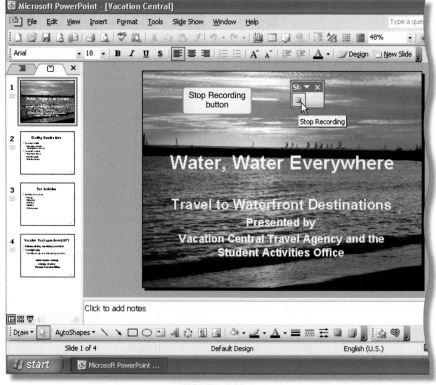

FIGURE 5-27

If you recorded the wrong actions, delete the macro and record it again. You delete a macro by clicking Tools on the menu bar, pointing to Macro on the Tools menu, and then clicking Macros on the Macro submenu. When the Macro dialog box is displayed, click the name of the macro (PrintHandout), and then click the Delete button. Then record the macro again.

Customizing a Menu

As you use PowerPoint to create presentations and print handouts, you may find yourself repeating many steps. It is convenient to simplify these repetitive processes by adding a button to a toolbar or a command to a menu that you can click to perform the tasks automatically. PowerPoint allows you to add commands to a button or to a menu. The following steps show how to add a command to the File menu to execute the PrintHandout macro.

More About

PowerPoint Features

The lead program manager for Microsoft PowerPoint 2003, Richard Bretschneider, says that performance is the most important feature in this version of the software. He says that the programmers worked diligently at making the product stable and eliminating crashes.

To Add a Command to a Menu, Assign the Command to a Macro, and Invoke the Command

1

• **Click Tools on the menu bar and then click Customize.**

• **If necessary, when the Customize dialog box is displayed, click the Commands tab.**

• **Scroll down in the Categories list and then click Macros.**

• **Click File on the menu bar to display the File menu.**

The Customize dialog box and File menu are displayed (Figure 5-28). A heavy border surrounds the File menu name, indicating PowerPoint is in edit mode.

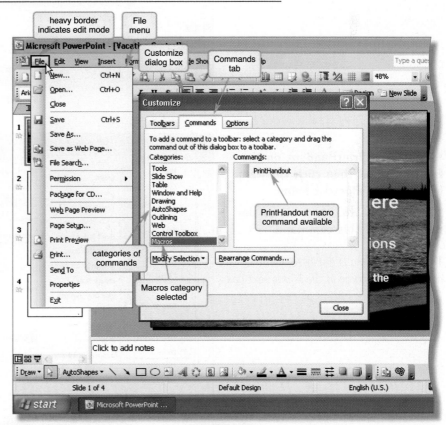

FIGURE 5-28

2

• **Drag the PrintHandout entry from the Commands list in the Customize dialog box immediately below the Print command on the File menu.**

PowerPoint adds PrintHandout to the File menu (Figure 5-29). The heavy border surrounding PrintHandout on the File menu indicates PowerPoint is in edit mode.

FIGURE 5-29

3

• **Right-click PrintHandout on the File menu and then click the Name label on the shortcut menu.**

• **Type** Print BW Handout **as the new name of this command.**

The shortcut menu is displayed with the new command name in the Name text box (Figure 5-30).

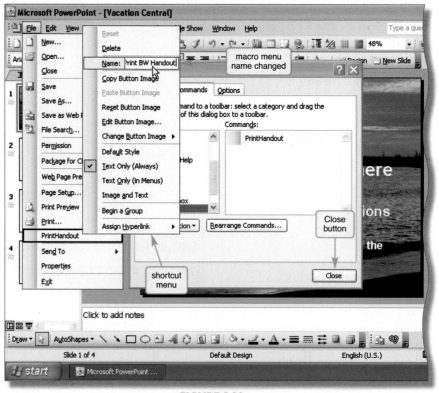

FIGURE 5-30

4

• **Click the Close button at the bottom of the Customize dialog box.**

• **Click File on the menu bar and then point to Print BW Handout.**

PowerPoint quits edit mode. The File menu is displayed with the new command, Print BW Handout, on the menu (Figure 5-31).

5

• **Click Print BW Handout on the File menu.**

The handout prints as shown in Figure 5-21 on page PPT 360. In addition, the four slides print in shades of gray (grayscale).

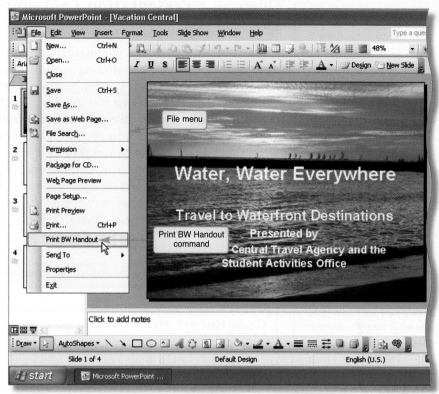

FIGURE 5-31

Other Ways

1. Right-click toolbar, click Customize on shortcut menu, click Commands tab
2. On View menu click Toolbars, click Customize, click Commands tab
3. In Voice Command mode, say "View, Toolbars, Customize, Commands"

You have the same customization capabilities with menus as you do with toolbars. All of the commands described in Table 5-1 on page PPT 359 apply to menus as well. Any command specific to buttons pertains to editing the button on the left side of a command on a menu.

An alternative to adding a command to a menu is to add a new menu name to the menu bar and add commands to its menu. You can add a new menu name to the menu bar by selecting New Menu in the Categories list of the Customize dialog box and dragging New Menu from the Commands list to the menu bar.

With the toolbar and macro added to the presentation, save the file and then close the presentation. The following steps show how to accomplish these tasks.

To Save and Close the Presentation

1 **Click the Save button on the Standard toolbar.**

2 **Click the presentation's Close Window button on the menu bar to close the presentation and leave PowerPoint open.**

PowerPoint saves the Vacation Central presentation to drive A and then closes the presentation.

Q: How can I protect my computer against macro viruses?

A: The best protection against macro viruses is to install specialized antivirus software. You also can make some adjustments in PowerPoint: click Options on the Tools menu, click the Security tab, click Macro Security, click the Trusted Publishers tab, and then click the Trust all installed add-ins and templates check box to remove the check mark. Microsoft has digitally signed all templates, add-ins, and macros shipped with Microsoft Office 2003, so you then should add Microsoft to the list of trusted publishers.

Opening a Presentation Containing a Macro and Executing the Macro

A **computer virus** is a potentially damaging computer program designed to affect a computer negatively by infecting it and altering the way it works without the user's knowledge or permission. Currently, more than 65,000 known computer viruses exist, and more than 500 viruses are discovered each month. The increased use of networks, the Internet, and e-mail has accelerated the spread of computer viruses.

To combat this evil, most computer users run antivirus programs that search for viruses and destroy them before they ever have a chance to infect the computer. Macros are a known carrier of viruses because people can add code easily to them. For this reason, each time you open a presentation with an associated macro with it, PowerPoint displays a Security Warning dialog box warning that a macro is attached and that macros can contain viruses. Table 5-2 summarizes the buttons users can choose to continue the process of opening a presentation with macros.

Table 5-2 Buttons in the Security Warning Dialog Box	
BUTTONS	**DESCRIPTION**
Disable Macros	Macros are unavailable to the user
Enable Macros	Macros are available to the user to execute
More Info	Opens the Microsoft PowerPoint Help window and displays information on viruses and macros

If you are confident of the source (author) of the presentation and macros, click the Enable Macros button. If you are uncertain about the reliability of the source, then click the Disable Macros button. For more information on this topic, click the More Info button.

The following steps open the Vacation Central presentation to illustrate the Security Warning dialog box that is displayed when a presentation contains a macro. The following steps also show how to execute the recorded macro, PrintHandout.

More About

Computer Viruses

More than one-half of the 1,400 companies surveyed in a 2003 Ernst & Young Global Information Security survey say they have deficient computer security measures. The corporate employees surveyed say insufficient funding is the reason why more attention is not being paid to increase corporate security.

To Open a Presentation with a Macro and Execute the Macro

1

• **With PowerPoint active, click File on the menu bar and then click Open.**

• **If necessary, when the Open dialog box is displayed, click the Look in box arrow, and navigate to the folder where your files are stored.**

• **Double-click the file name, Vacation Central.**

Depending upon the Macro Security settings on your system, the Security Warning dialog box may be displayed (Figure 5-32).

2

• **If the Security Warning dialog box is displayed, click the Enable Macros button.**

• **When Slide 1 of the Vacation Central presentation is displayed, click File on the menu bar and then click Print BW Handout.**

PowerPoint opens the Vacation Central presentation, executes the macro, and then prints the handout and the four slides shown in Figures 5-5 and 5-21 on pages PPT 349 and PPT 360.

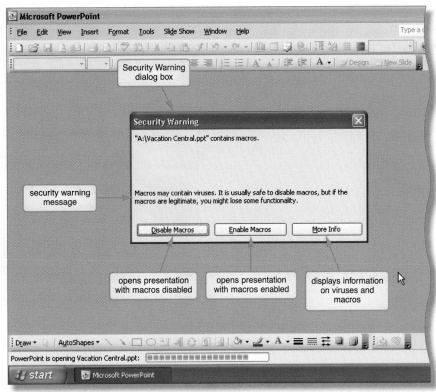

FIGURE 5-32

If you are running antivirus software, you may want to turn off the security warning shown in Figure 5-32. You can turn off the security warning by clicking Tools on the menu bar, pointing to Macro, and then clicking Security on the Macro submenu. When the Security dialog box is displayed, click the Low button. Then, the next time you open a presentation with an attached macro, PowerPoint will open the presentation immediately, rather than display the dialog box shown in Figure 5-32.

Viewing a Macro's VBA Code

As described earlier, a macro is composed of VBA code, which is created automatically by the macro recorder. You can view the VBA code through the **Visual Basic Editor**. The Visual Basic Editor is used by all Office applications to enter, modify, and view VBA code. The steps on the next page illustrate how to view a macro's VBA code.

To View a Macro's VBA Code

1

• **Click Tools on the menu bar, point to Macro, and then point to Macros on the Macro submenu.**

The Tools menu and Macro submenu are displayed (Figure 5-33).

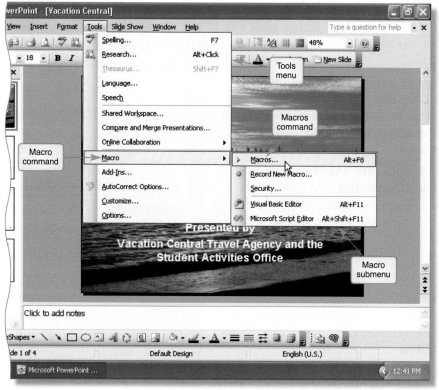

FIGURE 5-33

2

• **Click Macros.**

• **If necessary, when the Macro dialog box is displayed, click PrintHandout in the list.**

The Macro dialog box is displayed (Figure 5-34).

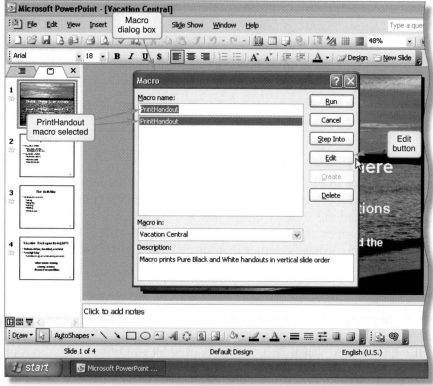

FIGURE 5-34

3

• **Click the Edit button.**

The Visual Basic Editor starts and displays the VBA code in the PrintHandout macro (Figure 5-35).

4

• **Scroll through the VBA code.**

• **When you are finished, click the Close button on the right side of the Microsoft Visual Basic - Vacation Central title bar.**

The Visual Basic Editor closes, and Slide 1 in the Vacation Central presentation is displayed.

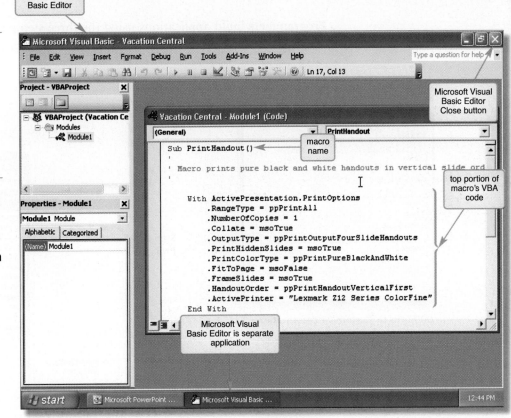

FIGURE 5-35

This set of instructions, beginning with line 1 in Figure 5-35 and continuing sequentially to the last line, executes when you invoke the macro. By scrolling through the VBA code, you can see that the macro recorder generates many instructions. In this case, 32 lines of code are generated to print the handout vertically using the Pure Black and White option.

Phase 3 — Creating a Form to Customize the Presentation

With a toolbar and buttons added and the macro recorded to print handouts, you are ready to develop a form that allows users to design custom presentations. This form, called a **user interface**, allows users to input data and then display results. The user interface and the step-by-step procedure for its implementation are called an **application**. Thus, Microsoft created the name Visual Basic for Applications (VBA) for its programming language used to customize PowerPoint and other Microsoft Office 2003 programs.

Other Ways

1. Click Visual Basic Editor button on Visual Basic toolbar

Q&A

Q: How can I learn more about VBA?

A: A wealth of information is provided on the Microsoft Visual Basic for Applications Web site. Included are product support, training events, technical chats, downloads, and articles. To learn more about VBA help, visit the PowerPoint 2003 More About Web page (scsite.com/ppt2003/more) and click Assistance.

Programmers build applications using the three-step process shown in Figures 5-36a through 5-36c: (1) create the user interface; (2) set the control properties; and (3) write the VBA code.

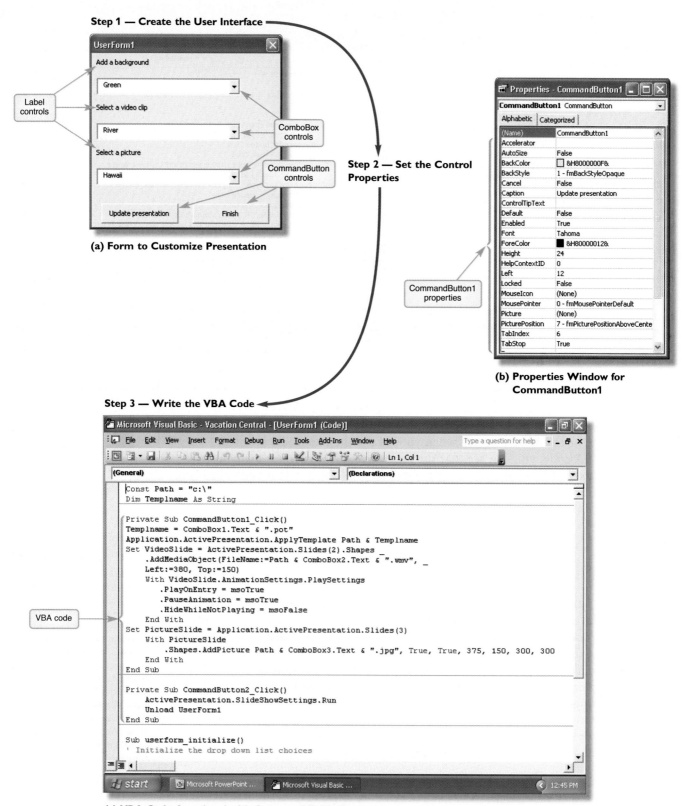

(a) Form to Customize Presentation

(b) Properties Window for CommandButton1

(c) VBA Code Associated with Command Buttons

FIGURE 5-36

Step 1 — Create the User Interface

The form shown Figure 5-36a displays the application's user **interface**. The interface allows the user to specify a template, a video clip, and a digital picture and place them in the presentation. The form contains three label controls, three combo box controls, and two command button controls. The **labels** identify the contents of the combo boxes. Each **combo box** allows a choice of two items. The **command buttons** update the presentation, close the interface form, and run the presentation.

The first three elements on the form are labels, each of which indicates the use of the combo box directly below the label. The first label instructs the user to select one of two slide design templates listed in the combo box. This label-and-combo-box set is repeated twice. The second set allows the user to select one of two video clips, and the final set tells the user to choose one of two photos. The two command buttons at the bottom of the form execute the VBA procedure. The Update presentation button applies the design template and inserts the video clip and picture into the slides, and the Finish button hides the user form, unloads it from memory, and runs the presentation.

Creating the interface consists of sizing the form, adding each of the controls to the form, and adjusting their sizes and positions. When beginning to create a user interface, position the controls as close as possible to their final locations on the form; after setting the properties, you can finalize their positions. As you create the form, try to locate the controls as shown in Figure 5-36a.

The Standard toolbar (Figure 5-37) is displayed when you use VBA. Alternately, you can right-click a toolbar and then click Standard on the shortcut menu to display it.

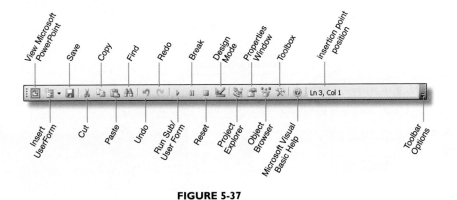

FIGURE 5-37

Opening the Visual Basic IDE and a New Form

Before you begin creating the interface, you must start the **Visual Basic integrated development environment (IDE)**, which contains nine different windows and four toolbars. The windows can be **docked**, or anchored, to other windows that are dockable, and the four toolbars can be docked or can float in their own windows. The steps on the next page open the Visual Basic IDE and open a new form.

To Open the Visual Basic IDE and a New Form

1

• **With the Vacation Central presentation still open, click Tools on the menu bar, point to Macro, and then point to Visual Basic Editor.**

The Tools menu and Macro submenu are displayed (Figure 5-38).

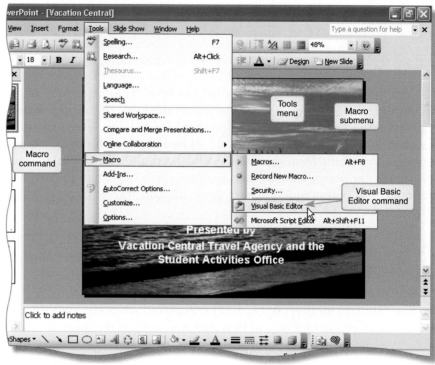

FIGURE 5-38

2

• **Click Visual Basic Editor.**

• **If the VBA code displays, click the Close button in the upper-right corner of the Vacation Central - Module 1 (Code) window. You may need to drag the window to the left to view this Close button.**

• **Click Insert on the menu bar and then point to UserForm.**

The Visual Basic Editor opens and displays a Project window and a Properties window. The Insert menu is displayed (Figure 5-39).

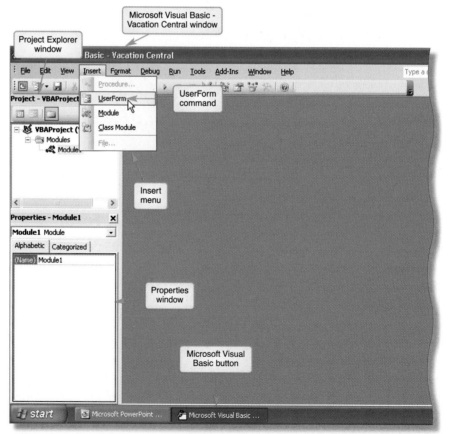

FIGURE 5-39

3

- **Click UserForm.**

- **If the Toolbox does not display, click the Toolbox button on the Standard toolbar.**

A new form, UserForm1, opens and the Toolbox is displayed (Figure 5-40). Your form may display in a different location, and your Toolbox may have a different shape.

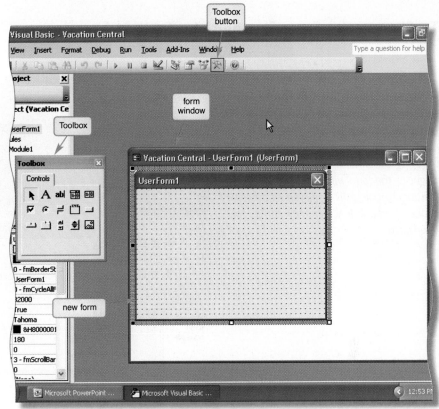

FIGURE 5-40

Changing the Form Size and the Toolbox Location

In design mode, you can resize a form by changing the values of its **Height property** and **Width property** in the Properties window, and you can change a form's location on the screen by changing the values of its **Top property** and **Left property**. You also can resize a form by dragging its borders and change its location by dragging and dropping. The steps on the next page describe how to set the size of the form by dragging its borders and set the location by dragging and dropping.

More About

Microsoft Feedback

Ever dreamt of an exciting new feature that would give PowerPoint pizzazz? Tell Microsoft via its Wish e-mail box. Every wish is read, studied, evaluated, and considered when Microsoft develops its next PowerPoint version. Send the message to mswish@microsoft.com and type the word, PowerPoint, in the Subject text box.

To Change the Form Size and the Toolbox Location

1

• **Without releasing the mouse button, drag the form window's bottom border down.**

Dragging the bottom border increases the height of the form window (Figure 5-41). The mouse pointer is displayed as a two-headed arrow. Your screen may display only UserForm1.

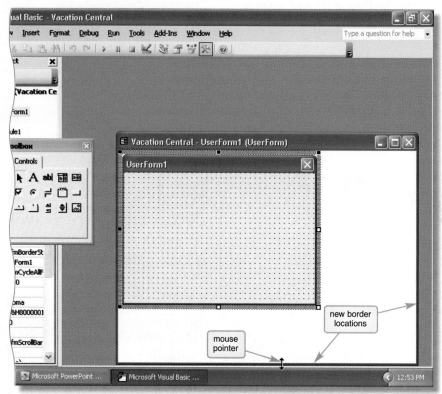

FIGURE 5-41

2

• **Release the mouse button.**

• **Without releasing the mouse button, drag the form's bottom-center sizing handle down.**

Dragging the border of the form increases the height of the form. The mouse pointer is displayed as a two-headed arrow (Figure 5-42).

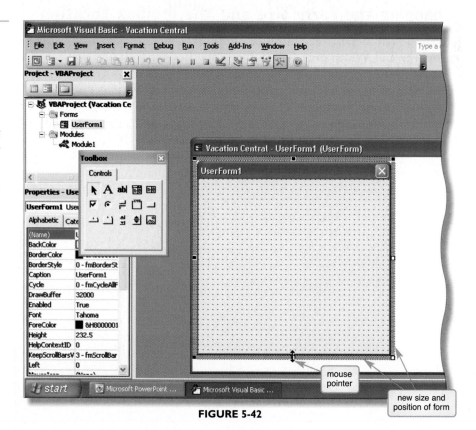

FIGURE 5-42

3

• **Release the mouse button.**

• **Click the Toolbox title bar and drag it to the lower-right side of the form window.**

The form's size is displayed as shown in Figure 5-43. The Toolbox is displayed to the right of the form window.

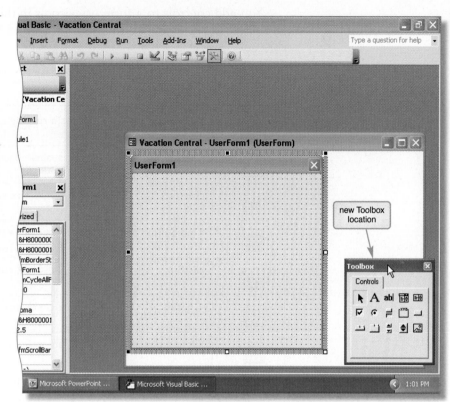

FIGURE 5-43

Adding Controls

Graphical images, or objects, in Windows applications include buttons, check boxes, tabs, and text boxes. Visual Basic calls these objects **controls**. The user form in this project contains three types of controls (see Figure 5-36a on page PPT 372). Table 5-3 describes these controls and their functions.

Table 5-3 VBA Controls Used in UserForm1	
CONTROL	**DESCRIPTION**
Label	Displays text such as the words, Company Name, on a form. At run time, the user cannot change the text on a label.
ComboBox	Presents a list of choices. When an item is selected from the list by clicking it, the item is displayed in a highlighted color.
CommandButton	Represents a button that initiates an action when clicked.

You add controls to a form using tools in the **Toolbox**. To use a tool, you click its respective button in the Toolbox. Table 5-4 identifies the Toolbox buttons.

Table 5-4	Summary of Buttons in the Toolbox	
BUTTON	**NAME**	**FUNCTION**
	Select Objects pointer	Draws a rectangle over the controls you want to select
	Label	Adds a label control
	TextBox	Adds a text box control
	ComboBox	Adds a custom edit box, drop-down list box, or combo box on a menu bar, toolbar, menu, submenu, or shortcut menu
	ListBox	Adds a list box control
	CheckBox	Adds a check box control
	OptionButton	Adds an option button control
	ToggleButton	Adds a toggle button control
	Frame	Creates an option group or groups controls with closely related contents
	CommandButton	Adds a command button control
	TabStrip	Contains a collection of one or more tabs
	MultiPage	Contains a collection of one or more pages
	ScrollBar	Adds a scroll bar control
	SpinButton	Adds a spin button control
	Image	Adds an image control

ADDING LABEL AND COMBO BOX CONTROLS The next steps are to add the three label and combo box controls shown in Figure 5-36a on page PPT 372. The following steps demonstrate how to add these controls to the form.

To Add Label and Combo Box Controls to a Form

1

• **Click the Label button in the Toolbox.**

• **Position the mouse pointer in the upper-left corner of the form.**

The Label button in the Toolbox is selected, and the mouse pointer changes to a cross hair and a copy of the Label button when it is over the form (Figure 5-44). The upper-left corner of the Label control will be positioned in this location.

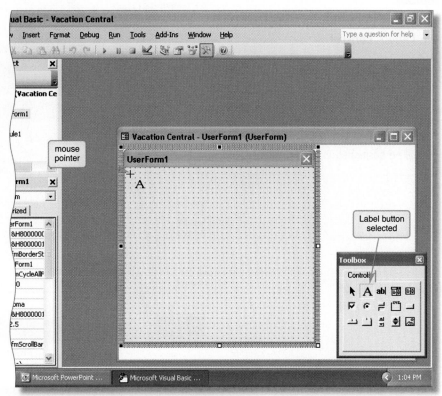

FIGURE 5-44

2

• **Click the mouse button.**

The label is displayed on the form with the default caption, Label1 (Figure 5-45). The label is surrounded by a selection rectangle and sizing handles.

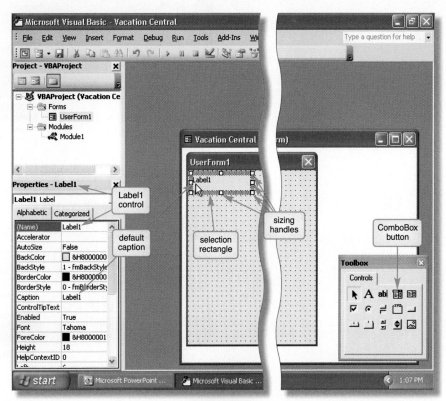

FIGURE 5-45

3

• **Click the ComboBox button in the Toolbox.**

• **Position the mouse pointer below the Label1 control.**

The ComboBox button in the Toolbox is selected, and the mouse pointer changes to a cross hair and a copy of the ComboBox button when it is over the form (Figure 5-46). The upper-left corner of the ComboBox control will be positioned in this location.

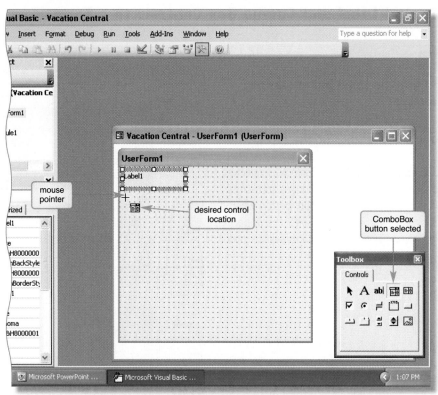

FIGURE 5-46

4

• **Click the mouse button.**

The ComboBox control is added to the form (Figure 5-47).

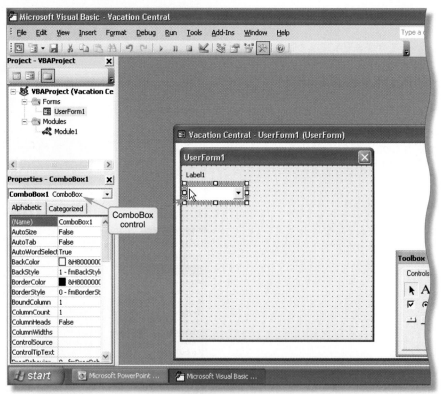

FIGURE 5-47

5

• **Repeat Steps 1 through 4 to add the second and third Label controls and second and third ComboBox controls to the form as shown in Figure 5-48.**

The three Label and ComboBox controls are displayed on the form (Figure 5-48).

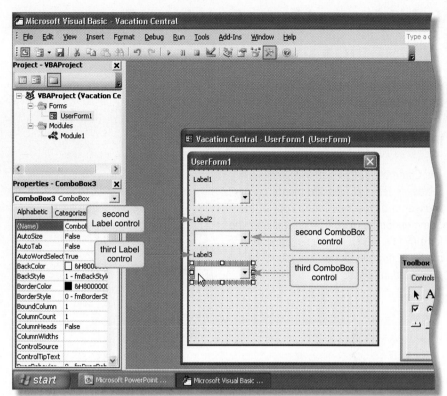

FIGURE 5-48

With the labels and combo boxes added to the form, the next step is to add the two CommandButton controls below the third ComboBox control.

ADDING COMMAND BUTTON CONTROLS When users finish making selections in the form, they can click the Update presentation button to assemble the presentation by applying the design template and inserting the video clip and picture into the slides. After clicking the Update presentation button, they can click the Finish button to hide the user form, unload it from memory, and run the presentation. The steps on the next page demonstrate how to add these two command button controls to the form.

To Add Command Button Controls to a Form

1

• **Click the CommandButton button in the Toolbox.**

• **Position the mouse pointer in the lower-left corner of the form.**

The CommandButton button in the Toolbox is selected, and the mouse pointer changes to a cross hair and a copy of the CommandButton button when it is over the form (Figure 5-49). The upper-left corner of the first CommandButton control will be positioned in this location.

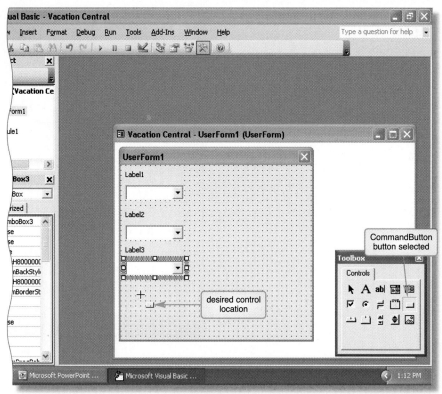

FIGURE 5-49

2

• **Click the mouse button.**

The CommandButton1 control is added to the form (Figure 5-50).

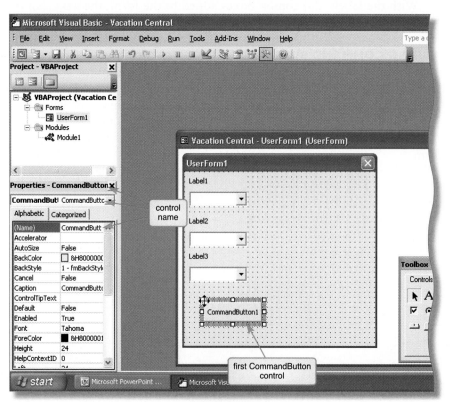

FIGURE 5-50

3

• **Repeat Steps 1 and 2 to add a second CommandButton control, CommandButton2, as shown in Figure 5-51.**

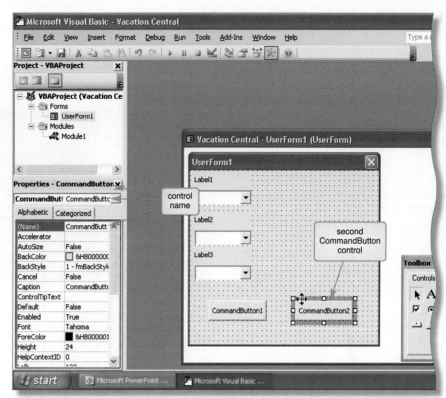

FIGURE 5-51

Step 2 — Set Control Properties

Controls have several different **properties** (Figure 5-52 on the next page), such as caption (the words on the face of the button), background color, foreground color, height, width, and font. Once you add a control to a form, you can change any property to improve its appearance and modify how it works.

SETTING THE CONTROL CAPTION PROPERTIES The controls on the form are not very informative because they do not state their functions. You want to provide meaningful descriptions of the choices the user can make when using the form. These descriptions are called **captions**. You type the captions in the Properties window. This window has two tabs, Alphabetic and Categorized. The **Alphabetic list** displays the properties in alphabetical order. The **Categorized list** displays the properties in categories, such as appearance, behavior, font, and miscellaneous. The steps on the next page change the controls' caption properties.

More About

Renaming Commands

Once you have added a command to a menu, you can change its name. To rename a command, click Customize on the Tools menu, click the menu that contains the command, right-click the command, type a name in the Name text box, and then press the ENTER key.

To Set the Controls' Caption Properties

1

• **Click the Label1 control.**

• **With the Label1 control selected, click Caption on the Alphabetic tab in the Properties window.**

The Properties window for the Label1 control is displayed (Figure 5-52). The default Caption property is Label1.

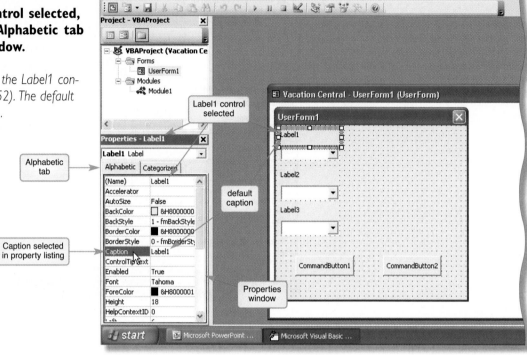

FIGURE 5-52

2

• **Double-click the current caption, Label1, to select it, type** Add a background **as the caption, and then press the ENTER key.**

Add a background is the new caption for the Label1 control (Figure 5-53). The new caption is displayed on the form.

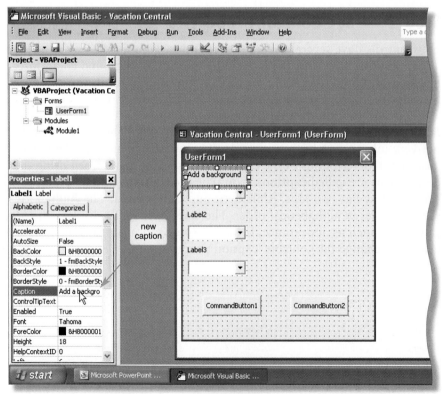

FIGURE 5-53

3

• **Change the captions for the remainder of the controls on the form using the information from Table 5-5.**

The captions for the form are displayed (Figure 5-54).

Alphabetic list displays properties in alphabetical order

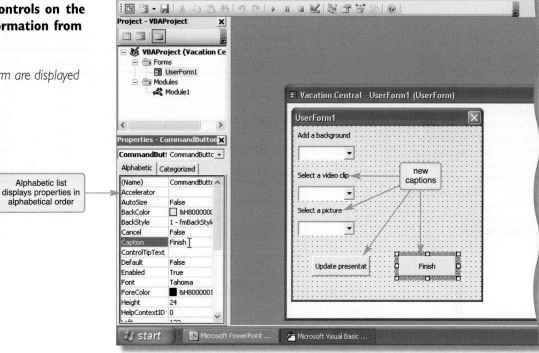

FIGURE 5-54

FINE-TUNING THE USER INTERFACE   After setting the properties for all the controls, you can fine-tune the size and location of the controls on the form. You can reposition a control in three ways:

1. Drag the control to its new location.
2. Select the control and use the arrow keys to reposition it.
3. Select the control and set the control's Top and Left properties in the Properties window.

Table 5-5	Control Captions
CONTROL CAPTION	NEW CAPTION
Label2	Select a video clip
Label3	Select a picture
CommandButton1	Update presentation
CommandButton2	Finish

To use the third technique, you need to know the distance the control is from the top of the form and the left edge of the form in points. One point is equal to 1/72 of an inch. Thus, if the Top property of a control is 216, then the control is 3 inches (216 / 72) from the top of the form.

Controls also may require resizing. You need to increase the size of the CommandButton1 control so the entire caption is displayed. You can resize a control in two ways:

1. Drag the sizing handles.
2. Select the control and set the control's Height and Width properties in the Properties window.

More About

Wireless Remotes

If you present PowerPoint slide shows on a regular basis, you might want to consider purchasing a wireless presentation remote. These devices generally are smaller than a credit card and fit in the palm of your hand. You often can stand as far as 100 feet away from your computer and advance your slides. To learn more about these remotes, visit the PowerPoint 2003 More About Web page (scsite.com/ppt2003/more) and click Remotes.

As with the Top and Left properties, the Height and Width properties are measured in points. Table 5-6 lists the exact points for the Top, Left, Height, and Width properties of each of the controls on the form.

Table 5-6	Exact Locations of Controls on the Form			
CONTROL	**TOP**	**LEFT**	**HEIGHT**	**WIDTH**
Label1	6	6	18	96
Label2	60	6	18	96
Label3	114	6	18	96
ComboBox1	30	6	20	180
ComboBox2	84	6	20	180
ComboBox3	138	6	20	180
CommandButton1	180	12	24	96
CommandButton2	180	126	24	96

The following steps resize and reposition the controls on the form using the values in Table 5-6.

To Resize and Reposition Controls on a Form

1

- **Click the Label1 control, Add a background.**

- **Change its Top, Left, Height, and Width properties in the Properties window to those listed in Table 5-6.**

The Label1 control Properties window is displayed (Figure 5-55).

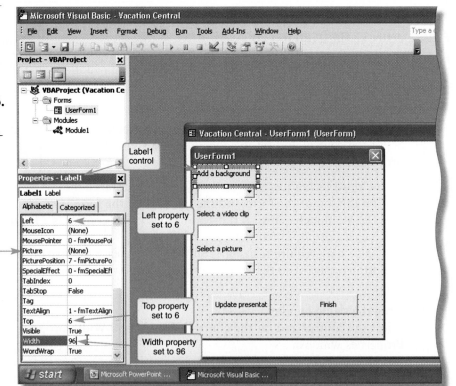

FIGURE 5-55

2

• **One at a time, select the controls and change their Top, Left, Height, and Width properties to those listed in Table 5-6.**

The form is displayed with the resized and repositioned controls (Figure 5-56).

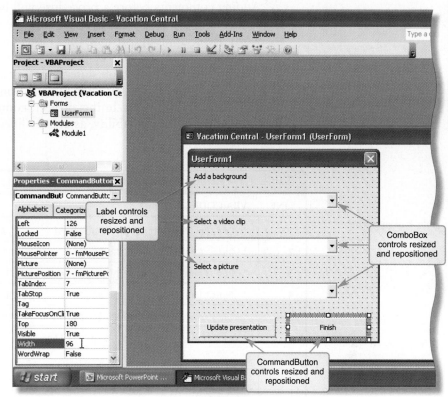

FIGURE 5-56

Step 3 — Write the VBA Code

The interface is created and the properties of the controls are set for this project. The next step is to write and then enter the procedure that will execute when you click the Create Presentation button on the Vacation toolbar. You will create this button near the end of this project. Clicking this button is the event that triggers execution of the procedure that assembles the custom presentation. As mentioned earlier, Visual Basic for Applications (VBA) is a powerful programming language that can automate many activities described thus far in this book. The code for this project will include events and modules. The events in this program are the buttons on the form. The process begins with writing a module that will serve as a macro to display the form.

PLANNING A PROCEDURE When you trigger the event that executes a procedure, PowerPoint steps through the Visual Basic statements one at a time, beginning at the top of the procedure. When you plan a procedure, therefore, remember that the order in which you place the statements in the procedure is important because the order determines the sequence of execution.

Once you know what you want the procedure to do, write the VBA code on paper in a format similar to that shown in Table 5-7 on the next page. Then, before entering the procedure into the computer, test it by putting yourself in the position of PowerPoint and stepping through the instructions one at a time. As you do so, think about how the instructions affect the slide show. Testing a procedure before entering it is called **desk checking**, which is an important part of the development process.

Adding comments before a procedure will help you remember its purpose at a later date. In Table 5-7, the first seven lines are comments. **Comments** begin with the word, Rem, or an apostrophe ('). These comments contain overall documentation about the procedure and may be placed anywhere in the procedure. Most developers place comments before the Sub statement. Comments have no effect on the execution of a procedure; they simply provide information about the procedure, such as name, creation date, and function. In this project, comments that are displayed on multiple lines are indented for readability, as are the lines that are displayed between Sub and End Sub statements.

Table 5-7 Create Presentation Procedure

LINE	VBA CODE
1	` ' Create Presentation Procedure        Author: Ramon Cruz`
2	` ' Date Created: 12/1/2005`
3	` ' Run from: Click Update presentation button`
4	` ' Function: When executed, this procedure accepts data that causes`
5	` '              PowerPoint to build a custom presentation that adds a`
6	` '              template, video clip, and digital picture.`
7	` '`
8	` Sub createpresentationtravel()`
9	`     UserForm1.userform_initialize`
10	`     UserForm1.Show`
11	` End Sub`

A procedure begins with a **Sub statement** and ends with an **End Sub statement** (lines 8 and 11 in Table 5-7). The Sub statement begins with the name of the procedure. The parentheses following the procedure name allow the passing of data values, or arguments, from one procedure to another. Passing arguments is beyond the scope of this project, but the parentheses still are required. The End Sub statement signifies the end of the procedure and returns PowerPoint to normal view.

The first executable statement in Table 5-7 is line 9, which calls the userform_initialize procedure on the form, indicated by the object name, UserForm1. You use the UserForm1 object name so VBA can find the userform_initialize procedure. Line 10 issues the command to display the form in the PowerPoint normal view window. Again, you must use the form name so VBA knows which form to display. Line 11 is the end of the procedure. Every procedure must conclude with an End Sub statement.

To enter a procedure, use the Visual Basic Editor. To activate the Visual Basic Editor, click the View Code button in the VBA Project window or click the Module command on the Insert menu.

The Visual Basic Editor is a full-screen editor, which allows you to enter a procedure by typing the lines of VBA code as if using word processing software. At the end of a line, press the ENTER key to move to the next line. If you make a mistake in a statement, you can use the arrow keys and the DELETE or BACKSPACE key to correct it. You also can move the insertion point to previous lines to make corrections.

USING THE VISUAL BASIC EDITOR TO ENTER A PROCEDURE The following steps activate the Visual Basic Editor and create the procedure for the Create Presentation module.

More About

Projectors

The newest projectors do more than display PowerPoint slides on a screen at work or school — they also can project DVD movies and video games on walls at home. These ultra-portable machines, called crossover or multi-use units, are designed for people who want their investment to do double-duty in business and entertainment environments. To learn more about these projectors, visit the PowerPoint 2003 More About Web page (scsite.com/ppt2003/more) and click Projectors.

To Enter the Create Presentation Procedure

1

• **Click the Insert UserForm button arrow on the Standard toolbar and then point to Module.**

The Insert UserForm list is displayed (Figure 5-57).

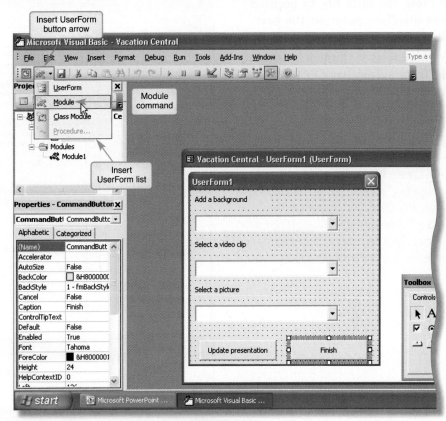

FIGURE 5-57

2

• **Click Module in the Insert UserForm list.**

• **When the Visual Basic Editor opens, click the Maximize button in the Vacation Central - [Module2 (Code)] window.**

• **Type the seven comment statements (lines 1 through 7) shown in Table 5-7. Be certain to enter an apostrophe at the beginning of each comment line.**

PowerPoint starts the Visual Basic Editor, adds Module2, and displays the Microsoft Visual Basic window (Figure 5-58). The comment lines are displayed in green. Module1 contains the code for the Print BW Handout macro you recorded in Phase 2 of this project.

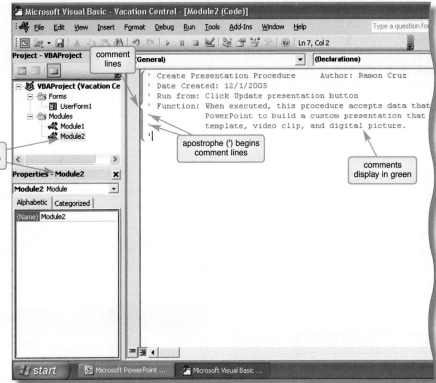

FIGURE 5-58

3

• **Press the ENTER key to position the insertion point on the next line.**

• **Enter lines 8 through 10 shown in Table 5-7 on page PPT 388. Do not enter the End Sub statement (line 11). For clarity, indent all lines between the Sub statement and End Sub statement by three spaces.**

The Create Presentation procedure is complete (Figure 5-59). You do not need to enter the End Sub statement in line 11 of Table 5-7 because the Visual Basic Editor displays that line automatically when you type the Sub statement in line 8.

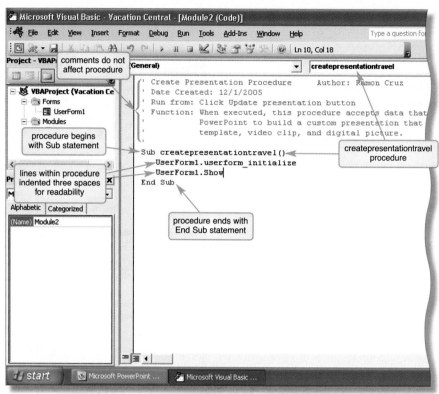

FIGURE 5-59

4

• **Click the Close Window button on the right side of the menu bar.**

The Module2 Code window closes, and the form is displayed in the UserForm1 window (Figure 5-60). The UserForm1 window is maximized.

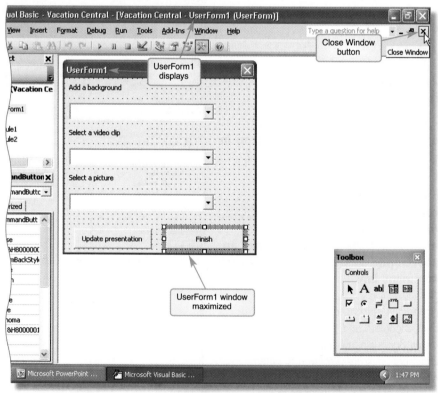

FIGURE 5-60

More About Visual Basic for Applications

Visual Basic for Applications uses many more statements than those presented here. Even this simple procedure, however, should help you understand the basic makeup of a Visual Basic statement. Lines 9 and 10 in the procedure shown in Figure 5-59 include a period. The entry on the left side of the period tells PowerPoint which object you want to affect.

An **object** is a real-world thing. Your textbook, your car, your pets, and even your friends are objects. Visual Basic uses objects in its association with applications. This technique is described as **object-oriented (OO)**. When it refers to programming, it is called **Object-Oriented Programming (OOP)**. The development of OOP provides a way to represent the world in conceptual terms that people understand. People relate to their everyday objects and easily can understand that these objects have properties and behaviors.

An object is described by its properties. Properties are attributes that help differentiate one object from another. For example, your car has a color, a certain body style, and a certain type of interior. These properties are used to describe the car. The Visual Basic programming language has specific rules, or **syntax**. In Visual Basic syntax, you separate an object and its property with a period. For example, car.color, specifies a car object and the property, color. You would write the statement, car.color = "red", to set the value of the color property to red.

An object also has certain behaviors, or methods. A **method** is a function or action you want the object to perform or an action that will be performed on an object. You can write your own functions, or use the built-in methods supplied with Visual Basic. Methods associated with car, pet, and friend objects might be drive, feed, and talk, respectively. The drive method would be written, car.drive, just as in the statement, UserForm1.Show, where UserForm1 is the object and Show is the method.

The following example shows that you can change an object's property value during execution of a procedure. Similar statements often are used to clear the properties of controls or to set them to initial values. This process is called **initialization**. The object in this case is a text box control.

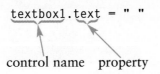

textbox1.text = " "

control name   property

WRITING THE FORM'S INITIALIZATION PROCEDURE The next step is to write the procedure to initialize some of the control properties. Recall in Step 2 — Set Control Properties that you added the controls to the form and then set some of the properties. With respect to VBA, PowerPoint has two modes: design mode and run mode. In **design mode**, you can resize controls, assign properties to controls, and enter VBA code. In **run mode**, all controls are active. That is, if you click a control, it triggers the event, and PowerPoint executes the procedure associated with the control.

Properties such as the label and command button caption properties were set in Step 2 of this project in design mode. The **AddItem method** is used in run mode to add data items to a combo box. Table 5-8 shows the general form of the AddItem method.

Table 5-8	AddItem Method Format
General Form:	ComboBox1.AddItem "item name"
Comment:	The AddItem method places the item name string into the text list of the combo box.
Example:	ComboBox1.AddItem "Blue" ComboBox2.AddItem "River" ComboBox3.AddItem "Hawaii"

Table 5-9   General Form of the Clear Method

General Form:	ComboBox1.Clear
Comment:	All the items in the combo box are deleted.
Example:	ComboBox2.Clear

A good practice is to issue the **Clear method** before adding items to a combo box. Table 5-9 shows the general form of the Clear method to clear all the items in a combo box.

The initialize procedure code in Table 5-10 sets some controls' property values during run mode. The **Initialize Form procedure** ensures the combo boxes are clear and adds the text items to the combo boxes. To add items to a combo box, use the AddItem method. Before adding items to a combo box, the Initialize Form procedure clears the entries in the combo boxes.

The statements in lines 3, 4, and 5 use the Clear method to make sure the combo boxes are empty. Lines 6 through 11 use the AddItem method to add the items to the combo boxes. To complete the section of code for the InitializeForm() procedure, an End Sub statement closes the procedure at line 12, as the following steps illustrate.

Table 5-10   Initialize Form Procedure

LINE	VBA CODE
1	Sub userform_initialize()
2	' Initialize the drop down list choices
3	ComboBox1.Clear
4	ComboBox2.Clear
5	ComboBox3.Clear
6	ComboBox1.AddItem "Green"
7	ComboBox1.AddItem "Blue"
8	ComboBox2.AddItem "River"
9	ComboBox2.AddItem "Fountain"
10	ComboBox3.AddItem "Hawaii"
11	ComboBox3.AddItem "Seattle"
12	End Sub

To Enter the InitializeForm() Procedure

1

• **With UserForm1 selected in the Project window, point to the View Code button at the top of the Project Explorer window (Figure 5-61).**

• **If UserForm1 is not selected, click the form.**

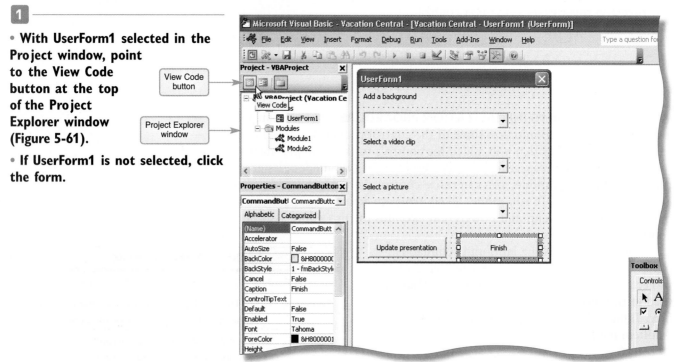

FIGURE 5-61

2

- **Click the View Code button.**
- **Enter the VBA code shown in Table 5-10.**

The initialize procedure is displayed in the Code window (Figure 5-62). The word, UserForm, is displayed in the Object box, and the word, initialize, is displayed in the Procedure box.

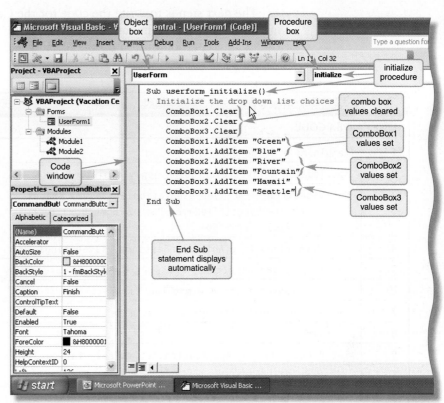

FIGURE 5-62

WRITING THE COMMANDBUTTON1 PROCEDURE Whenever you need to work with an object's properties or methods in more than one line of code, you can use the With statement to eliminate some coding. The **With statement** accepts an object as a parameter and is followed by several lines of code that pertain to this object. Therefore, you do not need to retype the object name in these lines. Table 5-11 describes the general form of the With statement.

Table 5-11	With Statement Format
General Form:	With object Visual Basic code End With
Comment:	Object is any valid Visual Basic or user-defined object.
Example:	With textbox1 .text = "" End With

More About

Inserting Video Files

A video file, also called a movie or media clip, can play automatically when the slide is displayed, play when the mouse is clicked, or play after a specific time delay. This file is added to a presentation by clicking Movies and Sounds on the Insert menu and then clicking Movie from File or Movie from Clip Organizer.

The next step is to write the code for the CommandButton1 procedure as shown in Table 5-12. The CommandButton1 procedure is activated when the user clicks the Update presentation button on the form. The code for this procedure is associated with the Click event.

Table 5-12	CommandButton1 Procedure
LINE	VBA CODE
1	`Templname = ComboBox1.Text & ".pot"`
2	`Application.ActivePresentation.ApplyTemplate Path & Templname`

3	`Set VideoSlide = ActivePresentation.Slides(2).Shapes _`
	`    .AddMediaObject(FileName:=Path & ComboBox2.Text & ".wmv", _`
	`    Left:=380, Top:=150)`

4	`  With VideoSlide.AnimationSettings.PlaySettings`
5	`      .PlayOnEntry = msoTrue`
6	`      .PauseAnimation = msoTrue`
7	`      .HideWhileNotPlaying = msoFalse`
8	`  End With`
9	`Set PictureSlide = Application.ActivePresentation.Slides(3)`
10	`  With PictureSlide`
11	`      .Shapes.AddPicture Path & ComboBox3.Text & ".jpg", True, True, 375, 150, 300, 300`
12	`  End With`

Line 1 defines the name of the template. Line 2 assigns the template to the presentation object. The Set statement in line 3 does several things. It sets an object name, VideoSlide, that represents Slide 2. The statement then assigns the video file selected in ComboBox2 to Slide 2 using the **AddMediaObject() method**. Table 5-13 shows the general form of the AddMediaObject() method. The method places the video at a specific location on the slide using the Left and Top coordinates. The underscore at the end of the line indicates that the statement continues on the next line.

Table 5-13	AddMediaObject() Method Format
General Form:	`Shape_Object.AddMediaObject(FileName, Left, Top, Width, Height)`
Comment:	Shape_Object is the name of the shape on the slide. The file name is required and is the name of the media file. If a path is not specified, the current working folder is the path. Left and Top are the positions (in points) of the upper-left corner of the media location relative to the upper-left corner of the document. You also may supply optional Width and Height positions.
Example:	`ActivePresentation.Slides(2).Shapes.AddMediaObject(FileName:= "river.wmv", Left:=380, Top:=150)`

Lines 4 through 8 use the same object, VideoSlide, and assign the animation and play settings. The **PauseAnimation property** set to True indicates the animation will pause when the user clicks the shape. When the user clicks the shape again, the animation will continue to play. The **HideWhileNotPlaying property** is set to False, so the video is displayed on the slide and stays on the slide even when not running.

Line 9 sets Slide 3 to a new object called PictureSlide. Lines 10 through 12 add the picture selected from the Picture combo box to the specific coordinates using the AddPicture method. Table 5-14 shows the general form of the **AddPicture method**.

Table 5-14	AddPicture Method Format
General Form:	`Shape_Object.AddPicture(FileName, LinkToFile, SaveWithDocument, Left, Top, Width, Height)`
Comment:	The file name is required and represents the file from which the OLE object is created. LinkToFile value is True to link the picture to the file or False to make the picture an independent copy of the file. SaveWithDocument value is True to save the linked picture with the presentation or False to store only the linked information in the document. If LinkToFile is False, this value must be True. Left and Top are the points location for the picture, and Width and Height are the width and height of the picture.
Example:	`.Shapes.AddPicture "mypicture.jpg", True, True, 375, 150, 300, 300`

To Enter the CommandButton1 Procedure

1

• **Click the Object box arrow at the top of the Code window, and then point to CommandButton1 in the Object list (Figure 5-63).**

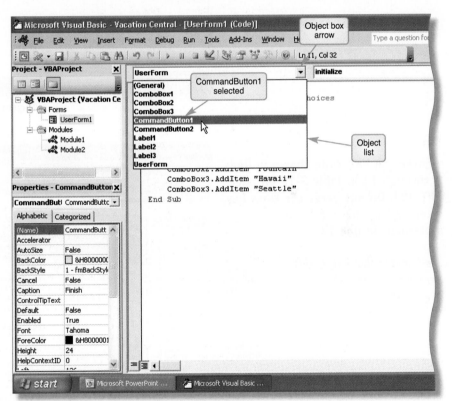

FIGURE 5-63

2

• **Click CommandButton1.**

• **Make sure Click is in the Procedure box.**

The Visual Basic Editor displays the Sub and End Sub statements for the CommandButton1 procedure and positions the insertion point between the two statements (Figure 5-64).

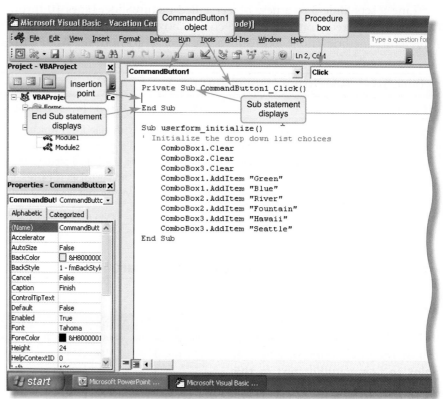

FIGURE 5-64

3

• **Enter the VBA code shown in lines 1 through 12 in Table 5-12 on page PPT 394. Do not press the ENTER key after typing the End With statement in line 12.**

The CommandButton1_Click() procedure is displayed (Figure 5-65).

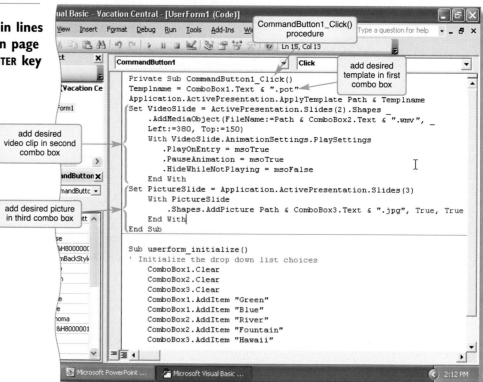

FIGURE 5-65

WRITING THE COMMANDBUTTON2 PROCEDURE The next step is to write the CommandButton2 procedure. Table 5-15 shows the procedure to execute when the user clicks the Finish button. The procedure hides and unloads the form and starts the presentation.

Table 5-15	CommandButton2 Procedure
LINE	**VBA CODE**
1	`ActivePresentation.SlideShowSettings.Run`
2	`Unload UserForm1`

Line 1 starts the current active presentation. Line 2 unloads the form (UserForm1).

More About

CommandButton Click Events

A user can press the ENTER key during run time instead of clicking a command button if you change the CommandButton control's Default property. Only one command button on a form can be the default command button. When Default is set to True for one command button, it automatically is set to False for all other command buttons on the form.

To Enter the CommandButton2 Procedure

1

• **Click the Object box arrow in the Code window, and then click CommandButton2 in the Object box.**

• **Make sure Click is in the Procedure box.**

The Visual Basic Editor displays the Sub and End Sub statements for the CommandButton2 procedure and positions the insertion point between the two statements (Figure 5-66).

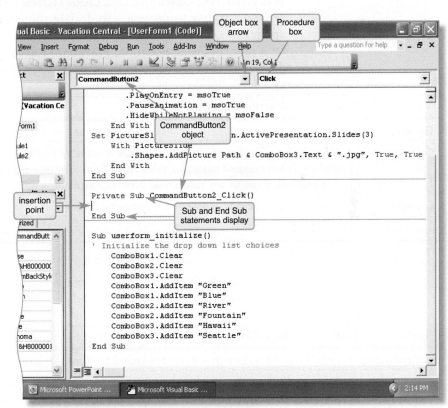

FIGURE 5-66

2

• **Enter the VBA code shown in Table 5-15 on the previous page.**

The CommandButton2_Click() procedure is displayed (Figure 5-67).

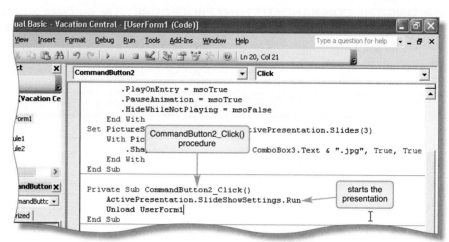

FIGURE 5-67

WRITING THE GENERAL DECLARATIONS   At the beginning of a Visual Basic program, it may be necessary to declare some variables or constant values. In this application, a **Path constant** is declared, which tells PowerPoint where to find files on a disk. In this application, PowerPoint needs to locate the templates, video, and digital images. The basic form of a **Constant statement** is shown in Table 5-16.

Table 5-16	Constant Statement Format
General Form:	`[Public	Private] Const constname [As type] = expression`
Comment:	Public or Private indicates whether the value is available to all Visual Basic modules or just the current module. The constname must be a valid Visual Basic identifier and type must be a valid Visual Basic data type. The expression can be any valid Visual Basic expression.
Example:	`Const Path = "c:\"   (Note: A \ must be placed at the end of the Path statement.)` `Const Tax = 0.065`

Similar to the Constant statement is the Dim statement. The general form of the Dim statement is shown in Table 5-17.

Table 5-17	Dim Statement Format
General Form:	`[Public	Private] Dim VariableName [As type] = expression`
Comment:	Public or Private indicates whether the value is available to all Visual Basic modules or just the current module. The VariableName must be a valid Visual Basic identifier and type must be a valid Visual Basic data type. The expression can be any valid Visual Basic expression.
Example:	`Dim Area As Single` `Dim Templname As String`

This project uses the Path constant because the video clip and digital images used are too large to fit on a floppy disk. By assigning the Path value once, the Path constant can be used in several modules as needed. If the location of the files changes, the programmer need only change the value of the Path constant. This procedure reduces the possibility of errors. The following steps describe how to initialize a Path constant.

To Initialize a Path Constant

1

• **Click the Object box arrow and then click (General).**

(General) is displayed in the Object box, and (Declarations) is displayed in the Procedure box (Figure 5-68).

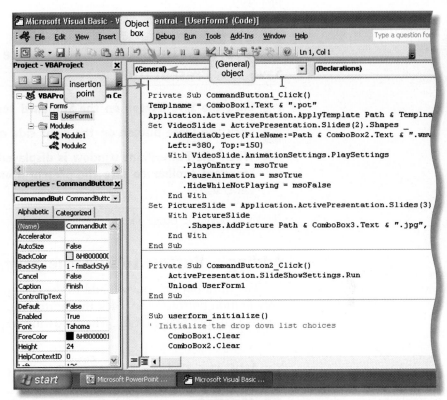

FIGURE 5-68

2

• **Type** Const Path = "c:\", **replacing c with the actual location of the video and photo files on your system. Make sure a \ is at the end of your path.**

• **Press the ENTER key.**

• **Type** Dim Templname As String **and then press the ENTER key.**

Be certain to enter the exact location of the travel files on your system in place of the letter c in the first statement. The constant and variable are declared for all procedures. A line is displayed and separates the General Declarations from the CommandButton1 procedure (Figure 5-69).

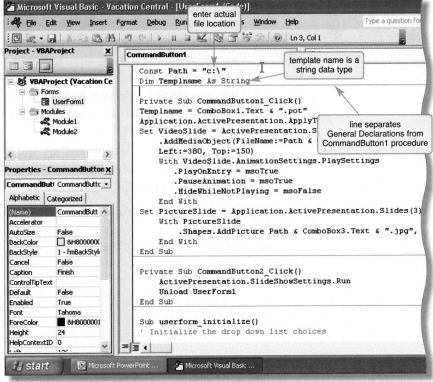

FIGURE 5-69

The VBA code is complete. The next step is to close the Visual Basic Editor and save the presentation. Before closing the Visual Basic Editor, you should verify your code by comparing it with Figures 5-58 through 5-69 on pages PPT 389 through PPT 399.

To Save the Visual Basic Code, Close the Visual Basic Editor, and Save the Presentation

1 Click the Save button on the Standard toolbar.

2 Click the Close button on the right side of the Visual Basic Editor title bar.

3 When the PowerPoint window is displayed, click the Save button on the Standard toolbar to save the presentation using the same file name, Vacation Central.

The Visual Basic IDE closes and the Vacation Central presentation displays.

Adding a Button to Run the Form

The third button you will add to the custom Vacation toolbar is the Create Presentation button. Users click this button and then make selections in the form to create a custom presentation. The following steps illustrate how to add this button.

To Add the Create Presentation Button

1 Click Tools on the menu bar and then click Customize.

2 If necessary, when the Customize dialog box opens, click the Commands tab. Scroll down in the Categories box and then click Macros. Click createpresentationtravel in the Commands box.

3 Drag the createpresentationtravel entry from the Commands list in the Customize dialog box to the right of the Package for CD button on the Vacation toolbar.

4 Click the Modify Selection button and then point to Change Button Image on the submenu. When the Change Button Image palette is displayed, click the button with footsteps (row 4, column 6).

5 Click the Modify Selection button and then click Name on the submenu. Type Create Presentation as the new name of this button.

6 Click Default Style on the submenu.

7 Click the Close button in the Customize dialog box.

The Create Presentation button is displayed with a footsteps image (Figure 5-70).

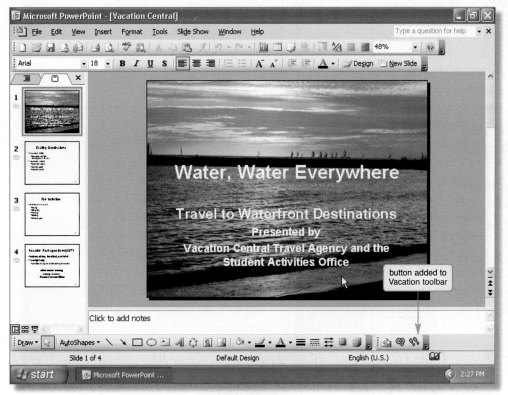

FIGURE 5-70

Saving the Presentation

The changes to the presentation are complete. The following step shows how to save the finished presentation before testing the controls.

To Save a Presentation

1 **Click the Save button on the Standard toolbar.**

PowerPoint saves the presentation by saving the changes made to the presentation since the last save.

Testing the Controls

The final step is to test the controls on the form. Use the following data: Blue design template; Fountain video clip; and Hawaii picture. The steps on the next page show how to test the controls.

To Test the Controls on the Form

• **Click the Create Presentation button on the Vacation toolbar.**

• **When the form is displayed, click the Add a background box arrow and then click Blue.**

• **Click the Select a video clip box arrow and then click Fountain.**

• **Click the Select a picture box arrow and then click Hawaii.**

The form is displayed as shown in Figure 5-71.

• **Click the Update presentation button.**

• **Click the Finish button.**

The Vacation Central slide show runs.

• **Click the black slide to end the slide show.**

• **Click File on the menu bar and then click Print BW Handout to print the four slides as a handout.**

The Vacation Central presentation will display automatically (Figures 5-1e through 5-1h on page PPT 347). The Blue design template is applied, the fountain video is displayed in Slide 2, and the Waikiki beach digital picture is displayed in Slide 3.

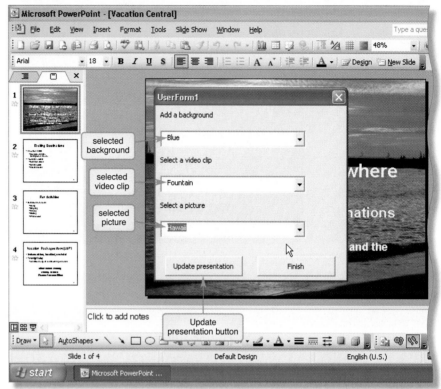

FIGURE 5-71

If the slides do not display as indicated here, then click Tools on the menu bar, point to Macro, and then click Visual Basic Editor. Click the View Code button on the VBA Project toolbar, and then check the controls' properties and VBA code. Save the presentation again and repeat Steps 1 and 2 above.

Quitting PowerPoint

The project is complete. The following steps show how to quit PowerPoint.

To Quit PowerPoint

1 **Click the Close button on the title bar.**

2 **If the Microsoft Office PowerPoint dialog box is displayed, click the Yes button to save changes made since the last save.**

PowerPoint closes.

Project Summary

Project 5 presented the principles of customizing a presentation. In Phase 1, you learned how to create a toolbar and add two buttons, Save as Web Page and Package for CD Wizard. In Phase 2, you learned how to use the macro recorder to create a macro that prints handouts displaying four slides per page and assign this macro to a command on the File menu. In Phase 3, you learned how to create a form composed of label controls, combo box controls, and command button controls. In this phase, you also learned how to write VBA code.

 If you have a SAM user profile, you may have access to hands-on instruction, practice, and assessment of the skills covered in this project. Log in to your SAM account and go to your assignments page to see what your instructor has assigned.

What You Should Know

Having completed this project, you should be able to perform the tasks below. The tasks are listed in the same order they were presented in this project. For a list of the buttons, menus, toolbars, and commands introduced in this project, see the Quick Reference Summary at the back of this book and refer to the Page Number column.

1. Open a Presentation and Save it with a New File Name   (PPT 349)
2. Create a Custom Toolbar   (PPT 352)
3. Add Two Buttons to the Vacation Toolbar (PPT 355)
4. Save a Presentation   (PPT 359, PPT 401)
5. Record a Macro to Print Handouts in Vertical Slide Order in Pure Black and White   (PPT 362)
6. Add a Command to a Menu, Assign the Command to a Macro, and Invoke the Command (PPT 365)
7. Save and Close the Presentation   (PPT 367)
8. Open a Presentation with a Macro and Execute the Macro   (PPT 369)
9. View a Macro's VBA Code   (PPT 370)
10. Open the Visual Basic IDE and a New Form (PPT 374)
11. Change the Form Size and the Toolbox Location (PPT 376)
12. Add Label and Combo Box Controls to a Form (PPT 379)
13. Add Command Button Controls to a Form (PPT 382)
14. Set the Controls' Caption Properties   (PPT 384)
15. Resize and Reposition Controls on a Form (PPT 386)
16. Enter the Create Presentation Procedure (PPT 389)
17. Enter the InitializeForm() Procedure   (PPT 392)
18. Enter the CommandButton1 Procedure (PPT 395)
19. Enter the CommandButton2 Procedure (PPT 397)
20. Initialize a Path Constant   (PPT 399)
21. Save the Visual Basic Code, Close the Visual Basic Editor, and Save the Presentation (PPT 400)
22. Add the Create Presentation Button   (PPT 400)
23. Test the Controls on the Form   (PPT 402)
24. Quit PowerPoint   (PPT 403)

Learn It Online

Instructions: To complete the Learn It Online exercises, start your browser, click the Address bar, and then enter the Web address scsite.com/ppt2003/learn. When the PowerPoint 2003 Learn It Online page is displayed, follow the instructions in the exercises below. Each exercise has instructions for printing your results, either for your own records or for submission to your instructor.

1 Project Reinforcement TF, MC, and SA

Below PowerPoint Project 5, click the Project Reinforcement link. Print the quiz by clicking Print on the File menu for each page. Answer each question.

2 Flash Cards

Below PowerPoint Project 5, click the Flash Cards link and read the instructions. Type 20 (or a number specified by your instructor) in the Number of playing cards text box, type your name in the Enter your Name text box, and then click the Flip Card button. When the flash card is displayed, read the question and then click the ANSWER box arrow to select an answer. Flip through Flash Cards. If your score is 15 (75%) correct or greater, click Print on the File menu to print your results. If your score is less than 15 (75%) correct, then redo this exercise by clicking the Replay button.

3 Practice Test

Below PowerPoint Project 5, click the Practice Test link. Answer each question, enter your first and last name at the bottom of the page, and then click the Grade Test button. When the graded practice test is displayed on your screen, click Print on the File menu to print a hard copy. Continue to take practice tests until you score 80% or better.

4 Who Wants To Be a Computer Genius?

Below PowerPoint Project 5, click the Computer Genius link. Read the instructions, enter your first and last name at the bottom of the page, and then click the PLAY button. When your score is displayed, click the PRINT RESULTS link to print a hard copy.

5 Wheel of Terms

Below PowerPoint Project 5, click the Wheel of Terms link. Read the instructions, and then enter your first and last name and your school name. Click the PLAY button. When your score is displayed, right-click the score and then click Print on the shortcut menu to print a hard copy.

6 Crossword Puzzle Challenge

Below PowerPoint Project 5, click the Crossword Puzzle Challenge link. Read the instructions, and then enter your first and last name. Click the SUBMIT button. Work the crossword puzzle. When you are finished, click the Submit button. When the crossword puzzle is redisplayed, click the Print Puzzle button to print a hard copy.

7 Tips and Tricks

Below PowerPoint Project 5, click the Tips and Tricks link. Click a topic that pertains to Project 5. Right-click the information and then click Print on the shortcut menu. Construct a brief example of what the information relates to in PowerPoint to confirm you understand how to use the tip or trick.

8 Newsgroups

Below PowerPoint Project 5, click the Newsgroups link. Click a topic that pertains to Project 5. Print three comments.

9 Expanding Your Horizons

Below PowerPoint Project 5, click the Expanding Your Horizons link. Click a topic that pertains to Project 5. Print the information. Construct a brief example of what the information relates to in PowerPoint to confirm you understand the contents of the article.

10 Search Sleuth

Below PowerPoint Project 5, click the Search Sleuth link. To search for a term that pertains to this project, select a term below the Project 5 title and then use the Google search engine at google.com (or any major search engine) to display and print two Web pages that present information on the term.

11 PowerPoint Online Training

Below PowerPoint Project 5, click the PowerPoint Online Training link. When your browser displays the Microsoft Office Online Web page, click the PowerPoint link. Click one of the PowerPoint courses that covers one or more of the objectives listed at the beginning of the project on page PPT 346. Print the first page of the course before stepping through it.

12 Office Marketplace

Below PowerPoint Project 5, click the Office Marketplace link. When your browser displays the Microsoft Office Online Web page, click the Office Marketplace link. Click a topic that relates to PowerPoint. Print the first page.

Apply Your Knowledge

1 Preventing Car Theft

Instructions: Start PowerPoint. Open the presentation, Apply 5-1 Car Theft Prevention, on the Data Disk. See the inside back cover of this book for instructions for downloading the Data Disk or see your instructor for information on accessing the files required for this book.

Save the presentation with the file name, Apply 5-1 Car Theft Update. Use the Record New Macro command to create a macro that prints Notes Pages using the Pure Black and White, Scale to fit paper, and Frame slides options. In addition, the macro should print an outline using the Pure Black and White and the Scale to fit paper options. Call the macro PrintPages. Change the name of the author in the Description box to your name. Make sure the Store macro in text box displays Apply 5-1 Car Theft Update. Click the OK button.

Add a button to the Standard toolbar (Figure 5-72a) and a command to the File menu (Figure 5-72b) that will run the macro. Use the image of a book (row 6, column 1) and the Default Style for the button. Change the macro name on the File menu to Print Pages.

View the PrintPages macro's VBA code. When the Visual Basic Editor displays the macro (Figure 5-72c), click File on the menu bar, click Print, and then click the OK button. Close the Visual Basic Editor.

Run the macro as follows: (a) click the button you added to the Standard toolbar; (b) click File on the menu bar and then click the Print Pages command.

Reset the toolbars to their installation settings (see Appendix D). Hand in the hard copies to your instructor.

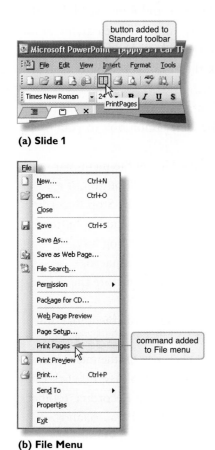

(a) Slide 1

button added to Standard toolbar

(b) File Menu

command added to File menu

(c) VBA Code Associated with Macro

```
Sub PrintPages()
'
' Student Name
'
    With ActivePresentation.PrintOptions
        .RangeType = ppPrintAll
        .NumberOfCopies = 1
        .Collate = msoTrue
        .OutputType = ppPrintOutputNotesPages
        .PrintHiddenSlides = msoTrue
        .PrintColorType = ppPrintPureBlackAndWhite
        .FitToPage = msoTrue
        .FrameSlides = msoTrue
        .HandoutOrder = ppPrintHandoutHorizontalFirst
        .ActivePrinter = "Okidata OL-400"
        .RangeType = ppPrintAll
        .NumberOfCopies = 1
        .Collate = msoTrue
        .OutputType = ppPrintOutputOutline
        .PrintHiddenSlides = msoTrue
        .PrintColorType = ppPrintPureBlackAndWhite
        .FitToPage = msoTrue
        .FrameSlides = msoTrue
        .HandoutOrder = ppPrintHandoutHorizontalFirst
        .ActivePrinter = "Okidata OL-400"
    End With
    ActivePresentation.PrintOut
```

PrintPages macro

FIGURE 5-72

1 Family Hiking

Problem: On weekends you volunteer at the nature center near your campus. You organize programs for families and also serve as a guide on the trails. Many families arrive at the nature center when a nature walk is not scheduled, and they ask for help in hiking safely and having fun identifying trees, plants, and animals. The nature center director has asked you to prepare a PowerPoint presentation for these families to view before they begin their hiking adventures. You agree to create this presentation and decide to write a macro that changes the slide backgrounds. You also add a button to save the presentation using the Package for CD Wizard. A third macro prints Notes Pages for handouts to distribute to these families. Two versions of Slide 1 and the new buttons display in Figure 5-73.

Instructions: Perform the following tasks:

1. Open the Lab 5-1 Family Hiking presentation on the Data Disk. See the inside back cover of this book for instructions for downloading the Data Disk or see your instructor for information on accessing the files required for this book. Save the presentation with the file name, Lab 5-1 Hiking Backgrounds.

2. Create a new toolbar and name it Hiking. Place the new toolbar next to the Drawing toolbar.

3. Use the Record New Macro command to create a macro that changes the backgrounds on Slides 1 and 4. Name the macro, Background, change the name of the author in the Description box to your name, and then store the macro in the Lab 5-1 Hiking Backgrounds file.

4. With the Stop Recording toolbar on the screen, do the following: (a) select Slides 1 and 4 on the Slides tab; (b) click Format on the menu bar and then click Background; (c) click the Background fill area arrow in the Background dialog box, click Fill Effects, click the Texture tab, click Medium wood, click the OK button, and then click the Apply button in the Background dialog box; and (d) click the Stop Recording button on the Stop Recording toolbar.

5. Use the Record New Macro command to create a macro that saves the presentation using the Package for CD Wizard. Call the macro, CreateCD, change the name of the author in the Description box to your name, and store the macro in the Lab 5-1 Hiking Backgrounds file.

6. With the Stop Recording toolbar displaying, perform the following steps: (a) click File on the menu bar and then click Package for CD; (b) name the CD Family Hiking and then click the Copy to CD button; if a Microsoft Office PowerPoint dialog box is displayed, click the Continue button; (c) click the Stop Recording button on the Stop Recording toolbar; and (d) when the copying process is complete, click the No button in the Microsoft Office PowerPoint dialog box and then click the Close button to close the dialog box.

7. Use the Record New Macro command to create a macro that prints Notes Pages. Call the macro, PrintNotes, change the name of the author in the Description box to your name, and then store the macro in the Lab 5-1 Hiking Backgrounds file.

8. With the Stop Recording toolbar displaying, perform the following steps: (a) click File on the menu bar and then click Print; (b) in the Print what box, click Handouts; (c) click 4 in the Slides per page box, make sure Order is Horizontal, and then click the OK button; (d) after the handouts print, click File on the menu bar and then click Print; (e) in the Slides per page box, click 6; (f) in the Print what box, click Slides; (g) click the OK button; and (h) after the four slides print, click the Stop Recording button on the Stop Recording toolbar.

9. Add the three macros to the new Hiking toolbar. Modify the selection for the Background macro, and change the image to the bell icon (row 2, column 3). On the Modify Selection menu, select Default Style. Change the image icon for the Package for CD macro to the floppy disk with the arrow pointing out (row 1, column 5). Select Default Style on the Modify Selection menu. Modify the selection for the PrintNotes macro and change the image to the pencil (row 4, column 4). Select Default Style on the Modify Selection menu.

In the Lab

10. Add the PrintNotes macro to the File menu above the Print menu command. Change the name of the command to Print Notes. Test the macros on the File menu and on the Hiking toolbar.

11. Save the presentation again. Print the macro code for all three macros. Reset the menus and toolbars to their installation settings (see Appendix D). Hand in the hard copies to your instructor.

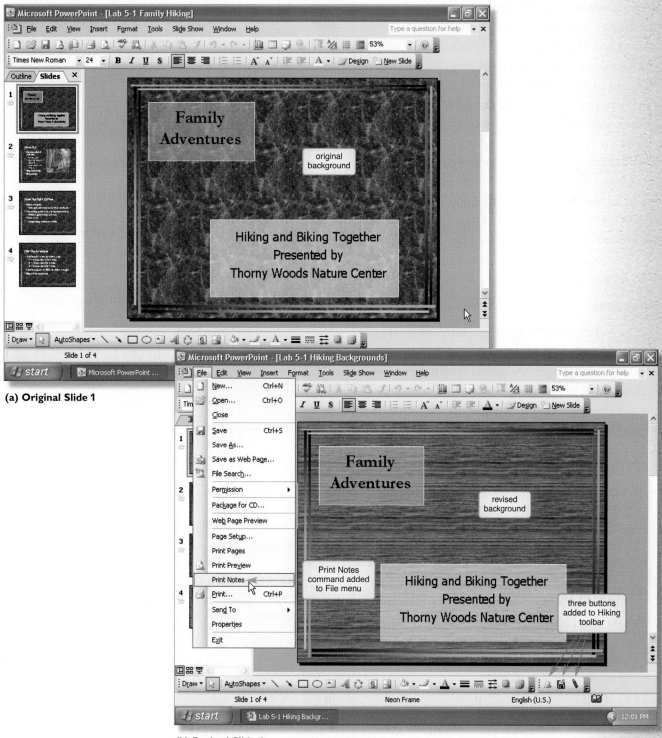

(a) Original Slide 1

(b) Revised Slide 1

FIGURE 5-73

In the Lab

2 Car Loan Computation

Problem: Buying a new or used car is an exciting experience. Obtaining financing for the vehicle, however, can be a confusing process. Accounting Club members at your college are planning monthly seminars on vehicle buying techniques, and one of their topics is securing a loan. They plan to show students how to determine the monthly payment on a particular loan amount, and they want to prepare a PowerPoint slide show to display a form, enter figures, and show the monthly payment amount. You agree to help the Accounting Club members with this project by developing the form shown in Figure 5-74a on page PPT 410 and the Display Loan Form command shown in Figure 5-74b on page PPT 410. The VBA code is shown in Figures 5-74c and 5-74d on page PPT 411.

Instructions: Perform the following tasks:

1. Open the Lab 5-2 Car Financing presentation on the Data Disk. See the inside back cover of this book for instructions for downloading the Data Disk or see your instructor for information on accessing the files required for this book.
2. Create the form shown in Figure 5-74a. Use Table 5-18 to set the properties that specify the locations of the controls.
3. Write the code for the Calculate command button using Table 5-19.
4. Write the code for the Clear command button using Table 5-20.
5. Write the code for the Close Button procedure using Table 5-21.
6. Insert a module, and use the code in Table 5-22 to enter the code for displaying the form.

Table 5-18 Form Controls Locations		
CONTROL	PROPERTY	VALUE
Label1	Caption	Loan Amount
	Left	12
	Top	12
	Width	72
Label2	Caption	Interest in Percent
	Left	12
	Top	42
	Width	72
Label3	Caption	Number of Years
	Left	12
	Top	72
	Width	72
Label4	Caption	Monthly Payment
	Left	12
	Top	102
	Width	72
Label5	Caption	(leave caption blank)
	Left	96
	Top	102
	Width	72
	Special Effect	2-fmSpecialEffectSunken
TextBox1	Left	96
	Top	12
	Width	72
TextBox2	Left	96
	Top	42
	Width	72
TextBox3	Left	96
	Top	72
	Width	72
CommandButton1	Caption	Calculate
	Left	18
	Top	132
	Width	54
CommandButton2	Caption	Clear
	Left	90
	Top	132
	Width	54
CommandButton3	Caption	Close
	Left	162
	Top	132
	Width	54

In the Lab

Table 5-19 Verify Values and Calculate Payment Procedure

LINE	VBA CODE
1	'Validate the text box fields
2	'If OK, then calculate loan
3	If TextBox1.Text = "" Then
4	MsgBox "Please enter a loan amount", vbOKOnly, "Loan Amount"
5	TextBox1.SetFocus
6	ElseIf TextBox2.Text = "" Then
7	MsgBox "Please enter an interest rate", vbOKOnly, "Interest Rate"
8	TextBox2.SetFocus
9	ElseIf TextBox3.Text = "" Then
10	MsgBox "Please enter the number of years for the loan", vbOKOnly, "Years"
11	TextBox3.SetFocus
12	Else
13	Label5.Caption = FormatCurrency(Pmt(TextBox2.Text / 1200, TextBox3.Text * 12, -TextBox1.Text, 0, 0), 2)
14	End If

7. Add the module to the shortcut menu for the slide show by using the Customize command on the Tools menu. Click the Toolbars tab and click Shortcut Menus in the Customize dialog box. Click the Commands tab and select Macros in the Categories list. Click the DisplayLoanForm macro in the Commands list, drag it to the SlideShow menu on the Shortcut Menus bar, drag it to the Slide Show command, and then place it below the Go to Slide command.

8. Change the command name to Display Loan Form.

9. Save the presentation as Lab 5-2 Car Financing Update. Run the slide show, right-click a slide, and then click Display Loan Form on the shortcut menu. Enter values and then click Calculate to see the results. Close the form. Print the form and the Visual Basic code. Close the presentation. Hand in the hard copies to your instructor.

Table 5-20 Clear Procedure

LINE	VBA CODE
1	'Clear all text boxes and monthly payment
2	'Set insertion point in first text box
3	TextBox1.Text = ""
4	TextBox1.SetFocus
5	TextBox2.Text = ""
6	TextBox3.Text = ""
7	Label5.Caption = ""

Table 5-21 Close Button Procedure

LINE	VBA CODE
1	UserForm1.Hide
2	Unload UserForm1

Table 5-22 Display Loan Form Procedure

LINE	VBA CODE
1	Sub DisplayLoanForm()
2	UserForm1.Show
3	End Sub

(continued)

In the Lab

Car Loan Computation (continued)

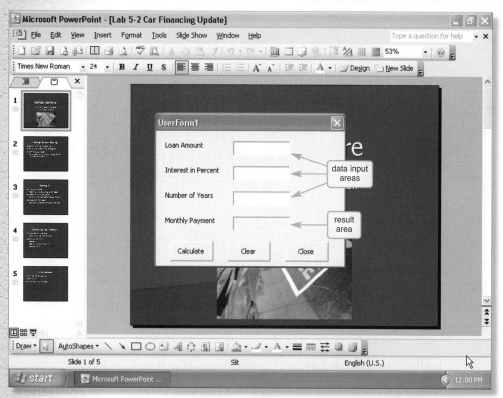

(a) Payment Form

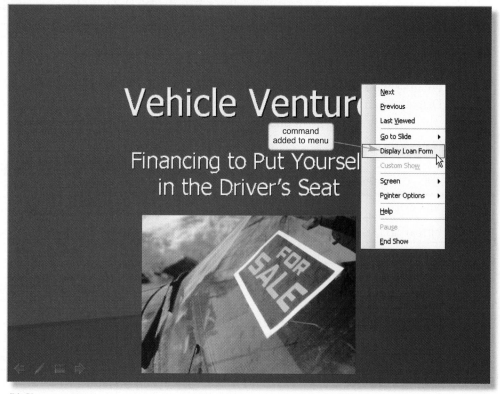

(b) Shortcut Menu

FIGURE 5-74

In the Lab

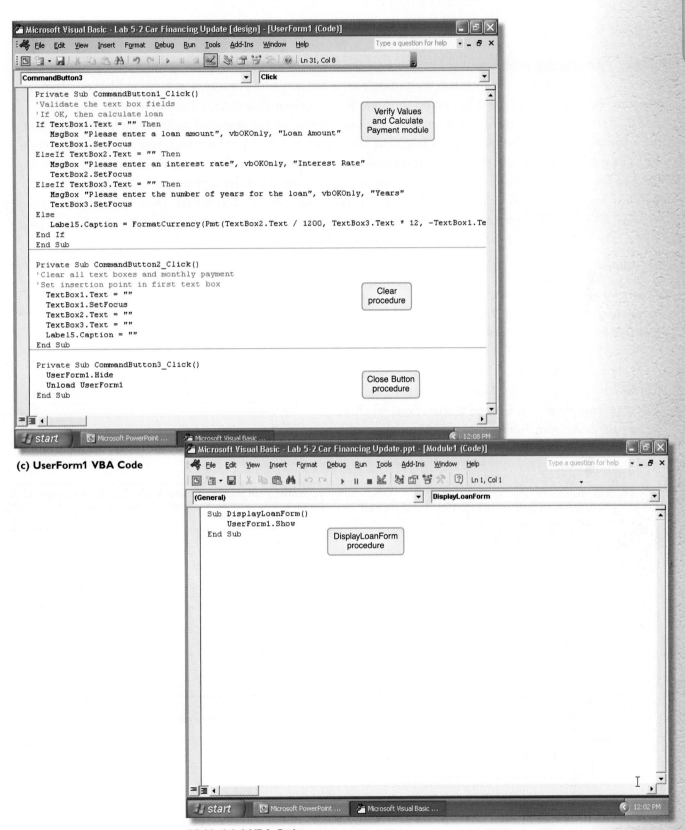

(c) UserForm1 VBA Code

(d) Module1 VBA Code

FIGURE 5-74 *(continued)*

3 Cash for College Summary Slide

Problem: An effective public speaker knows that a conclusion is an important component of the total presentation. This aspect of the speech helps audience members remember the critical facts and leaves a lasting impression. PowerPoint includes a button on the Slide Sorter toolbar that creates a summary slide, but you decide that adding a Summary Slide command to the Insert menu on the Standard toolbar would be convenient. Using a Visual Basic module that contains For/Next statements and the Count method, you can create this command. The module adds a new blank slide at the end of a presentation and then reads the title text of each slide other than the title slide. The local credit union employees use slide shows to supplement speeches they give to community residents, so you decide to enhance one of their presentations, Better Save Than Sorry, with a summary slide. The original presentation and new summary slide are shown in Figures 5-75a through 5-75e on page PPT 414. The VBA code is shown in Figure 5-75f on page PPT 415.

Instructions: Perform the following tasks:

1. Start PowerPoint. Open the Lab 5-3 Credit Union presentation on the Data Disk. See the inside back cover of this book for instructions for downloading the Data Disk or see your instructor for information on accessing the clips and files required for this book.

2. Start a new module called SummarySlide() by creating a new subroutine. In the General Declarations window, enter the code from Table 5-23 to declare the variables used in the module.

Table 5-23	General Declarations
LINE	**VBA CODE**
1	`Dim mySlide As Integer`
2	`Dim SumText As String`
3	`Dim SummarySlideLines(4) As String`

3. Click line 4. Type `Sub Summary_Slide()` and then press the ENTER key. The End Sub statement should display automatically.

4. Enter lines 5 through 9 of the Visual Basic code from Table 5-24 to determine the total number of slides in the presentation.

5. Enter the Visual Basic code from Table 5-25 to collect the titles from every slide.

Table 5-24	Determine Slide Count Procedure
LINE	**VBA CODE**
4	`Sub SummarySlide()`
5	`Dim SlideCount As Integer`
6	`With ActivePresentation.Slides`
7	`'Determine the number of total slides`
8	`SlideCount = .Count + 1`
9	`End With`

Table 5-25	Collect Titles Procedure
LINE	**VBA CODE**
10	`For mySlide = 2 To SlideCount - 1`
11	`'Collect the titles from every slide`
12	`Set myPresentation = ActivePresentation.Slides(mySlide)`
13	`SummarySlideLines(mySlide) = myPresentation.Shapes.Title.TextFrame.TextRange.Text`
14	`Next mySlide`

6. Add the Visual Basic code from Table 5-26 to add a slide at the end of the presentation and then insert the slide title.

Table 5-26	Add Summary Slide Procedure
LINE	**VBA CODE**
15	`'Add the summary slide`
16	`Set SumSlide = ActivePresentation.Slides.Add(SlideCount, ppLayoutText).Shapes`
17	`'Insert the title for the summary slide`
18	`SumSlide.Title.TextFrame.TextRange.Text = "In Conclusion"`

7. Using the For/Next loop from Table 5-27, collect the slide titles into one long string of text. The Chr(13) function acts as the ENTER key at the end of each title so the titles will display on separate lines in the slide.

Table 5-27	Collect Slide Titles Procedure
LINE	**VBA CODE**
19	`'Collect the Slide titles into one long string of text`
20	`'inserting a carriage return at the end of each title`
21	`'so the titles will display on separate lines`
22	`For mySlide = 2 To SlideCount - 1`
23	`    SumText = SumText & SummarySlideLines(mySlide) & Chr(13)`
24	`Next mySlide`

8. Insert the SumText module from Table 5-28 to place text into the text placeholder.

Table 5-28	Insert Summary Text Procedure
LINE	**VBA CODE**
25	`'Now insert the titles in the Text list placeholder of the slide`
26	`SumSlide.Placeholders(2).TextFrame.TextRange.Text = SumText`
27	`End Sub`

9. Add a Summary Slide command to the Insert menu to execute the Summary_Slide() module, as shown in Figure 5-75g on page PPT 415.
10. Save the Visual Basic code, and then save the presentation with the file name, Lab 5-3 Credit Union Update.
11. Execute the Visual Basic program. Print the Visual Basic code and the slides using the Pure Black and White option. Hand in the hard copies to your instructor.

(continued)

In the Lab

Cash for College Summary Slide *(continued)*

Credit Union Presentation

Better Save Than Sorry

Start Saving Today
At Your Credit Union

Take This Quiz...

(a) Slide 1

Credit Union Services

1) Your credit union offers which services?
   a) Low-interest credit cards
   b) Certificates of deposit
   c) Retirement planning
   d) All of the above

d) All of the above

(b) Slide 2

Accessing Your Account

2) When is the telephone information line available?
   a) 24 hours a day
   b) Only when the lobby is closed
   c) Only on weekends
   d) From midnight until 9 a.m.

a) 24 hours a day

(c) Slide 3

Your Credit Union...

Working in your best interest

Visit us today

**324 State Street
Hometown, IL
(607) 555-0909**

(d) Slide 4

In Conclusion

- Credit Union Services
- Accessing Your Account
- Your Credit Union...

new summary slide

(e) Slide 5

FIGURE 5-75

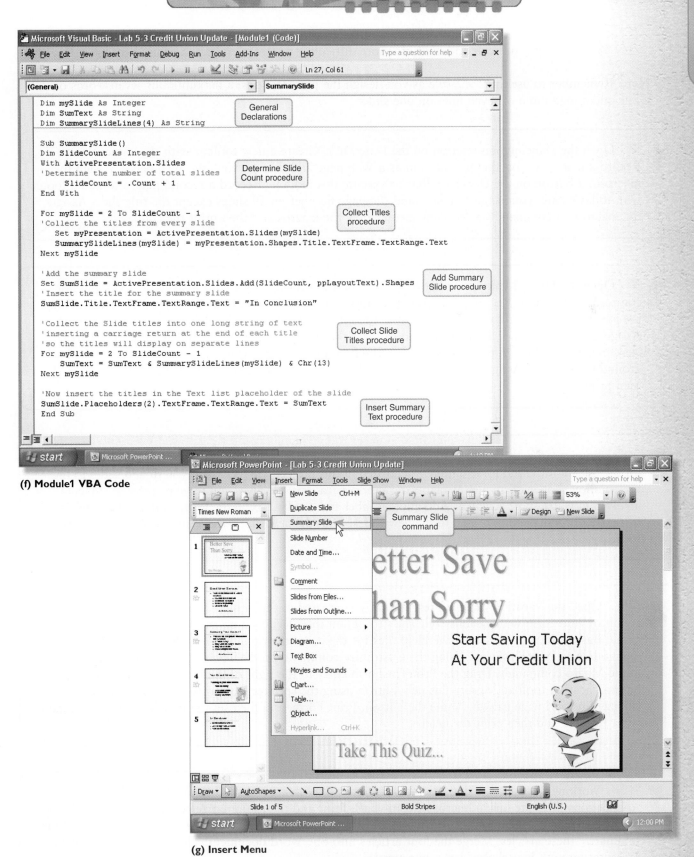

(f) Module1 VBA Code

(g) Insert Menu

FIGURE 5-75 *(continued)*

Cases and Places

The difficulty of these case studies varies:
■ are the least difficult and ■■ are more difficult. The last exercise is a group exercise.

Note: Remember to use the 7 × 7 rule as you design the presentations: a maximum of seven words on a line and a maximum of seven lines on one slide.

1 ■ Open the Dancing presentation on the Data Disk. Create a new toolbar with the name, Dance. Record a macro to save the presentation as a Web page and then preview the Web pages. Assign the macro to a button on the Dance toolbar to execute this module. Record a second macro to add a footer with today's date, your school's name, and the page number on all slides except the title slide. Assign the macro to a command on the View menu. View the macros and then print the code.

2 ■ Open the Hidden Lake presentation you created in Project 3. See your instructor if you did not complete this project. Record a macro that changes the Slide 3 background to a preset gradient. Name the macro, Gradient. On the Gradient tab in the Fill Effects dialog box, click the Two colors option. Assign Color 1 the color, light green, and Color 2 the color, light yellow. In the Shading styles area, click the Diagonal down title style and click the first Variants style (row 1, column 1). Apply the background to all slides. Assign the macro to a new button on the Standard toolbar. View the macro and then print the code.

3 ■■ Ramon Cruz, the Student Activities Office director at your college, wants to generate more interest for the Vacation Central presentation you created in this project. He has asked you to add slides to the presentation showing activities available during the vacations. He gives you three pictures of students involved in water sport activities. Add another label and combo box to the form so Ramon can select from one of these pictures to add to the new slides. Print the new slides, the Visual Basic code, and the form.

4 ■■ Open the Vacation Central presentation you created in this project. You would like to share the layout of your form with various colleagues to obtain their feedback on the form's layout. With the Visual Basic Editor open, search the Help files for the code to write a module that prints the form. Save the module as PrintThisForm. Using the Customize command on the Tools menu, locate your module in the Macro commands. Drag the PrintThisForm entry to the right of the Create Presentation button on the Vacation toolbar. Modify this new button using the speaker icon (row 2, column 2) on the Change Button Image palette. Name the button, Print Form, and then set the new button to the default style. Execute and then print the macro.

5 ■■ **Working Together** Using Microsoft Internet Explorer, go to the Microsoft Visual Basic for Applications Web site (msdn.microsoft.com/vba/). Print and then summarize two articles. Using Google or another search engine, search for two forums or instructional articles discussing VBA. Print and then summarize these articles. Merge the four articles into one Word document. Then create a PowerPoint presentation with hyperlinks to the four articles.

Creating a Self-Running Presentation Containing Shapes

PROJECT

6

CASE PERSPECTIVE

Family reunions are an exciting means of uniting people spanning several generations for a few hours with memories that last a lifetime. The event can range from an afternoon in a community park to a weeklong cruise. Wherever the venue, the time together instills a respect for the past, a sense of identity, and a hope for the future.

Reunions are extremely popular events today. Their origin, however, is found in early civilizations. More than 300,000 years ago, prehistoric clans celebrated the rewards of a successful hunt. Thousands of years later, royalty in the Middle Ages held reunions to entertain, celebrate, and share their nobility. Many historians consider Thanksgiving as the first family reunion in the United States.

A successful reunion requires planning. At least one person needs to conceptualize the event and execute the plans. The result is an outstanding event with an atmosphere of excitement and historical significance. You have organized several reunions for your family, and you want to share your expertise with students in your speech class. Your professor has assigned an informative speech, and you decide to develop a PowerPoint presentation to accompany your speech. You had prepared another PowerPoint presentation as an extra-credit assignment in your accounting class, and that slide show analyzed the budget for a one-day family reunion. You decide to use one of the slides from that presentation in your new presentation. You also want the slide show to run unattended at an open house at your school designed to showcase the top student assignments.

As you read through this project, you will learn how to use PowerPoint to insert a slide from another presentation, use the Format Painter, insert and format a Venn diagram and an AutoShape, and create and start a self-running presentation.

MICROSOFT
Office PowerPoint 2003

Creating a Self-Running Presentation Containing Shapes

P R O J E C T

6

Objectives

You will have mastered the material in this project when you can:

- Insert a slide from another presentation
- Insert and format an AutoShape
- Add and format AutoShape text
- Apply a motion path animation effect to an AutoShape

- Insert, size, and format a Venn diagram
- Add text to a Venn diagram
- Use the Format Painter
- Create and start a self-running presentation

Introduction

People thirst for information. From catching the breaking news on cable television to downloading their latest e-mail messages, individuals constantly are faced with keeping up with the day's events.

One method used for disseminating information is a **kiosk**. This freestanding, self-service structure is equipped with computer hardware and software and is used to provide information or reference materials to the public. Some have a touch screen or keyboard that serves as an input device and allows users to select various options to browse through or find specific information. Advanced kiosks allow customers to place orders, make payments, and access the Internet. Many kiosks have multimedia devices for playing sound and video clips.

Kiosks frequently are found in public places, such as shopping centers, hotels, museums, libraries, and airport terminals, where customers or visitors may have questions about community events, local hotels, and rental cars. Military bases have installed kiosks that allow soldiers to conduct personal business and communicate with friends and family back home by sending video clips and photographs. Governments worldwide have installed kiosks that provide Internet access to public services and information.

In this project, you will create a slide show to accompany an informative speech you will deliver in your speech class. This show will run automatically while you are giving your five-minute talk. In addition, you will set the presentation to run at a kiosk so that the slides will display unattended at the showcase of top student projects during your school's open house. When the last slide in the presentation is viewed, the slide show will restart at Slide 1. The six presentation slides are shown in Figures 6-1a through 6-1f.

More About

Reunions

Family reunions have grown in popularity in recent years, and many Web sites provide excellent help with organizing the event. To learn more about these Web sites, view the PowerPoint 2003 More About Web page (scsite.com/ppt2003/more) and click Reunions.

(a) Slide 1

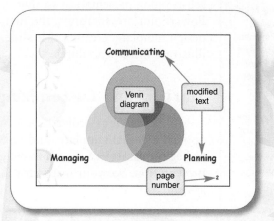

(b) Slide 2

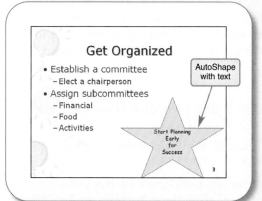

(c) Slide 3

(d) Slide 4

(e) Slide 5

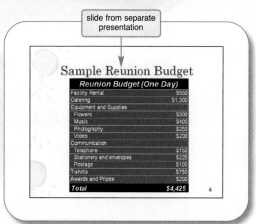

(f) Slide 6

FIGURE 6-1

Project Six — Planning a Family Reunion

The self-running, five-minute presentation created in Project 6 contains several visual elements, including a Venn diagram and an AutoShape that emphasize the need to start making plans as early as possible. Automatic slide timings are set so these slides display after a desired period of time. The presentation then is designated to be a self-running presentation so that it restarts when it is finished. As with other PowerPoint presentations, the first steps are to create a new presentation, select a design template, create a title slide, and save the presentation. The following steps illustrate these procedures.

Starting and Customizing a New Presentation

In the previous projects, you started a presentation document, chose layouts, applied a design template, and reset your toolbars. You need to repeat the same steps to begin this project. The following steps show how to start and customize a new presentation. See your instructor if the Balloons template is not available on your system.

To Start and Customize a New Presentation

1 Click the Start button on the Windows taskbar, point to All Programs on the Start menu, point to Microsoft Office on the All Programs submenu, and then click Microsoft Office PowerPoint 2003 on the Microsoft Office submenu.

2 If the PowerPoint window is not maximized, double-click its title bar to maximize it.

3 If the Language bar appears, right-click it and then click Close the Language bar on the shortcut menu.

4 If the Getting Started task pane appears in the PowerPoint window, click its Close button in the upper-right corner.

5 If the Standard and Formatting toolbars are positioned on the same row, click the Toolbar Options button and then click Show Buttons on Two Rows.

6 Click the Slide Design button on the Formatting toolbar. When the Slide Design task pane is displayed, click the down scroll arrow in the Apply a design template list, and then double-click the Balloons template in the Available For Use area.

7 Click the Close button in the Slide Design task pane.

The PowerPoint window with the Standard and Formatting toolbars on two rows appears as shown in Figure 6-2. PowerPoint displays the Title Slide slide layout and the Balloons template on Slide 1 in normal view.

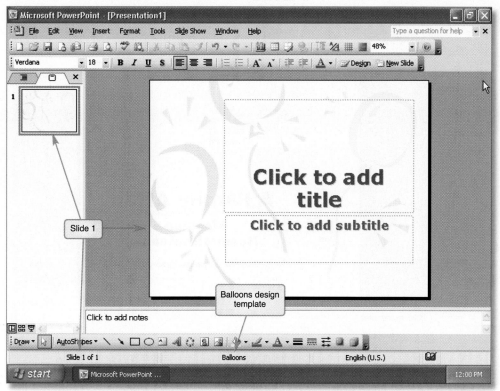

FIGURE 6-2

Developing the Core Presentation Slides

Many tasks are involved when organizing a family reunion. They involve appointing a planning committee, selecting a location and date, contacting family members, developing a theme, sending invitations, planning activities and games, decorating the site, cleaning the site, and, if all goes well, preparing for the next reunion. Four slides in your presentation give details about these tasks.

Creating a Title Slide

The purpose of this presentation is to help classmates understand the steps required to plan a successful reunion. The slide show will give helpful pointers to help get organized, select a date and location, establish a budget, and plan activities. The opening slide should introduce this concept. Perform the following steps to create a title slide.

To Create a Title Slide

1. **Click the title text placeholder.**

2. **Type** A Family Affair **in the title text placeholder.**

3. **Press CTRL+ENTER to move the insertion point to the subtitle text placeholder.**

4. **Type** Planning a **and then press SHIFT+ENTER to create a line break.**

5. **Type** Memorable Reunion **but do not press the ENTER key.**

The title text and subtitle text are displayed on Slide 1 as shown in Figure 6-3 on the next page.

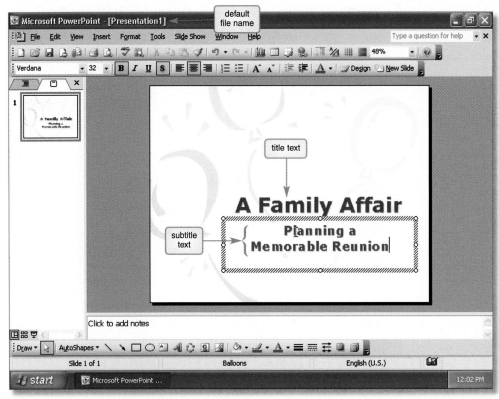

FIGURE 6-3

Saving the Presentation

You now should save the presentation because you applied a design template and created a title slide. The following steps summarize how to save the presentation.

To Save the Presentation

1 **Click the Save button on the Standard toolbar.**

2 **Type** Family Reunion **in the File name text box.**

3 **Click the Save in box arrow. Click 3½ Floppy (A:) in the Save in list.**

4 **Click the Save button in the Save As dialog box.**

The presentation is saved on the floppy disk in drive A with the file name, Family Reunion. This file name is displayed on the title bar.

Creating Slide 2

People who have organized family reunions emphasize that early planning is essential to success. Two years should be sufficient time to arrange the multitude of details. Each step in the planning process requires help, and the most efficient means of coordinating plans is to establish a committee who then elects a chairperson. Once the committee is in place, committee members are assigned to various subcommittees. Slide 2 in the presentation lists these organization tips. The following steps describe how to create this slide.

More About

Embedding Fonts

If you frequently show your presentation on different computers, you may want to embed your fonts to ensure they are available when you are at a remote site. You can embed TrueType fonts that come with Microsoft Windows; other TrueType fonts can be embedded only if they have no license restrictions. You can embed all font characters or just the characters used in your presentation. To embed the fonts, click Save As on the File menu, click the Tools button on the toolbar, click Save Options, click Embed TrueType Fonts, and then click either Embed characters in use only or Embed all characters.

To Create Slide 2

1 Click the **New Slide** button on the Formatting toolbar.

2 Type `Get Organized` in the title text placeholder.

3 Press CTRL+ENTER to move the insertion point to the body text placeholder.

4 Type `Establish a committee` and then press the ENTER key.

5 Press the TAB key. Type `Elect a chairperson` and then press the ENTER key.

6 Press the SHIFT+TAB keys. Type `Assign subcommittees` and then press the ENTER key.

7 Press the TAB key. Type `Financial` and then press the ENTER key.

8 Type `Food` and then press the ENTER key.

9 Type `Activities` but do not press the ENTER key.

The Slide 2 title text and body text are displayed (Figure 6-4).

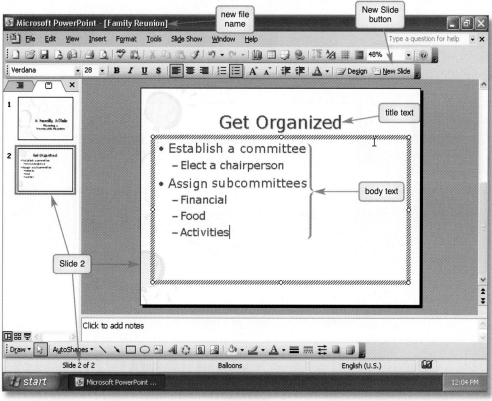

FIGURE 6-4

Creating Slide 3

The reunion date and location depend upon many factors. If the family has many school-age children, consider holding the reunion during vacations or long holiday weekends. Birthdays, anniversaries, local festivals, and weather may help determine when and where to set the venue. Popular locations include dude ranches, historic sites, theme parks, sporting events, national and state parks, and campgrounds. The third slide in the presentation describes selecting dates and locations. The steps on the next page describe how to create this slide.

To Create Slide 3

1 **Click the New Slide button on the Formatting toolbar.**

2 **Type** Select a Date and Location **in the title text placeholder.**

3 **Press CTRL+ENTER to move the insertion point to the body text placeholder.**

4 **Type** Date **and then press the ENTER key.**

5 **Press the TAB key. Type** Can range from one day to one week **and then press the ENTER key.**

6 **Press the SHIFT+TAB keys. Type** Location **and then press the ENTER key.**

7 **Press the TAB key. Type** Dude ranch; historic site **and then press the ENTER key.**

8 **Type** Theme park; sporting event **and then press the ENTER key.**

9 **Type** National or state park; campground **but do not press the ENTER key.**

The Slide 3 title text and body text are displayed (Figure 6-5).

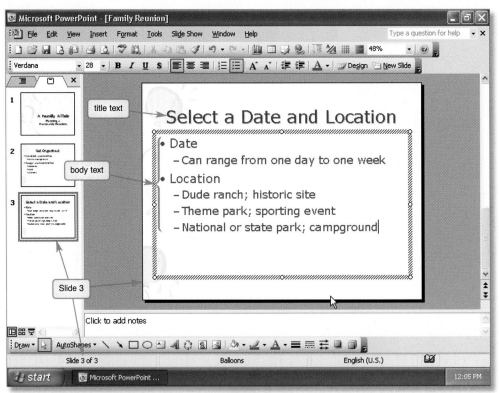

FIGURE 6-5

Creating Slide 4

Once the reunion committee, date, and location have been determined, the next step is to prepare the activities that will help guests meet, reminisce, and bond. Audience participation begins with icebreakers to help family members unwind and feel comfortable. Games and sports such as tug-of-war, three-legged races, tag, swimming, or golfing may provide fun and exercise. Another popular event is

More About

Footers

Once you have developed the footer information for your slides, you can choose to have these details display on all or just selected slides. To remove footer information from several, but not all, slides, select the slides that should display the information, click Header and Footer on the View menu, click the Slide tab, and then click the Apply button. To remove the footer from only the title slide, click Don't show on title slide.

storytelling; children enjoy hearing the adults talk about when they were children, and children enjoy sharing stories of playing with their friends and school activities. Distribute disposable cameras, and have each person take a photo of himself or herself. Then arrange for a group photo and video. After the reunion, these images can be recorded on a DVD to distribute as birthday or holiday presents. Another fun activity is to share the participants' skills by scheduling talent shows and skits. Slide 4 in the presentation lists these activities and games, and the following steps describe how to create this slide.

To Create Slide 4

1 Click the **New Slide** button on the Formatting toolbar.

2 **Type** Plan Activities and Games **in the title text placeholder.**

3 **Press CTRL+ENTER to move the insertion point to the body text placeholder.**

4 **Type** Icebreakers **and then press the ENTER key.**

5 **Type** Sports **and then press the ENTER key.**

6 **Type** Storytelling **and then press the ENTER key.**

7 **Type** Group photograph and video **and then press the ENTER key.**

8 **Type** Talent show and skits **but do not press the ENTER key.**

The Slide 4 title text and body text are displayed (Figure 6-6).

More About

Changing Fonts

Changing the fonts on the title slide and all text slides is an easy task when you apply the changes to both the slide master and the title master. When you change the font on the master, this change is reflected throughout the presentation. To make this change, point to Master on the View menu and then click Slide Master. On the slide, select the title text or the level of body text to which you want to apply the new font style. Click a new font name in the Font box on the Formatting toolbar. Click the other slide thumbnail displayed on the left edge of the screen and then make the desired font changes. To apply the font changes to your presentation, click the Close Master View button on the Slide Master View toolbar.

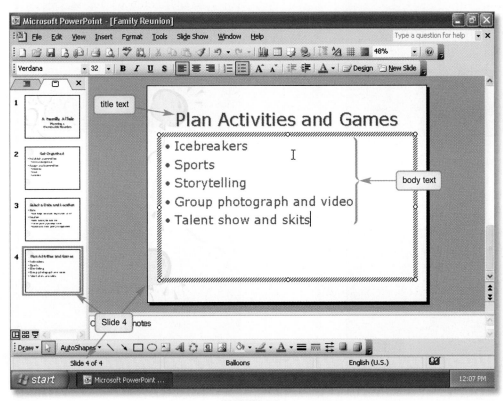

FIGURE 6-6

The four core slides in the presentation are created. You now want to add one slide from another presentation on the topic of budgeting a reunion.

Adding a Presentation within a Presentation

Occasionally, you may need a slide from another presentation in the presentation you are creating. PowerPoint makes it easy to insert one or more slides from other presentations.

Inserting a Slide from Another Presentation

The PowerPoint presentation with the file name, Reunion Budget, describes various expenses associated with a family reunion. It contains four slides, and the second slide, shown in Figure 6-7b, contains a spreadsheet with average costs for essential reunion expenses. The Reunion Budget file is on your Data Disk. See the inside back cover of this book for instructions for downloading the Data Disk or see your instructor for information on accessing the files required for this book. An inserted slide is placed in the presentation directly after the current slide and inherits the styles of this current slide; in this case, Slide 4 is active, so the budget slide will be placed after Slide 4 and will become Slide 5. The following steps demonstrate how to insert Slide 2 from the Reunion Budget file as the last slide in your presentation.

(a) Slide 1

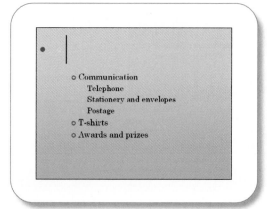

(b) Slide 2

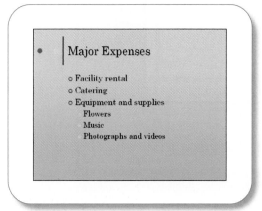

(c) Slide 3

(d) Slide 4

FIGURE 6-7

To Insert a Slide from Another Presentation

1

• **With Slide 4 selected and your Data Disk in drive A, click Insert on the menu bar and then point to Slides from Files.**

The Insert menu is displayed (Figure 6-8). The Slides from Files command allows you to insert a slide from another PowerPoint file.

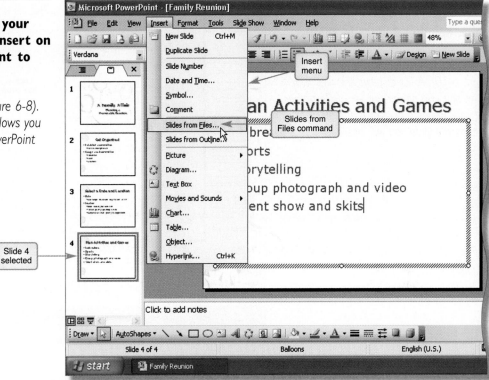

FIGURE 6-8

2

• **Click Slides from Files.**

• **If necessary, when the Slide Finder dialog box is displayed, click the Find Presentation tab.**

The Slide Finder dialog box is displayed (Figure 6-9). If you use several presentations on a regular basis, you can add them to your List of Favorites so you can find them easily.

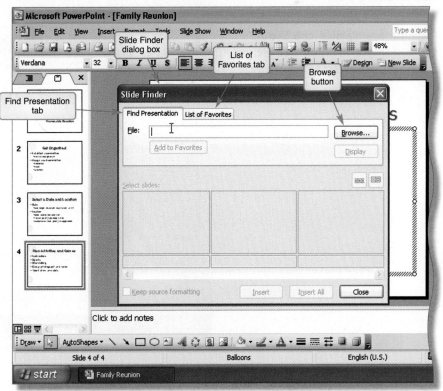

FIGURE 6-9

3

• **Click the Browse button.**

• **Click the Look in box arrow and then click 3½ Floppy (A:).**

• **Click Reunion Budget in the list.**

The Browse dialog box is displayed (Figure 6-10). A list displays the files that PowerPoint can open. Your list of file names may vary. Reunion Budget is the file that contains the slide you will insert.

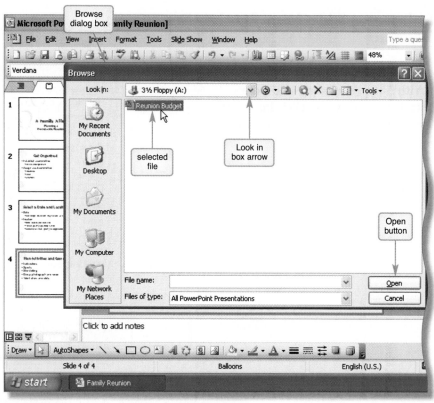

FIGURE 6-10

4

• **Click the Open button in the Browse dialog box.**

• **When the Slide Finder dialog box is visible again, click the Slide 2 image, Sample Reunion Budget, in the Select slides area.**

The Slide Finder dialog box is visible again (Figure 6-11). The selected file, A:\Reunion Budget.ppt, is displayed in the File text box. Slide 2 of this presentation is the slide to insert in your new presentation.

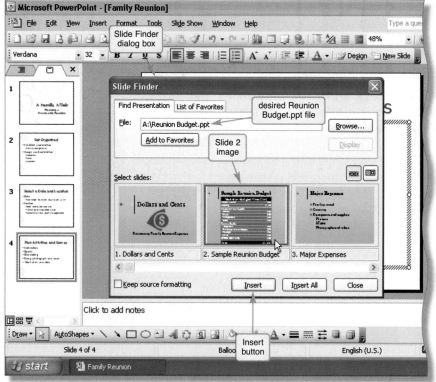

FIGURE 6-11

5

• **Click the Insert button.**

PowerPoint inserts the Reunion Budget Slide 2 in your presentation (Figure 6-12). The Slide Finder dialog box remains open to allow you to insert additional slides.

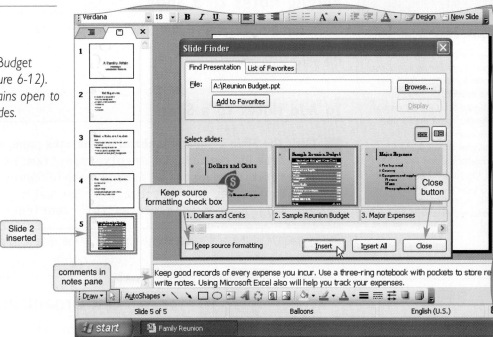

FIGURE 6-12

6

• **Click the Close button in the Slide Finder dialog box.**

Your presentation consists of five slides (Figure 6-13). Slide 4 had been displayed prior to inserting the new slide; the new slide is added after Slide 4.

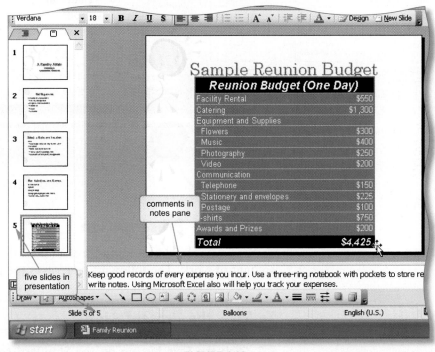

FIGURE 6-13

Other Ways

1. In Voice Command mode, say "Insert, Slides from Files, Browse, [type file name], Open, [select slide], Insert, Close"

The Balloons design template is applied to the newly inserted slide. To retain the Echo design template that is applied to the Reunion Budget slides, you would click Keep source formatting in the Slide Finder dialog box. If desired, you could have selected additional slides from the Reunion Budget presentation or from other slide shows. If you might use the Reunion Budget file later, you can add that file to your Favorites folder so it is accessible readily.

More About

Coloring Bullets

The template color scheme determines the default bullet styles and colors. To change the bullet color, select the bulleted list, click Bullets and Numbering on the Format menu, and then click the Bulleted tab. Click the Color arrow and either select one of the eight colors associated with the color scheme or click More Colors for additional color choices.

Adding Notes to a Slide

In this project, Slides 2 and 5 have comments. Slide 5 retains the comments that were inserted for the Reunion Budget presentation. The following step adds text to the notes pane on Slide 2.

To Add Notes to a Slide

1 **Click the Slide 2 slide thumbnail in the tabs pane, click the notes pane, and then type** Be certain to involve many family members in the organization process. If many people contribute their talents and expertise, the outcome will be tailored to their interests and will result in a successful experience for everyone.

The information in this note supplements the text in the slide (Figure 6-14).

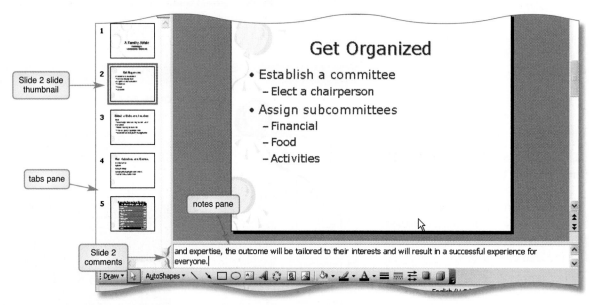

FIGURE 6-14

Saving the Presentation

You now should save your presentation because you have done a substantial amount of work. The following step saves the presentation.

To Save the Presentation

1 **Click the Save button on the Standard toolbar.**

The presentation is saved on the floppy disk in drive A with the file name, Family Reunion.

The presentation contains five slides. The next section inserts and modifies a clip.

Inserting, Sizing, and Moving a Clip

With all the desired text added to the slides in the presentation, the next step is to add a clip to Slide 3. The following steps add and size this clip and then move it to the lower-right corner of the slide.

To Insert, Size, and Move a Clip

1 Click the Slide 3 slide thumbnail in the tabs pane. Click the Insert Clip Art button on the Drawing toolbar. When the Clip Art task pane is displayed, type calendar in the Search for text box and then click the Go button. Click the animated yellow calendar or another appropriate clip. Click the Close button on the Clip Art task pane title bar. If the Picture toolbar is displayed, click the Close button on the toolbar.

2 Right-click the clip and then click Format Picture on the shortcut menu. If necessary, click the Size tab when the Format Picture dialog box is displayed. Double-click the Height text box in the Scale area and then type 60 in the box. Click the OK button.

3 Use the arrow keys to move the clip to the lower-right corner of the slide.

The selected clip is inserted into Slide 3, sized, and moved to the desired location (Figure 6-15).

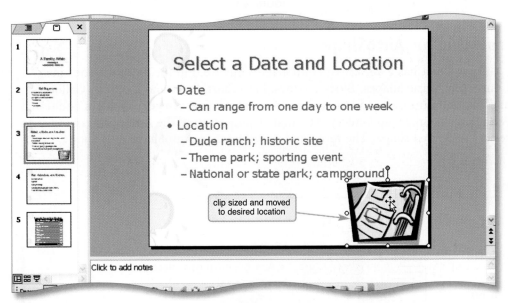

FIGURE 6-15

More About

Inserting Images

Microsoft provides thousands of clips in the Microsoft Clip Organizer, but you may want to add a personal or corporate image, such as a company logo or a photograph of your family. You can insert images saved with many popular graphics file formats into your presentation, including .jpg, .gif, and .bmp, without needing separate filters. Click the Insert Picture button on the Drawing toolbar, locate the folder that contains the picture you want to insert, and then click the Insert button.

Inserting and Formatting an AutoShape

One key element of planning a successful event is to start early. Considering all the details and the number of people involved, 18 to 24 months may be sufficient time to secure a choice location and allow guests to make travel plans. Early planning should be emphasized in the presentation, and one method of calling attention to this element is to add an AutoShape to a slide. An **AutoShape** is a ready-made object, such as a line, star, banner, arrow, connector, or callout. These shapes can be sized, rotated, flipped, colored, and combined to add unique qualities to a presentation.

Figure 6-16 shows the AutoShape you will create and add to Slide 2. Creating this object requires several steps. First, you must choose the desired AutoShape and insert it into the slide. You then add text and resize the AutoShape to accommodate this text. The next several sections explain how to create this AutoShape.

FIGURE 6-16

Inserting an AutoShape

PowerPoint has a variety of AutoShapes organized in the categories of Lines, Connectors, Basic Shapes, Block Arrows, Flowchart, Stars and Banners, Callouts, and Action Buttons. In addition, the More AutoShapes category displays additional AutoShapes in the Clip Gallery. The first step in creating the AutoShape object is to select the desired shape. The following steps insert an AutoShape into Slide 2.

To Insert an AutoShape

1

• **Click the Slide 2 slide thumbnail in the tabs pane.**

• **Click the AutoShapes button on the Drawing toolbar, point to Stars and Banners, and then point to 5-Point Star (row 1, column 4) on the Stars and Banners submenu.**

The Stars and Banners submenu is displayed (Figure 6-17). The desired AutoShape, 5-Point Star, is selected.

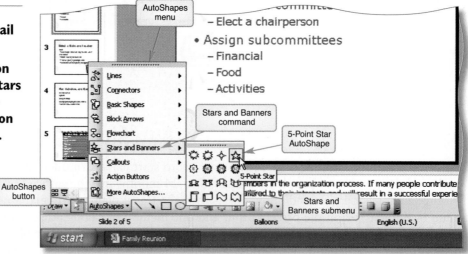

FIGURE 6-17

2

- **Click 5-Point Star.**
- **Point to the center of the white space in the lower-right corner of the slide, to the right of the word, Activities.**

The mouse pointer changes shape to a cross hair (Figure 6-18). The AutoShape will be inserted in this area of the slide.

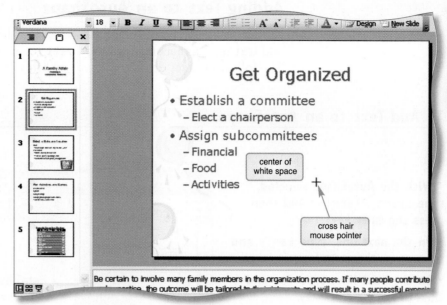

FIGURE 6-18

3

- **Click the white space area of the slide.**

The 5-Point Star AutoShape is inserted in the desired location (Figure 6-19).

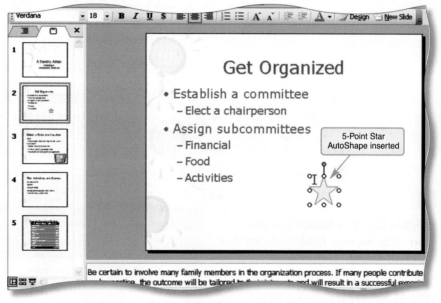

FIGURE 6-19

If desired, you now could add special effects and text to the AutoShape. One special effect, for example, is a shadow you can create by clicking Shadow Settings in the Shadow Style list. To allow you to accomplish this, PowerPoint displays the Shadow Settings toolbar containing buttons to turn the shadow on or off, to nudge the shadow up, down, left, or right, and to change the shadow color. Another addition is text. The next section describes adding text to the AutoShape.

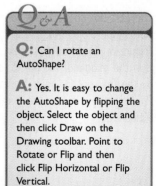

Q&A

Q: Can I rotate an AutoShape?

A: Yes. It is easy to change the AutoShape by flipping the object. Select the object and then click Draw on the Drawing toolbar. Point to Rotate or Flip and then click Flip Horizontal or Flip Vertical.

Adding Text to an AutoShape

The AutoShape is displayed on Slide 2 in the correct location. The next step is to add text stating that starting early in the reunion planning process is encouraged. The following steps describe how to add this information.

To Add Text to an AutoShape

1

• **With the AutoShape selected, type** Start Planning **and then press the ENTER key.**

• **On the next line, type** Early **and then press the ENTER key.**

• **On the next line, type** for **and then press the ENTER key.**

• **On the next line, type** Success **to complete the entry.**

The AutoShape text is displayed on four lines (Figure 6-20).

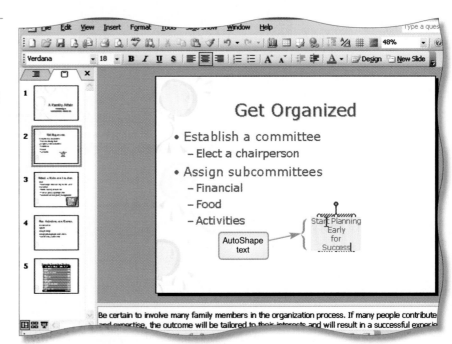

FIGURE 6-20

2

• **Right-click the AutoShape and then click Format AutoShape on the shortcut menu.**

• **Click the Text Box tab in the Format AutoShape dialog box.**

• **Click Resize AutoShape to fit text.**

The Text Box sheet in the Format AutoShape dialog box is displayed (Figure 6-21). The default text placement is in the middle of the object, as indicated by the Text anchor point. You can click the Preview button to see the resized AutoShape.

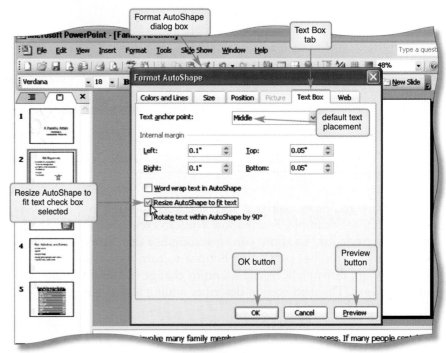

FIGURE 6-21

3 ——————

• **Click the OK button.**

• **If necessary, click the AutoShape border and drag the object so it is centered in the white space in the lower-right corner of the slide.**

PowerPoint changes the size of the AutoShape automatically based on the amount of text entered and the amount of space allocated for the AutoShape's margins. The AutoShape is displayed in the desired location (Figure 6-22). You also can press the arrow keys to adjust the location.

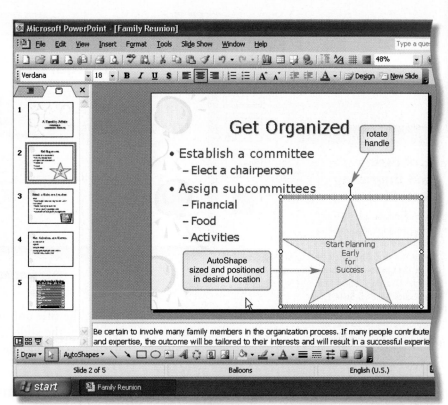

FIGURE 6-22

You can rotate the AutoShape by dragging the green **rotate handle** on the object in the desired direction.

Applying an AutoShape Entrance Animation Effect

The next step in creating Slide 2 is to animate the AutoShape object. The following steps apply an entrance effect.

To Apply an AutoShape Entrance Animation Effect

1 **With the AutoShape selected, click Slide Show on the menu bar, click Custom Animation, and then click the Add Effect button in the Custom Animation task pane.**

2 **Point to Entrance and then click Box on the Entrance menu.**

3 **Click the Start box arrow and then click After Previous on the Start menu.**

4 **Click the Speed box arrow and then click Slow.**

The AutoShape will be displayed slowly in the presentation using the Box animation effect during the slide show (Figure 6-23 on the next page).

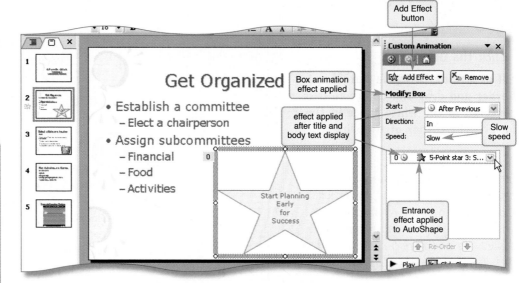

FIGURE 6-23

When you run the slide show, the title and body text will be displayed, and then the AutoShape slowly will appear on the slide. The next section describes how the AutoShape will move in a circular pattern around Slide 2.

Applying a Motion Path Animation Effect to an AutoShape

The next step is applying a motion path to the AutoShape. A **motion path** is a predetermined path the shape will follow. In this presentation, the shape will display and then move on the slide in a circular pattern. The following steps apply a motion path animation effect.

To Apply a Motion Path Animation Effect to an AutoShape

1

• **With the AutoShape selected, click the Add Effect button in the Custom Animation task pane.**

• **Point to Motion Paths and then point to More Motion Paths on the Motion Paths submenu.**

The effects in your list may differ (Figure 6-24).

FIGURE 6-24

2

• **Click More Motion Paths.**

• **When the Add Motion Path dialog box is displayed, click Circle in the Basic category.**

The Circle effect is previewed on Slide 5 behind the dialog box because the Preview Effect check box is selected (Figure 6-25).

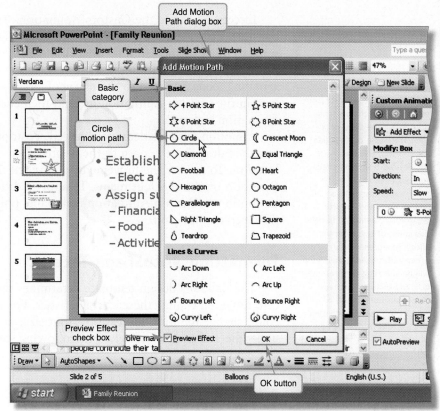

FIGURE 6-25

3

• **Click the OK button.**

• **Click the Start box arrow in the Custom Animation task pane and then click After Previous.**

• **Click the Speed box arrow and then click Very Slow.**

The Circle motion path is applied (Figure 6-26).

4

• **Click the Close button in the Custom Animation task pane.**

When the presentation runs, the 5-Point Star AutoShape will move very slowly in a circular path.

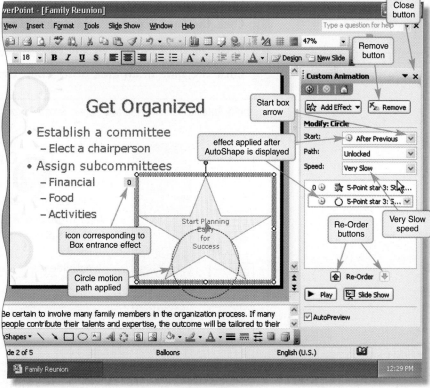

FIGURE 6-26

More About

Transition Effects

A single slide can have a transition effect separate from other slides in the presentation. Select the slide, click Slide Transition on the Slide Show menu, and then click the desired transition effect. Although each slide in the presentation can have a unique transition, graphic designers recommend using a maximum of two different effects in a presentation; otherwise, audience members will be watching the presentation and awaiting the next slide transition instead of focusing on the slide content and the information being presented.

Effects display in the Custom Animation list in the order they were applied to the slide. This animation sequence can be changed easily by clicking the item you want to move in the list and either dragging it to another position or clicking the Re-Order buttons. The changes are reflected in the renumbered list and in the corresponding icons attached to the placeholders. To remove an effect, click the animation item in the Custom Animation list and then click the Remove button in the Custom Animation task pane.

A motion path also can be changed. Positioning the mouse pointer over the path and then dragging the path to the desired area on the slide, for example, changes its location. To reverse the movement, right-click the path and then click Reverse Path Direction on the shortcut menu. To apply a different motion path, click the Change button in the Custom Animation task pane, point to Motion Paths, and then click the desired animation.

Formatting AutoShape Text

The Balloons design template determines the AutoShape's text attributes. You can, however, change these characteristics. For example, you can modify the font color, change the font, increase the font size, and add bold and italic styles and underline and shadow effects. The following steps change the AutoShape's font, font size, and style.

To Format AutoShape Text

1 Select the AutoShape text. Click the Font box arrow on the Formatting toolbar and then click Comic Sans MS.

2 Click the Font Size box arrow on the Formatting toolbar and then click 20.

3 Click the Bold button on the Formatting toolbar.

4 Click the slide in an area other than the AutoShape or placeholders.

The bold AutoShape text has the Comic Sans MS font and a font size of 20 (Figure 6-27).

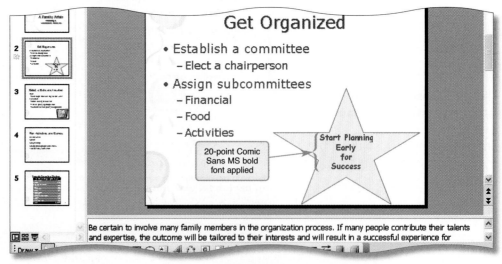

FIGURE 6-27

Text added to an AutoShape becomes part of the shape, which means that it increases font size if the AutoShape is enlarged or that it rotates or flips if the shape is rotated or flipped. If you do not want to attach text to the object, add text instead by using the Text Box button on the Drawing toolbar and then placing the text on top of the object.

Inserting, Formatting, and Animating a Diagram

Diagrams help users understand concepts by showing the relationship among parts of a process or visualizing how something works. One feature in PowerPoint is the capability of inserting predesigned diagrams by clicking the Insert Diagram or Organization Chart button on the Drawing toolbar or by selecting the slide layout with a content placeholder and then clicking the Insert Diagram or Organization Chart button in the content placeholder. The five diagram types are described in Table 6-1.

Table 6-1	**Diagram Types and Functions**	
BUTTON	**BUTTON NAME**	**FUNCTION**
⟳	Cycle	Shows process with continuous action
▲	Pyramid	Shows relationship between elements based on a foundation
❋	Radial	Shows elements relating to a core element
◎	Target	Shows steps leading to a goal
⚙	Venn	Shows overlap between and among different elements

Diagrams have a **drawing space** around them that extends to the nonprinting border and drawing handles. More drawing space can be added if additional objects are needed, or this space can be reduced to fit tightly around the diagram.

Inserting a Venn Diagram

PowerPoint inserts a **Venn diagram** composed of three related elements. While each individual element is important, the synergy of these components leads to overall success. You easily can add elements by using the Diagram toolbar buttons. The steps on the next page insert the Venn diagram.

More About

Adding Shadows

Shadows can give interesting effects to text on your slides. To add a shadow, select the text you want to change and then click the Shadow button on the Formatting toolbar. You then can change the shadow color by clicking the Shadow Style button on the Drawing toolbar, clicking Shadow Settings, and then clicking the Shadow Color button arrow on the Shadow Setting toolbar. You can click one of the color scheme colors under Automatic or use a color not in the color scheme by clicking More Shadow Colors and then clicking the desired color on the Standard tab or the Custom tab. To see through the shadow color, click the Shadow Color button arrow on the Shadow Settings toolbar and then click Semitransparent Shadow.

To Insert a Venn Diagram

1

• **Click the Slide 1 slide thumbnail in the tabs pane.**

• **Click the New Slide button on the Formatting toolbar to insert a new slide.**

• **Click Format on the menu bar and then click Slide Layout.**

• **When the Slide Layout task pane is displayed, point to the Content slide layout in the Content Layouts area.**

The Slide Layout task pane is displayed (Figure 6-28). The new Slide 2 is displayed with Title and Text layout.

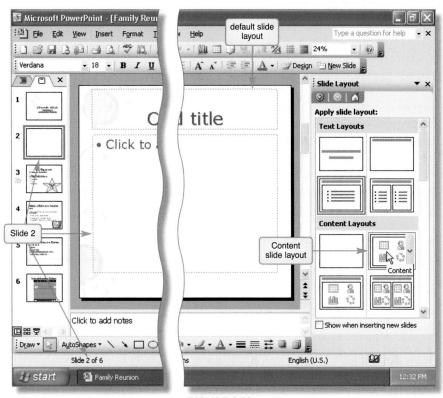

FIGURE 6-28

2

• **Click the Content slide layout.**

• **Click the Close button in the Slide Layout task pane.**

• **Point to the Insert Diagram or Organization Chart button in the content placeholder.**

The Insert Diagram or Organization Chart button is selected (Figure 6-29). A ScreenTip describes its function.

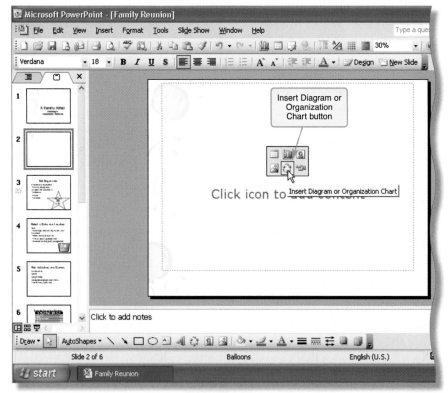

FIGURE 6-29

3

• **Click the Insert Diagram or Organization Chart button.**

• **When the Diagram Gallery dialog box is displayed, click the Venn Diagram diagram type.**

Venn Diagram is selected (Figure 6-30).

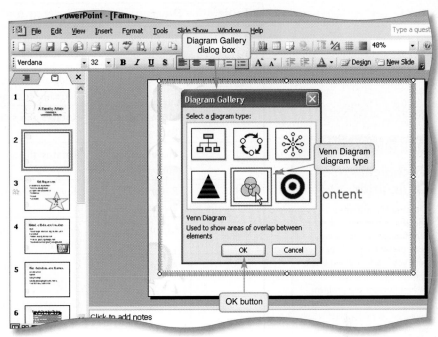

FIGURE 6-30

4

• **Click the OK button.**

The Venn diagram and Diagram toolbar are displayed (Figure 6-31).

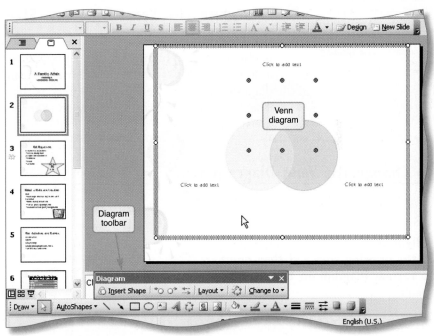

FIGURE 6-31

The Diagram toolbar is displayed automatically when you select any diagram other than an organization chart. It contains buttons that allow you to create and design a diagram. Table 6-2 on the next page describes the functions of each button on the Diagram toolbar.

Table 6-2   Diagram Toolbar Buttons and Functions

BUTTON	BUTTON NAME	FUNCTION
Insert Shape	Insert Shape	Adds a new shape next to the selected shape in the diagram, such as a new level to a pyramid diagram
⬩○	Move Shape Backward	Rotates the shape within the diagram
○⬩	Move Shape Forward	Rotates the shape within the diagram
⬅→	Reverse Diagram	Reverses the order of shapes in the diagram
Layout ▾	Layout	Adjusts the size of the drawing area containing the diagram
⟳	AutoFormat	Customizes the overall style of a diagram with a preset design scheme in the Diagram Style Gallery dialog box
Change to ▾	Change to	Converts the diagram to another type of diagram or chart, such as from a Venn diagram to a Radial diagram

More About

Technical Difficulties

Occasionally you may encounter computer or other technical problems during your presentation. Be open with your audience and briefly explain the trouble. If you cannot correct the problem within five minutes, ask your audience to take a brief break so that you can reboot the computer or take other measures. To learn more about public speaking pointers, view the PowerPoint 2003 More About Web page (scsite.com/ppt2003/more) and click Public Speaking.

Changing the Venn Diagram Size

Each object inserted into a slide is placed on a drawing layer. Each **drawing layer** is stacked on top of another and can be rearranged, in a manner similar to shuffling a deck of cards, so that it is displayed in front of or behind other objects. The Venn diagram drawing layer should display as the top layer of Slide 2, but it is too small. The diagram can be sized and scaled in the same manner as clip art and other objects are sized. The following steps scale the diagram.

To Change the Venn Diagram Size

1

• **Right-click the slide background in the drawing area and then point to Format Diagram on the shortcut menu.**

The shortcut menu is displayed, and a border is displayed around the drawing area (Figure 6-32).

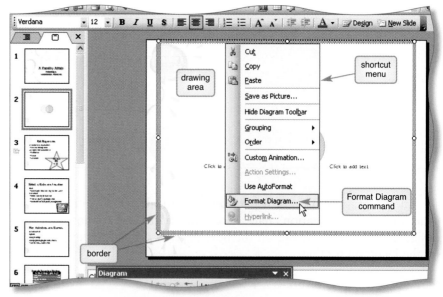

FIGURE 6-32

2

• **Click Format Diagram.**

• **If necessary, when the Format Diagram dialog box is displayed, click the Size tab.**

• **Click and hold down the Height box up arrow in the Scale area until 125 % is displayed.**

Both the Height and Width boxes in the Scale area display 125 % (Figure 6-33).

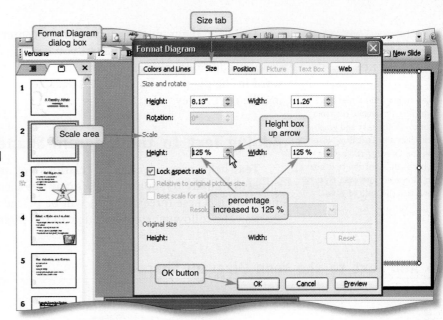

FIGURE 6-33

3

• **Click the OK button.**

• **Click the Layout button on the Diagram toolbar and then point to Fit Diagram to Contents.**

The Fit Diagram to Contents command reduces the unnecessary space around the diagram (Figure 6-34).

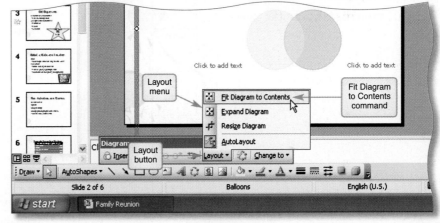

FIGURE 6-34

4

• **Click Fit Diagram to Contents.**

• **Click the border of the diagram and then drag the border so the top, left, and right borders align with the edges of the slide.**

The Venn diagram is the desired size and is positioned in the correct location (Figure 6-35).

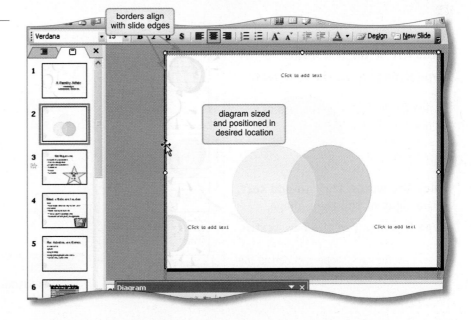

FIGURE 6-35

More About

Text Boxes

To add text outside of a placeholder, add a text box, which is a movable, resizable container for text and graphics. Click the Text Box button on the Drawing toolbar, click where you want the text box to be placed, and then type or paste the desired text.

The Venn diagram is displayed in the center of Slide 2. It consists of three overlapping elements. If necessary, you can use the Diagram toolbar to add and connect additional elements to the core element and to move them forward or backward in the diagram. You also can delete elements by selecting them and then pressing the DELETE key.

Adding Text to the Diagram Shapes

Text helps users identify the relationships among these objects. Planning a successful family reunion requires many key elements: planning, managing, and communicating. These three concepts will be placed adjacent to the three Venn diagram shapes. The following steps add text to the three shapes in the Venn diagram.

To Add Text to the Venn Diagram Shapes

1

• **Click the words, Click to add text, above the top shape.**

• **Type** Communicating **as the new text.**

The desired text is added to the text box above the top shape (Figure 6-36).

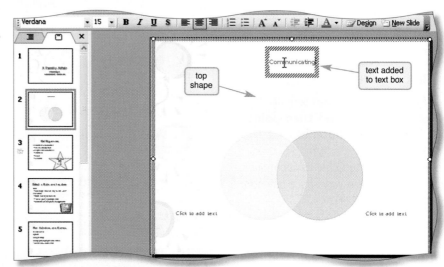

FIGURE 6-36

2

• **Click the words, Click to add text, to the left of the left shape.**

• **Type** Managing **as the new text.**

The text for the left shape is added to the text box.

3

• **Click the words, Click to add text, to the right of the right shape.**

• **Type** Planning **as the new text.**

The text for the right shape is added to the text box (Figure 6-37).

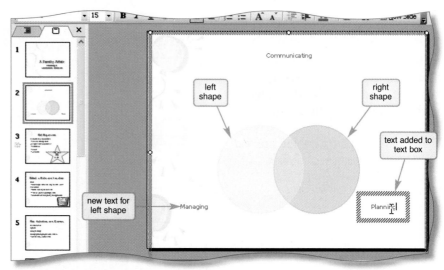

FIGURE 6-37

All elements of the Venn diagram have been added. Formatting the text would help emphasize these words on the slides. The next section describes how to format the three words easily using the Format Painter.

Formatting the Venn Diagram Text Using the Format Painter

Changing the characteristics of the Venn diagram text adds visual appeal. The following steps format the right text by changing the font to Comic Sans MS, increasing the font size to 32, bolding the letters, and changing the font color to green. Once you change these font attributes for one text box, you easily can apply these same changes to another text box by clicking the Format Painter button on the Standard toolbar. The **Format Painter** allows you to copy all formatting changes from one object to another.

To Format the Venn Diagram Text Using the Format Painter

1

• **If necessary, click the right Venn diagram text box that contains the word, Planning.**

• **Click Edit on the menu bar and then click Select All.**

The text is selected (Figure 6-38). The Select All command selects all letters in the text box.

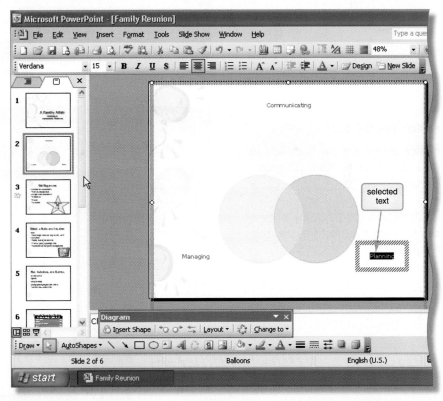

FIGURE 6-38

2

• **Right-click the text and then click Font on the shortcut menu.**

• **When the Font dialog box is displayed, scroll up to and then click Comic Sans MS in the Font list.**

• **Click Bold in the Font style list.**

• **Click 32 in the Size list.**

• **Click the Color box arrow and then click the color green (row 1, column 4).**

Comic Sans MS is displayed in the Font box, Bold is displayed in the Font style box, 32 is displayed in the Size box, and the color green is displayed in the Color box (Figure 6-39).

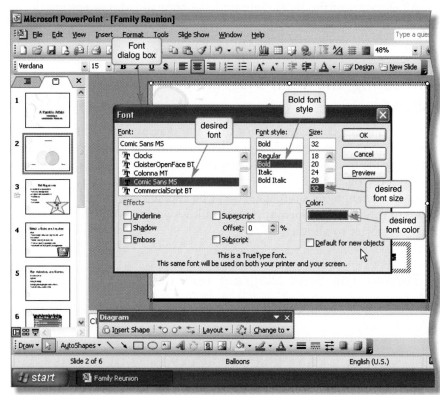

FIGURE 6-39

3

• **Click the OK button.**

• **Click anywhere on the slide other than the text or Venn diagram circles.**

PowerPoint displays the text with the new font, font style, font size, and color (Figure 6-40).

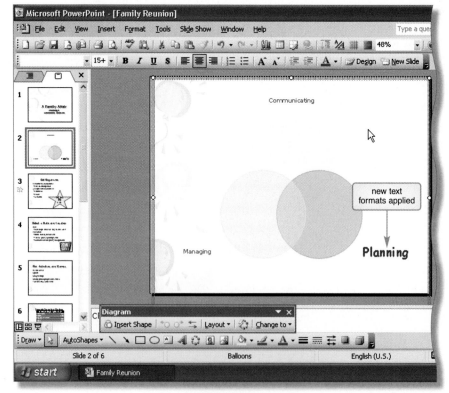

FIGURE 6-40

4

- **Click the word, Planning, to select it.**
- **Click the Format Painter button on the Standard toolbar.**
- **Position the mouse pointer on top of the text for the left Venn diagram element, Managing.**

A paintbrush is connected to the mouse pointer when the Format Painter button is selected (Figure 6-41).

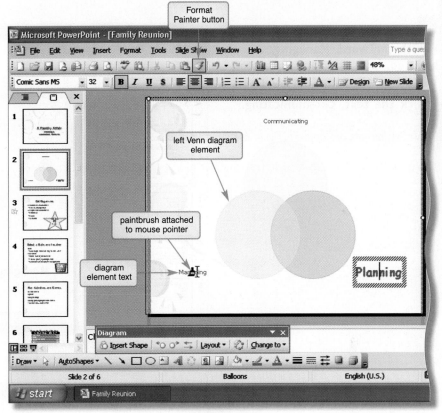

FIGURE 6-41

5

- **Click the text, Managing.**

New text formats are applied (Figure 6-42). These formats are identical to the font changes made to the word, Planning.

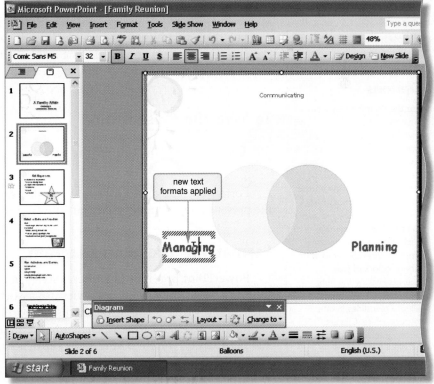

FIGURE 6-42

6

- **With the word, Managing, selected, click the Format Painter button on the Standard toolbar.**
- **Click the text, Communicating.**

New text formats are applied (Figure 6-43).

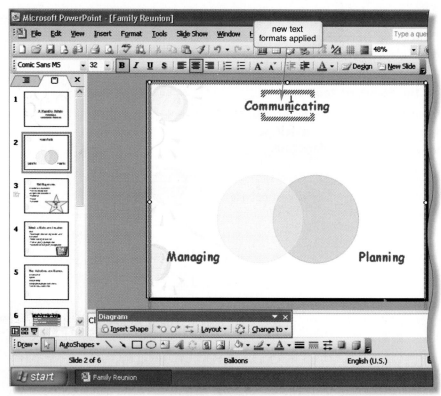

FIGURE 6-43

The three text elements on Slide 2 are formatted. You now should save your presentation because you have done a substantial amount of work. The following step saves the presentation.

To Save the Presentation

1 **Click the Save button on the Standard toolbar.**

Formatting the diagram would create visual interest. The next section describes the preset design schemes that can enliven a presentation.

Formatting the Venn Diagram

PowerPoint provides nine preset styles in addition to the default style in the **Diagram Style Gallery**. These styles use assorted colors, shadows, and lines to add interest and variety. You also can custom format the diagram by adding color, changing the line style and weight, changing the fill color, inserting a background, and adding texture. The following steps show how to format the diagram by applying the Primary Colors diagram style.

To Format the Venn Diagram

1

• **Click the AutoFormat button on the Diagram toolbar.**

• **When the Diagram Style Gallery dialog box is displayed, click Primary Colors in the Select a Diagram Style list.**

Diagram style names are displayed in the list. When you click a diagram style name, PowerPoint previews that style (Figure 6-44).

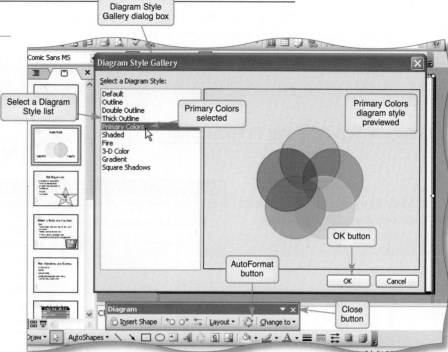

FIGURE 6-44

2

• **Click the OK button.**

• **Click the Close button on the Diagram toolbar.**

PowerPoint applies the Primary Colors diagram style to the Venn diagram (Figure 6-45).

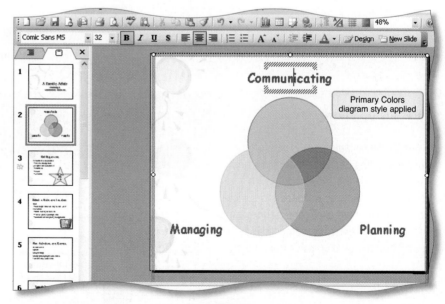

FIGURE 6-45

The elements of the Venn diagram are complete. If you want to move one of the shapes, select that shape and then click the Move Shape Forward or Move Shape Backward button on the Diagram toolbar.

All slide elements have been added to the presentation. The next section describes how to set the controls so the slide show runs automatically without user intervention.

Creating a Self-Running Presentation

You will run the Family Reunion presentation during your speech, but you also want it to run unattended at your school's open house. When the last slide in the presentation is displayed, the slide show **loops**, or restarts, at Slide 1.

PowerPoint has the option of running continuously until a user presses the ESC key. The following steps explain how to set the slide show to run in this manner.

To Create a Self-Running Presentation

1

• **Click Slide Show on the menu bar and then point to Set Up Show.**

The Set Up Show options let you decide how much control, if any, you will give to your audience (Figure 6-46).

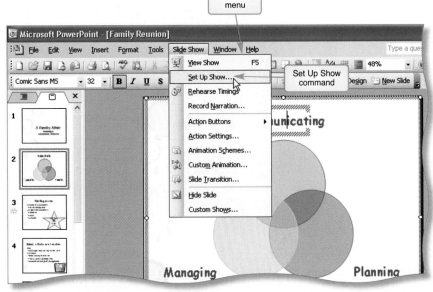

FIGURE 6-46

2

• **Click Set Up Show.**

The Set Up Show dialog box is displayed (Figure 6-47). The Set Up Show dialog box is used to specify the show type, which slides to display, how to advance slides, how multiple monitors are used, and performance enhancements. The default show type is Presented by a speaker (full screen).

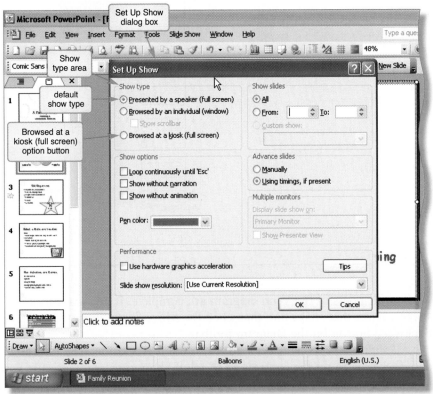

FIGURE 6-47

3

• **Click Browsed at a kiosk (full screen) in the Show type area.**

A check mark is displayed in the Loop continuously until 'Esc' check box, and the check box and label are dimmed (Figure 6-48). The slides will advance automatically based on the timings you specify.

4

• **Click the OK button.**

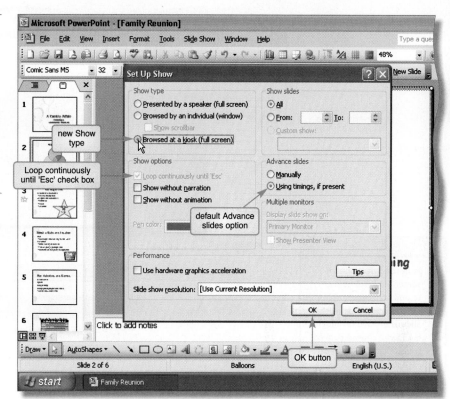

FIGURE 6-48

This slide show will run by itself without user intervention. The user can, however, advance through the slides manually.

Adding an Animation Scheme

The next step in preparing the Family Reunion presentation is to add an animation scheme. The following steps add the Float motion animation scheme.

To Add an Animation Scheme

1 Click Slide Show on the menu bar and then click Animation Schemes.

2 Scroll to and then click Float in the Exciting category.

3 Click the Apply to All Slides button.

4 Click the Close button on the Slide Design task pane title bar.

The Float motion animation scheme is applied to all slides in the presentation (Figure 6-49 on the next page).

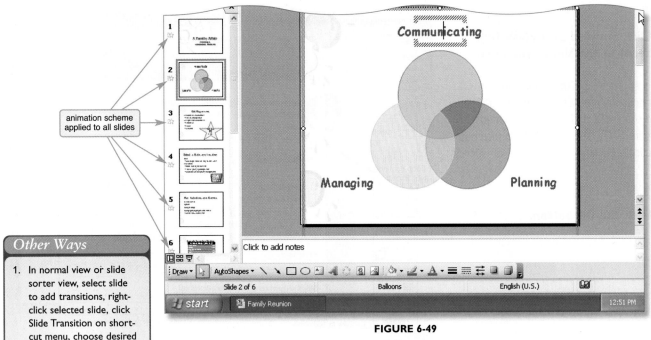

FIGURE 6-49

Setting Slide Show Timings Manually

The slide show is designed to loop continuously at a kiosk for five minutes unless the user moves through the slides manually. Consequently, you must determine the length of time each slide will be displayed on the screen. You can set these times in two ways. One method is to use PowerPoint's **rehearsal** feature, which allows you to advance through the slides at your own pace, and the amount of time you view each slide is recorded. The other method is to set each slide's display time manually. You will use this second technique in the following steps.

To Set Slide Show Timing Manually for Slide 1

1

• **Click the Slide Sorter View button.**

• **Right-click Slide 1 and then point to Slide Transition.**

Slide 1 is selected, and the shortcut menu is displayed (Figure 6-50).

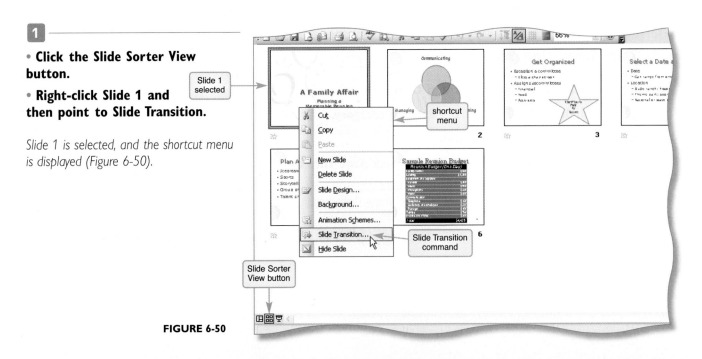

FIGURE 6-50

2

- **Click Slide Transition on the shortcut menu.**

The Slide Transition task pane is displayed (Figure 6-51). The On mouse click check box is selected in the Advance slide area. A speaker generally uses this default setting to advance through the slides in a presentation.

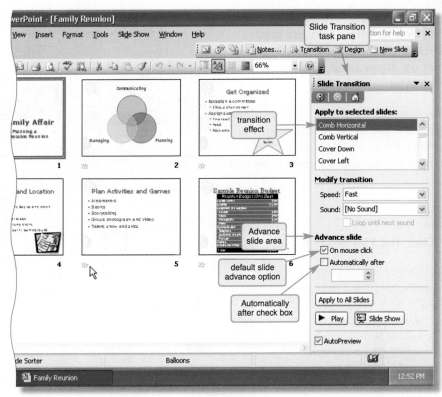

FIGURE 6-51

3

- **Click Automatically after in the Advance slide area.**

This slide show advances the slide automatically after it has displayed for a designated period or allows users to display the slides manually (Figure 6-52). You specify the length of time you want the slide to display in the Automatically after box.

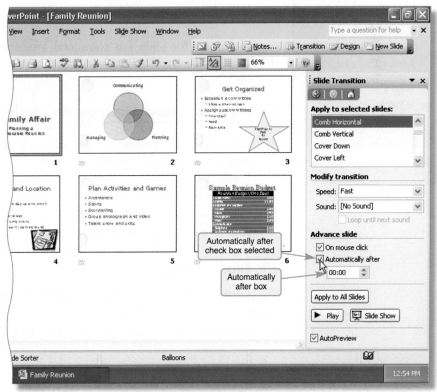

FIGURE 6-52

• **Click and hold down the mouse button on the Automatically after box up arrow until 00:30 is displayed.**

The Automatically after box displays 00:30 seconds (Figure 6-53). Another method of entering the time is to type the specific number of minutes and seconds in the text box.

5

• **Click the Play button.**

The Comb Horizontal slide transition is displayed in the Slide 1 slide thumbnail. Below Slide 1, 00:30 is displayed, indicating the designated slide timing.

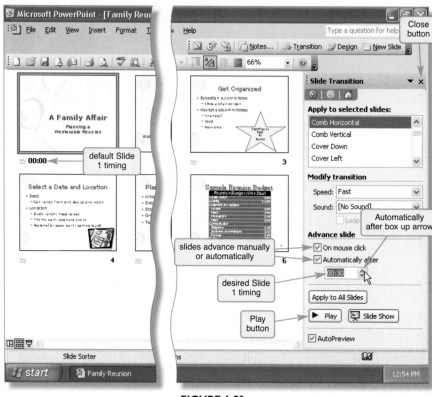

FIGURE 6-53

The timing for Slide 1 is complete. You need to repeat this procedure for Slides 2 through 6 in the Family Reunion presentation. The following steps set these timings.

To Set Slide Show Timings Manually for the Remaining Slides

1 Click the Slide 2 slide thumbnail, press and hold down the SHIFT key, and then click Slide 5. Click Automatically after in the Advance slide area in the Slide Transition task pane. Click and hold down the Automatically after box up arrow until 00:45 is displayed.

2 Click the Slide 6 slide thumbnail. Click Automatically after in the Advance slide area in the Slide Transition task pane. Click and hold down the Automatically after box up arrow until 01:30 is displayed.

3 Click the Play button.

4 Click the Close button on the Slide Transition task pane title bar.

Each slide's timing is displayed in the lower-left corner (Figure 6-54).

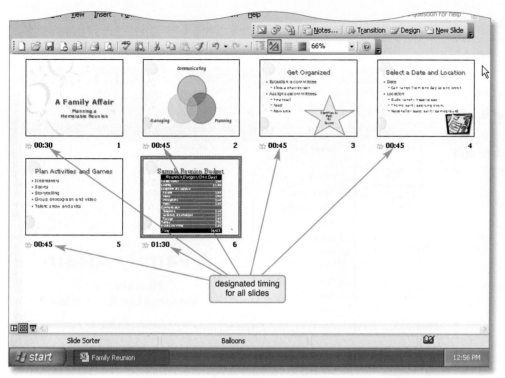

FIGURE 6-54

The Family Reunion slide timing is complete. The presentation will run for five minutes.

Adding and Formatting Slide Numbers

Slides can contain information at the top or bottom. The area at the top of a slide is called a **header**, and the area at the bottom is called a **footer**. As a default, no information is displayed in the header or footer. You can choose to apply only a header, only a footer, or both a header and footer. In addition, you can elect to have the header or footer display on single slides, all slides, or all slides except the title slide.

Adding Slide Numbers

Slide numbers help a presenter organize a talk. While few audience members are cognizant of this aspect of a slide, the presenter can glance at the number and know which slide contains particular information. If an audience member asks a question pertaining to information contained on a slide that had been displayed previously or is on a slide that has not been viewed yet, the presenter can jump to that slide in an effort to answer the question. In addition, the slide number helps pace the slide show. For example, a speaker could have the presentation timed so that Slide 4 is displaying three minutes into the talk. The steps on the next page describe how to add this number to a slide.

More About

Restoring Placeholders

The Title, Text, Date, Slide number, and Footer placeholders can be restored on the slide master if they have been deleted. To reinsert a placeholder, point to Master on the View menu and then click Slide Master. Click Master Layout on the Format menu. Under Placeholders, select the placeholder you want to restore. If you have moved or sized a placeholder and now want to move or size it to its original size and location, delete it and then follow the steps specified in this paragraph.

To Add Slide Numbers

1

• **Click the Normal View button.**

• **Click the Slide 1 slide thumbnail in the tabs pane.**

• **Click Insert on the menu bar and then point to Slide Number.**

The Insert menu is displayed (Figure 6-55).

FIGURE 6-55

2

• **Click Slide Number.**

• **If necessary, when the Header and Footer dialog box is displayed, click the Slide tab.**

The Slide sheet in the Header and Footer dialog box is displayed (Figure 6-56). The Date and time and Footer check boxes are selected in the Include on slide area. The left and center footer placeholders are selected in the Preview area, indicating the Date and time and Footer check boxes are selected.

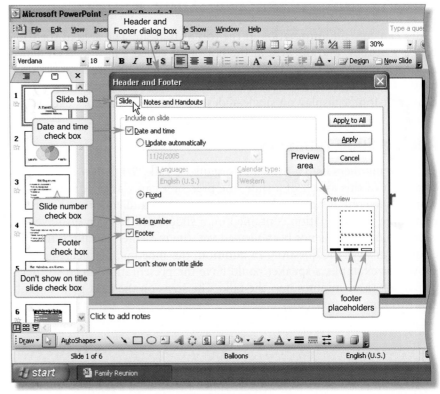

FIGURE 6-56

3

- **Click Date and time.**
- **Click Slide number.**
- **Click Footer.**
- **Click Don't show on title slide.**

Check marks are removed from the Date and time and the Footer check boxes. Check marks are placed in the Slide number and Don't show on title slide check boxes (Figure 6-57). The right footer place-holder is selected in the Preview area, indicating the Slide number check box is selected.

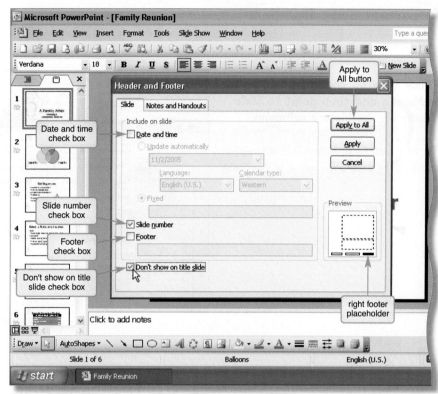

FIGURE 6-57

4

- **Click the Apply to All button.**
- **After verifying the slide number does not display on Slide 1, click the Next Slide button on the vertical scroll bar to display Slide 2.**

The slide number is displayed on Slide 2 and on all slides except Slide 1 (Figure 6-58).

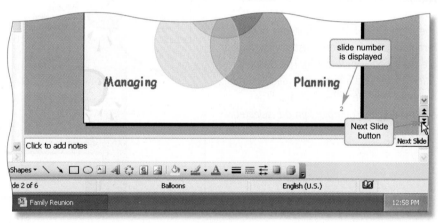

FIGURE 6-58

The slide number placeholder can be moved to a different location on the slide using the slide master. You also can add, modify, and delete headers and footers when you view the slides using the slide master.

Formatting Slide Numbers

Header or footer text can be formatted and sized. The easiest method of modifying these characteristics is to change the placeholders on the slide master. The following section describes how to format slide numbers.

Other Ways

1. On the Insert menu click Slide Number, click Slide tab, click Slide number, click Apply to All
2. Press ALT+I, press U, press N, press Y
3. In Voice Command mode, say "Insert, Slide Number, Slide number, Apply to All"

To Format Slide Numbers

1

• **Click View on the menu bar, point to Master, and then point to Slide Master on the Master submenu.**

The View menu and Master submenu are displayed (Figure 6-59).

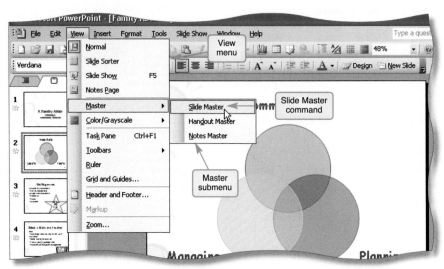

FIGURE 6-59

2

• **Click Slide Master.**

• **Click the number sign in the Number Area on the slide master.**

The Slide Master for the Balloons design template and the Slide Master View toolbar are displayed (Figure 6-60). The Balloons Title Master and Slide Master slide thumbnails are displayed. The Balloons Slide Master and the number sign are selected.

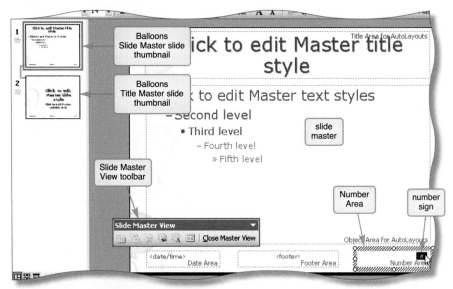

FIGURE 6-60

3

• **Click Format on the menu bar and then click Font.**

• **When the Font dialog box is displayed, change the font to Comic Sans MS, the font style to Bold, the font size to 18, and the font color to green (row 1, column 4).**

The new text attributes for the slide number are specified (Figure 6-61).

FIGURE 6-61

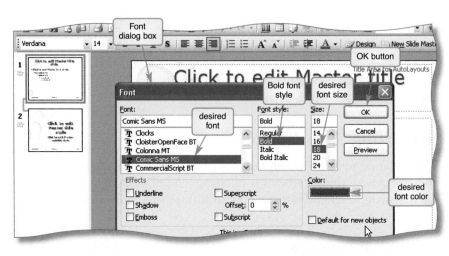

4

- **Click the OK button.**
- **Click the slide master anywhere except the Number Area.**

The number sign in the Number Area is displayed with the new text formatting (Figure 6-62).

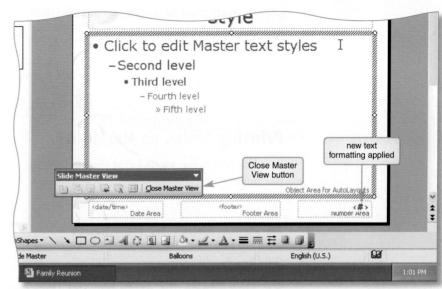

FIGURE 6-62

5

- **Click the Close Master View button on the Slide Master View toolbar.**

The slide number on Slide 2 is displayed with the new text formatting (Figure 6-63).

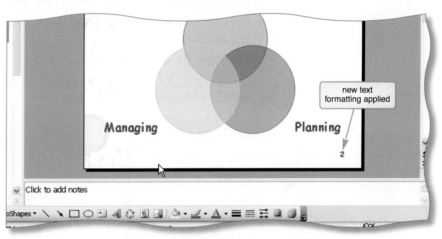

FIGURE 6-63

The presentation is complete. You now should save it again, as shown in the following step.

To Save the Presentation

1 Click the Save button on the Standard toolbar.

Starting the Self-Running Presentation

Starting a self-running slide show basically is the same as starting any other slide show. The following steps run the presentation.

To Start the Self-Running Presentation

1 Click the Slide 1 slide thumbnail in the tabs pane and then click the Slide Show from current slide button.

2 As each slide is displayed automatically, review the information.

3 When Slide 1 is displayed again, press the ESC key to stop the presentation.

The presentation will run for five minutes, and then it will loop back to the beginning and start automatically.

Printing Slides as Handouts

The following steps print the presentation slides as handouts, with three slides per page.

To Print Slides as Handouts

1 Ready the printer.

2 Click File on the menu bar and then click Print.

3 Click the Print what box arrow and then click Handouts in the list.

4 Click the Slides per page box arrow in the Handouts area and then click 3 in the list.

5 Click the OK button.

The handouts print as shown in Figure 6-64.

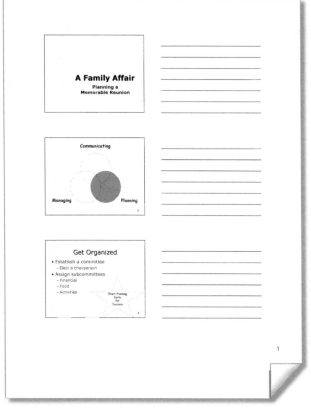

(a) Page 1

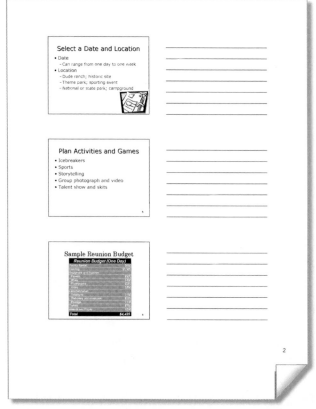

(b) Page 2

FIGURE 6-64

The Family Reunion presentation now is complete. If you made any changes to your presentation since your last save, you now should save it again before quitting PowerPoint, as shown in the following steps.

To Quit PowerPoint

1 Click the **Close** button on the **title bar**.

2 If prompted to save the presentation before quitting PowerPoint, click the **Yes** button in the Microsoft Office PowerPoint dialog box.

Project Summary

Project 6 presented the principles of creating a self-running presentation. You began the project by starting a new presentation and then inserting a slide from another presentation. You then inserted and formatted an AutoShape and added text and a motion path animation effect. Next, you inserted and formatted a Venn diagram and added meaningful text to that graphic. You then added an animation scheme and set automatic slide timings to display each slide for a designated period of time. After adding and formatting slide numbers, you printed your presentation slides as handouts with three slides displaying on each page.

 If you have a SAM user profile, you may have access to hands-on instruction, practice, and assessment of the skills covered in this project. Log in to your SAM account and go to your assignments page to see what your instructor has assigned.

What You Should Know

Having completed this project, you should be able to perform the tasks below. The tasks are listed in the same order they were presented in this project. For a list of the buttons, menus, toolbars, and commands introduced in this project, see the Quick Reference Summary at the back of this book and refer to the Page Number column.

1. Start and Customize a New Presentation (PPT 420)
2. Create a Title Slide   (PPT 421)
3. Save the Presentation   (PPT 422, PPT 430, PPT 448, PPT 459)
4. Create Slide 2   (PPT 423)
5. Create Slide 3   (PPT 424)
6. Create Slide 4   (PPT 425)
7. Insert a Slide from Another Presentation (PPT 427)
8. Add Notes to a Slide   (PPT 430)
9. Insert, Size, and Move a Clip   (PPT 431)
10. Insert an AutoShape   (PPT 432)
11. Add Text to an AutoShape   (PPT 434)
12. Apply an AutoShape Entrance Animation Effect   (PPT 435)
13. Apply a Motion Path Animation Effect to an AutoShape   (PPT 436)
14. Format AutoShape Text   (PPT 438)

15. Insert a Venn Diagram   (PPT 440)
16. Change the Venn Diagram Size   (PPT 442)
17. Add Text to the Venn Diagram Shapes   (PPT 444)
18. Format the Venn Diagram Text Using the Format Painter   (PPT 445)
19. Format the Venn Diagram   (PPT 449)
20. Create a Self-Running Presentation   (PPT 450)
21. Add an Animation Scheme   (PPT 451)
22. Set Slide Show Timing Manually for Slide 1 (PPT 452)
23. Set Slide Show Timings Manually for the Remaining Slides   (PPT 454)
24. Add Slide Numbers   (PPT 456)
25. Format Slide Numbers   (PPT 458)
26. Start the Self-Running Presentation   (PPT 459)
27. Print Slides as Handouts   (PPT 460)
28. Quit PowerPoint   (PPT 461)

Learn It Online

Instructions: To complete the Learn It Online exercises, start your browser, click the Address bar, and then enter the Web address scsite.com/ppt2003/learn. When the PowerPoint 2003 Learn It Online page is displayed, follow the instructions in the exercises below. Each exercise has instructions for printing your results, either for your own records or for submission to your instructor.

1 Project Reinforcement TF, MC, and SA

Below PowerPoint Project 6, click the Project Reinforcement link. Print the quiz by clicking Print on the File menu for each page. Answer each question.

Flash Cards

Below PowerPoint Project 6, click the Flash Cards link and read the instructions. Type 20 (or a number specified by your instructor) in the Number of playing cards text box, type your name in the Enter your Name text box, and then click the Flip Card button. When the flash card is displayed, read the question and then click the ANSWER box arrow to select an answer. Flip through Flash Cards. If your score is 15 (75%) correct or greater, click Print on the File menu to print your results. If your score is less than 15 (75%) correct, then redo this exercise by clicking the Replay button.

3 Practice Test

Below PowerPoint Project 6, click the Practice Test link. Answer each question, enter your first and last name at the bottom of the page, and then click the Grade Test button. When the graded practice test is displayed on your screen, click Print on the File menu to print a hard copy. Continue to take practice tests until you score 80% or better.

4 Who Wants To Be a Computer Genius?

Below PowerPoint Project 6, click the Computer Genius link. Read the instructions, enter your first and last name at the bottom of the page, and then click the PLAY button. When your score is displayed, click the PRINT RESULTS link to print a hard copy.

5 Wheel of Terms

Below PowerPoint Project 6, click the Wheel of Terms link. Read the instructions, and then enter your first and last name and your school name. Click the PLAY button. When your score is displayed, right-click the score and then click Print on the shortcut menu to print a hard copy.

6 Crossword Puzzle Challenge

Below PowerPoint Project 6, click the Crossword Puzzle Challenge link. Read the instructions, and then enter your first and last name. Click the SUBMIT button. Work the crossword puzzle. When you are finished, click the Submit button. When the crossword puzzle is redisplayed, click the Print Puzzle button to print a hard copy.

7 Tips and Tricks

Below PowerPoint Project 6, click the Tips and Tricks link. Click a topic that pertains to Project 6. Right-click the information and then click Print on the shortcut menu. Construct a brief example of what the information relates to in PowerPoint to confirm you understand how to use the tip or trick.

8 Newsgroups

Below PowerPoint Project 6, click the Newsgroups link. Click a topic that pertains to Project 6. Print three comments.

9 Expanding Your Horizons

Below PowerPoint Project 6, click the Expanding Your Horizons link. Click a topic that pertains to Project 6. Print the information. Construct a brief example of what the information relates to in PowerPoint to confirm you understand the contents of the article.

10 Search Sleuth

Below PowerPoint Project 6, click the Search Sleuth link. To search for a term that pertains to this project, select a term below the Project 6 title and then use the Google search engine at google.com (or any major search engine) to display and print two Web pages that present information on the term.

11 PowerPoint Online Training

Below PowerPoint Project 6, click the PowerPoint Online Training link. When your browser displays the Microsoft Office Online Web page, click the PowerPoint link. Click one of the PowerPoint courses that covers one or more of the objectives listed at the beginning of the project on page PPT 418. Print the first page of the course before stepping through it.

12 Office Marketplace

Below PowerPoint Project 6, click the Office Marketplace link. When your browser displays the Microsoft Office Online Web page, click the Office Marketplace link. Click a topic that relates to PowerPoint. Print the first page.

1 Academic Assistance Center

Instructions: The director of the Academic Assistance Center at your school wants to encourage students to visit the Center when they are having difficulties completing homework assignments or comprehending class material. The director asks you to help promote the Center's services by creating a PowerPoint presentation. Start PowerPoint and then perform the following tasks to create the title slide shown in Figure 6-65.

1. Create a new presentation using the Blank slide layout and the Network design template. Apply the color scheme in row 1, column 1.
2. Click the AutoShapes button on the Drawing toolbar, point to Stars and Banners, and then click Horizontal Scroll (row 4, column 2) on the Stars and Banners submenu. Click the slide to display the scroll object. Right-click the scroll and then click Format AutoShape on the shortcut menu. If necessary, when the Format AutoShape dialog box is displayed, click the Size tab and then change the Height to 3.0 and the Width to 8.0 in the Size and rotate area.
3. Display the drawing guides. Drag the horizontal guide to 2.75 inches above center and the vertical guide to 4.25 inches left of center. Drag the scroll so the top and left edges snap to the intersection of the guides.
4. Type the text for the scroll as shown in Figure 6-65. Increase the font size for the first two lines to 32 and last line to 28. Select the last line of text and then add a shadow by clicking the Shadow button on the Formatting toolbar. Italicize this last line.
5. Insert the professor clip, size it to 180 %, and then position it as shown in Figure 6-65. Ungroup the clip and then delete the pointer. Regroup the clip.
6. Click the AutoShapes button on the Drawing toolbar, point to Callouts, and then click Rounded Rectangular Callout (row 1, column 2) on the Callouts submenu. Click the slide to display the callout object. Right-click the callout and then click Format AutoShape on the shortcut menu. If necessary, when the Format AutoShape dialog box is displayed, click the Size tab, place a check mark in the Lock aspect ratio check box, and then scale the callout to 130 %. Add the text shown in the figure. Change the font to Bookman Old Style.

FIGURE 6-65

7. Drag the horizontal guide to 0.33 inches below center and the vertical guide to 0.75 inches right of center. Drag the scroll so the top and left edges snap to the intersection of the guides. With the callout selected, click the Fill Color button arrow on the Drawing toolbar and then click the color red (color 8 in the palette of available colors). Hide the drawing guides.
8. Apply the Rise up animation scheme. Save the presentation with the file name, Apply 6-1 Academic Assistance. Print the slide using the Pure Black and White option and then hand in the hard copy to your instructor.

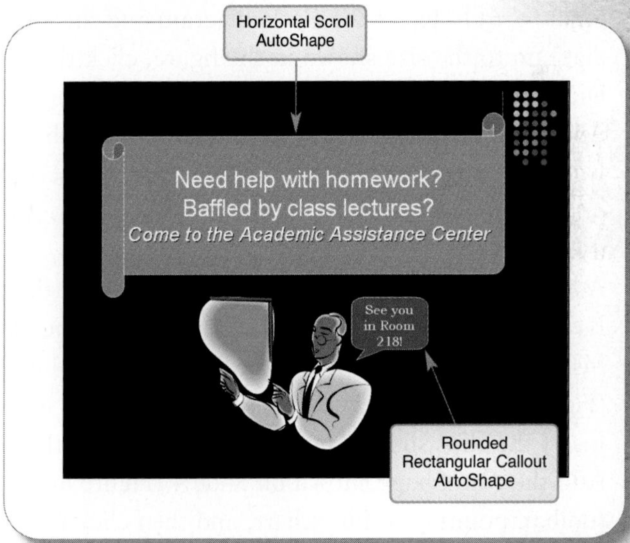

In the Lab

1 Television Buying Guide

Problem: Shopping for a television can be a confusing, frustrating affair. For starters, you will encounter such features as flat panel, flat screen, LCD, plasma, and high definition. The choice of television revolves around three key factors: flat panel or flat screen; standard or widescreen screen shape; and plasma or LCD. One assignment in your speech class is to deliver an informative presentation, and you decide to use your experience as a sales person at a local electronics store to prepare a five-minute talk on the topic of buying a television. You develop a self-running PowerPoint presentation to accompany your presentation. To make the slide show useful and interesting, you create a slide with a Cycle diagram to introduce these concepts. Create the presentation shown in Figures 6-66a through 6-66e.

Instructions: Perform the following tasks. If the clip art images are not available on your computer, see your instructor for copies of these files or substitute similar objects.

1. Open a new presentation and apply the Title Slide slide layout and the Satellite Dish design template. Create the title slide shown in Figure 6-66a by typing the text and moving the placeholder locations. Add the clip and size it to 245 %.

2. Insert a new slide and then apply the Title and Content slide layout. Type the title text shown in Figure 6-66b. Insert the Cycle diagram and then apply the Square Shadows AutoFormat. Scale the Cycle diagram to the size shown in the figure, click the Layout button on the Diagram toolbar, and then click Fit Diagram to Contents. Center the Cycle diagram on the slide.

3. Add the captions shown in Figure 6-66b to each of the areas marked, Click to add text. Change the font color for the upper-left box, Flat panel or flat screen?, to dark brown (color 6 in the palette of available colors), the font to Garamond, and the font size to 20, and then bold the text. Use the Format Painter to modify the text in the two other box captions.

4. Add the Curve Up entrance animation effect in the Exciting category and the Diamond motion path in the Basic category to the Cycle diagram. Change the Start settings for both animations to After Previous.

5. Insert a new slide and apply the Title and 2-Column Text slide layout. Type the text shown on Slide 3 (Figure 6-66c). Repeat this step to create Slides 4 and 5 (Figures 6-66d and 6-66e).

6. Insert the clips shown on Slides 3 and 5. Scale the clip on Slide 3 to 210 %.

7. Add the AutoShape shown on Slide 4 (Figure 6-66d) by clicking the AutoShapes button on the Drawing toolbar, pointing to Flowchart, and then clicking Flowchart: Punched Tape (row 4, column 4). Insert the AutoShape below the two columns of text. Type LCDs use both formats and then change the font to Garamond and the font size to 24. Bold this text. Right-click the AutoShape, click Format AutoShape on the shortcut menu, and then click the Text Box tab when the Format AutoShape dialog box is displayed. Place a check mark in the Resize AutoShape to fit text check box and then click the OK button.

8. Add the Rise Up entrance animation effect to the AutoShape. Change the Start setting to After Previous.

9. Apply the Shape Circle slide transition to all slides.

10. Save the presentation with the file name, Lab 6-1 Television Terminology.

11. Print the five presentation slides as a handout with two slides per page. Hand in the hard copy to your instructor.

In the Lab

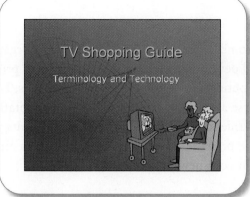

(a) Slide 1

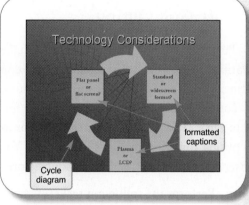

(b) Slide 2

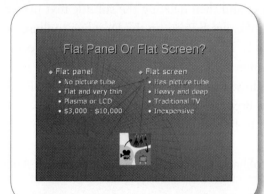

(c) Slide 3

(d) Slide 4

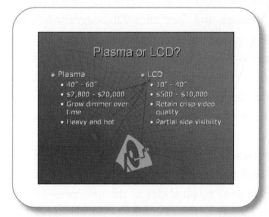

(e) Slide 5

FIGURE 6-66

2 Putt Putt Golf Outing

Problem: Putt Putt Golfing Extravaganza specializes in customizing golf outings for community organizations and corporations. You work as an agent for this company and develop PowerPoint presentations to promote various outings. Your company uses four golf courses for the outings: Over the Hill, Pines and Oaks, Lots of Lakes, and Timber Rocks, and the specifications for each course are part of the Golf Courses presentation that is on your Data Disk. The human resources director at Ability Athletics has called your office and wants you to develop an outing for the company's employees. You create the presentation shown in Figures 6-67a and 6-67b and then insert one slide from the Golf Courses presentation in your new presentation.

Instructions: Perform the following tasks:

1. Open a new presentation and apply the Title Slide slide layout and the Glass Layers design template. Create the title slide shown in Figure 6-67a by typing the title text and then deleting the subtitle text placeholder.

2. Add the AutoShape shown on Slide 1 by clicking the AutoShapes button on the Drawing toolbar, pointing to Basic Shapes, and then clicking Donut (row 5, column 2). Insert the AutoShape below the word, Golf. Type the text shown in the shape on Slide 1 and then change the font to Bookman Old Style or a similar font and the font size to 24. Bold this text and add a shadow. Right-click the AutoShape, click Format AutoShape on the shortcut menu, and then click the Text Box tab when the Format AutoShape dialog box is displayed. Place a check mark in the Resize AutoShape to fit text check box and then click the OK button.

3. Add the Dissolve In entrance animation effect to the AutoShape and change the Start setting to After Previous and the Speed setting to Medium.

4. Insert a new slide and apply the Title and Content slide layout. Type the title text shown on Slide 2 (Figure 6-67b). Insert the Target diagram. Click the Insert Shape button on the Diagram toolbar to add a fourth ring to the diagram. Apply the 3-D Color AutoFormat. Scale the Target diagram to 150 %, click the Layout button on the Diagram toolbar, and then click Fit Diagram to Contents. Center the Target diagram on the slide.

5. Add the captions shown in Figure 6-67b to each of the areas marked, Click to add text. Using the Format Painter, change the font color for the four captions to yellow (color 8 in the palette of available colors), the font to Century Schoolbook, and the font size to 24, and then italicize the text.

6. Add the Stretch entrance animation effect and the Octagon motion path to the Target diagram. Change the Start settings for both animations to After Previous.

7. Insert Slide 4 from the Golf Courses presentation on your Data Disk. Use the Format Painter to modify the Slide 3 title and body text to match the font and formatting on Slide 2.

8. Apply the Newsflash animation scheme to all slides in the new presentation. Save the presentation with the file name, Lab 6-2 Ability Golf Outing.

9. Print the presentation slides as Notes Pages. Hand in the hard copy to your instructor.

In the Lab

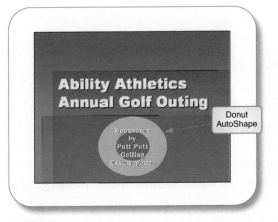

(a) Slide 1

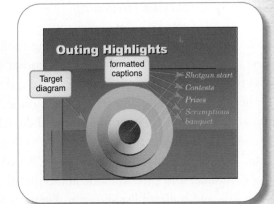

(b) Slide 2

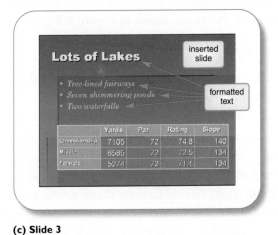

(c) Slide 3

FIGURE 6-67

3 Healthy Family Lifestyles

Problem: Families have hectic schedules, and their daily activities of school, work, sports, and commuting often do not allow time for healthy meals. A healthy lifestyle includes recreation and nutritious foods. Some simple steps can help balance exercise and eating, and you have offered to create a PowerPoint presentation to highlight these guidelines. The presentation will run at your college's fitness center, so you decide a self-running slide show would be the best vehicle to share information. Develop the presentation shown in Figures 6-68a through 6-68d on page PPT 469.

Instructions: Perform the following tasks:

1. Start PowerPoint, open a new presentation, and apply the Echo design template. Add the Fruit Basket picture on your Data Disk to the Slide 1 background and omit the background graphics from the master. Delete the title and subtitle text placeholders.

(continued)

Healthy Family Lifestyles *(continued)*

2. Click the AutoShapes button on the Drawing toolbar, point to Stars and Banners, and then click Explosion 2 (row 1, column 2). Click the lower-right corner of the slide and then add the text shown in Figure 6-68a. Increase the font size to 32 point and italicize the text. Change the font color to purple (color 3 in the palette of available colors) and the font to Comic Sans MS. Resize the AutoShape to fit the text. You may need to adjust the AutoShape to fit on the slide. Click the green rotate handle and turn the AutoShape to the left, as shown on Figure 6-68a. Add the Split entrance effect, and change the Start setting to After Previous. Add the Heart motion path to the AutoShape, and change the Start setting to After Previous.

3. Insert a new slide, and enter the title and bulleted list shown in Figure 6-68b. Insert another new slide and enter the title and bulleted list shown in Figure 6-68c.

4. Insert a new slide and apply the Blank slide layout. Click the AutoShapes button on the Drawing toolbar, point to Block Arrows, click the Right Arrow Callout shape (row 6, column 1), and then click the left-center side of the slide. Type Varied foods as shown in Figure 6-68d and scale the height and width of the arrow to 300 %.

5. Click the AutoShapes button on the Drawing toolbar, point to Block Arrows, click the Left Arrow Callout shape (row 6, column 2), and then click the right-center side of the slide. Type Small snacks as shown in Figure 6-68d and scale the height and width of the arrow to 300 %.

6. Click the AutoShapes button on the Drawing toolbar, point to Block Arrows, click the Up Arrow Callout shape (row 6, column 3), and then click the bottom-center side of the slide. Type Physical activity as shown in Figure 6-68d and scale the height and width of the arrow to 300 %.

7. Display the drawing guides. Drag the horizontal guide to 1.25 inches above center and the vertical guide to 3.75 inches left of center. Drag the Right Arrow Callout shape so the top and left edges snap to the intersection of the guides. Drag the vertical guide to 3.75 inches right of center. Drag the Left Arrow Callout shape so the top and right edges snap to the intersection of the guides. Drag the horizontal guide to 3.25 inches below center and the vertical guide to 1.00 inches right of center. Drag the Up Arrow Callout shape so the bottom and right edges snap to the intersection of the guides. Hide the drawing guides.

8. Using the Format Painter, change the font color for the three arrows to purple, the font to Century Schoolbook, and the font size to 36. Resize the three AutoShapes to fit the text.

9. Click the AutoShapes button on the Drawing toolbar, point to Basic Shapes, click the Sun shape (row 6, column 3), and then click the top-center side of the slide. Type Family health as shown in Figure 6-68d, scale the height and width of the AutoShape to 300 %, and then resize the AutoShape to fit the text. Change the font color to light green, the font to Comic Sans MS, the font size to 28, and the fill color to purple.

10. For the Left Arrow Callout shape, add the Fly In entrance animation effect, change the Start setting to After Previous, change the Direction to From Left, and change the Speed to Fast.

11. For the Right Arrow Callout shape, add the Fly In entrance animation effect, change the Start setting to After Previous, change the Direction to From Right, and change the Speed to Fast.

12. For the Up Arrow Callout shape, add the Fly In entrance animation effect, and change the Start setting to After Previous. If necessary, change the Direction to From Bottom, and change the Speed to Fast.

13. For the Sun shape, add the Dissolve In entrance animation effect, change the Start setting to After Previous, and change the Speed to Medium.

In the Lab

14. Change the background for Slides 2, 3, and 4 to the Blue tissue paper texture.
15. Set the slide timings to 15 seconds for Slide 1 and 30 seconds for the other three slides.
16. Set the show type as Browsed at a kiosk.
17. Add the slide number to the slide footer and display it on all slides except the title slide.
18. Apply the Split Horizontal Out animation scheme to all slides. Save the presentation with the file name, Lab 6-3 Healthy Family.
19. Run the slide show. When Slide 4 is displayed, review the information and wait for Slide 1 to be displayed. When Slide 1 is displayed, press the ESC key.
20. Print handouts with two slides per page. Hand in the hard copy to your instructor.

(a) Slide 1

(b) Slide 2

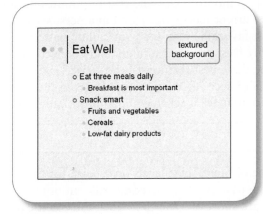

(c) Slide 3

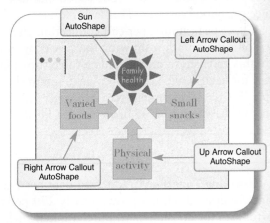

(d) Slide 4

FIGURE 6-68

Cases and Places

The difficulty of these case studies varies:
■ are the least difficult and ■■ are more difficult. The last exercise is a group exercise.

Note: Remember to use the 7 × 7 rule as you design the presentations: a maximum of seven words on a line and a maximum of seven lines on one slide.

1 ■ The Akita Rescue of Western New York, Inc. (ARWNY) is a not-for-profit organization that works to save neglected, abused, abandoned, and/or homeless Akitas and place them in supportive homes. An Akita is revered in its home country of Japan, where it is said to bring health, wealth, and good luck in a home. The dog's average lifespan is 10 to 13 years if raised properly, including eating a diet rich in natural meat, fish, and protein. ARWNY's devoted volunteers rescue, temperament test, rehab, and then rehome the dogs through an adoption process. They also provide educational services regarding proper Akita care, training, and health issues. An online application form is available on the organization's Web site, akitarescuewny.com. In addition, the Web site lists needed supplies, including grooming items, blankets, tarps, and dog food. Using the techniques introduced in this project, create a self-running presentation publicizing ARWNY's efforts. Include information about the breed of dog, the organization, and possible donations. ARWNY's Web site will provide additional information. Enhance the slide show with clips, an animation scheme, and an AutoShape urging people to donate to the organization or start the process to adopt a dog in need. One slide should have hyperlinks to the ARWNY Web site and to other animal anticruelty sites. Include the slide number in the footer of each slide.

2 ■■ Deciding on long distance service for your landline telephone can require much research to find the best plan for your needs. Your economics instructor has assigned a project comparing three long distance telephone services. This task requires you to research monthly fees, the cost of minutes during peak and off-peak hours, per-call connection charges, and current incentives. Develop a persuasive PowerPoint presentation showing the service with the most favorable plan for your calling patterns. Create this slide show, and include a table showing monthly fees, price per minute, and connection charges for each service. Add a Cycle diagram showing the three best features of the service you selected. Set the slide timings to 10 seconds for Slide 1 and 15 seconds for the other slides in the presentation. Set the show type as Browsed at a kiosk. Include an animation scheme and appropriate clips.

3 ■■ **Working Together** Credit card debt has risen to one of the highest levels on record, for the average credit card bill has grown nearly 270 percent in the past 10 years. Credit cards can offer opportunities for consumers to purchase items when they are short on cash. But when the credit card debt exceeds household income, credit cards can become a burden. Have each member of your team visit a bank, savings and loan, or credit union to gather data about the institution's services and savings plans, such as certificates of deposit, Individual Retirement Accounts, and debit cards. After coordinating the data, create a presentation with at least one slide featuring each institution's financial services. Add at least one AutoShape encouraging consumers to charge wisely and to take advantage of financial services offered, such as debt counseling. Enhance the presentation by adding slide transition effects, slide numbers, and an animation scheme.

MICROSOFT
Office PowerPoint 2003

Importing Files from the Microsoft Office Online Web Site

CASE PERSPECTIVE

Students and community residents can learn Microsoft Office skills by attending noncredit workshops at Midland Community College. As an assistant to one of the instructors for the PowerPoint Fundamentals class, you decide to issue certificates for the students who have completed the class.

You want to display these certificates in class as you present each student with a framed copy. You browse the templates in the AutoContent Wizard and do not find any certificates. Knowing that Internet access is built into Microsoft Office PowerPoint 2003, you decide to browse the Microsoft Office Templates Web site for a suitable certificate. In addition, you view the animated clips in the Microsoft Office Clip Art and Media Web site for a new clip of a computer mouse and a typing sound to add to this certificate.

As you read through this Microsoft Online Feature, you will learn to create a presentation and handout using a template from the Microsoft Office Online Web site and add an animated clip and sound clip from this Web site.

Objectives

You will have mastered the material in this Online Feature when you can:

- Connect to the Microsoft Office Templates Web site
- Locate and download a template from the Microsoft Office Templates Web site
- Connect to the Microsoft Office Clip Art and Media Web site
- Search for and copy Microsoft Office Clip Art and Media clips

Introduction

Although the design templates included in Microsoft Office PowerPoint 2003 are varied and versatile, they sometimes do not fit your needs. The Microsoft Clip Organizer likewise has a wide variety of picture images, but at times these images are not exactly to your liking. Microsoft has created Templates and Clip Art and Media Web pages on the Microsoft Office Online Web site, which are sources of additional templates, pictures, sounds, and movie clips on the World Wide Web.

To access the Templates Web page, you click the Templates on Office Online hyperlink in the New Presentation task pane. To access the Microsoft Office Clip Art and Media Web page, you click the Clip art on Office Online hyperlink in the Clip Art task pane. If you have an open connection to the Internet, PowerPoint connects you directly to the Microsoft Office Templates or the Microsoft Office Clip Art and Media Web pages (Figures 1a and 1b on the next page).

In this Microsoft Online Feature, you download the Certification of Completion for Course template and then modify the slide by adding an animated clip of a computer mouse and a sound file from the Microsoft Office Online Web site, as shown in Figure 1c.

(a) Microsoft Office Templates Web site

(b) Microsoft Office Clip Art and Media Web site

(c) Slide 1

FIGURE 1

Importing a Design Template from the Microsoft Office Templates Web Site

Downloading a template from the Microsoft Office Templates Web site, which is part of the Microsoft Office Online Web site, is an easy process. To begin, the following steps show how to start and customize PowerPoint.

To Start and Customize a New Presentation

1 Click the Start button on the Windows taskbar, point to All Programs on the Start menu, point to Microsoft Office on the All Programs submenu, and then click Microsoft Office PowerPoint 2003 on the Microsoft Office submenu.

2 If the PowerPoint window is not maximized, double-click its title bar to maximize it.

3 If the Language bar appears, right-click it and then click Close the Language bar on the shortcut menu.

4 If the Standard and Formatting toolbars are positioned on the same row, click the Toolbar Options button on the right side of either toolbar and then click Show Buttons on Two Rows on the Toolbar Options menu.

A new presentation titled Presentation1 is displayed in the PowerPoint window.

Content experts have developed hundreds of templates for PowerPoint, Word, Excel, and Access. The templates are arranged in a variety of categories, including Calendars and Planners, Holidays and Occasions, Finance and Accounting, and Your Career. These categories are subdivided into organized groupings. For example, the Education category is subdivided into the For Teachers, For Parents, and For Students categories. Several certificates are included in the Awards subcategory within the For Teachers category.

To use the Microsoft Office Templates and Microsoft Office Clip Art and Media Web sites, you must have access to the World Wide Web through an **Internet service provider (ISP)**. To use the Microsoft Office Templates Web site, you must have access to an ISP and then use **Web browser** software to find the Microsoft site. This project uses **Microsoft Internet Explorer** for the Web browser. If you do not have Internet access, your instructor will provide the template used in this part of the project. To simplify connecting to the Templates Web site, the New Presentation task pane contains a Templates on Office Online hyperlink to connect directly to the Templates Web site.

Connecting to the Microsoft Office Templates Web Site

You want to use a template with a certificate of completion. Once you connect to the Web, the Microsoft Office Templates Web site home page is displayed. A **home page** is a specially-designed page that serves as a starting point for a Web site. Microsoft updates this home page frequently to reflect additions and features.

The steps on the next page show how to open the New Presentation task pane; if necessary, connect to the World Wide Web; and then display the Microsoft Office Templates Web site home page.

More About

The Office Online Web Site

When Microsoft programmers created the new Microsoft Office Online Web site, they reviewed customer comments to help make decisions about content and features. Most of the changes you see have come about as the result of feedback from users.

More About

Supported Browsers

The Microsoft Office Online Web site officially supports Internet Explorer version 5.01 and later and Netscape Navigator version 6.0 and later. If you install Netscape Navigator after installing Microsoft Office 2003, some content may not display. To view this content, repair your Office 2003 installation by opening any Office 2003 program, clicking Detect and Repair on the Help menu, and then clicking the Start button. To learn more about browsers, visit the PowerPoint 2003 More About Web page (scsite.com/ppt2003/more) and click Browsers.

To Connect to the Microsoft Office Templates Web Site

1

• **Point to the Create a new presentation hyperlink in the Open area of the Getting Started task pane.**

The Getting Started task pane is displayed (Figure 2). You want to open the New Presentation task pane and then connect to the Microsoft Web site.

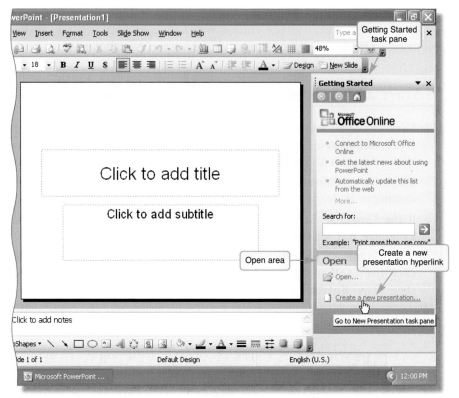

FIGURE 2

2

• **Click the Create a new presentation hyperlink.**

• **When the New Presentation task pane is displayed, point to the Templates on Office Online hyperlink in the Templates area.**

The New Presentation task pane is displayed (Figure 3).

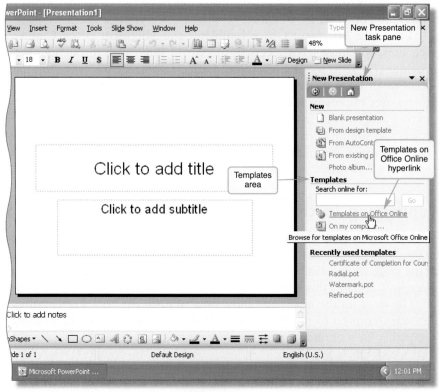

FIGURE 3

3

• Click Templates on Office Online.

• Connect to the World Wide Web as required by your browser software and ISP.

• Click the down arrow to scroll down and then point to the For Teachers hyperlink in the Education category.

If you are using a modem, a dialog box is displayed that connects you to the Web via your ISP. If you are connected directly to the Web through a computer network, the dialog box does not display. Microsoft Internet Explorer displays the Microsoft Office Templates home page, which is part of the Microsoft Office Online Web site. This page contains information about Microsoft Office Online Templates features. The For Teachers hyperlink is underlined and has the font color purple (Figure 4).

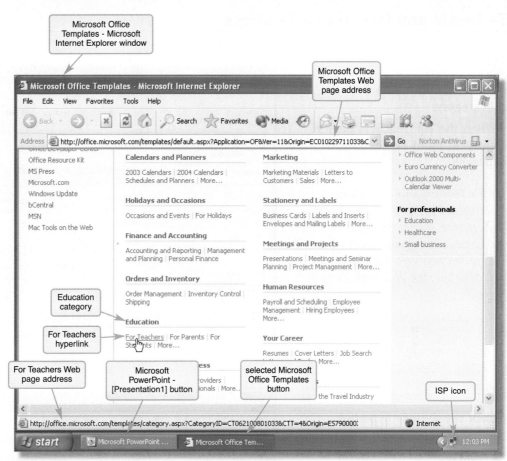

FIGURE 4

Hundreds of templates are available in the Templates category. The Microsoft Office Templates Web site also has links to related templates, Help topics about using Microsoft Office Online, features on the site, and sign-up information to learn about new templates. To find a specific template, you can browse the categories or perform a search by typing a description of the content you want to find. When you locate a desired template, you can preview the template and then download it to your computer. You then can customize and edit the template.

Locating and Downloading a Template

Templates are located by browsing the categories or by using keywords to search for a particular type of file. In this Microsoft Online Feature, you will locate a certificate template by browsing the For Teachers subcategory in the Education category.

When you find a template to add to your presentation, you can **download**, or copy, it instantly by previewing the template and then clicking the Download Now button. The steps on the next page show how to locate and download the Certificate of Completion for Course template.

To Locate and Download a Template

1

• **Click the For Teachers subcategory.**

• **When the For Teachers page is displayed, point to the Awards hyperlink.**

The For Teachers page has several subcategories: Lesson Planning, Classroom Management, Awards, Assessing Students, and Communicating with Parents (Figure 5). The For Teachers Web page you view may differ from the Web page shown in Figure 5.

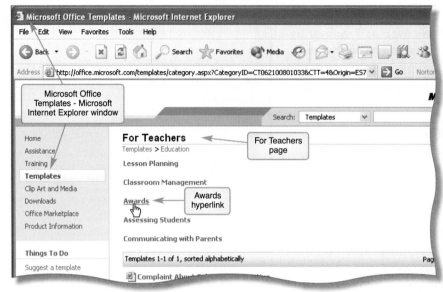

FIGURE 5

2

• **Click the Awards hyperlink.**

• **Point to Certificate of Completion for Course.**

The Certificate of Completion for Course template is required for this project (Figure 6). You may need to scroll through the list of templates to find the desired template. Among the other PowerPoint templates in the Awards subcategory are Certificate for Student of the Month and Certificate of Excellence for Student.

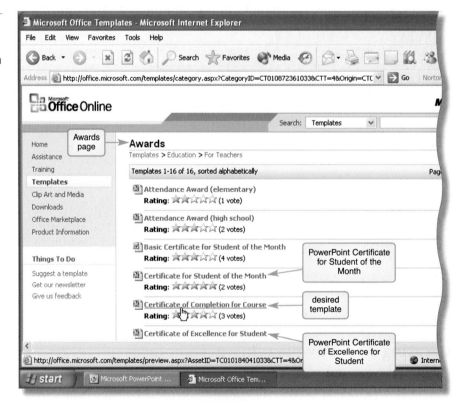

FIGURE 6

3

• **Click Certificate of Completion for Course.**

• **If the Security Warning dialog box is displayed asking you to install and run the Microsoft Office Tools on the Web Control, click the Yes button.**

• **If the Terms of Use Agreement for Templates is displayed, read the agreement and then click the Accept button.**

Once connected to the Web, the Microsoft Office Templates Web page may display the Terms of Use Agreement. When you click the Accept button, the agreement area no longer is displayed. The Certificate of Completion for Course template is displayed in the Web page (Figure 7). The file size is 48 kilobytes, and the download time is less than 1 minute.

FIGURE 7

4

• **Click the Download Now button.**

• **If the Security Warning dialog box is displayed, click the Yes button.**

• **If the Status box message states that `the Microsoft Office Template and Media Control has been installed successfully, click the Continue button.**

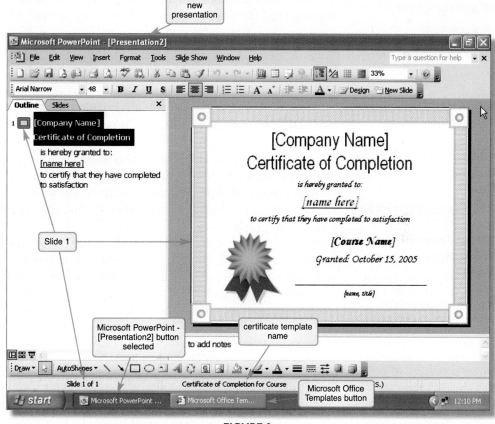

FIGURE 8

• **If the Microsoft Office Online dialog box is displayed asking if you want to download and display links automatically to additional assistance and resources, click the No button.**

• **Click the Close button in the New Presentation task pane.**

The Security Warning dialog box may display based on the security level set on your system. PowerPoint opens a new presentation, downloads the Certificate of Completion for Course template, and displays it in Slide 1 (Figure 8).

Saving the Presentation

You now should save the presentation because you applied a design template. The following steps summarize how to save a presentation.

To Save a Presentation

1 **Click the Save button on the Standard toolbar.**

2 **Type** Completion Certificate **in the File name text box.**

3 **Click the Save in box arrow. Click 3½ Floppy (A:) in the Save in list.**

4 **Click the Save button in the Save As dialog box.**

The presentation is saved on the floppy disk in drive A with the file name, Completion Certificate. This file name is displayed on the title bar.

The Completion Certificate is displayed in Slide 1. The next section describes copying clips from the Microsoft Office Clip Art and Media Web site.

Copying Clips from the Microsoft Office Clip Art and Media Web Site

Depending on the Microsoft Office product version installed on your computer, you access the Microsoft Clip Gallery or the Microsoft Clip Organizer for drawings, photographs, sounds, video, and other media files. Many companies provide clip art images on the Web; some sites offer clips free of charge, and others charge a fee.

For additional clips, Microsoft maintains a Web site called Microsoft Office Clip Art and Media on the Microsoft Office Online site. The site contains clips of pictures, photographs, sounds, and videos. To use the Microsoft Office Clip Art and Media Web site, as with the Microsoft Office Templates Web site, you must have access to an ISP and then use a Web browser. If you do not have Internet access, your instructor will provide the two clips used in this part of the project.

After you find and select a desirable clip, you can insert it into your slides using one of three methods. The first is to copy the clip from the Web site and then paste it into your slide. The second is to drag the clip from the Web site into your slide. These two methods are useful when you want to access and move the clip quickly.

If you will want to reuse the clip in another presentation, you can download it to your computer in the Microsoft Clip Gallery or the Microsoft Clip Organizer. Depending on the Microsoft Office product version installed on your computer, the clips are located in one of these two programs. One of these programs must be installed on your computer for you to obtain clips from the Microsoft Office Online Web site.

The first time you visit the Microsoft Office Online Web site and attempt to copy and paste or drag a clip to your presentation, you will need to take two actions. The first is to install the Microsoft ActiveX control, and the second is to accept the Terms of Use Agreement that will display.

More About

Copying and Pasting Clips

In previous versions of Microsoft PowerPoint, users needed to download clips to their hard drives before being able to use the clips in a presentation. The copy and paste technique used in this Online Feature simplifies finding and inserting clips in your presentation.

More About

The Terms of Use Agreement

When you view the Microsoft Office Online Web site for the first time, you may be asked to read the Terms of Use Agreement or the Addendum to the Microsoft End-User License Agreement. When you click the OK button, you agree to abide by the copyright restrictions Microsoft imposes to protect the use of its software. Read these agreements to see what rights and restrictions are connected with using the templates and clips found at this site. To learn more about copyright agreements, visit the PowerPoint 2003 More About Web page (scsite.com/ppt2003/more) and click Copyrights.

Connecting to the Microsoft Office Clip Art and Media Web Site

To simplify connecting to the Microsoft Office Clip Art and Media Web site, the Clip Art task pane contains a Clip art on Office Online hyperlink. You want to insert an animation clip of a computer mouse and a sound file into Slide 1. Once you connect to the Web, the Microsoft Office Clip Art and Media home page is displayed. Microsoft updates this home page frequently to reflect seasons, holidays, new collections, artists, special offers, and events.

The following steps show how to open the Clip Art task pane, connect to the World Wide Web, and then display the Microsoft Office Clip Art and Media home page.

Q & A

Q: How many clips are on the Microsoft Office Clip Art and Media Web site?

A: Around 130,000 clips are provided. More than 30,000 new images have been added to the Web site since the introduction of Microsoft Office 2003.

To Connect to the Microsoft Office Clip Art and Media Web Site

1

• **Click the Insert Clip Art button on the Drawing toolbar.**

• **Point to the Clip art on Office Online hyperlink in the Clip Art task pane.**

The Clip Art task pane is displayed (Figure 9).

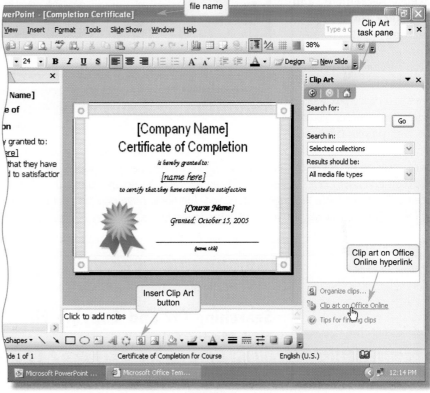

FIGURE 9

2

• **Click Clip art on Office Online.**

• **If necessary, click the OK button in the Connect to Web for More Clip Art, Photos, Sounds dialog box and connect to the Internet.**

• **If necessary, when the Microsoft Office Clip Art and Media Web site is displayed, read the Addendum to the Microsoft End-User License Agreement, and then click the Accept button.**

If you are using a modem and are not connected to the Web already, a dialog box is displayed that connects you to the Web via your ISP. If you are connected directly to the Web through a computer network, the dialog box does not display. Once connected to the Web, the Microsoft Office Online page may display the Addendum to the Microsoft End-User License Agreement. When you click the Accept button, the Microsoft End-User License Agreement area no longer is displayed. The home page displays information about Microsoft Office Clip Art and Media features and boxes to locate specific types of clips (Figure 10).

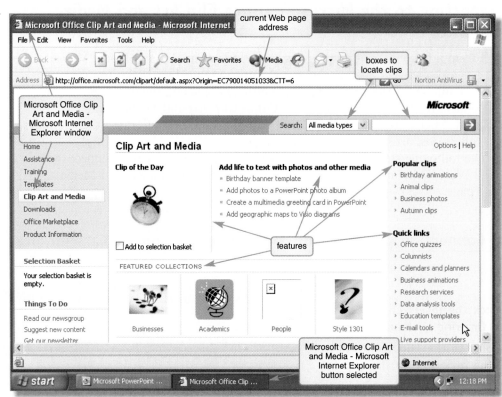

FIGURE 10

Q&A

Q: How many search terms should I use?

A: Fewer than eight. Microsoft recommends using at least two terms and no more than seven to return the most accurate results. If your search yields too many templates, narrow your search by selecting a scope in the Search scope list. For example, to search for only templates, click Templates in the Search scope list.

Searching for and Copying Microsoft Office Clip Art and Media Clips

The Microsoft Office Clip Art and Media Web site is similar to the Microsoft Office Templates Web site and the Microsoft Clip Organizer in that you can use keywords to search for clips. You want to locate an animation clip of a computer mouse and a sound clip containing a typing sound. You first will search the Microsoft Office Clip Art and Media Web site for animation files with the keyword, computer. Then, you will search for sound files with the same keyword.

When you find a clip to add to your presentation, you can copy it from the site and then paste it in your presentation. You also can download clips to the My Pictures folder in the Downloaded Clips category if you want to reuse these files in other presentations.

The following steps describe how to search for clips in the Clip Art and Media Web site.

To Search for and Copy Clip Art and Media Web Site Clips

1

• **Click the Search box arrow in the Clip Art and Media Web site.**

• **Point to Animations in the list.**

The default category is All media types. Microsoft groups all the clips in four categories: Clip art, Photos, Animations, and Sounds. You also can search for clips found only on the Office Online Web site (Figure 11).

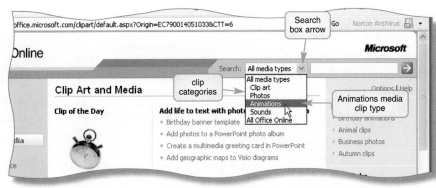

FIGURE 11

2

• **Click Animations.**

• **Click the Search text box and then type** computer mouse **in the box (Figure 12).**

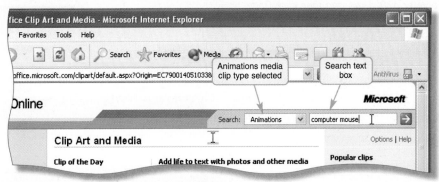

FIGURE 12

3

• **Click the Click to search button.**

• **When the search results display, click the Dropdown arrow on the thumbnail of the computer mouse eating a piece of cheese.**

• **Point to the Copy command on the shortcut menu.**

Microsoft Office Clip Art and Media executes the search and displays the results (Figure 13). If you want to select multiple clips and save them for later use, you would click the Add to Selection Basket command and then download the clips. If you click the Properties command, you would see the file name, dimensions, size, and keywords.

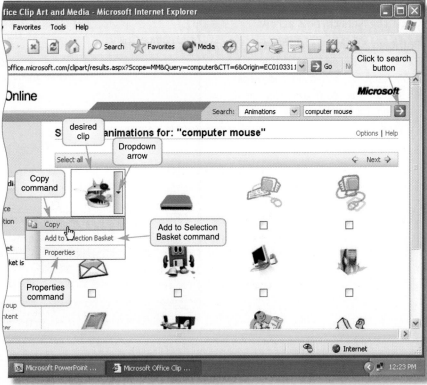

FIGURE 13

4

- **Click Copy.**

- **Click the Microsoft PowerPoint - [Completion Certificate] button on the taskbar.**

- **Right-click the Certificate of Completion and then click the Paste command.**

The computer mouse clip is copied into the slide (Figure 14). When you right-click a clip and then click Copy, the actual animation clip is placed on the Office Clipboard. You also could click the Dropdown arrow that is displayed when you place your mouse pointer over a clip and then click Copy, or you could click Properties and then click Copy.

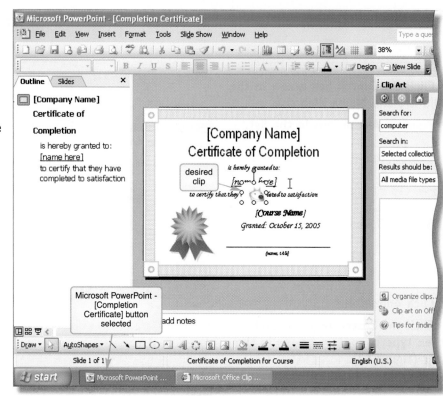

FIGURE 14

5

- **Click the Microsoft Office Clip Art and Media - Microsoft Internet Explorer button on the taskbar.**

- **Click the Search box arrow.**

- **Point to Sounds in the list.**

The Microsoft Office Clip Art and Media Web site is displayed (Figure 15). The results from the computer search still are displayed.

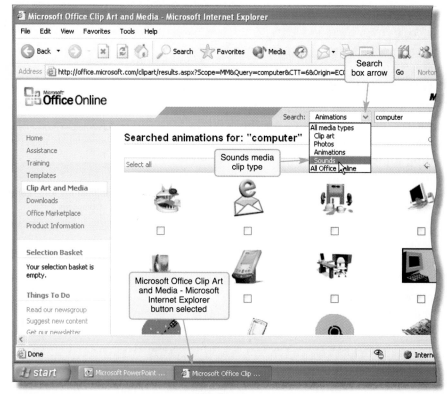

FIGURE 15

6

• **Click Sounds.**

• **Click the Click to search button.**

Microsoft Office Clip Art and Media executes the search. After a few moments, several speaker icons with the keyword, computer, display (Figure 16). The speaker icons identify the sound clips.

7

• **Click the Dropdown arrow of the clip with the file name, Computer Typing1.**

• **Click the Copy command on the shortcut menu.**

When you click the Copy command, a copy of the sound clip is stored on the Office Clipboard.

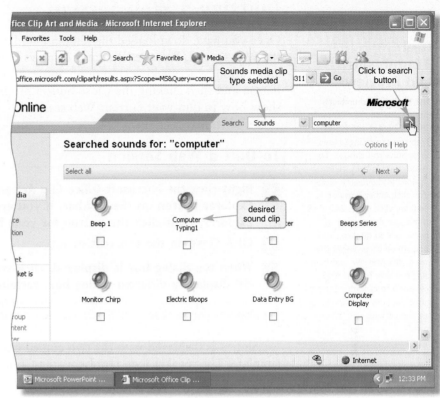

FIGURE 16

8

• **Click the Microsoft PowerPoint - [Completion Certificate] button on the taskbar.**

• **Right-click the certificate.**

• **Click Paste on the shortcut menu.**

• **When the Microsoft Office PowerPoint dialog box is displayed, click the Automatically button.**

• **If the Picture toolbar is displayed, click its Close button.**

• **Click the Close button on the Clip Art task pane title bar.**

The speaker icon, which represents the Computer Typing1 sound file, is displayed on top of the animated computer mouse (Figure 17). You want the sound to play automatically when Slide 1 is displayed. The Microsoft Office Clip Art and Media Design Web site still is open, and you still are connected to the ISP.

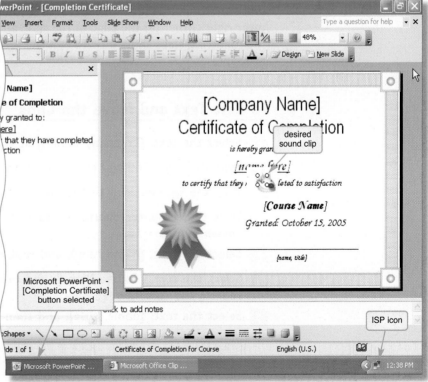

FIGURE 17

Quitting a Web Session

Once you have downloaded the template and copied the clips, you can quit the Web session. Because Windows displays buttons on the taskbar for each open application, you quickly can quit an application by right-clicking an application button and then clicking the Close button on the shortcut menu. The following steps show how to quit your current Web session.

To Quit a Web Session

1 Right-click the Microsoft Office Clip Art and Media - Microsoft Internet Explorer button on the taskbar. If you are not using Microsoft Internet Explorer, right-click the button for your browser.

2 Click Close on the shortcut menu.

3 When the dialog box is displayed, click the Yes button to disconnect. If your ISP displays a different dialog box, terminate your connection to your ISP.

The browser software closes, and the ISP connection is terminated.

Slide 1 is displayed with the two copied clips in the center of the certificate template. The speaker icon represents the Computer Typing1 sound file.

Editing Text and Moving the Clips

You want to edit the default certificate text and then move the speaker icon to the lower-right corner off the edge of the slide and the mouse to the upper-left corner. The following steps show how to edit the text and move the clips to these respective locations.

To Edit Text and Move the Clips

1 Select the text, [Company Name], at the top of the certificate.

2 Type Midland Community College to replace the current text.

3 Drag the speaker icon to the lower-right corner off the edge of Slide 1.

4 Scale the computer mouse clip to 110 % and then move it to the location shown in Figure 18.

5 Select the text, [name here], and replace the text with your name.

6 Select the text, [Course Name], and type PowerPoint Fundamentals to replace the current text.

7 Select the text, [name, title], and then click the Cut button.

The revised text and copied clips display in the appropriate locations in the Slide 1 certificate (Figure 18).

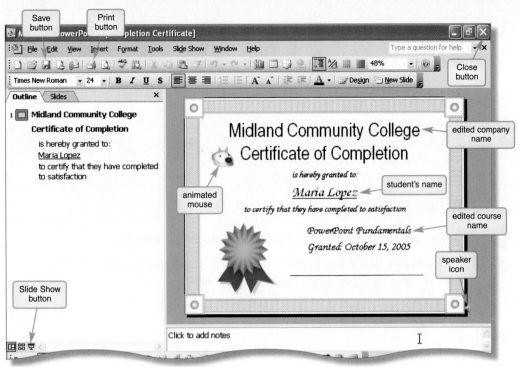

FIGURE 18

Running and Printing the Presentation

The changes to the presentation are complete. Save the presentation again before running the slide show.

Running a Slide Show

To verify the certificate looks as expected, run the presentation. The following steps illustrate how to run the Completion Certificate slide show.

To Run a Slide Show

1 Click the Slide Show button in the lower-left corner of the PowerPoint window.

2 When Slide 1 is displayed, view the information and then click the slide anywhere except on the Pop-up menu buttons.

3 Click the black slide.

The presentation displays the animated computer mouse, plays the sound file, and then returns to normal view when finished.

The presentation is complete. If the certificate elements do not display in the desired locations, you can move them on the slide. The next step is to print the presentation slide.

Printing a Presentation Slide

The step on the next page shows how to print the certificate.

More About

Using Copied Clips

The clips you copy while working on your PowerPoint presentation can be used in other Microsoft Office applications. For example, the mouse you import in this Online Feature can be part of a flyer created in Microsoft Word, and the typing sound can play while users view a Microsoft Excel chart. The clips also can be used and reused in Microsoft Publisher, Microsoft FrontPage, and Microsoft Works.

To Print a Presentation Slide

1 **Click the Print button on the Standard toolbar.**

Slide 1 prints.

Quitting PowerPoint

The following steps show how to quit PowerPoint.

To Quit PowerPoint

1 **Click the Close button on the Microsoft PowerPoint title bar.**

2 **If the Microsoft Office PowerPoint dialog box is displayed, click the Yes button to save changes made since the last save.**

PowerPoint closes.

Microsoft Online Feature Summary

This Microsoft Online Feature introduced importing design templates and sound and animation clips from the Microsoft Office Templates and the Microsoft Office Clip Art and Media Web sites on the World Wide Web. You began by opening a new presentation and then accessing the Microsoft Office Templates home page by clicking the Templates on Office Online hyperlink in the New Presentation task pane. You then downloaded the Certificate of Completion for Course design template. The next step was to access the Microsoft Office Clip Art and Media home page on the Microsoft Office Online Web site by clicking the Clip art on Office Online hyperlink in the Clip Art task pane. Once connected to the Microsoft Office Clip Art and Media home page, you searched for an animated mouse and a typing sound. Then, you copied these clips to the certificate template. You moved the clips to appropriate locations on Slide 1, edited the certificate text, and quit the Web session by closing the browser software and disconnecting from the ISP. Finally, you saved the presentation, ran the presentation in slide show view to check for continuity, printed the presentation slide, and quit PowerPoint.

 If you have a SAM user profile, you may have access to hands-on instruction, practice, and assessment of the skills covered in this feature. Log in to your SAM account and go to your assignments page to see what your instructor has assigned.

What You Should Know

Having completed this feature, you should be able to perform the tasks below. The tasks are listed in the same order they were presented in this feature. For a list of the buttons, menus, toolbars, and commands introduced in this feature, see the Quick Reference Summary at the back of this book and refer to the Page Number column.

1. Start and Customize a New Presentation (PPT 473)
2. Connect to the Microsoft Office Templates Web Site   (PPT 474)
3. Locate and Download a Template   (PPT 476)
4. Save a Presentation   (PPT 478)
5. Connect to the Microsoft Office Clip Art and Media Web Site   (PPT 479)
6. Search for and Copy Clip Art and Media Web Site Clips   (PPT 481)
7. Quit a Web Session   (PPT 484)
8. Edit Text and Move the Clips   (PPT 484)
9. Run a Slide Show   (PPT 485)
10. Print a Presentation Slide   (PPT 486)
11. Quit PowerPoint   (PPT 486)

In the Lab

1 Enhancing the Fruit and Nutrition Slide Show

Problem: The news is filled with stories about proper nutrition. Many stories report updates of the latest discoveries in healthy eating. Nancy Nataro, the nutritionist at your campus fitness center, is pleased with the Fruit and Vegetable Nutrition presentation you created in Project 3. She has asked you to enhance the presentation by adding information about the food pyramid. In addition, she believes the sound of a person eating and an animated clip from the Microsoft Office Clip Art and Media Web site would make the presentation even more impressive. You decide to use the Microsoft Office Online Web site to find information about the food pyramid and appropriate clips to modify Slides 2 and 3 of the Fruit and Vegetable Nutrition presentation.

Instructions: Perform the following tasks:

1. Open the Lab 3-2 Five a Day presentation shown in Figure 3-84 on page PPT 199 that you created in Project 3. (If you did not complete In the Lab Exercise 2, see your instructor for a copy of the presentation.)
2. Save the Fruit and Vegetable Nutrition presentation with the new file name, Lab OF-1 Five a Day.
3. Display Slide 2, click View on the menu bar, click Task Pane, and then click the Templates on Office Online hyperlink in the New Presentation task pane. If necessary, connect to the Internet. When the Microsoft Office Templates Web site is displayed, download the Food Pyramid Presentation from the Healthcare and Wellness category. Delete Slides 2, 11, and 12. Save the presentation with the file name, Food Pyramid.
4. Click the Microsoft PowerPoint - [Lab OF-1 Five a Day] button on the taskbar. Add an action button to the lower-right corner of Slide 2 and hyperlink it to the Food Pyramid file. Add the caption, Understanding the Food Pyramid. Center the caption and then format the caption font to Book Antiqua, the font size to 20 point, and the font color to red. Apply Shadow Style 3 to the action button with a 1-pt line.
5. Display Slide 3. Click the Insert Clip Art button on the Drawing toolbar, and then click the Clip art on Office Online hyperlink in the Clip Art task pane.
6. Search for animation clips with the keyword, fruit. Select a clip with a cornucopia. Copy it to Slide 3. Then search for sound clips with the keyword, eating. Select the Crunch and Eat clip, copy it to Slide 3, and have the sound play automatically.
7. Click the Microsoft PowerPoint - [Lab OF-1 Five a Day] button on the taskbar. Size the cornucopia to 300 %. Move the speaker icon to the lower-right corner of Slide 3, and move the cornucopia clip to the left of the Fruit Servings title.
8. Disconnect from the Web and save the file again.
9. Run the slide show and then print Slides 2 and 3. Print all the Food Pyramid slides as a handout. Quit PowerPoint.

2 Enhancing the U Travel 2 Travel Agency's European Tour Slide Show

Problem: Response to the European Adventures slide show you created in In the Lab Exercise 3 in Project 4 has been outstanding. Annie Airway, the manager of the U Travel 2 Travel Agency, has presented your slides at many community events. Annie says that many of the audience members have asked questions about flying overseas, so she asks you to add a travel checklist to the presentation that she can access by clicking an action button. She also wants you to add more clips. You decide to search the Microsoft Office Templates Web site for a checklist and the Microsoft Office Clip Art and Media Web site for the clips.

(continued)

Enhancing the U Travel 2 Travel Agency's European Tour Slide Show *(continued)*

Instructions: Perform the following tasks:

1. Open the Lab 4-3 Europe presentation shown in Figure 4-93 on pages PPT 282–283 that you created in Project 4. (If you did not complete In the Lab Exercise 3, see your instructor for a copy of the presentation.)
2. Save the European Adventures presentation with the new file name, Lab OF-2 Europe.
3. Click the Insert Clip Art button on the Drawing toolbar and then click Clip art on Office Online in the Clip Art task pane. Search for a photo clip with the keyword, airplane, and then copy this clip to Slide 1. Search for and select an animation clip of a camera, and copy this photo to Slide 2. Search for a sound clip of water, and then copy this clip to Slide 4 and have the sound play automatically.
4. Search the Microsoft Office Templates Web site for the Travel Checklist for Plane Trip template, which is located in the Travel Itineraries and Planners subcategory of the For Travelers subcategory of the Travel and Maps category. Download this document and then save the checklist with the file name, Travel Checklist.
5. Display Slide 1 and then scale the airplane photo to an appropriate size. Move the photo to the upper-left corner of the slide. Display Slide 2, scale the camera clip to an appropriate size, and then move the camera to the right of the slide title, Tour Highlights. Move the speaker icon to the lower-left corner of Slide 4.
6. Display Slide 3. Add an action button to the lower-left corner and hyperlink it to the Travel Checklist file. Add the caption, Travel Checklist, below the action button. Format the caption font to Times New Roman, the font size to 20 point, and the font color to blue. Bold and left-align the text. Apply Shadow Style 2 to the action button.
7. Disconnect from the Web and save the file again.
8. Run the slide show and then print Slides 1, 2, and 3 as a handout. Print the Travel Checklist. Quit PowerPoint.

3 Marketing Company Information

Problem: Your marketing instructor has assigned a project profiling the company where you currently work or desire to work after graduation. You decide to prepare a slide show to enhance your speech and search the Microsoft Office Templates Web site for an appropriate template. You download the Company Background Presentation. You add clips from the Microsoft Office Clip Art and Media Web site and then edit the text.

Instructions: Perform the following tasks:

1. Start a new presentation. Connect to the Microsoft Office Templates Web site and then locate and download the Company Background Presentation template, which is located in the Marketing Plans and Presentations subcategory of the Marketing category.
2. Search the Microsoft Office Clip Art and Media Web site for appropriate animation, picture, and sound clips. Add these clips to the slides.
3. Edit the slides to reflect the information from your actual or desired employer.
4. Save the presentation with the file name, Lab OF-3 Company Background.
5. Run the slide show and then print the slides. Quit PowerPoint.

Appendix A

Microsoft Office PowerPoint Help System

Using the PowerPoint Help System

This appendix shows you how to use the PowerPoint Help system. At any time while you are using PowerPoint, you can interact with its Help system and display information on any PowerPoint topic. It is a complete reference manual at your fingertips.

As shown in Figure A-1, five methods for accessing the PowerPoint Help system are available:

1. Microsoft Office PowerPoint Help button on the Standard toolbar
2. Microsoft Office PowerPoint Help command on the Help menu
3. Function key F1 on the keyboard
4. Type a question for help box on the menu bar
5. Office Assistant

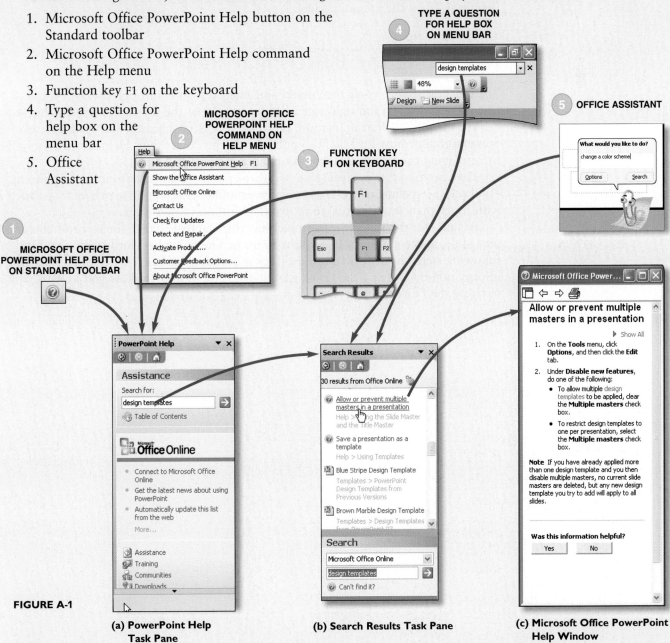

FIGURE A-1

(a) PowerPoint Help Task Pane

(b) Search Results Task Pane

(c) Microsoft Office PowerPoint Help Window

All five methods result in the PowerPoint Help system displaying a task pane on the right side of the PowerPoint window. The first three methods cause the **PowerPoint Help task** pane to appear (Figure A-1a on the previous page). This task pane includes a Search text box in which you can enter a word or phrase on which you want help. Once you enter the word or phrase, the PowerPoint Help system displays the Search Results task pane (Figure A-1b on the previous page). With the Search Results task pane displayed, you can select specific Help topics.

As shown in Figure A-1, methods 4 and 5 bypass the PowerPoint Help task pane and immediately display the **Search Results task pane** (Figure A-1b) with a list of links that pertain to the selected topic. Thus, the result of any of the five methods for accessing the PowerPoint Help system is the Search Results task pane. Once the PowerPoint Help system displays this task pane, you can choose links that relate to the word or phrase on which you searched. In Figure A-1, for example, design templates was the searched topic (Allow or prevent multiple masters in a presentation), which resulted in the PowerPoint Help system displaying the Microsoft Office PowerPoint Help window with information about design templates (Figure A-1c on the previous page).

Navigating the PowerPoint Help System

The quickest way to enter the PowerPoint Help system is through the Type a question for help box on the right side of the menu bar at the top of the screen. Here you can type words, such as animation, table, or bullets, or phrases, such as preview a presentation, or how do I do Web publishing. The PowerPoint Help system responds by displaying the Search Results task pane with a list of links.

Here are two tips regarding the words or phrases you enter to initiate a search: (1) check the spelling of the word or phrase; and (2) keep your search very specific, with fewer than seven words, to return the most accurate results.

Assume for the following example that you want to change the color of clip art on a slide, and you do not know how to do it. The likely keyword is clip art. The following steps show how to use the Type a question for help box to obtain useful information by entering the keyword, clip art. The steps also show you how to navigate the PowerPoint Help system.

To Obtain Help Using the Type a Question for Help Box

1

• **Click the Type a question for help box on the right side of the menu bar, type** `clip art` **and then press the ENTER key.**

The PowerPoint Help system displays the Search Results task pane on the right side of the window. The Search Results task pane includes 28 resulting links (Figure A-2). If you do not find what you are looking for, you can modify or refine the search in the Search area at the bottom of the Search Results task pane. The results returned in your Search Results task pane may be different.

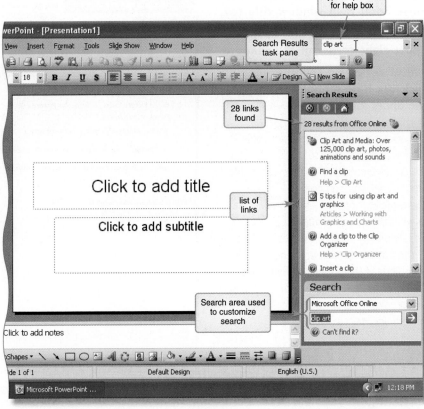

FIGURE A-2

2

• **Scroll down the list of links in the Search Results task pane and then click the Recolor a picture from the Clip Organizer link.**

• **If necessary, when the PowerPoint Help system displays the Microsoft Office PowerPoint Help window, click its Auto Tile button in the upper-left corner of the window to tile the windows.**

The PowerPoint Help system displays the Microsoft Office PowerPoint Help window with the desired information about recoloring a picture (Figure A-3). With the Microsoft Office PowerPoint Help window and Microsoft PowerPoint window tiled, you can read the information in one window and complete the task in the other window.

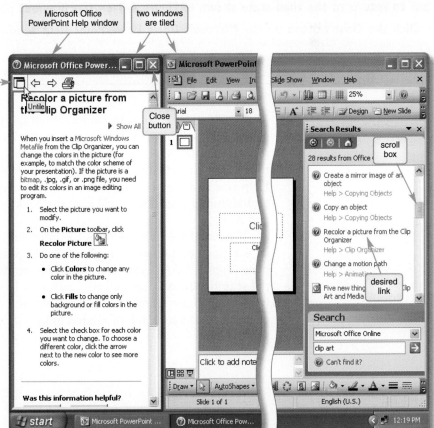

FIGURE A-3

3

• **Double-click the Microsoft Office PowerPoint Help window title bar.**

• **Click the Show All link in the upper-right corner of the window.**

• **After reviewing the information, click the Hide All link that replaced the Show All link.**

The Microsoft Office PowerPoint Help window is maximized so it fills the entire screen (Figure A-4). If you are connected to the Internet, you can give Microsoft your opinion as to whether the information was helpful by clicking the Yes or No button at the bottom of the page. The Show All link expands the coverage of information and the Hide all link condenses the information displayed on the topic in the PowerPoint Help window.

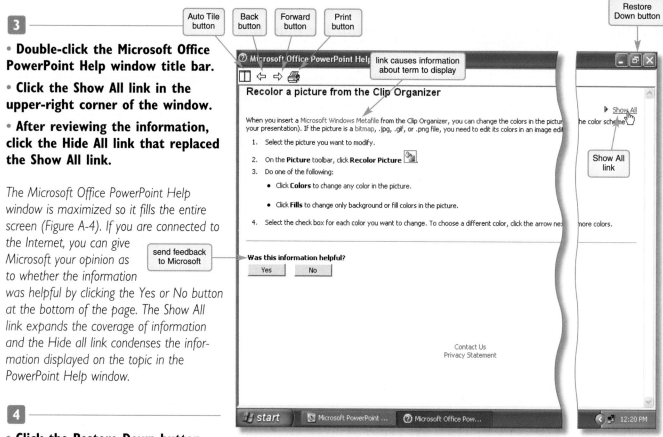

FIGURE A-4

4

• **Click the Restore Down button on the right side of the Microsoft Office PowerPoint Help window title bar to return to the tiled state shown in Figure A-3 on the previous page.**

• **Click the Close button on the Microsoft Office PowerPoint Help window title bar.**

The Microsoft Office PowerPoint Help window closes and the worksheet is active.

Use the four buttons in the upper-left corner of the Microsoft Office PowerPoint Help window (Figure A-4) to tile or untile, navigate through the Help system, or print the contents of the window. As you click links in the Search Results task pane, the PowerPoint Help system displays new pages of information. The PowerPoint Help system remembers the links you visited and allows you to redisplay the pages visited during a session by clicking the Back and Forward buttons (Figures A-3 and A-4).

If none of the links presents the information you want, you can refine the search by entering another word or phrase in the Search text box in the Search Results task pane (Figure A-5). If you have access to the Web, then the scope is global for the initial search. **Global** means all the categories listed in the Search box of the Search area in Figure A-5 are searched. For example, you can restrict the scope to **Offline Help**, which results in a search of related links only on your hard disk.

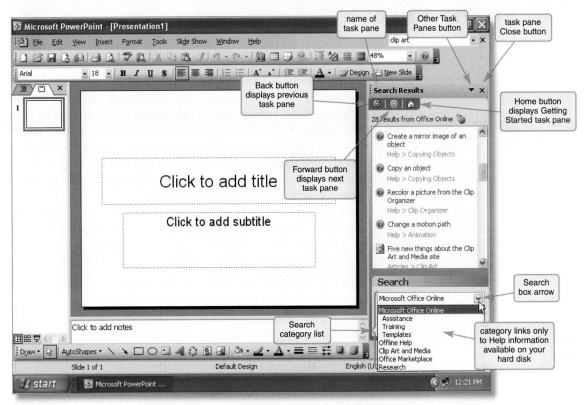

FIGURE A-5

Figure A-5 shows several additional features of the Search Results task pane with which you should be familiar. The buttons immediately below the name of the task pane allow you to navigate between task panes. The Other Task Panes button and the Close button on the Search Results task pane title bar let you change task panes and close the active task pane.

As you enter questions and terms in the Type a question for help box, the PowerPoint Help system adds them to its list. Thus, if you click the Type a question for help box arrow, a list of previously used words and phrases are displayed (Figure A-6).

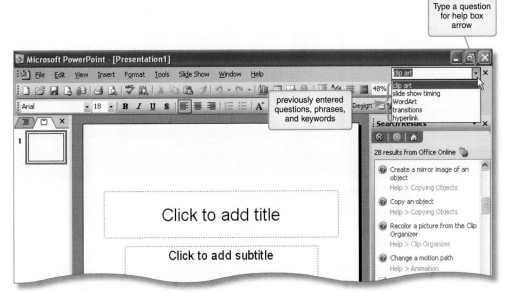

FIGURE A-6

The Office Assistant

The **Office Assistant** is an icon (middle of Figure A-7) that PowerPoint displays in the PowerPoint window while you work. For the Office Assistant to display, it must be activated by invoking the Show the Office Assistant command on the Help menu. This Help tool has multiple functions. First, it will respond in the same way as the Type a question for help box with a list of topics that relate to the entry you make in the text box at the bottom of the Office Assistant balloon. The entry can be in the form of a word or phrase as if you were talking to a person. For example, if you want to learn more about modifying a color scheme, in the balloon text box, you can type any of the following words or phrases: color scheme, change a color scheme, how do I change the color scheme, or anything similar.

In the example in Figure A-7, the phrase, change a color scheme, is entered into the Office Assistant balloon. The Office Assistant responds by displaying the Search Results task pane with a list of links from which you can choose. Once you click a link in the Search Results task pane, the PowerPoint Help system displays the information in the Microsoft Office PowerPoint Help window (Figure A-7).

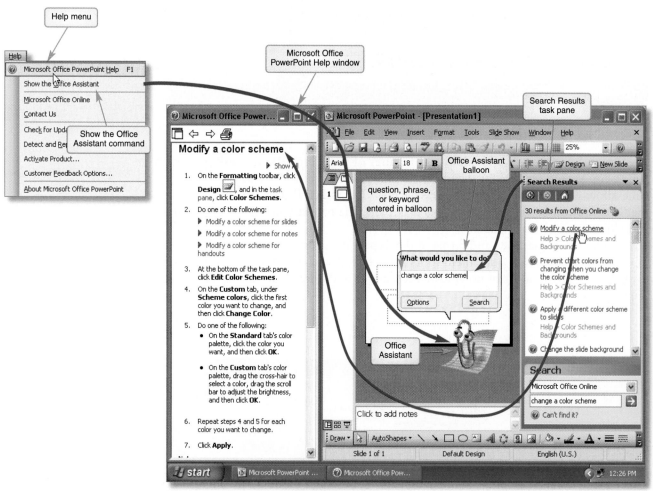

FIGURE A-7

Second, the Office Assistant monitors your work and accumulates tips during a session on how you might increase your productivity and efficiency. The accumulation of tips must be enabled. You enable the accumulation of tips by right-clicking the Office Assistant, clicking Options on the shortcut menu, and then selecting the types of tips you want accumulated. You can view the tips anytime. The accumulated tips appear when you activate the Office Assistant balloon. Also, if at any time you see a light bulb above the Office Assistant, click it to display the most recent tip. If the Office Assistant is hidden, then the light bulb shows on the Microsoft Office PowerPoint Help button on the Standard toolbar.

You hide the Office Assistant by invoking the Hide the Office Assistant command on the Help menu or by right-clicking the Office Assistant and then clicking Hide on the shortcut menu. The Hide the Office Assistant command shows on the Help menu only when the Office Assistant is active in the PowerPoint window. If the Office Assistant begins showing up on your screen without you instructing it to show, then right-click the Office Assistant, click Options on the shortcut menu, click the Use the Office Assistant check box to remove the check mark, and then click the OK button.

Third, if the Office Assistant is active in the PowerPoint window, then PowerPoint displays all program and system messages in the Office Assistant balloon.

You may or may not want the Office Assistant to display on the screen at all times. As indicated earlier, you can hide it and then show it later through the Help menu. For more information about the Office Assistant, type `office assistant` in the Type a question for help box and then click the links in the Search Results task pane.

Help Buttons in Dialog Boxes and Subsystem Windows

As you invoke commands that display dialog boxes or other windows, such as the Print Preview window, you will see buttons and links that offer helpful information. Figure A-8 shows two types of Help buttons you will see as you work with PowerPoint.

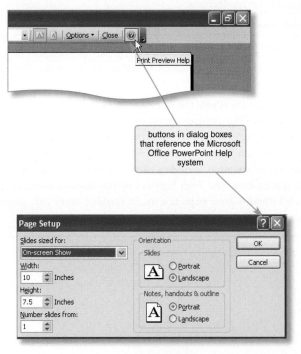

FIGURE A-8

Other Help Commands on the Help Menu

Thus far, this appendix has discussed the first two commands on the Help menu: (1) the Microsoft Office PowerPoint Help command (Figure A-1 on page APP 1) and (2) the Show the Office Assistant command (Figure A-7 on page APP 6). Several additional commands are available on the Help menu, as shown in Figure A-9. Table A-1 summarizes these commands.

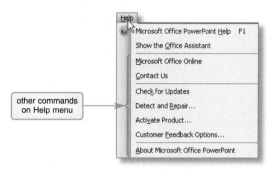

other commands
on Help menu

FIGURE A-9

Table A-1 Summary of Other Help Commands on the Help Menu	
COMMAND ON HELP MENU	**FUNCTION**
Microsoft Office Online	Activates your browser, which displays the Microsoft Office Online Home page. The Microsoft Office Online Home page contains links that can improve your Office productivity.
Contact Us	Activates your browser, which displays Microsoft contact information and a list of useful links.
Check for Updates	Activates your browser, which displays a list of updates to Office 2003. These updates can be downloaded and installed to improve the efficiency of Office or to fix an error in one or more of the Office applications.
Detect and Repair	Detects and repairs errors in the PowerPoint program.
Activate Product	Activates PowerPoint if it has not been activated already.
Customer Feedback Options	Gives or denies Microsoft permission to collect anonymous information about your hardware.
About Microsoft Office PowerPoint	Displays the About Microsoft Office PowerPoint dialog box. The dialog box lists the owner of the software and the product identification. You need to know the product identification if you call Microsoft for assistance. The three buttons below the OK button are the System Info button, the Tech Support button, and the Disabled Items button. The System Info button displays system information, including hardware resources, components, software environment, and applications. The Tech Support button displays technical assistance information. The Disabled Items button displays a list of disabled items that prevent PowerPoint from functioning properly.

1 Using the Type a Question for Help Box

Instructions: Perform the following tasks using the PowerPoint Help system.

1. Use the Type a question for help box on the menu bar to get help on custom shows.
2. Click About custom shows in the list of links in the Search Results task pane. Tile the windows. Double-click the Microsoft Office PowerPoint Help window title bar to maximize it. Click the Show All button. Read and print the information. At the top of the printout, write down the number of links the PowerPoint Help system found.
3. One at a time, click two additional links in the Search Results task pane and print the information. Hand in the printouts to your instructor. Use the Back and Forward buttons to return to the original page.
4. Use the Type a question for help box to search for information on design templates. Click the Apply a design template link in the Search Results task pane. When the Microsoft Office PowerPoint Help window is displayed, maximize the window. Read and print the information. One at a time, click the links on the page and print the information for any new page that displays. Close the Microsoft Office PowerPoint Help window.
5. For each of the following words and phrases, click one link in the Search Results task pane, click the Show All link, and then print the page: rotating objects; navigating; action button; creating tables; aligning text.

2 Expanding on the PowerPoint Help System Basics

Instructions: Use the PowerPoint Help system to understand the topics better and answer the questions listed below. Answer the questions on your own paper, or hand in the printed Help information to your instructor.

1. Show the Office Assistant. Right-click the Office Assistant and then click Animate! on the shortcut menu. Repeat invoking the Animate command to see various animations. Right-click the Office Assistant, click Options on the shortcut menu, click the Reset my tips button, and then click the OK button. Click the light bulb above the Office Assistant. When you see the light bulb, it indicates that the Office Assistant has a tip to share with you.
2. Use the Office Assistant to find help on undoing tasks. Print the help information for three links in the Search Results task pane. Close the Microsoft Office PowerPoint Help window. Hand in the printouts to your instructor. Hide the Office Assistant.
3. Press the F1 key. Search for information on Help. Click the first two links in the Search Results task pane. Read and print the information for both.
4. One at a time, invoke the first three commands in Table A-1. Print each page. Click two links on one of the pages and print the information. Hand in the printouts to your instructor.
5. Click About Microsoft Office PowerPoint on the Help menu. Click the Tech Support button and print the resulting page. Click the System Info button. Below the Components category, print the CD-ROM and Display information. Hand in the printouts to your instructor.

Appendix B

Speech and Handwriting Recognition

Introduction

This appendix discusses the Office capability that allows users to create and modify slide shows using its alternative input technologies available through **text services**. Office provides a variety of text services, which enable you to speak commands and enter text in an application. The most common text service is the keyboard. Other text services include speech recognition and handwriting recognition.

The Language Bar

The **Language bar** allows you to use text services in the Office applications. You can utilize the Language bar in one of three states: (1) in a restored state as a floating toolbar in the Word window (Figure B-1a or Figure B-1b if Text Labels are enabled); (2) in a minimized state docked next to the notification area on the Windows taskbar (Figure B-1c); or (3) hidden (temporarily closed and out of the way). If the Language bar is hidden, you can activate it by right-clicking the Windows taskbar, pointing to Toolbars on the shortcut menu (Figure B-1d), and then clicking Language bar on the Toolbars submenu. If you want to close the Language bar, right-click the Language bar and then click Close the Language bar on the shortcut menu (Figure B-1e).

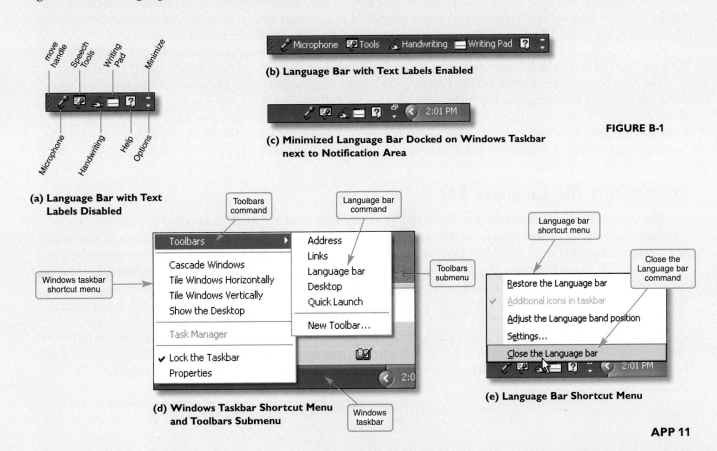

(b) **Language Bar with Text Labels Enabled**

(c) **Minimized Language Bar Docked on Windows Taskbar next to Notification Area**

FIGURE B-1

(a) **Language Bar with Text Labels Disabled**

(d) **Windows Taskbar Shortcut Menu and Toolbars Submenu**

(e) **Language Bar Shortcut Menu**

When Windows was installed on your computer, the installer specified a default language. For example, most users in the United States select English (United States) as the default language. You can add more than 90 additional languages and varying dialects such as Basque, English (Zimbabwe), French (France), French (Canada), German (Germany), German (Austria), and Swahili. With multiple languages available, you can switch from one language to another while working in PowerPoint. If you change the language or dialect, then text services may change the functions of the keys on the keyboard, adjust speech recognition, and alter handwriting recognition. If a second language is activated, then a Language icon appears immediately to the right of the move handle on the Language bar and the language name is displayed on the Word status bar. This appendix assumes that English (United States) is the only language installed. Thus, the Language icon does not appear in the examples in Figure B-1 on the previous page.

Buttons on the Language Bar

The Language bar shown in Figure B-2a contains seven buttons. The number of buttons on your Language bar may be different. These buttons are used to select the language, customize the Language bar, control the microphone, control handwriting, and obtain help.

The first button on the left is the Microphone button, which enables and disables the microphone. When the microphone is enabled, text services adds two buttons and a balloon to the Language bar (Figure B-2b). These additional buttons and the balloon will be discussed shortly.

The second button from the left is the Speech Tools button. The Speech Tools button displays a menu of commands (Figure B-2c) that allow you to scan the current document looking for words to add to the speech recognition dictionary; hide or show the balloon on the Language bar; train the Speech Recognition service so that it can interpret your voice better; add and delete specific words to and from its dictionary, such as names and other words not understood easily; and change the user profile so more than one person can use the microphone on the same computer.

The third button from the left on the Language bar is the Handwriting button. The Handwriting button displays the Handwriting menu (Figure B-2d), which lets you choose the Writing Pad (Figure B-2e), Write Anywhere (Figure B-2f), or the on-screen keyboard (Figure B-2g). The On-Screen Symbol Keyboard command on the Handwriting menu displays an on-screen keyboard that allows you to enter special symbols that are not available on a standard keyboard. You can choose only one form of handwriting at a time.

The fourth button indicates which one of the handwriting forms is active. For example, in Figure B-2a, the Writing Pad is active. The handwriting recognition capabilities of text services will be discussed shortly.

The fifth button from the left on the Language bar is the Help button. The Help button displays the Help menu. If you click the Language Bar Help command on the Help menu, the Language Bar Help window appears (Figure B-2h). On the far right of the Language bar are two buttons stacked above and below each other. The top button is the Minimize button and the bottom button is the Options button. The Minimize button minimizes the Language bar so that it appears on the Windows taskbar. The next section discusses the Options button.

Customizing the Language Bar

The down arrow icon immediately below the Minimize button in Figure B-2a is called the Options button. The Options button displays a menu of text services options (Figure B-2i). You can use this menu to hide the Speech Tools, Handwriting, and Help buttons on the Language bar by clicking their names to remove the check mark to the left of each button. You also can show the Correction, Speak Text, and Pause Speaking buttons on the Language bar by clicking their names to place a check mark to the left of the respective command. When you select text and then click the Correction button, a list of correction alternatives is displayed in the Word window. You can use the Corrections button to correct both speech recognition and handwriting recognition errors. The Speak Text and Pause Speaking buttons are discussed at the end of this Appendix. The Settings command on the Options menu displays a dialog box that lets you customize the Language bar. This command will be discussed shortly. The Restore Defaults command redisplays hidden buttons on the Language bar.

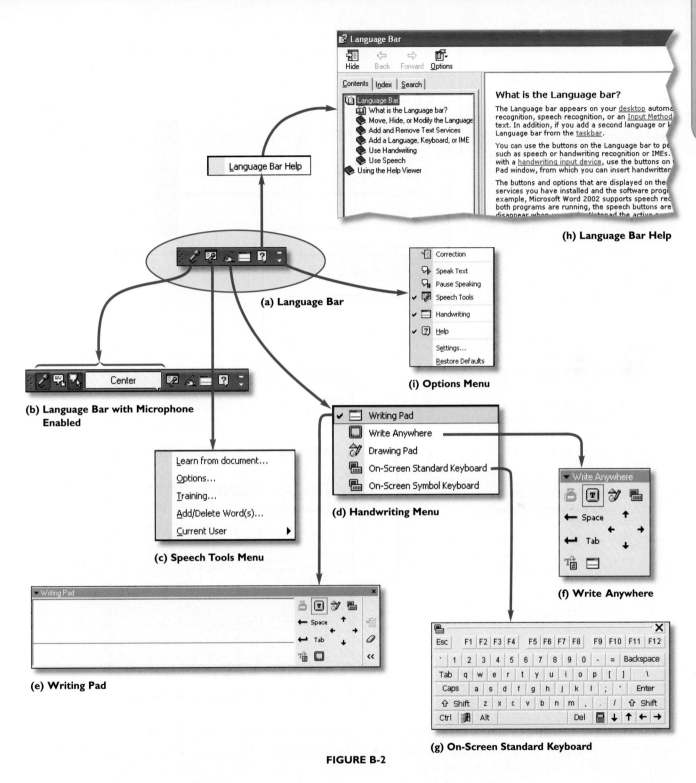

(a) Language Bar

(b) Language Bar with Microphone Enabled

(c) Speech Tools Menu

(d) Handwriting Menu

(e) Writing Pad

(f) Write Anywhere

(g) On-Screen Standard Keyboard

(h) Language Bar Help

(i) Options Menu

FIGURE B-2

If you right-click the Language bar, a shortcut menu appears (Figure B-3a on the next page). This shortcut menu lets you further customize the Language bar. The Minimize command on the shortcut menu docks the Language bar on the Windows taskbar. The Transparency command in Figure B-3a toggles the Language bar between being solid and transparent. You can see through a transparent Language bar (Figure B-3b). The Text Labels command toggles on text labels on the Language bar (Figure B-3c) and off (Figure B-3b). The Vertical command displays the Language bar vertically on the screen (Figure B-3d).

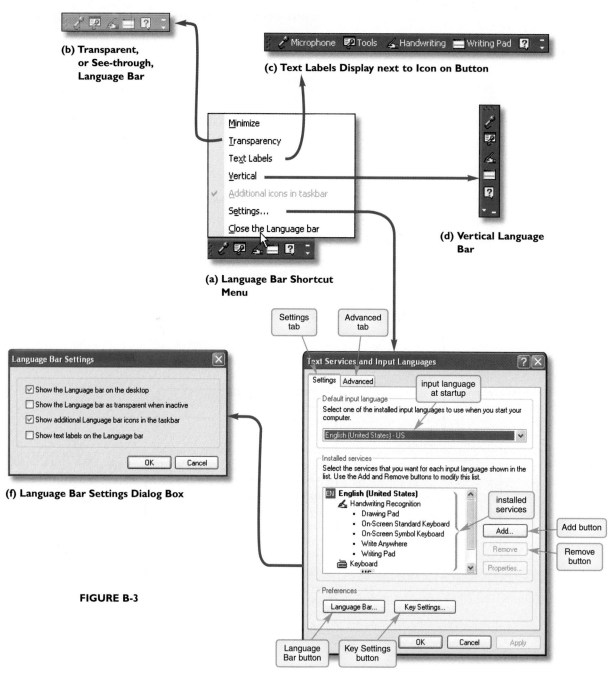

(b) Transparent, or See-through, Language Bar

(c) Text Labels Display next to Icon on Button

(a) Language Bar Shortcut Menu

(d) Vertical Language Bar

(f) Language Bar Settings Dialog Box

FIGURE B-3

(e) Text Services and Input Languages Dialog Box

The Settings command in Figure B-3a displays the Text Services and Input Languages dialog box (Figure B-3e). The Text Services and Input Languages dialog box allows you to add additonal languages, add and remove text services, modify keys on the keyboard, modify the Language bar, and extend support of advanced text services to all programs, including Notepad and other programs that normally do not support text services (through the Advanced tab). If you want to remove any one of the services in the Installed services list, select the service, and then click the Remove button. If you want to add a service, click the Add button. The Key Settings button allows you to modify the keyboard. If you click the Language Bar button in the Text Services and Input Languages dialog box, the Language Bar Settings dialog box appears (Figure B-3f). This dialog box contains Language bar options, some of which are the same as the commands on the Language bar shortcut menu shown in Figure B-3a.

The Close the Language bar command on the shortcut menu shown in Figure B-3a closes or hides the Language bar. If you close the Language bar and want to redisplay it, see Figure B-1d on page APP 11.

Speech Recognition

The **Speech Recognition service** available with Office enables your computer to recognize human speech through a microphone. The microphone has two modes: dictation and voice command (Figure B-4). You switch between the two modes by clicking the Dictation button and the Voice Command button on the Language bar. These buttons appear only when you turn on Speech Recognition by clicking the Microphone button on the Language bar (Figure B-5a on the next page). If you are using the Microphone button for the very first time in PowerPoint, it will require that you check your microphone settings and step through voice training before activating the Speech Recognition service.

The Dictation button places the microphone in Dictation mode. In **Dictation mode**, whatever you speak is entered as text at the location of the insertion point. The Voice Command button places the microphone in Voice Command mode. In **Voice Command mode**, whatever you speak is interpreted as a command. If you want to turn off the microphone, click the Microphone button on the Language bar or in Voice Command mode say, "Mic off" (pronounced mike off). It is important to remember that minimizing the Language bar does not turn off the microphone.

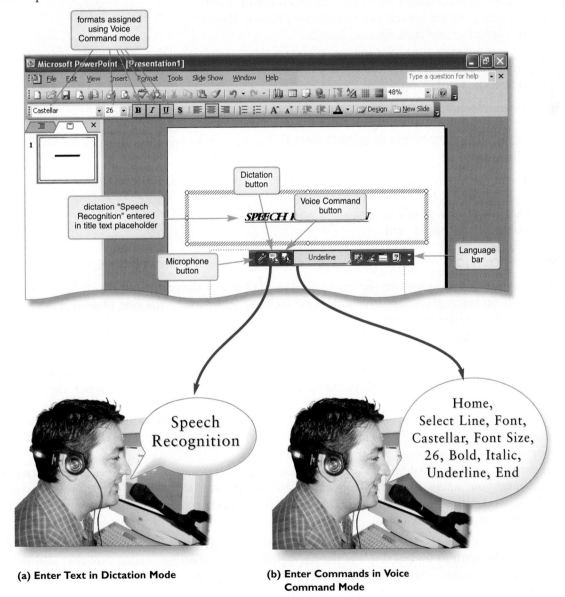

(a) Enter Text in Dictation Mode

(b) Enter Commands in Voice Command Mode

FIGURE B-4

The Language bar speech message balloon shown in Figure B-5b displays messages that may offer help or hints. In Voice Command mode, the name of the last recognized command you said appears. If you use the mouse or keyboard instead of the microphone, a message will appear in the Language bar speech message balloon indicating the word you could say. In Dictation mode, the message, Dictating, usually appears. The Speech Recognition service, however, will display messages to inform you that you are talking too soft, too loud, or too fast, or to ask you to repeat what you said by displaying, What was that?

Getting Started with Speech Recognition

For the microphone to function properly, you should follow these steps:

1. Make sure your computer meets the minimum requirements.
2. Start Word. Activate Speech Recognition by clicking Tools on the menu bar and then clicking Speech.
3. Set up and position your microphone, preferably a close-talk headset with gain adjustment support.
4. Train Speech Recognition.

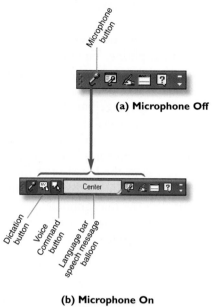

FIGURE B-5

The following sections describe these steps in more detail.

SPEECH RECOGNITION SYSTEM REQUIREMENTS   For Speech Recognition to work on your computer, it needs the following:

1. Microsoft Windows 98 or later or Microsoft Windows NT 4.0 or later
2. At least 128 MB RAM
3. 400 MHz or faster processor
4. Microphone and sound card

SET UP AND POSITION YOUR MICROPHONE   Set up your microphone as follows:

1. Connect your microphone to the sound card in the back of the computer.
2. Position the microphone approximately one inch out from and to the side of your mouth. Position it so you are not breathing into it.
3. On the Language bar, click the Speech Tools button and then click Options on the Speech Tools menu (Figure B-6a).
4. When text services displays the Speech input settings dialog box (Figure B-6b), click the Advanced Speech button. When text services displays the Speech Properties dialog box (Figure B-6c), click the Speech Recognition tab.
5. Click the Configure Microphone button. Follow the Microphone Wizard directions as shown in Figures B-6d, B-6e, and B-6f. The Next button will remain dimmed in Figure B-6e until the volume meter consistently stays in the green area.
6. If someone else installed Speech Recognition, click the New button in the Speech Properties dialog box and enter your name. Click the Train Profile button and step through the Voice Training dialog boxes. The Voice Training dialog boxes will require that you enter your gender and age group. It then will step you through voice training.

You can adjust the microphone further by clicking the Settings button in the Speech Properties dialog box (Figure B-6c). The Settings button displays the Recognition Profile Settings dialog box that allows you to adjust the pronunciation sensitivity and accuracy versus recognition response time.

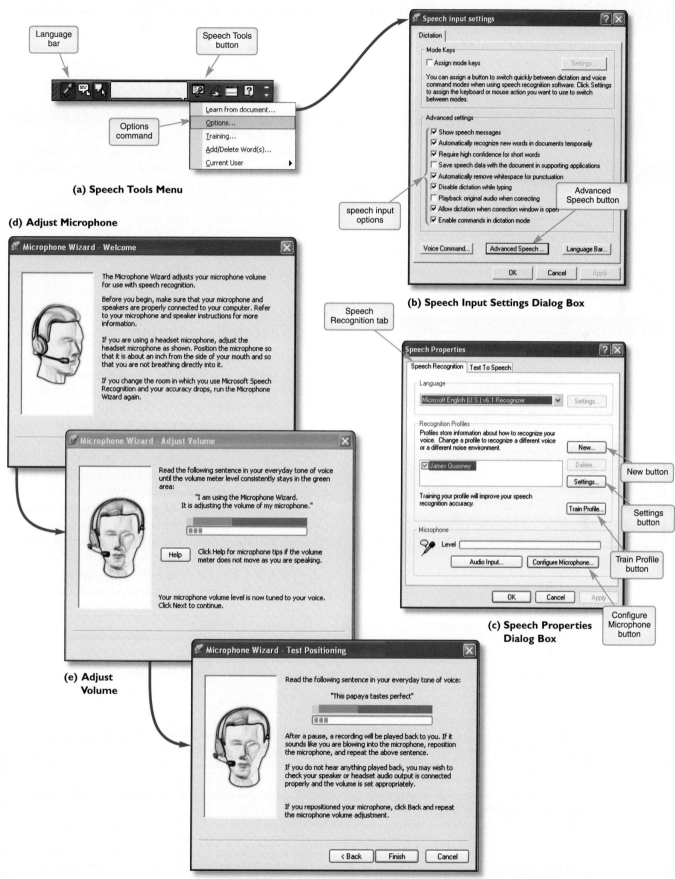

(a) **Speech Tools Menu**

(d) **Adjust Microphone**

(b) **Speech Input Settings Dialog Box**

(c) **Speech Properties Dialog Box**

(e) **Adjust Volume**

(f) **Test Microphone**

FIGURE B-6

TRAIN THE SPEECH RECOGNITION SERVICE   The Speech Recognition service will understand most commands and some dictation without any training at all. It will recognize much more of what you speak, however, if you take the time to train it. After one training session, it will recognize 85 to 90 percent of your words. As you do more training, accuracy will rise to 95 percent. If you feel that too many mistakes are being made, then continue to train the service. The more training you do, the more accurately it will work for you. Follow these steps to train the Speech Recognition service:

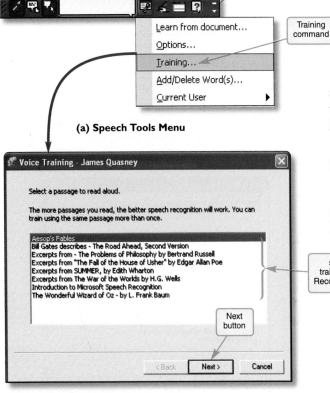

(a) **Speech Tools Menu**

(b) **Voice Training Dialog Box**

FIGURE B-7

1. Click the Speech Tools button on the Language bar and then click Training (Figure B-7a).
2. When the Voice Training dialog box appears (Figure B-7b), click one of the sessions and then click the Next button.
3. Complete the training session, which should take less than 15 minutes.

If you are serious about using a microphone to speak to your computer, you need to take the time to go through at least three of the eight training sessions listed in Figure B-7b.

Using Speech Recognition

Speech recognition lets you enter text into a document similarly to speaking into a tape recorder. Instead of typing, you can dictate text that you want to be displayed in the document, and you can issue voice commands. In Voice Command mode, you can speak menu names, commands on menus, toolbar button names, and dialog box option buttons, check boxes, list boxes, and button names. Speech recognition, however, is not a completely hands-free form of input. Speech recognition works best if you use a combination of your voice, the keyboard, and the mouse. You soon will discover that Dictation mode is far less accurate than Voice Command mode. Table B-1 lists some tips that will improve the Speech Recognition service's accuracy considerably.

Table B-1	Tips to Improve Speech Recognition
NUMBER	**TIP**
1	The microphone hears everything. Though the Speech Recognition service filters out background noise, it is recommended that you work in a quiet environment.
2	Try not to move the microphone around once it is adjusted.
3	Speak in a steady tone and speak clearly.
4	In Dictation mode, do not pause between words. A phrase is easier to interpret than a word. Sounding out syllables in a word will make it more difficult for the Speech Recognition service to interpret what you are saying.
5	If you speak too loudly or too softly, it makes it difficult for the Speech Recognition service to interpret what you said. Check the Language bar speech message balloon for an indication that you may be speaking too loudly or too softly.
6	If you experience problems after training, adjust the recognition options that control accuracy and rejection by clicking the Settings button shown in Figure B-6c on the previous page.
7	When you are finished using the microphone, turn it off by clicking the Microphone button on the Language bar or in Voice Command mode, say "Mic off." Leaving the microphone on is the same as leaning on the keyboard.
8	If the Speech Recognition service is having difficulty with unusual words, then add the words to its dictionary by using the Add/Delete Word(s) command on the Speech Tools menu (Figure B-8a). The last names of individuals and the names of companies are good examples of the types of words you should add to the dictionary.
9	Training will improve accuracy; practice will improve confidence.

The last command on the Speech Tools menu is the Current User command (Figure B-8a). The Current User command is useful for multiple users who share a computer. It allows them to configure their own individual profiles, and then switch between users as they use the computer.

For additional information about the Speech Recognition service, enter `speech recognition` in the Type a question for help box on the menu bar.

Handwriting Recognition

Using the Office **Handwriting Recognition service**, you can enter text and numbers into PowerPoint by writing instead of typing. You can write using a special handwriting device that connects to your computer or you can write on the screen using your mouse. Four basic methods of handwriting are available by clicking the Handwriting button on the Language bar: Writing Pad; Write Anywhere; Drawing Pad; and On-Screen Keyboard. Although the on-screen keyboard does not involve handwriting recognition, it is part of the Handwriting menu and, therefore, will be discussed in this section.

If your Language bar does not include the Handwriting button, then, for installation instructions, enter `install handwriting recognition` in the Type a question for help box on the menu bar.

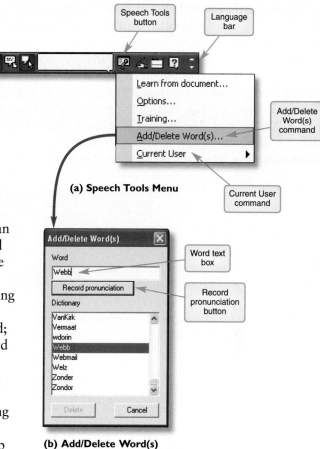

(a) Speech Tools Menu

(b) **Add/Delete Word(s) Dialog Box**

FIGURE B-8

Writing Pad

To display the Writing Pad, click the Handwriting button on the Language bar and then click Writing Pad (Figure B-9). The **Writing Pad** resembles a notepad with one or more lines on which you can use freehand to print or write in cursive. With the Text button enabled, you can form letters on the line by moving the mouse while holding down the mouse button. To the right of the notepad is a rectangular toolbar. Use the buttons on this toolbar to adjust the Writing Pad, select cells, and activate other handwriting applications.

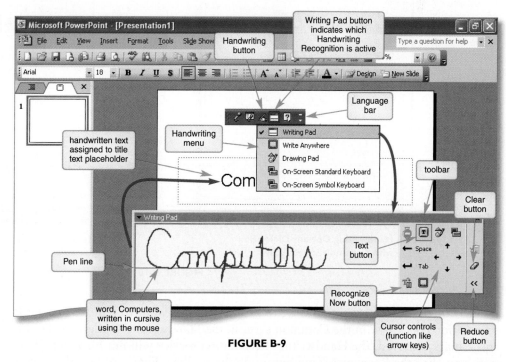

FIGURE B-9

Consider the example in Figure B-9 on the previous page. With the title text placeholder selected, the word, Computers, is written in cursive on the **Pen line** in the Writing Pad. As soon as the word is complete, the Handwriting Recognition service automatically assigns the word to the title text placeholder.

You can customize the Writing Pad by clicking the Options button on the left side of the title bar and then clicking the Options command (Figure B-10a). Invoking the Options command causes the Handwriting Options dialog box to display. The Handwriting Options dialog box contains two sheets: Common and Writing Pad. The Common sheet lets you change the pen color and pen width, adjust recognition, and customize the toolbar area of the Writing Pad. The Writing Pad sheet allows you to change the background color and the number of lines that are displayed in the Writing Pad. Both sheets contain a Restore Default button to restore the settings to what they were when the software was installed initially.

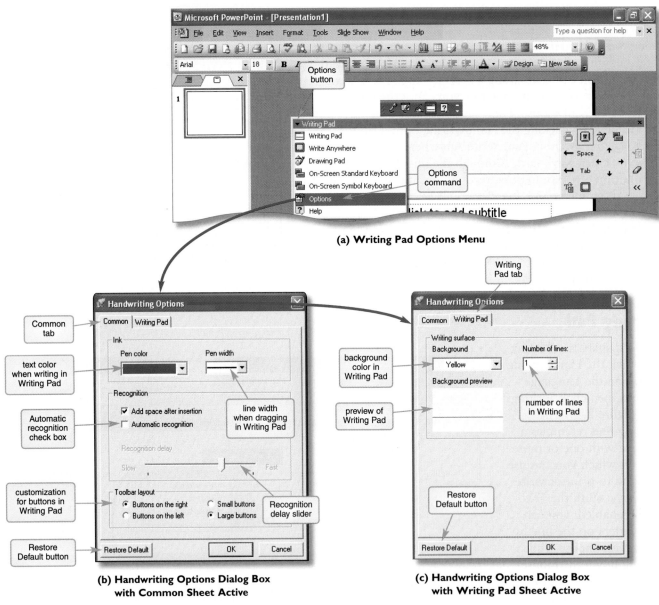

(a) Writing Pad Options Menu

(b) Handwriting Options Dialog Box with Common Sheet Active

(c) Handwriting Options Dialog Box with Writing Pad Sheet Active

FIGURE B-10

When you first start using the Writing Pad, you may want to remove the check mark from the Automatic recognition check box in the Common sheet in the Handwriting Options dialog box (Figure B-10b). With the check mark removed, the Handwriting Recognition service will not interpret what you write in the Writing Pad until you click the Recognize Now button on the toolbar (Figure B-9 on the previous page). This allows you to pause and adjust your writing.

The best way to learn how to use the Writing Pad is to practice with it. Also, for more information, enter `handwriting recognition` in the Type a question for help box on the menu bar.

Write Anywhere

Rather than use Writing Pad, you can write anywhere on the screen by invoking the Write Anywhere command on the Handwriting menu (Figure B-11) that appears when you click the Handwriting button on the Language bar. In this case, the entire window is your writing pad.

In Figure B-11, the word, `Budget`, is written in cursive using the mouse button. Shortly after the word is written, the Handwriting Recognition service interprets it, assigns it to the active cell, and erases what was written.

It is recommended that when you first start using the Writing Anywhere service that you remove the check mark from the Automatic recognition check box in the Common sheet in the Handwriting Options dialog box (Figure B-10b). With the check mark removed, the Handwriting Recognition service will not interpret what you write on the screen until you click the Recognize Now button on the toolbar (Figure B-11).

Write Anywhere is more difficult to use than the Writing Pad, because when you click the mouse button, PowerPoint may interpret the action as selecting a placeholder rather than starting to write. For this reason, it is recommended that you use the Writing Pad.

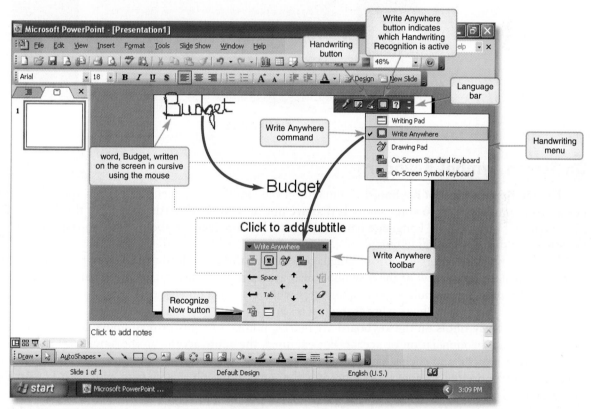

FIGURE B-11

On-Screen Standard Keyboard

The On-Screen Standard Keyboard command on the Handwriting menu (Figure B-12) displays an on-screen keyboard. The **On-Screen Standard Keyboard** lets you enter data into a cell by using your mouse to click the keys. This on-screen keyboard is similar to the type found on handheld computers.

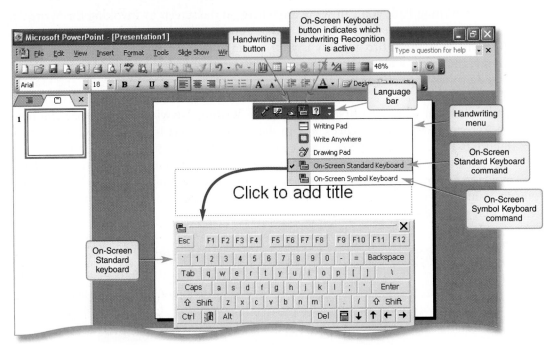

FIGURE B-12

On-Screen Symbol Keyboard

The **On-Screen Symbol Keyboard** command on the Handwriting menu displays a special on-screen keyboard that allows you to enter symbols that are not on your keyboard. To display this keyboard, click the Handwriting button on the Language bar and then click On-Screen Symbol Keyboard (Figure B-13). Clicking the SHIFT key displays capital letters.

Some symbols are letters in various languages, such as the Latin Þ (thorn), Greek β (beta) and the Latin letter o with slash (Ø). A few of these symbols also are used in mathematical and scientific applications. For example, Ø represents the null set in mathematics when a set has no elements. It also is used to indicate a zero reading when current or voltage is measured on a scale.

The **diacritic symbols** on the keyboard are marks, points, or signs printed above or below a letter to indicate its exact pronunciation or accent. For example, the acute accent on the letter e (é) is used in French words such as attaché and cliché. The cedilla (¸) and circumflex accent (^) are used in the French translation for the phrase, the more that changes, the more it is the same thing: plus ça change, plus c'est la même chose, shown in Figure B-13.

The **ligature symbols** on the keyboard are characters consisting of two or more letters joined together. The Latin small ligature œ, for example, is used in the French word cœur, meaning heart.

Three currency abbreviations also are located on the On-Screen Symbol Keyboard. They include the Euro (€), the British pound (£), and the Japanese yen (¥).

Table B-2 lists some of the symbols on the On-Screen Symbol Keyboard and their uses.

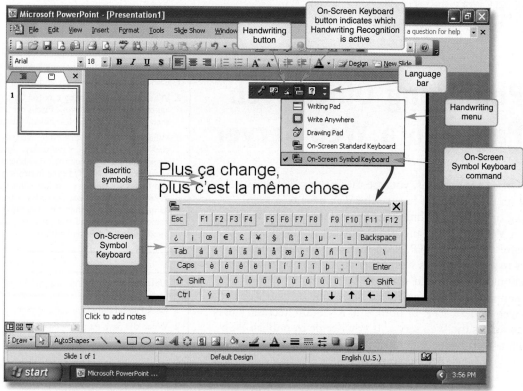

FIGURE B-13

Table B-2	On-Screen Symbol Keyboard Keys	
SYMBOL	**NAME**	**EXAMPLE**
Currency		
€	Euro sign	€875
£	Pound sign	£250
¥	Yen sign	¥500
Mathematics and Science		
β	Beta	$\beta = \omega * c / \lambda$
Ø	Empty (null) set	$A \cap B = \emptyset$
/	Fraction slash	4/2
µ	Micro sign (mu)	µ-inches
δ	Partial differential (delta)	$\delta y/\delta x$
±	Plus-minus sign	12 ± 2 inches
Diacritic		
´	Acute accent	Attaché, cliché
ç	Cedilla	Façade
^	Circumflex accent	Même
`	Grave accent	À la mode
~	Tilde	Niño
¨	Umlaut	Naïve
Ligature		
æ	Latin small ligature æ	Encyclopædia Britannica
œ	Latin small ligature œ	Cœur
Miscellaneous		
¿	Inverted question mark	¿Qué pasa?
§	Section	15 U.S. Code §1601

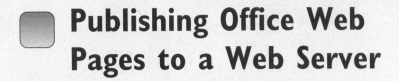

Appendix C

Publishing Office Web Pages to a Web Server

With the Office applications, you use the Save as Web Page command on the File menu to save the Web page to a Web server using one of two techniques: Web folders or File Transfer Protocol. A **Web folder** is an Office shortcut to a Web server. **File Transfer Protocol** (**FTP**) is an Internet standard that allows computers to exchange files with other computers on the Internet.

You should contact your network system administrator or technical support staff at your ISP to determine if their Web server supports Web folders, FTP, or both, and to obtain necessary permissions to access the Web server. If you decide to publish Web pages using a Web folder, you must have the Office Server Extensions (OSE) installed on your computer.

Using Web Folders to Publish Office Web Pages

When publishing to a Web folder, someone first must create the Web folder before you can save to it. If you are granted permission to create a Web folder, you must obtain the URL of the Web server, a user name, and possibly a password that allows you to access the Web server. You also must decide on a name for the Web folder. Table C-1 explains how to create a Web folder.

Office adds the name of the Web folder to the list of current Web folders. You can save to this folder, open files in the folder, rename the folder, or perform any operations you would to a folder on your hard disk. You can use your Office program or Windows Explorer to access this folder. Table C-2 explains how to save to a Web folder.

Using FTP to Publish Office Web Pages

When publishing a Web page using FTP, you first must add the FTP location to your computer before you can save to it. An FTP location, also called an **FTP site**, is a collection of files that reside on an FTP server. In this case, the FTP server is the Web server.

To add an FTP location, you must obtain the name of the FTP site, which usually is the address (URL) of the FTP server, and a user name and a password that allows you to access the FTP server. You save and open the Web pages on the FTP server using the name of the FTP site. Table C-3 explains how to add an FTP site.

Office adds the name of the FTP site to the FTP locations list in the Save As and Open dialog boxes. You can open and save files using this list. Table C-4 explains how to save to an FTP location.

Table C-1   Creating a Web Folder

1. Click File on the menu bar and then click Save As (or Open).
2. When the Save As dialog box (or Open dialog box) appears, click My Network Places on the My Places bar, and then click the Create New Folder button on the toolbar.
3. When the Add Network Place Wizard dialog box appears, click the Next button. If necessary, click Choose another network location. Click the Next button. Click the View some examples link, type the Internet or network address, and then click the Next button. Click Log on anonymously to deselect the check box, type your user name in the User name text box, and then click the Next button. Enter the name you want to call this network place and then click the Next button. Click the Finish button.

Table C-2   Saving to a Web Folder

1. Click File on the menu bar and then click Save As.
2. When the Save As dialog box appears, type the Web page file name in the File name text box. Do not press the ENTER key.
3. Click My Network Places on the My Places bar.
4. Double-click the Web folder name in the Save in list.
5. If the Enter Network Password dialog box appears, type the user name and password in the respective text boxes and then click the OK button.
6. Click the Save button in the Save As dialog box.

Table C-3   Adding an FTP Location

1. Click File on the menu bar and then click Save As (or Open).
2. In the Save As dialog box, click the Save in box arrow and then click Add/Modify FTP Locations in the Save in list; or in the Open dialog box, click the Look in box arrow and then click Add/Modify FTP Locations in the Look in list.
3. When the Add/Modify FTP Locations dialog box appears, type the name of the FTP site in the Name of FTP site text box. If the site allows anonymous logon, click Anonymous in the Log on as area; if you have a user name for the site, click User in the Log on as area and then enter the user name. Enter the password in the Password text box. Click the OK button.
4. Close the Save As or the Open dialog box.

Table C-4   Saving to an FTP Location

1. Click File on the menu bar and then click Save As.
2. When the Save As dialog box appears, type the Web page file name in the File name text box. Do not press the ENTER key.
3. Click the Save in box arrow and then click FTP Locations.
4. Double-click the name of the FTP site to which you wish to save.
5. When the FTP Log On dialog box appears, enter your user name and password and then click the OK button.
6. Click the Save button in the Save As dialog box.

Appendix D

Changing Screen Resolution and Resetting the PowerPoint Toolbars and Menus

This appendix explains how to change your screen resolution in Windows to the resolution used in this book. It also describes how to reset the PowerPooint toolbars and menus to their installation settings.

Changing Screen Resolution

The **screen resolution** indicates the number of pixels (dots) that your system uses to display the letters, numbers, graphics, and background you see on your screen. The screen resolution usually is stated as the product of two numbers, such as 800 × 600. An 800 × 600 screen resolution results in a display of 800 distinct pixels on each of 600 lines, or about 480,000 pixels. The figures in this book were created using a screen resolution of 800 × 600.

The screen resolutions most commonly used today are 800 × 600 and 1024 × 768, although some Office specialists operate their computers at a much higher screen resolution, such as 2048 × 1536. The following steps show how to change the screen resolution from 1024 × 768 to 800 × 600.

To Change the Screen Resolution

1

• **If necessary, minimize all applications so that the Windows desktop appears.**

• **Right-click the Windows desktop.**

Windows displays the Windows desktop shortcut menu (Figure D-1).

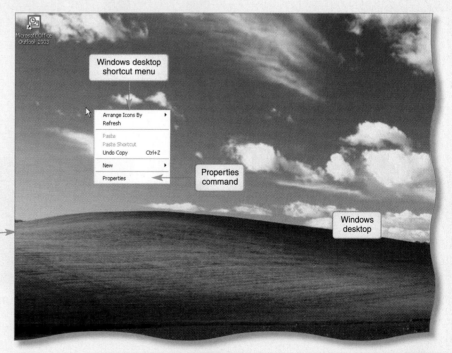

2

• **Click Properties on the shortcut menu.**

• **When Windows displays the Display Properties dialog box, click the Settings tab.**

Windows displays the Settings sheet in the Display Properties dialog box (Figure D-2). The Settings sheet shows a preview of the Windows desktop using the current screen resolution (1024 × 768). The Settings sheet also shows the screen resolution and the color quality settings.

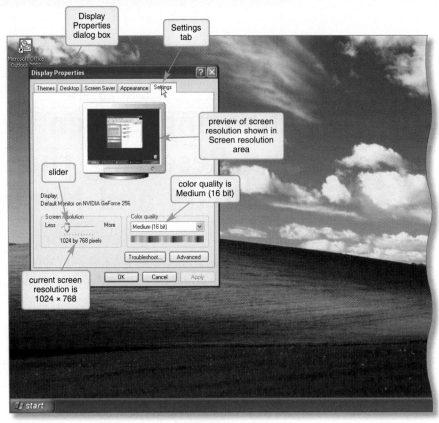

FIGURE D-2

3

• **Drag the slider in the Screen resolution area to the left so that the screen resolution changes to 800 × 600.**

The screen resolution in the Screen resolution area changes to 800 × 600 (Figure D-3). The Settings sheet shows a preview of the Windows desktop using the new screen resolution (800 × 600).

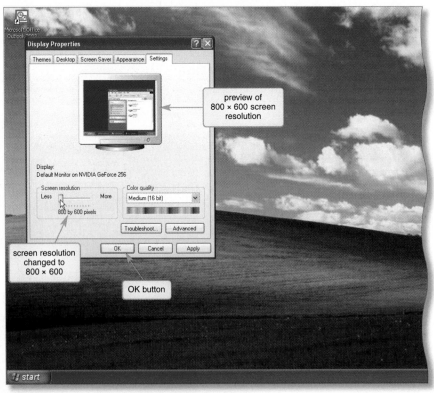

FIGURE D-3

4

• **Click the OK button.**

• **If Windows displays the Monitor Settings dialog box, click the Yes button.**

Windows changes the screen resolution from 1024 × 768 to 800 × 600 (Figure D-4).

800 x 600
screen resolution

FIGURE D-4

As shown in the previous steps, as you decrease the screen resolution, Windows displays less information on your screen, but the information increases in size. The reverse also is true: as you increase the screen resolution, Windows displays more information on your screen, but the information decreases in size.

Resetting the PowerPoint Toolbars and Menus

PowerPoint customization capabilities allow you to create custom toolbars by adding and deleting buttons and to personalize menus based on their usage. Each time you start PowerPoint, the toolbars and menus display using the same settings as the last time you used it. The figures in this book were created with the PowerPoint toolbars and menus set to the original, or installation, settings.

Resetting the Standard and Formatting Toolbars

The steps on the next page show how to reset the Standard and Formatting toolbars.

To Reset the Standard and Formatting Toolbars

1

• **Start PowerPoint following the steps outlined at the beginning of Project 1.**

• **Click the Toolbar Options button on the Standard toolbar and then point to Add or Remove Buttons on the Toolbar Options menu.**

PowerPoint displays the Toolbar Options menu and the Add or Remove Buttons submenu (Figure D-5).

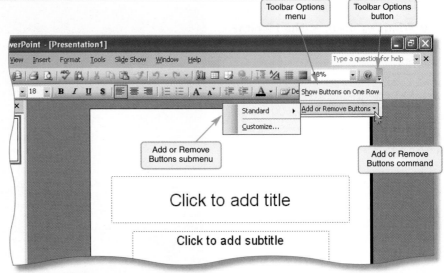

FIGURE D-5

2

• **Point to Standard on the Add or Remove Buttons submenu.**

• **When the Standard submenu displays, scroll down and then point to Reset Toolbar.**

PowerPoint displays the Standard submenu indicating the buttons and boxes that display on the Standard toolbar (Figure D-6). To remove a button from the Standard toolbar, click a button name with a check mark to the left of the name to remove the check mark.

3

• **Click Reset Toolbar.**

• **If PowerPoint displays the Microsoft Office PowerPoint dialog box, click Yes.**

PowerPoint resets the Standard toolbar to its original settings.

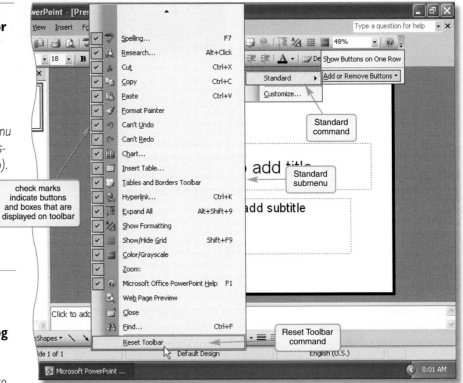

FIGURE D-6

4

• **Reset the Formatting toolbar by following Steps 1 through 3 and replacing any reference to the Standard toolbar with the Formatting toolbar.**

Not only can you use the Standard submenu shown in Figure D-6 to reset the Standard toolbar to its original settings, but you also can use it to customize the Standard toolbar by adding and deleting buttons. To add or delete buttons, click the button name on the Standard submenu to add or remove the check mark. Buttons with a check mark to the left currently are displayed on the Standard toolbar; buttons without a check mark are not displayed on the Standard toolbar. You can complete the same tasks for the Formatting toolbar, using the Formatting submenu to add and delete buttons from the Formatting toolbar.

Resetting the PowerPoint Menus

The following steps show how to reset the PowerPoint menus to their original settings.

To Reset the PowerPoint Menus

Other Ways

1. On View menu point to Toolbars, click Customize on Toolbars submenu, click Toolbars tab, click toolbar name, click Reset button, click OK button, click Close button
2. Right-click toolbar, click Customize on shortcut menu, click Toolbars tab, click toolbar name, click Reset button, click OK button, click Close button
3. In Voice Command mode, say "View, Toolbars, Customize, Toolbars, [desired toolbar name], Reset, OK, Close"

1

• **Click the Toolbar Options button on the Standard toolbar and then point to Add or Remove Buttons on the Toolbar Options menu.**

The Toolbar Options menu and Add or Remove Buttons submenu display (Figure D-7).

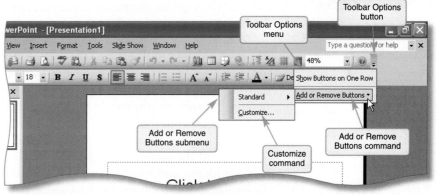

FIGURE D-7

2

• **Click Customize on the Add or Remove Buttons submenu.**

• **If necessary, when PowerPoint displays the Customize dialog box, click the Options tab.**

PowerPoint displays the Customize dialog box (Figure D-8). The Customize dialog box contains three sheets used for customizing the PowerPoint toolbars and menus.

3

• **Click the Reset menu and toolbar usage data button.**

• **When PowerPoint displays the Microsoft Office PowerPoint dialog box, click the Yes button.**

• **Click the Close button in the Customize dialog box.**

PowerPoint resets the menus to the original settings.

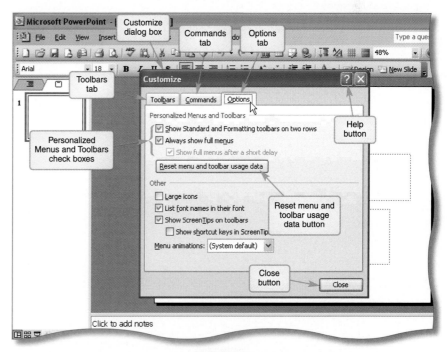

FIGURE D-8

Other Ways

1. On View menu point to Toolbars, click Customize on Toolbars submenu, click Options tab, click Reset menu and toolbar usage data button, click Yes button, click Close button
2. Right-click toolbar, click Customize on shortcut menu, click Options tab, click Reset menu and toolbar usage data button, click Yes button, click Close button
3. In Voice Command mode, say "View, Toolbars, Customize, Options, Reset menu and toolbar usage data, Yes, Close"

Using the Options sheet in the Customize dialog box, as shown in Figure D-8 on the previous page, you can select options to personalize menus and toolbars. For example, you can select or deselect a check mark that instructs PowerPoint to display the Standard and Formatting toolbars on two rows. You also can select whether PowerPoint always displays full menus or displays short menus followed by full menus after a short delay. Other options available on the Options sheet including settings to instruct PowerPoint to display toolbars with large icons; to use the appropriate font to display font names in the Font list; and to display a ScreenTip when a user points to a toolbar button. Clicking the Help button in the lower-left corner of the Customize dialog box displays Help topics that will assist you in customizing toolbars and menus.

Using the Commands sheet in the Customize dialog box, you can add buttons to toolbars and commands to menus. Recall that the menu bar at the top of the PowerPoint window is a special toolbar. To add buttons to a toolbar, click a category name in the Categories list and then drag the command name in the Commands list to a toolbar. To add commands to a menu, click a category name in the Categories list, drag the command name in the Commands list to a menu name on the menu bar, and then, when the menu displays, drag the command to the desired location in the list of menu commands.

Using the Toolbars sheet in the Customize dialog box, you can add new toolbars and reset existing toolbars and the menus. To add a new toolbar, click the New button, enter a toolbar name in the New Toolbar dialog box, and then click the OK button. Once the new toolbar is created, you can use the Commands sheet to add or remove buttons, as you would with any other toolbar. If you add one or more buttons to an existing toolbar and want to reset the toolbar to its original settings, click the toolbar name in the Toolbars list on the Toolbars sheet so a check mark displays to the left of the name and then click the Reset button. If you add commands to one or more menus and want to reset the menus to their default settings, click Worksheet Menu Bar in the Toolbars list so a check mark displays to the left of the name and then click the Reset button. When you have finished, click the Close button to close the Customize dialog box.

Appendix E

Microsoft Office Specialist Certification

What Is Microsoft Office Specialist Certification?

Microsoft Office Specialist certification provides a framework for measuring your proficiency with the Microsoft Office 2003 applications, such as Microsoft Office Word 2003, Microsoft Office Excel 2003, Microsoft Office Access 2003, Microsoft Office PowerPoint 2003, and Microsoft Office Outlook 2003. The levels of certification are described in Table E-1.

Table E-1 Levels of Microsoft Office Specialist Certification

LEVEL	DESCRIPTION	REQUIREMENTS	CREDENTIAL AWARDED
Microsoft Office Specialist	Indicates that you have an understanding of the basic features in a specific Microsoft Office 2003 application	Pass any ONE of the following: Microsoft Office Word 2003 Microsoft Office Excel 2003 Microsoft Office Access 2003 Microsoft Office PowerPoint 2003 Microsoft Office Outlook 2003	Candidates will be awarded one certificate for each of the Specialist-level exams they have passed: Microsoft Office Word 2003 Microsoft Office Excel 2003 Microsoft Office Access 2003 Microsoft Office PowerPoint 2003 Microsoft Office Outlook 2003
Microsoft Office Expert	Indicates that you have an understanding of the advanced features in a specific Microsoft Office 2003 application	Pass any ONE of the following: Microsoft Office Word 2003 Expert Microsoft Office Excel 2003 Expert	Candidates will be awarded one certificate for each of the Expert-level exams they have passed: Microsoft Office Word 2003 Expert Microsoft Office Excel 2003 Expert
Microsoft Office Master	Indicates that you have a comprehensive under-standing of the features of four of the five primary Microsoft Office 2003 applications	Pass the following: Microsoft Office Word 2003 Expert Microsoft Office Excel 2003 Expert Microsoft Office PowerPoint 2003 And pass ONE of the following: Microsoft Office Access 2003 or Microsoft Office Outlook 2003	Candidates will be awarded the Microsoft Office Master certificate for fulfilling the requirements.

Why Should You Be Certified?

Being Microsoft Office certified provides a valuable industry credential — proof that you have the Office 2003 applications skills required by employers. By passing one or more Microsoft Office Specialist certification exams, you demonstrate your proficiency in a given Office 2003 application to employers. With more than 400 million people in 175 nations and 70 languages using Office applications, Microsoft is targeting Office 2003 certification to a wide variety of companies. These companies include temporary employment agencies that want to prove the expertise of their workers, large corporations looking for a way to measure the skill set of employees, and training companies and educational institutions seeking Microsoft Office 2003 teachers with appropriate credentials.

The Microsoft Office Specialist Certification Exams

You pay $50 to $100 each time you take an exam, whether you pass or fail. The fee varies among testing centers. The **Microsoft Office Expert** exams, which you can take up to 60 minutes to complete, consist of between 40 and 60 tasks that you perform on a personal computer in a simulated environment. The tasks require you to use the application just as you would in doing your job. The **Microsoft Office Specialist** exams contain fewer tasks, and you will have slightly less time to complete them. The tasks you will perform differ on the two types of exams. After passing designated Expert and Specialist exams, candidates are awarded the **Microsoft Office Master** certificate (see the requirements in Table E-1 on the previous page).

How to Prepare for the Microsoft Office Specialist Certification Exams

The Shelly Cashman Series offers several Microsoft-approved textbooks that cover the required objectives of the Microsoft Office Specialist certification exams. For a listing of the textbooks, visit the Shelly Cashman Series Microsoft Office Specialist Center at scsite.com/winoff2003/cert. Click the link Shelly Cashman Series Microsoft Office 2003-Approved Microsoft Office Textbooks (Figure E-1). After using any of the books listed in an instructor-led course, you should be prepared to take the indicated Microsoft Office Specialist certification exam.

How to Find an Authorized Testing Center

To locate a testing center, call 1-800-933-4493 in North America, or visit the Shelly Cashman Series Microsoft Office Specialist Center at scsite.com/winoff2003/cert. Click the link Locate an Authorized Testing Center Near You (Figure E-1). At this Web site, you can look for testing centers around the world.

Shelly Cashman Series Microsoft Office Specialist Center

The Shelly Cashman Series Microsoft Office Specialist Center (Figure E-1) lists more than 15 Web sites you can visit to obtain additional information about certification. The Web page (scsite.com/winoff2003/cert) includes links to general information about certification, choosing an application for certification, preparing for the certification exam, and taking and passing the certification exam.

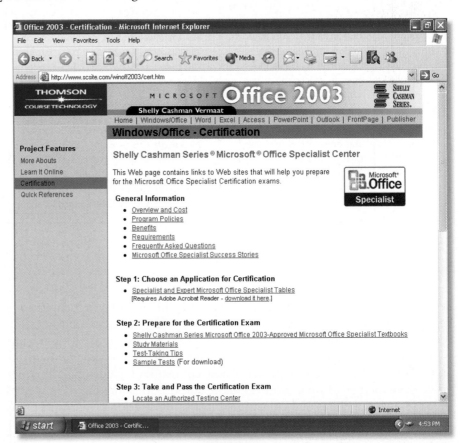

FIGURE E-1

Microsoft Office Specialist Certification Maps for Microsoft Office PowerPoint 2003

This book has been approved by Microsoft as courseware for the Microsoft Office Specialist certification. After completing the first four projects and corresponding exercises in this book, students will be prepared to take the specialist-level examination for Microsoft Office PowerPoint 2003. Table E-2 lists the specialist-level examination skill sets, activities, page numbers where the activities are demonstrated, and page numbers where the activities can be practiced. There is no expert-level examination for Microsoft Office PowerPoint 2003.

Table E-2 Specialist-Level Skill Sets, Activities, and Locations in Book for Microsoft Office PowerPoint 2003			
SKILL SET	**SKILL BEING MEASURED**	**SKILL DEMONSTRATED IN BOOK**	**SKILL EXERCISE IN BOOK**
I. Creating Content	A. Create new presentations from templates	PPT 18-43, PPT 85-111, PPT 163-210, PPT 228-231	PPT 69-71 (In the Lab 1 Steps 1-3), PPT 132-133 (In the Lab 1 Steps 1-4), PPT 297-298 (In the Lab 1 Step 1), PPT 299-301 (In the Lab 2 Steps 1-10), PPT 302-303 (In the Lab 3 Steps 1-11)
	B. Insert and edit text-based content	PPT 20-24, PPT 31-42, PPT 53-56, PPT 88-94, PPT 165-167, PPT 247, PPT 257, PPT 260, PPT 266-268	PPT 69-71 (In the Lab 1 Steps 2-4), PPT 72-73 (In the Lab 2 Step 4), PPT 74-77 (In the Lab 3 Part 1 Step 2, Part 2 Step 6), PPT 132-134 (In the Lab 1 Steps 2-4), PPT 218-219 (In the Lab 2 Step 1), PPT 220-221 (In the Lab 3 Step 1), PPT 222 (Cases and Places 3), PPT 299-301 (In the Lab 2 Steps 4, 6-8, 13), PPT 302-304 (In the Lab 3 Step 14), PPT 305 (Cases and Places 1 and 2)
	C. Insert tables, charts, and diagrams	PPT 190-195, PPT 195-207, PPT 246-251	PPT 218-219 (In the Lab 2 Steps 5-6), PPT 220-221 (In the Lab 3 Steps 5-6), PPT 222-223 (Cases and Places 1-2, 4), PPT 305-306 (Cases and Places 2-4), PPT 297-298 (In the Lab 1 Step 5), PPT 299-301 (In the Lab 2 Step 9)
	D. Insert pictures, shapes, and graphics	PPT 99-106, PPT 170-172, PPT 175-177	PPT 132-134 (In the Lab 1 Steps 2-3, 5-6), PPT 134-135 (In the Lab 2 Steps 2-5), PPT 217 (In the Lab 1 Steps 3, 5), PPT 297-298 (In the Lab 1 Step 2), PPT 299-301 (In the Lab 2 Step 3), PPT 302-303 (In the Lab 3 Step 2)
	E. Insert objects	PPT 243-244, PPT 251-255, PPT 256-258	PPT 296-297 (Apply Your Knowledge 1 Step 6), PPT 299-301 (In the Lab 2 Steps 5, 7), PPT 302-303 (In the Lab 3 Steps 4, 9, 11)
II. Formatting Content	A. Format text-based content	PPT 23-27, PPT 173-175, PPT 186-190, PPT 193-195	PPT 69-71 (In the Lab 1 Step 2), PPT 72-73 (In the Lab 2 Step 2), PPT 217 (In the Lab 1 Step 2), PPT 220-221 (In the Lab 3 Step 3), PPT 297-298 (In the Lab 1 Step 3), PPT 299-301 (In the Lab 2 Steps 2, 4, 11), PPT 302-304 (In the Lab 3 Steps 9, 11)
	B. Format pictures, shapes, and graphics	PPT 108-111, PPT 116-119, PPT 178-184, PPT 239-240, PPT 255-256, PPT 258-259, PPT 274-278	PPT 132-134 (In the Lab 1 Steps 2-3, 5-6), PPT 132-134 (In the Lab 1 Steps 2, 5-6), PPT 134-135 (In the Lab 2 Steps 2-5, 8), PPT 136-137 (In the Lab 3 Steps 2-5), PPT 216 (Apply Your Knowledge 1 Step 2), PPT 217 (In the Lab 1 Step 7), PPT 220-221 (In the Lab 3 Steps 6, 8), PPT 296-297 (Apply Your Knowledge 1 Step 6), PPT 302-304 (In the Lab 3 Step 12)
	C. Format slides	PPT 17-20, PPT 85, PPT 144, PPT 97-99, PPT 169-172, PPT 207-208, PPT 232-233, PPT 248, PPT 285, PPT 289	PPT 69-71 (In the Lab 1 Step 1), PPT 131-132 (Apply Your Knowledge 1 Steps 3, 5), PPT 132-134 (In the Lab 1 Steps 3, 5-6), PPT 134-135 (In the Lab 2 Step 1), PPT 217 (In the Lab 1 Step 1), PPT 218-219 (In the Lab 2 Steps 5-6), PPT 220-221 (In the Lab 3 Step 3), PPT 297-298 (In the Lab 1 Step 1), PPT 299-301 (In the Lab 2 Steps 6-8), PPT 302-304 (In the Lab 3 Steps 5, 18)

Table E-2   Specialist-Level Skill Sets, Activities, and Locations in Book for Microsoft Office PowerPoint 2003 *(continued)*

SKILL SET	SKILL BEING MEASURED	SKILL DEMONSTRATED IN BOOK	SKILL EXERCISE IN BOOK
	D. Apply animation schemes	PPT 114-116, PPT 210	PPT 131-132 (Apply Your Knowledge 1 Step 6), PPT 136-137 (In the Lab 3 Step 7), PPT 218-219 (In the Lab 2 Step 9), PPT 299-300 (In the Lab 2 Step 12), PPT 302-304 (In the Lab 3 Step 13)
	E. Apply slide transitions	PPT 278-281	PPT 296-297 (Apply Your Knowledge 1 Step 8), PPT 297-298 (In the Lab 1 Step 6), PPT 299-301 (In the Lab 2 Step 12)
	F. Customize slide templates	PPT 268-270	PPT 296-297 (Apply Your Knowledge 1 Step 2), PPT 297-298 (In the Lab 1 Step 1), PPT 299-301 (In the Lab 2 Step 1), PPT 305 (Cases and Places 1)
	G. Work with masters	PPT 112-113, PPT 184-190, PPT 223-236, PPT 248, PPT 252, PPT 257, PPT 270-278, PPT 283-285	PPT 132-134 (In the Lab 1 Step 7), PPT 134-135 (In the Lab 2 Step 6), PPT 136-137 (In the Lab 3 Step 6), PPT 218-219 (In the Lab 2 Step 7), PPT 220-221 (In the Lab 3 Step 7), PPT 223 (Cases and Places 4), PPT 296-297 (Apply Your Knowledge 1 Steps 2-3, 6), PPT 297-298 (In the Lab 1 Steps 2, 4), PPT 299-301 (In the Lab 2 Steps 1, 3, 11)
III. Collaborating	A. Track, accept, and reject changes in a presentation	PPT 314-316, PPT 321-329	PPT 338-340 (In the Lab 1 Steps 3-7), PPT 341-342 (In the Lab 2 Step 2), PPT 343 (In the Lab 3 Step 4)
	B. Add, edit, and delete comments in a presentation	PPT 310-314, PPT 321-329	PPT 338-340 (In the Lab 1 Steps 2-7), PPT 341-342 (In the Lab 2 Step 2), PPT 343 (In the Lab 3 Steps 2, 4)
	C. Compare and merge presentations	PPT 316-317	PPT 338-340 (In the Lab 1 Step 2), PPT 341-342 (In the Lab 2 Step 2), PPT 343 (In the Lab 3 Step 3)
IV. Managing and Delivering Presentations	A. Organize a presentation	PPT 30-31, PPT 89-97, PPT 209-210, PPT 240-243, PPT 245, PPT 261-263, PPT 275-276, PPT 285-286, PPT 330	PPT 69-71 (In the Lab 1 Step 3), PPT 132-134 (In the Lab 1 Steps 3-4), PPT 218-219 (In the Lab 2 Step 4), PPT 220-221 (In the Lab 3 Step 4), PPT 296-297 (Apply Your Knowledge 1 Step 4), PPT 297-298 (In the Lab 1 Steps 2, 5, 7), PPT 299-301 (In the Lab 2 Steps 7, 9-10), PPT 302-304 (In the Lab 3 Steps 2, 6-7, 9-12, 16), PPT 306 (Cases and Places 3-5), PPT 338-340 (In the Lab 1 Step 2)
	B. Set up slide shows for delivery	PPT 212-213, PPT 263-265, PPT 272-278	PPT 218-219 (In the Lab 2 Step 11), PPT 220-221 (In the Lab 3 Step 10), PPT 222-223 (Cases and Places 2, 5), PPT 299-301 (In the Lab 2 Step 14), PPT 302-304 (In the Lab 3 Steps 6-7, 11, 13), PPT 305-306 (Cases and Places 2-3)
	C. Rehearse timing	PPT 281-283	PPT 302-304 (In the Lab 3 Step 15), PPT 306 (Cases and Places 4-5)
	D. Deliver presentations	PPT 46-50, PPT 292-293	PPT 74-77 (In the Lab 3 Part 1 Step 2, Part 2 Step 6), PPT 296-297 (Apply Your Knowledge 1 Step 9), PPT 299-301 (In the Lab 2 Step 16), PPT 302-304 (In the Lab 3 Step 17), PPT 305 (Cases and Places 1-2)
	E. Prepare presentations for remote delivery	PPT 333-335	PPT 338-340 (In the Lab 1 Step 10), PPT 341-342 (In the Lab 2 Steps 3-4)
	F. Save and publish presentations	PPT 146-149, PPT 154-157, PPT 231-232, PPT 336, Appendix C	PPT 158 (In the Lab 1 Steps 2-3, 6), PPT 158 (In the Lab 2 Steps 2-3, 8), PPT 159 (In the Lab 3 Steps 2-3), PPT 299-301 (In the Lab 2 Step 15), PPT 341-342 (In the Lab 2 Step 3), PPT 343 (In the Lab 3 Step 4)

SKILL SET	SKILL BEING MEASURED	SKILL DEMONSTRATED IN BOOK	SKILL EXERCISE IN BOOK
	G. Print slides, outlines, handouts, and speaker notes	PPT 56-59, PPT 60-61, PPT 122-126, PPT 211, PPT 286-288, PPT 316-321	PPT 69-71 (In the Lab 1 Step 7), PPT 72-73 (In the Lab 2 Steps 6-8), PPT 158 (In the Lab 1 Step 7), PPT 296-297 (Apply Your Knowledge 1 Step 9), PPT 297-298 (In the Lab 1 Step 9), PPT 299-301 (In the Lab 2 Step 17), PPT 302-304 (In the Lab 3 Step 18), PPT 338-340 (In the Lab 1 Steps 2, 9), PPT 341-342 (In the Lab 2 Steps 2-3), PPT 343 (In the Lab 3 Step 3)
	H. Export a presentation to another Microsoft Office program	PPT 289	PPT 299-301 (In the Lab 2 Step 15), PPT 302-304 (In the Lab 3 Step 18)

Table E-2   Specialist-Level Skill Sets, Activities, and Locations in Book for Microsoft Office PowerPoint 2003

Index

Quick Reference Summary

In Microsoft Office PowerPoint 2003, you can accomplish a task in a number of ways. The following table provides a quick reference to each task presented in this textbook. The first column identifies the task. The second column indicates the page number on which the task is discussed in the book. The subsequent four columns list the different ways the task in column one can be carried out. You can invoke the commands listed in the MOUSE, MENU BAR, and SHORTCUT MENU columns using Voice commands.

Microsoft Office PowerPoint 2003 Quick Reference Summary

TASK	PAGE NUMBER	MOUSE	MENU BAR	SHORTCUT MENU	KEYBOARD SHORTCUT
Action Button, Add	PPT 272	AutoShapes button on Drawing toolbar | Action Buttons	Slide Show | Action Buttons		ALT+D | I
Action Button, Fill Color	PPT 275	Fill Color button on Drawing toolbar	Format | AutoShape | Colors and Lines tab	Format AutoShape | Colors and Lines tab	ALT+O | O | Colors and Lines tab
Action Button, Scale	PPT 274		Format | AutoShape	Format AutoShape	ALT+O | O
Animate Text	PPT 114		Slide Show | Custom Animation | Add Effect button		ALT+D | M
Animation Scheme, Add to Selected Slides	PPT 210		Slide Show | Animation Schemes	Slide Design | Animation Schemes	ALT+D | C
AutoContent Wizard	PPT 229		View | Task Pane | From AutoContent Wizard		
AutoShape, Add Text	PPT 434		Type desired text | Format | AutoShape | Text Box tab | Resize AutoShape to fit text	Type desired text | Format | AutoShape | Text Box tab | Resize AutoShape to fit text	Type desired text | ALT+O | O | CTRL+TAB | TAB | SPACEBAR
AutoShape, Apply Animation Effect	PPT 435-436		Slide Show | Custom Animation | Add Effect button	Custom Animation | Add Effect button	ALT+D | M
AutoShape, Insert	PPT 432	AutoShapes button on Drawing toolbar	Insert | Picture | AutoShapes		ALT+U
Black Slide, End Show	PPT 42		Tools | Options | End with black slide		ALT+T | O | E
Bullet Character, Change	PPT 187		Format | Bullets and Numbering | Bulleted tab | Customize	Bullets and Numbering | Bulleted tab | Customize	ALT+O | B | ALT+U
Bullet Color, Change	PPT 189		Format | Bullets and Numbering | Bulleted tab | Color box	Bullets and Numbering | Bulleted tab | Color box	
Chart, Insert	PPT 249	Insert Chart button in content placeholder or on Standard toolbar	Insert | Chart		ALT+I | H
Chart, Insert Excel	PPT 253		Insert | Object | Create from file		ALT+I | O | ALT+F
Chart, Scale	PPT 256		Format | Object	Format Object	ALT+O | O
Check Spelling	PPT 54	Spelling button on Standard toolbar	Tools | Spelling		F7

Microsoft Office PowerPoint 2003 Quick Reference Summary *(continued)*

TASK	PAGE NUMBER	MOUSE	MENU BAR	SHORTCUT MENU	KEYBOARD SHORTCUT
Clip, Add Animation Effects	PPT 117		Slide Show | Custom Animation		ALT+D | M
Clip, Change Size	PPT 109	Format Picture button on Picture toolbar | Size tab	Format | Picture | Size tab	Format Picture | Size tab	ALT+O | I | Size tab
Clip, Insert	PPT 101, PPT 104	Insert Clip Art button on Drawing toolbar	Insert | Picture | Clip Art		ALT+I | P | C
Clip, Move	PPT 108	Drag			
Clip, Ungroup	PPT 178	Draw button on Drawing toolbar | Ungroup		Grouping | Ungroup	SHIFT+F10 | G | U
Color, Change PowerPoint Object	PPT 180		Format | AutoShape	Format AutoShape	ALT+O | O | ALT+C
Color Scheme, Change	PPT 269	Slide Design button on Formatting toolbar | Color Schemes	Format | Slide Design | Color Schemes		ALT+O | D | DOWN ARROW
Comment, Accept	PPT 321	Apply button on Reviewing toolbar			
Comment, Insert	PPT 312	Insert Comment button on Reviewing toolbar	Insert | Comment		ALT+I | M
Comment, Reject	PPT 326	Delete Comment button on Reviewing toolbar			
Comment, Review	PPT 321	Next Item button on Reviewing toolbar			
Control, Add to Form	PPT 379	Click Control in Toolbox			
Custom Background, Insert Picture	PPT 170		Format | Background	Background	ALT+O | K
Delete Slide	PPT 168	Click slide icon | Cut button on Standard toolbar	Edit | Delete Slide	Delete Slide	ALT+E | D
Delete Text	PPT 56	Cut button on Standard toolbar	Edit | Cut	Cut	CTRL+X or BACKSPACE or DELETE
Demote a Paragraph on Outline tab	PPT 90	Demote button on Outlining toolbar			TAB or ALT+SHIFT+ RIGHT ARROW
Design Template	PPT 18	Slide Design button on Formatting toolbar	Format | Slide Design	Slide Design	ALT+O | D
Design Template, Apply to Single Slide	PPT 208	Slide Design button on Formatting toolbar | Arrow button on template | Apply to Selected Slides	Format | Slide Design | Arrow button on template | Apply to Selected Slides	Slide Design | Arrow button on template | Apply to Selected Slides	ALT+O | D Arrow button on template | S
Diagram, AutoFormat	PPT 449	AutoFormat button on Diagram toolbar			
Diagram, Change Size	PPT 442		Format | Diagram | Size tab	Format Diagram | Size tab	ALT+O | D | D | Size tab
Diagram, Insert	PPT 440	Insert Diagram or Organization Chart button on Drawing toolbar	Insert | Diagram		ALT+I | G
Display a Presentation in Black and White	PPT 57	Color/Grayscale button on Standard toolbar	View | Color/Grayscale | Pure Black and White		ALT+V | C | U
Edit Web Page through Browser	PPT 152	Edit button on Internet Explorer Standard Buttons toolbar	File on browser menu bar | Edit with Microsoft PowerPoint in browser window		ALT+F | D in browser window
E-Mail from PowerPoint	PPT 127	E-mail button on Standard toolbar	File | Send To | Mail Recipient		ALT+F | D | A
End Slide Show	PPT 50			End Show	ESC
Find and Replace Text	PPT 265		Edit | Replace		CTRL+H or ALT+E | E
Find Text	PPT 265		Edit | Find		CTRL+E or ALT+E | F

Microsoft Office PowerPoint 2003 Quick Reference Summary

TASK	PAGE NUMBER	MOUSE	MENU BAR	SHORTCUT MENU	KEYBOARD SHORTCUT
Folder, Create	PPT 232	Save button on Standard toolbar | Create New Folder button on Save As dialog box toolbar			
Font	PPT 24	Font box arrow on Formatting toolbar	Format | Font | Font tab	Font | Font tab	ALT+O | F or CTRL+SHIFT+F
Font Color	PPT 24	Font Color button arrow on Formatting toolbar, desired color	Format | Font	Font | Color	ALT+O | F | ALT+C | DOWN ARROW
Font Size, Decrease	PPT 27	Decrease Font Size button on Formatting toolbar	Format | Font	Font | Size	CTRL+SHIFT+LEFT CARET (<)
Font Size, Increase	PPT 25	Increase Font Size button on Formatting toolbar	Format | Font	Font | Size	CTRL+SHIFT+RIGHT CARET (>)
Footer, Modify on Title Master	PPT 271	Normal View button + SHIFT | Footer Area | type text | Close Master View button on Slide Master View toolbar	View | Master | Slide Master		ALT+V | M | S | type text | ALT+C
Format Painter	PPT 445	Format Painter button on Standard toolbar			
Grid and Guides, Display	PPT 241	Show/Hide Grid button on Standard toolbar	View | Grid and Guides	Grid and Guides	ALT+V | I | D | I
Grid and Guides, Hide	PPT 243	Show/Hide Grid button on Standard toolbar	View | Grid and Guides	Grid and Guides	ALT+V | I | D | I
Header and Footer, Add to Outline Page	PPT 112		View | Header and Footer | Notes and Handouts tab		ALT+V | H | Notes and Handouts tab
Help	PPT 62 and Appendix A	Microsoft PowerPoint Help button on Standard toolbar	Help | Microsoft PowerPoint Help		F1
Hide Slide	PPT 264	Hide Slide button on Slide Sorter toolbar	Slide Show | Hide Slide	Hide Slide	ALT+D | H
Highlight Items	PPT 292	Pointer arrow button on Slide Show toolbar | Highlighter		Pointer Options | Highlighter	
Hyperlink, Add	PPT 261	Hyperlink button on Standard toolbar	Insert | Hyperlink		ALT+I | I or CTRL+K
Insert Slide from Another Presentation	PPT 427		Insert | Slides from Files | Find Presentation tab | Browse | Open | Insert | Close		ALT+I | F | ALT+B | select desired file | ALT+O | select desired slide | ALT+I | ESC
Italicize	PPT 24	Italic button on Formatting toolbar	Format | Font | Font style	Font | Font style	CTRL+I
Ink Color, Change	PPT 292	Pointer arrow button on Slide Show toolbar | Ink Color		Pointer Options | Ink Color	
Language Bar	PPT 16 and Appendix B	Language Indicator button in tray	Tools | Speech | Speech Recognition		ALT+T | H | H
Macro, Create by Using Macro Recorder	PPT 362	Record Macro button on Visual Basic toolbar	Tools | Macro | Record New Macro		ALT+T | M | R
Macro, View VBA Code	PPT 370	Visual Basic Editor button on Visual Basic toolbar	Tools | Macro | Macros | Edit		ALT+T | M | V
Menu, Customize by Adding a Command	PPT 365	More Buttons button on Standard toolbar | Add or Remove Buttons | Customize | Commands tab	Tools | Customize | Commands tab	Customize | Commands tab	
Merge Slide Shows	PPT 316		Tools | Compare and Merge Presentations		ALT+T | P

Microsoft Office PowerPoint 2003 Quick Reference Summary *(continued)*

TASK	PAGE NUMBER	MOUSE	MENU BAR	SHORTCUT MENU	KEYBOARD SHORTCUT
Microsoft Office Clip Art and Media Web Site, Connect to	PPT 479	Insert Clip Art button on Drawing toolbar | Clip art on Office Online in Clip Art task pane	Insert | Picture | Clip Art | Clip art on Office Online in Clip Art task pane		ALT+I | P | C | TAB
Microsoft Office Templates Web Site, Connect to	PPT 474		File | New | Templates on Office Online in New Presentation task pane		ALT+F | N | TAB
Mouse Pointer, Constantly Display	PPT 273	Pointer arrow button on Slide Show toolbar | Arrow Options | Visible		Pointer Options | Arrow Options | Visible	
Mouse Pointer, Hide	PPT 293	Pointer arrow button on Slide Show toolbar | Arrow Options | Hidden		Pointer Options | Arrow Options | Hidden	
Move a Paragraph Down	PPT 87	Move Down button on Outlining toolbar			ALT+SHIFT+DOWN ARROW
Move a Paragraph Up	PPT 87	Move Up button on Outlining toolbar			ALT+SHIFT+UP ARROW
New Slide	PPT 30	New Slide button on Formatting toolbar	Insert | New Slide		CTRL+M
Next Slide	PPT 45	Next Slide button on vertical scroll bar			PAGE DOWN
Normal View	PPT 96	Normal View button at lower-left PowerPoint window	View | Normal		ALT+V | N
Online Broadcast, Set Up and Schedule	PPT 330		Slide Show | Online Broadcast | Schedule a Live Broadcast		ALT+D | O | S
Open an Outline as a Presentation	PPT 166		Insert | Slides from Outline | Insert		ALT+I | L
Open Presentation	PPT 52	Open button on Standard toolbar	File | Open		CTRL+O
Open Presentation and Execute Macro	PPT 369	Run Macro button on Visual Basic toolbar	File | Open | double-click file name | Enable Macros | File | click macro command		ALT+F8, double-click macro name
Organization Chart Design Scheme, Change	PPT 205	Autoformat button on Organization Chart toolbar			ALT+SHIFT+C | RIGHT ARROW
Organization Chart Diagram, Display	PPT 196	Insert Diagram or Organization Chart button on Drawing toolbar	Insert | Picture | Organization Chart		ALT+I | P | O
Organization Chart, Insert Subordinate and Coworker Shapes	PPT 200	Insert Shape button on Organization Chart toolbar			ALT+SHIFT+N
Organization Chart, Scale	PPT 207			Format Organization Chart	
Organization Chart Shape Layout, Change	PPT 203	Layout button on Organization Chart toolbar			ALT+SHIFT+L
Package for CD	PPT 334		File | Package for CD		ALT+F | K
Paragraph Indent, Decrease	PPT 37	Decrease Indent button on Formatting toolbar			SHIFT+TAB or ALT+ SHIFT+LEFT ARROW
Paragraph Indent, Increase	PPT 36	Increase Indent button on Formatting toolbar			TAB or ALT+SHIFT+ RIGHT ARROW
Preview Presentation as Web Page	PPT 144		File | Web Page Preview		ALT+F | B
Previous Slide	PPT 45	Previous Slide button on vertical scroll bar			PAGE UP

Microsoft Office PowerPoint 2003 Quick Reference Summary

TASK	PAGE NUMBER	MOUSE	MENU BAR	SHORTCUT MENU	KEYBOARD SHORTCUT
Print a Presentation	PPT 60	Print button on Standard toolbar	File | Print		CTRL+P
Print an Outline	PPT 122		File | Print | Print what box arrow | Outline View		CTRL+P | TAB | TAB | DOWN ARROW | Outline View
Print Comments	PPT 316		File | Print | Include comment pages		CTRL+P | TAB
Print Speaker Notes	PPT 287		File | Print | Print what box arrow | Notes Pages		CTRL+P | ALT+W | DOWN ARROW
Promote a Paragraph on Outline tab	PPT 89	Promote button on Outlining toolbar			SHIFT+TAB or ALT+ SHIFT+LEFT ARROW
Publish a Presentation	PPT 154		File | Save as Web Page | Publish | Publish		ALT+F | G | ALT+P | ALT+P
Quit PowerPoint	PPT 50	Close button on title bar or double-click control icon on title bar	File | Exit		ALT+F4 or CTRL+Q
Rearrange Slides	PPT 209	Drag slide thumbnail or slide icon to new location			
Redo Action	PPT 22	Redo button on Standard toolbar	Edit | Redo		CTRL+Y or ALT+E | R
Regroup Objects	PPT 183	Drag through objects | Draw button on Drawing toolbar | Regroup		Grouping | Regroup	SHIFT+F10 | G | O
Save a Presentation	PPT 27	Save button on Standard toolbar	File | Save		CTRL+S
Save as Web Page	PPT 147		File | Save as Web Page		ALT+F | G
Save in Rich Text Format	PPT 289		File | Save As | Save as type box arrow | Outline/RTF		ALT+F | A | ALT+T, DOWN ARROW
Self-Running Presentation, Create	PPT 450		Slide Show | Set Up Show | Browsed at a kiosk (full screen)		ALT+D | S | ALT+K
Send Presentation for Review	PPT 315		File | Sent To | Mail Recipient (for Review)		ALT+F | D | C
Slide Layout	PPT 98		Format | Slide Layout	Slide Layout	ALT+O | L
Slide Master, Display	PPT 185		View | Master | Slide Master		SHIFT | Normal View
Slide Numbers, Add	PPT 456		Insert | Slide Number | Slide tab | Slide number		ALT+I | U | N
Slide Numbers, Format Using Slide Master	PPT 458		View | Master | Slide Master		ALT+V | M | S
Slide Show Timing, Set Manually	PPT 452		Slide Show | Slide Transition | Automatically after | Automatically after box up arrow	Slide Transition | Automatically after | Automatically after box up arrow	ALT+D | T | TAB | type desired time
Slide Show View	PPT 47	Slide Show button at lower-left PowerPoint window	View | Slide Show		F5 or ALT+V | W
Slide Sorter View	PPT 95	Slide Sorter View button at lower-left PowerPoint window	View | Slide Sorter		ALT+V | D
Slide Transition, Add	PPT 279		Slide Show | Slide Transition	Slide Transition	ALT+D | T
Sound Effect, Add	PPT 243		Insert | Movies and Sounds | Sound from File		ALT+I | V | N
Spelling Check	PPT 54	Spelling button on Standard toolbar	Tools | Spelling	Spelling	F7
Table, Format Cell	PPT 193	Click cell			
Table, Insert	PPT 191, PPT 258	Insert Table button on Standard toolbar	Insert | Table Insert | Object | Create from file		ALT+I | B, ALT+I | O | ALT+F
Table, Scale	PPT 259		Format | Object	Format Object	ALT+O | O
Task Pane	PPT 11		View | Task Pane		ALT+V | K

Microsoft Office PowerPoint 2003 Quick Reference Summary *(continued)*

TASK	PAGE NUMBER	MOUSE	MENU BAR	SHORTCUT MENU	KEYBOARD SHORTCUT
Text Placeholder, Delete	PPT 234	Cut button on Standard toolbar	Edit | Cut		CTRL+X or DELETE
Thesaurus	PPT 267		Tools | Thesaurus		SHIFT+F7 or ALT+T | T
Timings, Rehearse	PPT 282		Slide Show | Rehearse Timings		ALT+D | R
Toolbar, Add Button	PPT 355	Toolbar Options button on toolbar | Add or Remove Buttons | Customize | Commands tab	Tools | Customize | Commands tab	Customize | Commands tab	
Toolbar, Create	PPT 352	More Buttons button on Standard toolbar | Add or Remove Buttons | Customize | Toolbars tab | New button	Tools | Customize | Toolbars tab | New button	Customize | Toolbars tab | New button	
Toolbar, Display Reviewing	PPT 312		View | Toolbars | Reviewing	Any toolbar | Reviewing	ALT+V | T
Toolbar, Reset	Appendix D	Toolbar Options button on toolbar | Add or Remove Buttons | Customize | Toolbars tab		Customize | Toolbars tab	ALT+V | T | C | B
Toolbar, Show Entire	PPT 9	Double-click move handle			
Undo Action	PPT 22	Undo button on Standard toolbar	Edit | Undo		CTRL+Z or ALT+E | U
Visual Basic Editor, Close and Return to Microsoft PowerPoint	PPT 400	Save button on Standard toolbar | Close button on Visual Basic Editor title bar	File | Close and Return to Microsoft PowerPoint		ALT+Q
Visual Basic IDE, Open	PPT 374		Tools | Macro | Visual Basic Editor		ALT+F11
Web Session, Close	PPT 484			Microsoft Internet Explorer button on taskbar | Close | Yes	
Word Table, Insert	PPT 258		Insert | Object | Create from file | Browse		ALT+I | O | ALT+F | B
WordArt, Change Height and Width	PPT 239	Format WordArt button on WordArt toolbar | Size tab	Format | WordArt | Size tab	Format WordArt | Size tab	ALT+O | O | ALT+E
WordArt, Style	PPT 236	Insert WordArt button on Drawing toolbar	Insert | Picture | WordArt		ALT+I | P | W
Zoom Percentage, Increase	PPT 44	Zoom Box arrow on Standard toolbar	View | Zoom		ALT+V | Z

SHELLY CASHMAN SERIES®

A few of the exercises in this book require that you begin
by opening a data file from a Data Disk. Choose one
of the following to obtain a copy of the Data Disk.

Instructors

☞ A copy of the Data Disk is on the Instructor Resources CD-ROM below the category
Data Files for Students, which you can copy to your school's network for student use.

☞ Download the Data Disk via the World Wide Web by following the instructions below.

☞ Contact us via e-mail at reply@course.com.

☞ Call Thomson Course Technology's Customer Service department for fast and efficient
delivery of the Data Disk.

Students

☞ Check with your instructor to determine the best way to obtain a copy of the Data Disk.

☞ Download the Data Disk via the World Wide Web by following the instructions below.

Instructions for Downloading the Data Disk from the World Wide Web

1 Insert your removable media (USB flash drive, floppy disk, or Zip disk) into your
computer.

2 Start your browser. Enter the URL scsite.com in the Address box.

3 When the scsite.com Web page displays, scroll down to the Browse by Subject area and
click the category to which your book belongs (for example, Office Suites).

4 When the category list expands, click the title of your textbook (for example, Microsoft
Office 2003: Introductory Concepts and Techniques).

5 When the Textbook page displays, scroll down to the Data Files for Students area and
click the appropriate link.

6 If Windows displays a File Download - Security Warning dialog box, click the Run
button. If Windows displays an Internet Explorer - Security Warning dialog box, click
the Run button.

7 When Windows displays the WinZip Self-Extractor dialog box, type in the Unzip to
folder box the portable storage media drive letter followed a colon, backslash, and a sub-
folder name of your choice (for example, f:/Office 2003).

8 Click the Unzip button.

9 When Windows displays the WinZip Self-Extractor dialog box, click the OK button.

10 Click the Close button on the right side of the title bar in the WinZip Self-Extractor
dialog box.

11 Start Windows Explorer and display the contents of the folder to which you unzipped the
Data Disk files in Step 7 to view the results.

Keep Your Skills Fresh with Quick Reference CourseCards!

Thomson Course Technology CourseCards allow you to easily learn the basics of new applications or quickly access tips and tricks long after your class is complete.

Each highly visual, four-color, six-sided CourseCard features:

- **Basic Topics** enable users to effectively utilize key content.

- **Tips and Solutions** reinforce key subject matter and provide solutions to common situations.

- **Menu Quick References** help users navigate through the most important menu tools using a simple table of contents model.

- **Keyboard Shortcuts** improve productivity and save time.

- **Screen Shots** effectively show what users see on their monitors.

- **Advanced Topics** provide advanced users with a clear reference guide to more challenging content.

Over 75 CourseCards are available on a variety of topics! To order, please visit *www.courseilt.com/ilt_cards.cfm*